AF207889

MUSÉE D'ORSAY

KÖNEMANN

© 2018 koenemann.com GmbH

www.koenemann.com

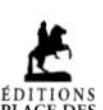

© Éditions Place des Victoires

6, rue du Mail – 75002 Paris

www.victoires.com

ISBN : 978-2-8099-1693-5

Dépôt légal : 2ᵉ trimestre 2019

Concept, Project Management: koenemann.com GmbH

Text: Valentin Grivet

Editorial coordination: Laurence Piault

Layout: Mathilde Decorbez

Color separation: Nord Compo

Translations into English, German, Spanish, Portuguese, Dutch:

TEXTCASE Translation Agency

info@textcase.nl

textcase.de   textcase.eu

Picture credits: akg-images gmbh, except pp. 12, 14, 25, 48, 53, 59, 82, 88, 195, 222, 246, 248, 252, 268, 260 Bridgeman Images

ISBN: 978-3-7419-2422-4

Printed in China by Shenzen Hua Xin Colour-printing & Platemaking Co., Ltd

VALENTIN GRIVET

MUSÉE D'ORSAY

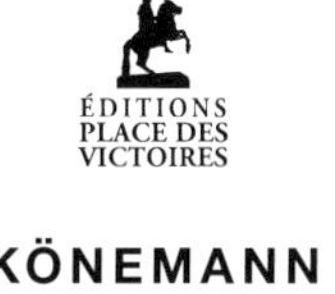

ÉDITIONS
PLACE DES
VICTOIRES

KÖNEMANN

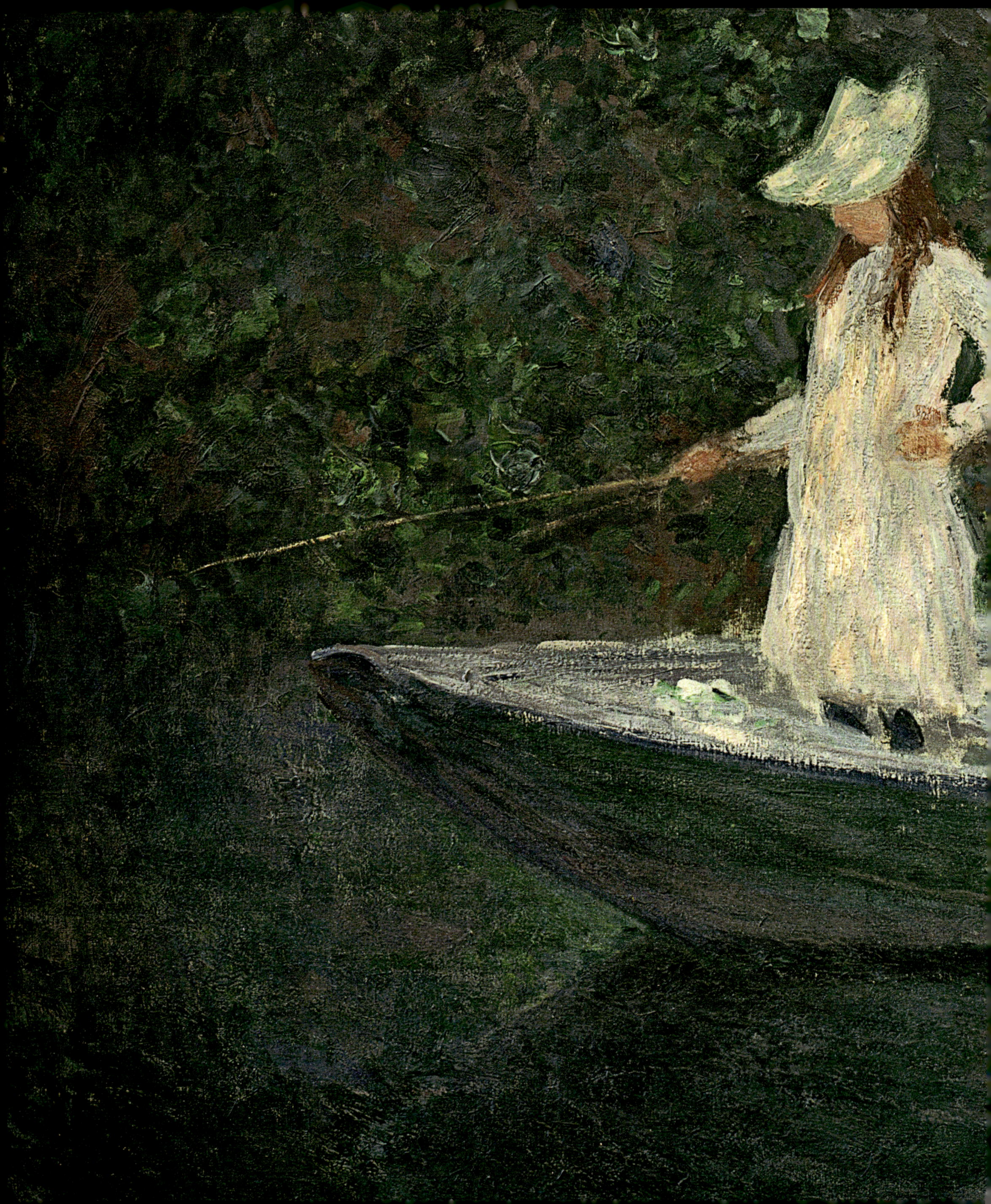

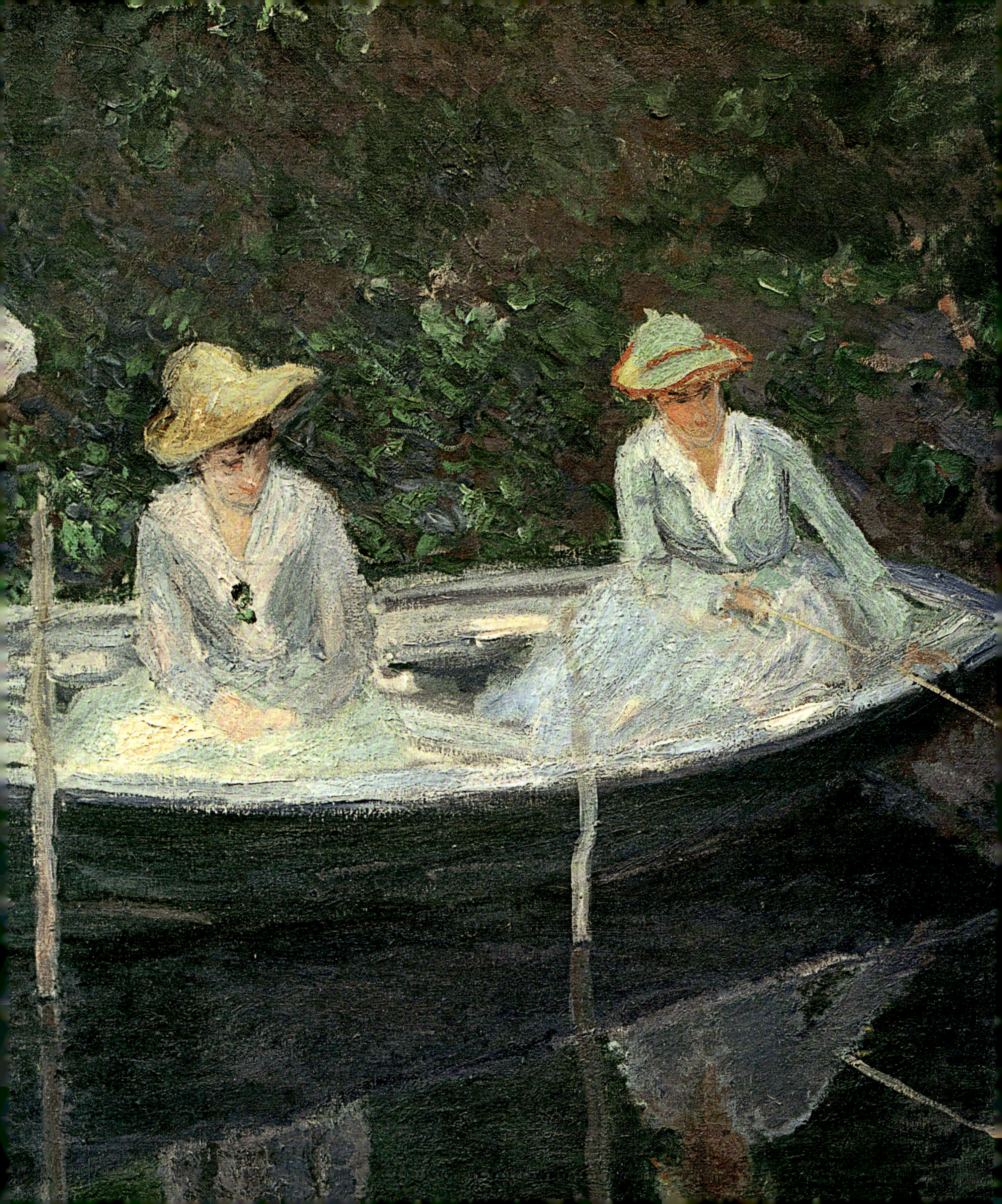

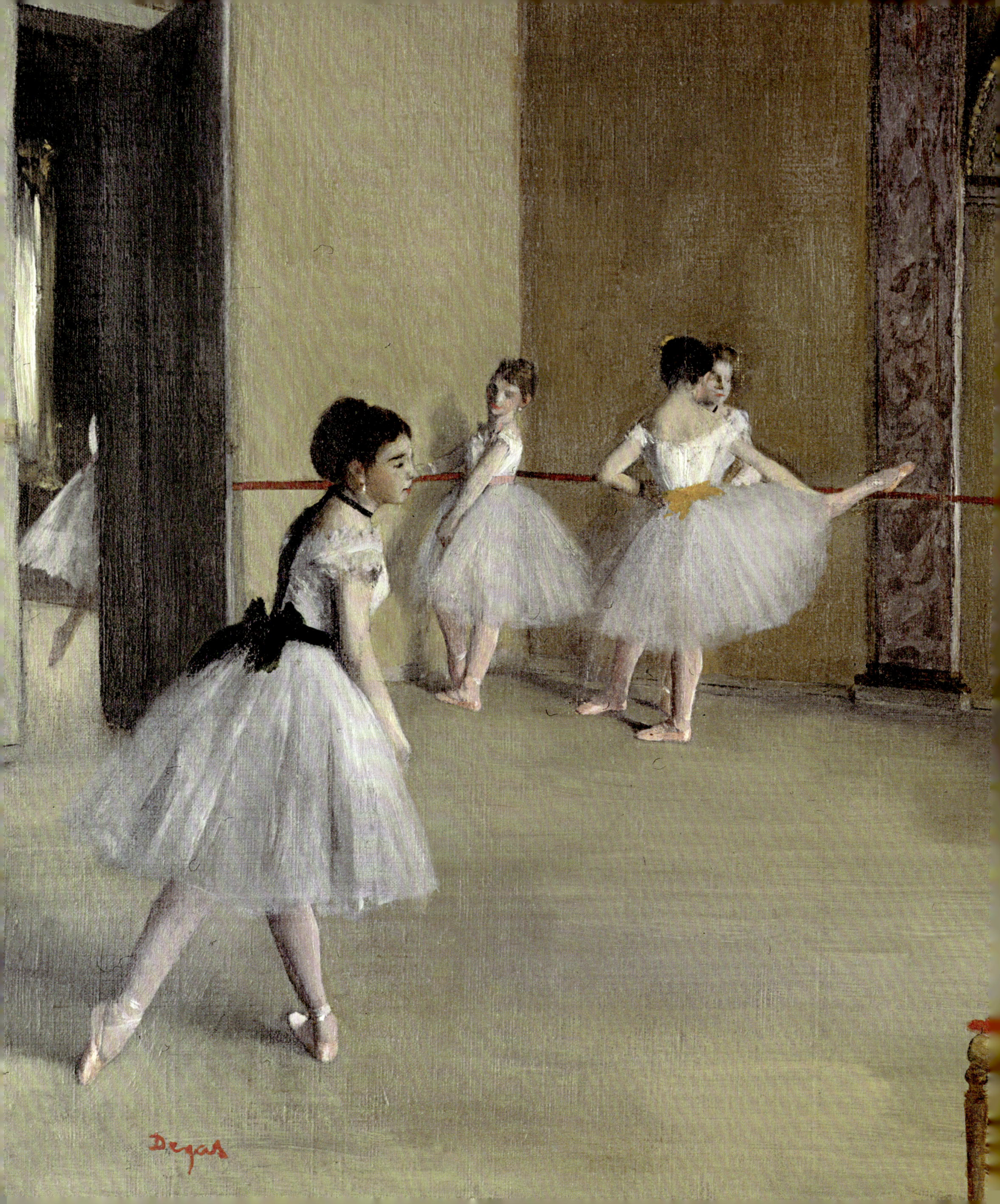
Degas

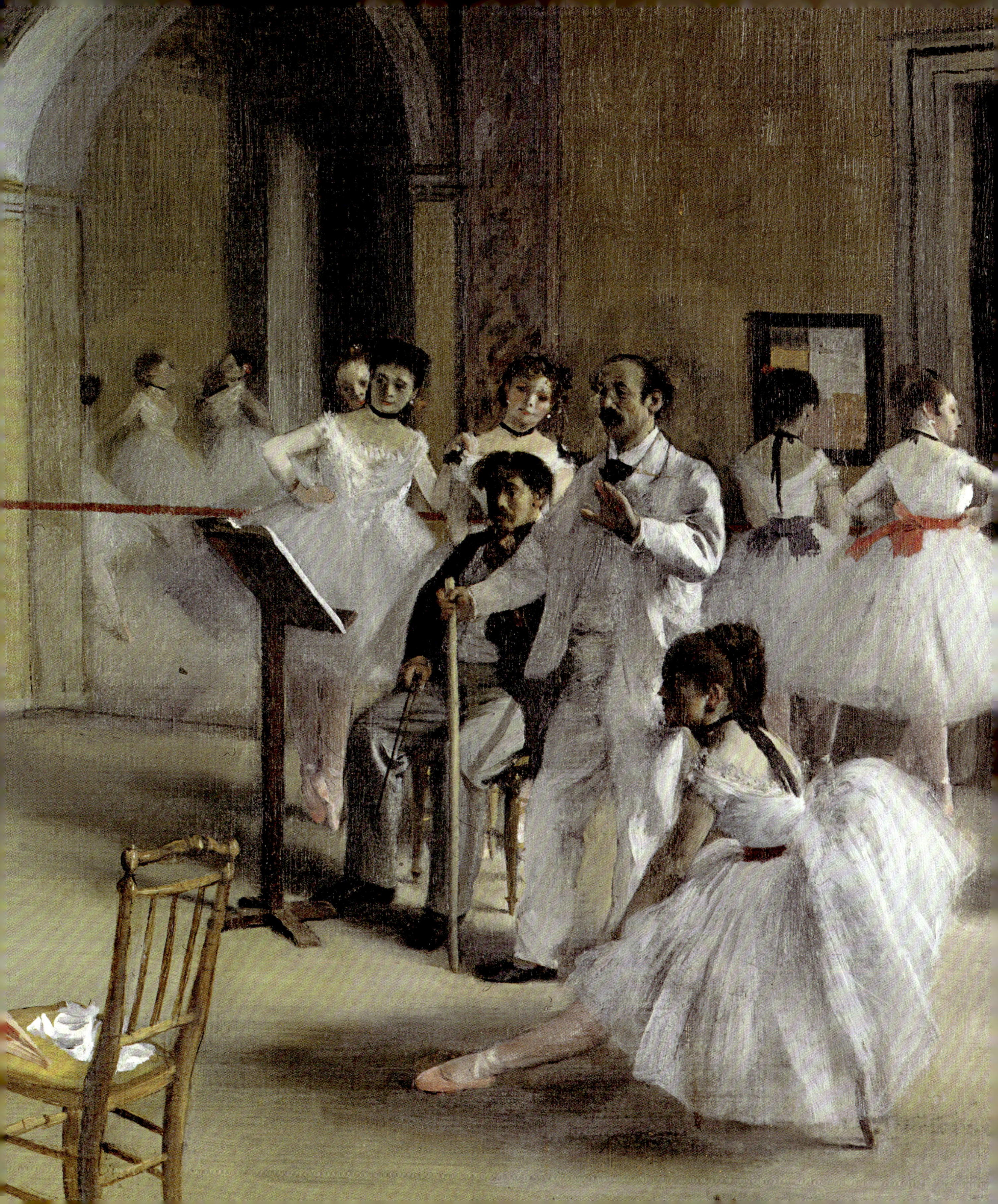

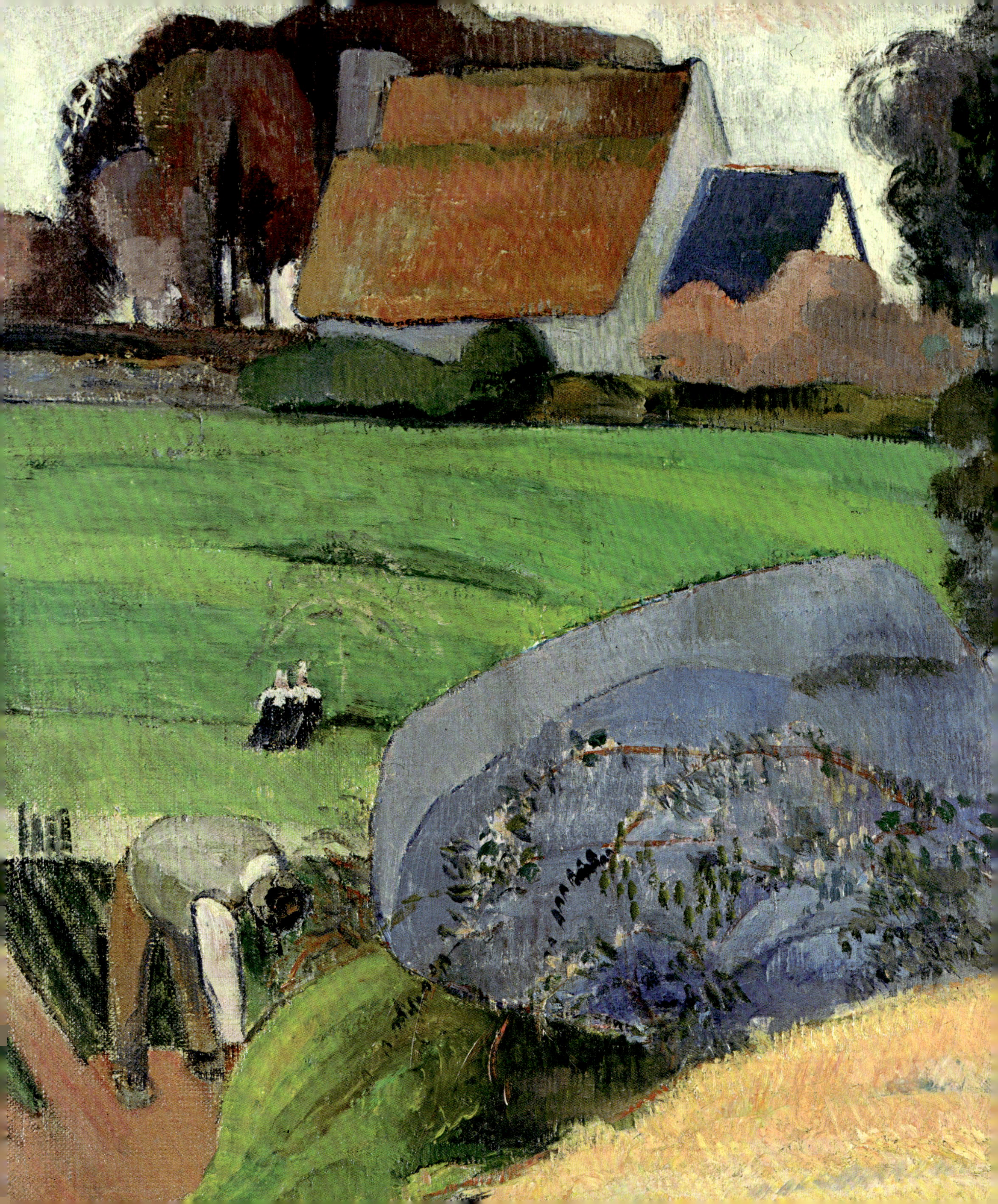

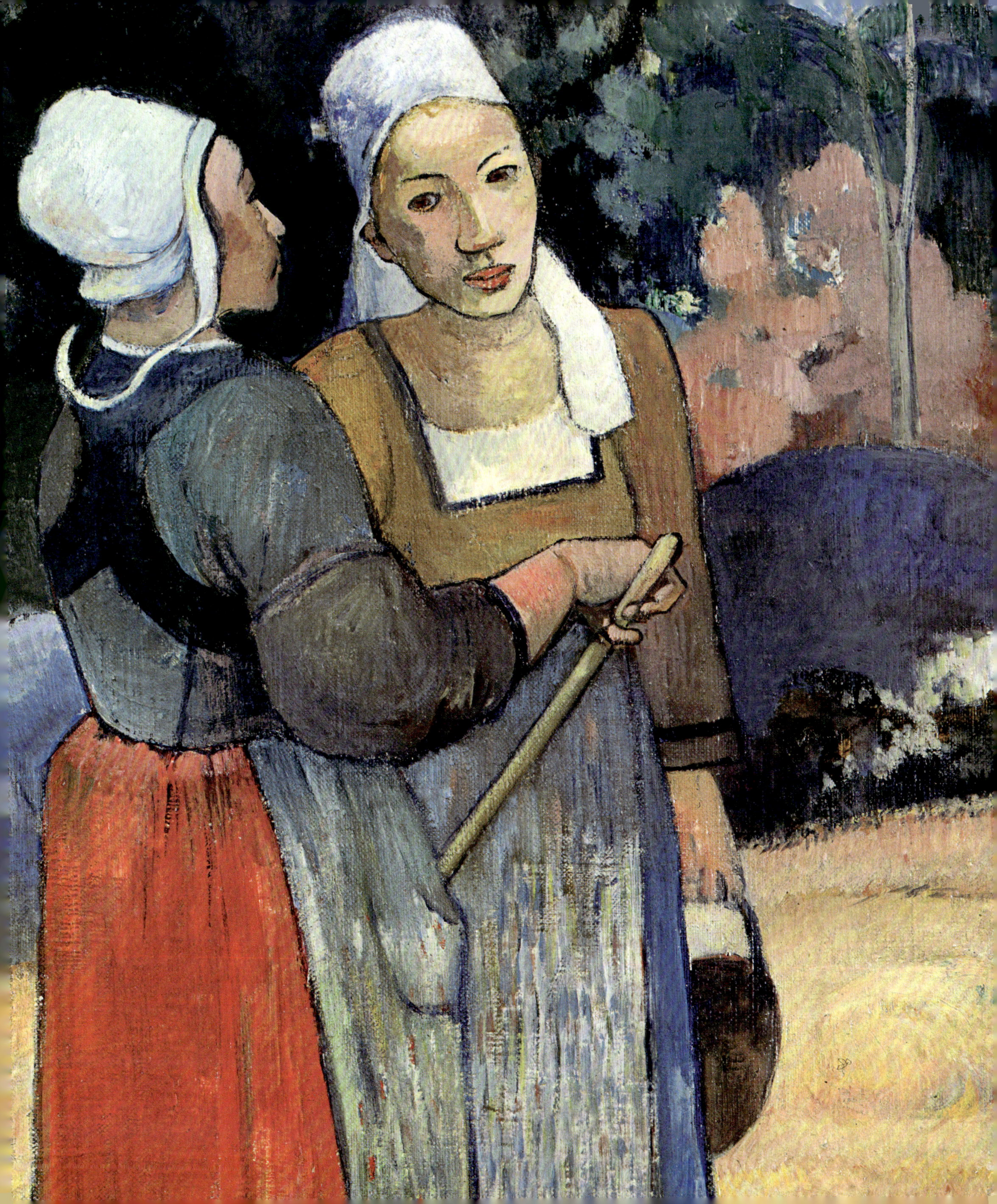

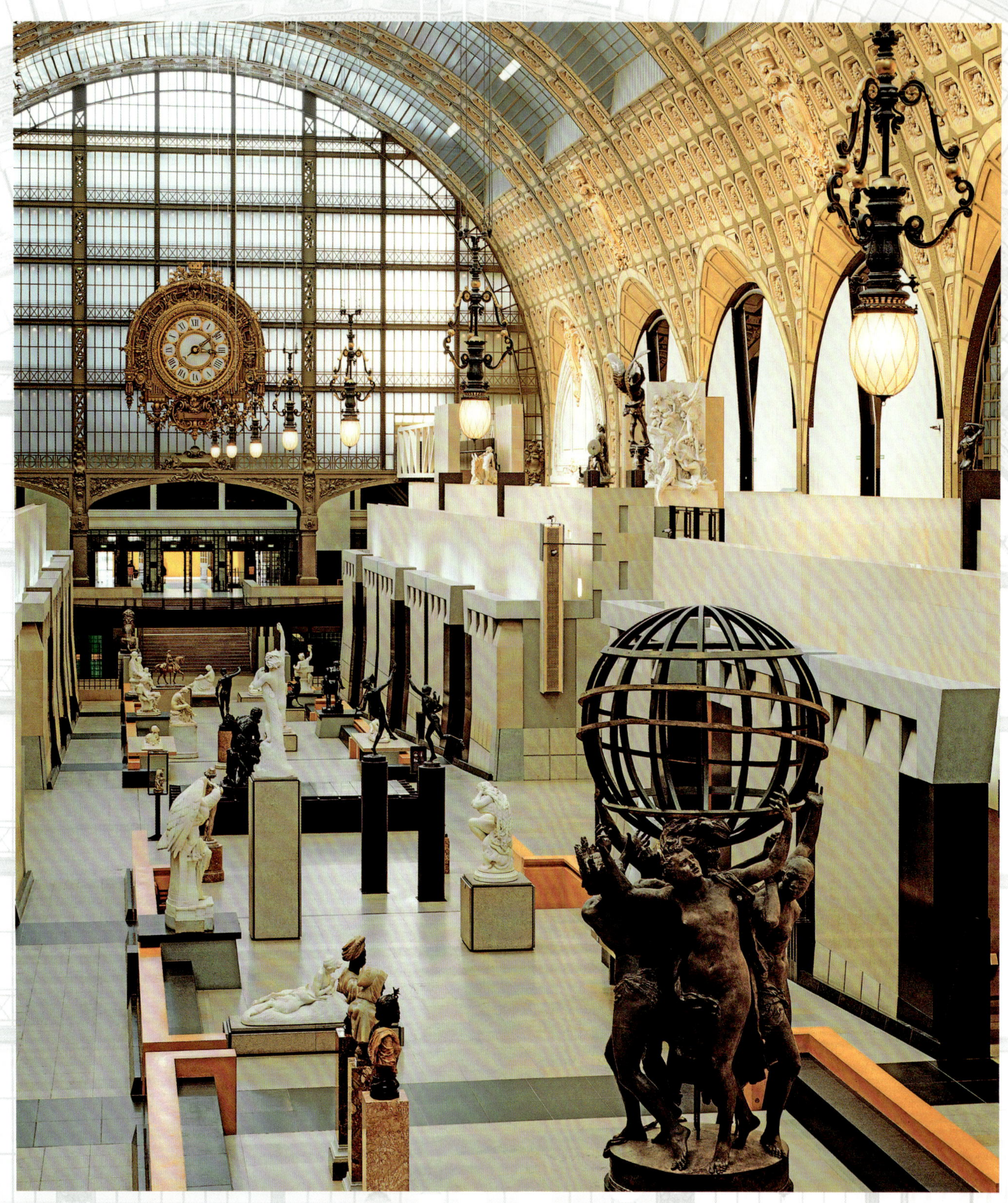

Contents Sommaire Inhalt Índice Indice Inhoud

View of the large nave of the Musée d'Orsay
Vue de la grande Nef du musée d'Orsay
Ansicht des Hauptschiffs des Musée d'Orsay
Vista de la nave principal del museo de Orsay
Veduta della grande navata del museo d'Orsay
De grote hal van het Musée d'Orsay

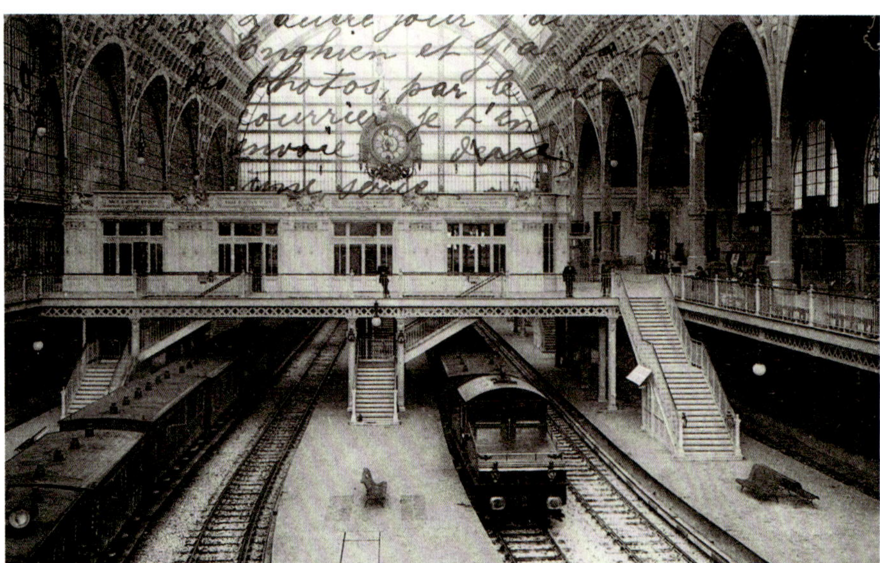

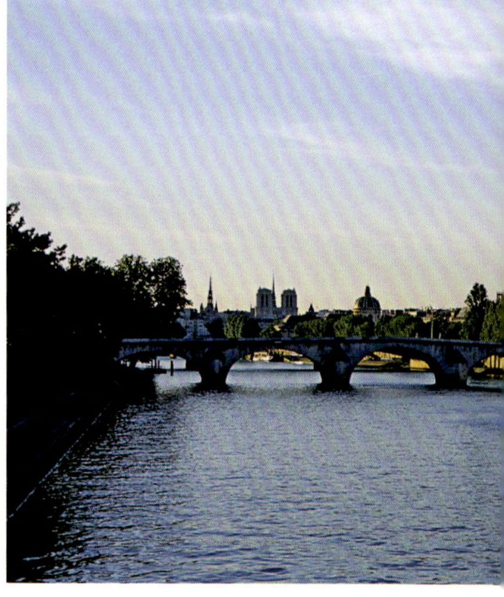

View of the Orsay station designed by the architect Victor Laloux (1850–1937)
Vue de la gare d'Orsay conçue par l'architecte Victor Laloux (1850–1937)
Ansicht des Bahnhofs von Orsay, entworfen vom Architekten Victor Laloux (1850–1937)
Vista de la estación de Orsay diseñada por el arquitecto Victor Laloux (1850–1937)
Veduta della stazione ferroviaria d'Orsay progettata dall'architetto Victor Laloux (1850–1937)
Het Gare d'Orsay naar het ontwerp van architect Victor Laloux (1850–1937)
c. 1904, Postcard/Carte postale

From its inception, the Musée d'Orsay intended to offer a global depiction of Western art between 1848 and 1914, covering all movements, currents, schools and styles including those that had been neglected during the 20th century—symbolism, orientalism, Art Nouveau—and even those that had been despised by critics, such as academicism and Pompier art.

Of course, the millions of visitors who flock every year to Orsay come first to revel in the paintings of Monet, Degas, Lautrec, Cézanne, Van Gogh, Gauguin or Vuillard. But ignoring previous tradition and retaining only the avant-garde would be nonsense. In the first place because in painting, as in anything else, nothing exists without that which preceded it. Consciously or not, artists feed on their elders, taking in their lessons, or rejecting them. And in second place, because the academic painters

Dès sa création, le musée d'Orsay avait pour vocation d'offrir une vision globale de l'art occidental entre 1848 et 1914, en balayant tous les mouvements, courants, écoles et styles, y compris ceux qui, au cours du xxe siècle, avaient pu être négligés – le symbolisme, l'orientalisme, l'Art nouveau… –, voire méprisés par la critique, comme l'académisme et l'art pompier.

Bien sûr, les millions de visiteurs qui se pressent chaque année à Orsay viennent d'abord pour se délecter des tableaux de Monet, Degas, Lautrec, Cézanne, Van Gogh, Gauguin ou Vuillard. Mais faire abstraction de la tradition et ne retenir que les avant-gardes serait un non-sens. D'abord, parce qu'en peinture comme ailleurs, rien n'existe sans ce qui l'a précédé. Consciemment ou non, les artistes se nourrissent de leurs aînés, en assimilent les leçons, ou les rejettent. Ensuite, parce que les peintres académiques (Cabanel, Gérôme…), furent

Bereits mit seiner Entstehung hatte das Musée d'Orsay die Berufung, einen Gesamtüberblick zu geben über die westliche Kunst zwischen 1848 und 1914 und alle Bewegungen, Strömungen, Schulen und Stile abzudecken, so auch diejenigen, die im Laufe des 20. Jahrhunderts unter Umständen vernachlässigt (Symbolismus, Orientalismus, Jugendstil …) oder sogar von den Kritikern verachtet worden waren, wie der Akademismus und die Art Pompier („Feuerwehrmann-Kunst").

Die Millionen an Besuchern, die jedes Jahr ins Musée d'Orsay strömen, kommen selbstverständlich, um sich die Gemälde von Monet, Degas, Lautrec, Cézanne, van Gogh, Gauguin und Vuillard anzuschauen. Aber die Tradition außer Acht zu lassen und nur den Avantgarden Beachtung zu schenken, wäre unsinnig. Zunächst einmal, weil in der Malerei, wie auch in anderen Bereichen, nichts existiert, ohne das, was vorausgegangen ist. Bewusst

View to Musée d'Orsay from the Seine
Vue du musée d'Orsay depuis les quais de Seine
Blick auf das Musée d'Orsay von der Seine aus
Vista del museo de Orsay desde el Sena
Vista del museo d'Orsay dalla Senna
Uitzicht op het Musée d'Orsay vanaf de Seine

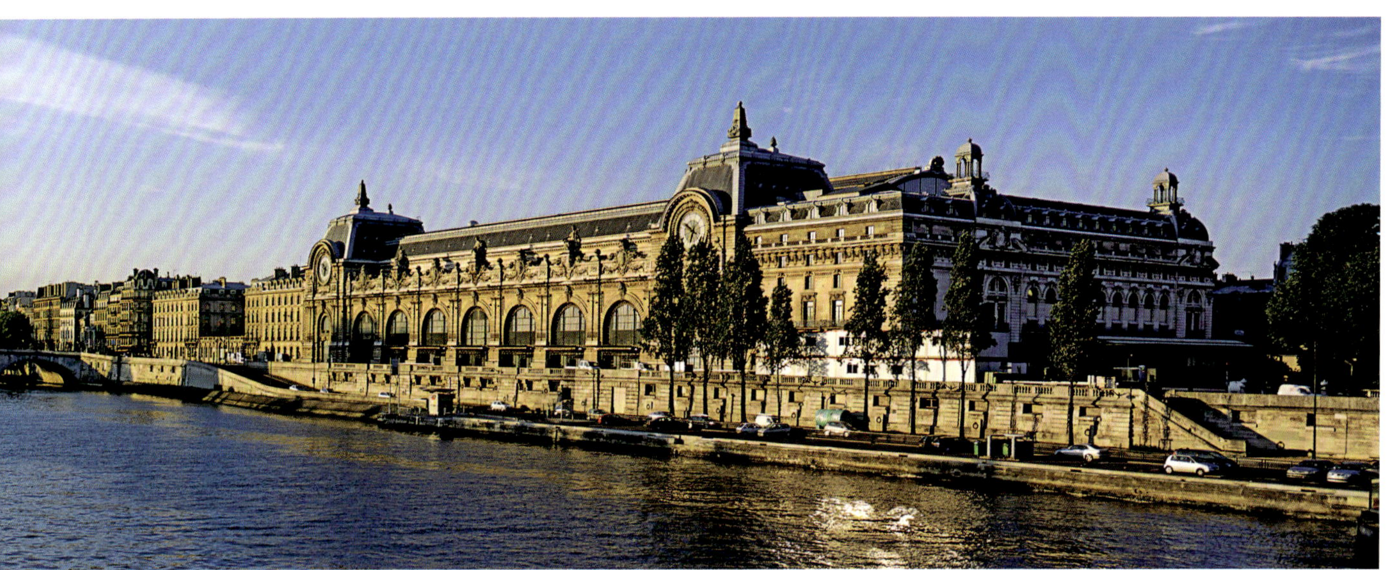

Desde su creación, el museo de Orsay tenía por objeto proporcionar una visión general del arte occidental entre 1848 y 1914, barriendo todos los movimientos, corrientes, escuelas y estilos, incluyendo aquellos que, durante el siglo XX había sido pasados por alto – el simbolismo, el orientalismo, el modernismo… – o incluso despreciado por los críticos, como el academicismo y el art pompier.

Por supuesto, los millones de visitantes que acuden cada año a Orsay vienen fundamentalmente para deleitarse con las pinturas de Monet, Degas, Lautrec, Cézanne, Van Gogh, Gauguin o Vuillard. Pero ignorar la tradición y mantener sólo las vanguardias sería un sin sentido. En primer lugar, porque en la pintura como en otros ámbitos, no existe nada sin aquello que lo ha precedido. Conscientemente o no, los artistas se alimentan de sus mayores, asimilan sus lecciones, o bien las

Fin dalla sua creazione, il museo d'Orsay si è proposto di fornire una panoramica dell'arte occidentale tra il 1848 e il 1914, includendovi tutti i movimenti, le correnti, le scuole e gli stili, compresi quelli che, nel corso del XX secolo, erano stati trascurati (ad esempio il Simbolismo, l'Orientalismo e l'Art Nouveau) o addirittura disprezzati dalla critica, come l'Accademismo e l'Art pompier.

Naturalmente, i milioni di visitatori che percorrono ogni anno le sale del museo d'Orsay sono attratti in primo luogo dalle opere di Monet, Degas, Lautrec, Cézanne, Van Gogh, Gauguin o Vuillard. Tuttavia, ignorare la tradizione a favore esclusivo delle avanguardie sarebbe un controsenso. In primo luogo perché, sia nella pittura sia in altri campi, non esisterebbe nulla senza ciò che l'ha preceduto. Consapevolmente o meno, gli artisti si nutrono dei loro predecessori, ne assimilano gli insegnamenti o li rifiutano. In secondo luogo, perché

Een globale visie bieden op de westerse kunst uit de periode 1848-1914, waarbij alle bewegingen, stromingen, scholen en stijlen zijn vertegenwoordigd, ook die die in de loop van de 20e eeuw vergeten hadden kunnen worden – symbolisme, oriëntalisme, nieuwe kunst… – of door critici werden veracht, zoals de academische en bombastische kunst: dat was al bij de oprichting de missie van het Musée d'Orsay.

Zeker, de miljoenen bezoekers die zich elk jaar weer voor de ingang van Orsay verdringen, komen in eerste instantie voor de schilderijen van Monet, Degas, Lautrec, Cézanne, Van Gogh, Gauguin en Vuillard. Maar de traditie buiten beschouwing laten en de avant-garde behouden, zou onzinnig zijn. Allereerst omdat niets kan bestaan zonder wat eraan is voorafgegaan, ook niet in de schilderkunst. Bewust of onbewust, voeden kunstenaars zich met hun voorgangers, profiteren ze van hun lessen, of

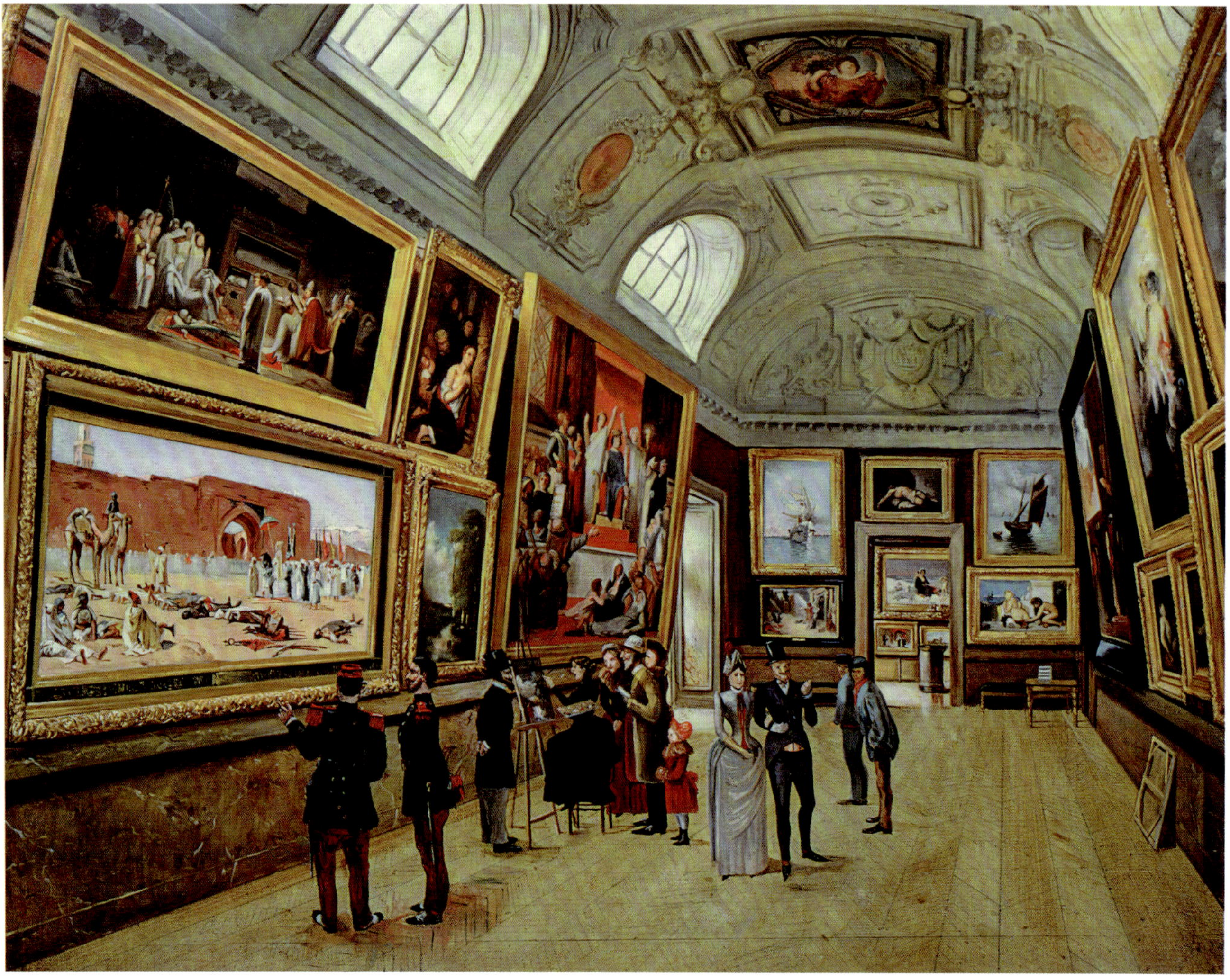

(Cabanel, Gérôme, …) were the stars of their time, whereas Manet and the impressionists suffered severe criticism.

The project for creating a museum entirely dedicated to the second half of the 19th century dates back to 1977. It took place in the ancient Orsay railway station built by Victor Laloux and inaugurated in 1900. Rehabilitation of the site was entrusted to the ACT-Architecture group, and the museum opened its doors on the 9th of December 1986.

les stars de leur époque, tandis que Manet et les impressionnistes essuyèrent des critiques acerbes.

Le projet de créer un musée entièrement dédié à la seconde moitié du XIXᵉ siècle, remonte à 1977. Il prendra place dans l'ancienne gare d'Orsay, construite par Victor Laloux, inaugurée en 1900. La réhabilitation du lieu est confiée au groupe ACT-Architecture, et le musée d'Orsay ouvre ses portes le 9 décembre 1986.

Claude Monet considérait les gares comme des « cathédrales de la modernité ». Orsay lui a donné

oder unbewusst orientieren sich die Künstler an ihren Vorgängern, eignen sich deren Lehren an oder lehnen sie ab. Des Weiteren waren die akademischen Maler (Cabanel, Gérôme …) die Stars ihrer Zeit, während Manet und die Impressionisten heftige Kritik einstecken mussten.

Das Projekt, ein vollständig der zweiten Hälfte des 19. Jahrhunderts gewidmetes Museum zu schaffen, geht auf das Jahr 1977 zurück. Es wird seinen Platz im ehemaligen, von Victor Laloux erbauten und im Jahr 1900 eingeweihten Bahnhof

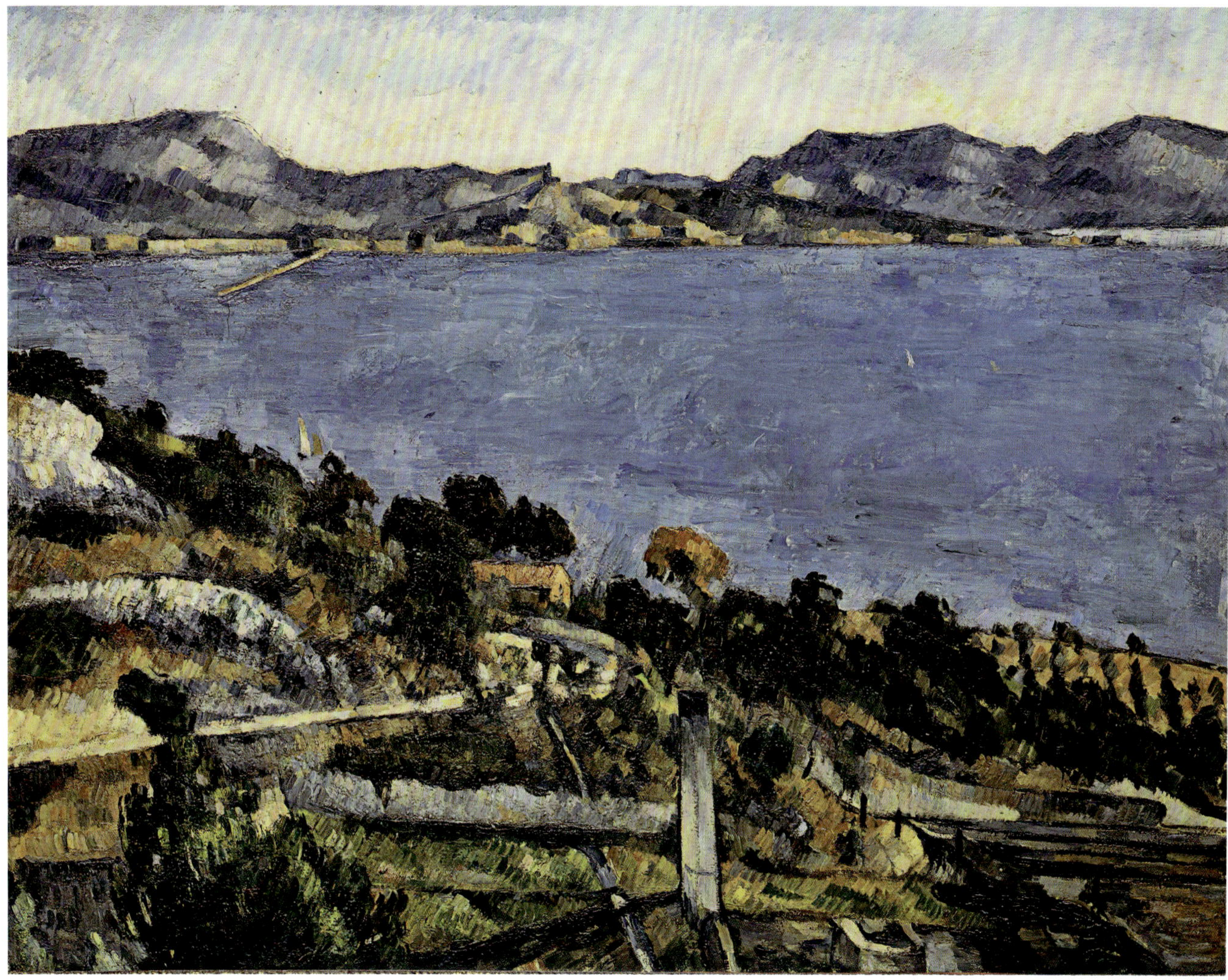

Paul Cézanne (1839–1906)

The Gulf of Marseille seen from L'Estaque
Le Golfe de Marseille vu de l'Estaque

Der Golf von Marseille, von L'Estaque aus gesehen
El golfo de Marsella visto desde l'Estaque

Il golfo di Marsiglia visto dall'Estaque
De Golf van Marseille gezien vanaf L'Estaque

c. 1878–1879, Oil on canvas/Huile sur toile, 59,5 × 73 cm

rechazan. De esta manera, los pintores académicos (Cabanel, Gérôme…) fueron las estrellas de su época, mientras que Manet y los impresionistas se enfrentaban a duras críticas.

El proyecto de crear un museo completamente dedicado a la segunda mitad del siglo XIX se remonta a 1977. Se llevó a cabo en la antigua estación de Orsay construida por Victor Laloux, inaugurada en 1900. La rehabilitación del lugar se confió al Grupo ACT-Architecture, y el museo de Orsay abría sus puertas el 9 de diciembre de 1986.

i pittori accademici (Cabanel, Gérôme…) furono quelli più apprezzati al loro tempo, mentre Manet e gli impressionisti ricevettero dure critiche.

Il progetto di creare un museo interamente dedicato alla seconda metà del XIX risale al 1977, quando si decise che esso avrebbe avuto sede presso l'ex stazione ferroviaria d'Orsay costruita da Victor Laloux e inaugurata nel 1900. La riabilitazione dell'edificio fu affidata al gruppo ACT-Architecture, e il museo d'Orsay aprì le sue porte il 9 dicembre 1986.

verwerpen ze die. En op de tweede plaats omdat academische schilders (Cabanel, Gérôme…) in hun tijd beroemdheden waren, terwijl Manet en de impressionisten scherp werden bekritiseerd.

Het plan voor een kunstmuseum dat volledig aan de tweede helft van de 19e eeuw is gewijd, dateert van 1977. Het voormalige treinstation Gare d'Orsay dat door Victor Laloux gebouwd en in 1900 in gebruik werd genomen, zal het museum gaan huisvesten. Na de verbouwing door ACT-Architecture opent het Musée d'Orsay op 9 december 1986 zijn deuren.

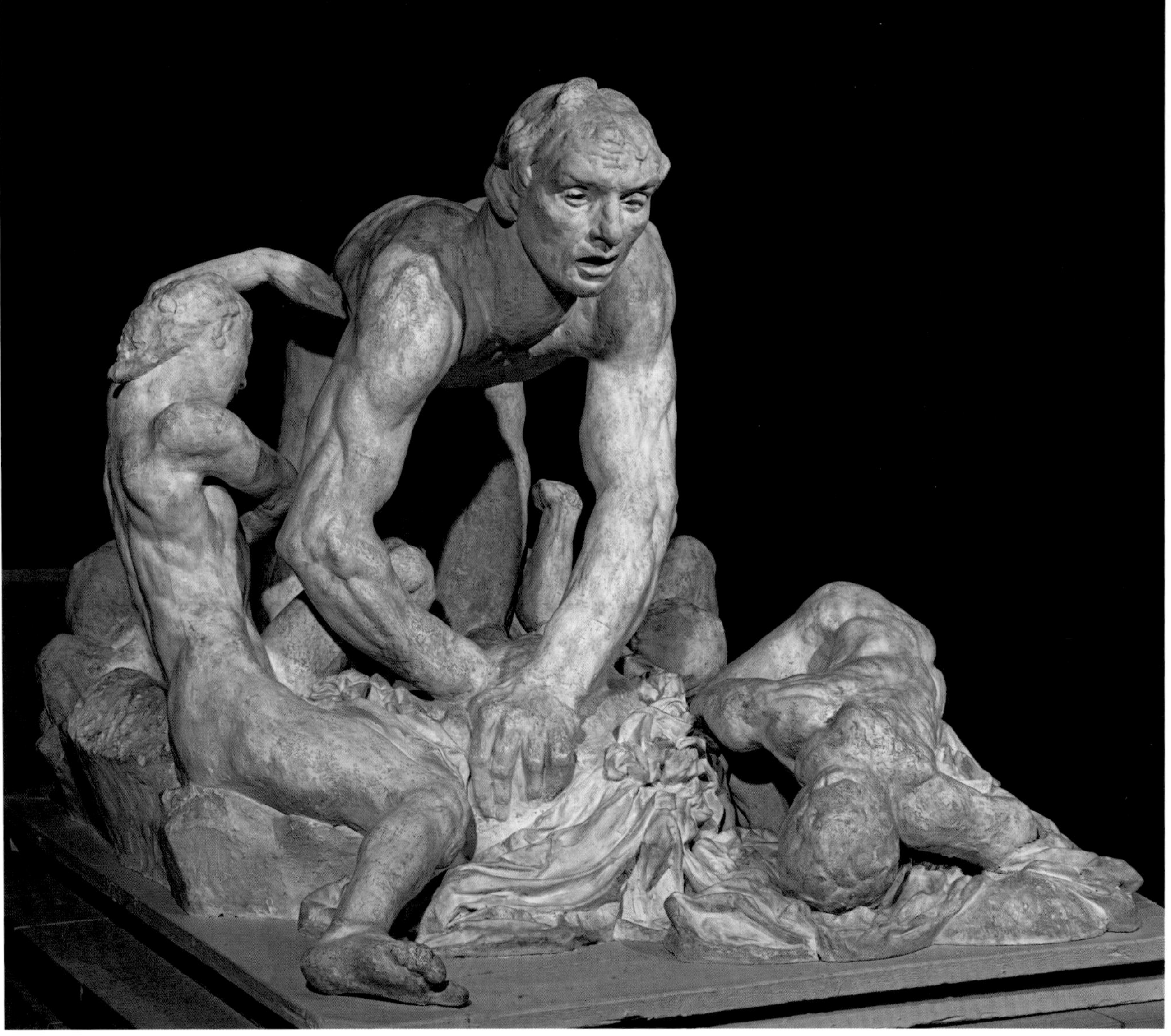

Auguste Rodin (1840–1917)

Ugolino

Ugolin

Ugolino und seine Söhne

Ugolino y sus hijos

Il Conte Ugolino

Ugolin

c. 1882–1906, Plaster, gypsum, stone/Plâtre, gypse, pierre, 139,2 × 173 × 278,6 cm

Claude Monet considered railway stations to be "cathedrals of modernity". Orsay justified this by sheltering the masterpieces of this pivotal and fertile period which tossed conventions and certitudes out to the wind.

raison, en abritant les chefs-d'œuvre de cette période charnière et si féconde qui fit voler en éclat conventions et certitudes.

von Orsay finden. Mit der Umgestaltung des Ortes wird die Gruppe ACT-Architecture beauftragt und das Musée d'Orsay öffnet schließlich am 9. Dezember 1986 seine Pforten.

Claude Monet betrachtete Bahnhöfe als „Kathedralen der Modernität". Orsay hat ihm Recht gegeben, indem es unter seinem Dach die Meisterwerke dieser so fruchtbaren Übergangsperiode ausstellt, in der Konventionen und Gewissheiten zerbrachen.

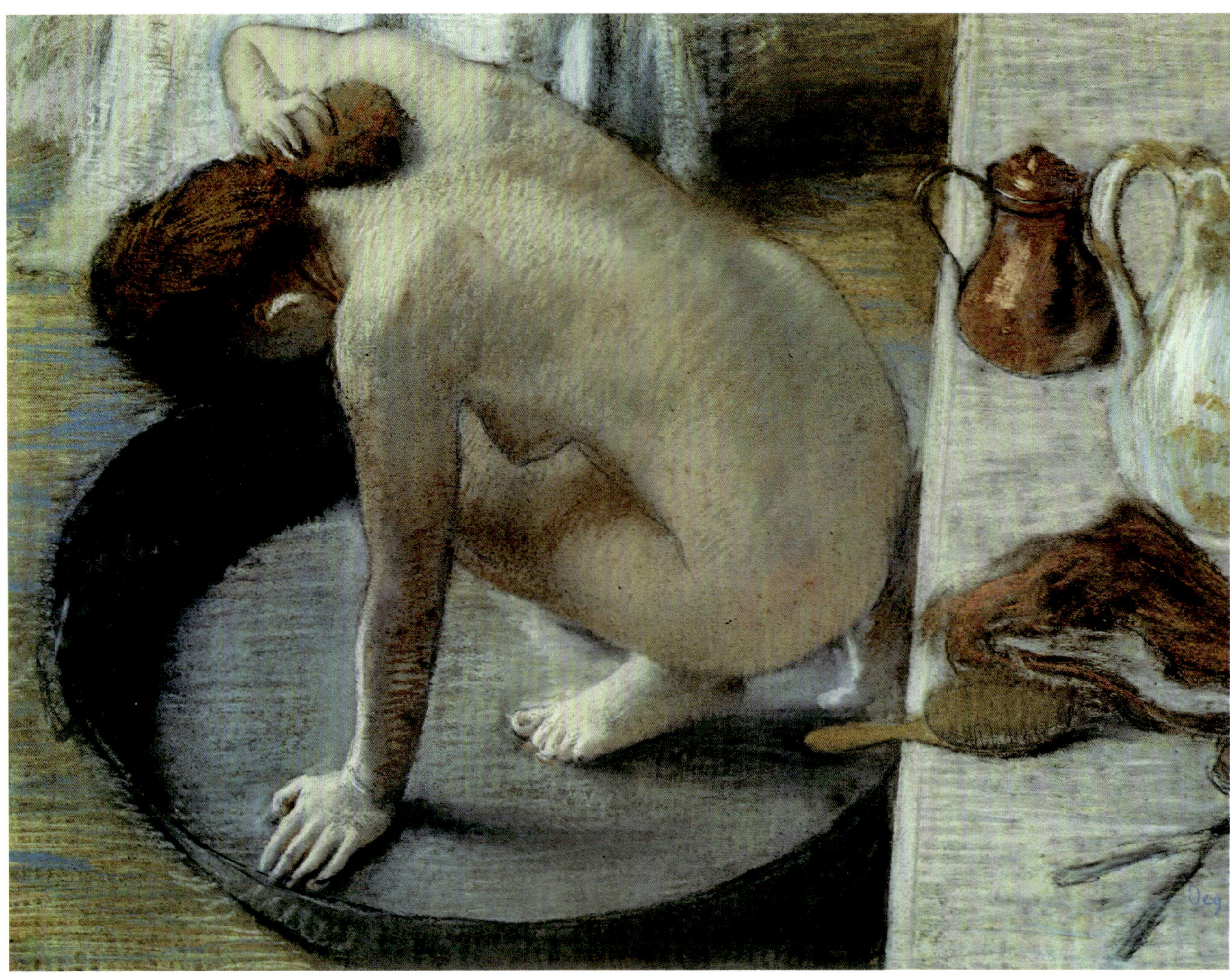

Claude Monet consideraba las estaciones como "catedrales de la modernidad". Orsay le dio la razón, al albergar obras maestras de este periodo crucial y tan fructífero que se hizo añicos las convenciones y certezas.

Claude Monet riteneva che le stazioni ferroviarie fossero "cattedrali della modernità". Orsay gli ha dato ragione, ospitando i capolavori di questo periodo cruciale e così fruttuoso che mandò in frantumi convenzioni e certezze.

Voor Claude Monet waren treinstations 'kathedralen van de moderniteit'. Door onderdak te bieden aan de meesterwerken uit deze zeer vruchtbare periode die een keerpunt markeerde en waarin conventies en zekerheden verdwenen, stelt het Musée d'Orsay hem in het gelijk.

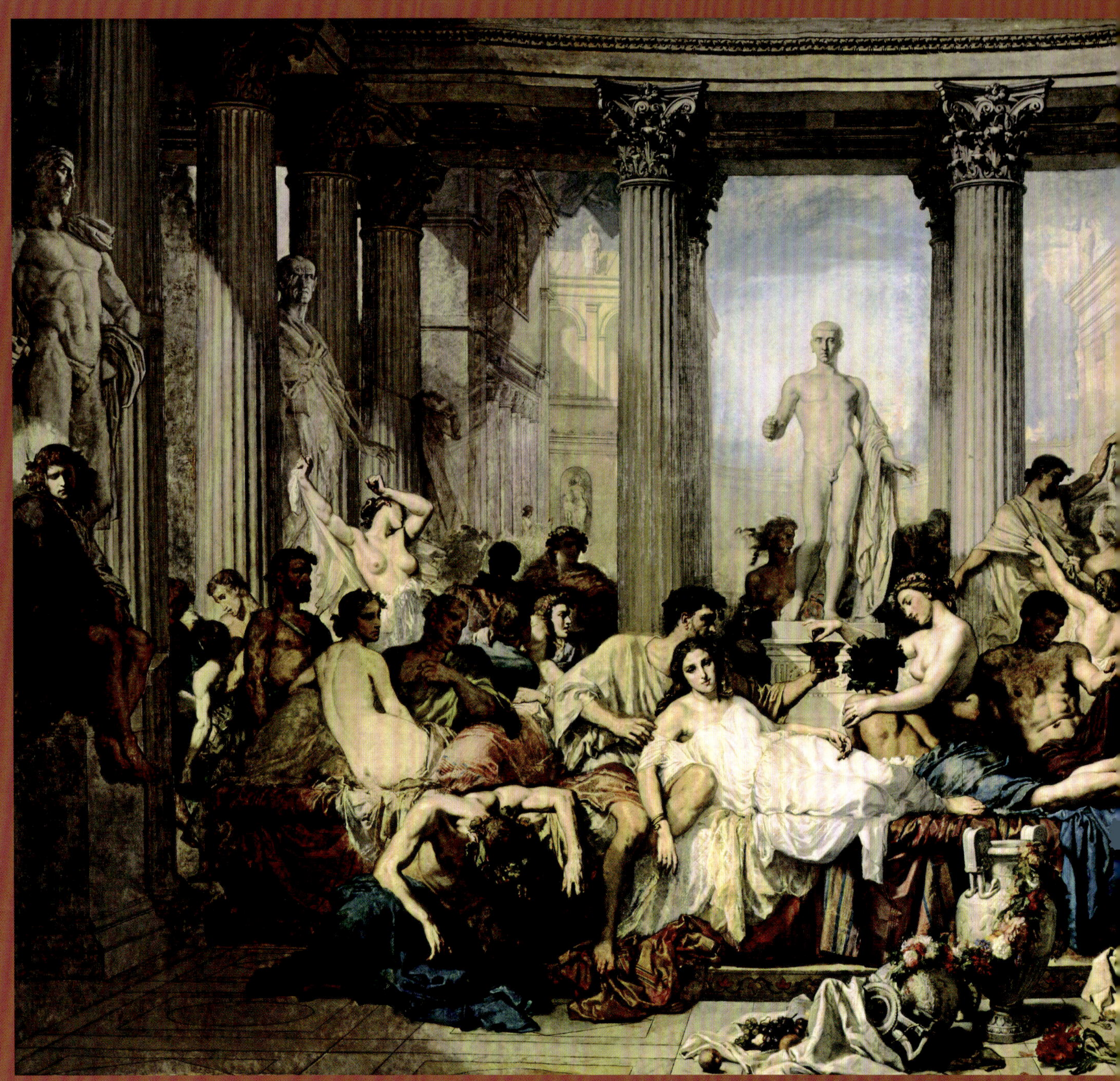

Thomas Couture (1815–1879)

Romans of the Decadence

Romains de la décadence

Die Römer der Verfallszeit

1847, Oil on canvas/Huile sur toile, 472 × 772 cm

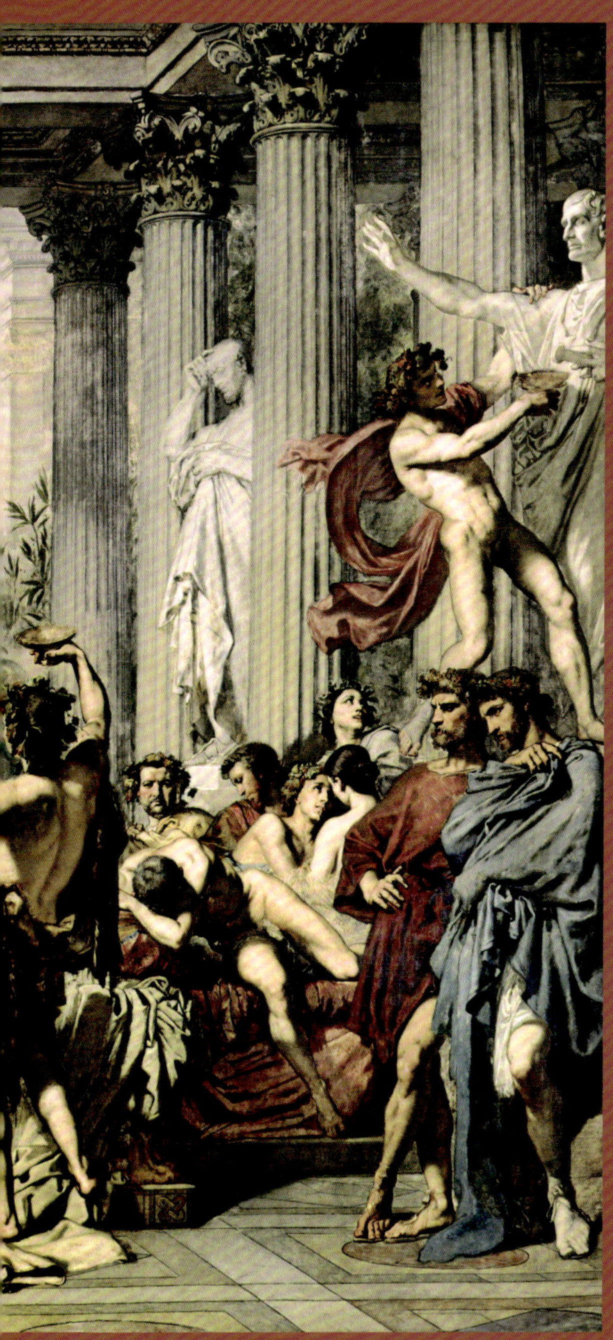

Academicism

During the second half of the 19th century, artistic life was governed by the Annual Salon, fond of historical paintings, mythological narratives, portraits and allegorical nudes. Cabanel Bouguereau or Gérôme are at the time esteemed for their sense of staging and mastery of technique which enabled them to play with the truth by conveying the illusion of perfect realism.

Académisme

Dans la seconde moitié du XIXe siècle, la vie artistique est régie par le Salon annuel, friand de peintures d'histoire, de récits mythologiques, de portraits et de nus allégoriques. Cabanel, Bouguereau ou Gérôme sont alors appréciés pour leur sens de la mise en scène et leur maîtrise technique qui leur permettait de jouer avec la vérité, en donnant l'illusion d'un réalisme parfait.

Akademismus

Während der zweiten Hälfte des 19. Jahrhunderts wird das künstlerische Leben von dem jährlich stattfindenden Salon bestimmt, wo man gierig ist nach historischen Gemälden, mythologischen Erzählungen, Porträts und allegorischen Aktdarstellungen. Cabanel, Bouguereau und Gérôme werden für ihren Gestaltungssinn und ihr fachliches Können geschätzt, das es ihnen erlaubt, mit der Wahrheit zu spielen, indem sie die Illusion eines perfekten Realismus erzeugen.

Academicismo

En la segunda mitad del siglo XIX la vida artística se rige por el Salón anual, aficionado a los cuadros de historia, de historias mitológicas, retratos y desnudos alegóricos. Cabanel, Bouguereau o Gérôme eran muy apreciados por su sentido de la puesta en escena y dominio de la técnica que les permitía jugar con la verdad, dando la ilusión de un realismo perfecto.

Accademismo

Nella seconda metà del XIX secolo la vita artistica era governata dal Salón annuale, amante dei dipinti storici, delle storie mitologiche, dei ritratti e dei nudi allegorici. Cabanel, Bouguereau e Gérôme erano a quel tempo molto apprezzati per il loro senso della composizione e la loro maestria tecnica, che permetteva loro di giocare con la verità creando l'illusione di un realismo perfetto.

Academisme

In de tweede helft van de 19de eeuw wordt het kunstleven beheerst door de jaarlijkse Salon met zijn vele historiestukken, mythologische verhalen, portretten en allegorische naakten. Cabanel, Bouguereau en Gérôme worden gewaardeerd om hun gevoel voor compositie en hun technisch meesterschap waardoor ze met de werkelijkheid konden spelen en de illusie van perfect realisme creëerden.

Romanos de la decadencia   I Romani della decadenza   Romeinen in tijd van verval

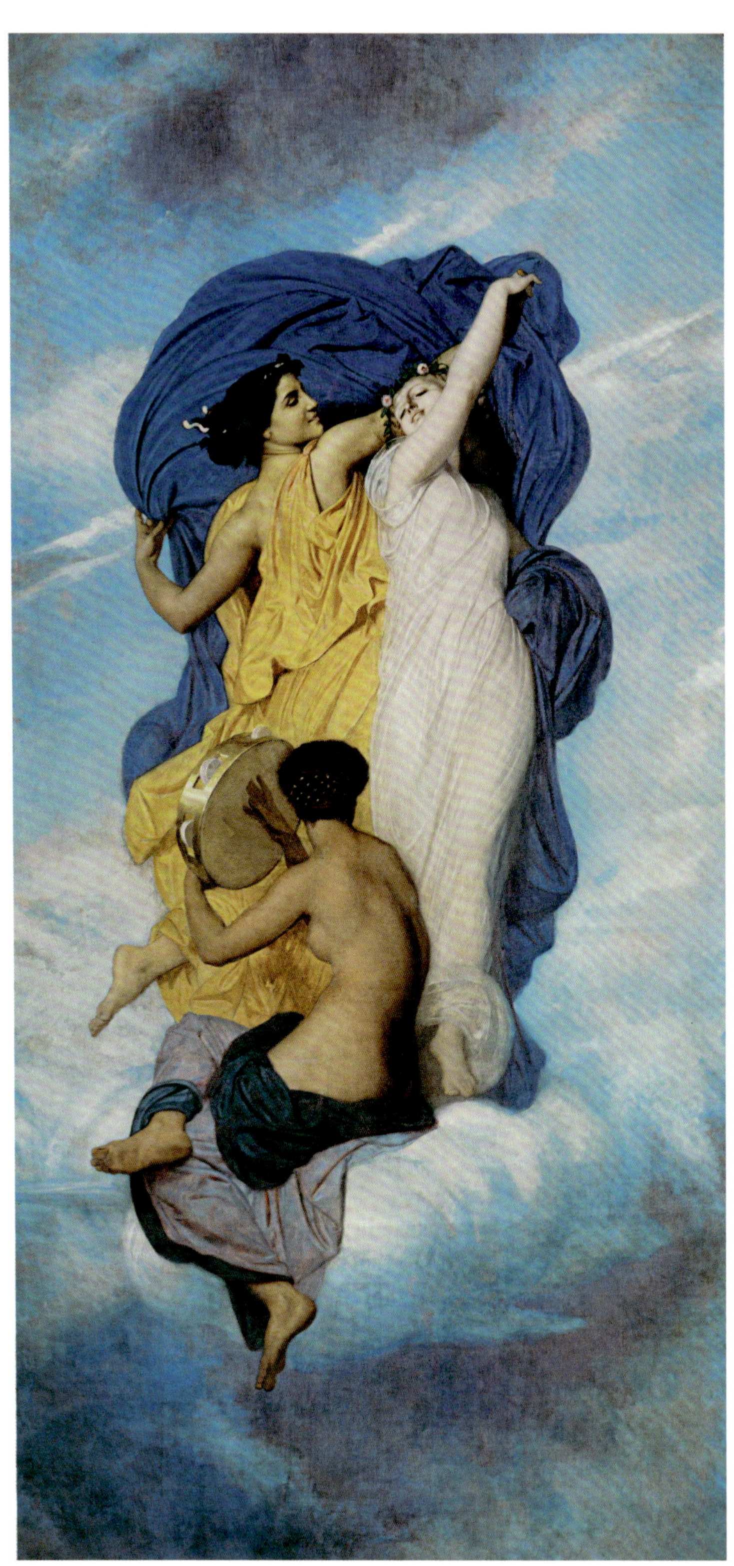

William Bouguereau
(1825–1905)

The Dance

La Danse

Der Tanz

La Danza

La Danza

De dans

1856, Oil and wax on canvas
with cut-off corners/Huile
et cire sur toile aux coins
abattus, 366 × 181 cm

William Bouguereau
(1825–1905)

The Birth of Venus

La Naissance de Vénus

Die Geburt der Venus

El nacimiento de Venus

La nascita di Venere

De geboorte de Venus

1879, Oil on canvas/Huile
sur toile, 300 × 215 cm

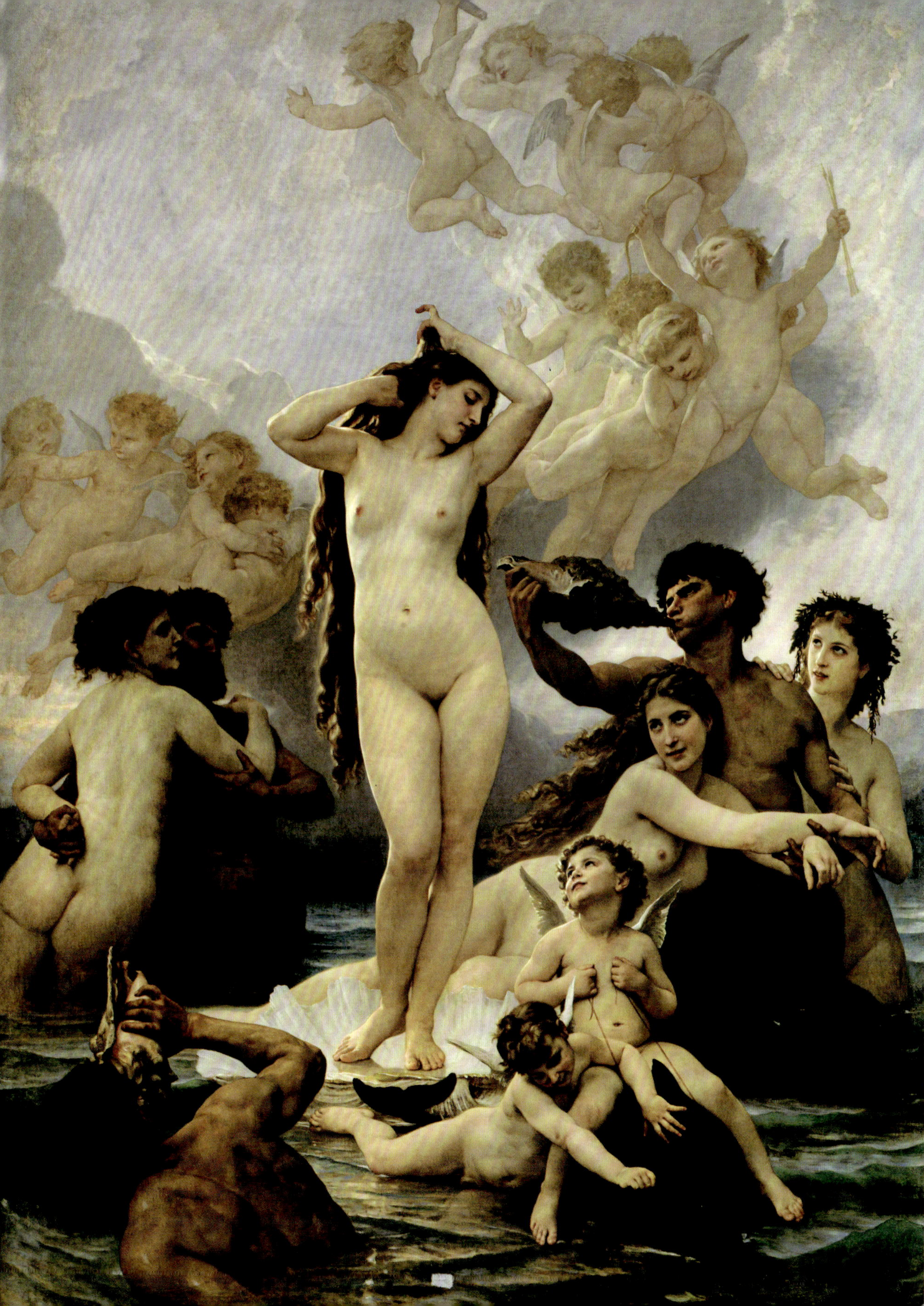

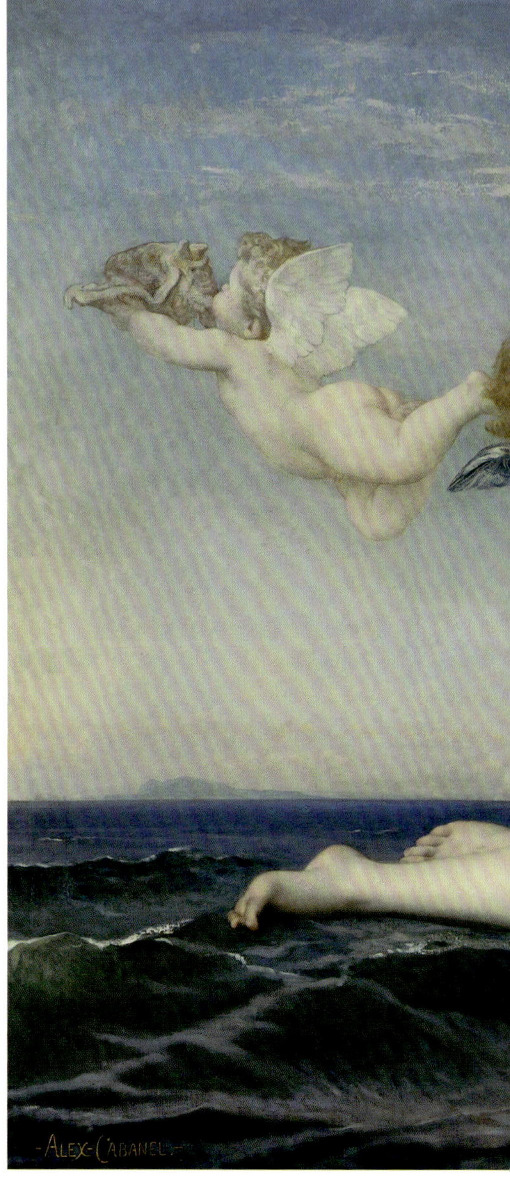

Like that of William Bouguereau, *The Birth of Venus* from the master of academicism Alexandre Cabanel is a true exponent of Pompier art. This nude, strangely laid on the waves and accompanied by cherubs, triumphed in the salon of 1863 and counts among the acquisitions of Napoleon III.

À l'instar de celle de William Bouguereau, *La Naissance de Vénus* du maître de l'académisme Alexandre Cabanel est un véritable manifeste de l'art pompier. Ce nu allégorique, étrangement posé sur les flots et survolé d'angelots, triomphe au salon de 1863 et compte parmi les acquisitions de Napoléon III.

Die Geburt der Venus vom Meister des Akademismus Alexandre Cabanel ist, genauso wie die *Venus* von William Bouguereau, ein wahrhaftes Manifest der *Art Pompier* (Feuerwehrmann-Kunst). Dieser allegorische Akt, der in seltsamer Weise auf den Wellen positioniert ist und über dem Engelchen schweben, feiert auf dem Salon von 1863 Triumphe und zählt zu den Erwerbungen von Napoleon III.

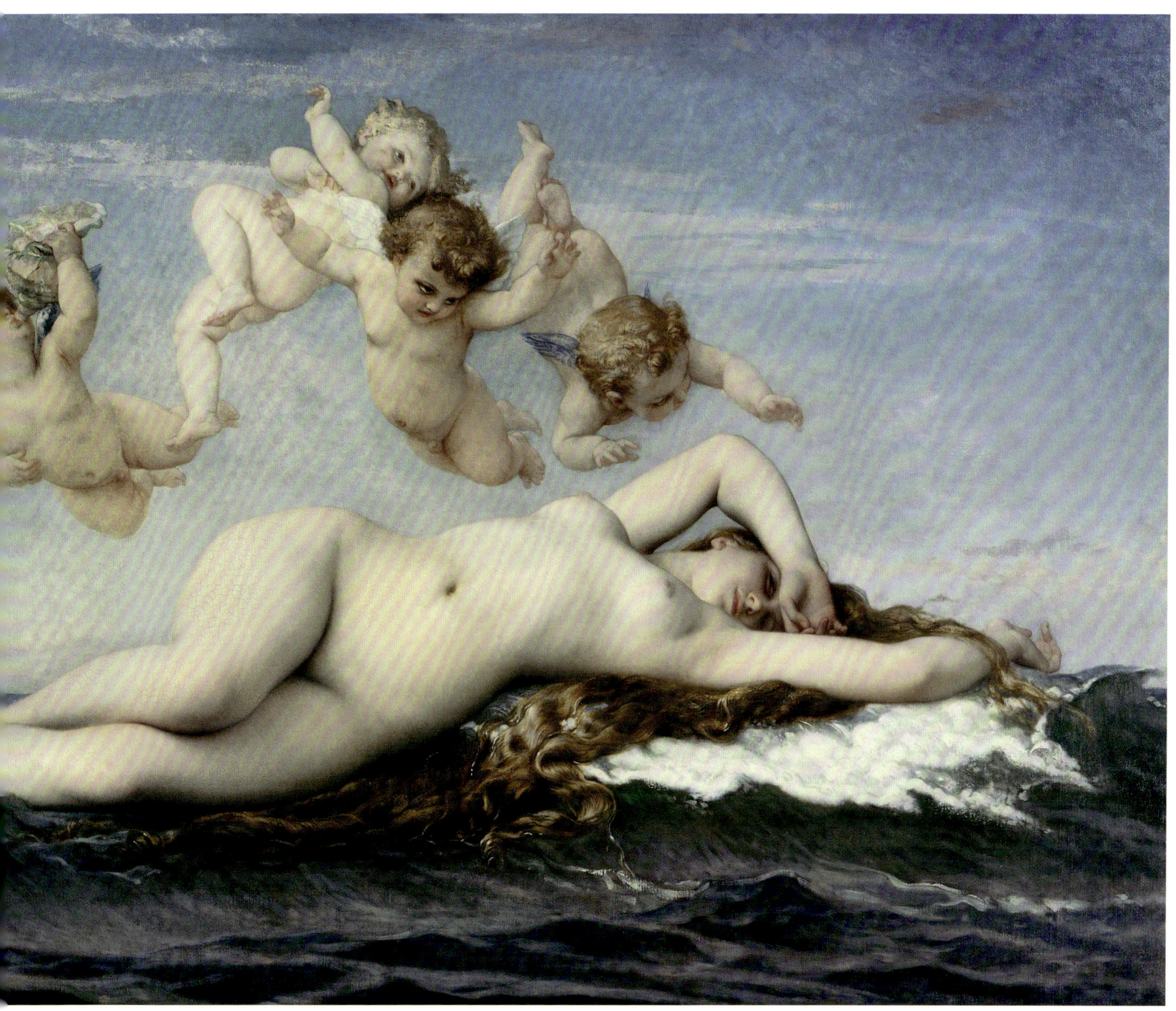

Al igual que el de William Bouguereau, *El nacimiento de Venus* del maestro del academicismo, Alexandre Cabanel, es un verdadero manifiesto del *art pompier*. Este desnudo alegórico, extrañamente colocado en el agua y sobrevolado por querubines, triunfó en el Salón de 1863 y se cuenta entre las adquisiciones de Napoléon III.

Analogamente a quella di William Bouguereau, *La nascita di Venere* di Alexandre Cabanel, maestro dell'Accademismo, è un vero e proprio manifesto dell'Art pompier. Questo nudo allegorico, curiosamente adagiato sulle acque e sorvolato da cherubini, ebbe un enorme successo al Salon del 1863 e fu una delle opere acquistate da Napoleone III.

Net als de *Venus* van William Bouguereau is *De Geboorte van Venus* van Alexandre Cabanel, de meester van het academisme, een illustratief voorbeeld van academische kunst. Dit allegorische naakt, dat merkwaardig op de schuimende golven ligt en waarboven engeltjes zweven, wordt juichend ontvangen op de Salon van 1863 en wordt – naast ander werk – door Napoleon III aangekocht.

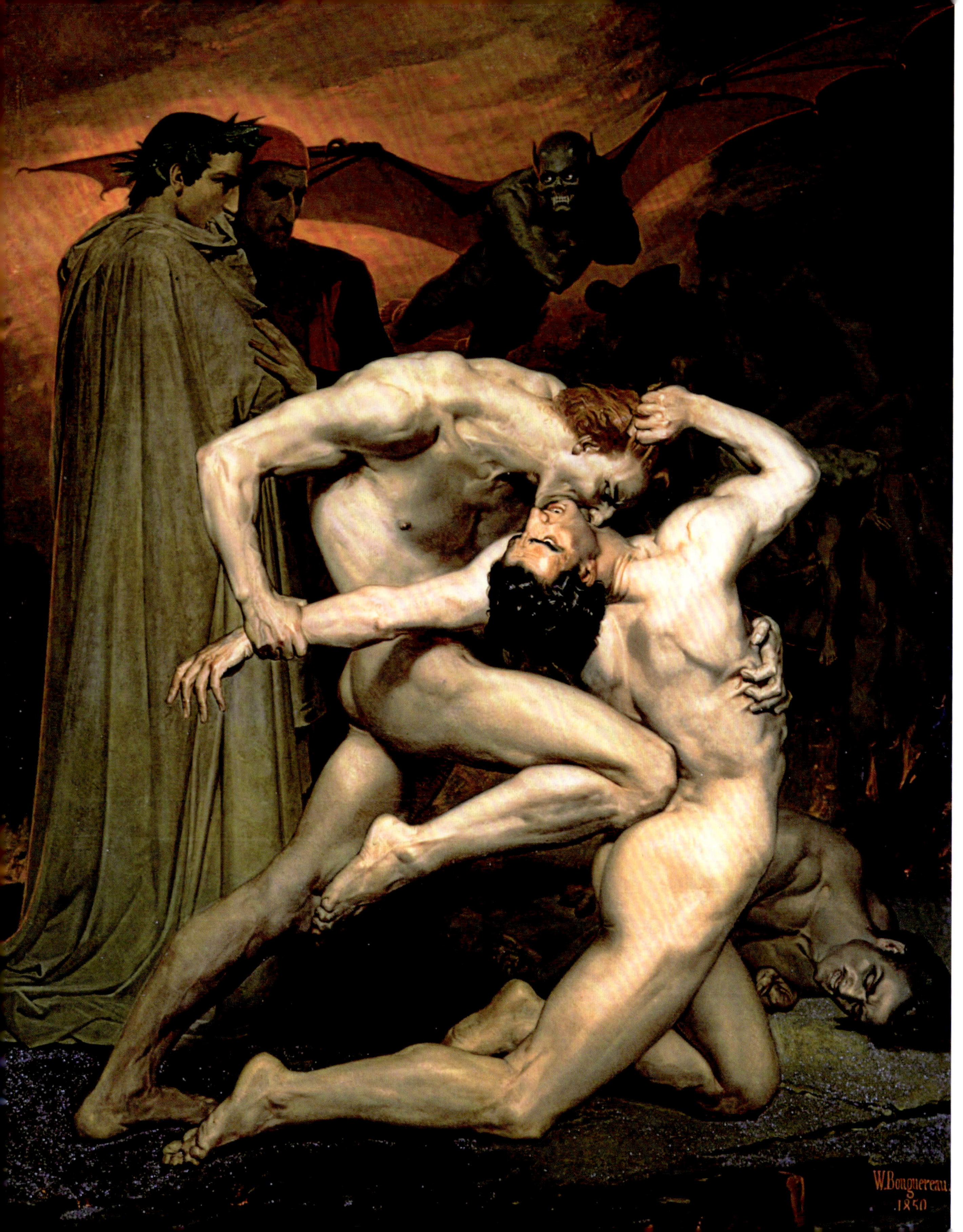

W.Bouguereau
1850

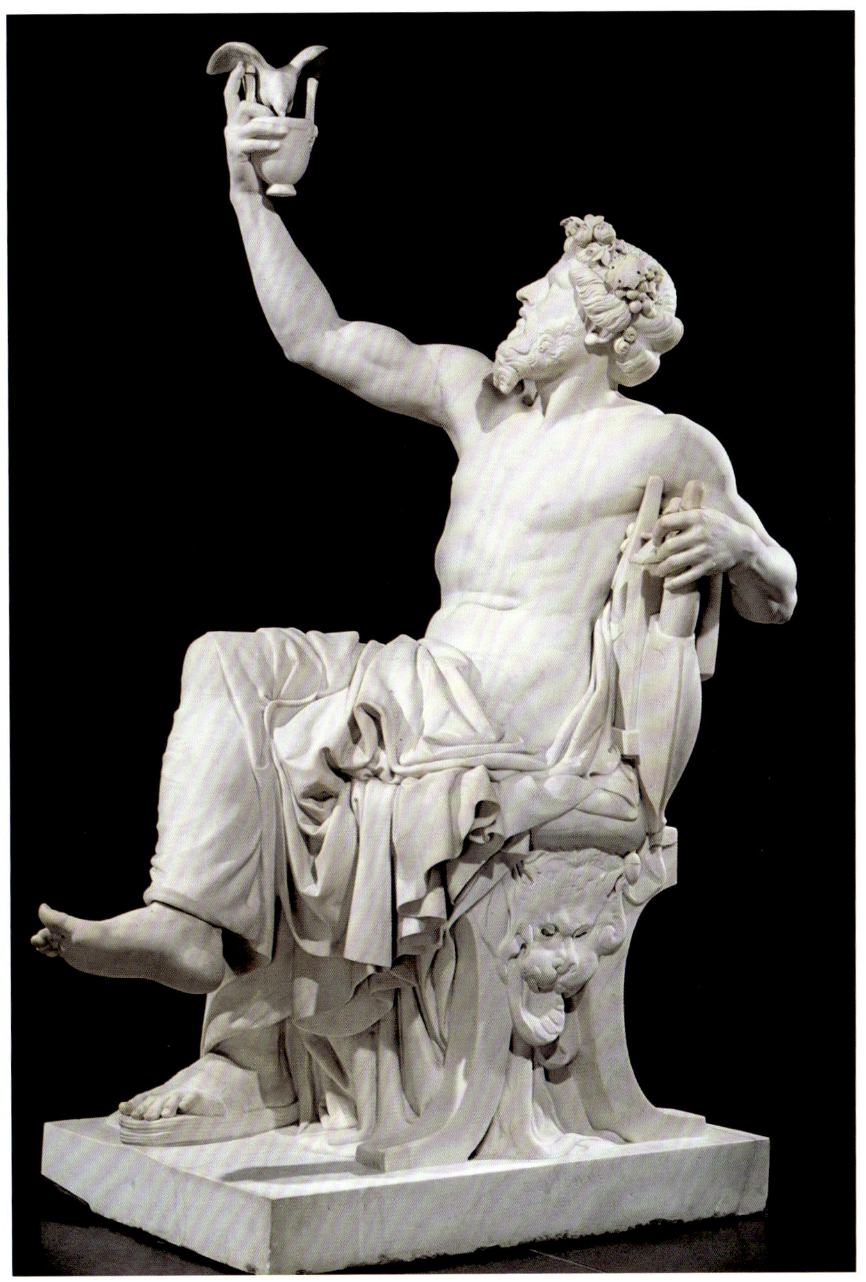

William Bouguereau (1825–1905)

Dante and Virgil

Dante et Virgile

Dante und Virgile

Dante y Virgilio en el infierno

Dante e Virgilio

Dante en Virgilius

1850, Oil on canvas/Huile sur toile, 280,5 × 225,3 cm

Guillaume Eugène (1822–1905)

Anacreon

Anacréon

Anakreon

Anacreonte

Anacreonte

Anacreon

1851, Marble/Marbre, 185 × 80 × 122 cm

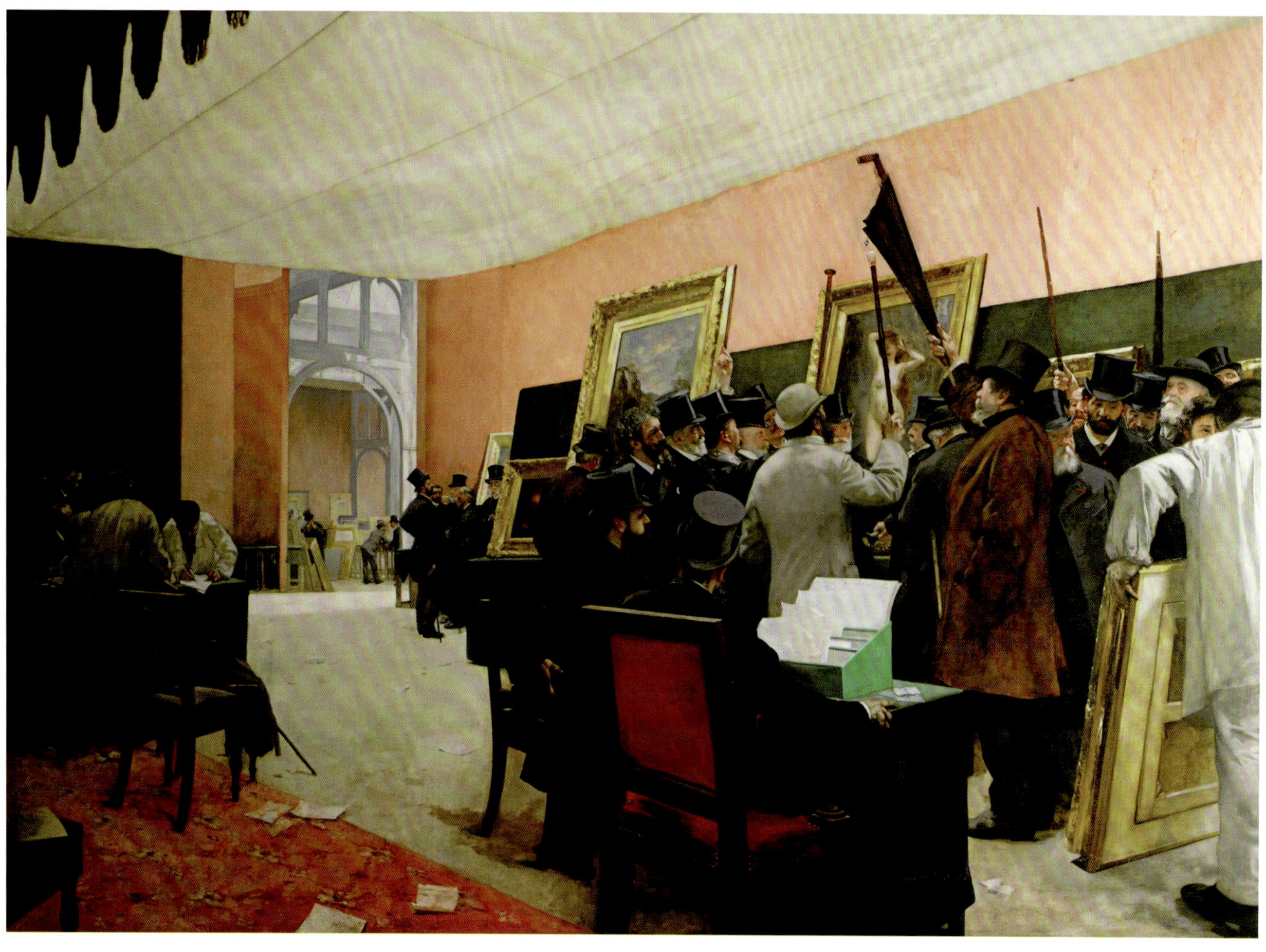

Henri Gervex (1852–1929)

A session of the painting jury
Une séance du jury de peinture
Die Sitzung der Jury für Malerei
Una reunión del jurado de pintura
Seduta della Giuria di pittura
Een zitting van de schilderijenjury
c. 1885, Oil on canvas/Huile sur toile, 300 × 419,5 cm

Alexandre Cabanel (1823–1889)

Countess Keller
La Comtesse de Keller
Komtesse de Keller
La condesa de Keller
La contessa di Keller
Gravin Keller
1873, Oil on canvas/Huile sur toile, 99 × 77 cm

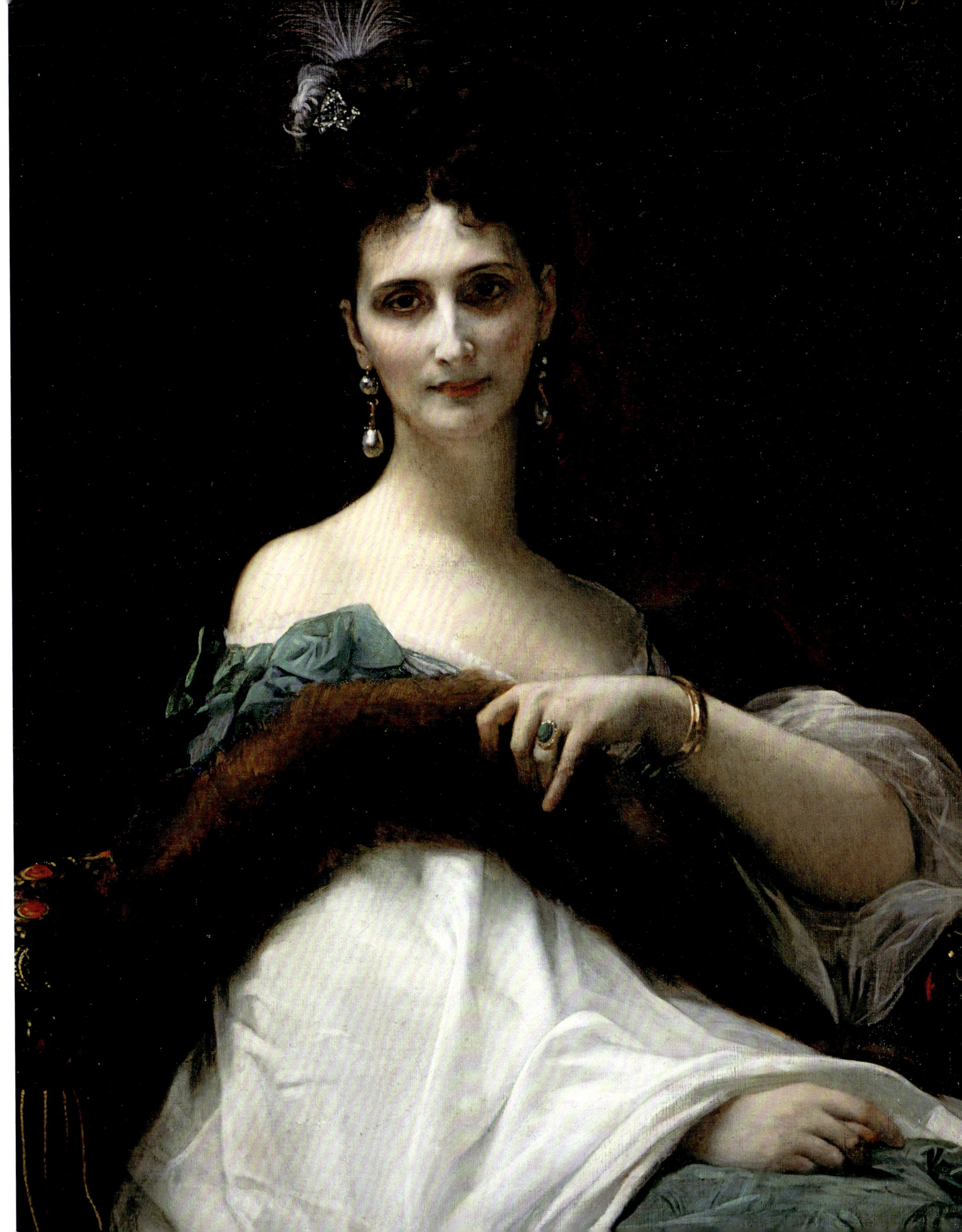

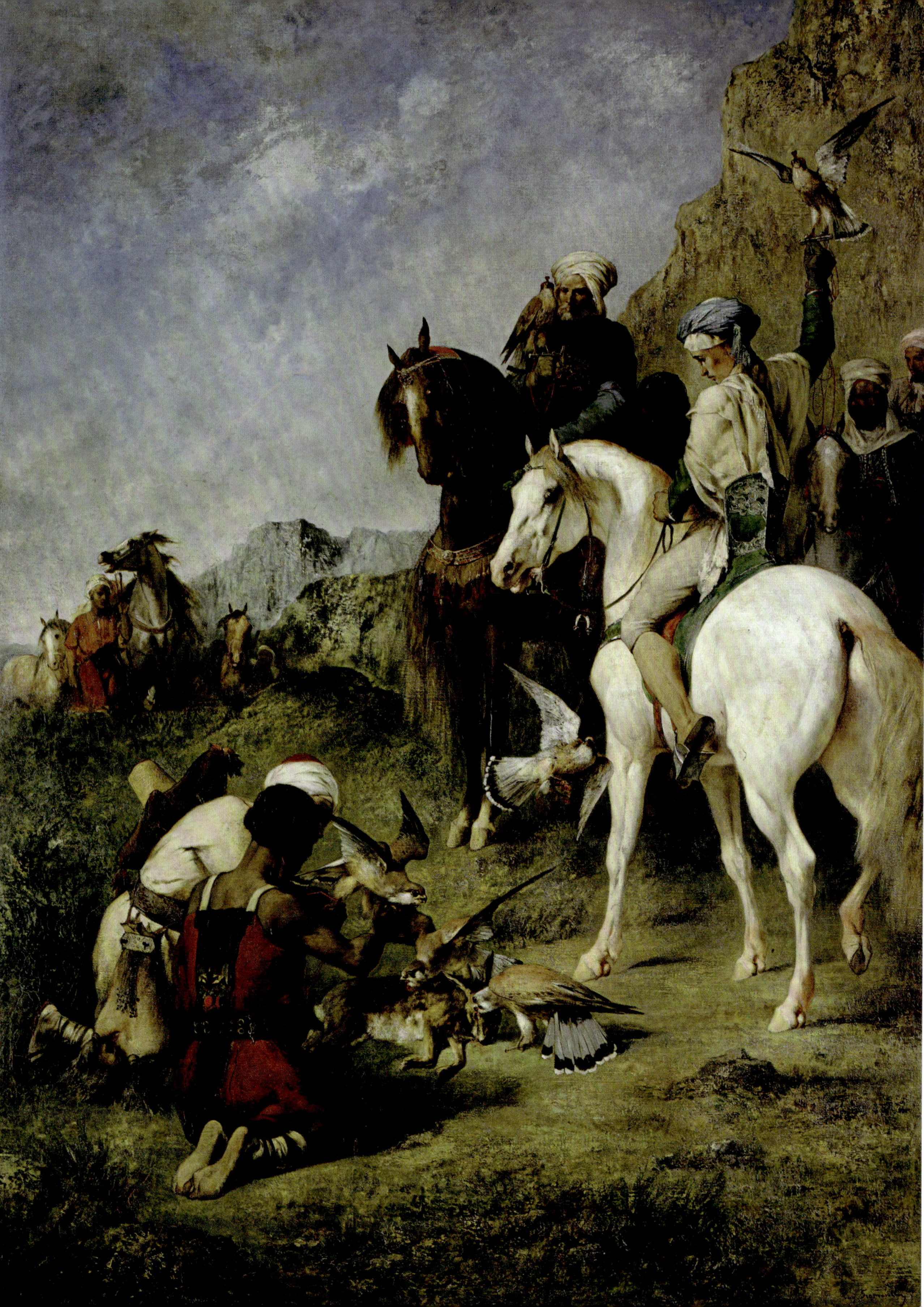

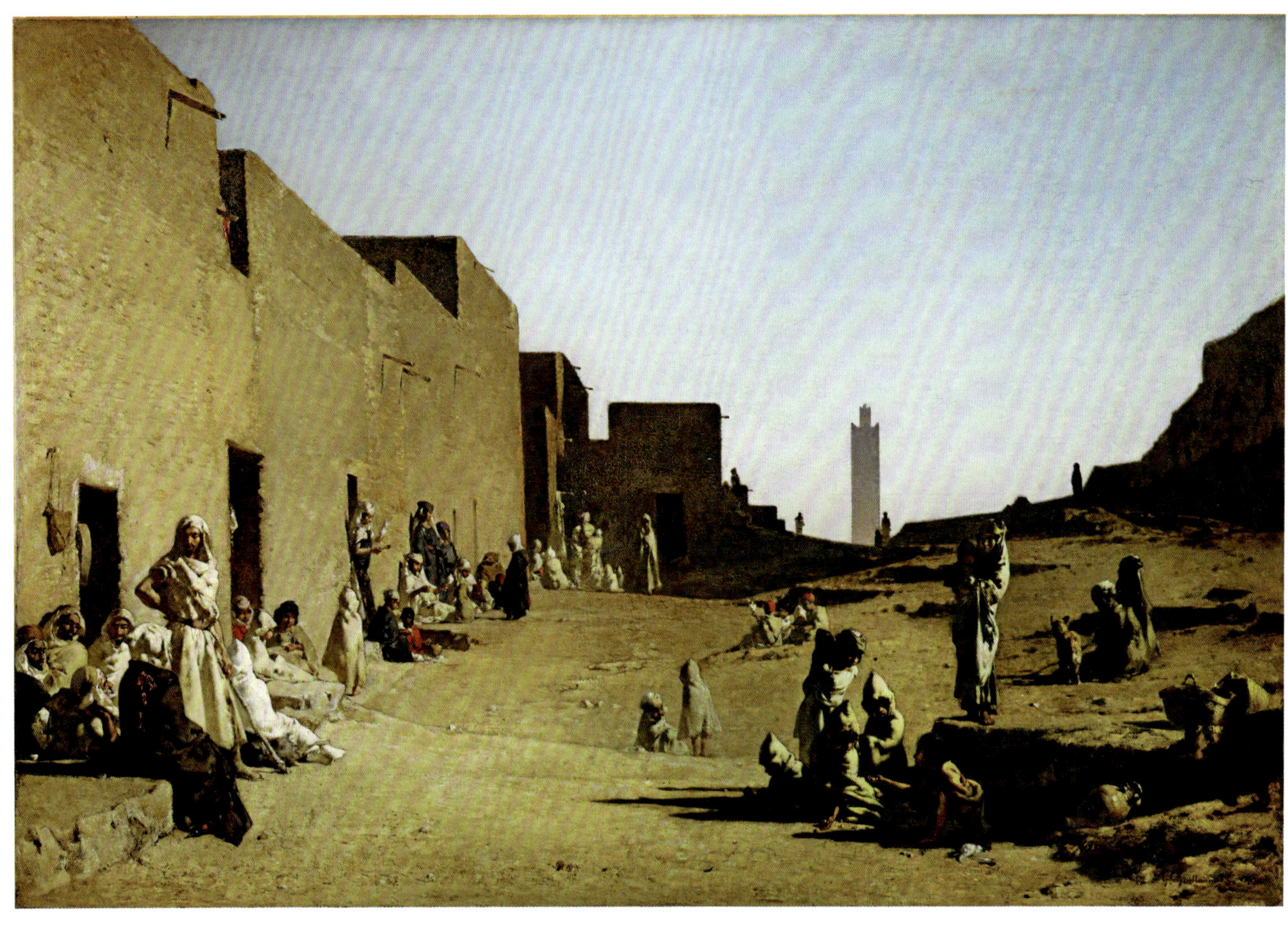

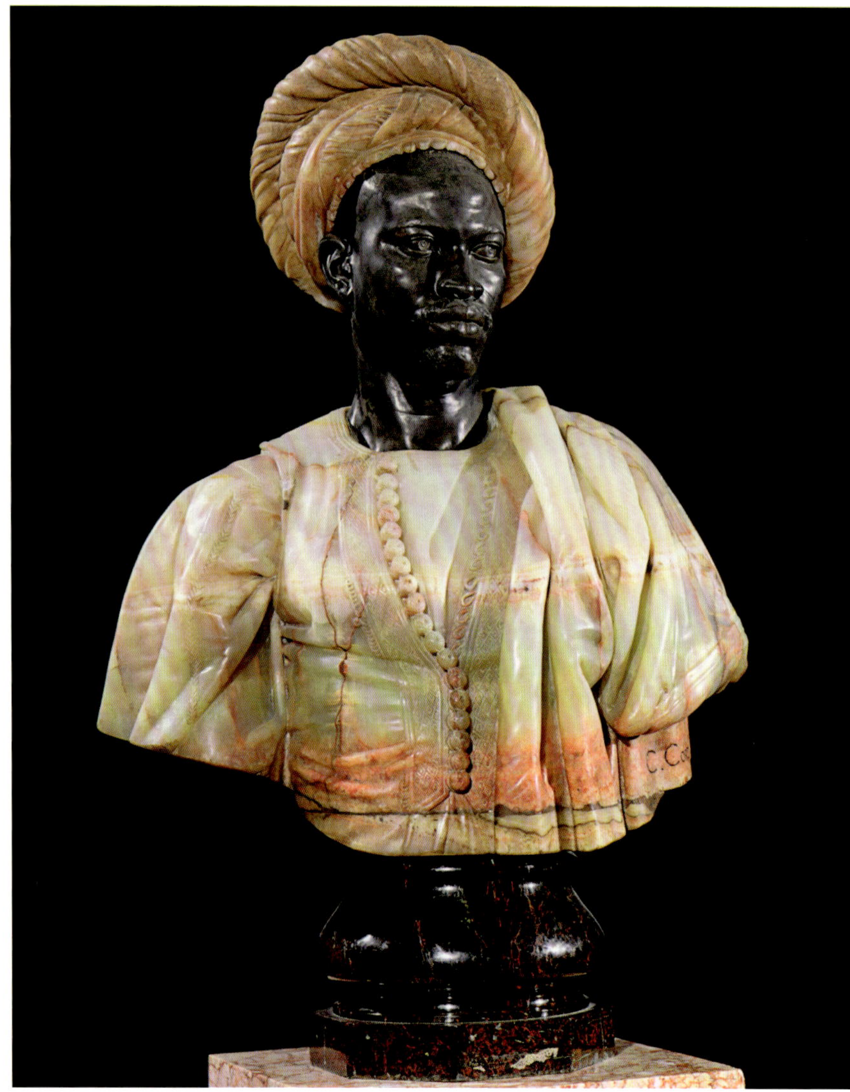

*Charles Henri Joseph
Cordier (1827–1905)*

Negro of the Sudan

Nègre du Soudan

Neger aus dem Sudan

Negro de Sudán

Negro del Sudan

Neger uit Soedan

c. 1856–1857, Bronze and
onyx bust on a pedestal
of Vosges porphyry/Buste
en bronze et onyx sur
piédouche en porphyre des
Vosges, 96 × 66 × 36 cm

*Léon-Auguste-Adolphe
Belly (1827–1877)*

Pilgrims Going to Mecca

Pèlerins allant à La Mecque

Pilgerkarawane auf dem
Weg nach Mekka

Peregrinos yendo
a La Meca

Pellegrini diretti
alla Mecca

Pelgrims op weg
naar Mekka

1861, Oil on canvas/Huile
sur toile, 160 × 242 cm

Charles Cordier devoted most of his career to the
study of the human figure. Through his ethnographic
busts (*Negro of the Sudan, Jew of Algiers, Black
Moor…*), he aims to "capture the different human
types at the moment of merging into one and
the same people". These polychrome figures
simultaneously portray the subject's visage and the
specifics of his costume. The objective? To show
the differences while extolling respect for the other
through aesthetically refined and very decorative,
seductive humanistic works.

Charles Cordier a consacré l'essentiel de sa
carrière à l'étude de la figure humaine. Par ses
bustes ethnographiques (*Nègre du Soudan, Juive
d'Alger, Mauresque noire…*), il entend « fixer les
différents types humains qui sont au moment de
se fondre dans un seul et même peuple ». Ces
figures polychromes rendent à la fois compte de
la physionomie du modèle et des spécificités de
son costume. L'objectif ? Montrer les différences
en prônant le respect de l'autre, par des œuvres
humanistes séduisantes, à l'esthétique soignée et
très décorative.

Charles Cordier widmete seine Karriere im
Wesentlichen dem Studium der menschlichen
Gestalt. Mit seinen ethnografischen Büsten (*Neger
aus dem Sudan, Jüdin aus Algier, Schwarze Maurin…*)
möchte er „die verschiedenen menschlichen
Typen, die im Begriff sind, in einem einzigen Volk
zu verschmelzen, festhalten". Seine polychromen
Figuren zeigen zugleich das Erscheinungsbild des
Modells und die Besonderheiten seiner Bekleidung.
Das Ziel? Durch reizvolle humanistische Werke
von gepflegter und dekorativer Ästhetik die
Unterschiede aufzeigen und dabei den Respekt des
Anderen preisen.

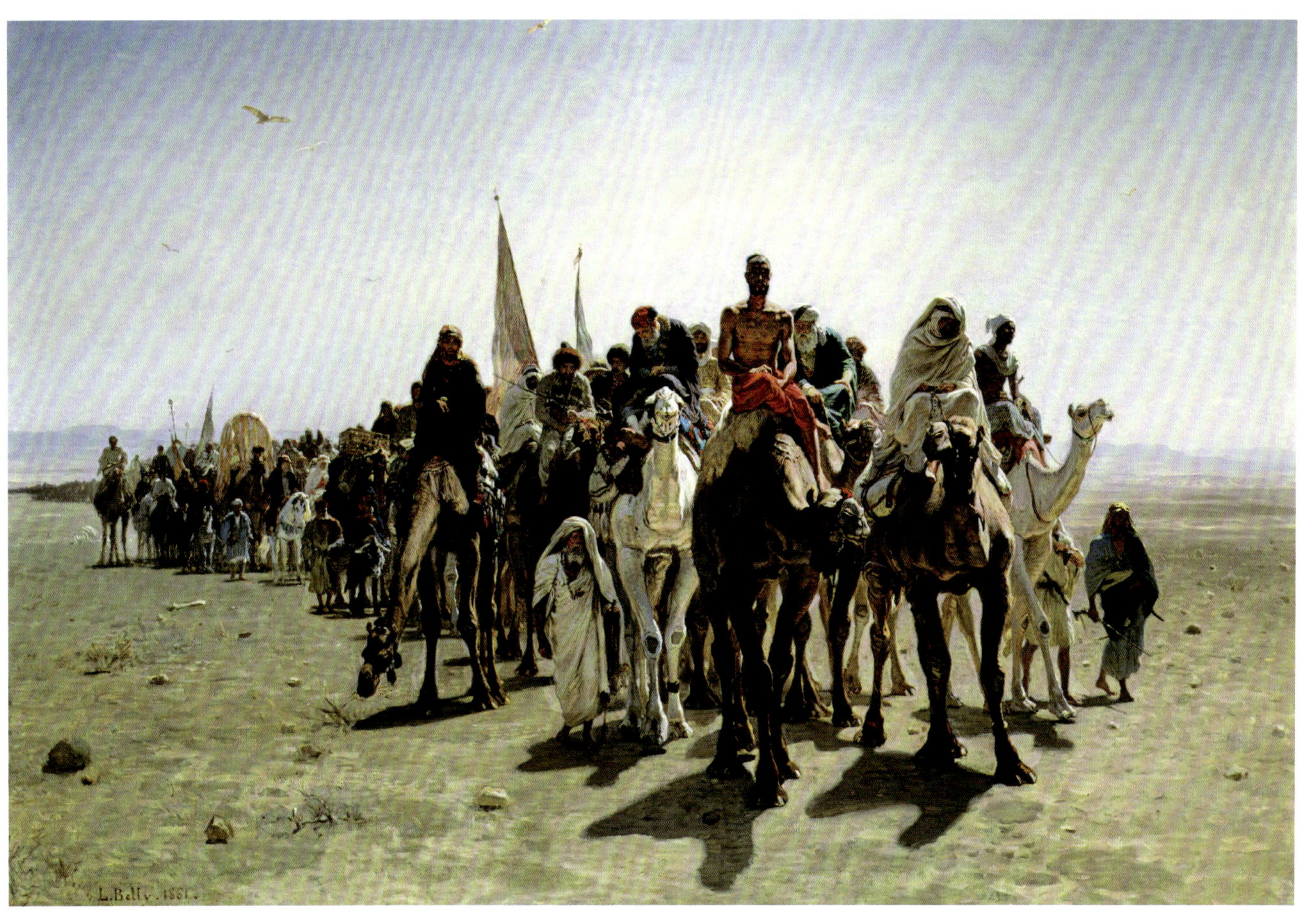

Charles Cordier consagró la mayor parte de su carrera al estudio de la figura humana. Con sus bustos etnográficos (*Negro del Sudán*, *La judía de Argel*, *Busto de árabe…*), tiene la intención de "fijar los diferentes tipos humanos que se encuentran fundidos en un solo pueblo". Estas figuras polícromas toman en consideración tanto el aspecto del modelo como los detalles de su traje. ¿El objetivo? Mostrar las diferencias promoviendo el respeto por el otro, mediante las obras humanísticas seductoras, a la estética soñada y muy decorativa.

Charles Cordier dedicò gran parte della sua carriera allo studio della figura umana. Mediante i suoi busti etnografici (*Negro del Sudan*, *Ebrea di Algeri*, *Araba nera…*), il pittore intendeva "immortalare i diversi tipi umani che si stanno fondendo in un unico popolo". Queste figure policrome immortalano allo stesso tempo la fisionomia del modello e le caratteristiche distintive del suo costume, con l'obiettivo di mostrare le differenze sostenendo il rispetto per l'altro mediante opere umanistiche seducenti, con un'estetica curata e molto decorativa.

Charles Cordier besteedde het grootste deel van zijn carrière aan de studie van het menselijk gezicht. Zijn etnografische bustes (*Neger uit Soedan*, *Jood uit Algiers*, *Zwarte Moor…*) verbeelden "verschillende typen mensen die op het punt staan in een en hetzelfde volk te versmelten". De polychrome gezichten tonen zowel de fysionomie van het model als de bijzonderheden van zijn kleding. Het doel? Door verschillen te tonen respect afdwingen, middels aanlokkelijke humanistische werken die esthetisch verzorgd en zeer decoratief zijn.

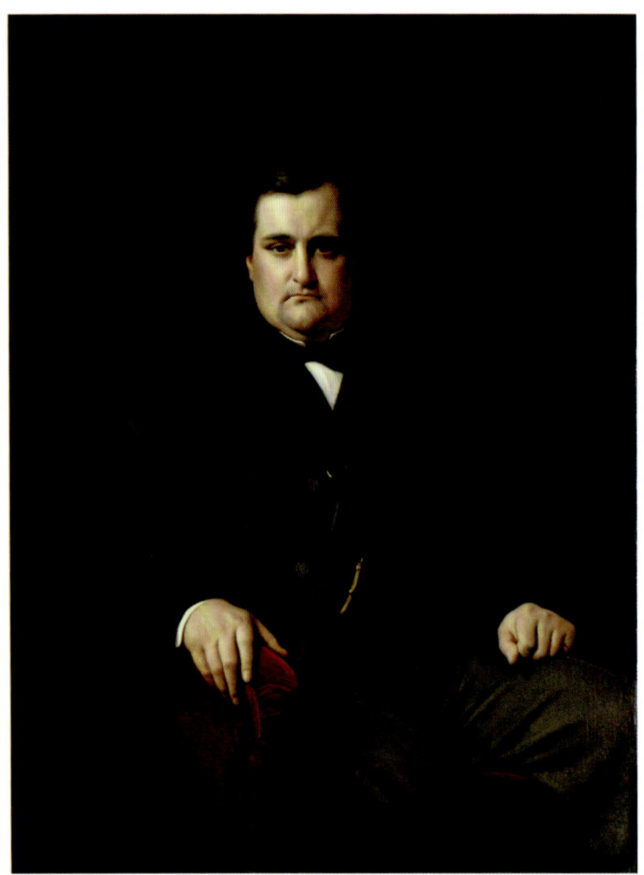

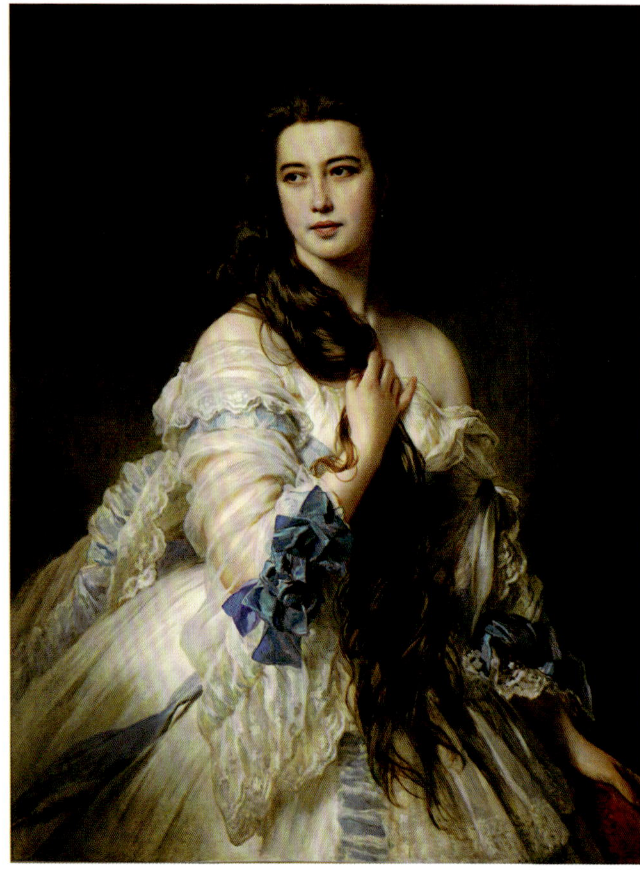

Hippolyte Flandrin (1809–1864)

Joseph Charles Paul Bonaparte, Prince Napoleon

Napoléon-Joseph-Charles-Paul Bonaparte, prince Napoléon

Napoleon-Joseph-Charles-Paul Bonaparte, Prinz Napoleon

Napoleón José Carlos Bonaparte, príncipe Napoleón

Joseph-Charles-Paul, principe Napoleone

Napoleon-Joseph-Charles-Paul Bonaparte, prins Napoleon

1860, Oil on canvas/Huile sur toile, 117 × 89 cm

Franz Xaver Winterhalter (1805–1873)

Madame Rimsky-Korsakov

Madame Rimski-Korsakov

Madame Rimski-Korsakow

Madame Rimski-Kórsakov

Madame Rimskij-Korsakov

Mevrouw Rimski-Korsakov

1864, Oil on canvas/Huile sur toile, 117 × 90 cm

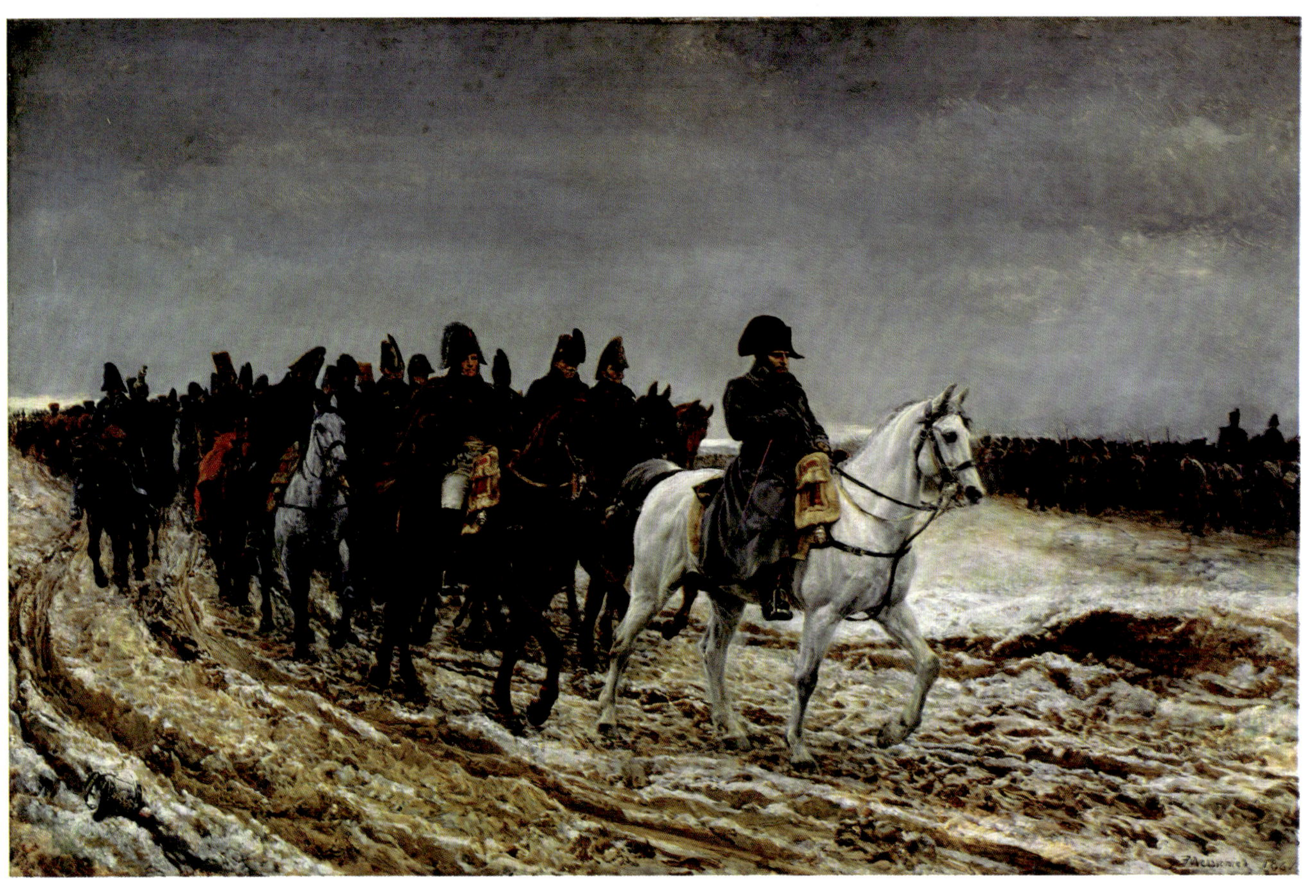

Ernest Meissonier (1815–1891)

Campaign of France, 1814

Campagne de France, 1814

Französischer Feldzug, 1814

Campaña de Francia, 1814

Campagna di Francia, 1814

De Franse veldtocht, 1814

1864, Oil on wood/Huile sur bois, 51,5 × 76,5 cm

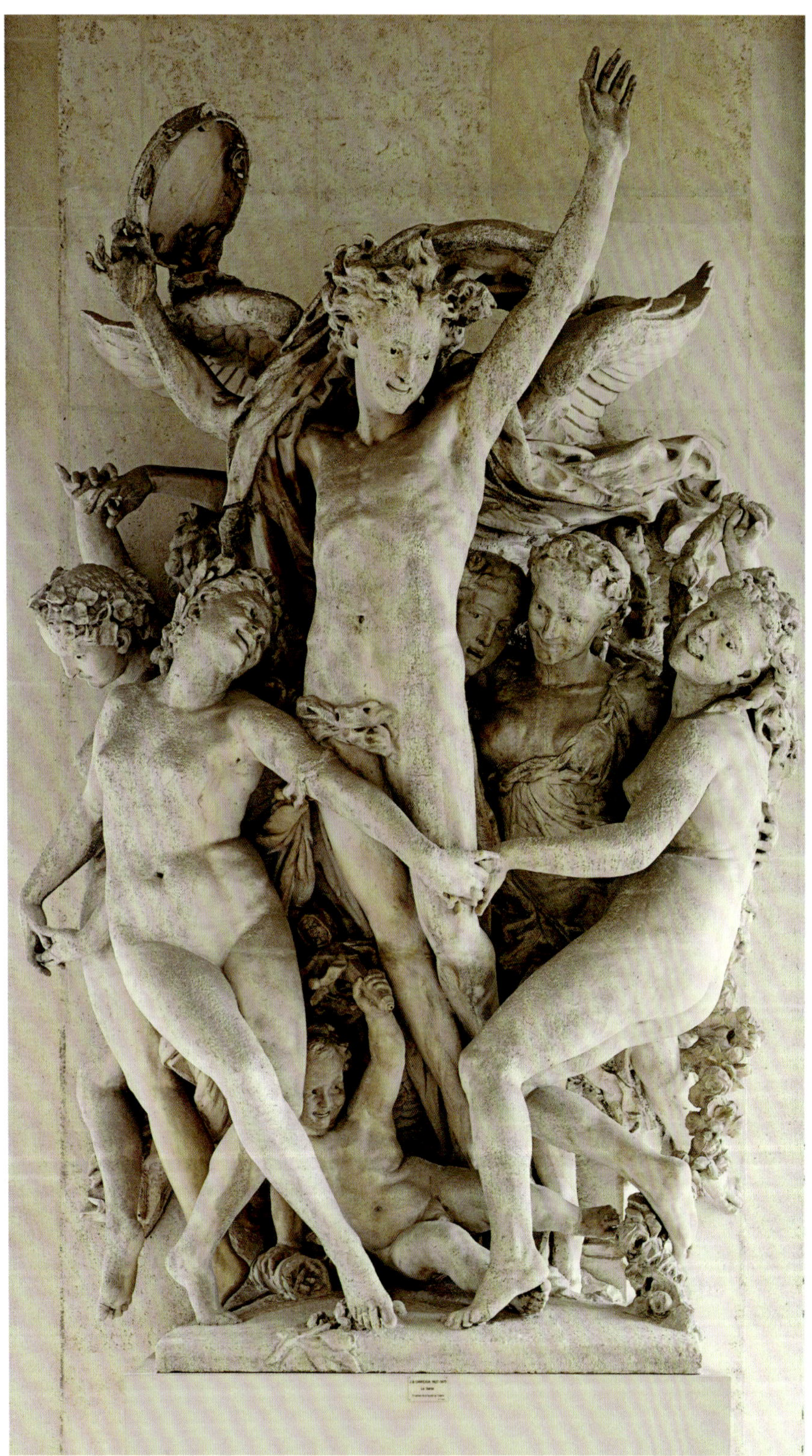

Jean-Baptiste Carpeaux (1827–1875)

The Dance
La Danse
Der Tanz
La Danza
La Danza
De dans

1868, Plaster/Plâtre, 232 × 148 × 115 cm

Jean-Baptiste Carpeaux is at the same time the privileged portraitist of Napoleon III and a free artist who endeavours to flout academic rules. *The Dance* was commissioned in 1863 by Charles Garnier to adorn the façade of the Paris opera. This monumentally sculpted group stages a scene with young ladies spinning around the genie of dance who is holding a tambourine in his hand.

Jean-Baptiste Carpeaux est à la fois le portraitiste privilégié de Napoléon III, et un artiste libre, qui s'applique à contredire les règles académiques. *La Danse* lui été commandée en 1863 par Charles Garnier, pour orner la façade de l'Opéra de Paris. Ce groupe sculpté monumental met en scène une ronde de jeunes femmes tournoyant autour du génie de la danse, qui tient dans sa main un tambourin.

Jean-Baptiste Carpeaux ist zugleich der bevorzugte Porträtist von Napoleon III. und ein freier Künstler, der beharrlich den akademischen Regeln widerspricht. *Der Tanz* wurde 1863 von Charles Garnier in Auftrag gegeben, um die Fassade der Pariser Oper zu schmücken. Die monumentale Skulpturengruppe zeigt einen schwungvollen Reigen von jungen Frauen um den Genius des Tanzes, der in seiner Hand ein Tamburin hält.

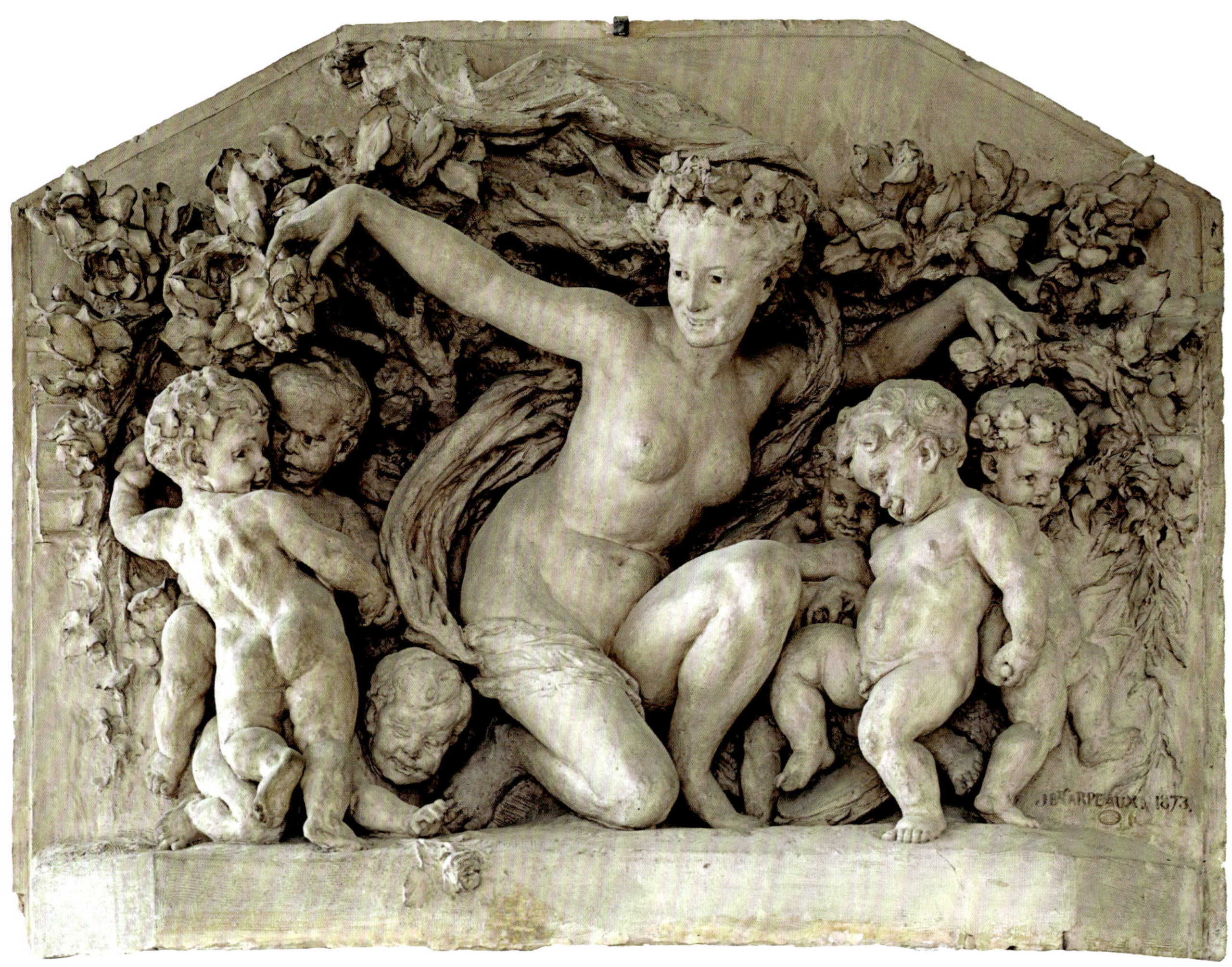

Jean-Baptiste Carpeaux (1827–1875)

The Triumph of Flora | Der Triumph der Flora | Il trionfo di Flora
Le Triomphe de Flore | El triunfo de Flora | De triomf van Flora

c. 1866, Plaster/Plâtre, 151 × 180 × 46 cm

Jean-Baptiste Carpeaux es a la vez el retratista privilegiado de Napoleón III, y un artista libre, que se aplica a contradecir las reglas académicas. *La Danza* fue encargado en 1863 por Charles Garnier, para adornar la fachada de la Opera de París. Este grupo monumental escultórico representa a un grupo de mujeres jóvenes girando alrededor de un genio central que sostiene en su mano una pandereta.

Jean-Baptiste Carpeaux fu al tempo stesso il ritrattista prediletto di Napoleone III e un artista libero, che contraddisse le regole accademiche. *La Danza* gli fu commissionata nel 1863 da Charles Garnier per la facciata dell'Opéra di Parigi. Questo gruppo scultoreo monumentale raffigura un gruppo di giovani donne che volteggiano attorno al genio della danza, che tiene in mano un tamburello.

Jean-Baptiste Carpeaux is zowel de favoriete portretschilder van Napoleon III als een vrij kunstenaar met een afkeur van de academische regels. *De Dans* maakte hij in 1863 in opdracht van Charles Garnier ter versiering van de gevel van de Parijse Opera. De monumentale beeldengroep toont een kring van jonge vrouwen rond de beschermgod van de dans die een tamboerijn in zijn hand houdt.

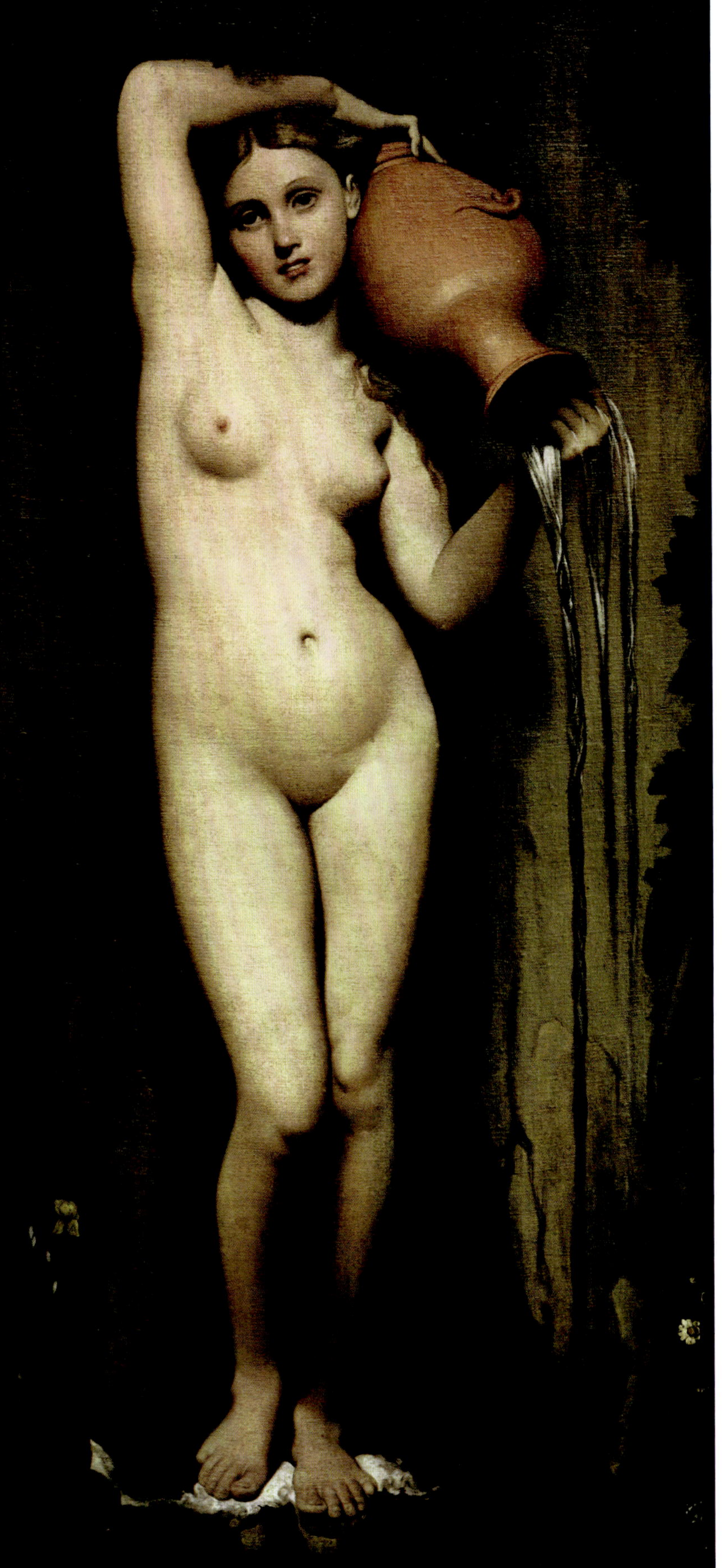

Jean Auguste Dominique Ingres (1780–1867)

The Source

La Source

Die Quelle

El manantial

La Sorgente

De bron

1856, Oil on canvas/Huile sur toile, 163 × 80 cm

The biblical theme of Susanna and the elders
inspired numerous artists, including Tintoretto,
Rembrandt, Carrache, Rubens and Delacroix. In
this painting made in Rome, Jean-Jacques Hennes
paints with the precision of Ingres a very realistic
nude, a voluptuous body with pale skin, observed by
an old man concealed in the vegetation.

Le thème biblique de Suzanne et les vieillards a
inspiré nombre d'artistes, dont Tintoret, Rembrandt,
Carrache, Rubens et Delacroix. Dans ce tableau
réalisé à Rome, Jean-Jacques Henner peint avec
une précision ingresque un nu très réaliste, un corps
voluptueux à la peau claire, qu'observe un vieil
homme dissimulé dans la végétation.

Das biblische Thema der Susanna und der Greise hat
zahlreiche Künstler inspiriert, darunter Tintoretto,
Rembrandt, Carracci, Rubens und Delacroix. Bei
diesem in Rom entstandenen Bild malt Jean-
Jacques Henner mit einer Präzision à la Ingres einen
sehr realistischen Akt, einen sinnlichen Körper mit
heller Haut, den ein alter Mann aus seinem Versteck
in der Vegetation beobachtet.

El tema bíblico de Susana y los viejos ha inspirado a
muchos artistas, incluyendo a Tintoretto, Rembrandt,
Carracci, Rubens y Delacroix. En esta pintura, hecha
en Roma, Jean-Jacques Henner pintó con una
precisión típica de Ingres un desnudo realista, un
cuerpo voluptuoso con la piel clara, observado por
un anciano escondido entre la vegetación.

Il tema biblico di Susanna e i vecchi ispirò molti
artisti, tra cui Tintoretto, Rembrandt, Carracci,
Rubens e Delacroix. In questo quadro dipinto a
Roma, Jean-Jacques Henner raffigurò, con una
precisione che ricorda quella di Ingres, un nudo
molto realistico: un corpo voluttuoso con la pelle
chiara osservato da un vecchio nascosto nella
vegetazione.

Het Bijbelse thema van Susanna en de oude mannen
heeft een groot aantal kunstenaars geïnspireerd,
onder wie Tintoretto, Rembrandt, Carrache, Rubens
en Delacroix. Op dit doek, dat Jean-Jacques Henner
in Rome maakte, schildert hij met een precisie à la
Ingres een realistisch naakt, een wellustig lichaam
met een bleke huid dat vanuit de bosjes door een
grijsaard wordt bespied.

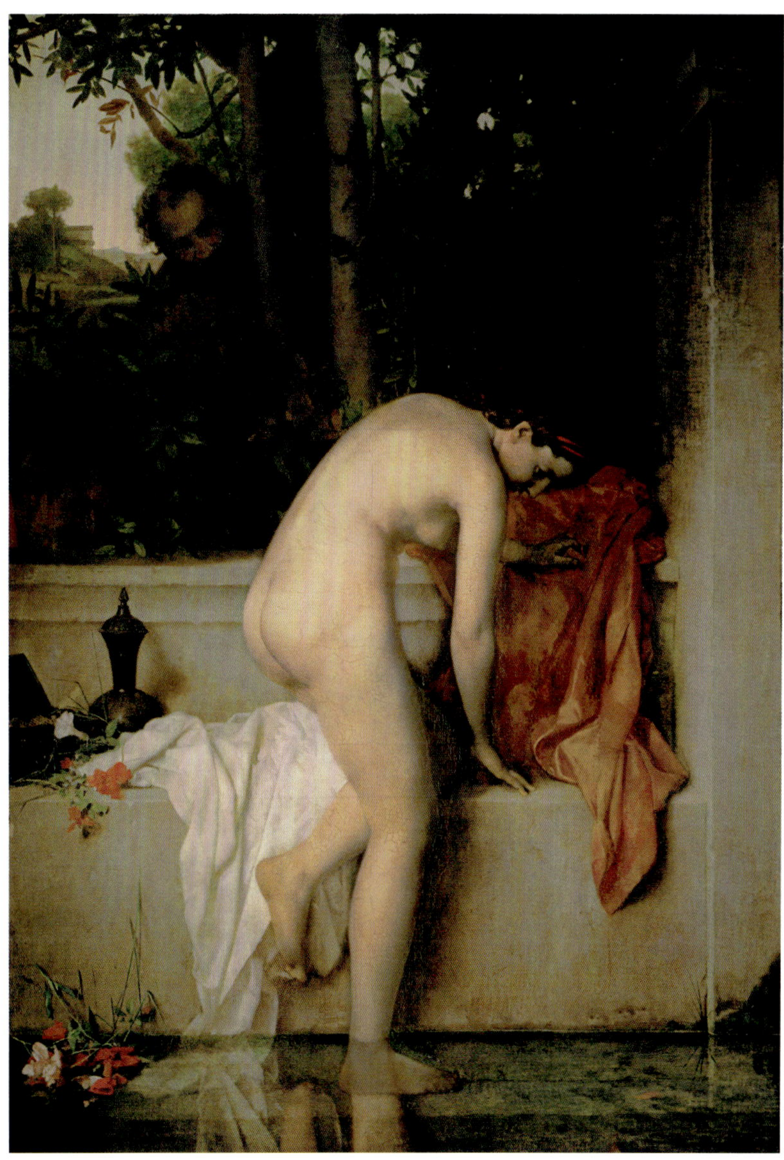

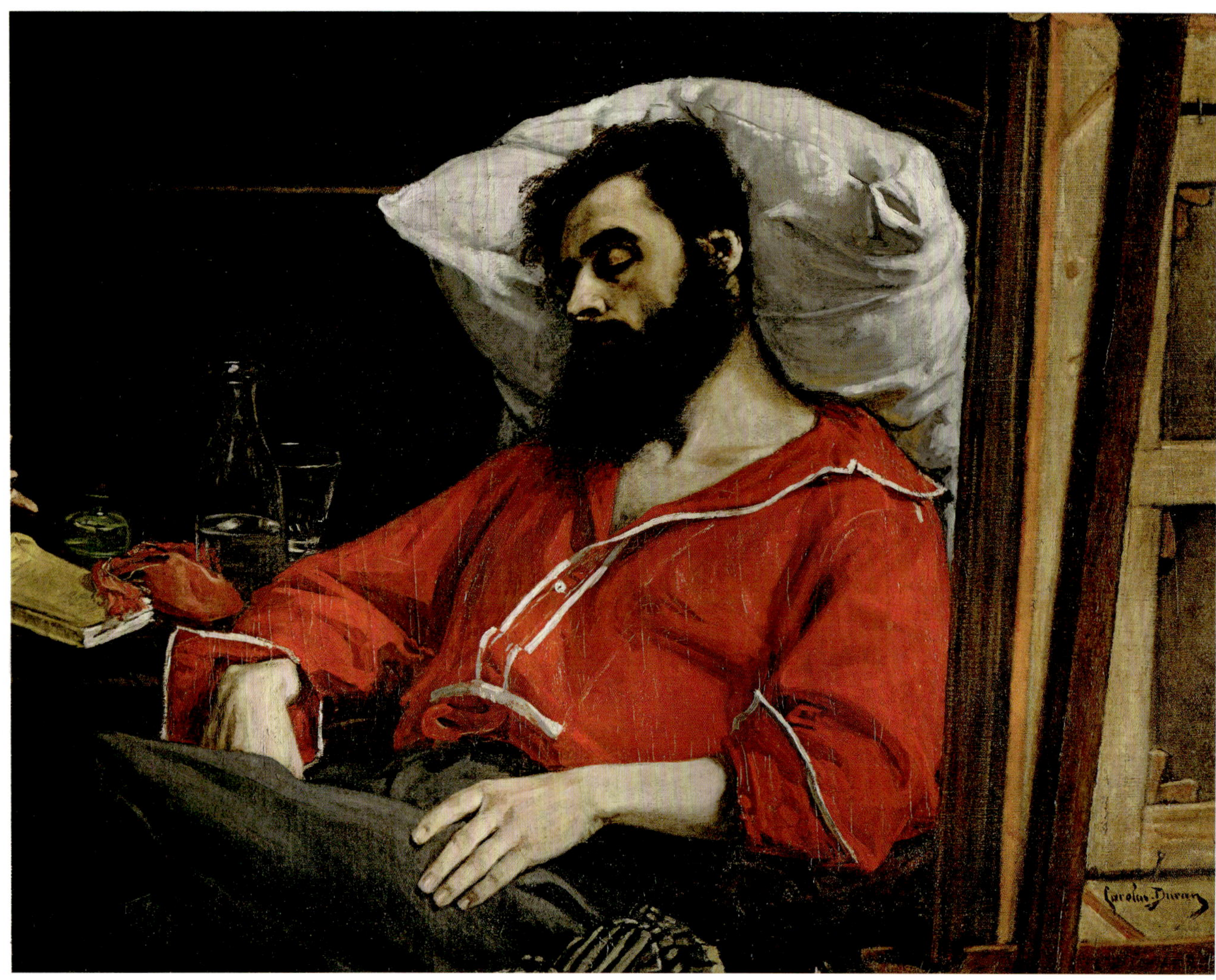

Carolus-Duran (1837–1917)

Le Convalescent

Le Convalescent

Der Genesende

El convaleciente

Il convalescente

De reconvalescente

c. 1860, Oil on canvas/Huile sur toile, 99 × 125,5 cm

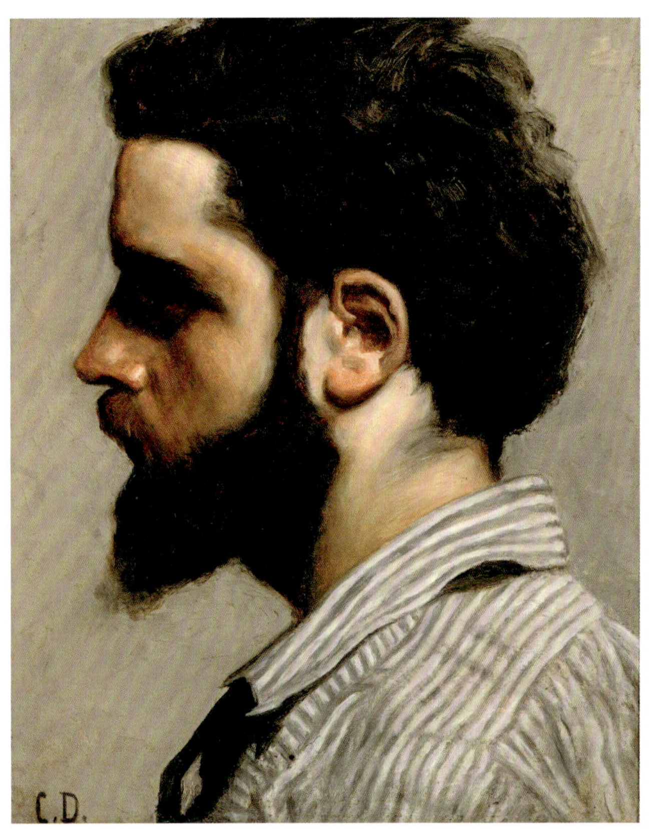

Carolus-Duran (1837–1917)
Zacharie Astruc
1861, Huile sur bois, 40,8 × 31,4 cm

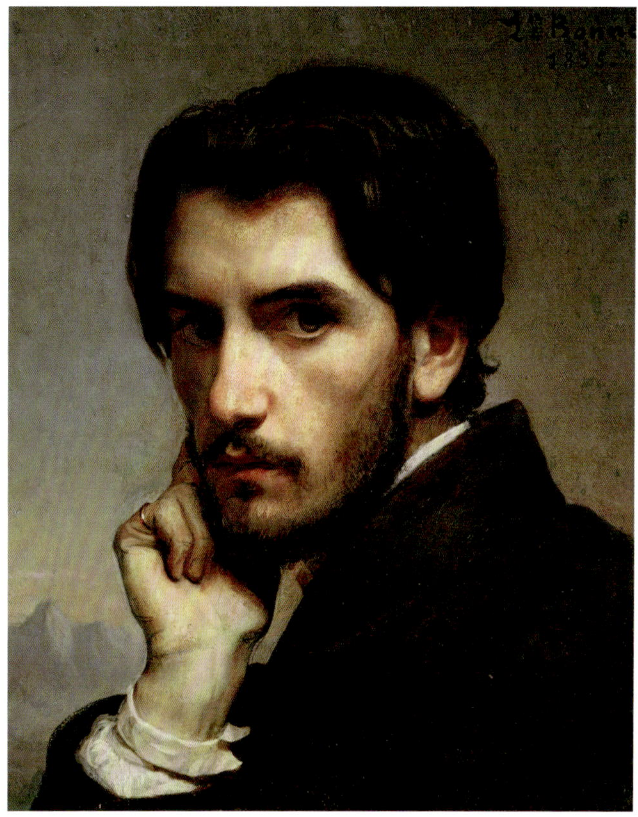

Léon Bonnat (1833–1922)
Portrait of the Artist
Portrait de l'artiste
Selbstbildnis
Autorretrato
Autoritratto
Portret van de kunstenaar
1855, Oil on canvas on wood/Huile sur toile sur bois, 46 × 37,5 cm

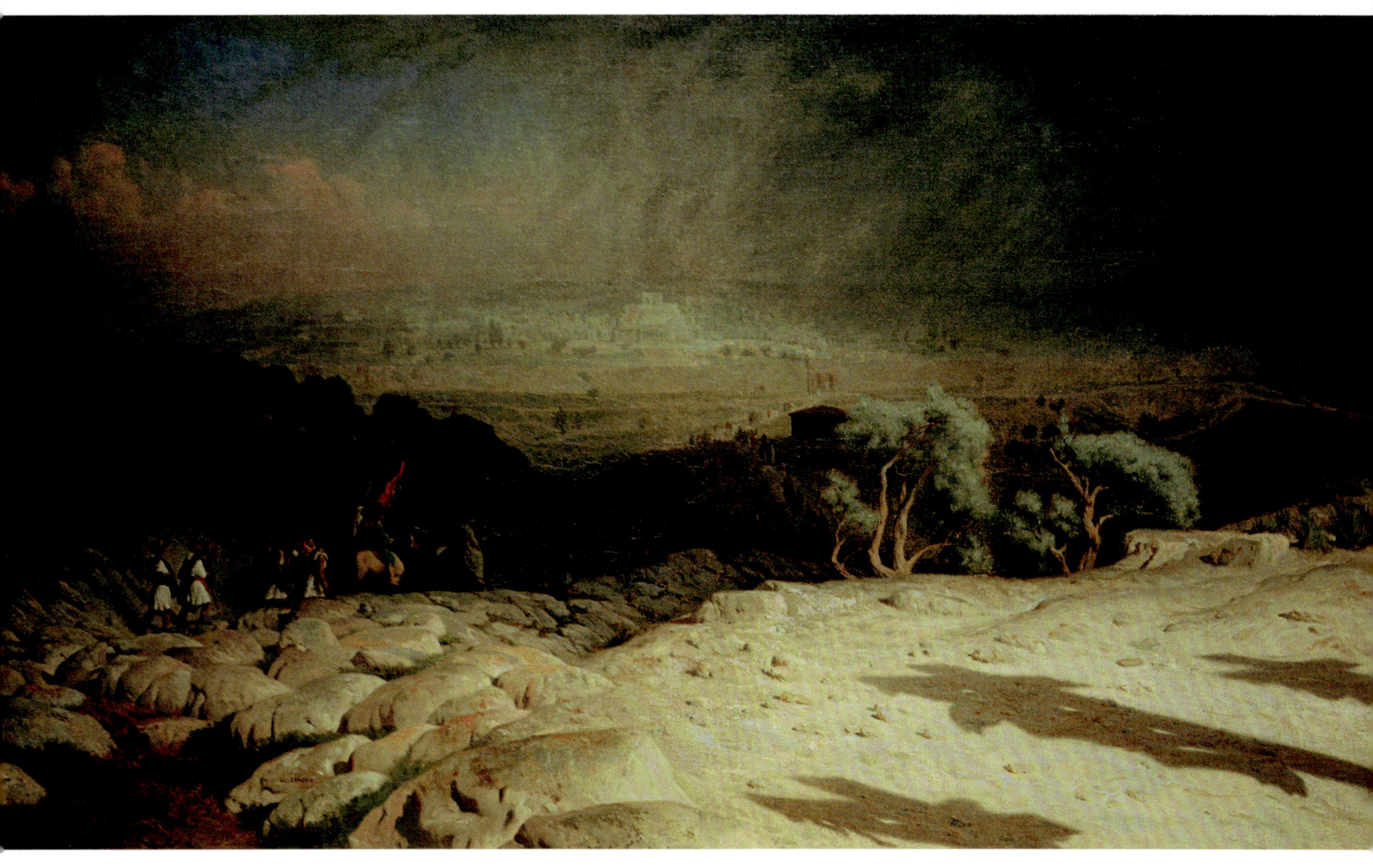

Jean-Léon Gérôme (1824–1904)

Jerusalem *or* Golgotha, Consummatum est

Jérusalem *ou* Golgotha, Consummatum est

Jerusalem *oder* Golgotha, Es ist vollbracht

Jerusalén *o* Golgotha, Consummatum est

Gerusalemme *o* Golgotha, Consummatum est

Jeruzalem *of* Golgotha, Consummatum est

1867, Oil on canvas/Huile sur toile, 82 × 144,5 cm

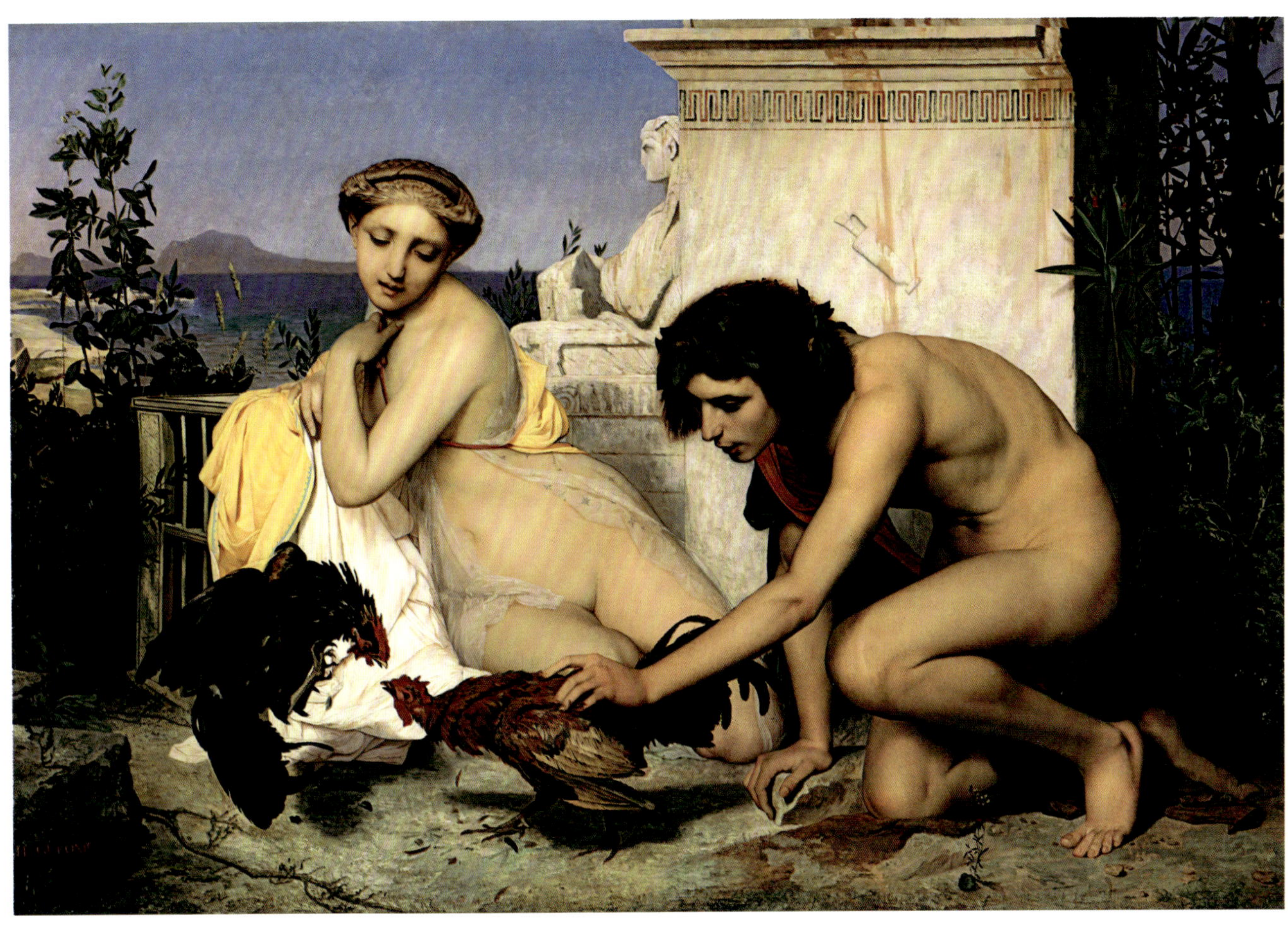

Jean-Léon Gérôme (1824–1904)

Young Greeks Attending A Cock Fight

Jeunes Grecs faisant battre des coqs

Junge Griechen lassen Hähne gegeneinander kämpfen

Jóvenes griegos presenciando una pelea de gallos

Giovani Greci assistono ad un combattimento di galli

Jonge Grieken bij het hanengevecht

1846, Oil on canvas/Huile sur toile, 143 × 204 cm

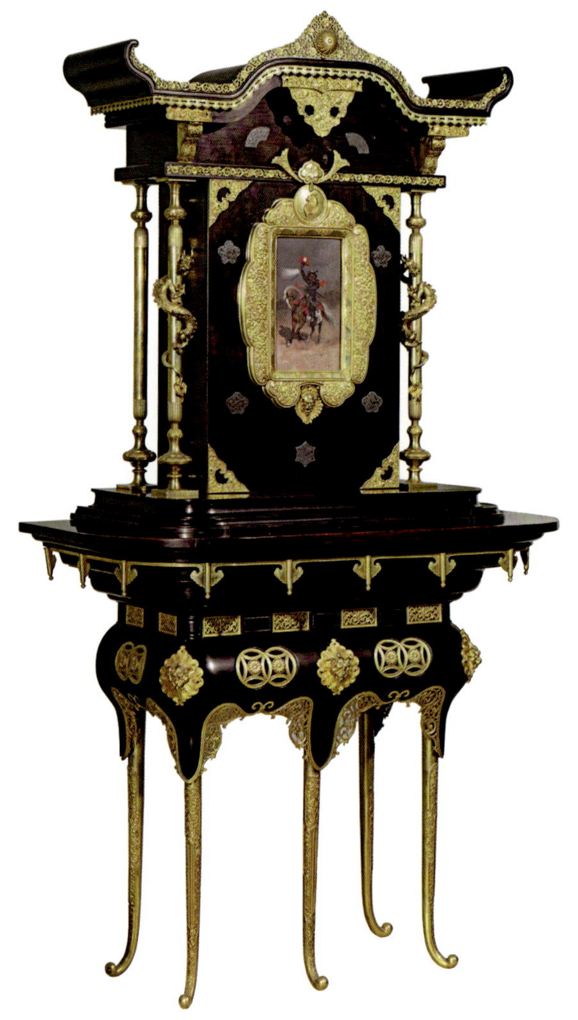

Eclecticism and the reinterpretation of neogothic, neoclassic and other styles—in architecture as well as in the decorative arts—characterizes the period under the Second Empire. The aesthetics is overdone, at times pompous, as evidenced by this medallion adorned with an imposing relief in silver-plated bronze depicting a historical motif. However, the materials are of high quality and the workmanship is impeccable. In his two-component piece of furniture, Édouard Lièvre revisits the forms of a far east pagoda, which he embellished with gilded bronze.

Sous le Second Empire, le temps est à l'éclectisme et à la réinterprétation des styles néogothique, néoclassique…, en architecture aussi bien que dans les arts décoratifs. L'esthétique est chargée, parfois pompeuse, comme en témoigne ce médailler orné d'un imposant relief en bronze argenté à motif historique. Mais les matériaux sont de qualité, et le savoir-faire irréprochable. Dans son meuble à deux corps, Édouard Lièvre revisite les formes d'une pagode extrême-orientale, qu'il agrémente de bronzes dorés.

Das Zweite Kaiserreich ist die Zeit des Eklektizismus und der Neuinterpretation der neugotischen bis klassizistischen Stile, sowohl in der Architektur als auch im Kunstgewerbe. Die Ästhetik ist üppig, manchmal pompös, wie dieser Münzschrank bezeugt, der mit einem imposanten Relief mit historischen Motiven aus versilberter Bronze geschmückt ist. Die Materialien sind jedoch von hoher Qualität und das Können einwandfrei. Sein zweiteiliges Möbelstück mit den Formen einer fernöstlichen Pagode verziert Édouard Lièvre mit vergoldeter Bronze.

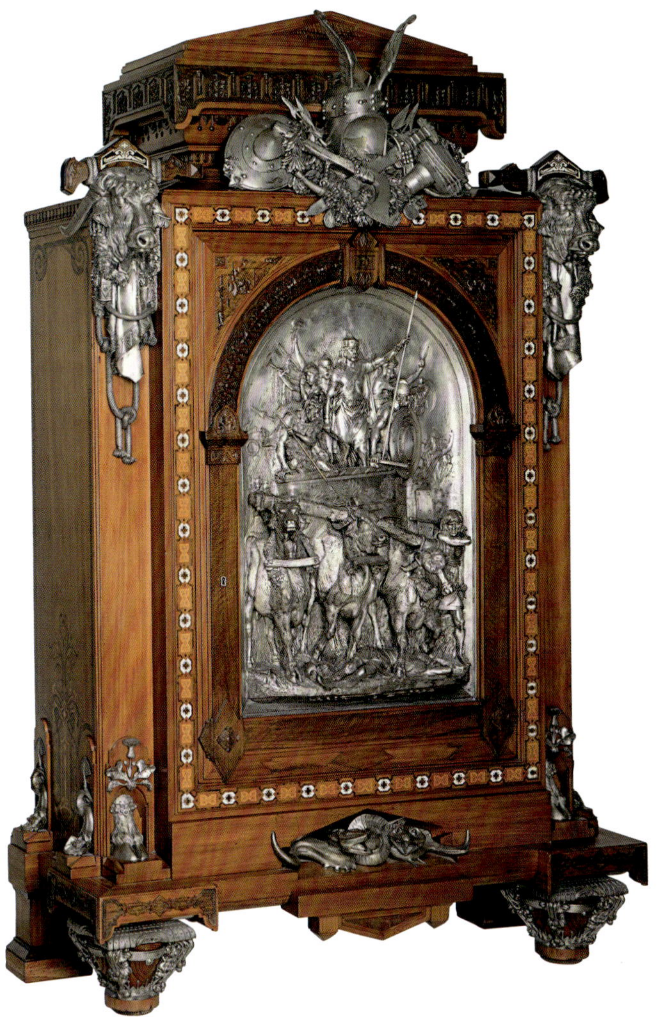

Bajo el Segundo Imperio, se llevó a cabo el eclecticismo y la reinterpretación de estilos gótico, neoclásico…, tanto en arquitectura, así como en las artes decorativas. La estética es recargada, a veces pomposa, como lo demuestra este medallón adornado con un imponente relieve de tema histórico en bronce plateado. Los materiales son de alta calidad y la técnica impecable. En su mueble de dos cuerpos, Édouard Lièvre revisita las formas de una pagoda del extremo oriental, embellecidas con bronces dorados.

Durante il Secondo Impero predominarono l'eclettismo e la reinterpretazione di vari stili, quali il Neogotico e il Neoclassico, sia nell'architettura sia nelle arti decorative. L'estetica era carica e a volte pomposa, come testimonia questo armadio delle medaglie ornato con un imponente bassorilievo di argomento storico in bronzo argentato. Tuttavia, i materiali erano di alta qualità e l'esecuzione impeccabile. Nel suo mobile a doppio corpo, Édouard Lièvre rivisita le forme di una pagoda dell'Estremo Oriente, impreziosendola con bronzi dorati.

Tijdens het Tweede Keizerrijk vieren het eclecticisme en de herinterpretatie van de neogotiek en het neoclassicisme hoogtij, zowel in de bouwkunst als in de toegepaste kunsten. Esthetisch was de kunst beladen, soms bombastisch, zie dit muntenkabinet met een groots historisch reliëf van verzilverd brons. Niettemin zijn de materialen van uitstekende kwaliteit en is de uitvoering onberispelijk. Met deze kast in twee delen biedt Édouard Lièvre een nieuwe kijk op de oosterse pagode, die hij versiert met vergulde bronzen beelden.

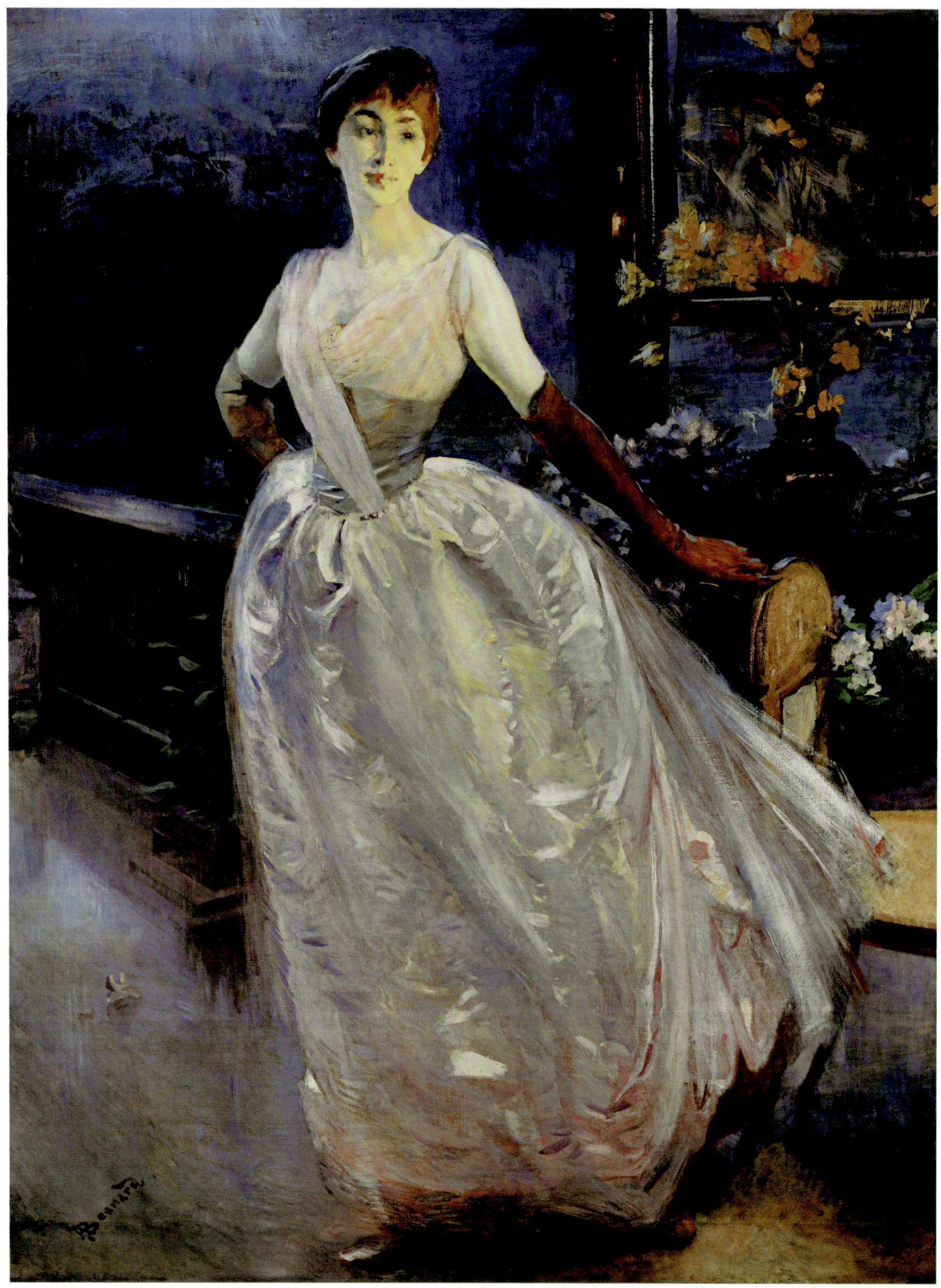

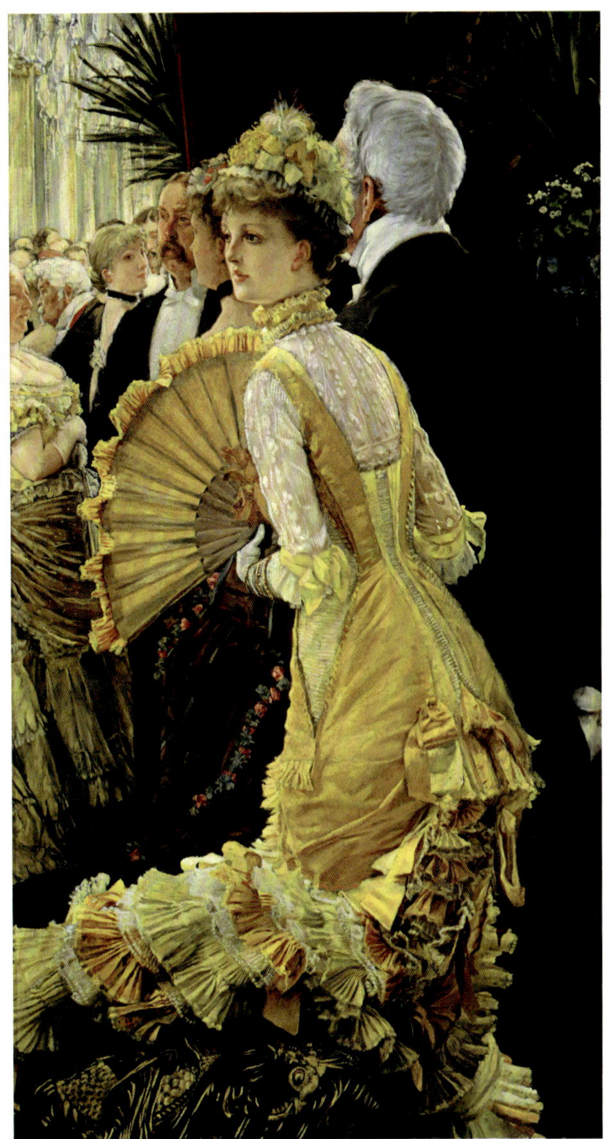

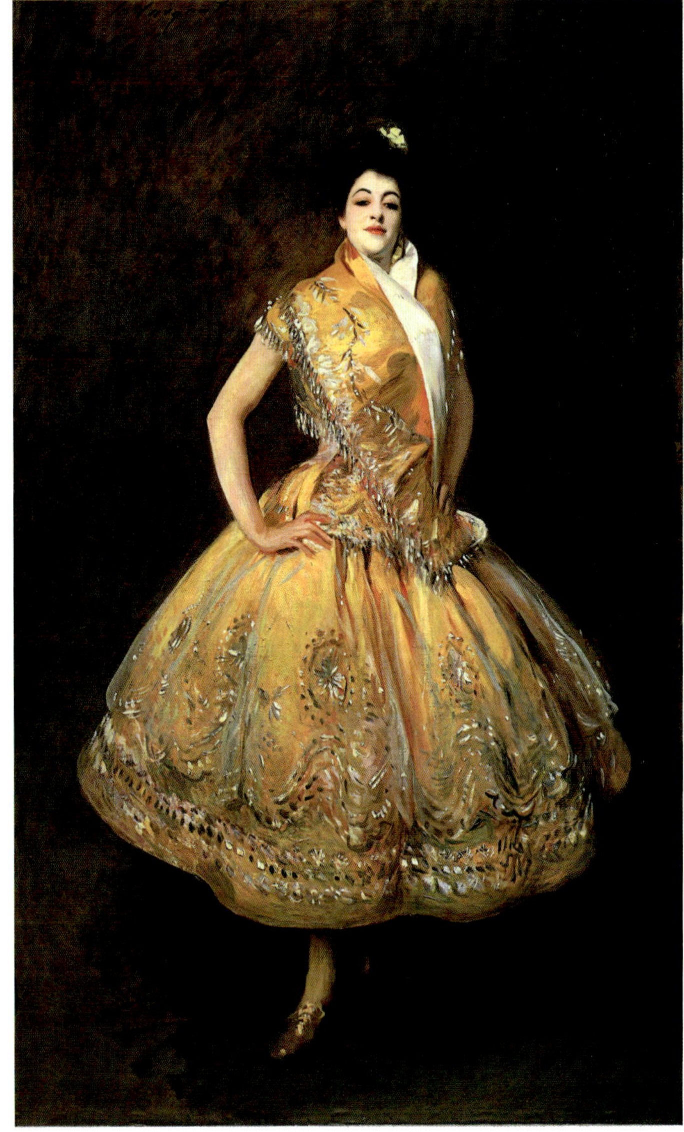

James Tissot (1836–1902)

Evening

Evening

Der Ball

Evening

Evening *detto anche* Il Ballo

Evening

1878, Oil on canvas/Huile sur toile, 91 × 51 cm

Albert Besnard (1849–1934)

Madame Roger Jourdain

1886, Oil on canvas/Huile sur toile, 199 × 150,5 cm

John Singer Sargent (1856–1925)

La Carmencita

c. 1890, Oil on canvas/Huile sur toile, 229 × 140 cm

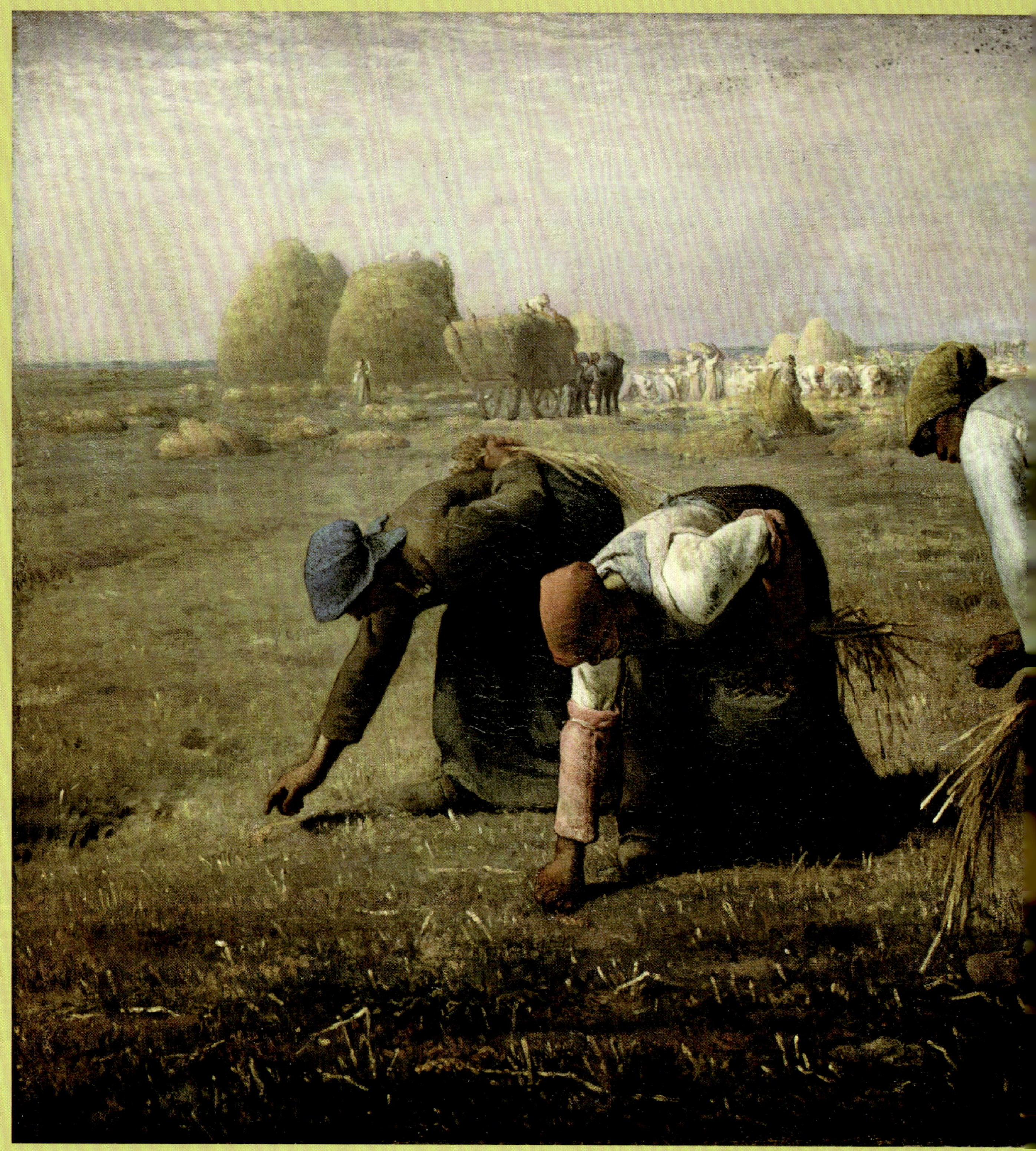

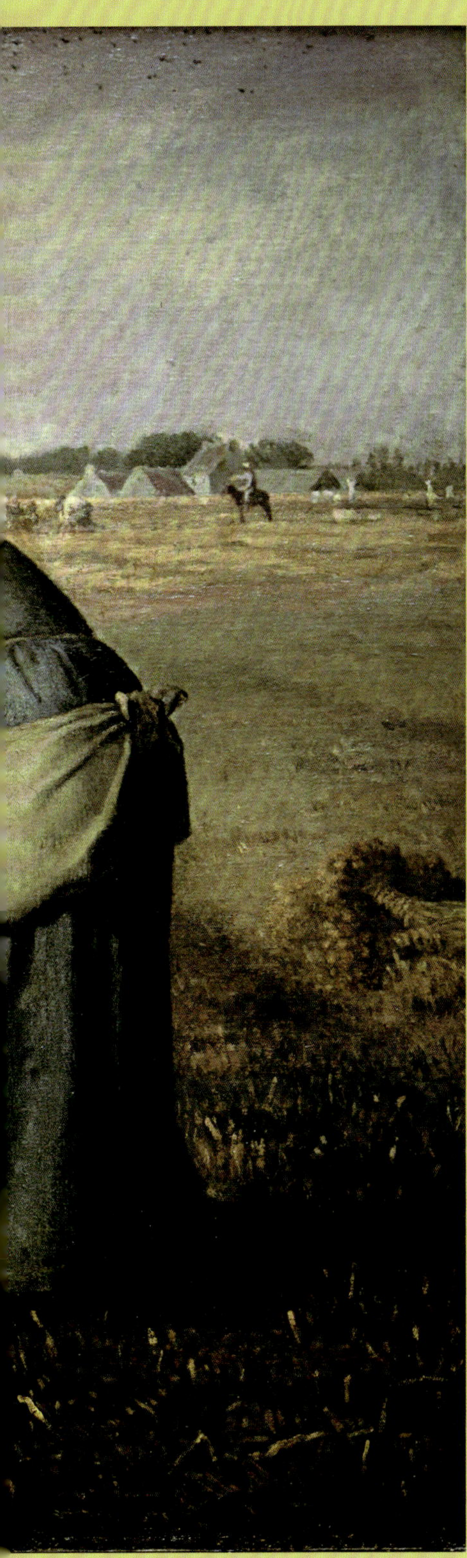

Naturalism and Realism

Working in the fields, everyday life, landscapes, constituted the new painting subjects. Courbet is the proponent of realism, while Manet will appear in the years 1860–1870 as the representative of the "new painting". Torn between his taste for the past masters and his desire to be an artist of his time, he will pave the way for the experiments of the impressionists.

Naturalisme et Réalisme

Les travaux des champs, la vie quotidienne, le paysage, constituent de nouveaux sujets de peinture. Courbet est le chantre du réalisme, tandis que Manet va apparaître, dans les années 1860–1870, comme le représentant de la « nouvelle peinture ». Tiraillé entre son goût pour les maîtres du passé et sa volonté d'être un artiste de son temps, il ouvrira la voie aux recherches des impressionnistes.

Naturalismus und Realismus

Die Feldarbeit, das Alltagsleben und die Landschaft sind neue Themen der Malerei. Courbet ist der Verfechter des Realismus, während Manet in den Jahren 1860–1870 zum Repräsentanten der „neuen Malerei" wird. Mit seiner Zerrissenheit zwischen seiner Vorliebe für die Meister der Vergangenheit und seinem Willen, ein Künstler seiner Zeit zu sein, ebnet er schließlich den Impressionisten den Weg.

Naturalismo y realismo

Las labores del campo, la vida cotidiana, el paisaje, son temas nuevos para la pintura. Courbet es el adalid del realismo, mientras que Manet aparecerá, en los años 1860–1870, como representante de la "nueva pintura". Dividido entre su amor por los maestros del pasado y su deseo de ser un artista de su tiempo, abrirá el camino a la investigación de los impresionistas.

Naturalismo e Realismo

Il lavoro nei campi, la vita quotidiana e il paesaggio erano soggetti nuovi per la pittura. Courbet è considerato il maestro per eccellenza del Realismo, mentre Manet si consolidò, negli anni Sessanta e Settanta dell'Ottocento, come il rappresentante della "nuova pittura". Combattuto tra il suo amore per i maestri del passato e il suo desiderio di essere un artista del suo tempo, aprirà infatti la strada agli studi degli impressionisti.

Naturalisme en realisme

Boerenarbeid, het dagelijks leven en landschappen vormen nieuwe schilderkunstige thema's. Courbet bezingt het realisme, terwijl Manet zich in de jaren 1860–1870 ontpopt als representant van de 'nieuwe schilderkunst'. Verscheurd tussen zijn voorliefde voor grote meesters uit het verleden en zijn streven een eigentijds kunstenaar te zijn, wordt hij de wegbereider voor de impressionisten.

Jean-François Millet (1814–1875)
The Gleaners
Des glaneuses
Die Ährenleserinnen
Cosechadoras
Alcune spigolatrici
De arenleessters
1857, Oil on canvas/Huile sur toile, 83,5 × 110 cm

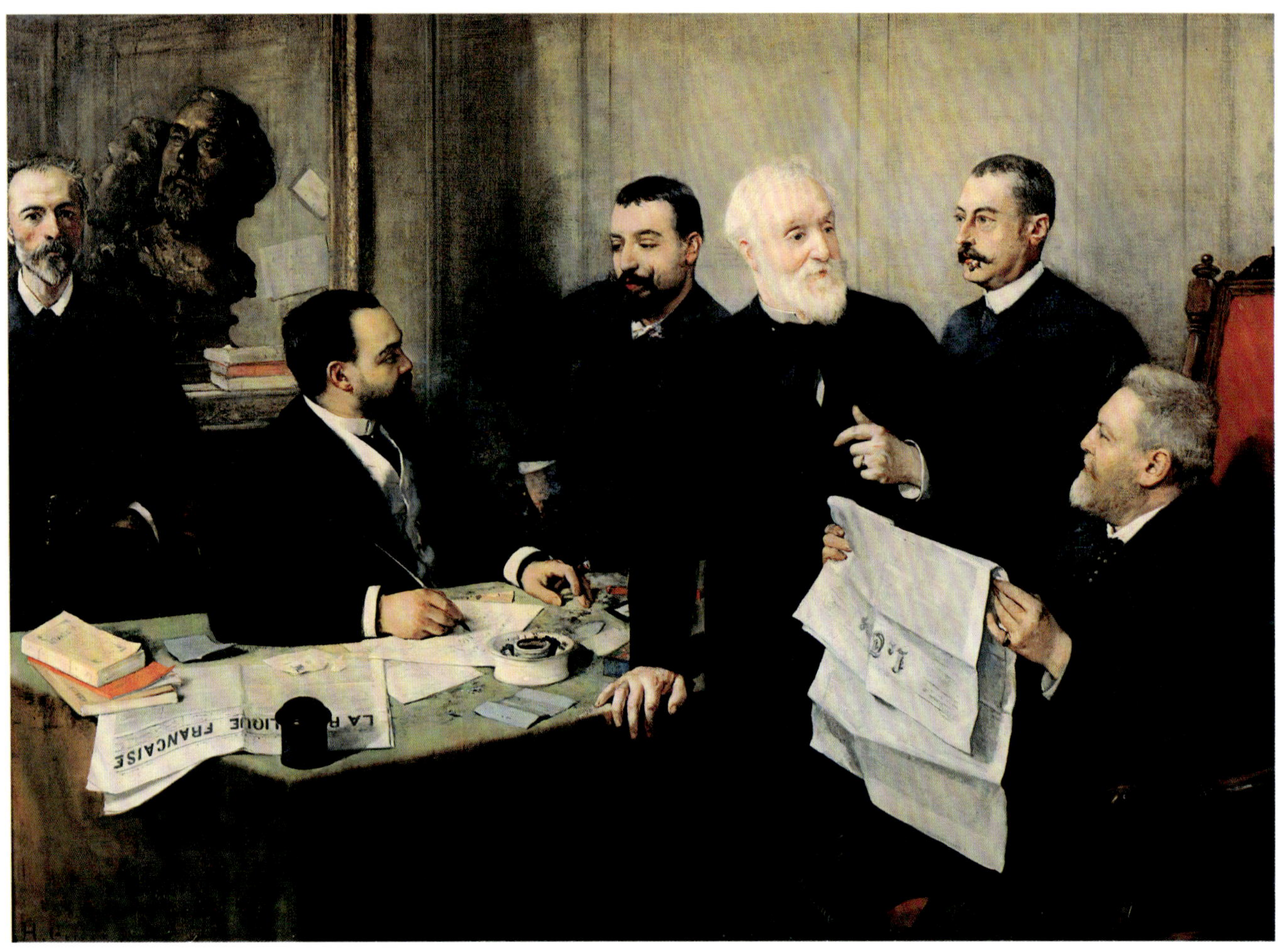

Henri Gervex (1852–1929)

At *La République française*

À *La République française*

Bei *La République française*

En *La République française*

I direttori de *La République française*

De directie van *La République française*

1890, Oil on canvas/Huile sur toile, 156 × 217,4 cm

Henri Gervex (1852–1929)

Before The Operation *or* Doctor Péan Teaching His Discovery of
the Compression of Blood Vessels at St Louis Hospital

Avant l'opération *dit aussi* Le docteur Péan enseignant à l'hôpital
Saint-Louis sa découverte du pincement des vaisseaux

Vor der Operation *oder* Dr. Péan führt im Hospital Saint-Louis
seine Entdeckung des Abklemmens von Blutgefäßen vor

Antes de la operación *también llamado* El doctor Péan enseñando en el hospital
San Luis su descubrimiento de la compresión de los vasos sanguíneos

Prima dell'operazione *detto anche* Il Dottore Péan mentre illustra la
sua scoperta sul pizzicamento dei vasi all'ospedale Saint-Louis

Voor de operatie *of* Dokter Péan onderwijst zijn ontdekking van
het afknijpen van de aders in het ziekenhuis Saint-Louis

1887, Oil on canvas/Huile sur toile, 242 × 188 cm

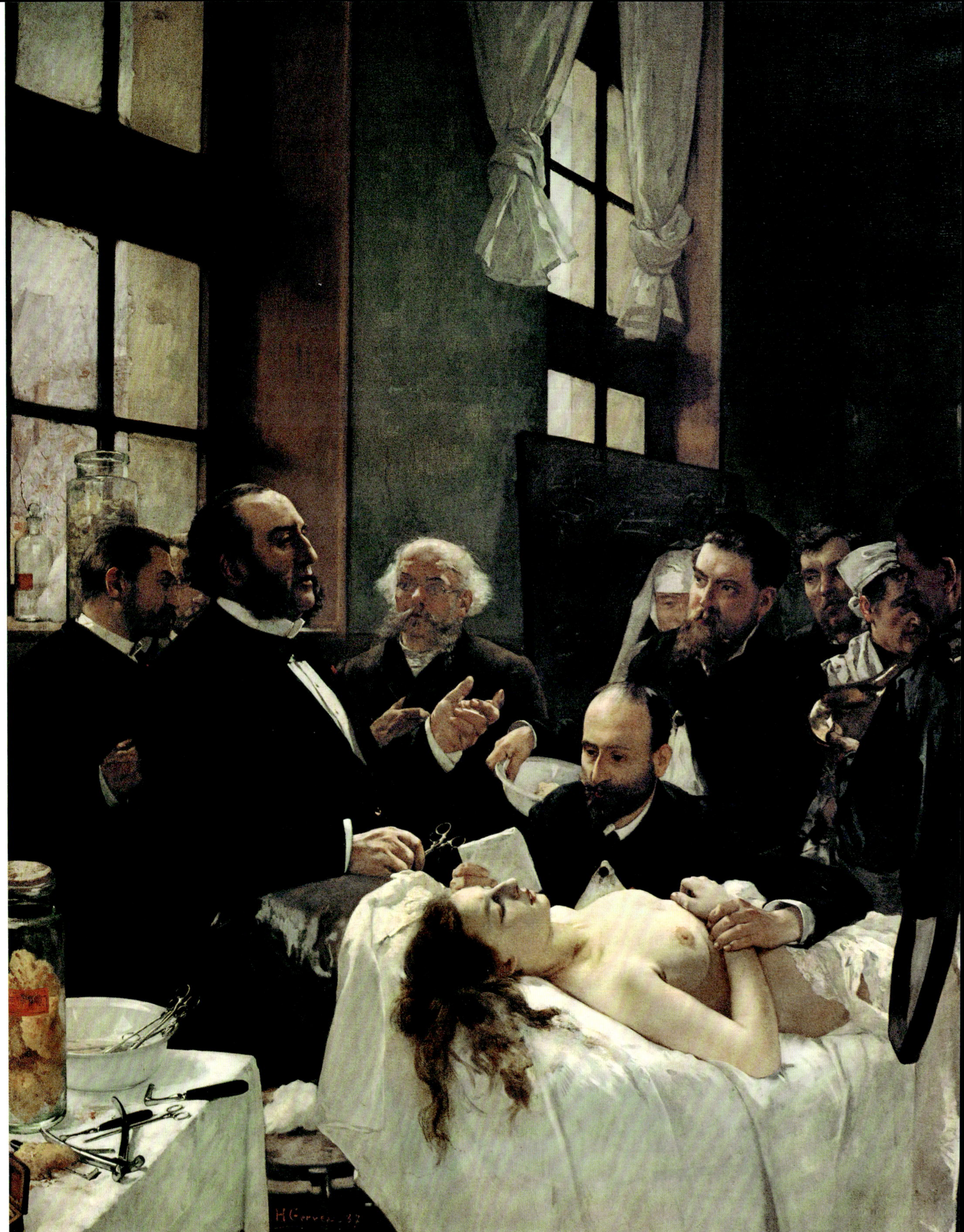

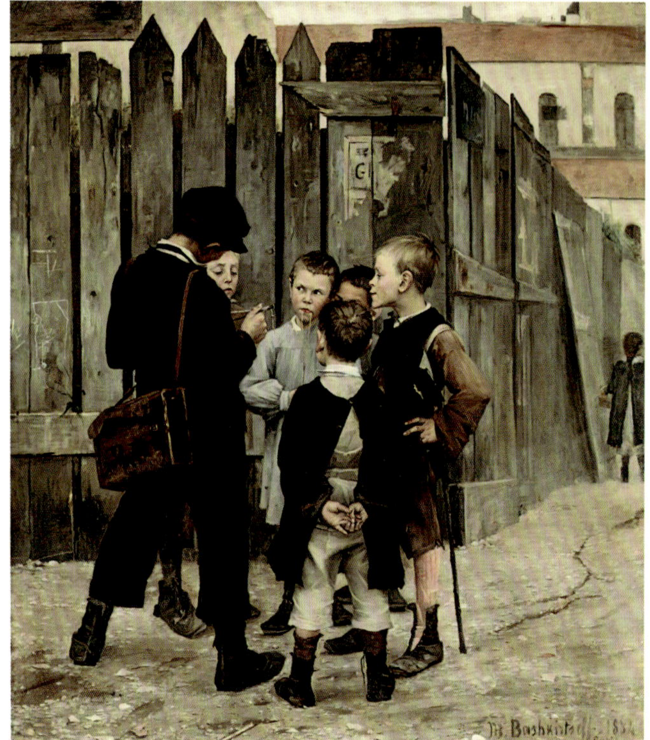

Marie-François Firmin-Girard (1838–1921)

The Convalescents

Les Convalescents

Die Rekonvaleszenten

Los convalecientes

I Convalescenti

De reconvalescenten

1861, Oil on canvas/Huile sur toile, 100,3 × 188 cm

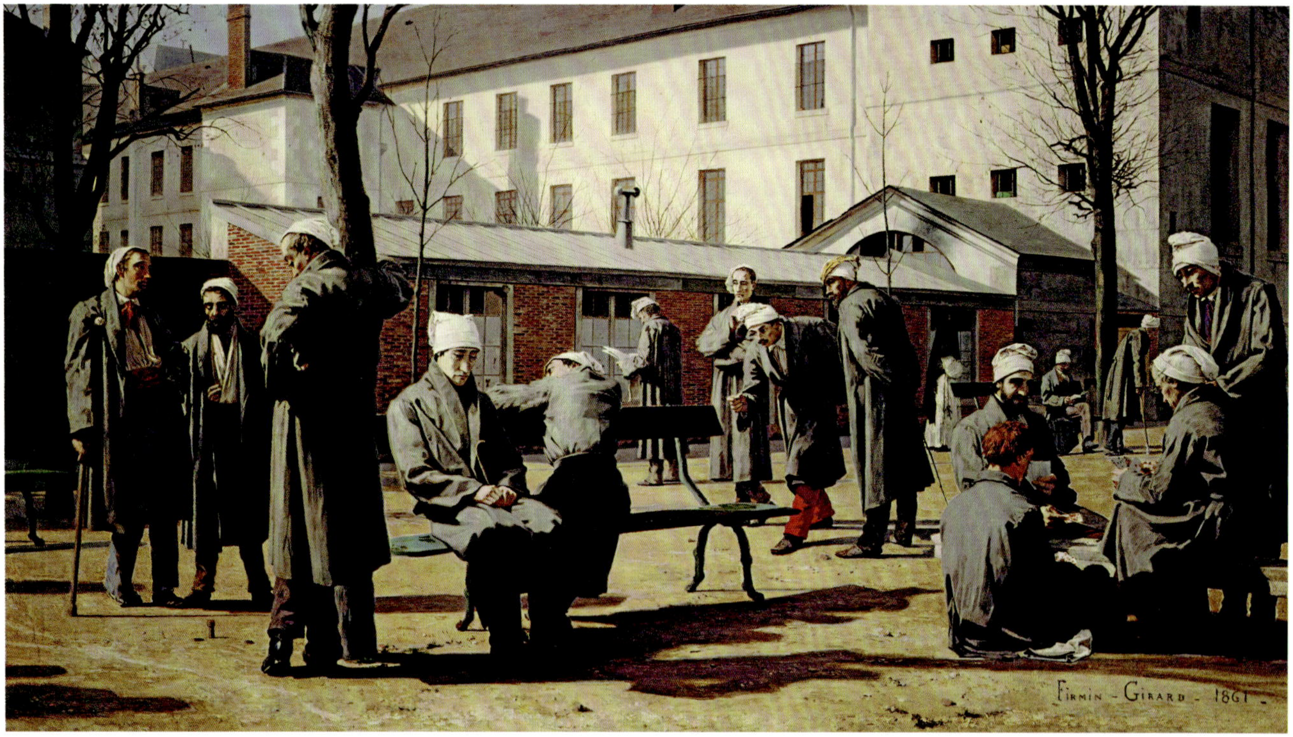

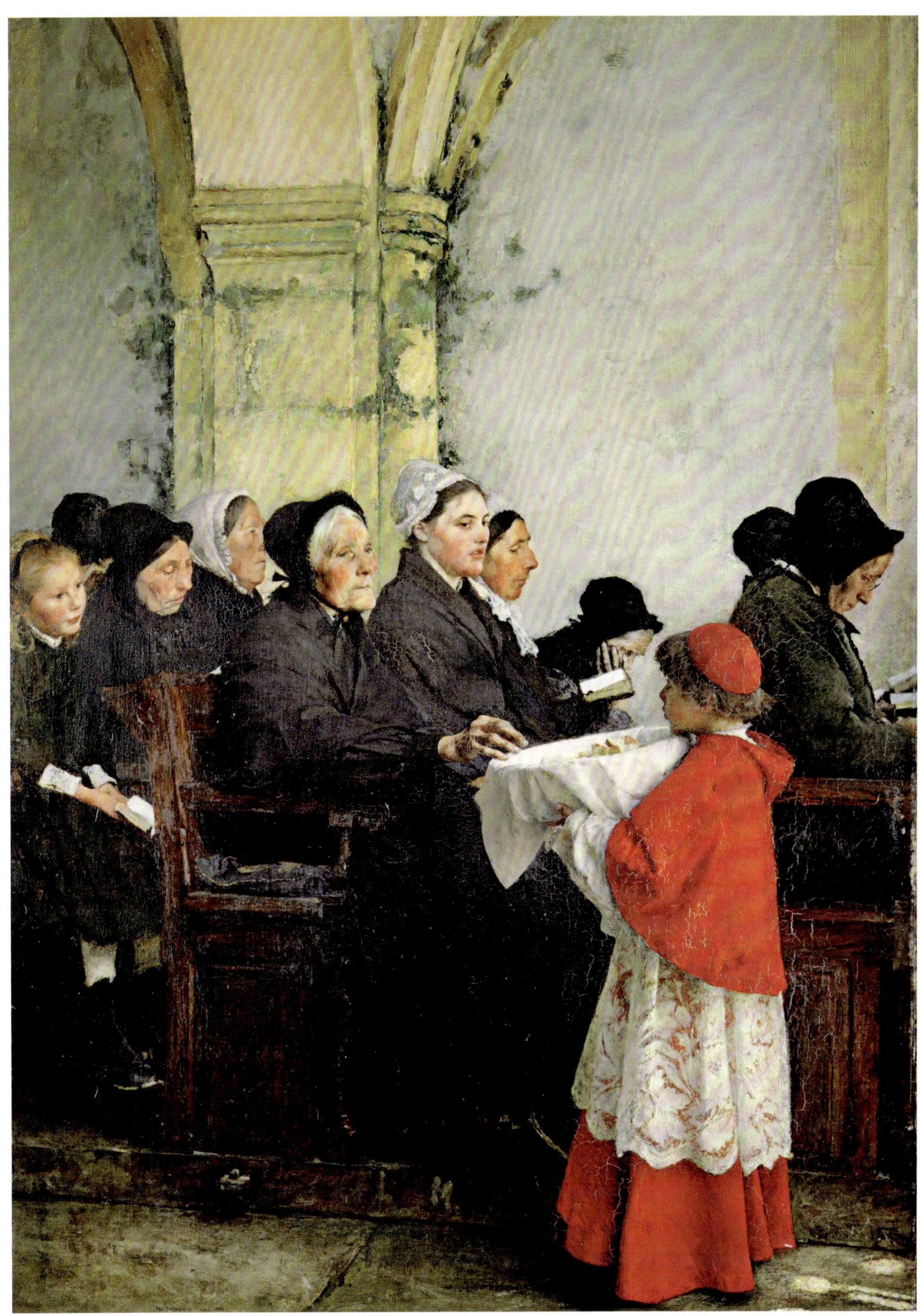

Pascal Dagnan-Bouveret
(1852–1929)

The Blessed Bread

Le Pain bénit

Geweihtes Brot

El pan bendito

Il Pane benedetto

Het gewijde brood

1885, Oil on canvas/Huile
sur toile, 121 × 84,5 cm

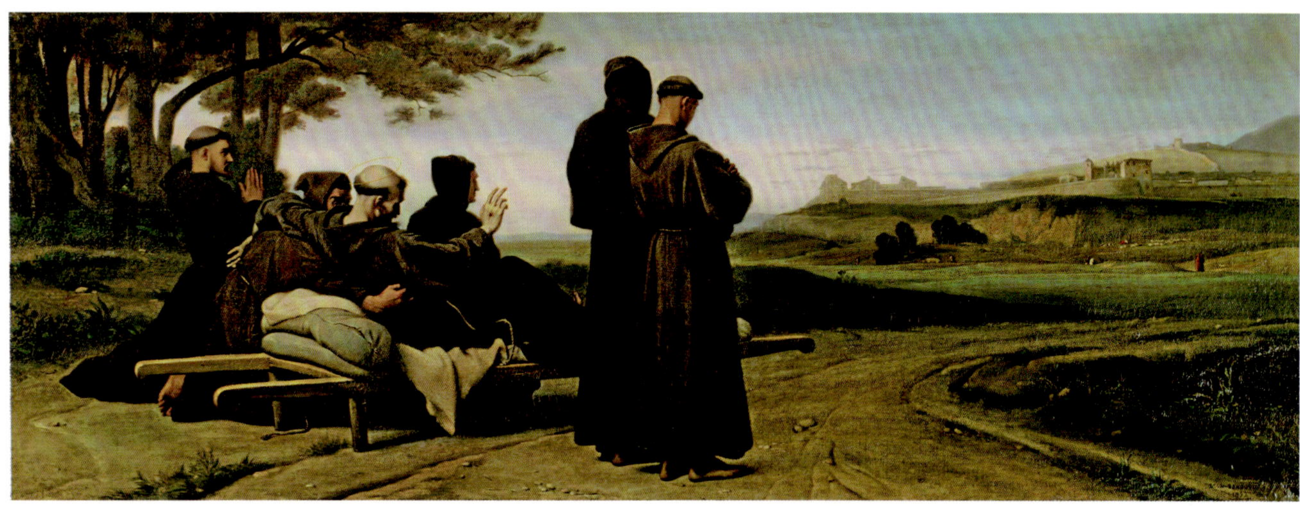

Léon Benouville (1860–1903)

St. Francis of Assisi, while being carried to his final resting place at Santa Maria degli Angeli, blesses the town of Assisi

Saint François d'Assise, transporté mourant à Sainte-Marie-des-Anges, bénit la ville d'Assise

Der sterbende Franz von Assisi wird zur Santa Maria degli Angeli transportiert und segnet Assisi

San Francisco de Asís, transportado muriendo a Santa María de los Ángeles, bendice la villa de Asís

San Francesco, trasportato in fin di vita a Santa Maria degli Angeli, benedice la città di Assisi

Franciscus van Assis, stervend onderweg naar Sta. Maria degli Angeli, zegent de stad Assisi

1853, Oil on canvas/Huile sur toile, 91 × 241,3 cm

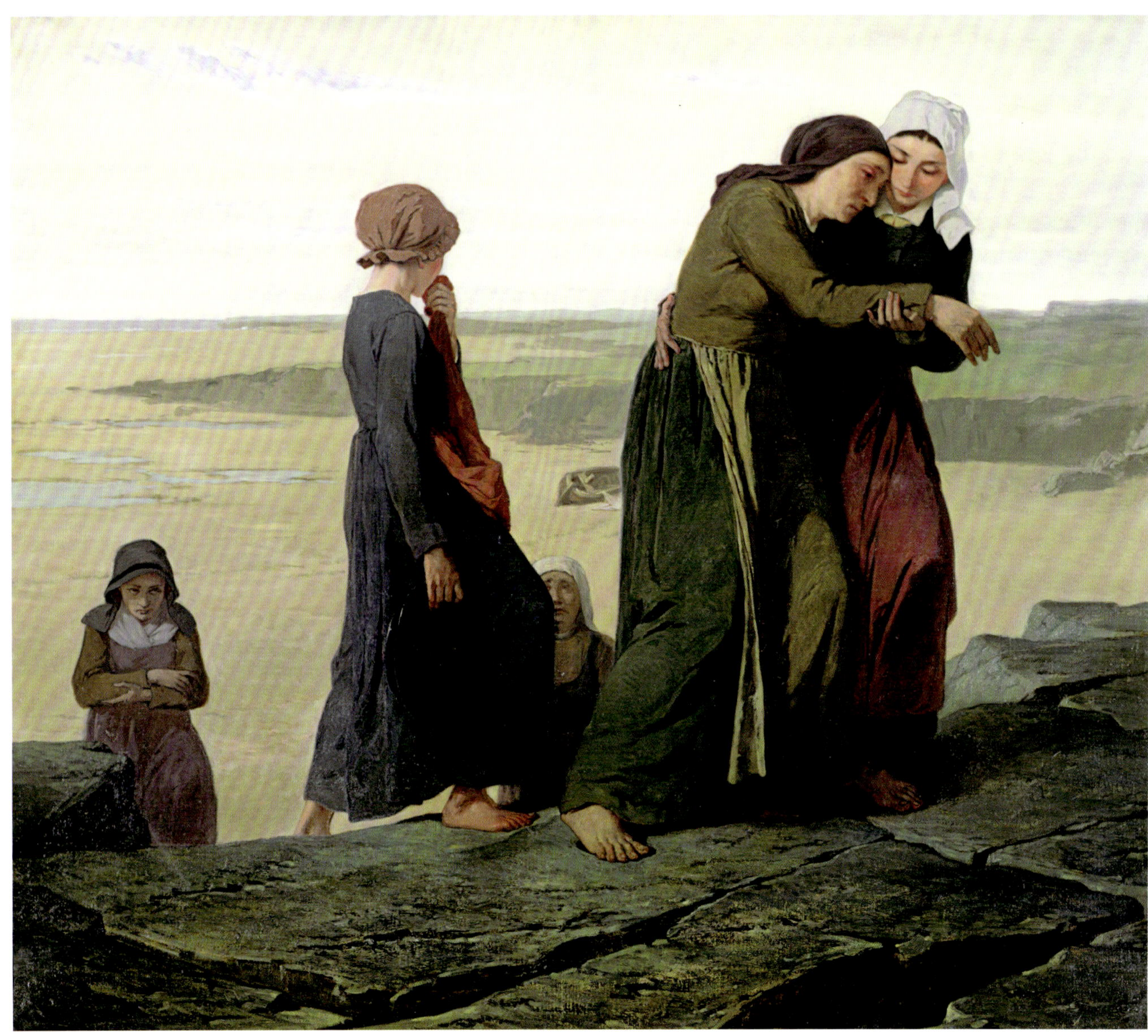

Évariste Vital Luminais (1822–1896)

The Widow

La Veuve

Die Witwe

La viuda

La Vedova

De weduwe

c. 1865, Oil on canvas/Huile sur toile, 90,5 × 104,5 cm

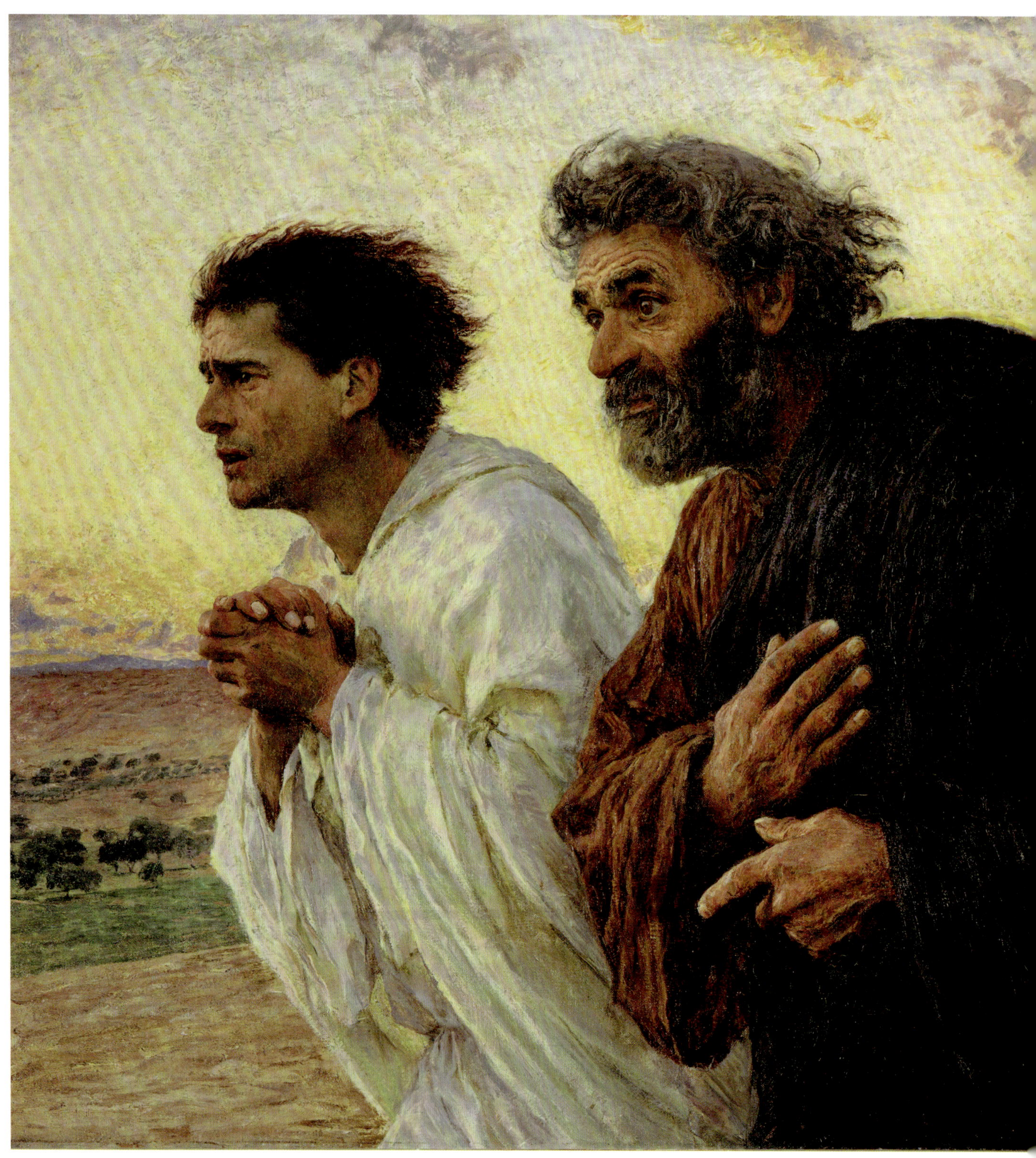

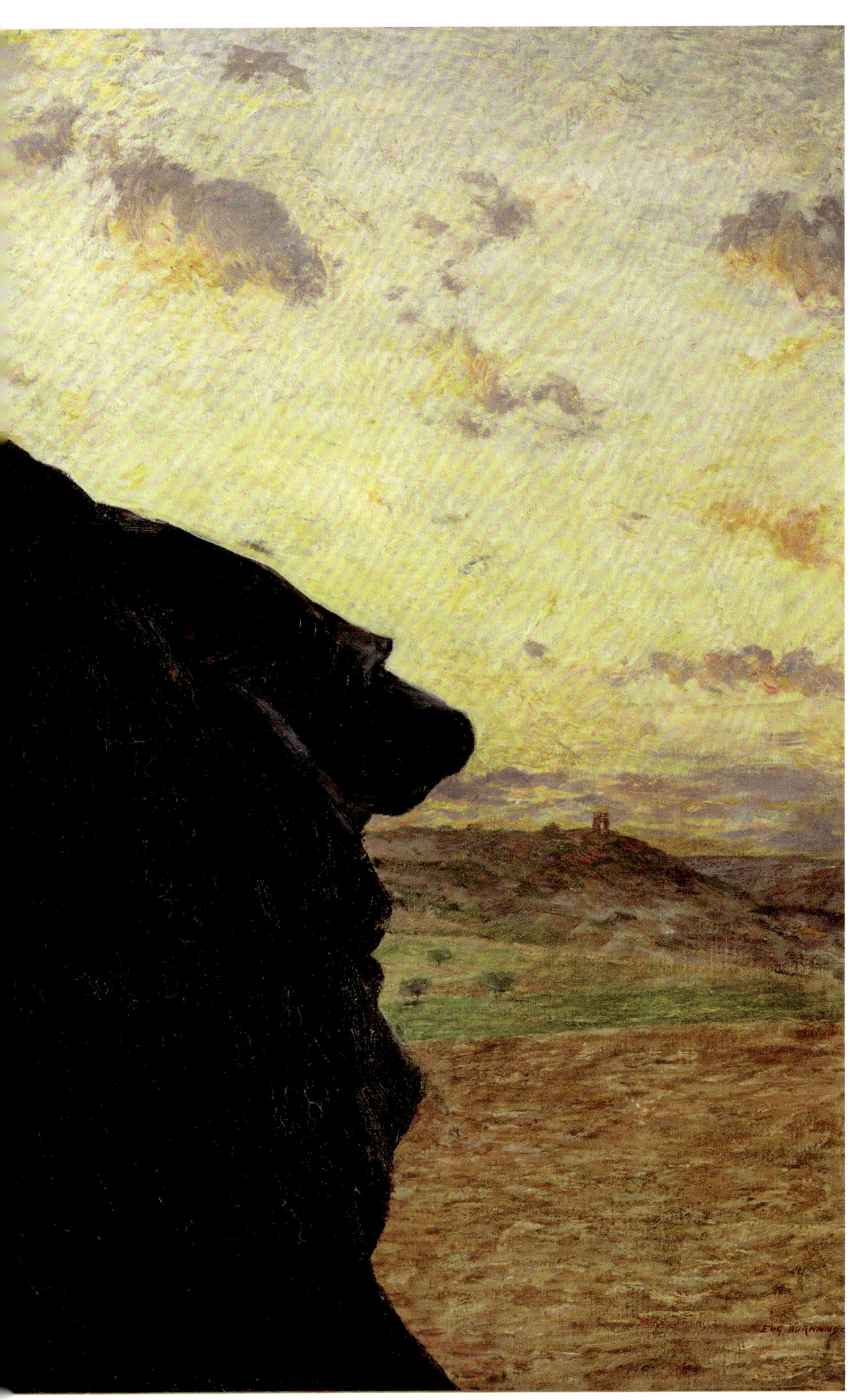

Eugène Burnand (1850–1921)

Disciples Peter and John running to the Sepulcher
on the Morning of the Resurrection

Les Disciples Pierre et Jean courant au
Sépulcre le matin de la Résurrection

Die Jünger Petrus und Johannes am
Auferstehungsmorgen auf dem Weg zum Grabe

Los discípulos Pedro y Juan corren al
sepulcro la mañana de la Resurrección

I discepoli Pietro e Giovanni accorrono al
sepolcro la mattina della Resurrezione

De discipelen Petrus en Johannes rennen naar
het graf op de ochtend van de Verrijzenis

1898, Oil on canvas/Huile sur toile, 83 × 135,5 cm

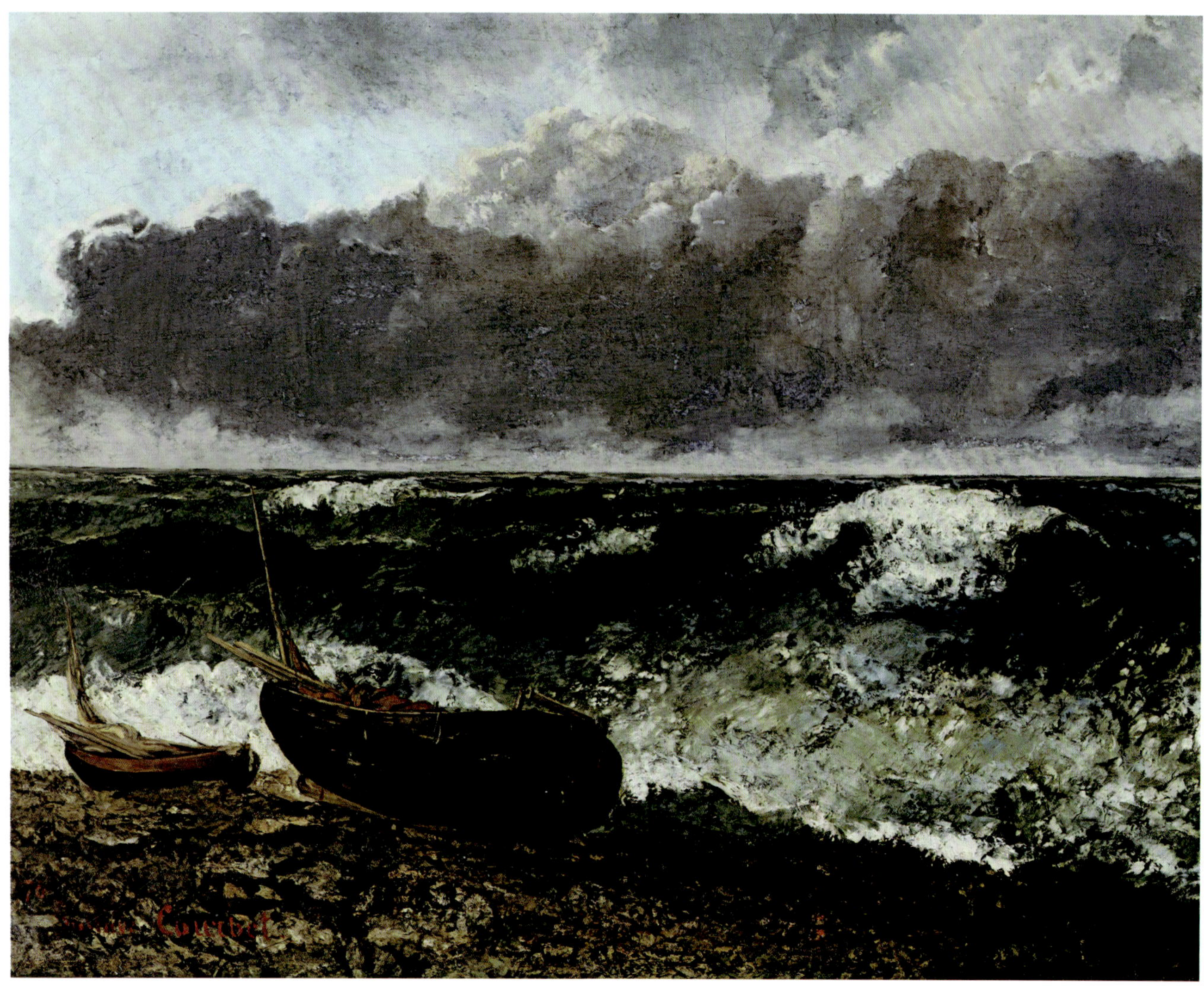

Gustave Courbet (1819–1877)

Stormy Sea

La Mer orageuse

Stürmische See

El mar tormentoso

Il mare in burrasca

De golf

1870, Oil on canvas/Huile sur toile, 116,5 × 160 cm

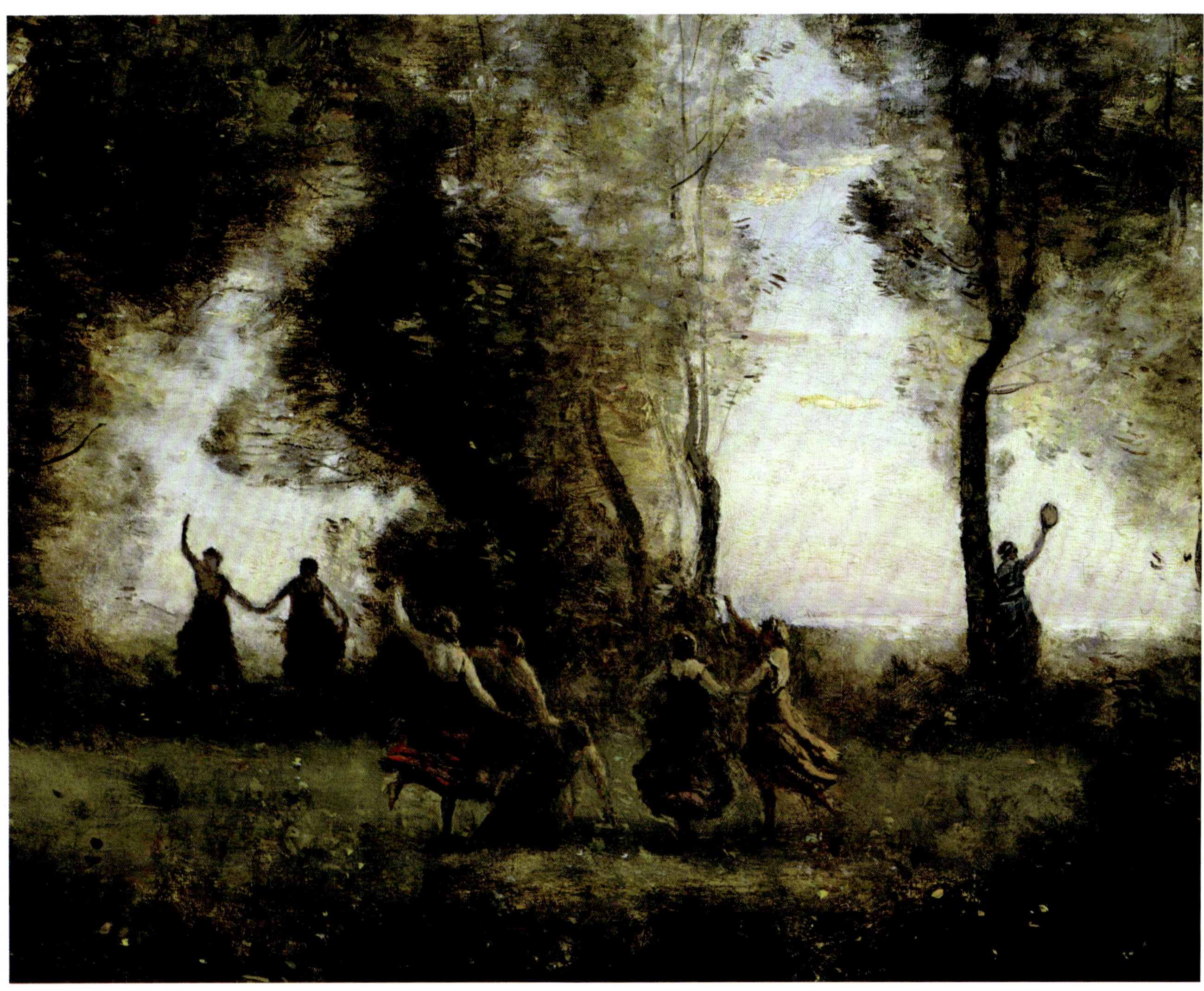

Camille Corot (1796–1875)
Dance of the Nymphs
La Danse des nymphes
Tanz der Nymphen
La danza de las ninfas
La danza delle ninfe
De dans van de nimfen
1860, Oil on canvas/Huile sur toile, 48,1 × 77,2 cm

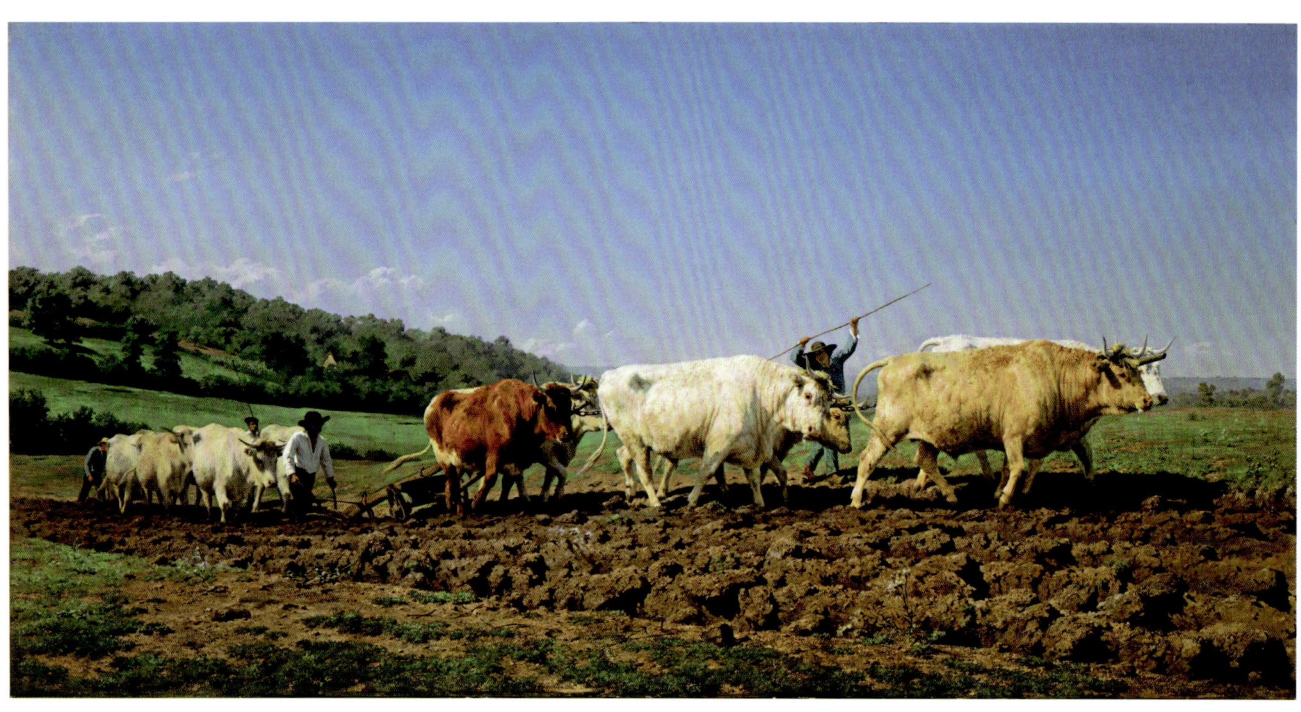

Rosa Bonheur (1822–1899)

Ploughing in the Nivernais

Labourage nivernais

Ackerbau im Nivernais

Labranza en Nivernés

Aratura nivernese

Landarbeid in de Nivernais

1849, Oil on wood/Huile sur bois, 133 × 260 cm

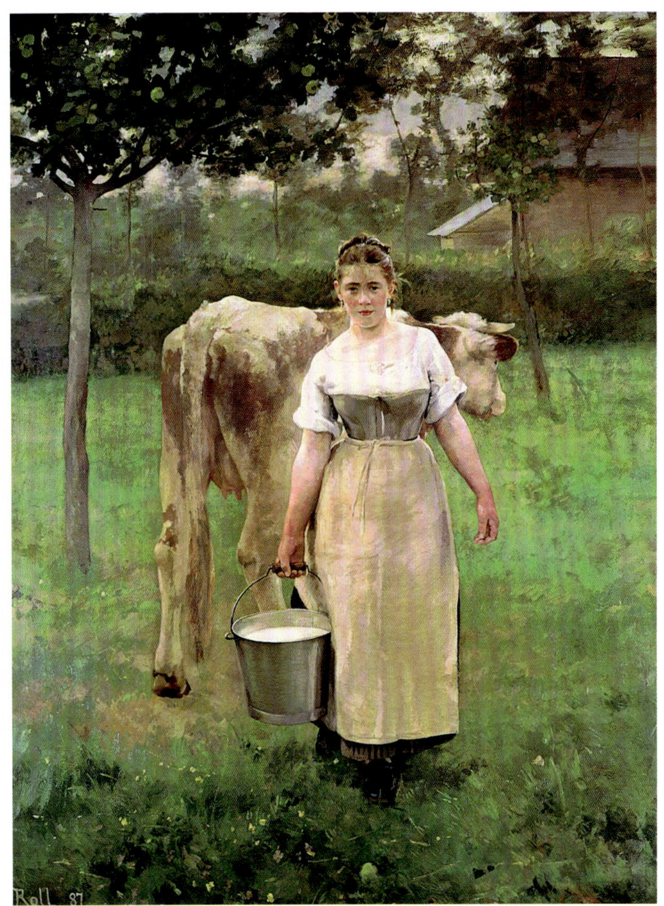

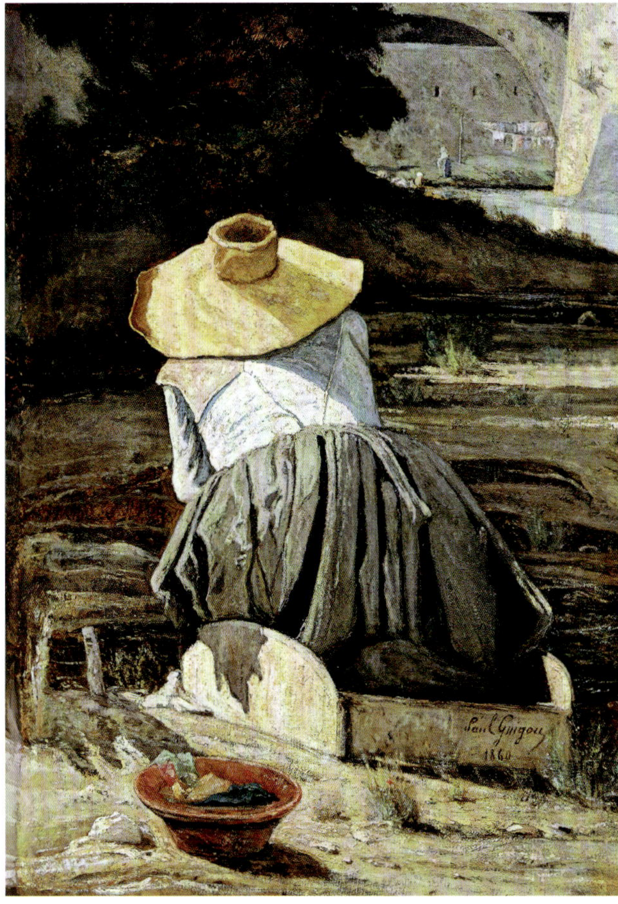

Paul Guigou (1834–1871)

The Laundress

Lavandière

Wäscherin

Cosechadora de lavanda

Lavandaia

De wasvrouw

1860, Oil on canvas/Huile sur toile, 81 × 59 cm

Alfred Roll (1846–1919)

Manda Lametrie, the Farm Maid

Manda Lamétrie, fermière

Manda Lamétrie, Bäuerin

Manda Lamétrie, granjera

Manda Lamétrie, lattaia

Manda Lamétrie, boerin

1887, Oil on canvas/Huile sur toile, 214,3 × 160 cm

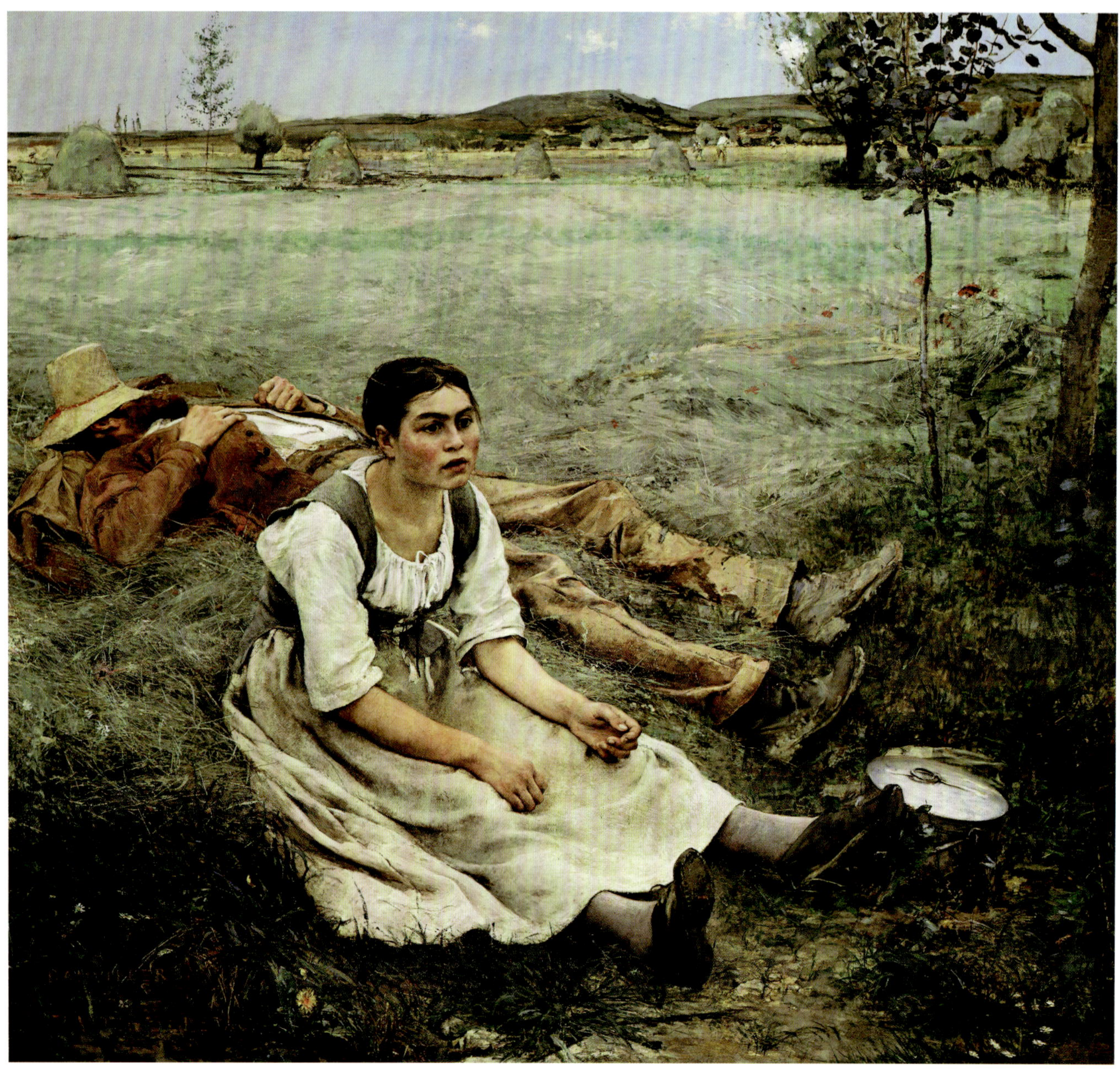

Jules Bastien-Lepage (1848–1884)

The Hay

Les Foins

Die Heuhaufen

La cosecha

I Fieni

De hooibergen

1877, Oil on canvas/Huile sur toile, 180 × 195 cm

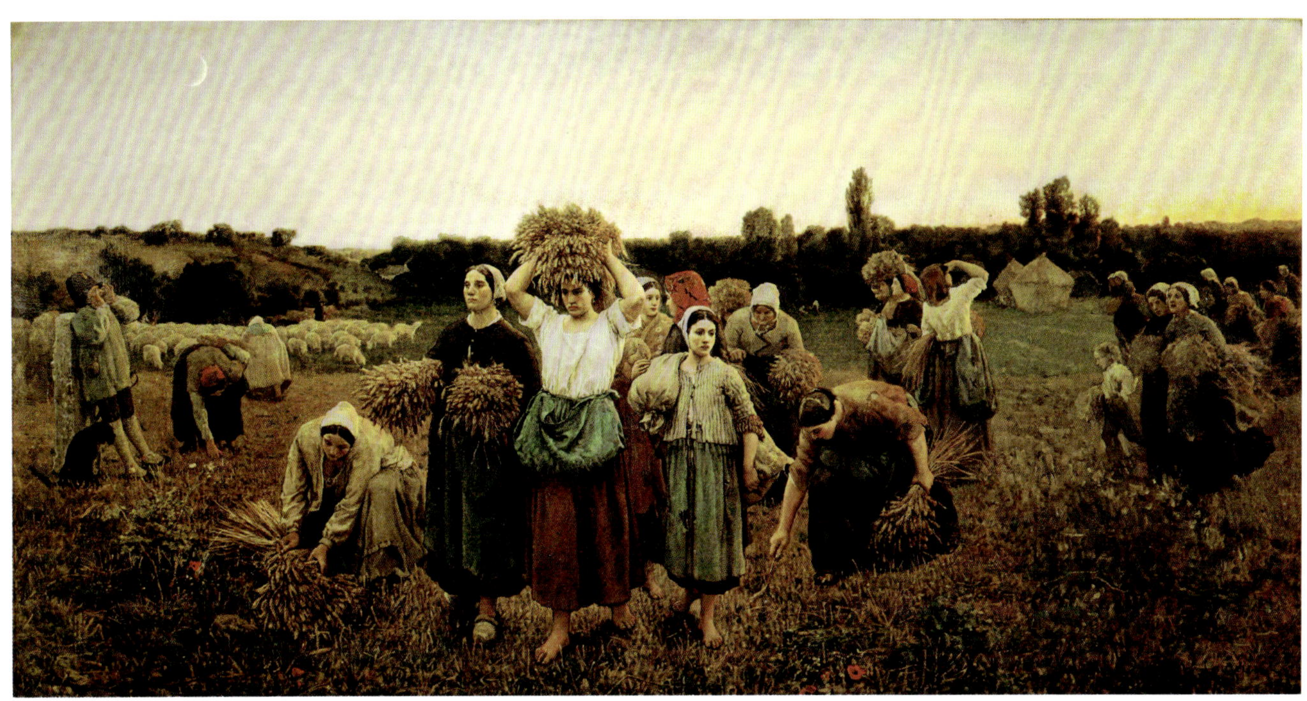

Jules Breton (1827–1906)

Recall of the Gleaners

Le Rappel des glaneuses

Die Heimkehr der Schnitterinnen

El llamamiento de las espigadoras

Il richiamo delle spigolatrici

De terugkeer van de arenleessters

1859, Oil on canvas/Huile sur toile, 90,5 × 176 cm

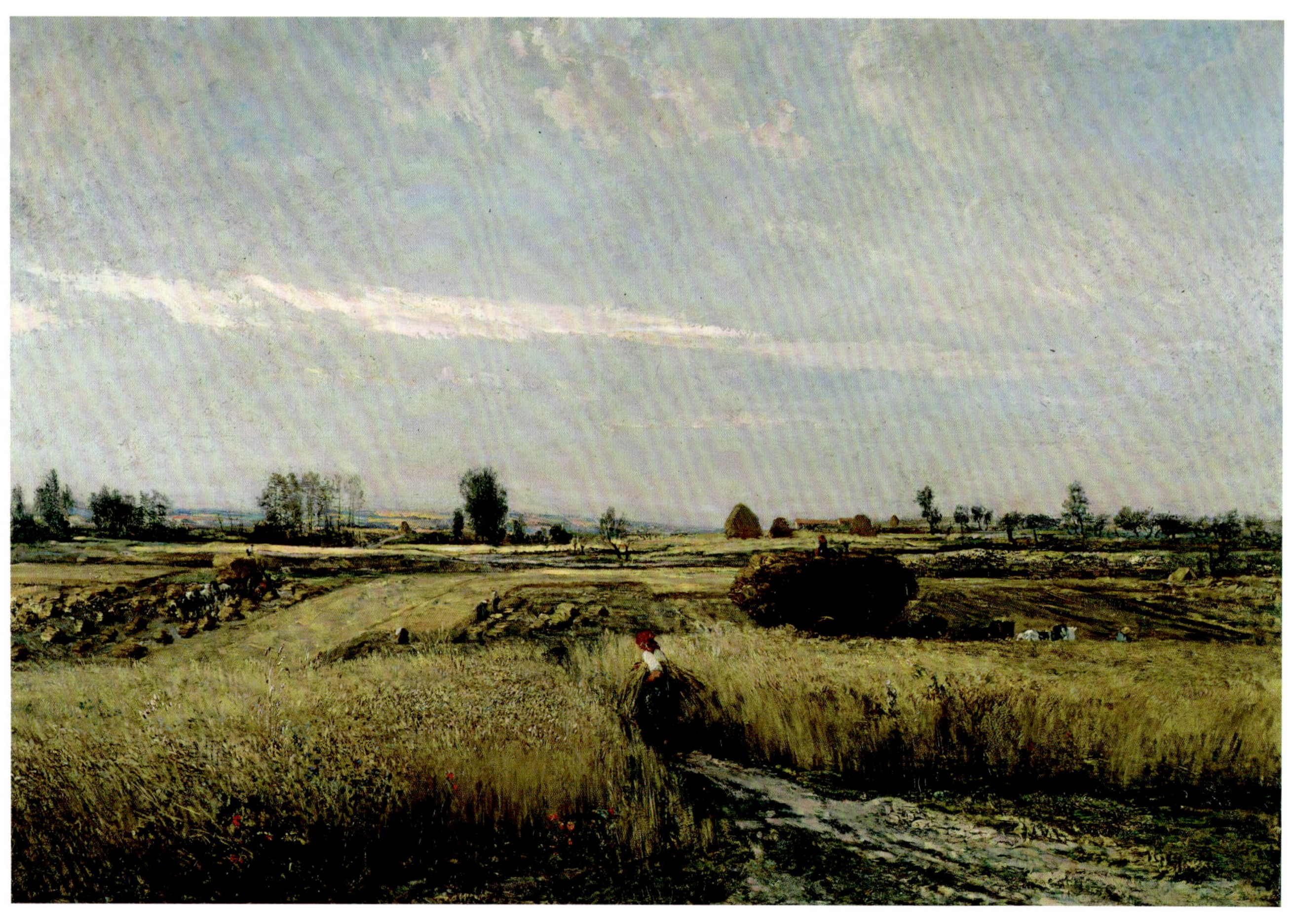

Charles-François Daubigny (1817–1878)

Harvest

Moisson

Ernte

Cosecha

La Mietitura

Oogst

1851, Oil on canvas/Huile sur toile, 135 × 196 cm

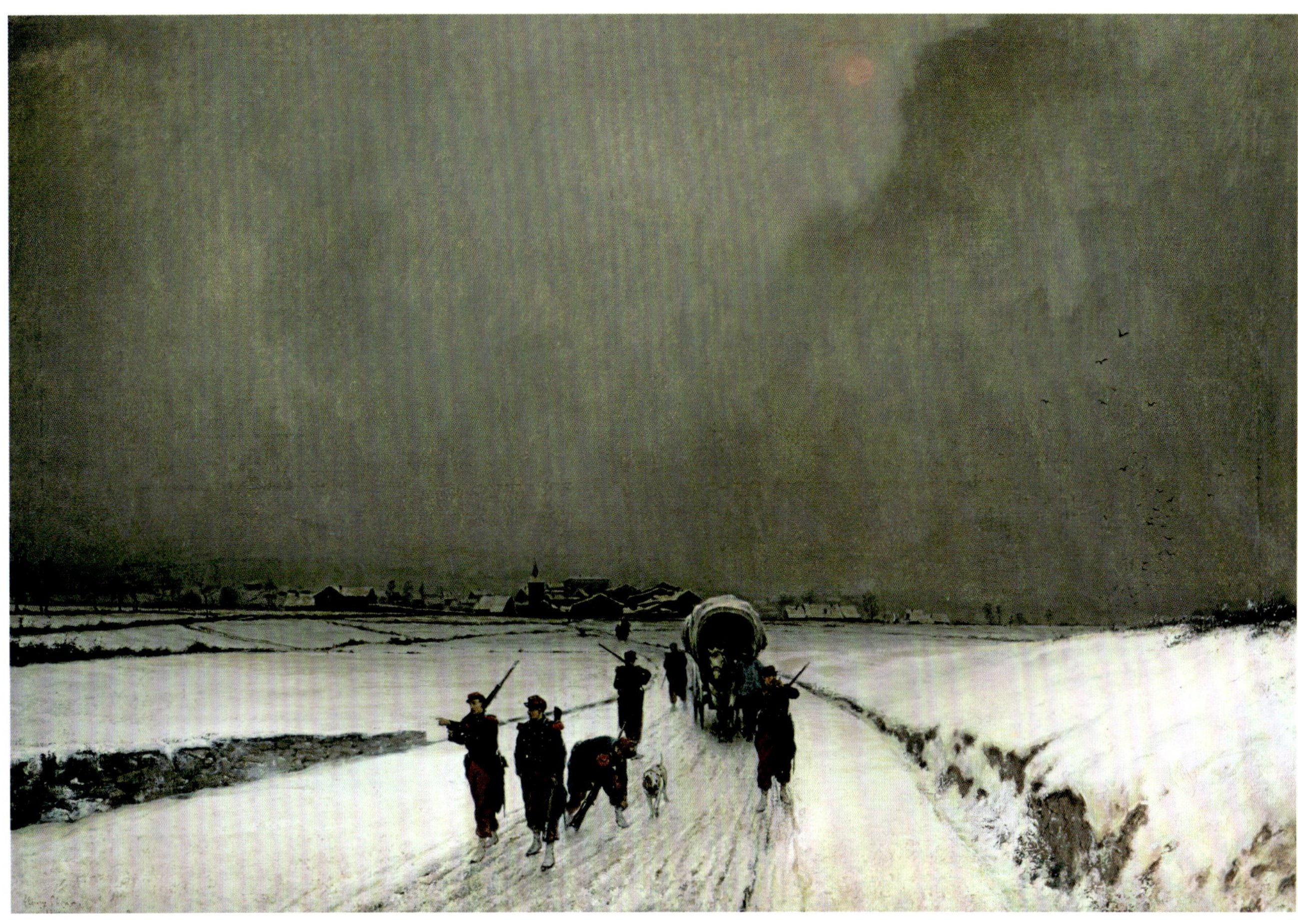

Fleury Chenu (1833–1875)

The Stragglers, Snow Effect

Les Traînards : effet de neige

Die Nachzügler im Schnee

Los rezagados: efecto de nieve

I ritardatari: effetto di neve

De achterblijvers in de sneeuw

1870, Oil on canvas/Huile sur toile, 170 × 152,5 cm

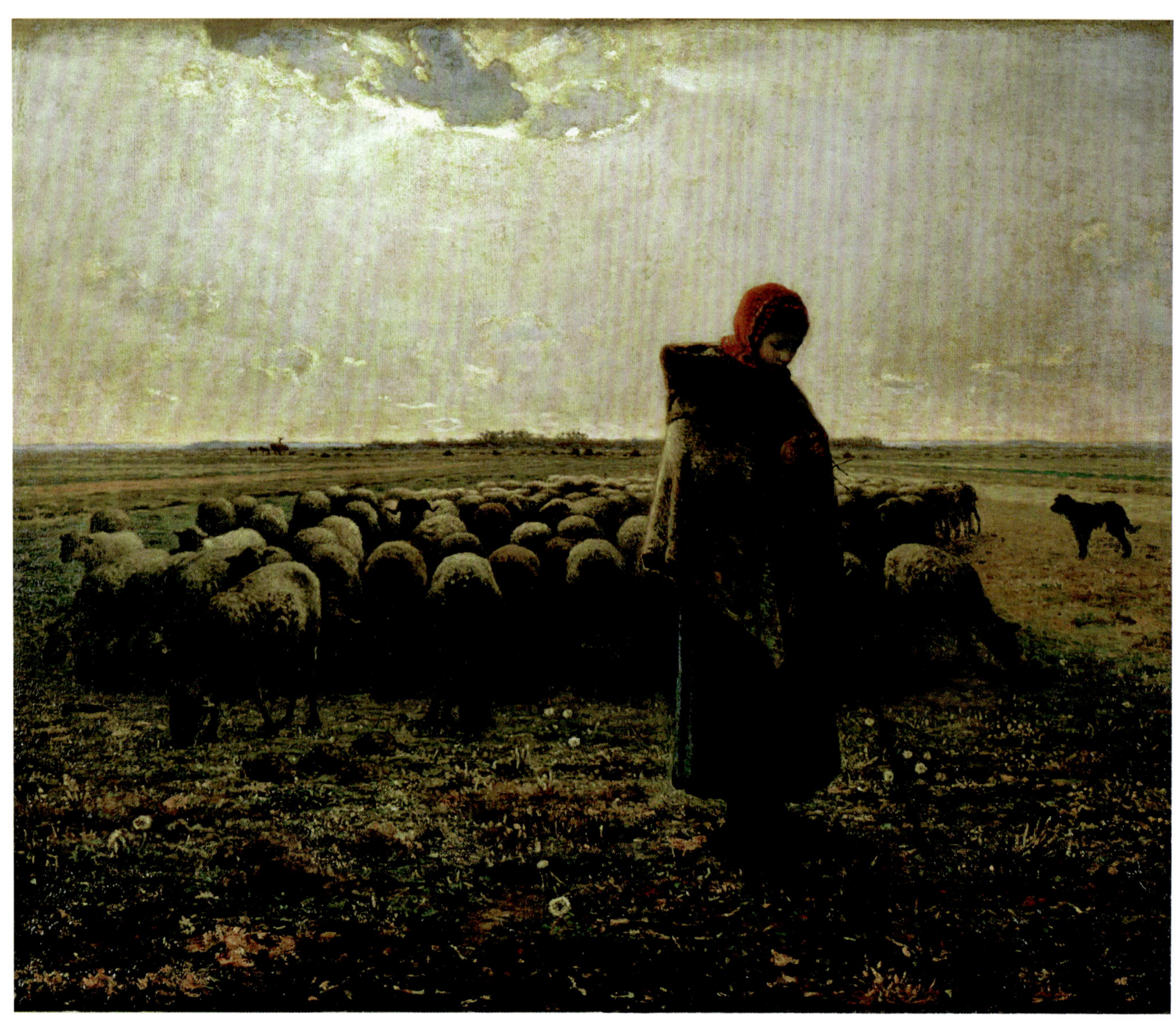

tJean-François Millet (1814–1875)

Shepherdess with her Flock

Bergère avec son troupeau

Schafhirtin mit ihrer Herde

Pastora con su rebaño

Pastorella con il suo gregge

Herderin met kudde

1863, Oil on canvas/Huile sur toile, 81 × 101 cm

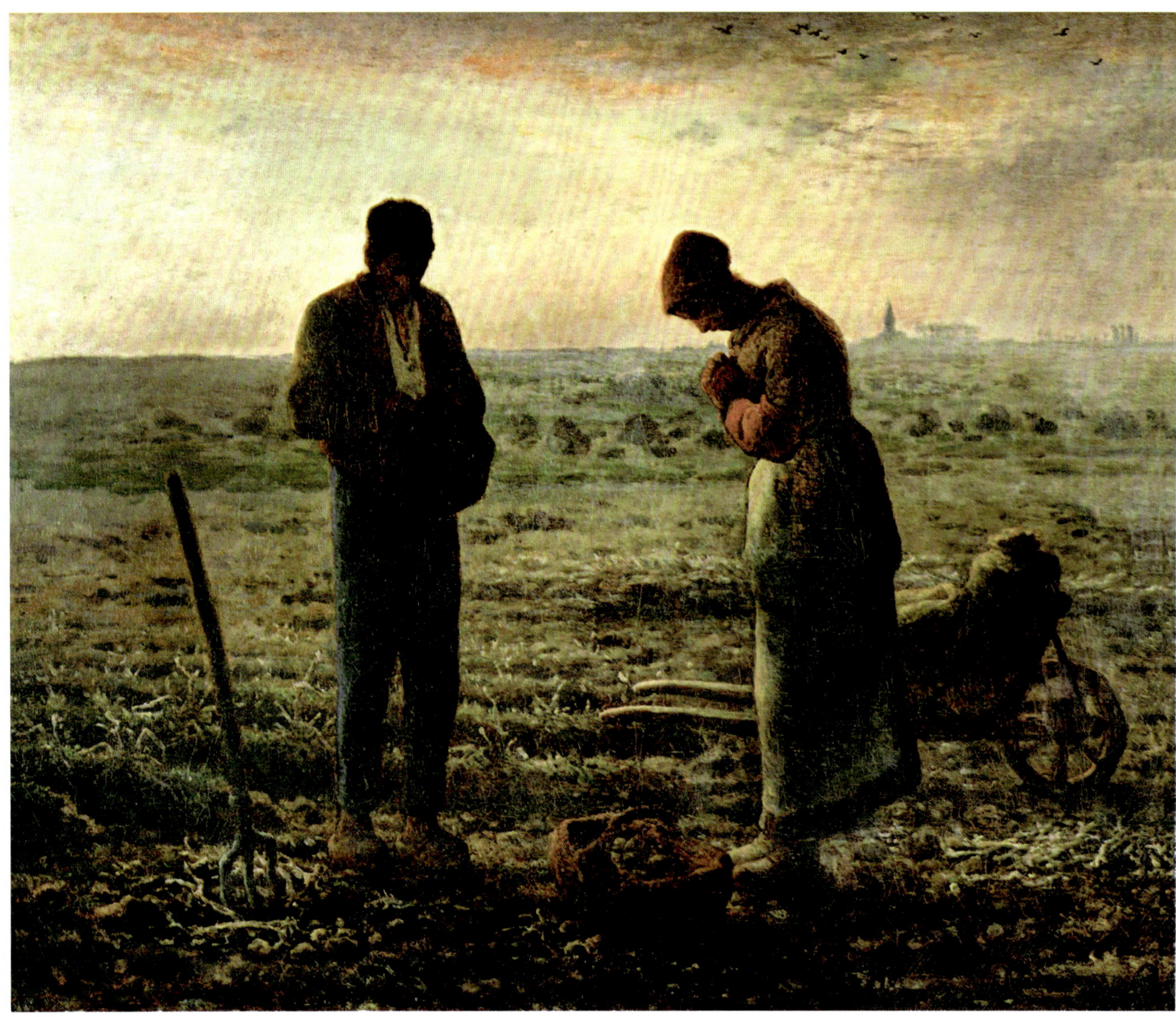

Jean-François Millet (1814–1875)
The Angelus
L'Angélus
Beim Angelusläuten
El Ángelus
L'Angelus
Het angelus
c. 1857–1859
Oil on canvas/Huile sur toile, 55,5 × 66 cm

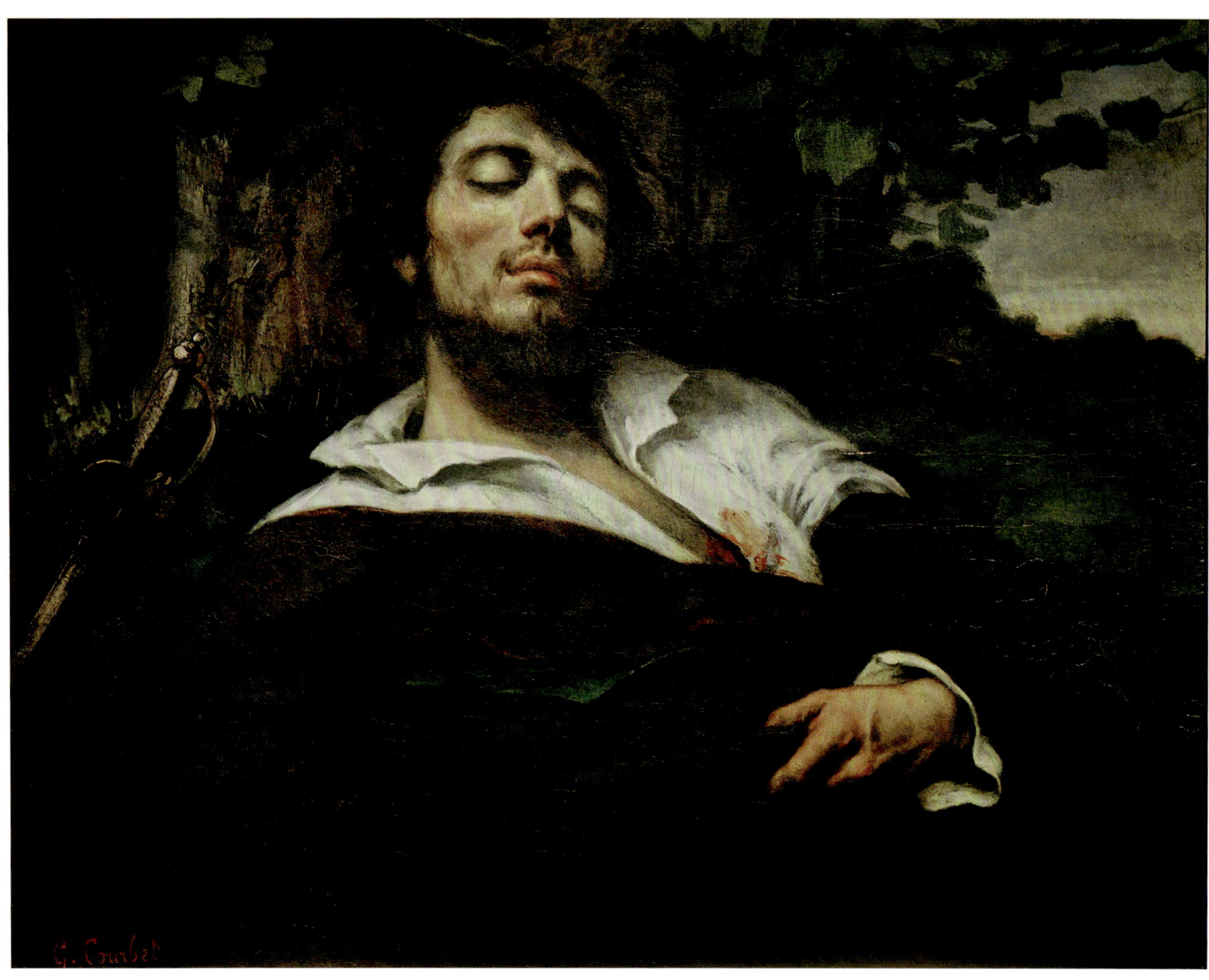

Gustave Courbet (1819–1877)

The Wounded Man

L'Homme blessé

Der Verwundete

El hombre herido

L'Uomo ferito

Gewonde man

c. 1844–1854, Oil on canvas/Huile sur toile, 81,5 × 97,5 cmt

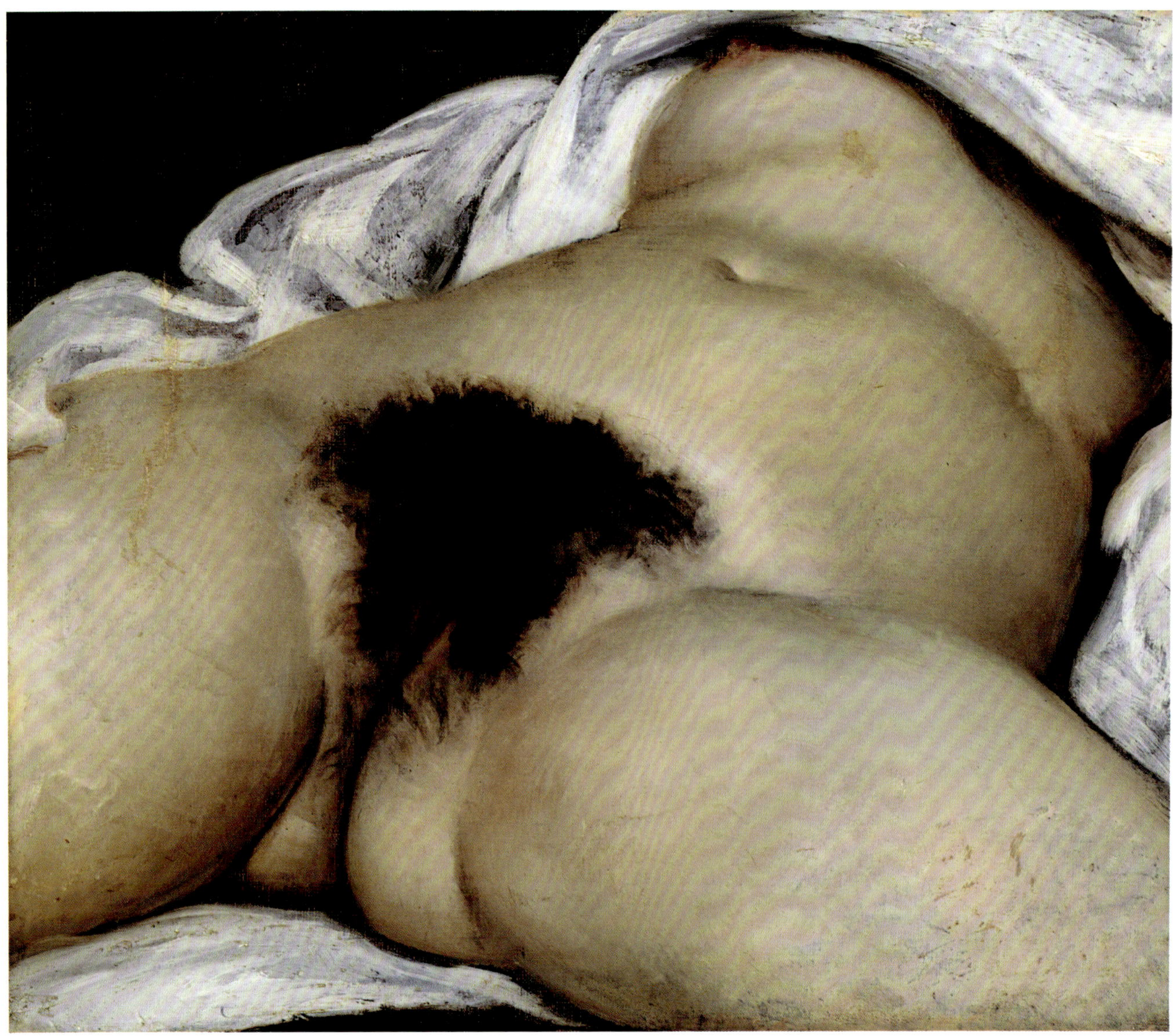

Gustave Courbet (1819–1877)

The Origin of the World

L'Origine du monde

Der Ursprung der Welt

El origen del mundo

L'Origine del mondo

De oorsprong van de wereld

1866, Oil on canvas/Huile sur toile, 46,3 × 55,4 cm

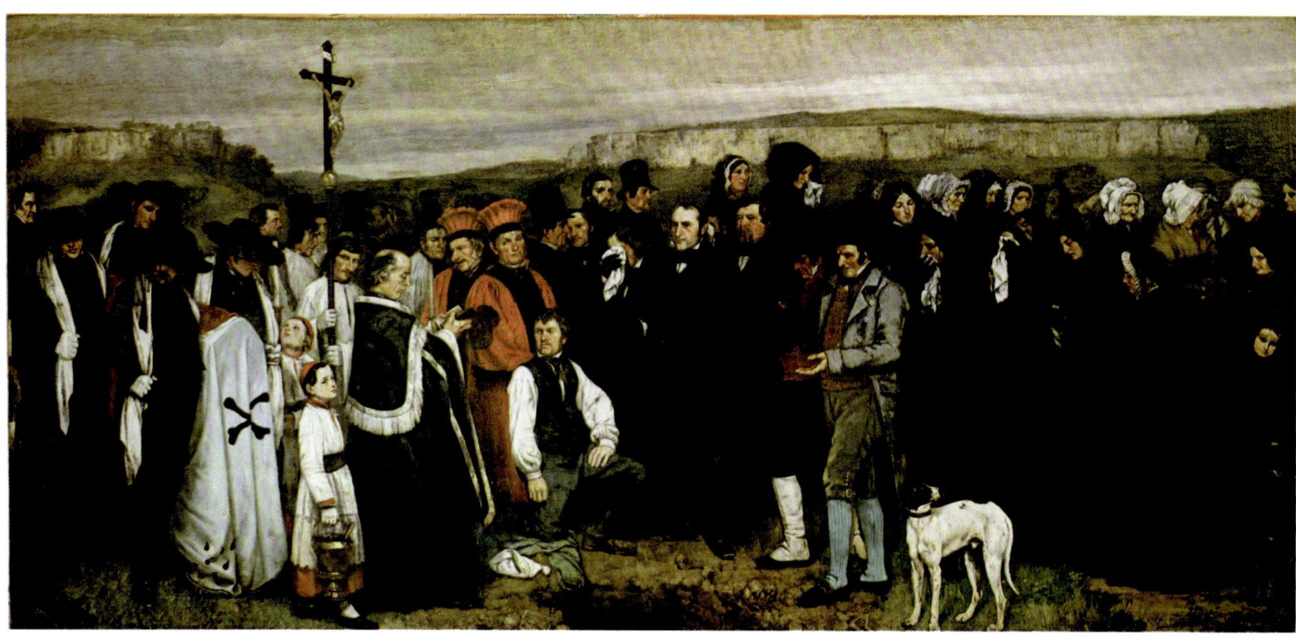

Gustave Courbet (1819–1877)
Burial at Ornans
Un enterrement à Ornans
Begräbnis in Ornans
Entierro en Ornans
Un funerale a Ornans
Begrafenis in Ornans
c. 1849–1850, Oil on canvas/Huile sur toile, 315 × 668 cm

A manifesto of the realism of Gustave Courbet, *Burial at Ornans* elicited the most extreme criticism at the Salon of 1850. Judged to be "trivial", even "ignoble", the painting has the audacity of staging a daily scene within a monumental format normally reserved for historical painting. Courbet uses the inhabitants of Ornans as models, whom he had pose in his studio, and whom he assembles into two distinct groups in the painting—the men on one side and the women on the other.

Œuvre manifeste du réalisme de Gustave Courbet, *Un enterrement à Ornans* essuya les critiques les plus violentes au salon de 1850. Jugé « trivial », voire « ignoble », le tableau a l'audace de mettre en scène un sujet du quotidien dans un format monumental habituellement réservé à la peinture d'histoire. Courbet prend pour modèles des habitants d'Ornans, qu'il fait poser un par un dans son atelier, et qu'il réunit sur la toile en deux groupes distincts, les hommes d'un côté, les femmes de l'autre.

Begräbnis in Ornans ist ein Manifest des Realismus von Gustave Courbet und wurde auf dem Salon von 1850 heftig kritisiert. Mit dem als „trivial" und sogar „schändlich" bezeichneten Gemälde wagt es Courbet, ein Alltagsthema in einem monumentalen Format in Szene zu setzen, welches gewöhnlich der Historienmalerei vorbehalten ist. Courbet lässt die Einwohner von Ornans einzeln in seinem Atelier Modell stehen und vereint sie dann in seinem Gemälde in zwei verschiedenen Gruppen: die Männer auf der einen, die Frauen auf der anderen Seite.

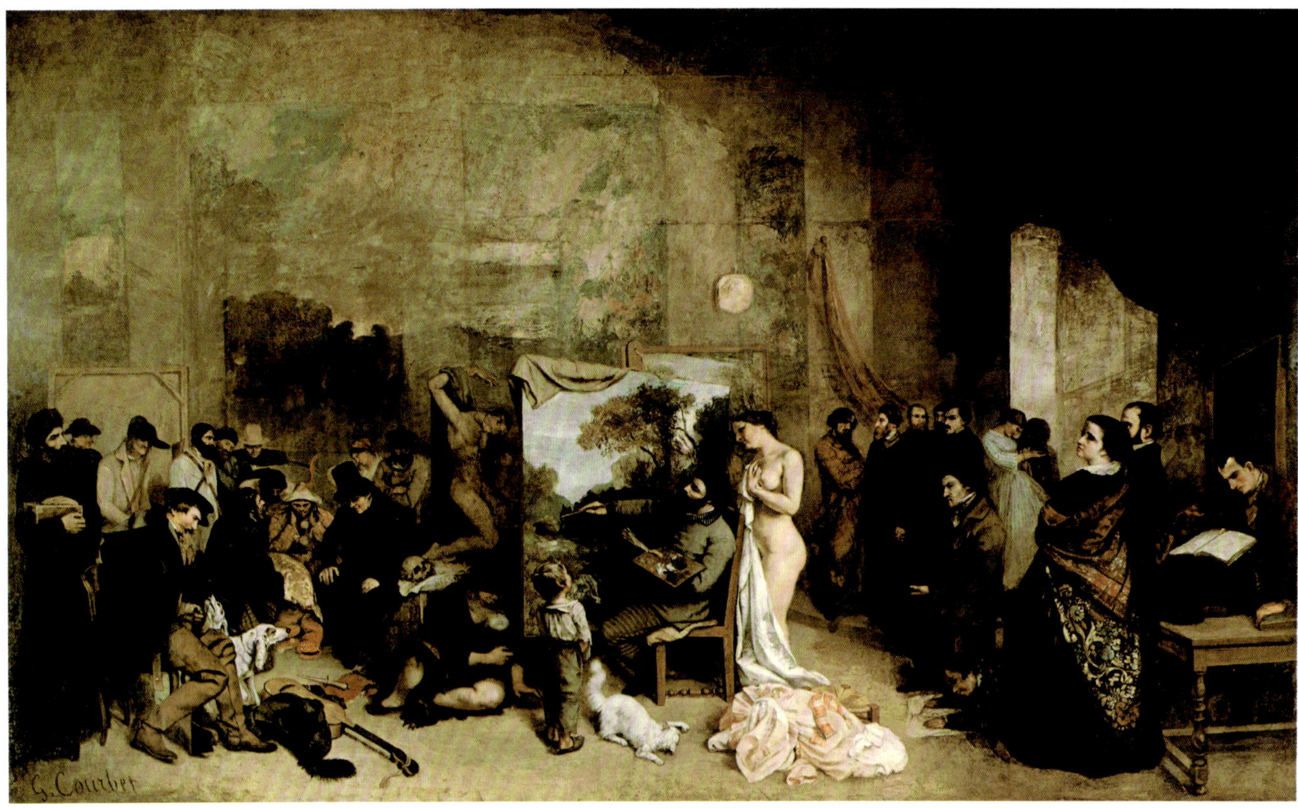

Gustave Courbet (1819–1877)

The Artist's Studio

L'Atelier du peintre

Das Atelier

El taller del pintor

La bottega del pittore

Het schildersatelier

c. 1854–1855, Oil on canvas/Huile sur toile, 361 × 598 cm

Obra de realismo manifiesto de Gustave Courbet, *Entierro en Ornans* recibe las críticas más violentas del Salón de 1850. Juzgado como "trivial" o "despreciable", el cuadro tiene la audacia de poner en escena un tema de la vida cotidiana en un formato monumental generalmente reservado para la pintura histórica. Courbet toma como modelos a los habitantes de Ornans, les hace posar uno por uno en su estudio, y los lleva al lienzo en dos grupos distintos, los hombres a un lado, las mujeres al otro.

Manifesto del Realismo di Gustave Courbet, *Un funerale a Ornans* suscitò le critiche più dure in occasione del Salon del 1850. Giudicato "banale" e "ignobile", il quadro osa rappresentare un tema della vita quotidiana in un formato monumentale, di solito riservato alla pittura storica. Courbet prese come modelli gli abitanti di Ornans, che fece posare uno per uno nel suo studio e che portò poi sulla tela in due gruppi distinti: gli uomini da una parte e le donne dall'altra.

Begrafenis in Ornans, een uitgesproken realistisch werk van Gustave Courbet, werd op de Salon van 1850 hevig bekritiseerd. Het schilderij, dat als 'triviaal' en zelfs 'afgrijselijk' werd afgedaan, getuigt van de moed om een alledaags tafereel te tonen op een monumentaal formaat dat tot dan toe aan historieschilders was voorbehouden. Courbet neemt de inwoners van Ornans als model en laat hen een voor een in zijn atelier poseren, waarna hij ze op het doek in twee verschillende groepen samenbrengt: mannen links, vrouwen rechts.

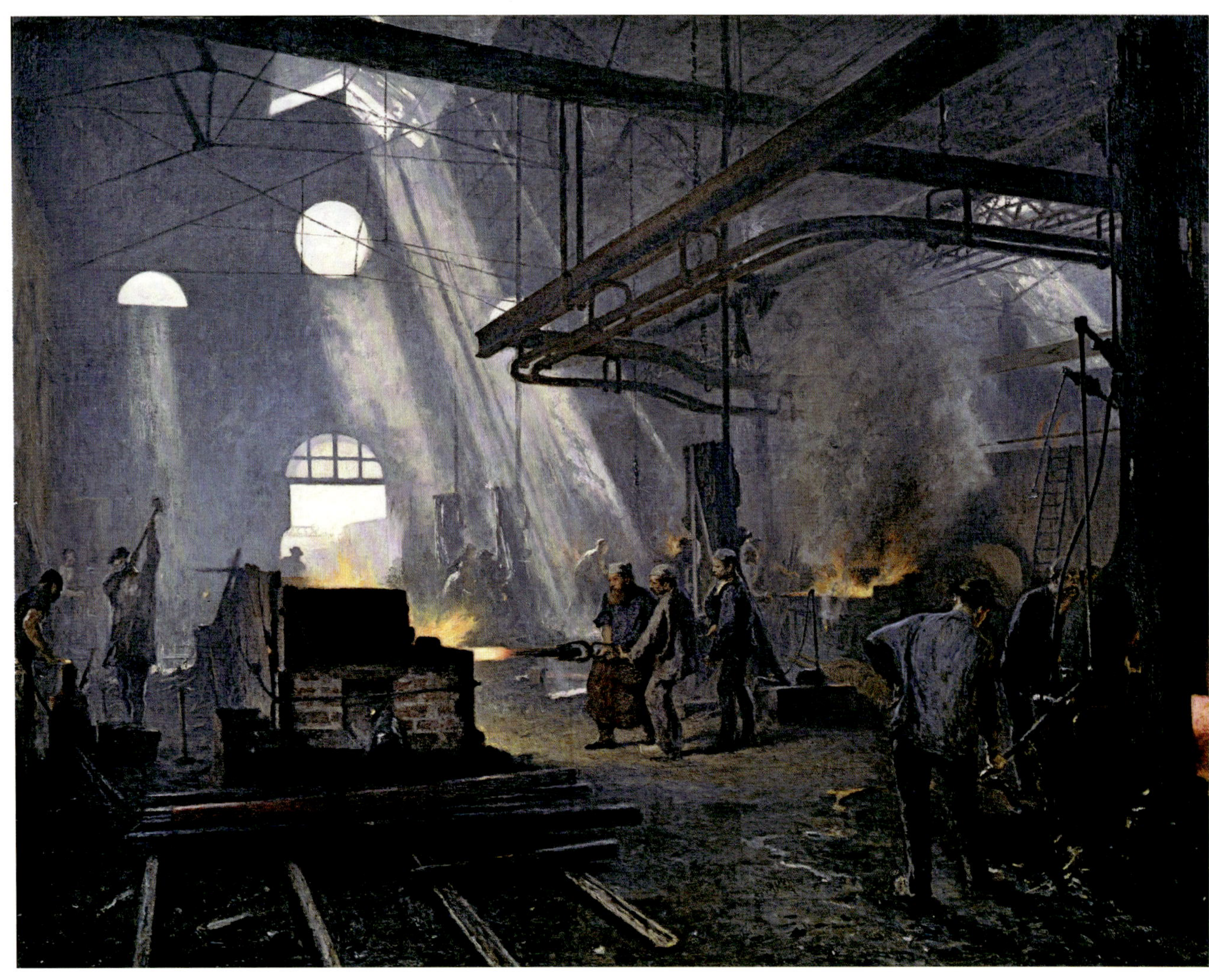

Fernand Cormon (1845–1924)

A Forge

Une forge

Hüttenwerk

Una fragua

La fonderia

Een smelterij

1893, Oil on canvas/Huile sur toile, 70,5 × 90,7 cm

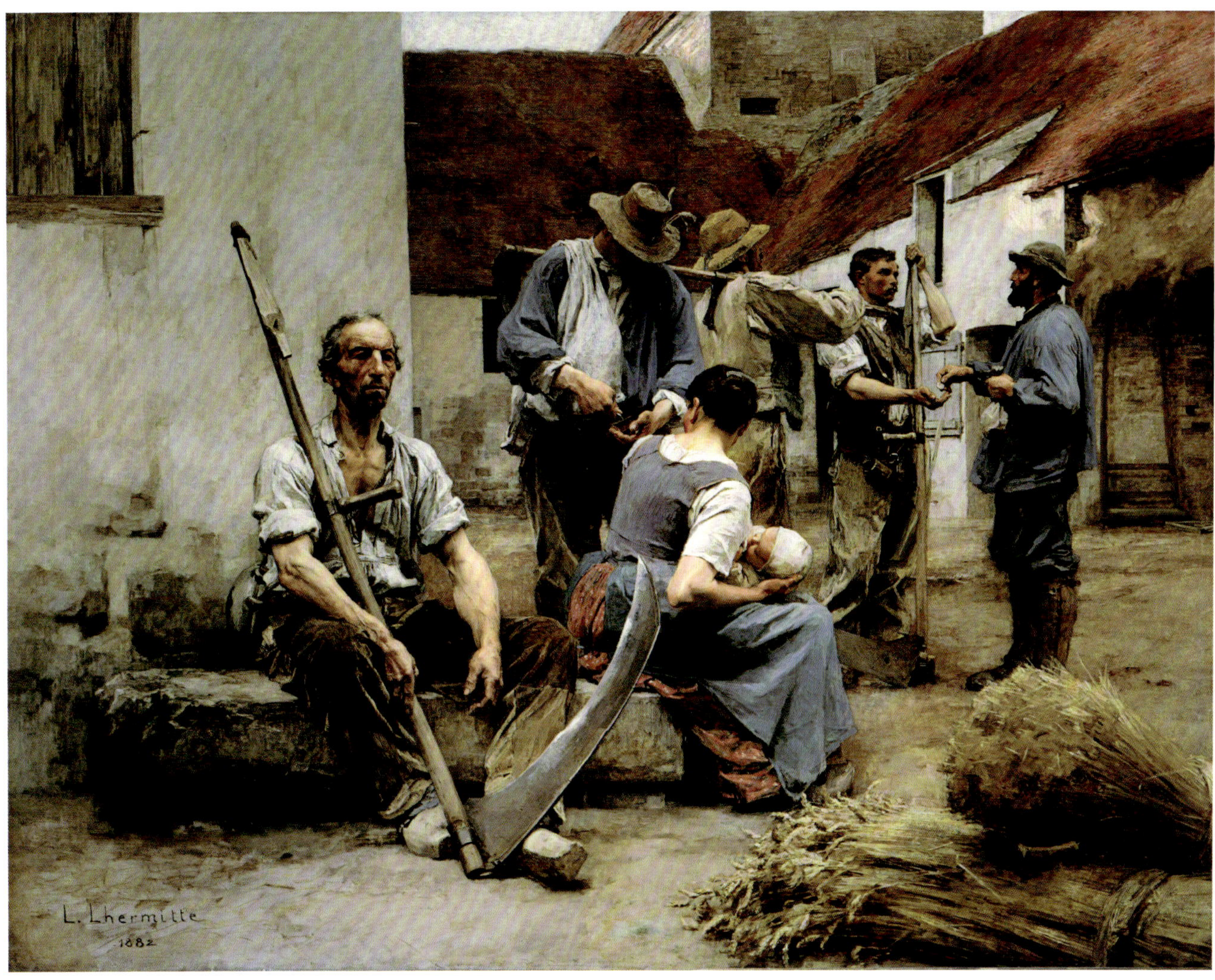

Léon Lhermitte (1844–1925)

Paying the Harvesters

La Paye des moissonneurs

Die Bezahlung der Schnitter

La paga de los cosechadores

La paga dei mietitori

Betaling van de maaiers

1882, Oil on canvas/Huile sur toile, 215 × 272 cm

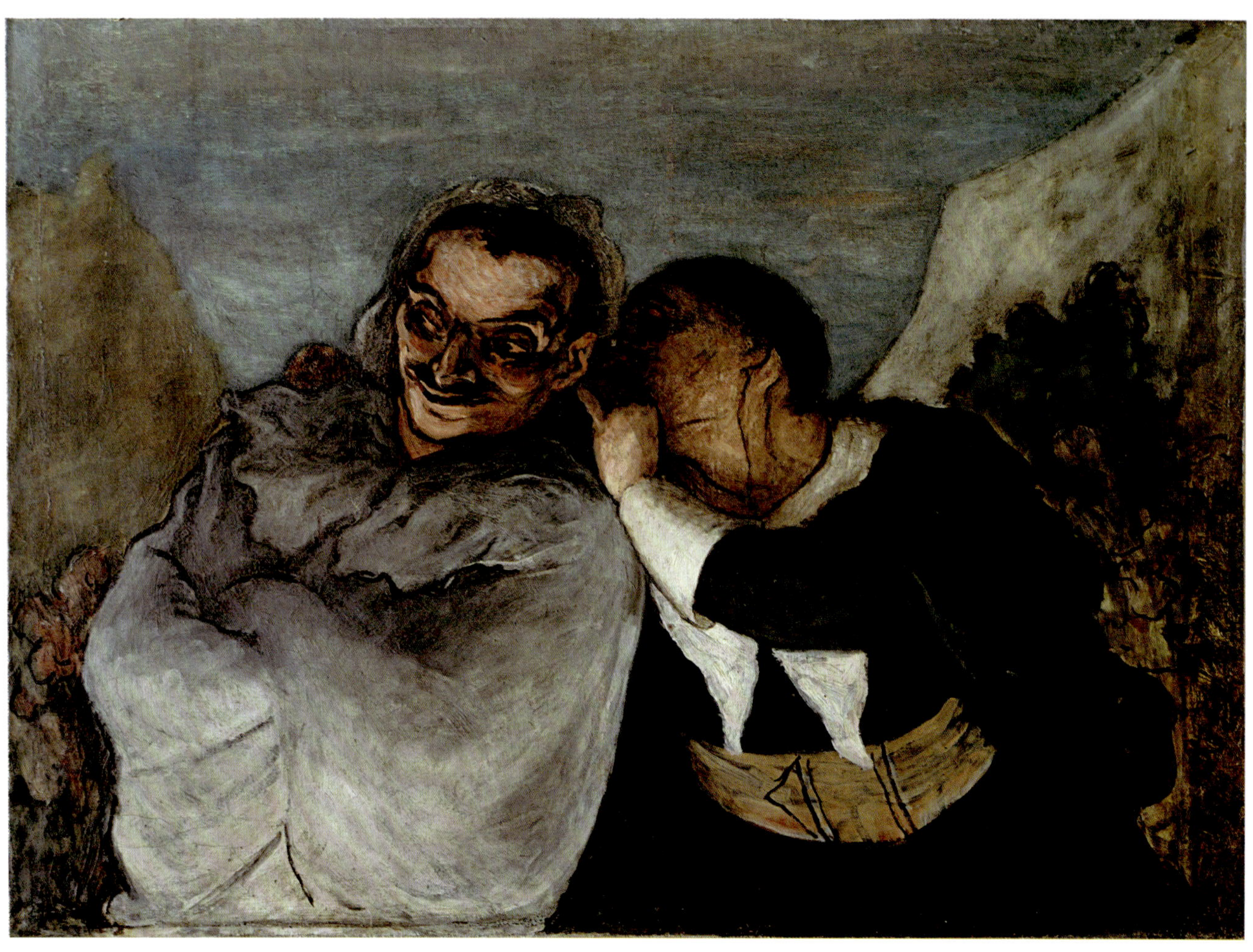

Honoré Daumier (1808–1879)

Crispin and Scapin

Crispin et Scapin

Crispin und Scapin

Crispin y Scapin

Crispino e Scapino

Crispin en Scapin

c. 1864, Oil on canvas/Huile sur toile, 61 × 83 cm

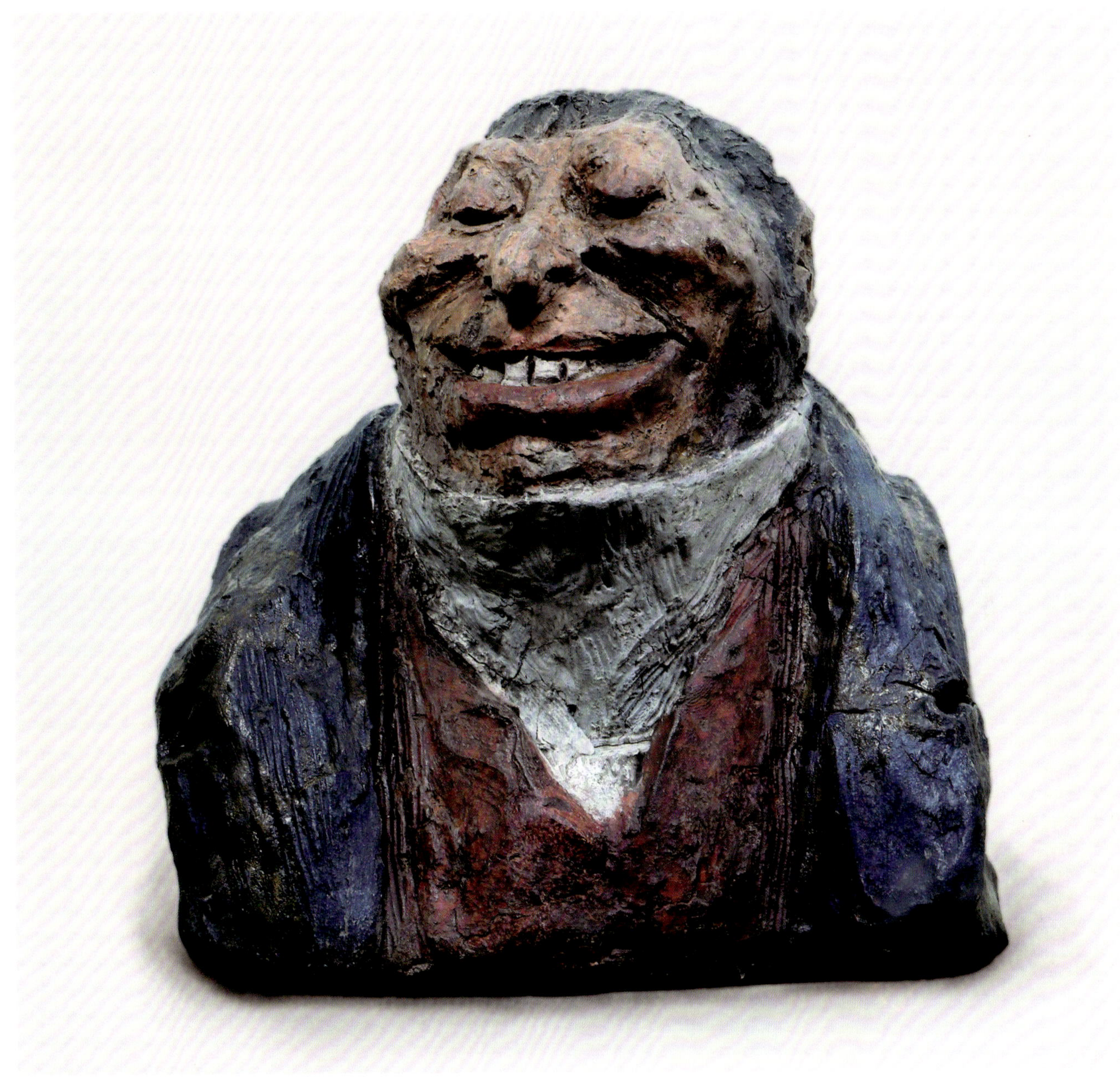

Honoré Daumier (1808–1879)

Count Auguste Hilarion de Kératry

Auguste Hilarion, comte de Kératry

Auguste Hilarion de Kératry

Auguste Hilarion, conde de Kératry

Auguste Hilarion, conte di Kératry

Graaf Auguste Hilarion de Kératry

1833, Raw painted earth/Terre crue peinte, 12,9 × 12,9 × 17,5 cm

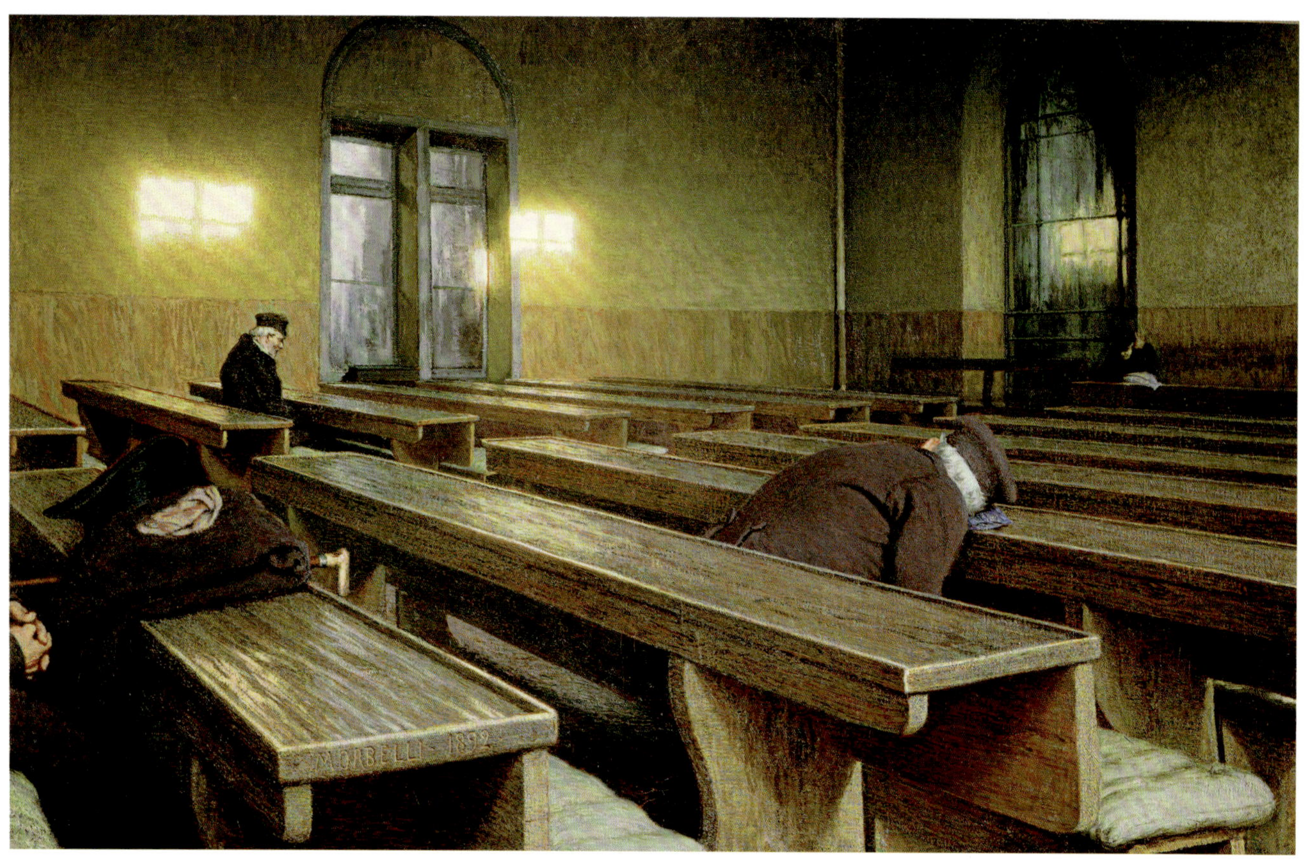

Angelo Morbelli (1853–1919)

High Day in the Trivulzio Hospice in Milan

Jour de fête à l'hospice Trivulzio à Milan

Feiertag im Hospiz Trivulzio in Mailand

Día de fiesta en el hospicio Trivulzio

Giorno di festa al Pio Albergo

Feestdag in het hospice Trivulzio in Milaan

1892, Oil on canvas/Huile sur toile, 78 × 123 cm

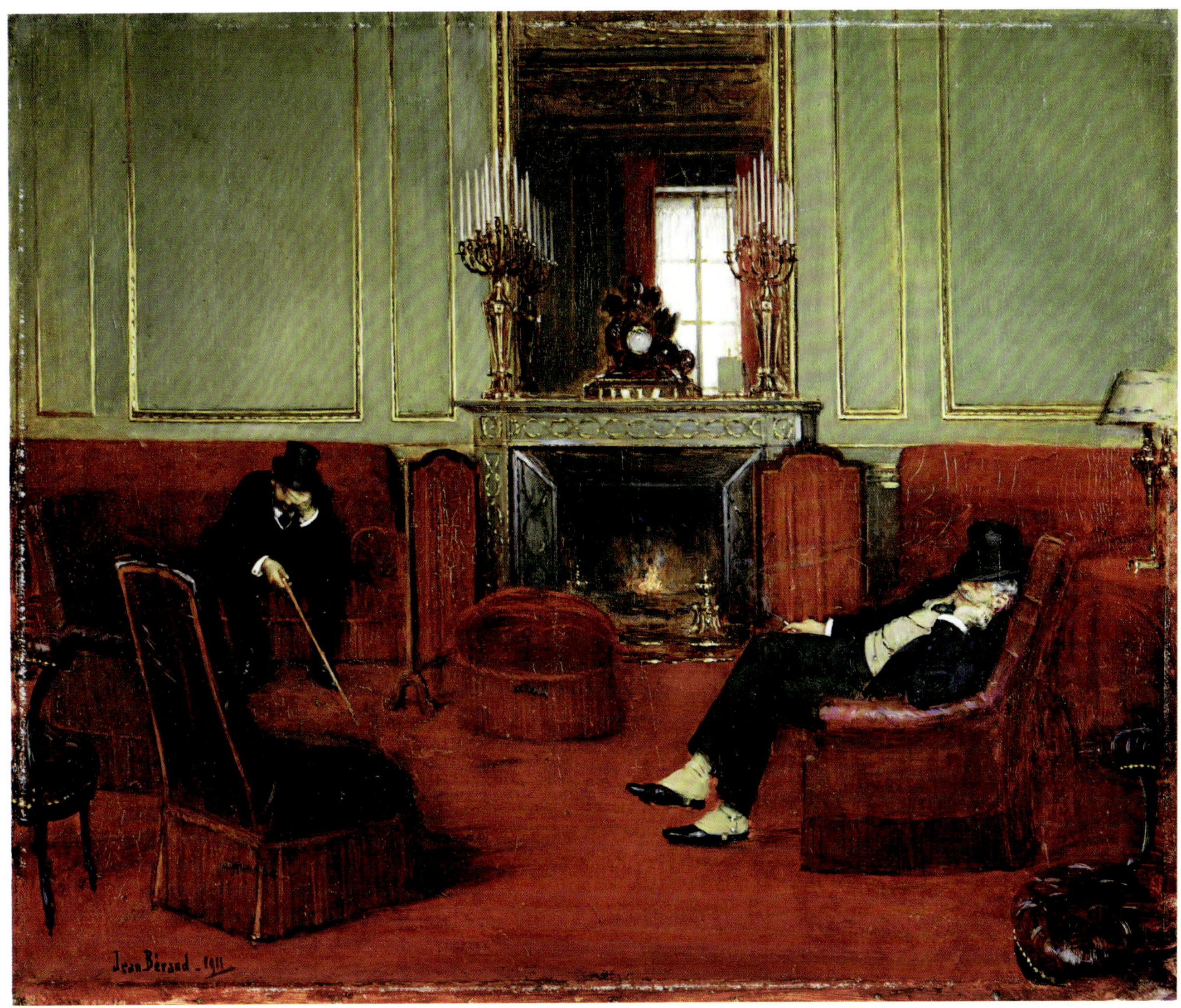

Jean Béraud (1848–1935)
The Club
Le Cercle
Club. „Le Cercle“
El Círculo
Il club
De cirkel
1911, Oil on canvas/Huile sur toile, 61 × 73,5 cm

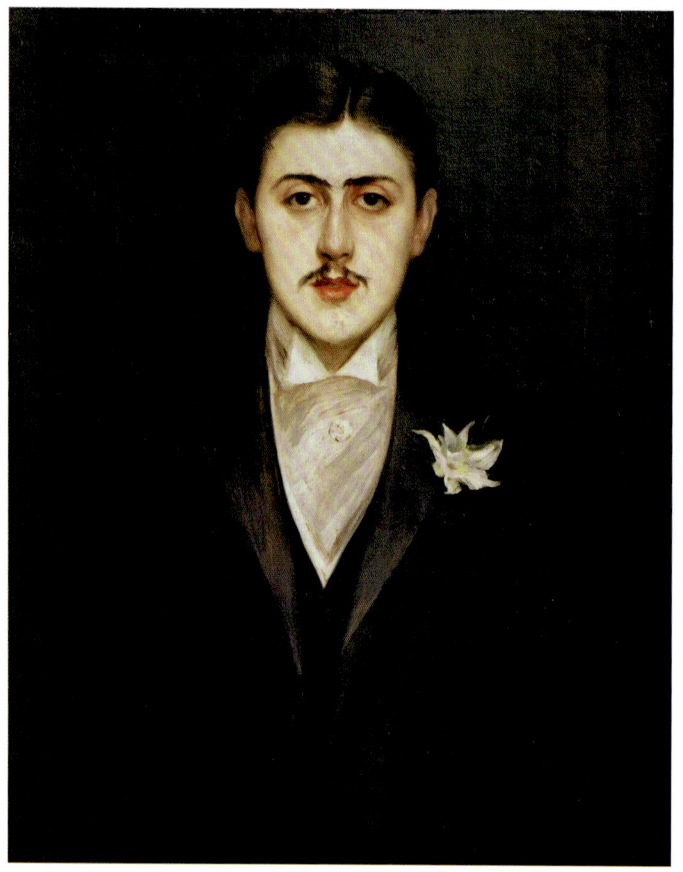

Jacques-Émile Blanche (1861–1942)
Marcel Proust
1892, Oil on canvas/Huile sur toile, 73,5 × 60,5 cm

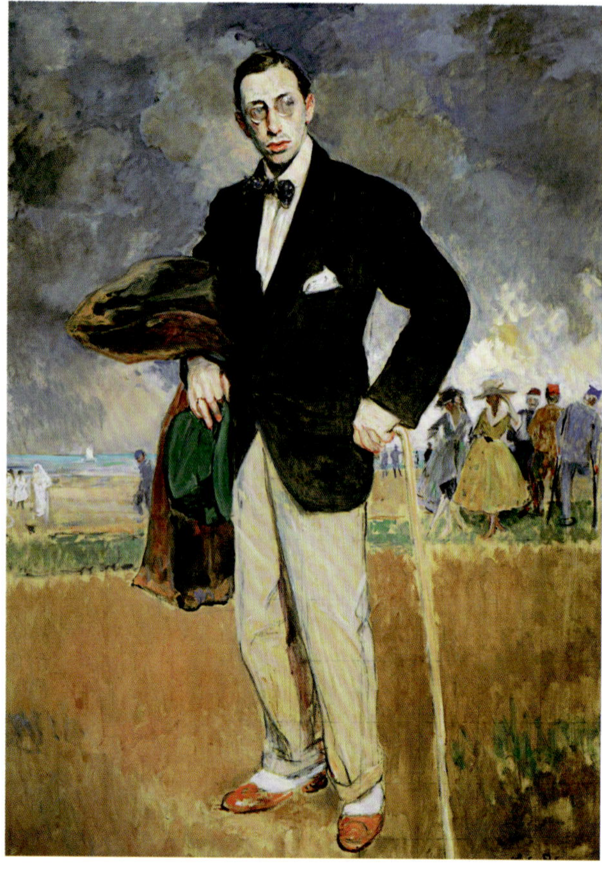

Jacques-Émile Blanche (1861–1942)

Igor Stravinsky	Igor Strawinsky	Igor Stravinskij
Igor Stravinsky	Igor Stravinski	Igor Stravinsky

1915, Oil on canvas/Huile sur toile, 175 × 124 cm

Friend of the artists of the Belle Époque, Jacques-Émile Blanche immortalises Marcel Proust at twenty-one. He is not yet the author of *Remembrance of Things Past* but is already a noted social chronicler. This portrait in a very interior setting is rather austere. Against an unadorned background the author's visage stands out—a pale complexion and a fine mustache—as well as the neckline of his shirt and the flower round his buttonhole. Proust kept the work until his death in 1922.

Ami des artistes de la Belle Époque, Jacques-Émile Blanche immortalise Marcel Proust à vingt-et-un ans. Il n'est pas encore l'auteur d'*À la recherche du Temps perdu,* mais déjà un chroniqueur mondain remarqué. Ce portrait, très intérieur, est plutôt austère. Sur un fond sans décor, se détachent le visage de l'écrivain – teint blafard et moustache fine –, l'encolure de sa chemise et la fleur de sa boutonnière. Proust a conservé l'œuvre jusqu'à sa mort, en 1922.

Jacques-Émile Blanche ist ein Freund der Belle Époque-Künstler und verewigt Marcel Proust im Alter von 21 Jahren. Der zukünftige Autor von *Auf der Suche nach der verlorenen Zeit* ist bereits ein beachteter mondäner Chronist. Dieses sehr intime Porträt wirkt relativ streng. Von einem Hintergrund ohne Dekor heben sich das Gesicht des Schriftstellers – blasser Teint, feiner Schnurrbart –, der Halsausschnitt seines Hemds und die Blume im Knopfloch ab. Proust bewahrte dieses Werk bis zu seinem Tod im Jahr 1922 auf.

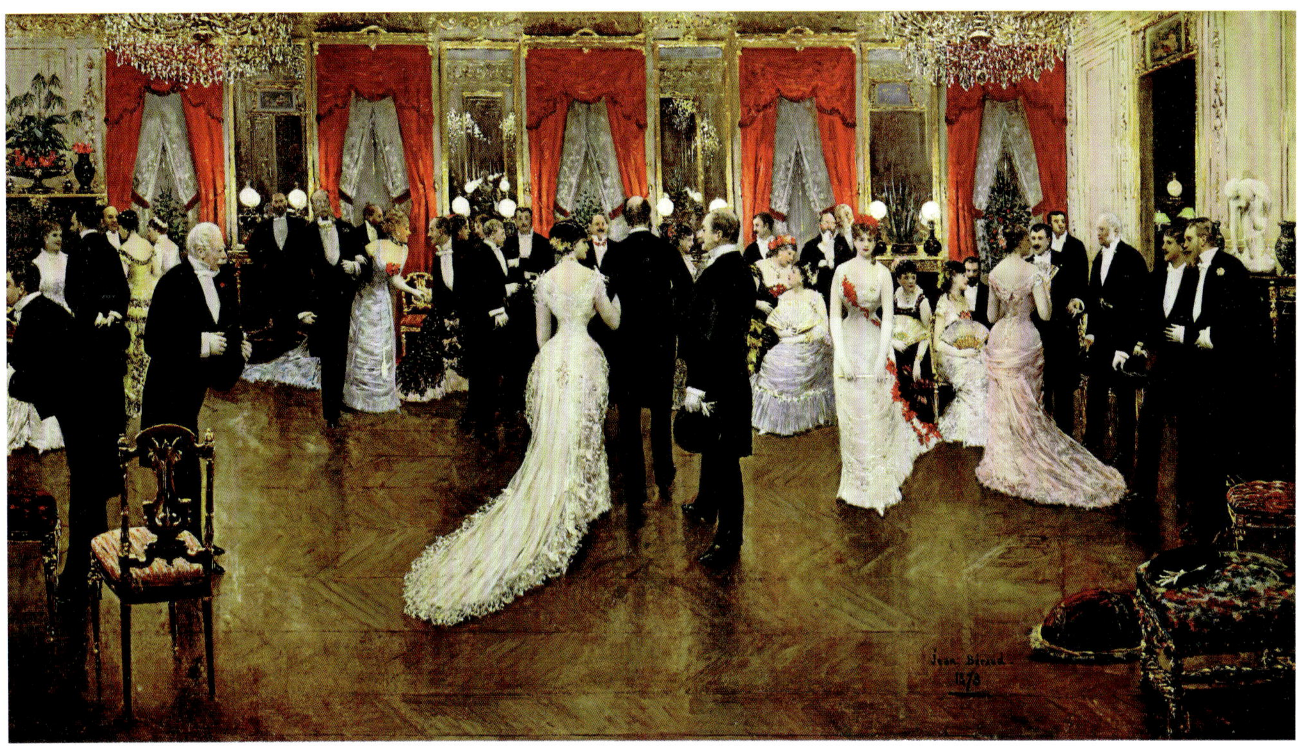

Jean Béraud (1848–1935)

| The Soirée | Ein Abend | Una serata |
| Une soirée | Soirée | Soirée |

1878, Oil on canvas/Huile sur toile, 65 × 117 cm

Amigo de artistas de la Belle Époque, Jacques-Émile Blanche inmortalizó a un Marcel Proust de veintiún años. Aún no había escrito *En busca del tiempo perdido,* pero ya era un cronista conocido. Este retrato, muy intimista, es más bien austero. Sobre un fondo sin decoración, destaca el rostro del escritor – pálida tez y fino bigote –, el cuello de la camisa y la flor en el ojal. Proust conservó la obra hasta su muerte en 1922.

Amico di artisti della Belle Époque, Jacques-Émile Blanche immortalò in questo quadro Marcel Proust all'età di ventuno anni, quando lo scrittore non era ancora l'autore di *Alla ricerca del tempo perduto* ma era già un noto cronista mondano. Il ritratto è molto intimo e piuttosto austero. Dallo sfondo liscio spiccano il volto dello scrittore, con un incarnato pallido e sottili baffi, il collo della camicia e il fiore all'occhiello. Proust restò in possesso dell'opera fino alla sua morte, nel 1922.

Jacques-Émile Blanche, een vriend van de kunstenaars uit de Belle Époque, vereeuwigt Marcel Proust op 21-jarige leeftijd. Proust heeft zijn *Op zoek naar de verloren tijd* dan nog niet geschreven, maar is al wel als mondain kroniekschrijver opgemerkt. Dit zeer naar binnen gekeerde portret is vooral streng. Het gezicht van de schrijver – vale teint en smalle snor –, het boord van zijn overhemd en de bloem in zijn knoopsgat tekenen zich af tegen een kale achtergrond. Proust had het werk tot zijn dood in 1922 in bezit.

Unjustly unrecognized, Charles Cottet excelled at rendering the atmosphere of intimate scenes, often dramatic ones. He is particularly interested in the condition of seafarers, and of their widows when the former disappear tragically at sea. In an almost Biblical scene, he shows here the return of a drowned body on the Île de Sein. The white houses in the background are the only source of light in a composition with crepuscular tones.

Injustement méconnu, Charles Cottet excelle à rendre l'atmosphère de scènes intimistes, souvent dramatiques. Il s'intéresse particulièrement à la condition des marins, et à celle de leurs veuves lorsqu'ils disparaissent tragiquement en mer. Dans une scène quasi biblique, il montre ici le retour du corps d'un noyé sur l'île de Sein. Les maisons blanches, en arrière-plan, sont le seul point de lumière d'une composition aux tonalités crépusculaires.

Der ungerechterweise unbekannte Charles Cottet stellt hervorragend die Atmosphäre intimer, oft dramatischer Szenen dar. Er interessiert sich insbesondere für die Lebensbedingungen der Matrosen und ihrer Witwen, wenn Erstere auf tragische Weise auf See umgekommen sind. In einer beinahe biblischen Szene zeigt er hier die Bergung eines Ertrunkenen auf der Île de Sein. Die weißen Häuser im Hintergrund sind der einzige Lichtpunkt in einer in dämmrigen Farbtönen gehaltenen Komposition.

Injustamente subestimado, Charles Cottet destaca al conseguir la atmósfera de escenas íntimas, a menudo dramáticas. Está particularmente interesado en la condición de los marineros y de las viudas de los que desaparecen trágicamente en el mar. En una escena casi bíblica, muestra aquí la devolución del cuerpo de un ahogado en la isla de Sein. Las casas blancas, como fondo, son el único punto de luz en una composición de tonalidades crepusculares.

Ingiustamente sottovalutato, Charles Cottet eccelse nella resa dell'atmosfera di scene intime e spesso drammatiche. Si interessò in special modo alla condizione dei marinai e delle loro vedove quando essi scompaiono tragicamente in mare. In una scena quasi biblica, il pittore mostra in questo quadro il ritorno del corpo di un uomo annegato sull'isola di Sein. Le case bianche sullo sfondo sono l'unico punto di luce di questa composizione dai toni crepuscolari.

De onterecht miskende Charles Cottet kan meesterlijk de sfeer van intieme, vaak dramatische taferelen weergeven. Hij interesseert zich vooral voor het tragische lot van vissers, en voor dat van hun weduwen nadat de mannen op zee het leven hebben gelaten. In een bijna Bijbels tafereel toont hij hier de aankomst van het levenloze lichaam van een drenkeling op het Île de Sein. De witte huisjes op de achtergrond vormen het enige lichtpuntje in een compositie van schermerachtige grijstinten.

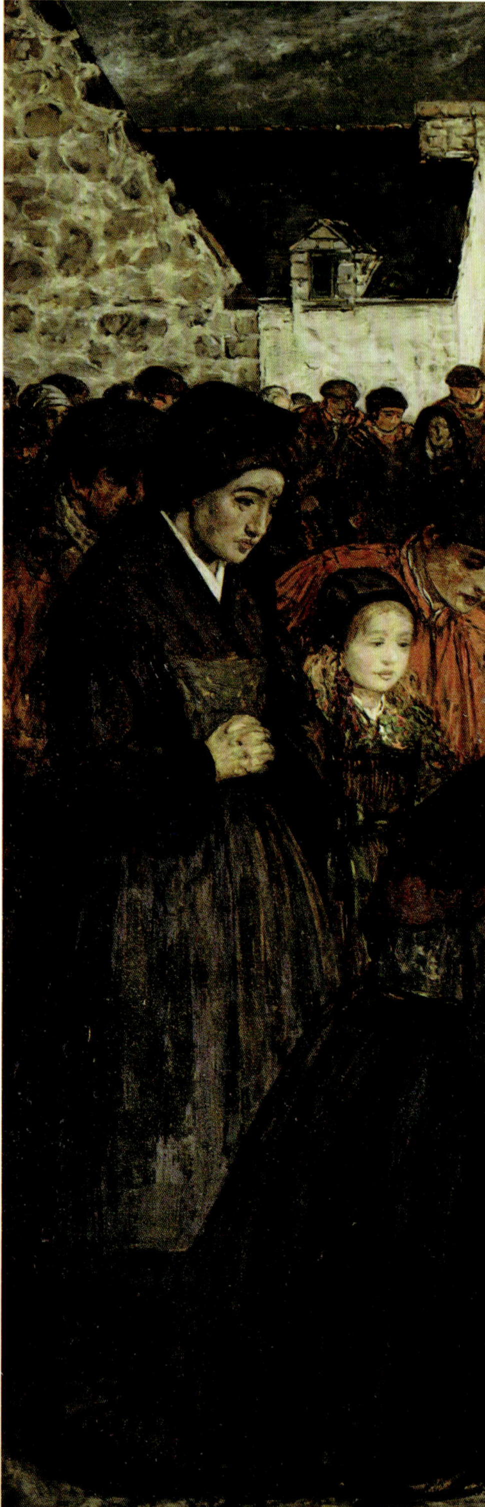

Charles Cottet (1863–1925)
In the Land of the Sea, Grief
Au Pays de la mer. Douleur
Im Land des Meeres, Schmerz
En el país del mar: Dolor
Nel paese del mare. Dolore
In het land van de zee. Verdriet
c. 1908–1909, Oil on canvas/Huile sur toile, 264 × 345 cm

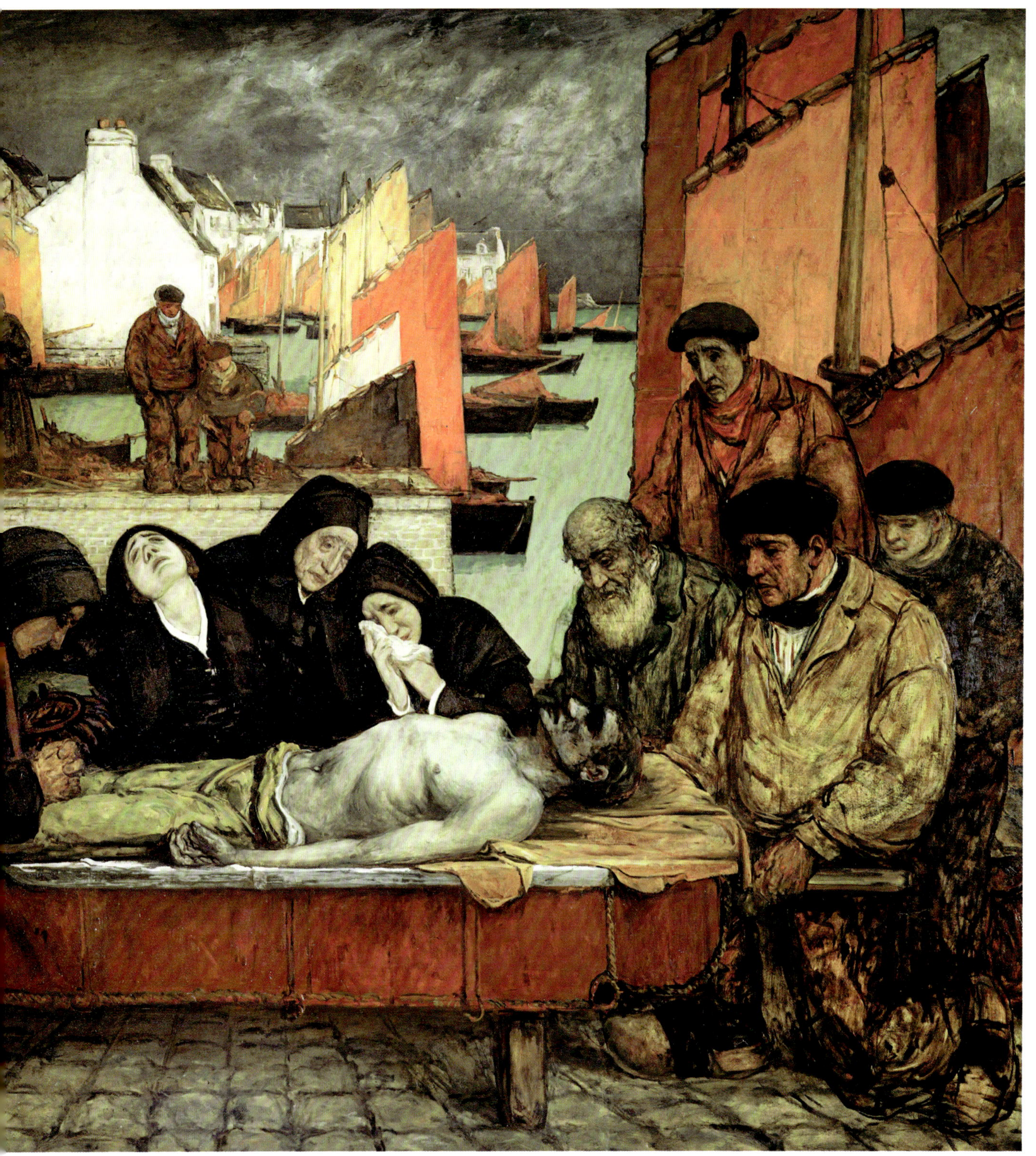

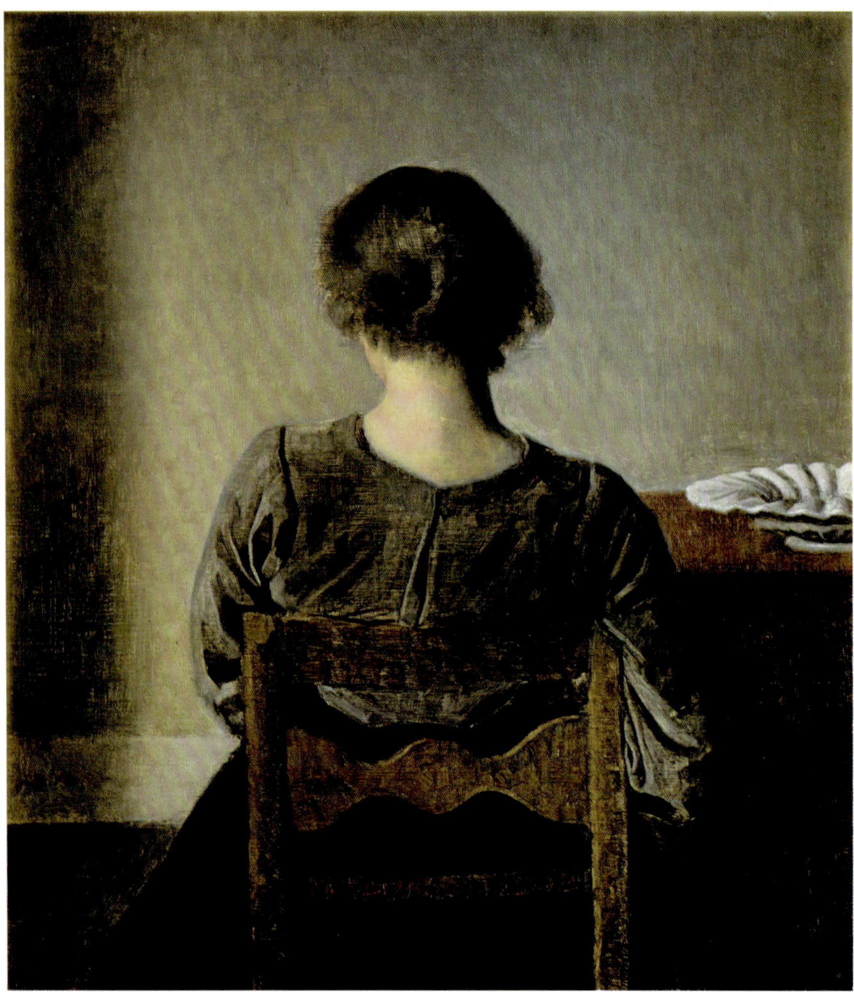

Henri Fantin-Latour
(1836–1904)

The Reader

La Liseuse

Die Leserin

La lectora

La lettrice

Lezende vrouw

1861, Oil on canvas/Huile
sur toile, 100 × 83 cm

Fernand Khnopff
(1858–1921)

Marie Monnom

1887, Oil on canvas/Huile
sur toile, 52,5 × 52,4 cm

Vilhelm Hammershøi (1864–1916)

Rest

Repos

Die Ruhe

Reposo

Riposo

Rust

1905, Oil on canvas/Huile sur toile, 49,5 × 46,5 cm

James Abbott McNeill
Whistler (1834–1903)

Arrangement in Grey
and Black No. 1

Arrangement en
gris et noir nº 1

Arrangement in Grau
und Schwarz № 1

Arreglo en gris y negro nº 1

Arrangiamento in
grigio e nero n. 1

Arrangement in grijs
en zwart nr. 1

1871, Oil on canvas/Huile
sur toile, 144,3 × 163 cm

John Everett Millais
(1829–1896)

Mrs Heugh

1872, Oil on canvas/Huile
sur toile, 120,5 × 104,5 cm

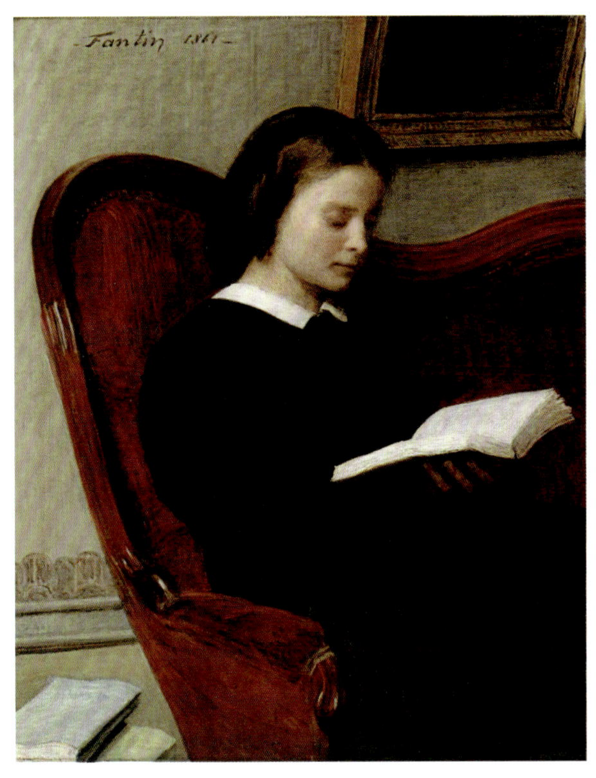 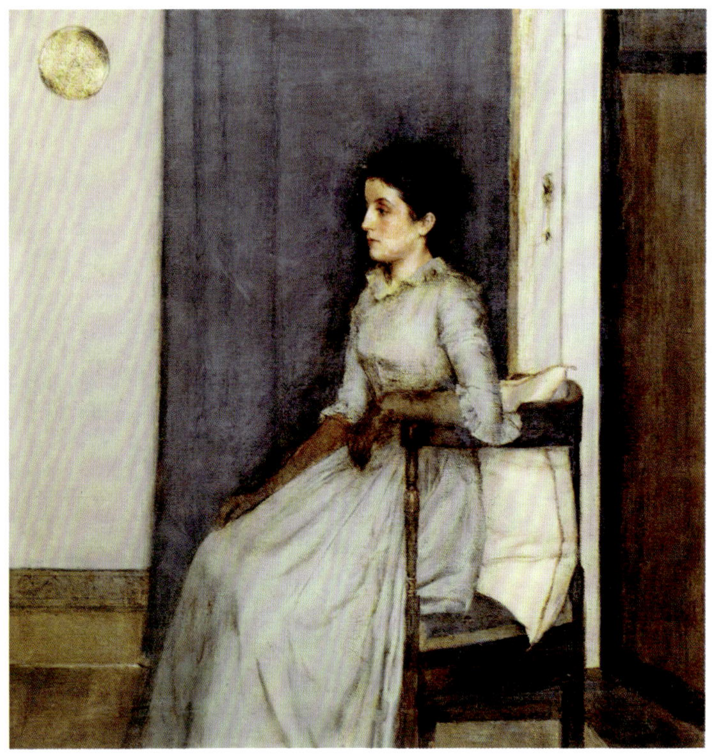

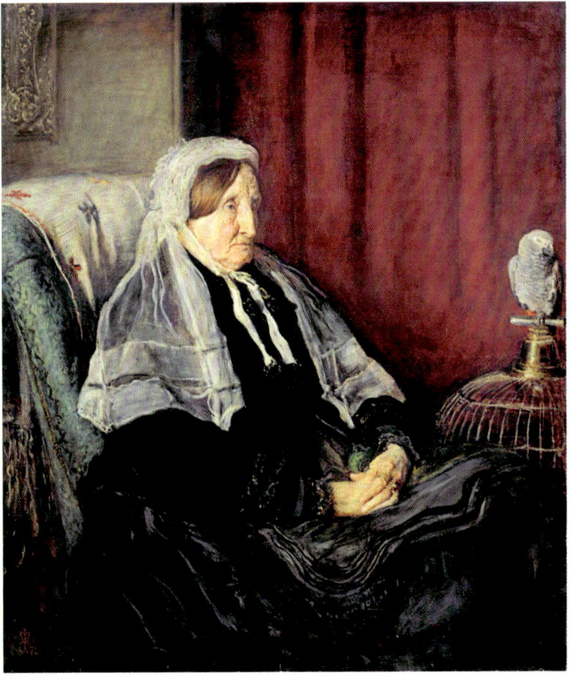 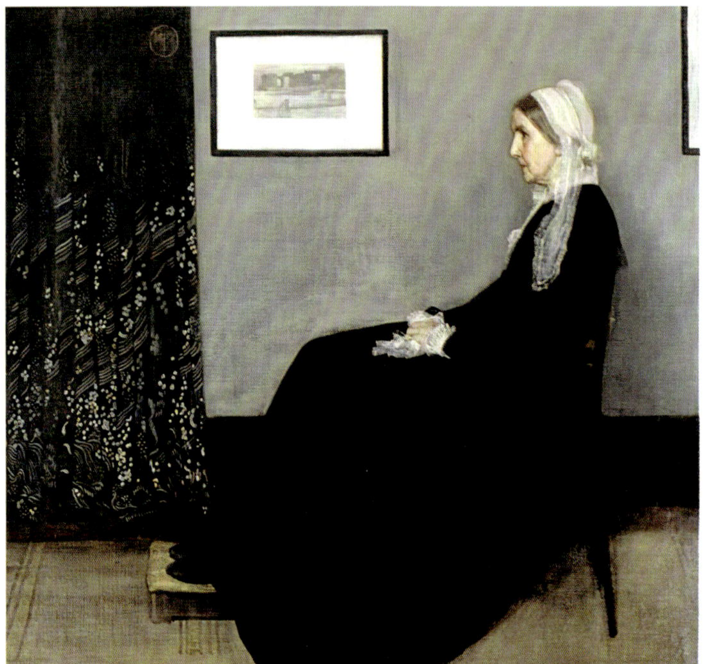

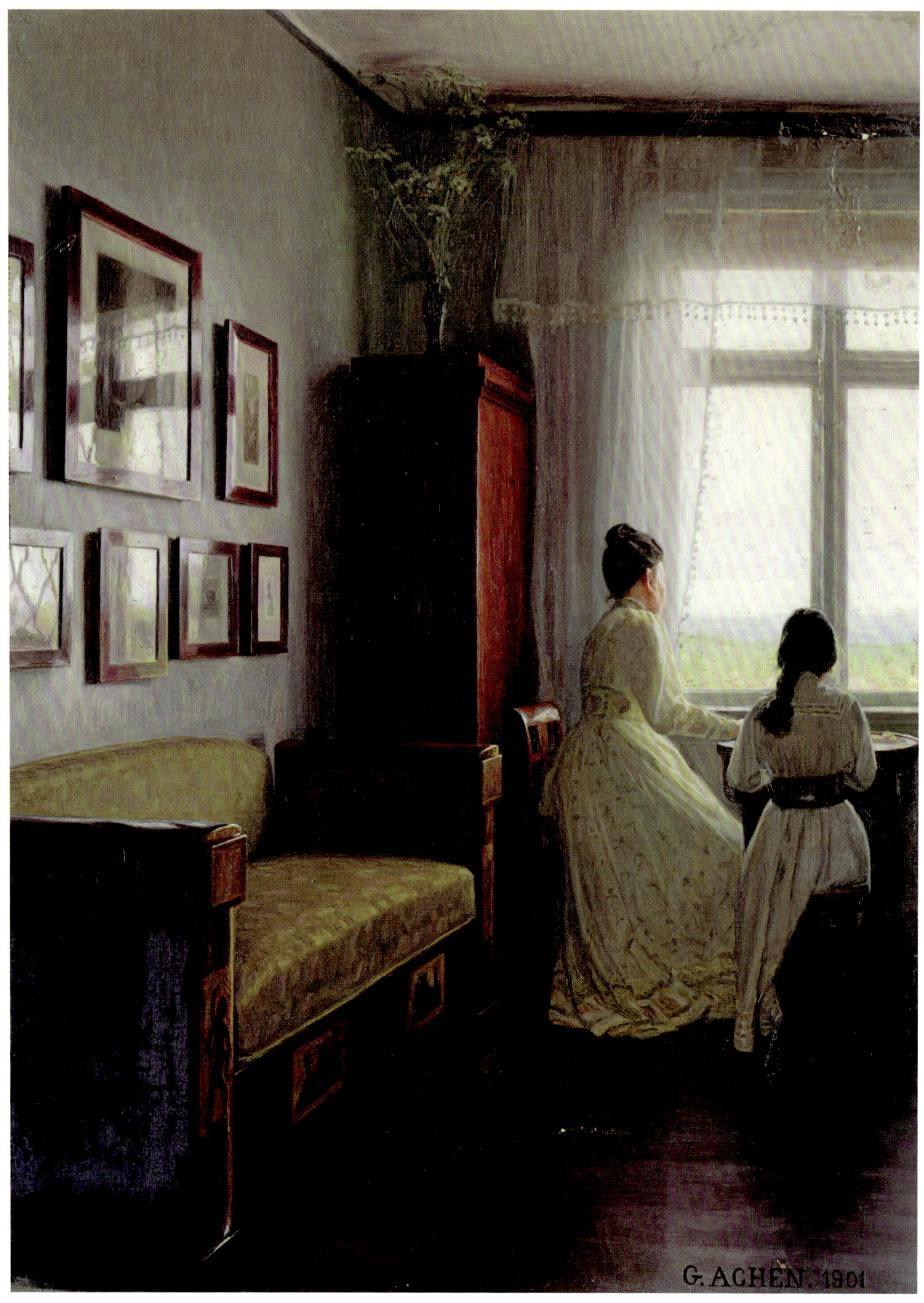
G. ACHEN. 1901

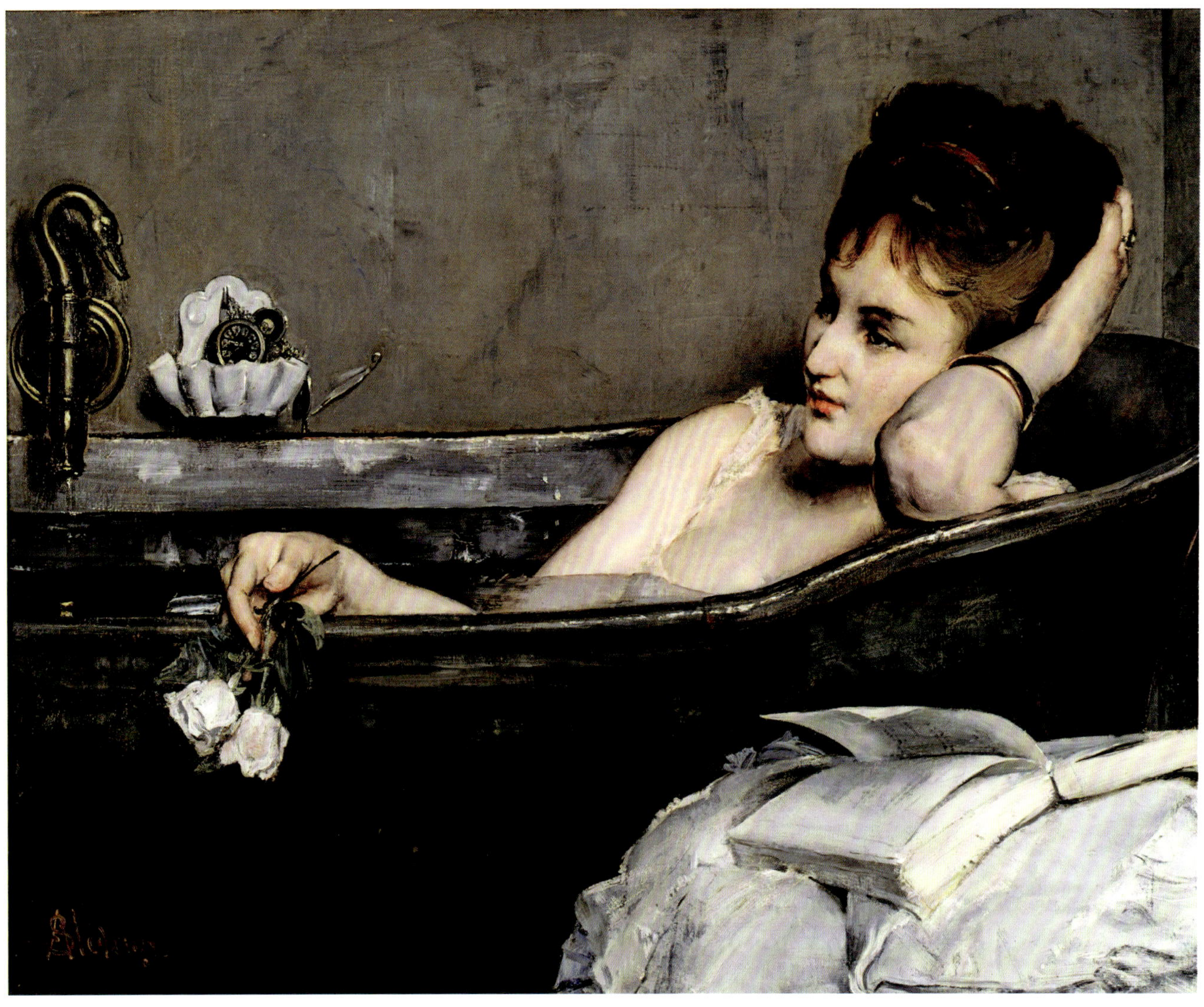

Georg Achen (1860–1912)

Interior

Intérieur

Interieur

Interior

Interno

Interieur

1901, Oil on canvas/Huile sur toile, 65,5 × 48,5 cm

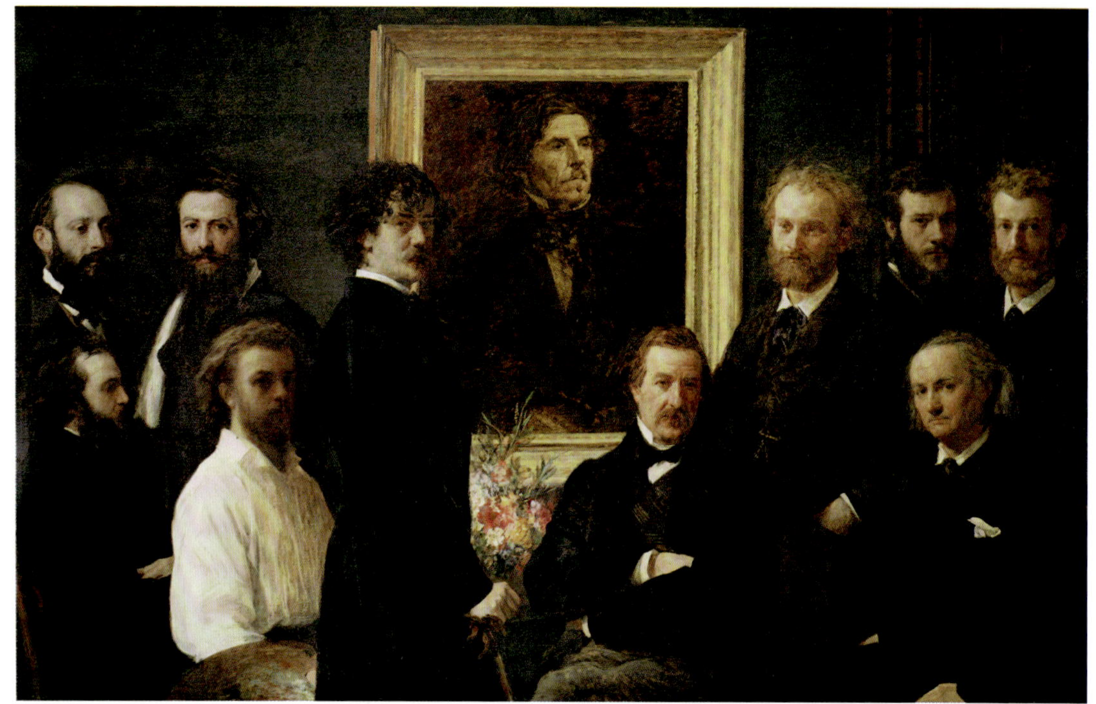

Henri Fantin-Latour
(1836–1904)

Homage to Delacroix

Hommage à Delacroix

Hommage an Delacroix

Homenaje a Delacroix

Omaggio a Delacroix

Hommage aan Delacroix

1864, Oil on canvas/Huile
sur toile, 160 × 250 cm

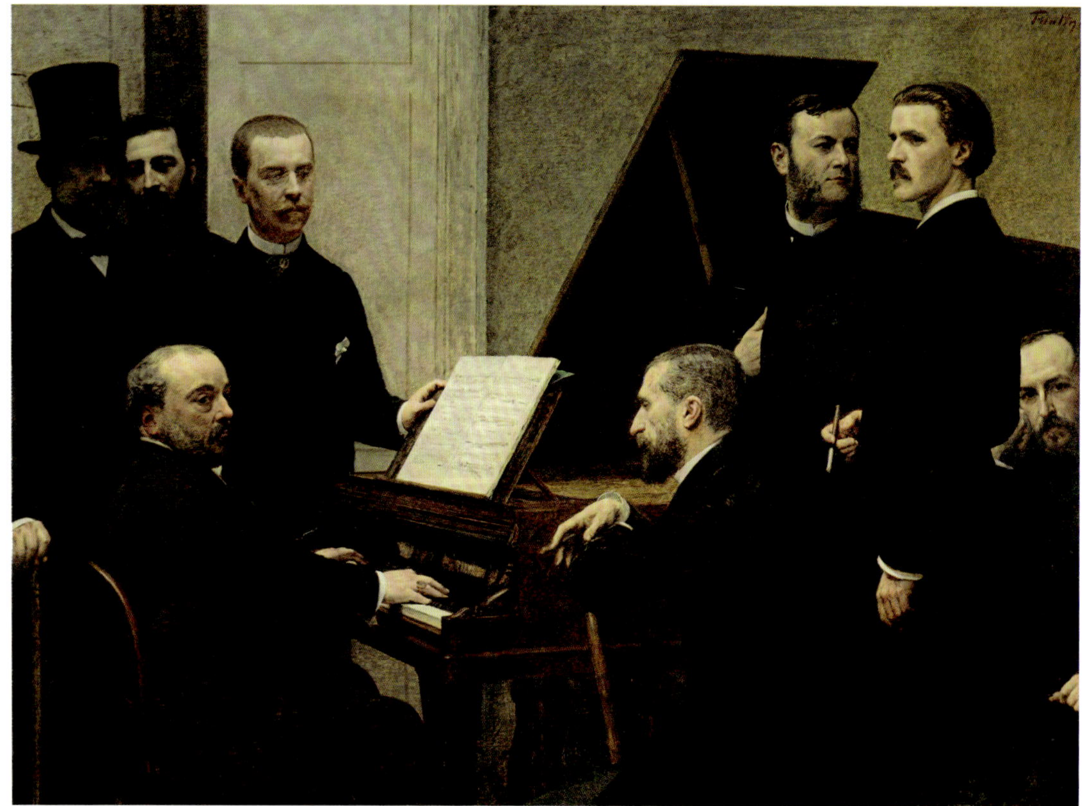

Henri Fantin-Latour
(1836–1904)

Around the Piano

Autour du piano

Um das Klavier

Alrededor del piano

Intorno al pianoforte

Rond de piano

1885, Oil on canvas/Huile
sur toile, 160 × 222 cm

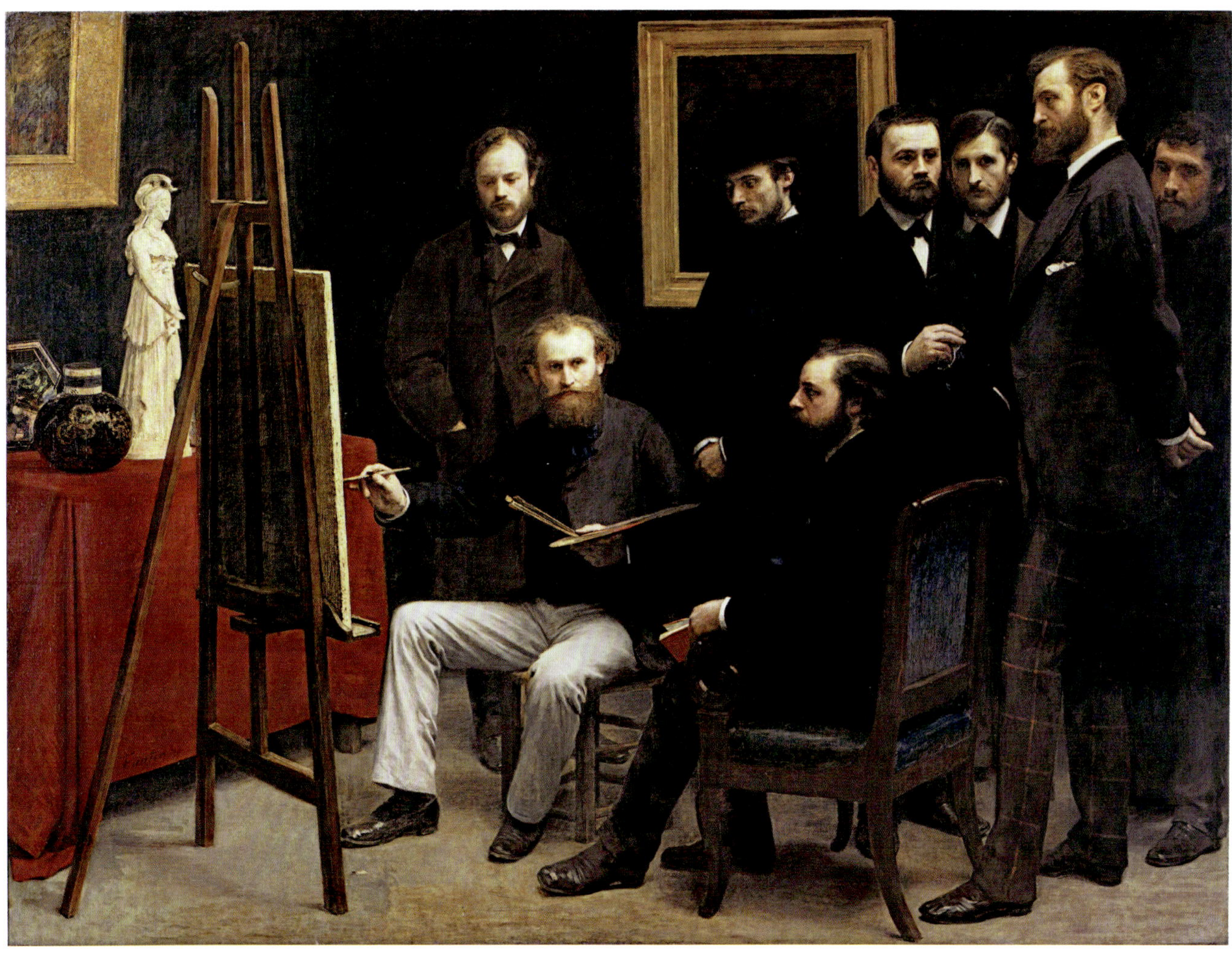

Henri Fantin-Latour (1836–1904)

A Studio at Les Batignolles

Un atelier aux Batignolles

Ein Atelier in Batignolles

Un taller en las Batignolles

Studio a Batignolles

Een atelier in Batignolles

1870, Oil on canvas/Huile sur toile, 204 × 273,5 cm

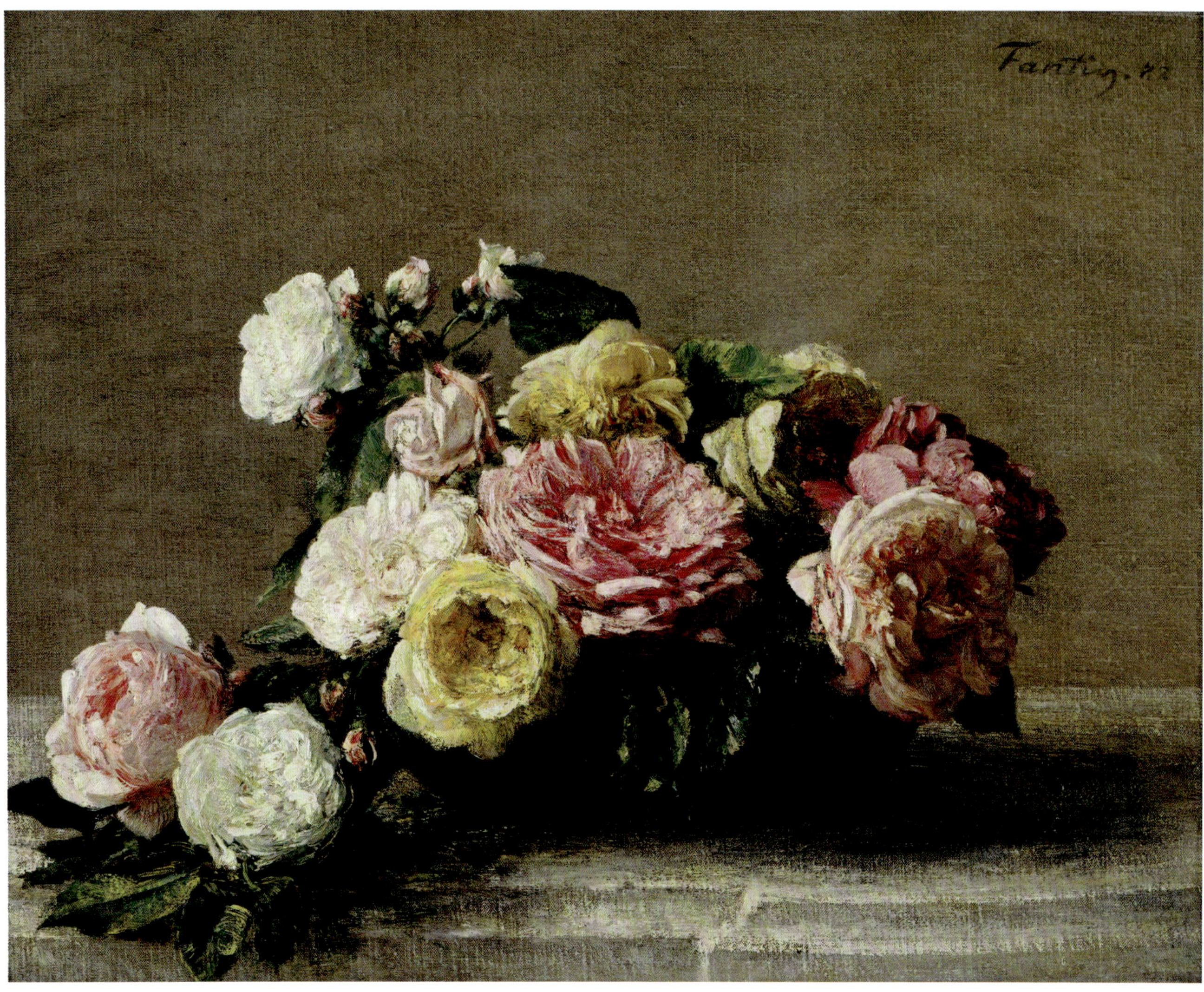

Henri Fantin-Latour (1836–1904)

Roses in a Bowl   Rosen in einer Schale   Cesto di rose

Roses dans une coupe   Cesta de rosas   Rozen in een kelk

1882, Oil on canvas/Huile sur toile, 36,5 × 46 cm

Dominated by grey and black, this somber painting is one of five large group portraits painted by Henri Fantin-Latour. Very photographic with its assembly of taciturn, immobile, and almost petrified men, *By the Table* unites, at the end of a meal, a circle of young parnassian poets, including the volatile couple Paul Verlaine and Arthur Rimbaud (to the left of the scene).

Dominé par le gris et le noir, ce tableau sombre est l'un des cinq grands portraits de groupes peints par Henri Fantin-Latour. Très photographique, avec son assemblée d'hommes taciturnes, immobiles, presque pétrifiés, *Coin de table* réunit, en fin de repas, un cercle de jeunes poètes parnassiens, dont le couple sulfureux Paul Verlaine et Arthur Rimbaud (à gauche de la scène).

Dieses dunkle Gemälde, in dem Grau und Schwarz dominieren, ist eines der fünf großen Gruppenbildnisse, die Henri Fantin-Latour gemalt hat. *Französische Dichter an einem Tisch* wirkt mit seiner Versammlung von schweigsamen, unbeweglichen, fast versteinerten Männern sehr fotografisch und vereint nach dem Essen mehrere junge Parnassien-Dichter, darunter die Rebellen Paul Verlaine und Arthur Rimbaud (links im Bild).

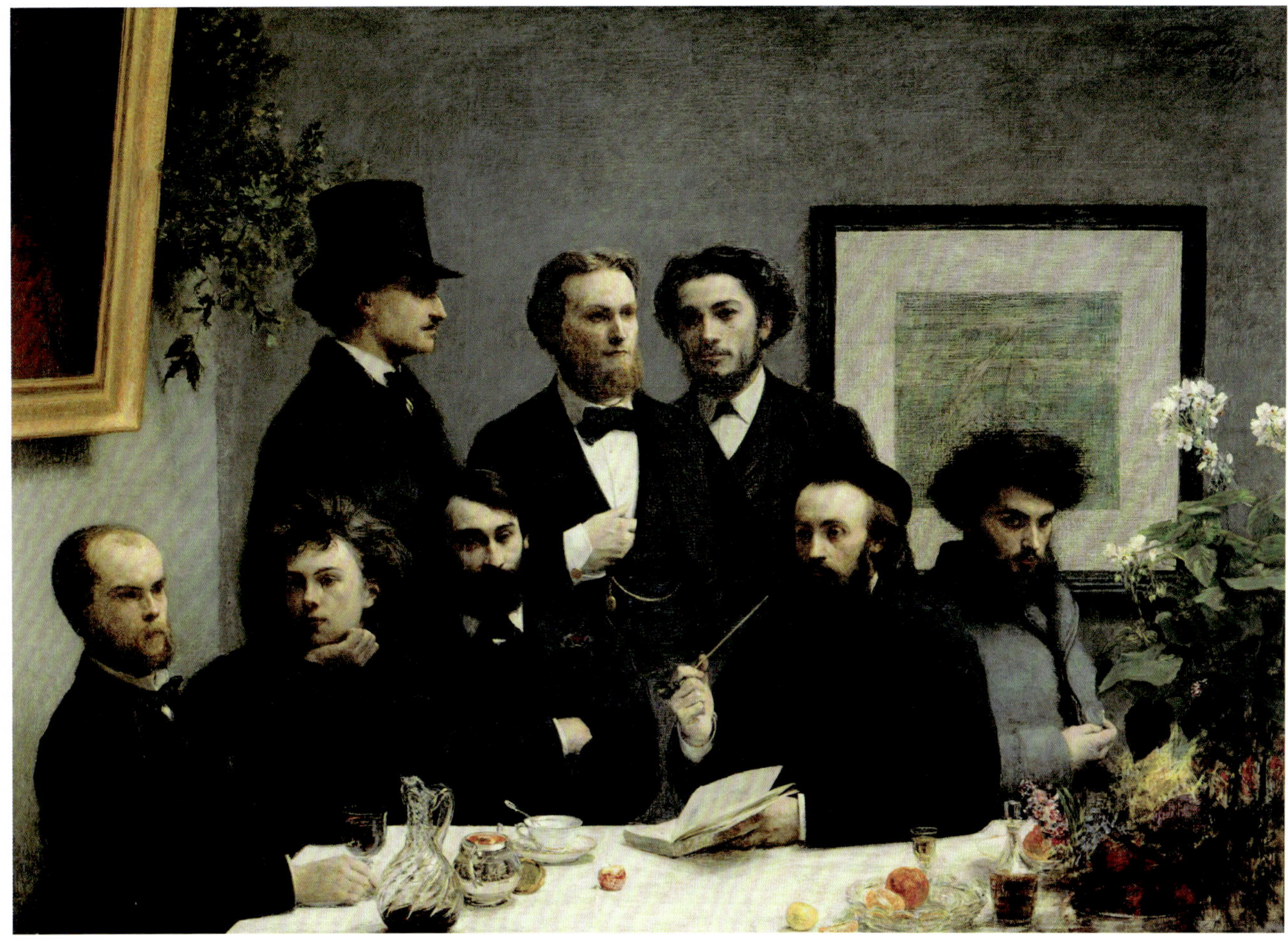

Henri Fantin-Latour (1836–1904)

By the Table

Coin de table

1872, Oil on canvas/Huile sur toile, 161 × 223,5 cm

Französische Dichter an einem Tisch

Un rincón de mesa

Gruppo di poeti riuniti intorno ad un tavolo

Hoek van de tafel

Dominado por el gris y el negro, este sombrío cuadro es uno de los cinco grandes grupos de retratos pintados por Henri Fantin-Latour. Muy fotográfico, con su asamblea de hombres taciturnos, inmóviles, casi petrificados, *Un rincón de mesa* reúne, después de una comida, un círculo de jóvenes del Parnaso, con los sulfurosos Paul Verlaine y Arthur Rimbaud (a la izquierda de la escena).

Dominato dal grigio e dal nero, questo quadro cupo è uno dei cinque grandi ritratti di gruppo dipinti da Henri Fantin-Latour. Opera molto fotografica, con la sua riunione di uomini taciturni, immobili e quasi pietrificati, il *Gruppo di poeti riuniti intorno ad un tavolo* raffigura, nel momento che segue a un pasto, un circolo di giovani poeti parnassiani, tra cui si riconoscono Paul Verlaine e Arthur Rimbaud (sulla sinistra della scena).

Dit sombere schilderij in vooral grijs- en zwarttinten is een van de vijf grote groepsportretten van Henri Fantin-Latour. De zeer fotorealistisch geschilderde groep zwijgende, onbeweeglijke, bijna versteende mannen op *Hoek van de tafel*, na de maaltijd, wordt gevormd door de Parnassiens, een groep jonge Franse dichters onder wie het licht ontvlambare duo Paul Verlaine en Arthur Rimbaud (links).

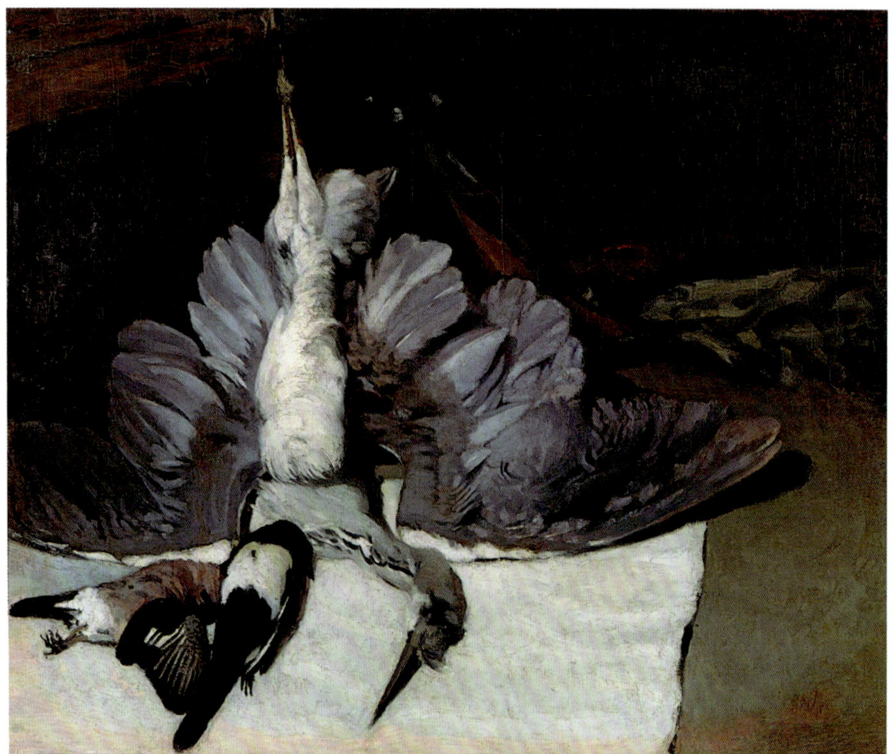

Alfred Sisley (1839–1899)
Heron with Spread Wings
Le Héron aux ailes déployées
Der Reiher mit ausgebreiteten Flügeln
La garza con las alas extendidas
L'airone con le ali spiegate
Reiger met gespreide vleugels
1865, Oil on canvas/Huile sur toile, 80 × 100 cm

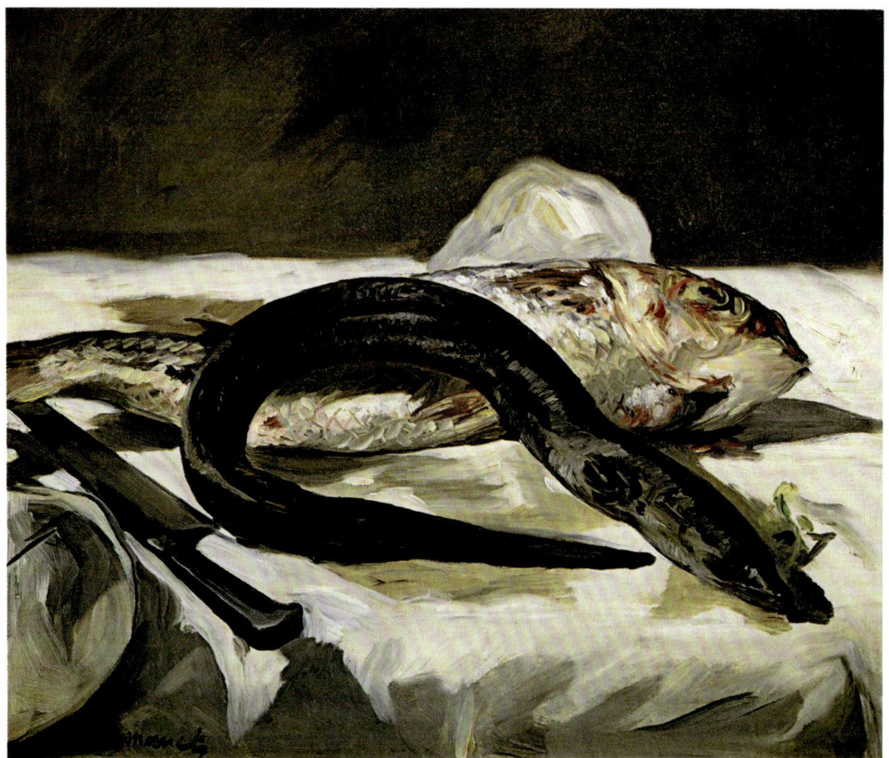

Édouard Manet (1832–1883)
Eel and Red Mullet
Anguille et rouget
Aal und Barbe
Bodegón con salmonete y anguila
Anguilla e triglia
Aal en rode poon
1864, Oil on canvas/Huile sur toile, 38 × 46 cm

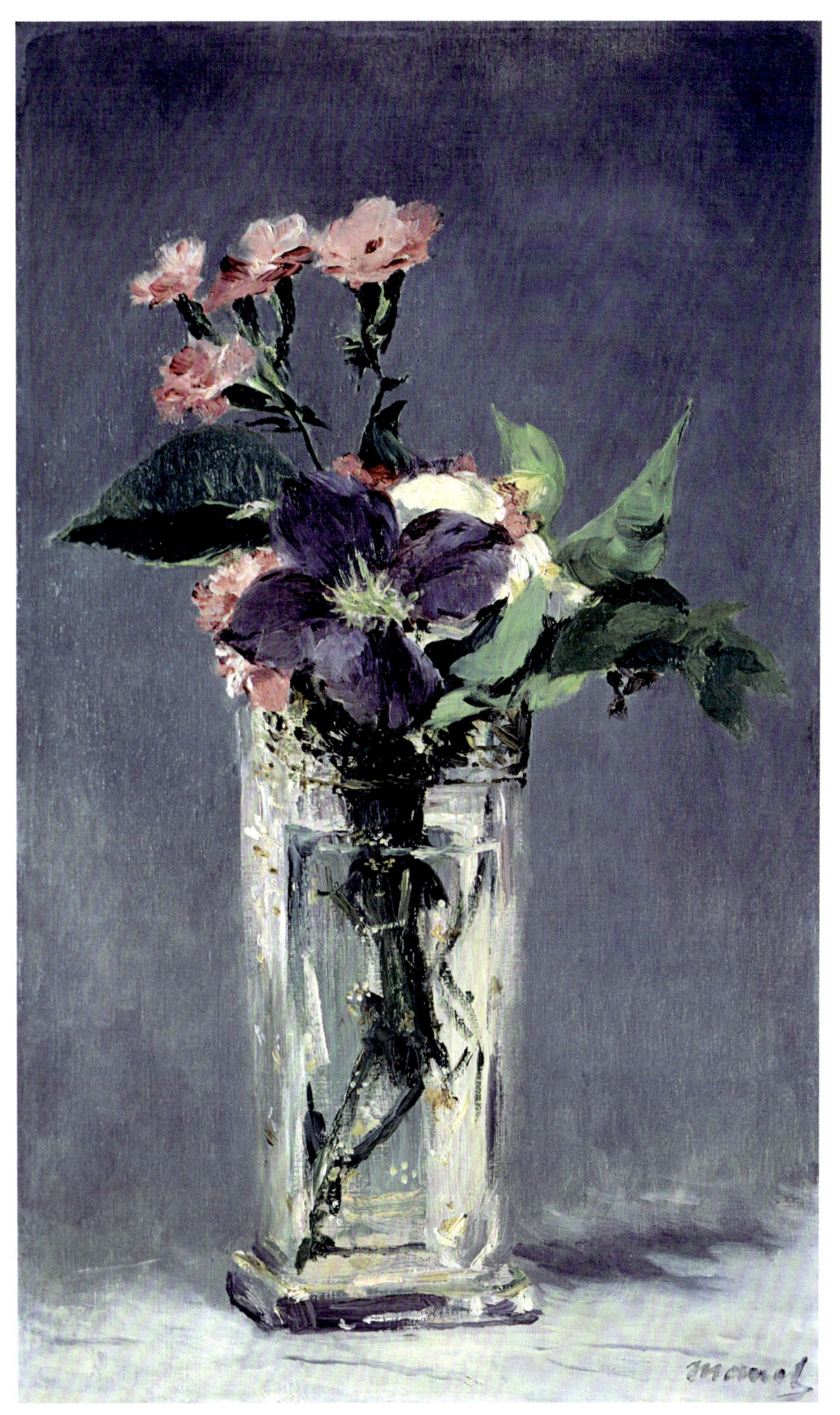

*Édouard Manet
(1832–1883)*

Pinks and Clematis
in a Crystal Vase

Œillets et clématite
dans un vase de cristal

Nelken und Klematis
in einer Kristallvase

Claveles y clemátide en
un florero de cristal

Garofani e clematide
in un vaso di cristallo

Anjers en clematis in
een kristallen vaas

c. 1882, Oil on
canvas/Huile sur
toile, 56 × 35,5 cm

Freely inspired by Titian's *Pastoral Concert,* and by an engraving of the *Judgment of Paris* by Raphael, Édouard Manet's *Luncheon on the Grass* is notorious for the scandal it provoked at the *salon des Refusés* in 1863. The artist had the gall to paint a life-sized naturalist nude without resorting to an allegorical or mythological pretext. Accompanied by clothed men, the young lady stares seemingly defiantly or provocatively at the viewer.

Librement inspiré du *Concert champêtre* du Titien et d'une gravure du *Jugement de Pâris* par Raphaël, *Le Déjeuner sur l'herbe* d'Édouard Manet est célèbre pour le scandale qu'il a provoqué lors du salon des Refusés, en 1863. L'artiste a l'audace de peindre un nu naturaliste, en grandeur réelle, sans se cacher derrière un prétexte allégorique ou mythologique. Accompagnée d'hommes habillés, la jeune femme regarde le spectateur, comme pour le défier, et le provoquer.

Das Frühstück im Grünen greift auf *Ländliches Konzert* von Tizian und den Kupferstich *Das Urteil des Paris* von Raffael zurück und ist berühmt für den Skandal, den es 1863 auf dem Salon der Zurückgewiesenen auslöste. Der Künstler wagt es, einen naturalistischen Akt in Lebensgröße zu malen, ohne sich hinter einem allegorischen oder mythologischen Vorwand zu verstecken. Die junge Frau inmitten bekleideter Männer schaut den Betrachter an, als ob sie ihn herausfordern und provozieren wolle.

Basado libremente en el *Concierto campestre* de Tiziano y en un grabado del *Juicio de París* de Rafael, el *Almuerzo sobre la hierba* de Édouard Manet es famoso por el escándalo que causó en el Salón de los Rechazados de 1863. El artista tiene la audacia de pintar un desnudo naturalista, tamaño real, sin esconderse detrás de un pretexto alegórico o mitológico. Acompañado por hombres vestidos, la joven mira al espectador, como para desafiarlo y provocarlo.

Liberamente ispirata al *Concerto campestre* di Tiziano e ad un'incisione del *Giudizio di Paride* di Raffaello, *La colazione sull'erba* di Édouard Manet è famosa per lo scandalo che causò al Salone dei Rifiutati del 1863. L'artista osò dipingere un nudo naturalista in dimensioni reali, senza nascondersi dietro un pretesto allegorico o mitologico. Accompagnata da uomini vestiti, la giovane donna rivolge lo sguardo all'osservatore, a mo' di sfida, e lo provoca.

Lunch op het gras van Édouard Manet is losjes geïnspireerd op het *Landelijk concert* van Titiaan en een ets van *Het oordeel van Paris* van Rafaël. Het doek is bekend geworden vanwege het schandaal dat het tijdens de Salon des Refusés in 1863 veroorzaakte. De kunstenaar heeft lef: hij schildert een naturalistisch naakt op ware grootte, zonder voor te wenden dat het een allegorisch of mythologisch tafereel betreft. De jonge vrouw tussen de keurig geklede mannen kijkt de toeschouwer recht in de ogen, alsof ze hem wil uitdagen, en provoceren.

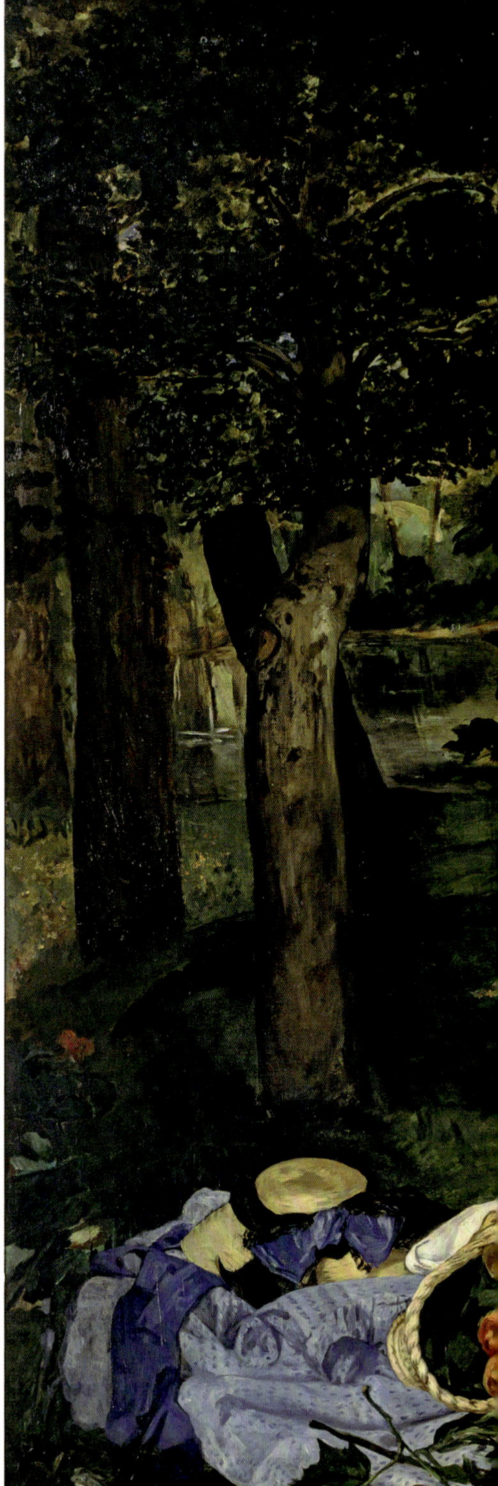

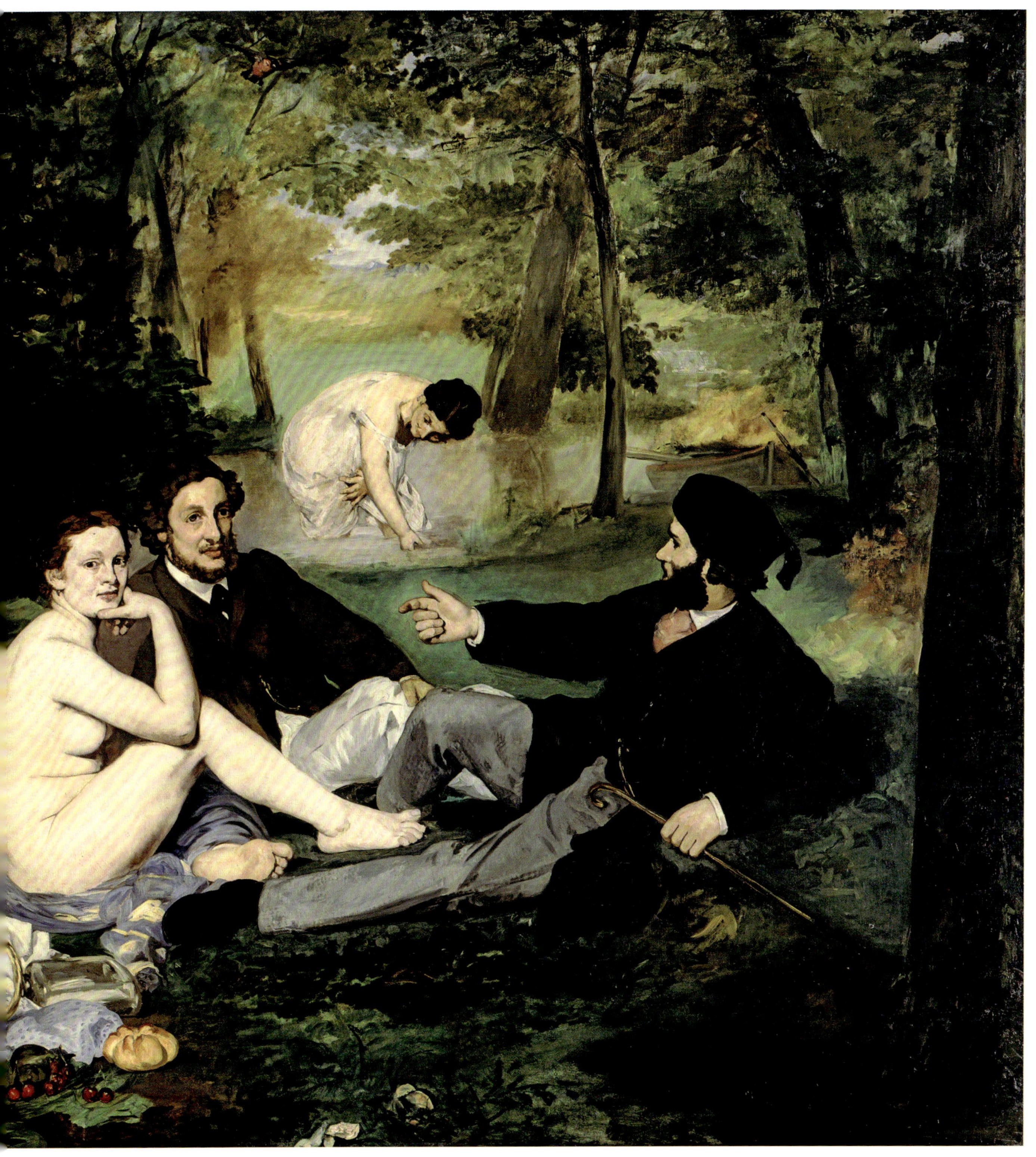

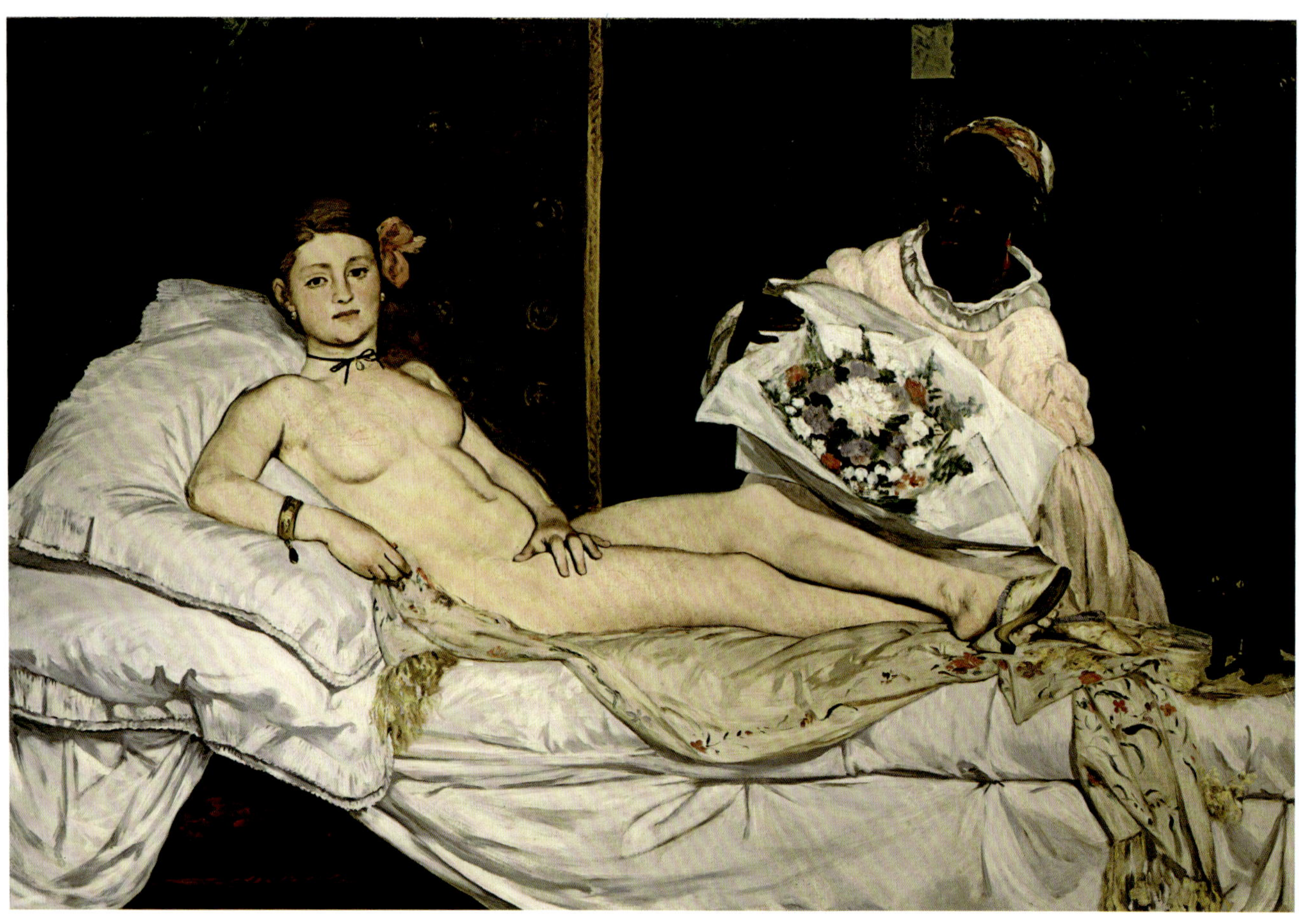

Édouard Manet (1832–1883)

Olympia

t1863, Oil on canvas/Huile sur toile, 130,5 × 191 cm

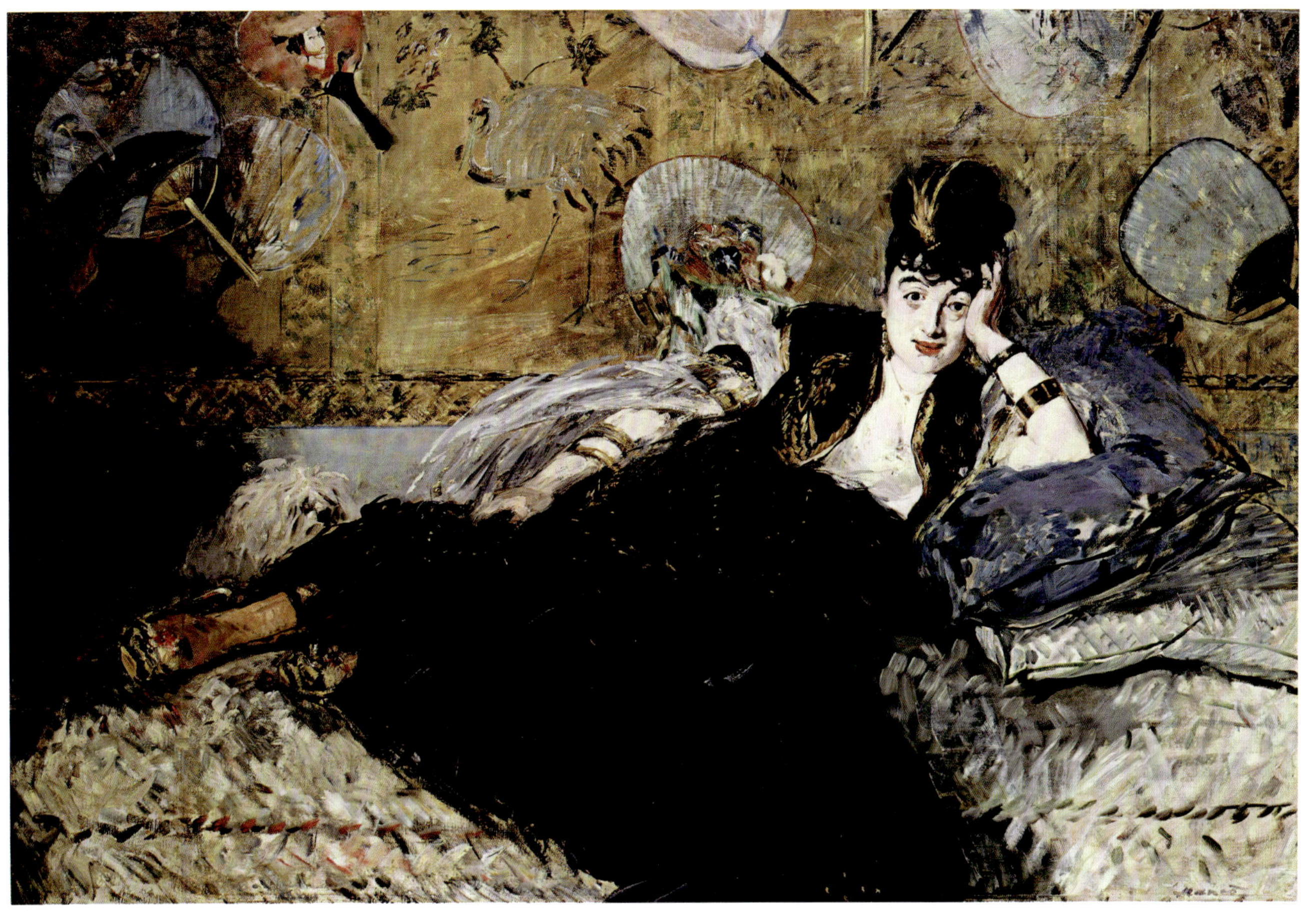

Édouard Manet (1832–1883)

The Lady with Fans

La Dame aux éventails

Die Dame mit den Fächern

La dama de los abanicos

La dama con ventagli

De dame met de waaiers

1873, Oil on canvas/Huile sur toile, 113 × 166,5 cm

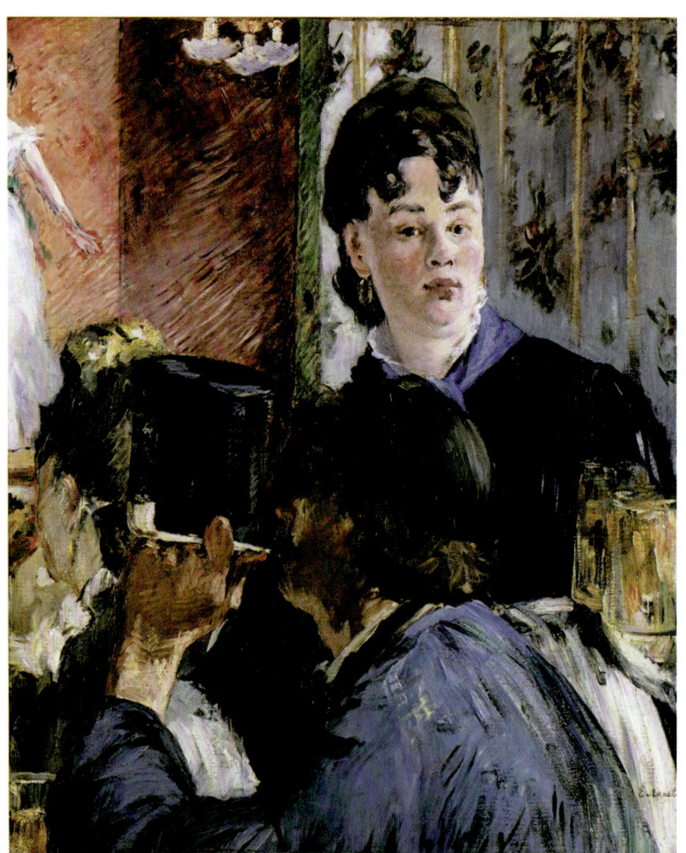

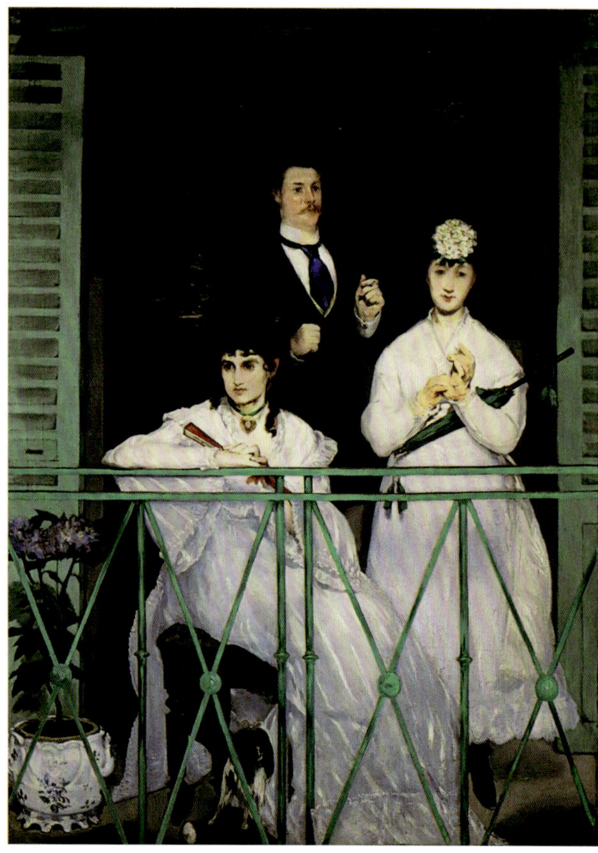

Édouard Manet (1832–1883)

Waitress Serving Bocks

La Serveuse de bocks

Die Kellnerin

Camarera

La cameriera della birreria

De serveerster

c. 1878–1879, Oil on canvas/Huile sur toile, 77 × 64,5 cm

Édouard Manet (1832–1883)

The Balcony

Le Balcon

Der Balkon

El balcón

Il balcone

Het balkon

c. 1868–1869, Oil on canvas/Huile sur toile, 170 × 125 cm

Édouard Manet (1832–1883)

Émile Zola

1868, Oil on canvas/Huile sur toile, 146 × 114 cm

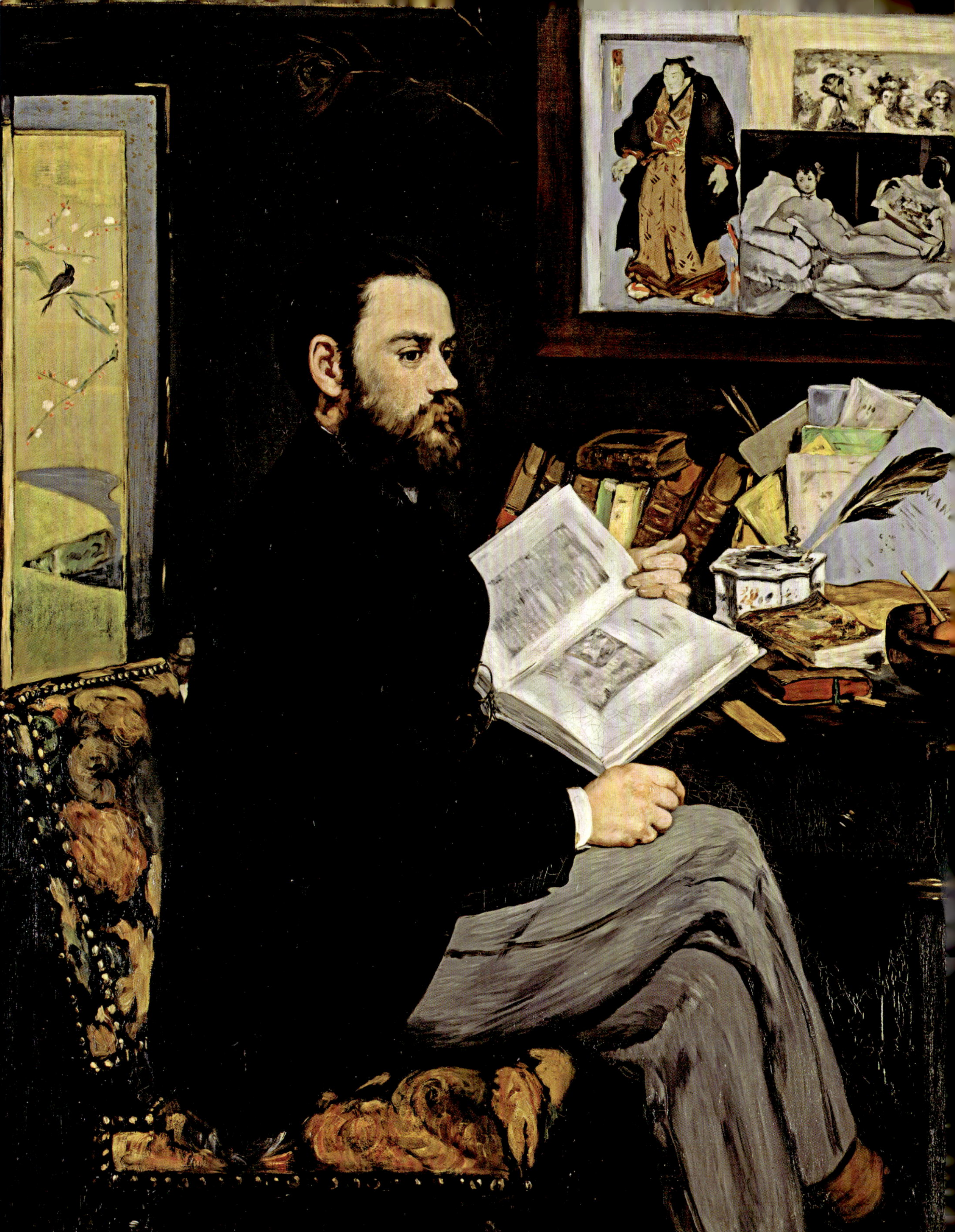

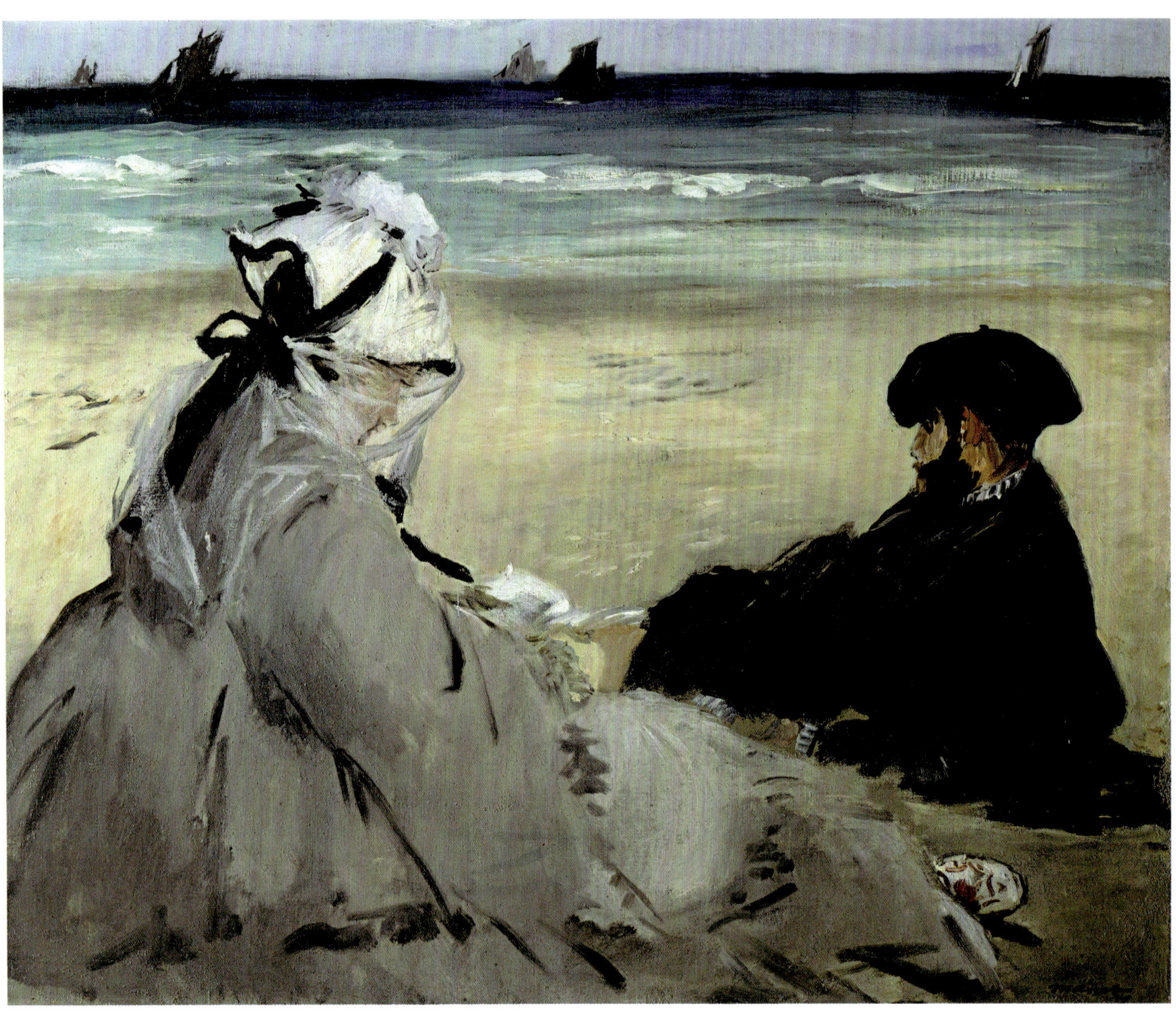

Édouard Manet (1832–1883)

On the Beach

Sur la plage

Am Strand

En la playa

Sulla spiaggia

Op het strand

1873, Oil on canvas/Huile sur toile, 60 × 73,5 cm

Édouard Manet (1832–1883)

Rochefort's Escape

L'évasion de Rochefort

Die Flucht des Henri Rochefort

La fuga de Rochefort

Fuga di Rochefort

De ontsnapping van Henri Rochefort

c. 1881, Oil on canvas/Huile sur toile, 79 × 72 cm

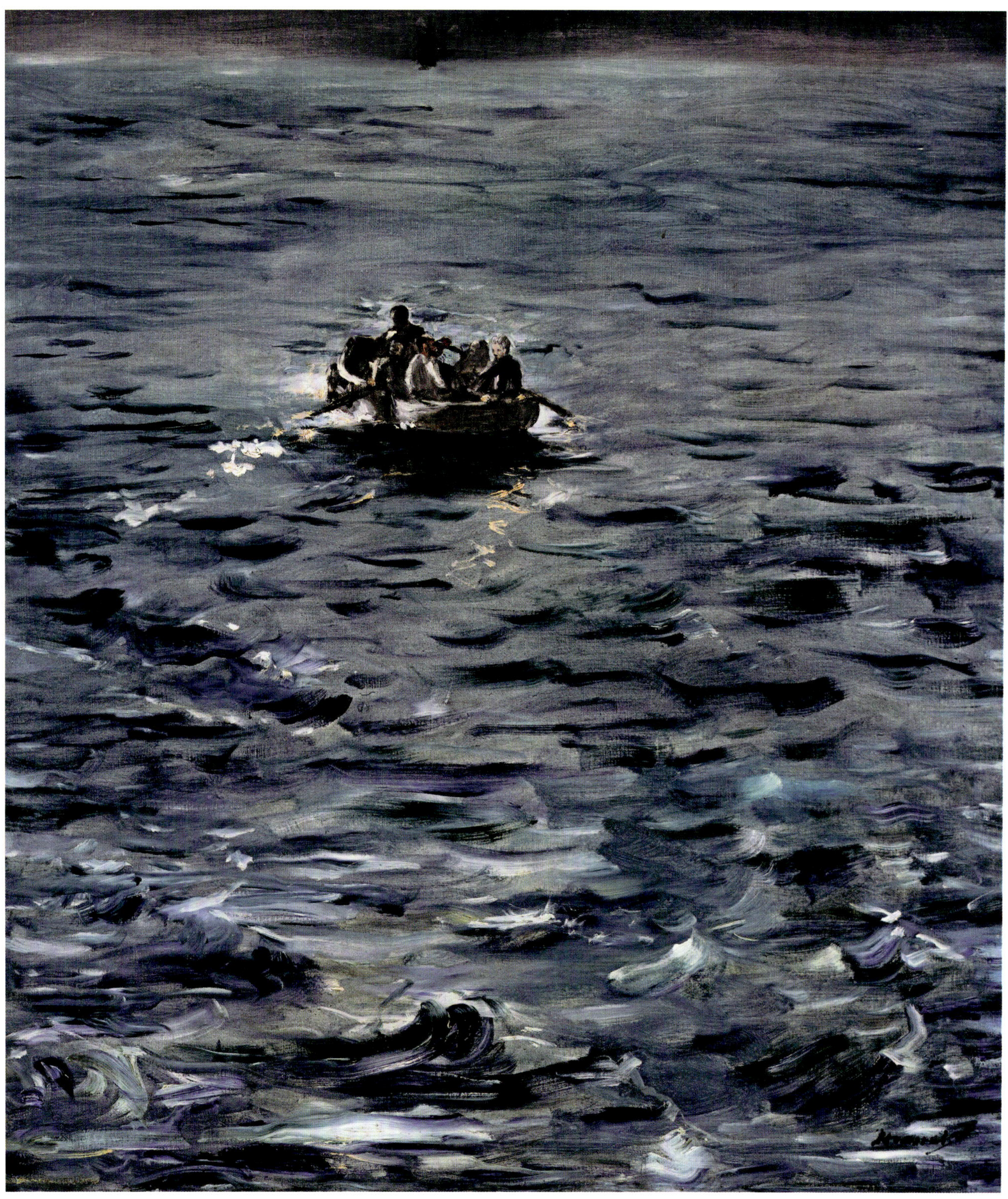

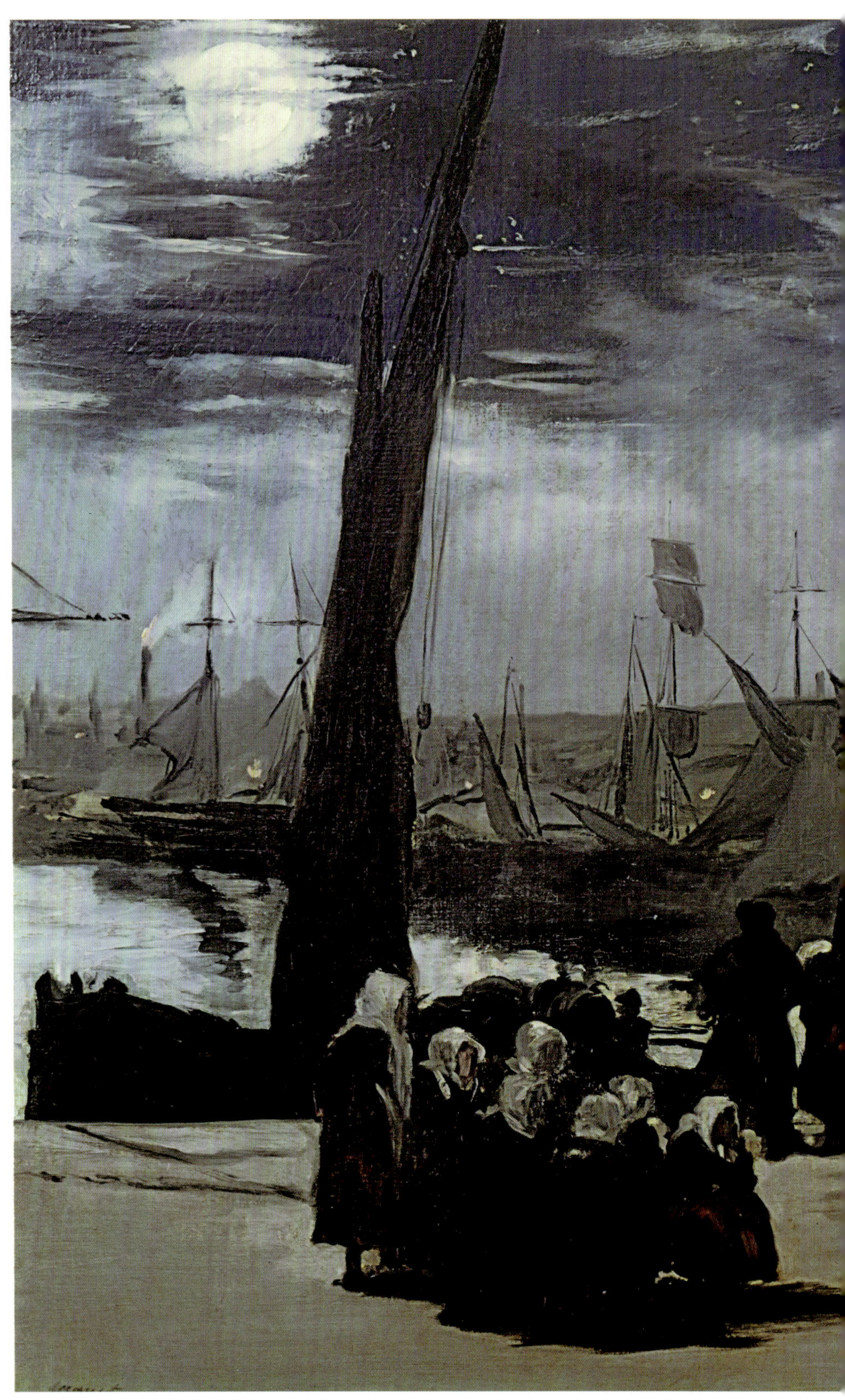

Édouard Manet (1832–1883)

Moonlight at the Port of Boulogne
Clair de lune sur le port de Boulogne
Der Hafen von Boulogne im Mondlicht
Claro de luna en el puerto de Boulogne
Chiaro di luna sul porto di Boulogne
De haven van Boulogne in het maanlicht

1869, Oil on canvas/Huile sur toile, 81,5 × 101 cm

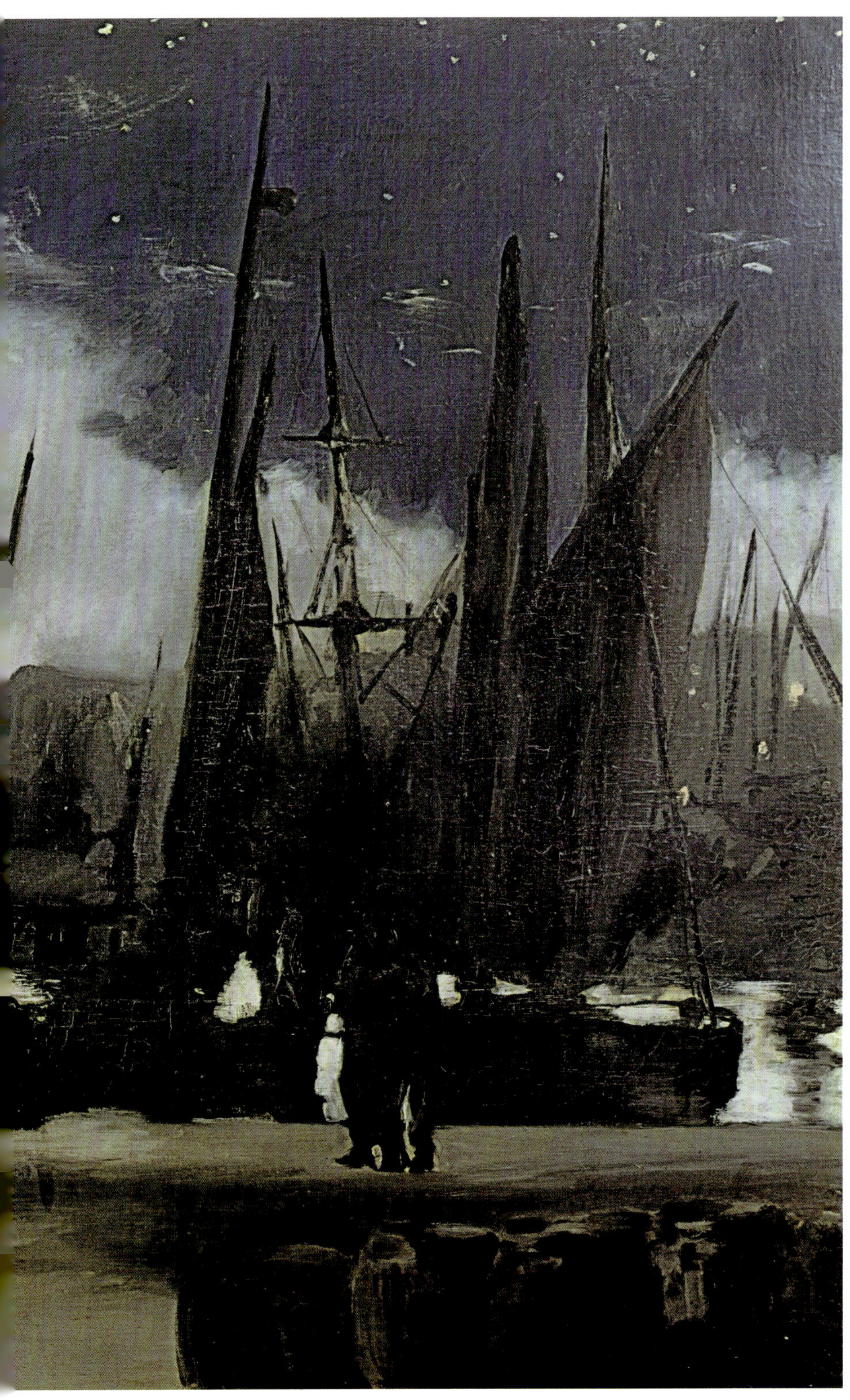

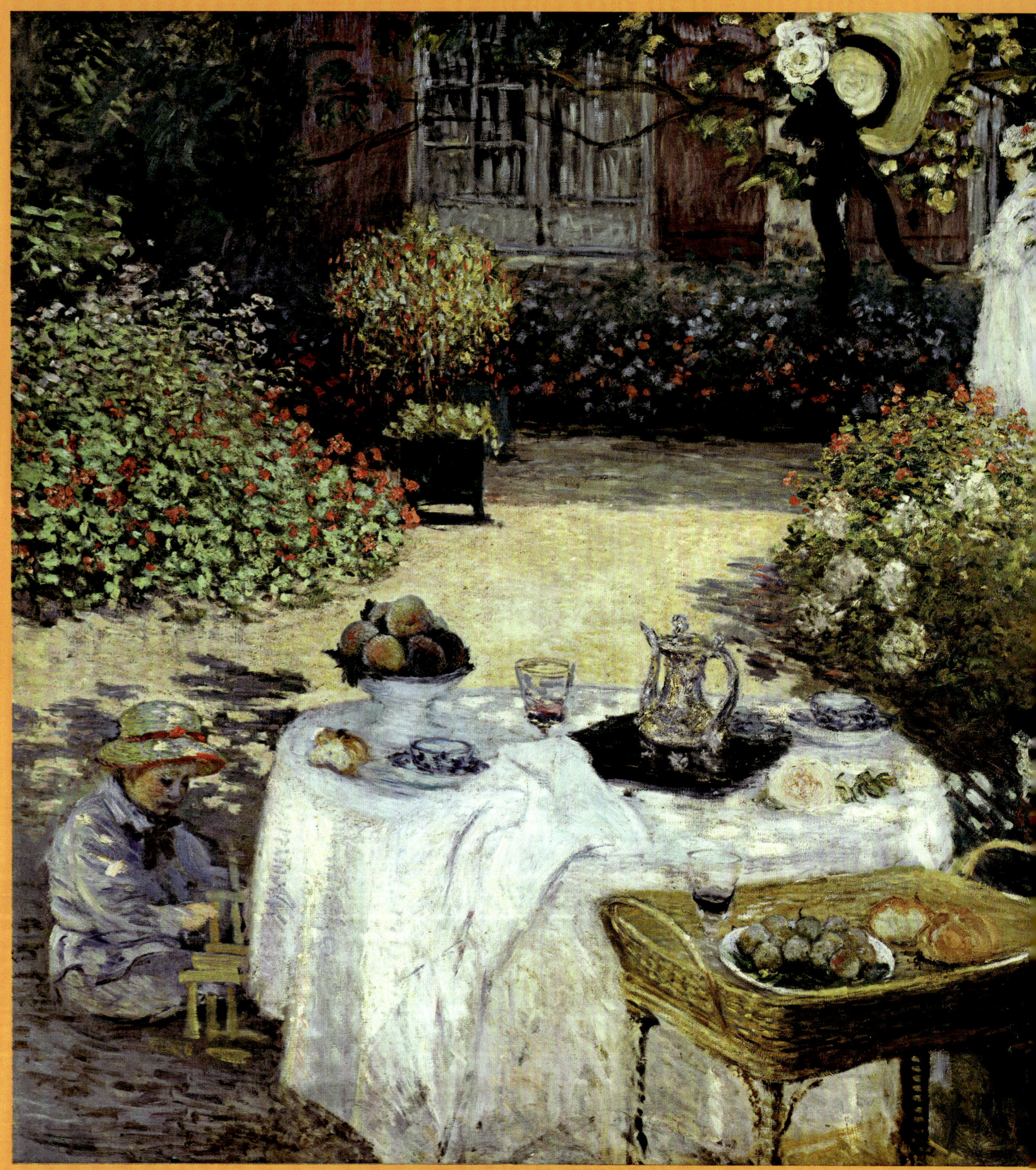

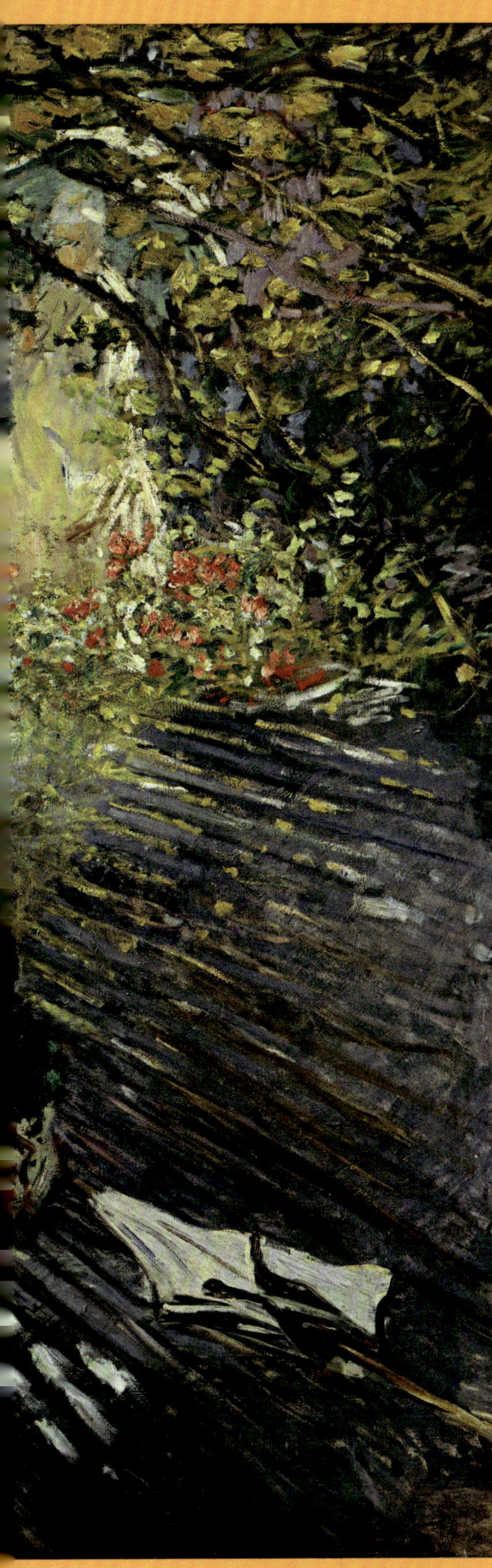

Impressionism

The term "impressionism" first appeared in 1874 in the writings of the critic Louis Leroy who mocked the painting entitled *Impression, Sunrise* by Claude Monet. Using a lively and fragmented touch, the impressionists (Renoir, Pissarro, Morisot, Caillebotte…) were mainly interested in landscapes, daily life, and leisure, preferring natural light to that of the studio.

Impressionnisme

Le terme « impressionnisme » apparaît en 1874 sous la plume du critique Louis Leroy, qui raille le tableau *Impression, soleil levant* de Claude Monet. Usant d'une touche vive et fragmentée, les impressionnistes (Renoir, Pissarro, Morisot, Caillebotte…) s'intéresseront principalement au paysage, à la vie quotidienne, aux loisirs, en préférant la lumière naturelle à celle de l'atelier.

Impressionismus

Der Begriff „Impressionismus" wird im Jahre 1874 von dem Kunstkritiker Louis Leroy verwendet, der das Gemälde *Impression, Sonnenaufgang* von Claude Monet verspottet. Die Impressionisten (Renoir, Pissarro, Morisot, Caillebotte…) arbeiten mit flinken und kurzen Pinselstrichen und interessieren sich im Wesentlichen für Landschaften, Alltagsleben und Freizeitvergnügen, wobei sie das natürliche Licht dem im Atelier vorziehen.

Impresionismo

El término "impresionismo" aparece en 1874 bajo la pluma del crítico Louis Leroy, que se burla de la impresión del cuadro *Impresión, sol naciente* de Claude Monet. Con una pincelada viva y fragmentada, los impresionistas (Renoir, Pissarro, Morisot, Caillebotte…) se interesarán principalmente por el paisaje, la vida cotidiana, el ocio, prefiriendo la luz natural a la del taller.

Impressionismo

Il termine "Impressionismo" fu coniato nel 1874 dal critico Louis Leroy per schernire il quadro *Impressione, levar del sole* di Claude Monet. Gli impressionisti (Renoir, Pissarro, Morisot, Caillebotte…) utilizzavano pennellate vivaci e frammentate, erano interessati principalmente al paesaggio, alla vita quotidiana e allo svago, e preferivano la luce naturale a quella dello studio.

Impressionisme

De term 'impressionisme' vloeit in 1874 uit de pen van criticus Louis Leroy, als die zich spottend uitlaat over Monets schilderij *Impressie, opkomende zon.* Met levendige, gefragmenteerde penseelstreken en een voorkeur voor natuurlijk licht boven kunstlicht in het atelier, schilderen de impressionisten (Renoir, Pissarro, Morisot, Caillebotte…) vooral landschappen, het gewone leven en openluchtactiviteiten.

Claude Monet (1840–1926)
Breakfast: decorative panel
Le Déjeuner: panneau décoratif
Das Mittagessen
El desayuno: panel decorativo
La colazione: pannello decorativo
De lunch: decoratief paneel
c. 1873, Oil on canvas/Huile sur toile, 160 × 201 cm

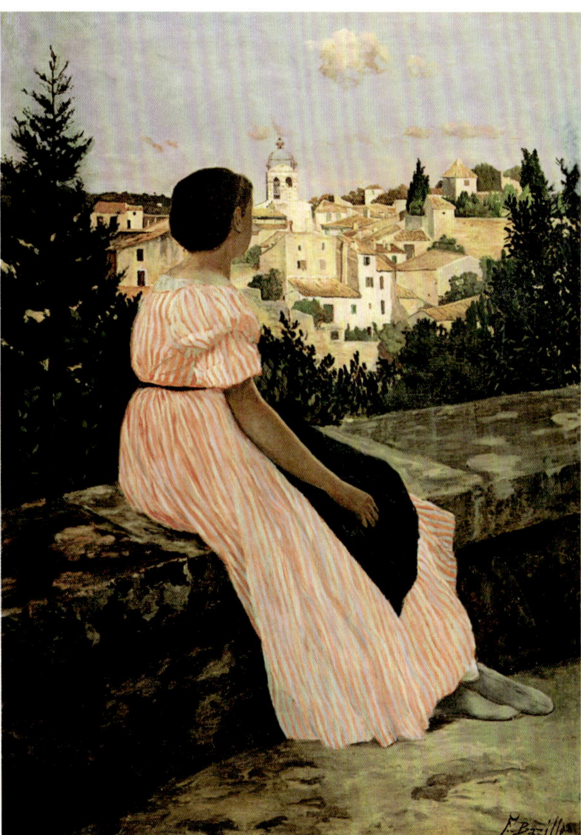

Trained in Charles Gleyre's academic panting studio and a friend of the future impressionists, Frédéric Bazille has left a handful of portraits of male nudes and very successful family scenes. For *The Pink Dress* he chose as his model his cousin Thérèse des Hours. With her back to the spectator and slightly in the shade while the sun illuminates the roofs, she poses on the low wall located at the edge of the terrace of their family property of Méric near Montpellier.

Formé dans l'atelier du peintre académique Charles Gleyre et ami des futurs impressionnistes, Frédéric Bazille a laissé une poignée de portraits, de nus masculins et de scènes familiales très aboutis. Pour *La Robe rose,* il a choisi pour modèle sa cousine Thérèse des Hours. Tournant le dos au spectateur, et légèrement dans l'ombre tandis que le soleil éclaire les toits, celle-ci pose sur le muret situé au bord de la terrasse de leur propriété familiale de Méric, près de Montpellier.

Frédéric Bazille, im Atelier des akademischen Malers Charles Gleyre ausgebildet und Freund der späteren Impressionisten, hat eine Handvoll sehr gelungener Porträts, männlicher Aktdarstellungen und Familienszenen hinterlassen. Für *Das rosa Kleid* wählte er seine Cousine Thérèse des Hours als Modell. Sie sitzt auf einer kleinen Mauer am Rande der Terrasse des Familienanwesens Méric, in der Nähe von Montpellier, mit dem Rücken zum Betrachter und leicht im Schatten, während die Dächer von der Sonne beleuchtet werden.

Formado en el taller del pintor académico Charles Gleyre y amigo de futuros impresionistas, Frédéric Bazille dejó un puñado de retratos de desnudos masculinos y escenas familiares muy logrado. En *El vestido rosa,* optó por modelar a su prima Thérèse des Hours. Dando la espalda al espectador, y un poco a la sombra mientras el sol ilumina los tejados, se apoya en un murete situado al borde de la terraza de la propiedad familiar en Meric, cerca de Montpellier.

Formatosi nella bottega del pittore accademico Charles Gleyre e amico dei futuri impressionisti, Frédéric Bazille ha lasciato una manciata di ritratti, di nudi maschili e di scene di famiglia molto felici. Nel quadro *L'abito rosa* scelse come modella la cugina Thérèse des Hours, la quale, di spalle all'osservatore e leggermente all'ombra mentre il sole illumina i tetti, posa sul muro situato al bordo della terrazza della loro tenuta familiare di Méric, vicino a Montpellier.

Frédéric Bazille, leerling van de academische schilder Charles Gleyre en bevriend met de latere impressionisten, liet een handvol zeer geslaagde portretten, mannelijke naakten en familietaferelen na. Voor *De roze jurk* stond zijn nicht Thérèse des Hours model. Met haar rug naar de toeschouwer gekeerd en enigszins in de schaduw van de zon die in het dorp de daken beschijnt, zit ze op het muurtje van het terras van het familielandhuis in Méric, niet ver van Montpellier.

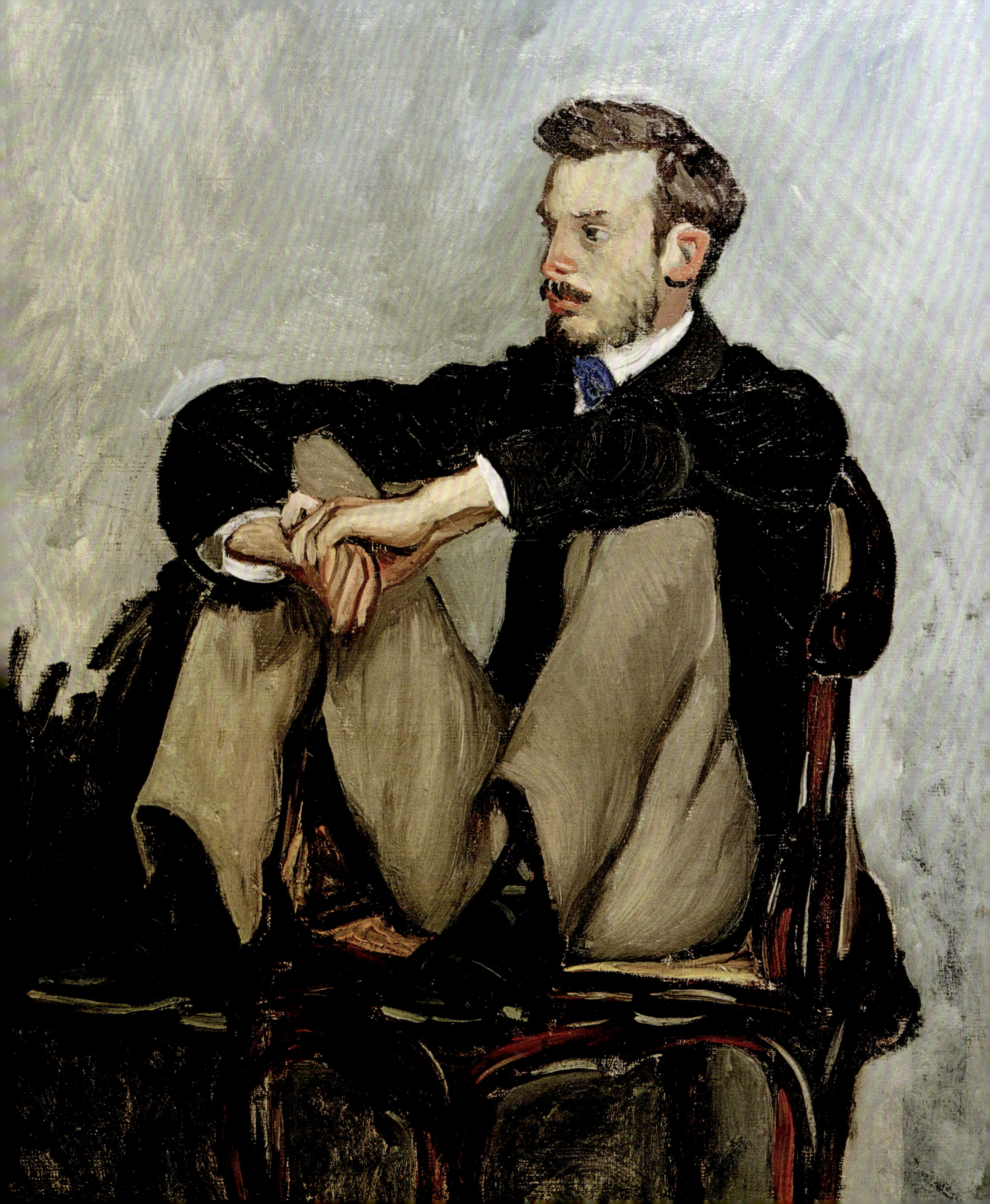

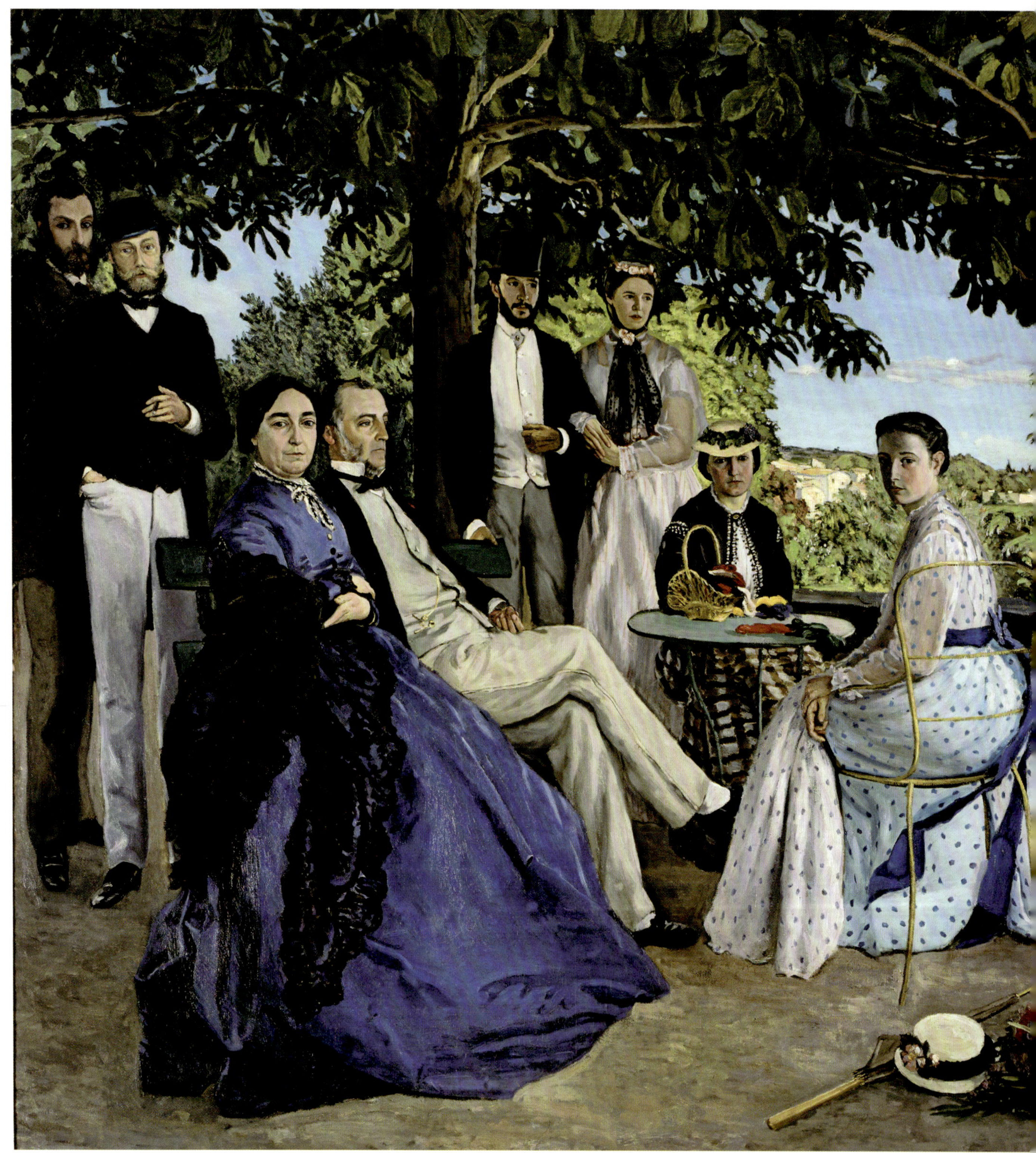

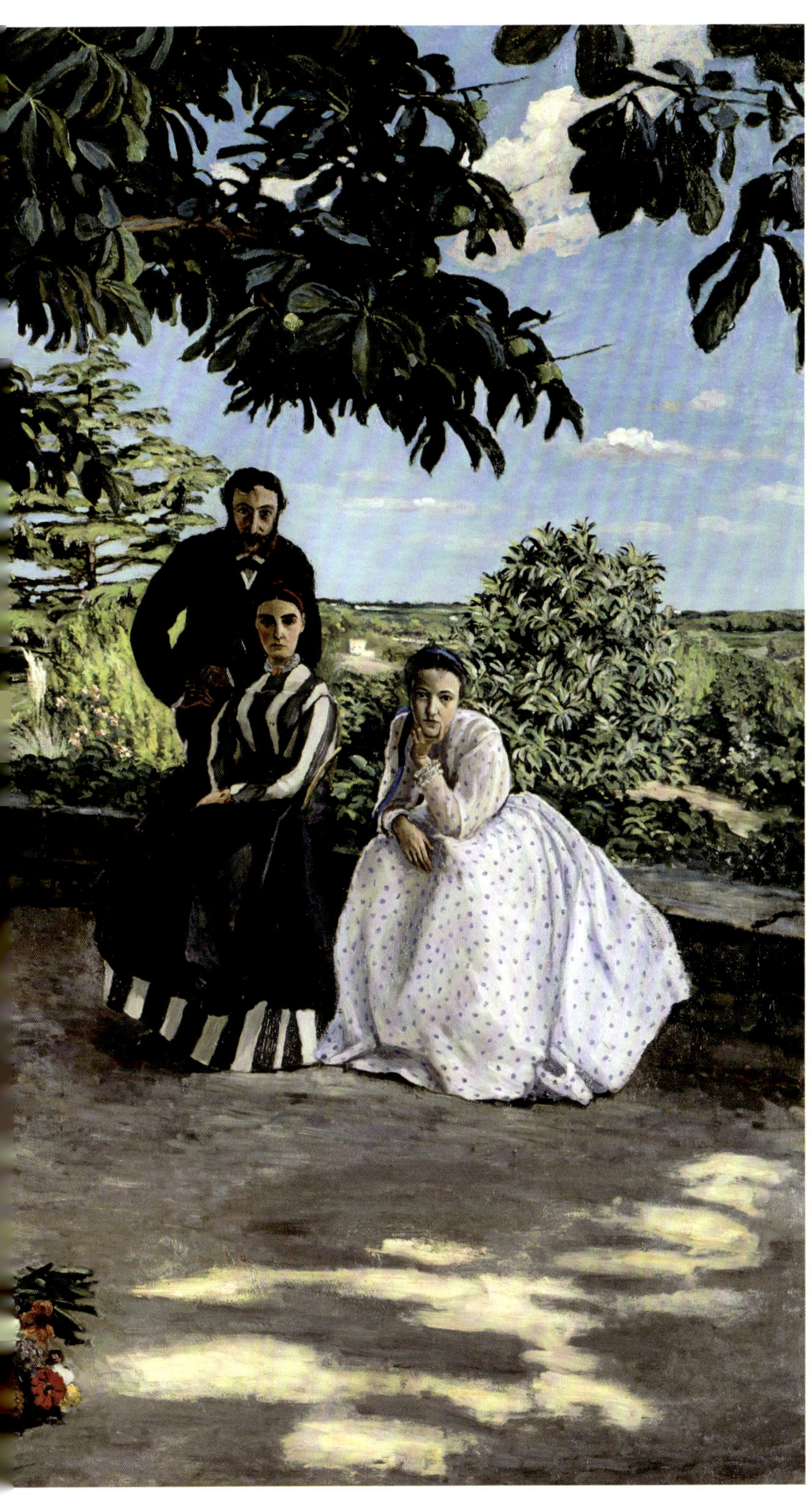

Frédéric Bazille (1841–1870)

Family Reunion

Réunion de famille

Familienbild

Reunión de familia

Riunione di famiglia

Familiereünie

c. 1867–1868, Oil on canvas/Huile sur toile, 152 × 230 cm

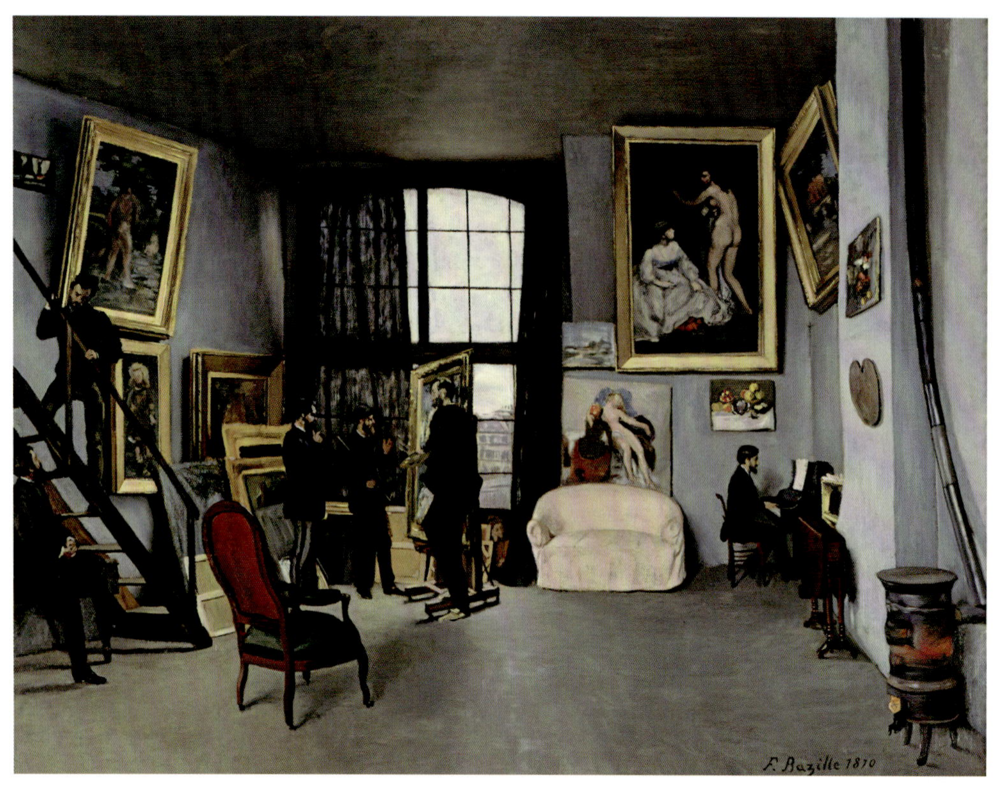

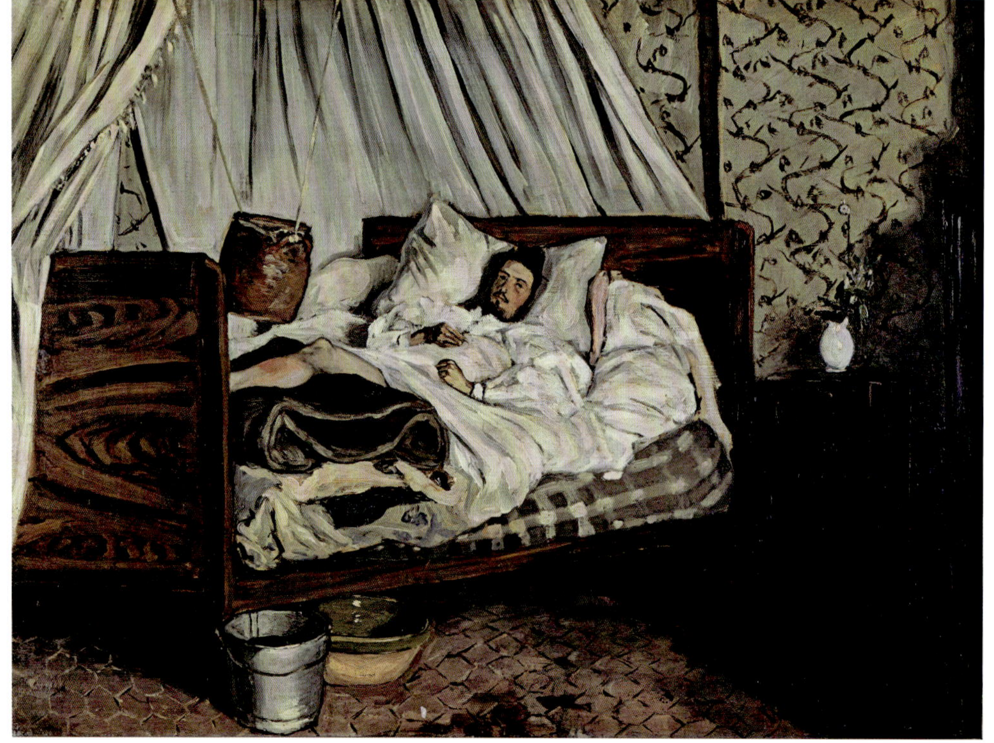

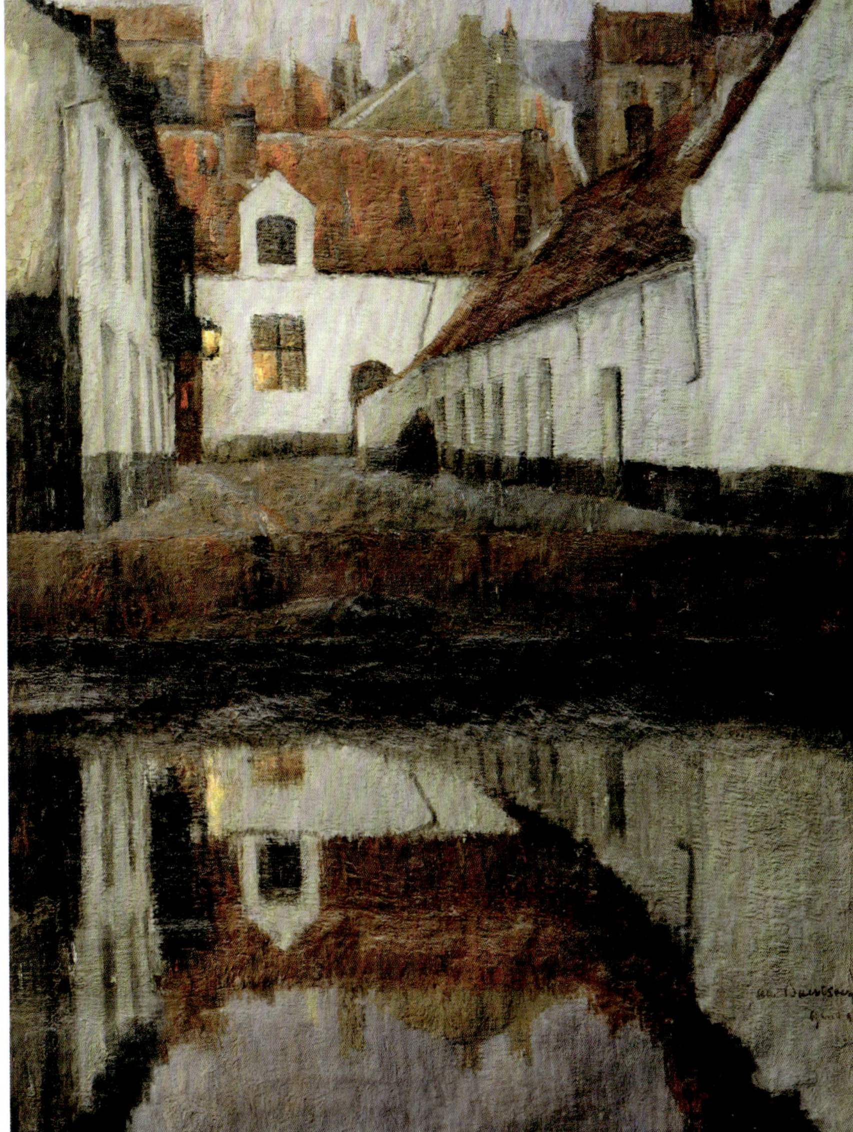

Frédéric Bazille (1841–1870), Édouard Manet (1832–1883)

Bazille's Studio

L'Atelier de Bazille

Das Atelier von Bazille

El taller de Bazille

L'atelier di Bazille

Het atelier in Bazille

1870, Oil on canvas/Huile sur toile, 98 × 128 cm

Albert Baertsoen (1866–1922)

The Pink Dress

Petite Cour en Flandre au crépuscule

Kleinstadt am Wasser am Abend

Pequeño patio en Flandes al atardecer

Piccolo cortile nelle Fiandre al crepuscolo

Hofje in Vlaanderen in de schemering

1899, Oil on canvas/Huile sur toile, 141 × 108,5 cm

Frédéric Bazille (1841–1870)

The Improvised Ambulance

L'Ambulance improvisée

Claude Monet verwundet

La ambulancia improvisada

L'ospedale da campo improvvisato

De geïmproviseerde ambulance

1865, Oil on canvas/Huile sur toile, 47 × 62 cm

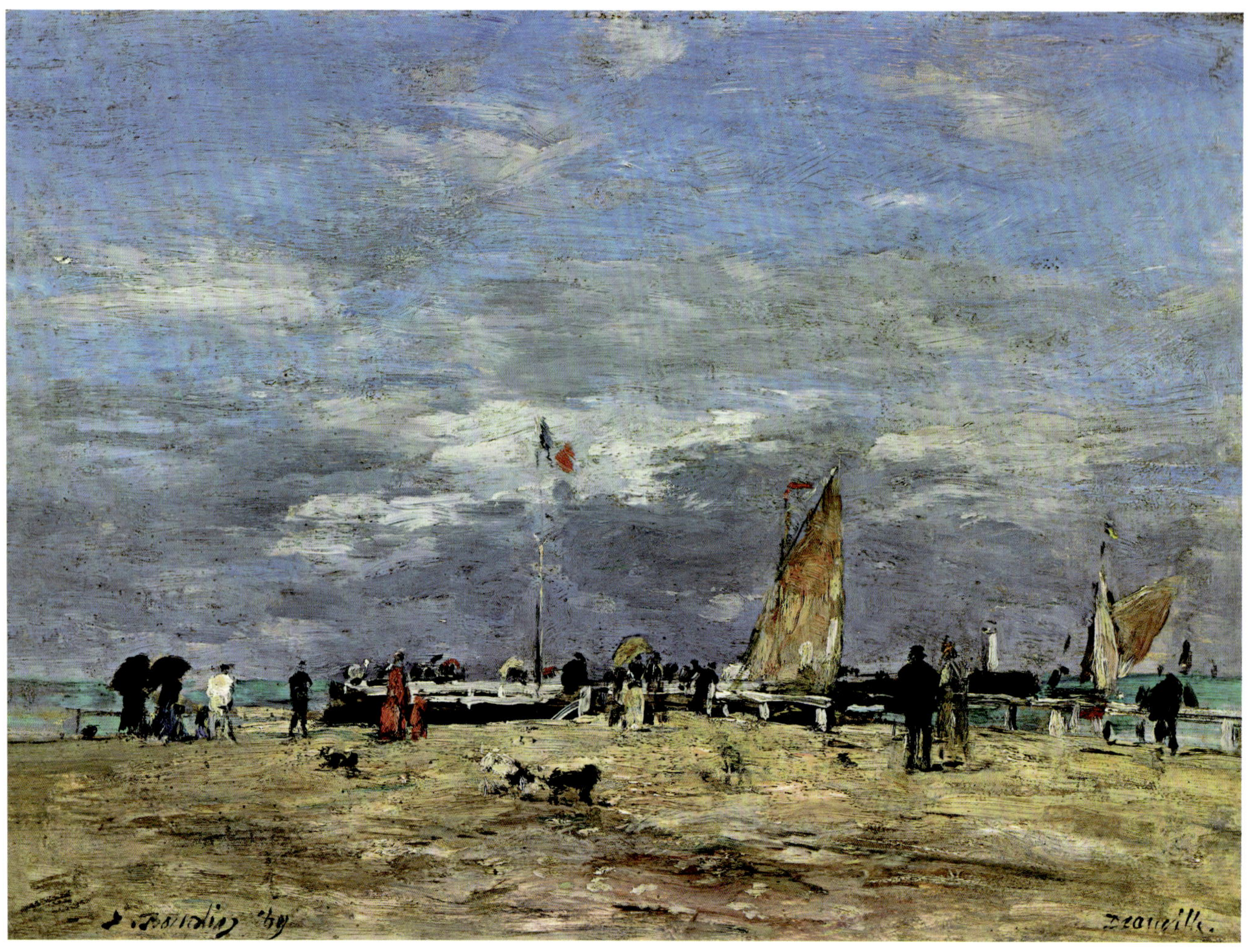

Eugène Boudin (1824–1898)

The Deauville Pier	Mole von Deauville	Il molo di Deauville
La Jetée de Deauville	El muelle de Deauville	De pier van Deauville

1869, Oil on canvas/Huile sur toile, 23,5 × 32,5 cm

"Follow the clouds with the brush in hand"—such is the objective of Eugène Boudin, this outdoor enthusiast fascinated by the study of atmospheric effects. While he may paint beach scenes with a myriad animated details of characters who made his reputation, the rocks of the Normandy coast, or the waltz of sailboats at sea, his true subject is ultimately the sky, which often occupies most of the space of his paintings.

« Suivre les nuages le pinceau à la main », tel est l'objectif d'Eugène Boudin, cet adepte du plein air fasciné par l'étude des effets atmosphériques. Qu'il peigne ces scènes de plage aux mille détails animées de personnages qui ont fait sa réputation, les rochers des côtes normandes, ou la valse des voiliers sur l'océan, son vrai sujet est finalement le ciel, qui occupe souvent la majeure partie de l'espace de ses tableaux.

„Den Wolken folgen mit dem Pinsel in der Hand" ist das Ziel von Eugène Boudin, einem vom Studium der atmosphärischen Einflüsse faszinierten Anhänger der Freilichtmalerei. Wenn er die detailreichen, von Figuren bevölkerten Strandszenen malt, die ihn berühmt gemacht haben, die Felsen der Normandieküste oder den Walzer der Segelschiffe auf dem Ozean, ist sein eigentliches Thema der Himmel, der oft den größten Platz auf seinen Gemälden einnimmt.

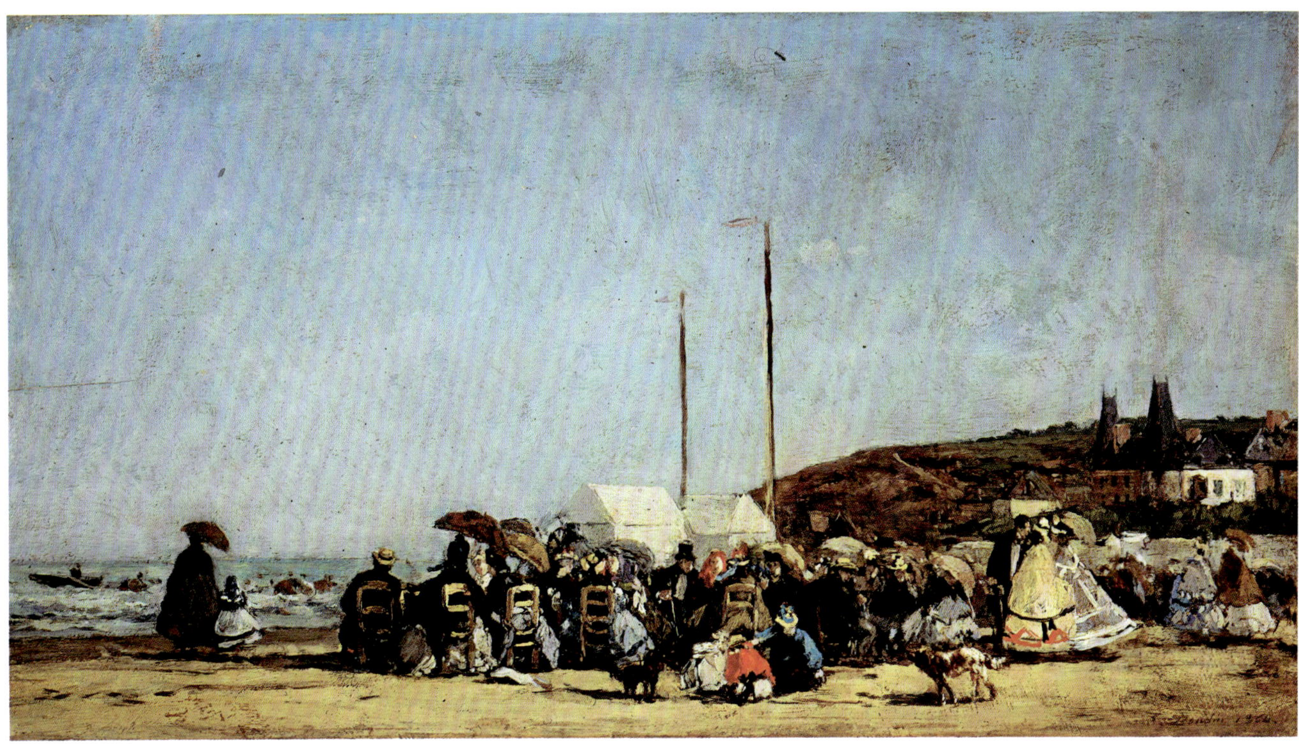

Eugène Boudin (1824–1898)

The Beach at Trouville
La Plage de Trouville
Der Strand in Trouville
La playa de Trouville
La spiaggia di Trouville
Het strand van Trouville

1864, Oil on canvas/Huile sur toile, 25,7 × 48 cm

"Sigue a las nubes con el pincel en la mano", es el objetivo de Eugène Boudin, este aficionado al aire libre fascinado por el estudio de los efectos atmosféricos. Aunque pinte escenas de playa con miles de animados detalles de sus personajes, que forjaron su reputación, las rocas de la costa de Normandía, o el vals de los barcos de vela en el océano, su tema real es en última instancia el cielo que a menudo ocupa la mayor parte del espacio de sus pinturas.

"Seguire le nuvole con il pennello in mano" era l'obiettivo di Eugène Boudin, un appassionato della pittura en plein air affascinato dallo studio degli effetti atmosferici. Sia nei dipinti di scene di spiaggia dai mille dettagli e popolati da personaggi animati, che lo hanno reso famoso, sia nei quadri raffiguranti le scogliere della costa della Normandia o il valzer delle barche a vela sul mare, il suo vero soggetto è in ultima istanza il cielo, che spesso occupa la maggior parte della tela.

"Met het penseel in de hand de wolken volgen", dat is het doel van Eugène Boudin, een fervent aanhanger van schilderen in de openlucht met een fascinatie voor atmosferische effecten. Of hij nu tot in detail uitgewerkte en met badgasten verlevendigde strandtaferelen schildert, of de Normandische rotskust of de dans van een zeilschip op de golven, uiteindelijk is het de lucht die vaak het grootste deel van zijn doeken beslaat.

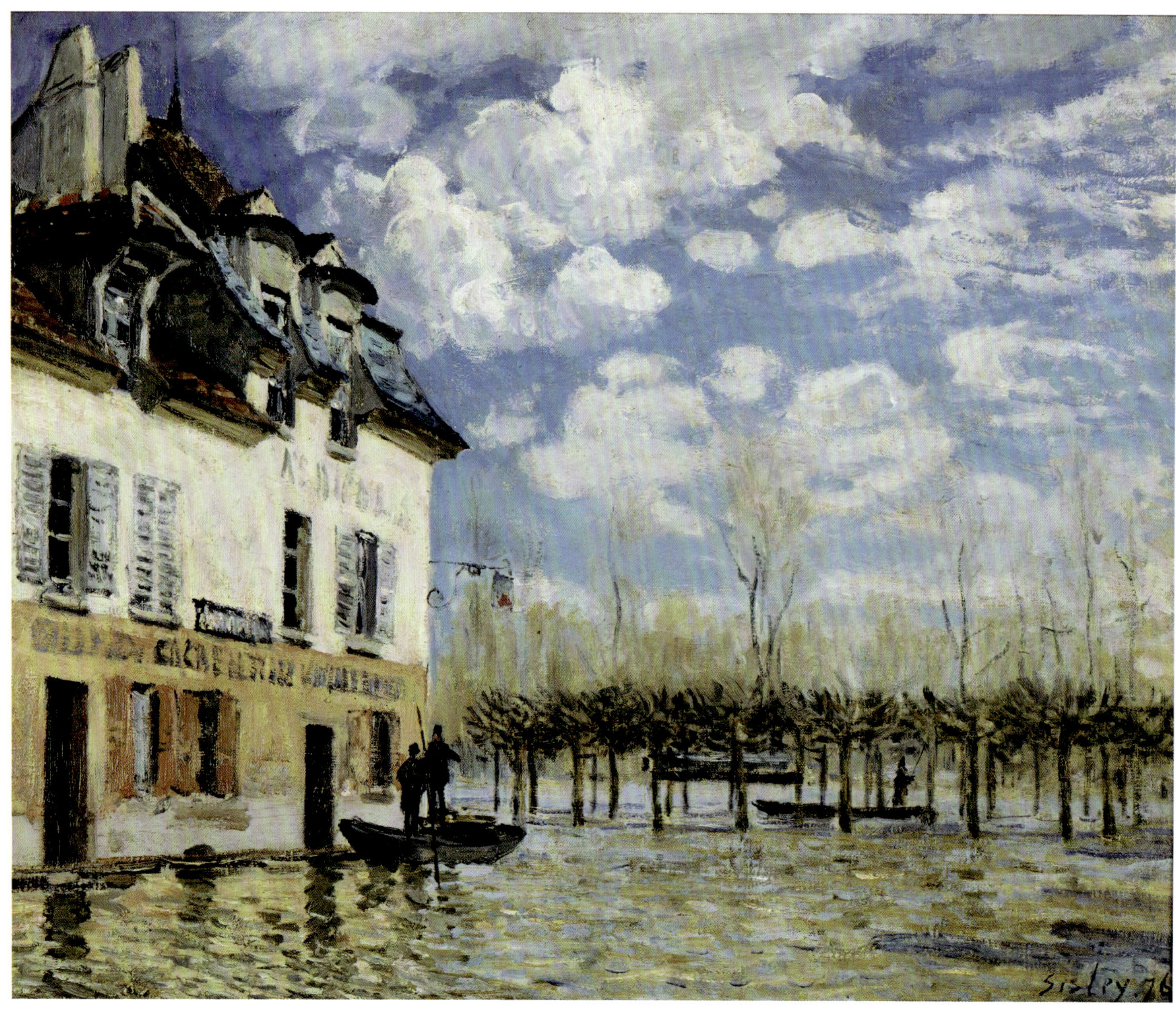

Alfred Sisley (1839–1899)

Boat in the Flood at Port Marly

La Barque pendant l'inondation, Port-Marly

Überschwemmung in Port-Marly

La barca durante la inundación

La barca durante l'inondazione, Port-Marly

Roeibootje tijdens de overstroming, Port-Marly

1876, Oil on canvas/Huile sur toile, 50,4 × 61 cm

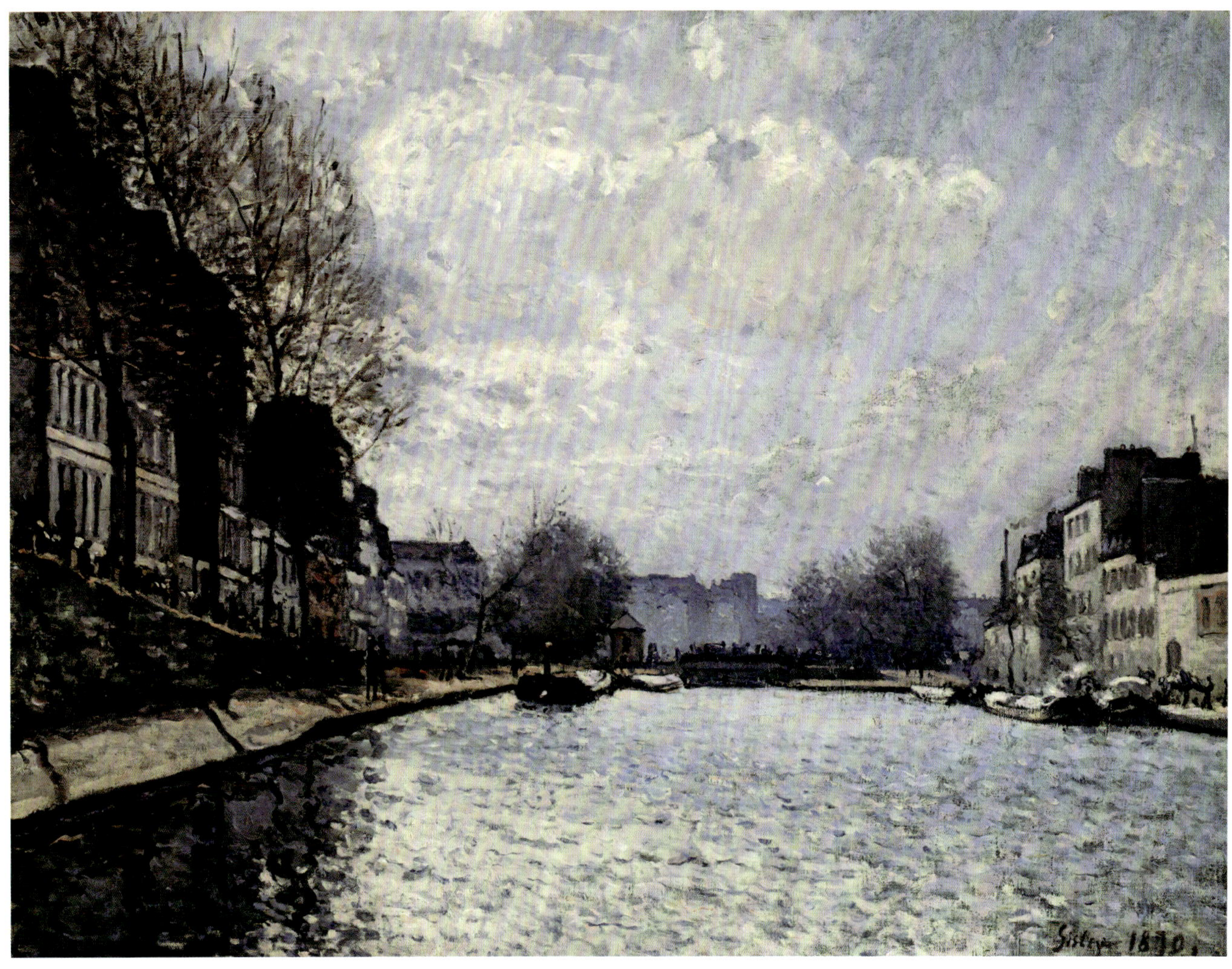

Alfred Sisley (1839–1899)

View of the Canal Saint Martin

Vue du canal Saint-Martin

Ansicht des Kanals Saint-Martin in Paris

Vista del canal de Saint Martin

Vista del canale Saint-Martin

Gezicht op het Canal Saint-Martin

1870, Oil on canvas/Huile sur toile, 50 × 65 cm

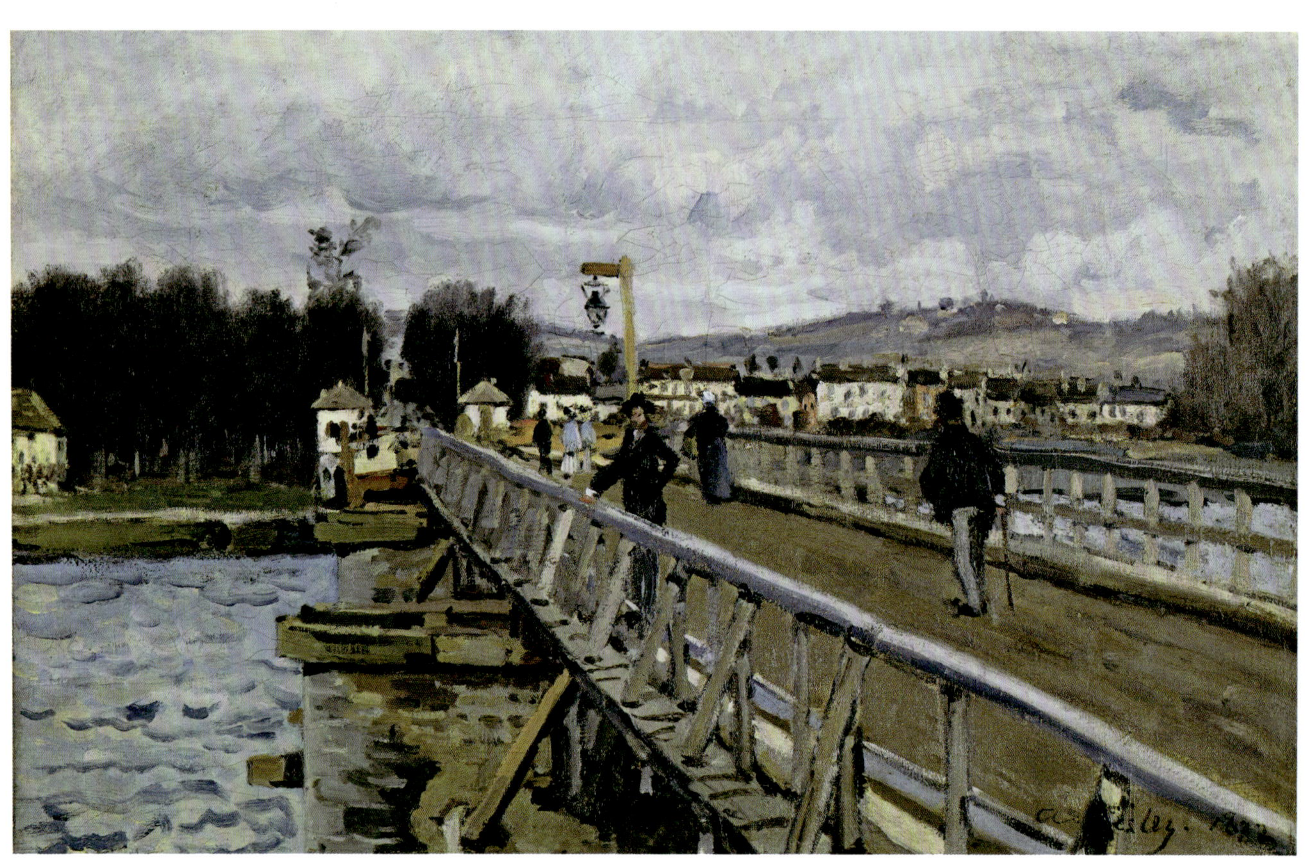

Alfred Sisley (1839–1899)

Footbridge at Argenteuil

Passerelle d'Argenteuil

Fußgängerbrücke in Argenteuil

Pasarela de Argenteuil

Passerella di Argenteuil

Voetgangersbrug in Argenteuil

1872, Oil on canvas/Huile sur toile, 39 × 60 cm

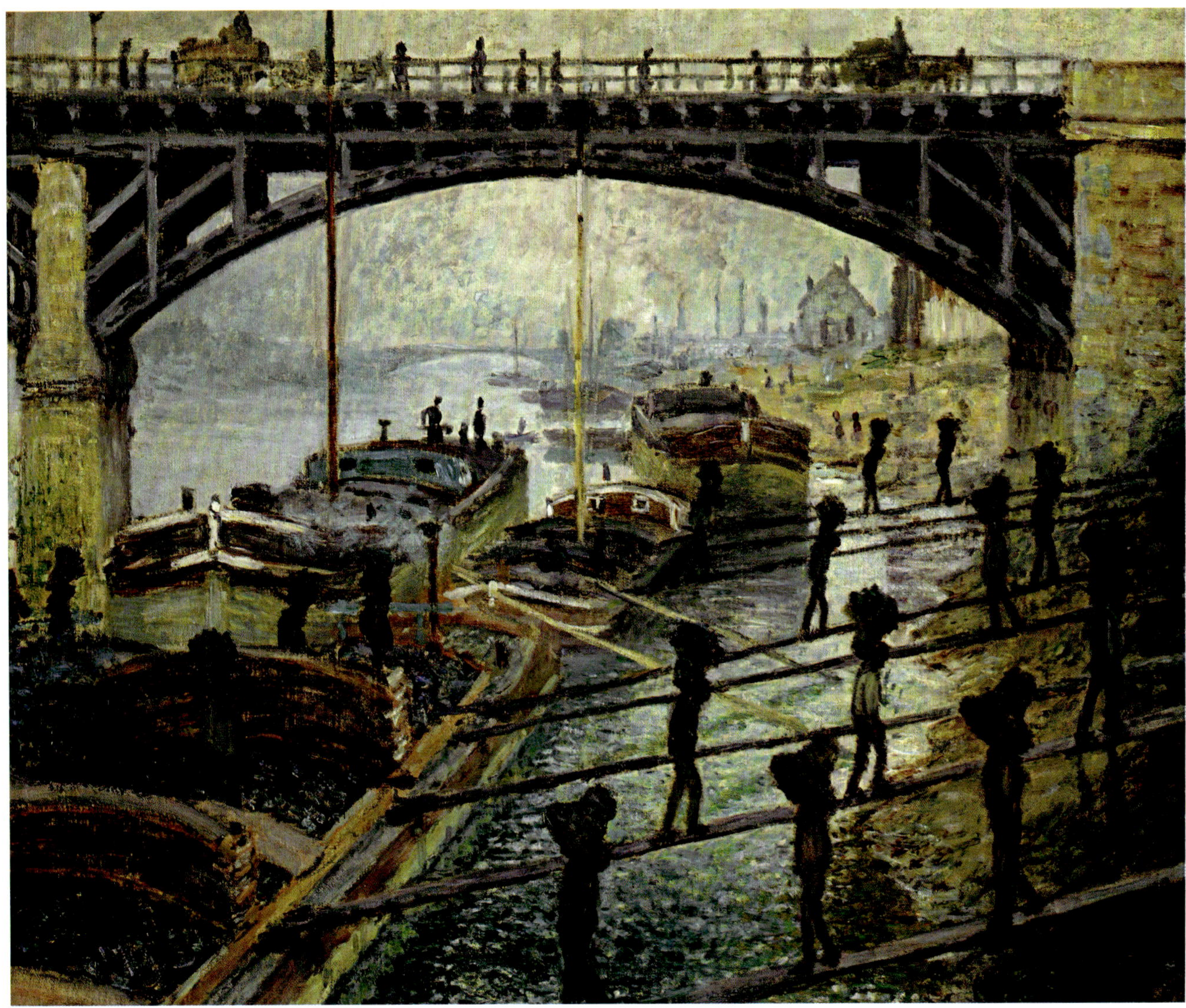

Claude Monet (1840–1926)

Unloading Coal or The Coal Dockers

Les Déchargeurs de charbon

Die Kohlenträger

Los descargadores de carbón

I carbonai

De kolensjouwers

c. 1875, Oil on canvas/Huile sur toile, 54 × 65,5 cm

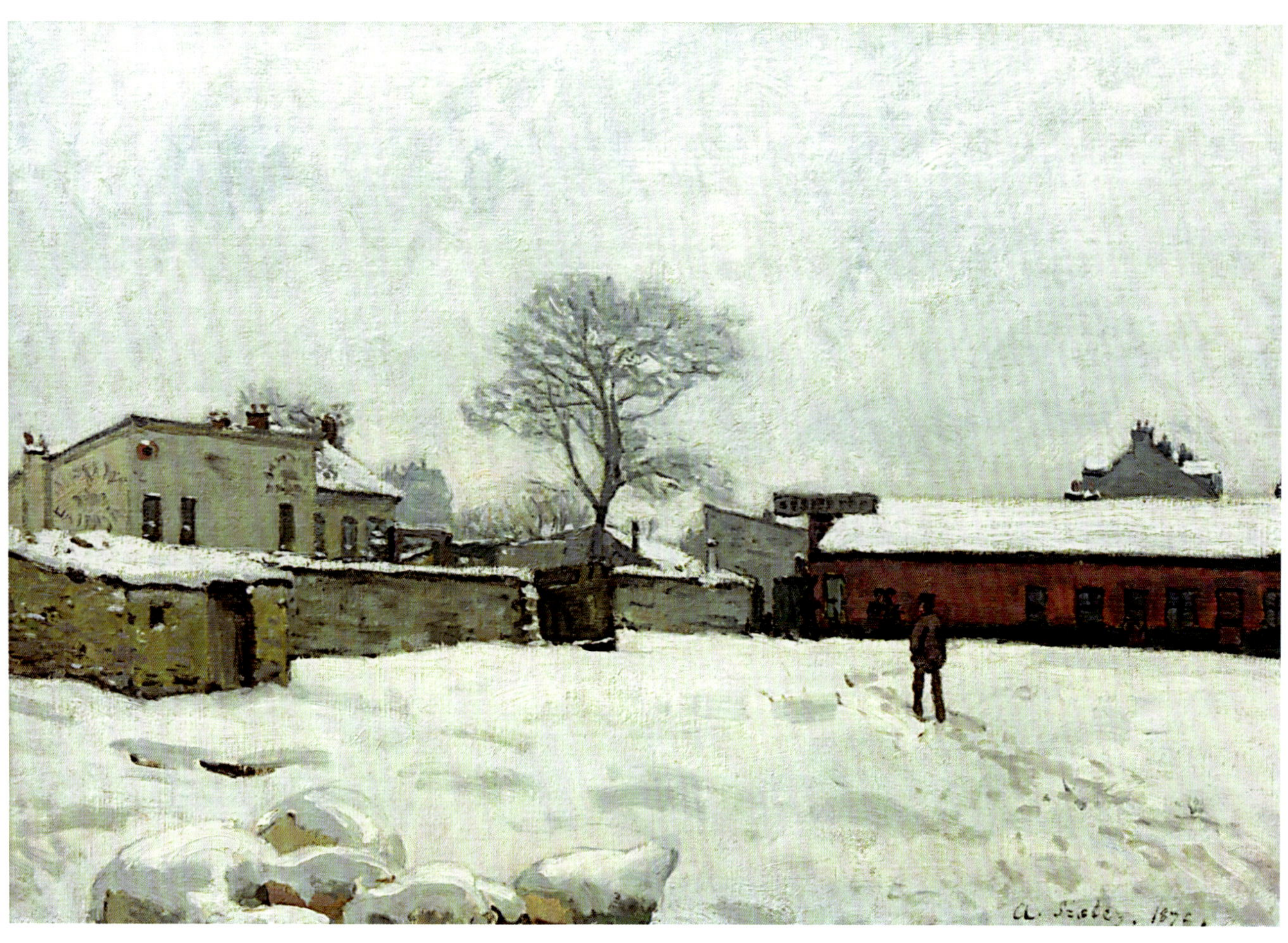

Alfred Sisley (1839–1899)
Snow at Marly le Roi
Sous la neige : cour de ferme à Marly-le-Roi
Gutshof in Marly-le-Roi im Schnee
Bajo la nieve: corral en Marly-le-Roi
Sotto la neve: cortile a Marly-le-Roi
Boerderij in Marly-le-Roi in de sneeuw
1876, Oil on canvas/Huile sur toile, 38,5 × 55,7 cm

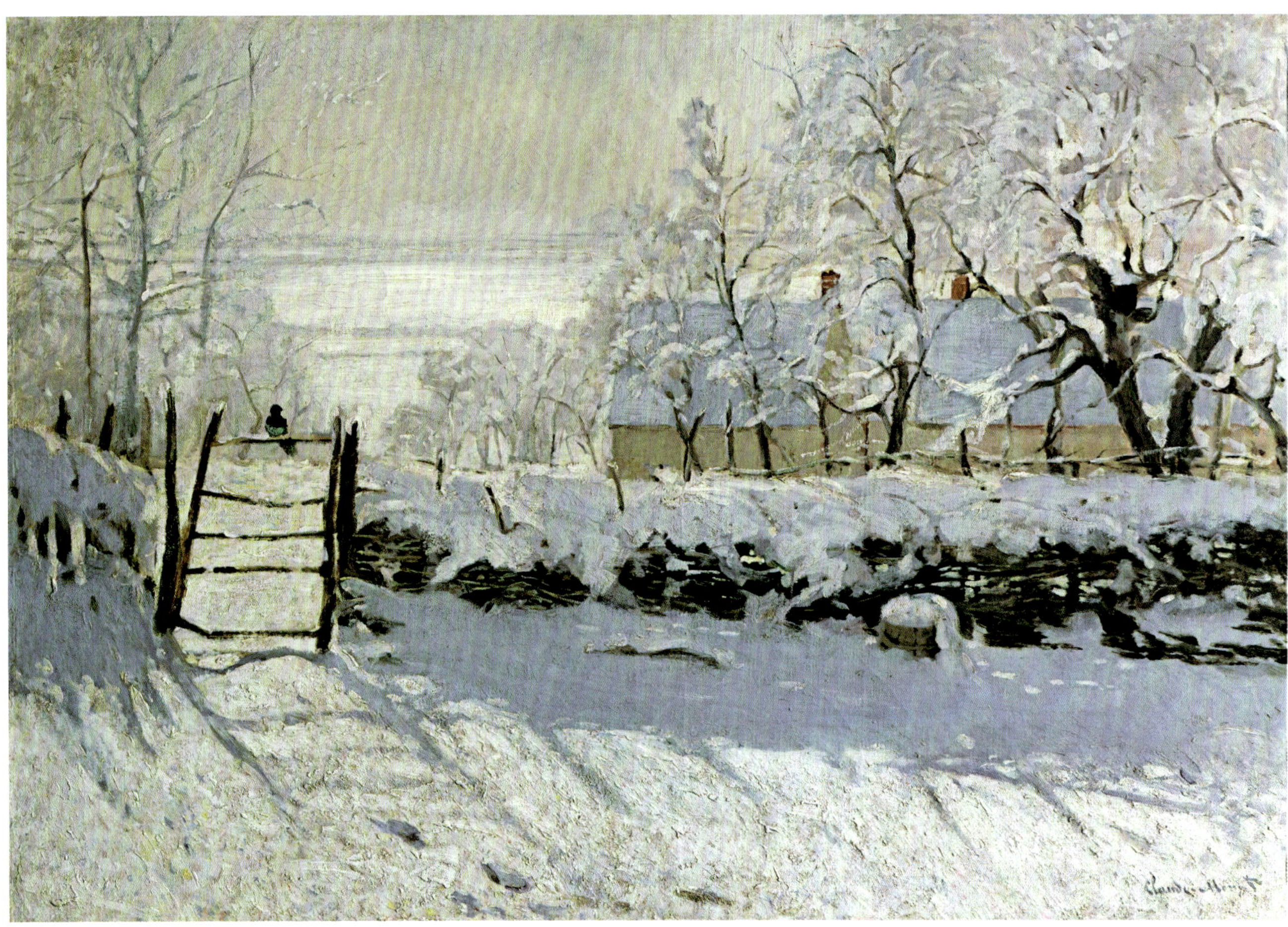

Claude Monet (1840–1926)

The Magpie

La Pie

Die Elster

La urraca

La Gazza

De ekster

c. 1868–1869, Oil on canvas/Huile sur toile, 89 × 130 cm

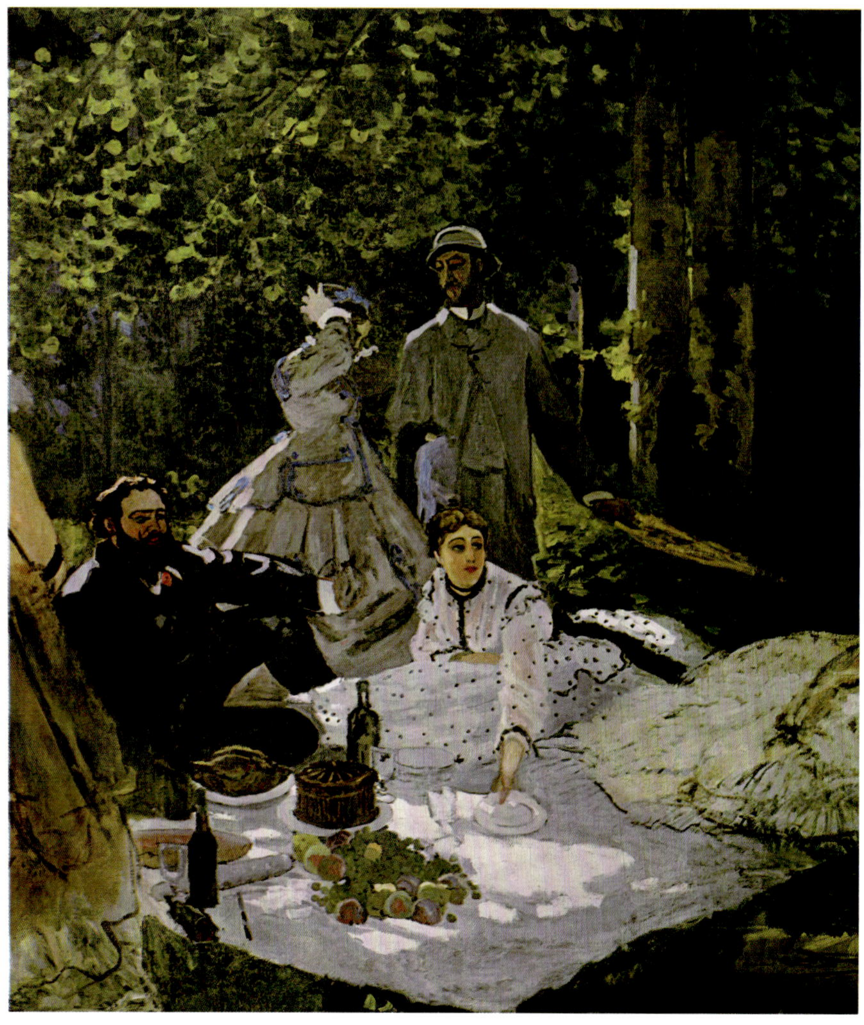

Claude Monet (1840–1926)

Luncheon on the Grass, *central panel*

Le Déjeuner sur l'herbe, *panneau central*

Frühstück im Grünen, *Mittelteil*

El almuerzo sobre la hierba, *panel central*

La colazione sull'erba, *sezione centrale*

Lunch op het gras, *middenpaneel*

c. 1865–1866, Oil on canvas/Huile sur toile, 248,7 × 218 cm

Claude Monet (1840–1926)

Women in the Garden

Femmes au jardin

Frauen im Garten

Mujeres en el jardín

Donne in giardino

Vrouwen in de tuin

c. 1866, Oil on canvas/Huile sur toile, 25,5 × 20,5 cm

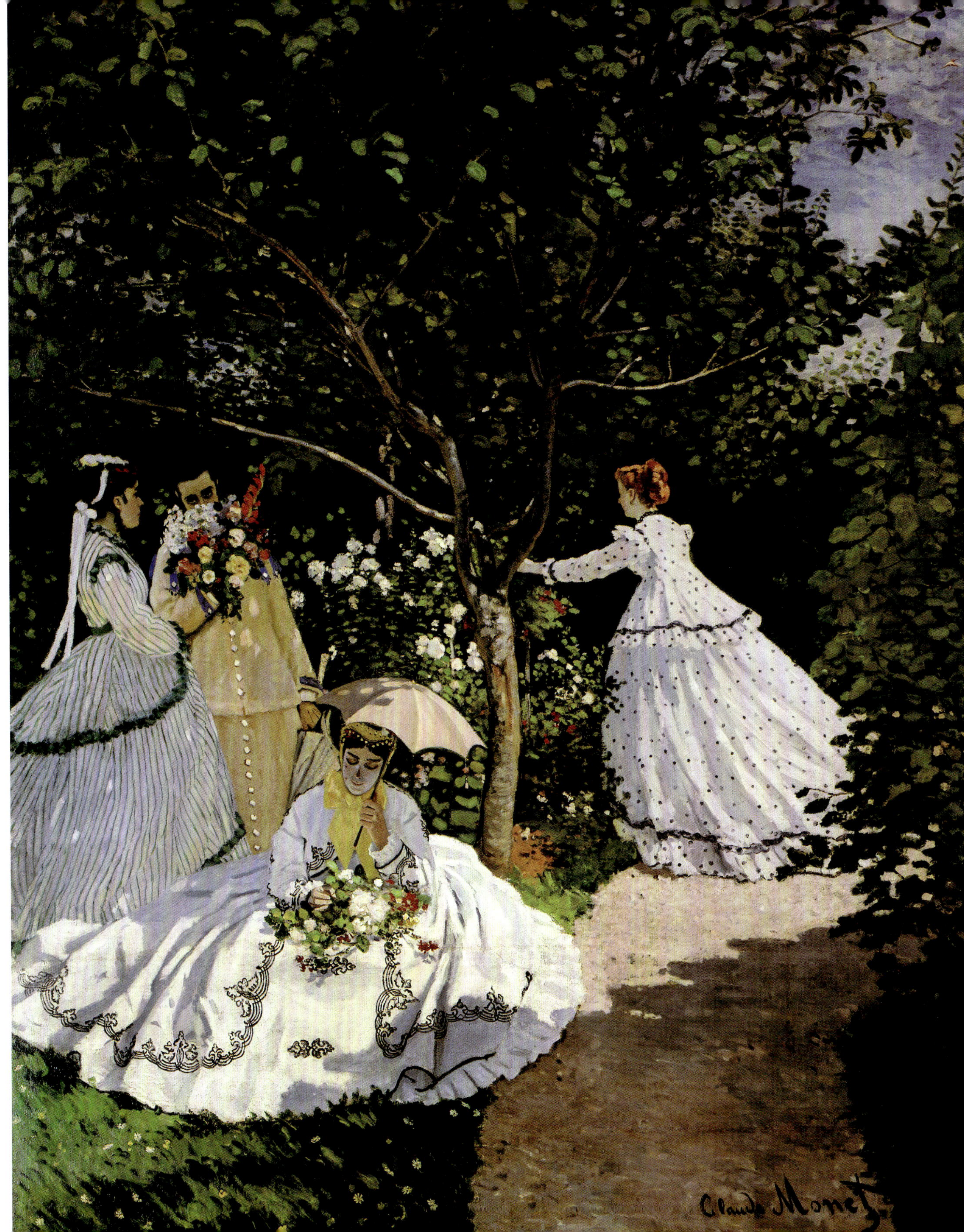

Claude Monet

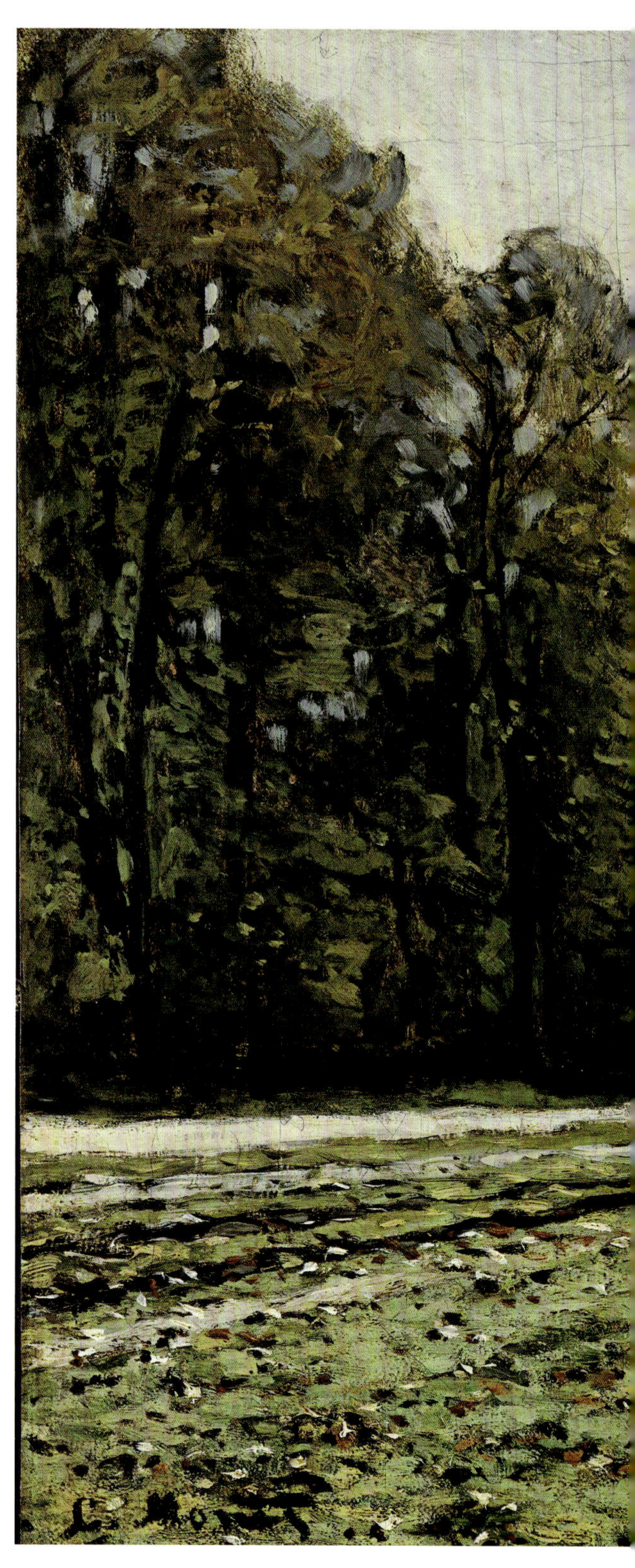

Claude Monet (1840–1926)
The Pavé de Chailly
Le Pavé de Chailly
Die Straße von Chailly
El camino de Chailly a Fontainebleau
Il lastricato di Chailly
De weg naar Chailly
c. 1865, Oil on canvas/Huile sur toile, 43,5 × 59,3 cm

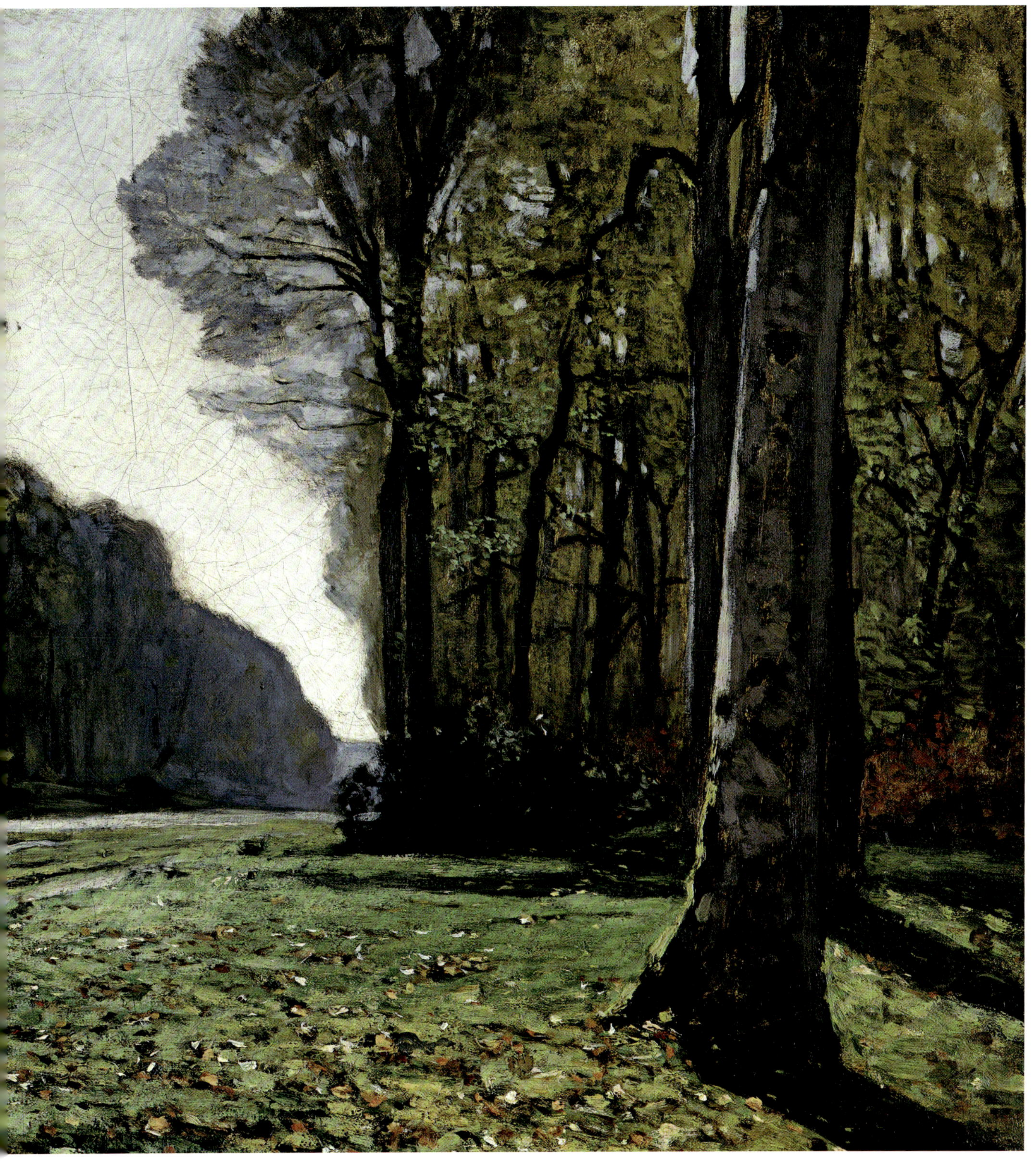

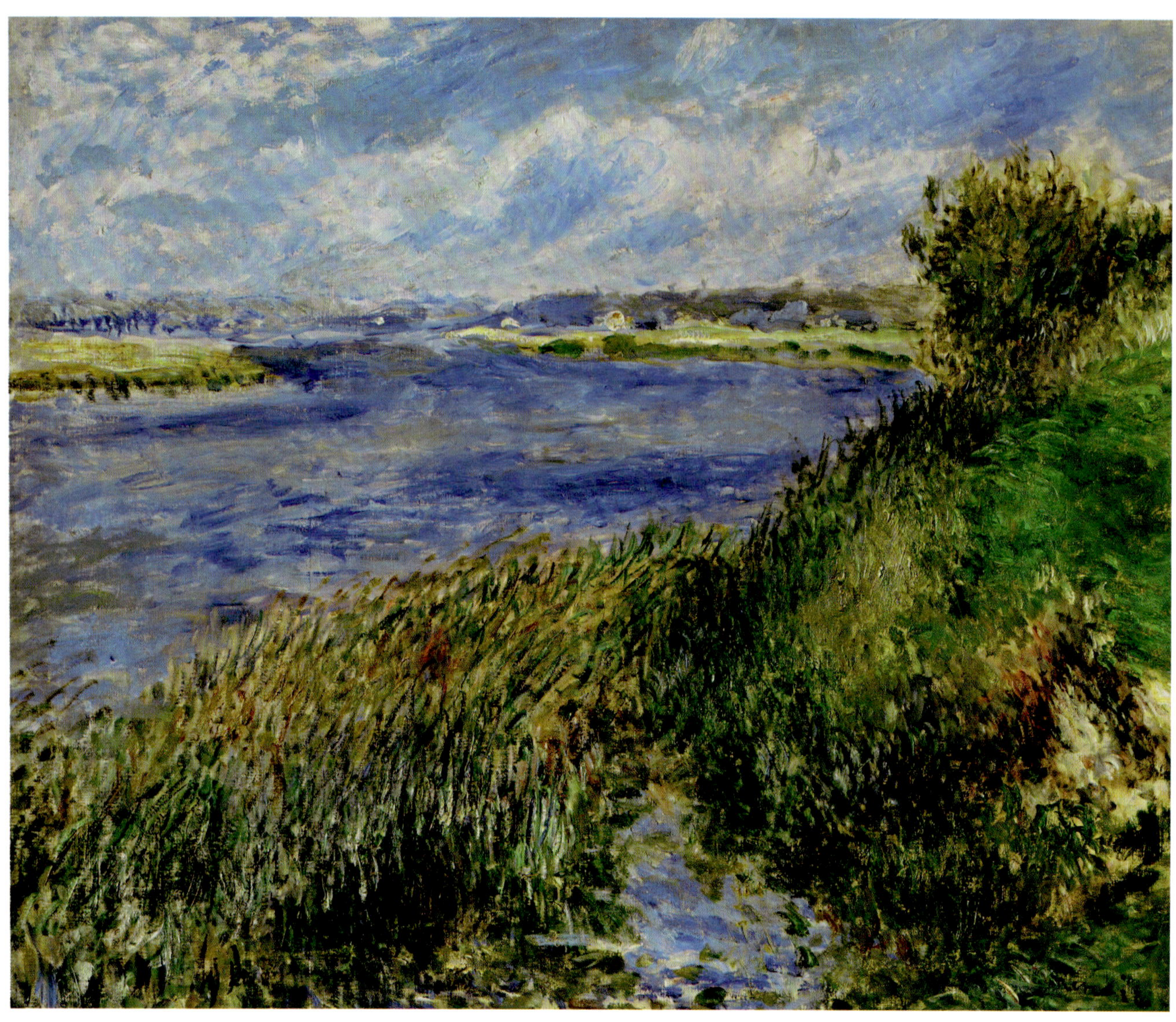

Auguste Renoir (1841–1919)

Banks of the Seine River at Champrosay

La Seine à Champrosay

Die Seine bei Champrosay

El Sena en Champrosay

La Senna a Champrosay

De Seine in Champrosay

1876, Oil on canvas/Huile sur toile, 54,6 × 66 cm

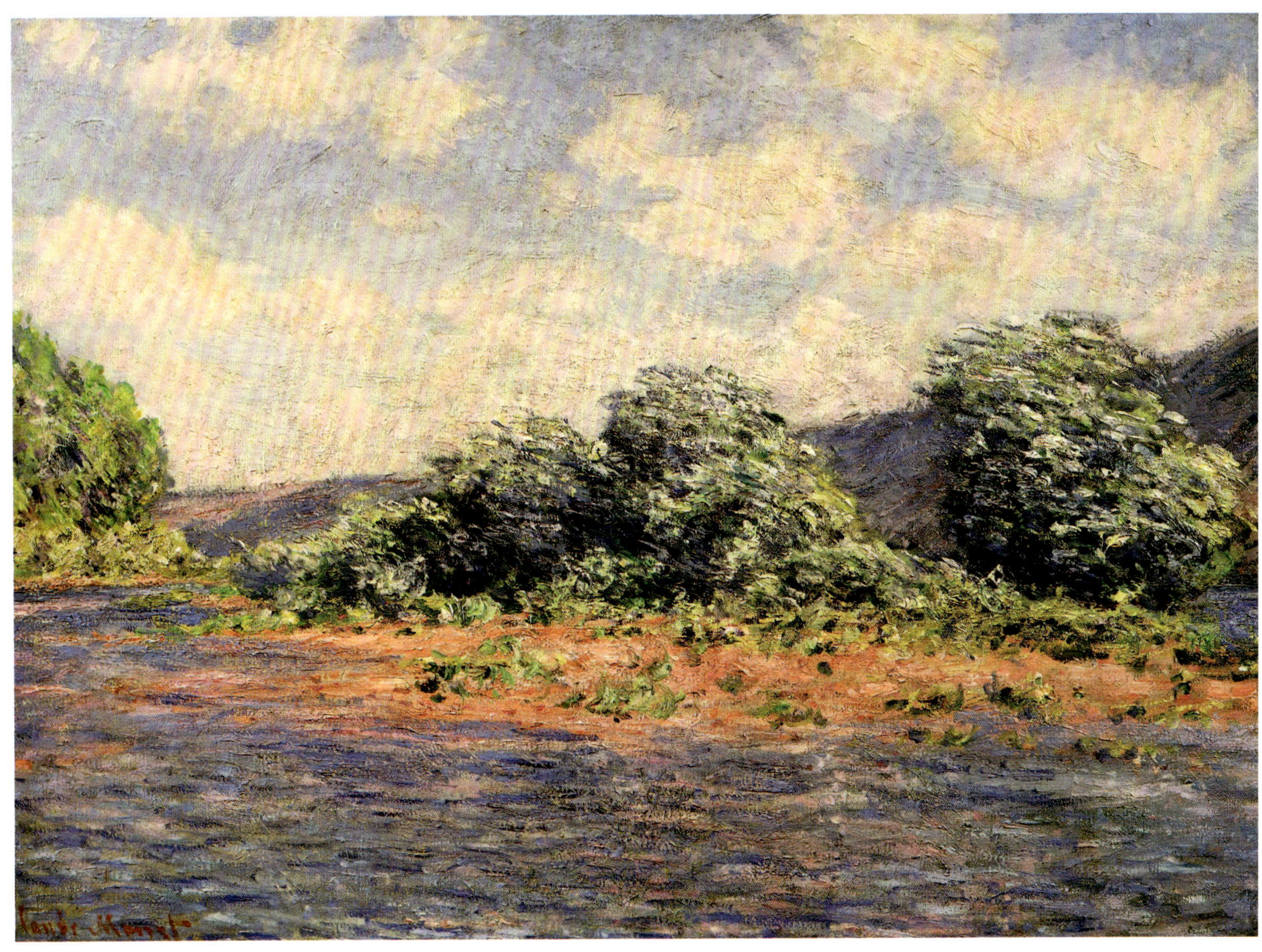

Claude Monet (1840–1926)

The Seine at Port Villez

La Seine à Port-Villez

Die Seine bei Port-Villez

El Sena en Port-Villez

La Senna a Port-Villez

De Seine in Port-Villez

c. 1890, Oil on canvas/Huile sur toile, 65,5 × 92,5 cm

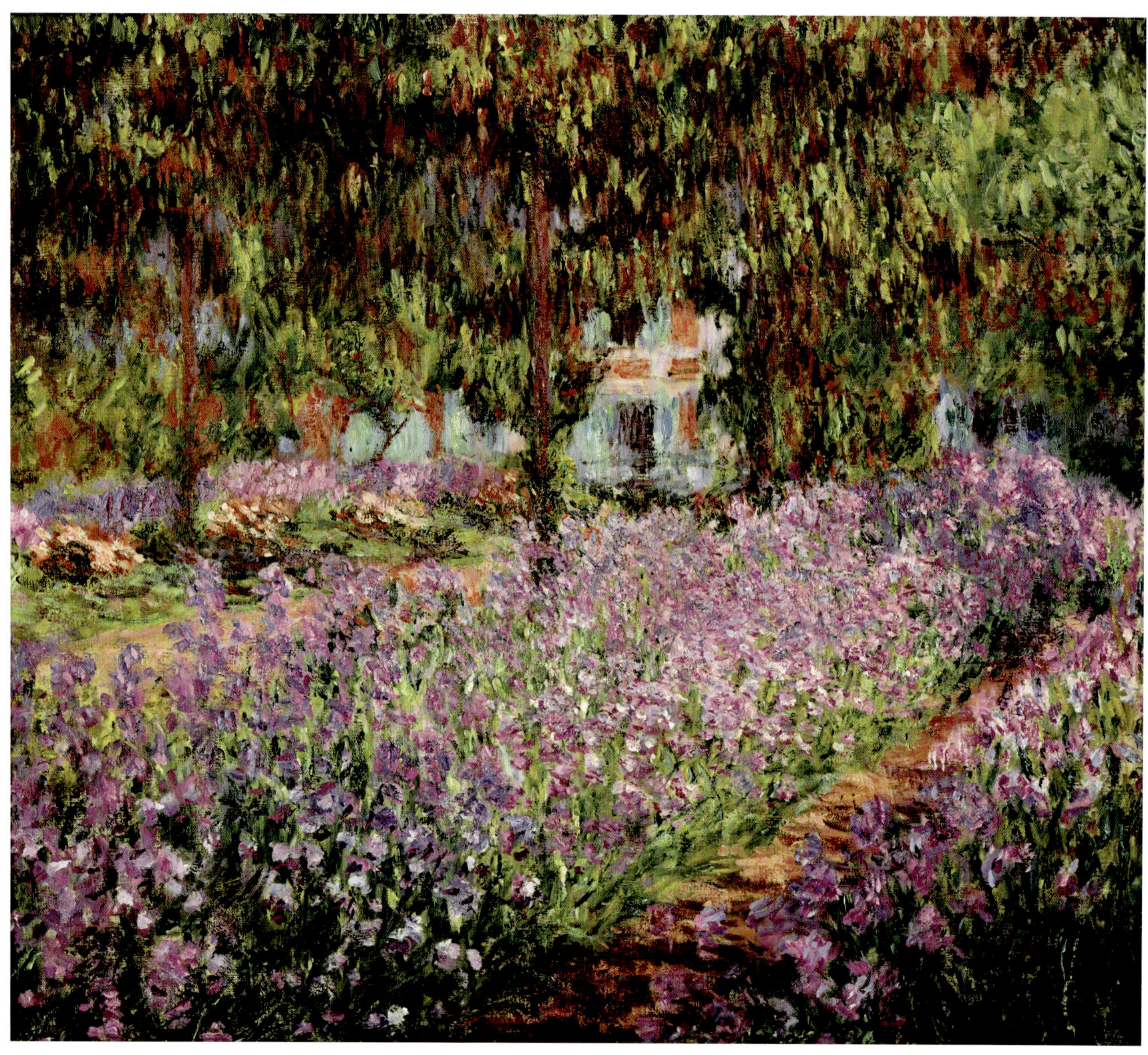

Claude Monet (1840–1926)

The Artist's Garden at Giverny
Le Jardin de l'artiste à Giverny
Der Garten des Künstlers in Giverny
El jardín del artista en Giverny
Il giardino dell'artista a Giverny
De tuin van de kunstenaar in Giverny
1900, Oil on canvas/Huile sur toile, 81,6 × 92,6 cm

Claude Monet (1840–1926)

Corner of the Apartment
Un coin d'appartement
Wohnungsinterieur
Un rincón de apartamento
Un angolo di appartamento
Hoek van het appartement
1875, Oil on canvas/Huile sur toile, 81,5 × 60 cm

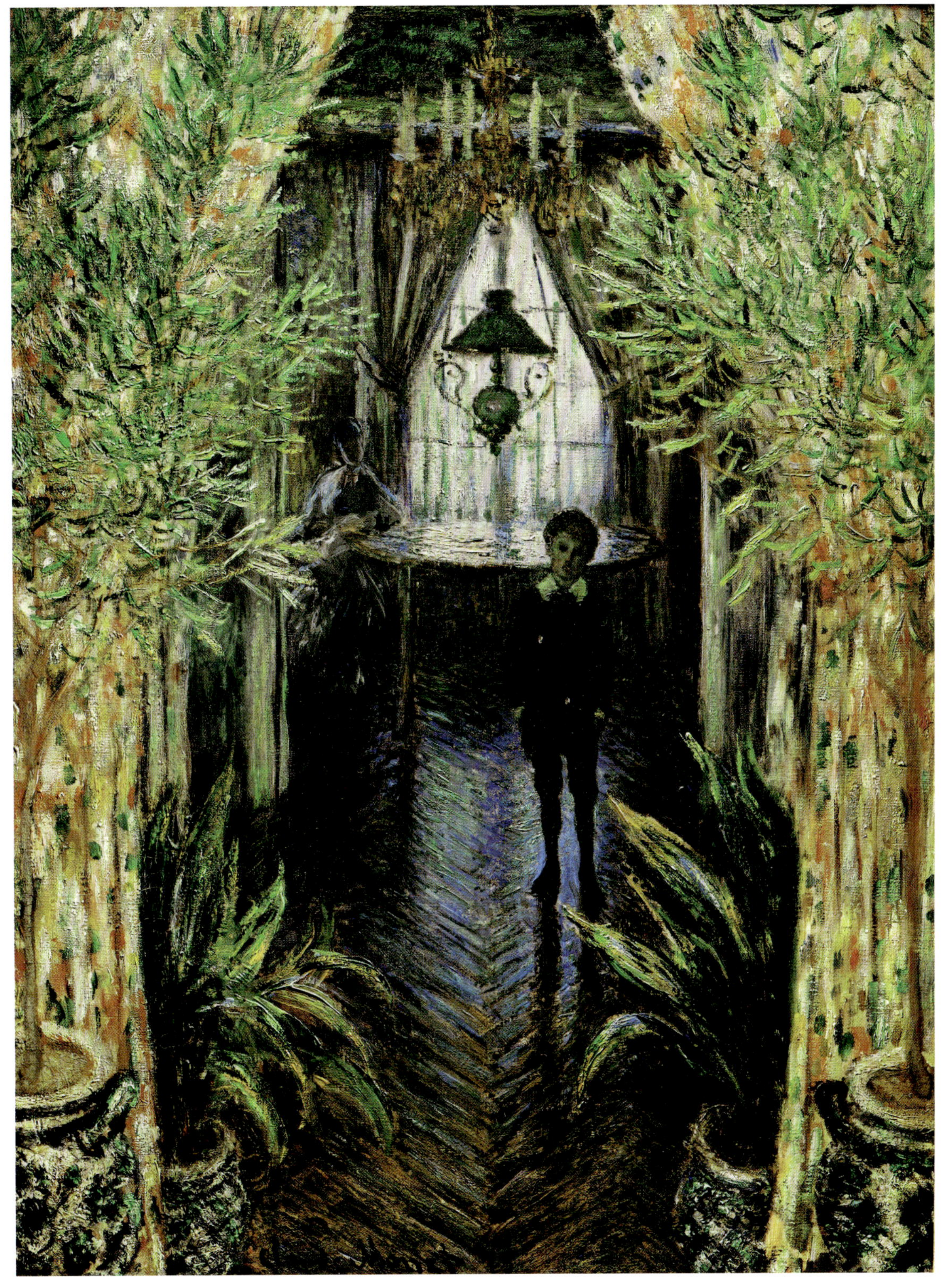

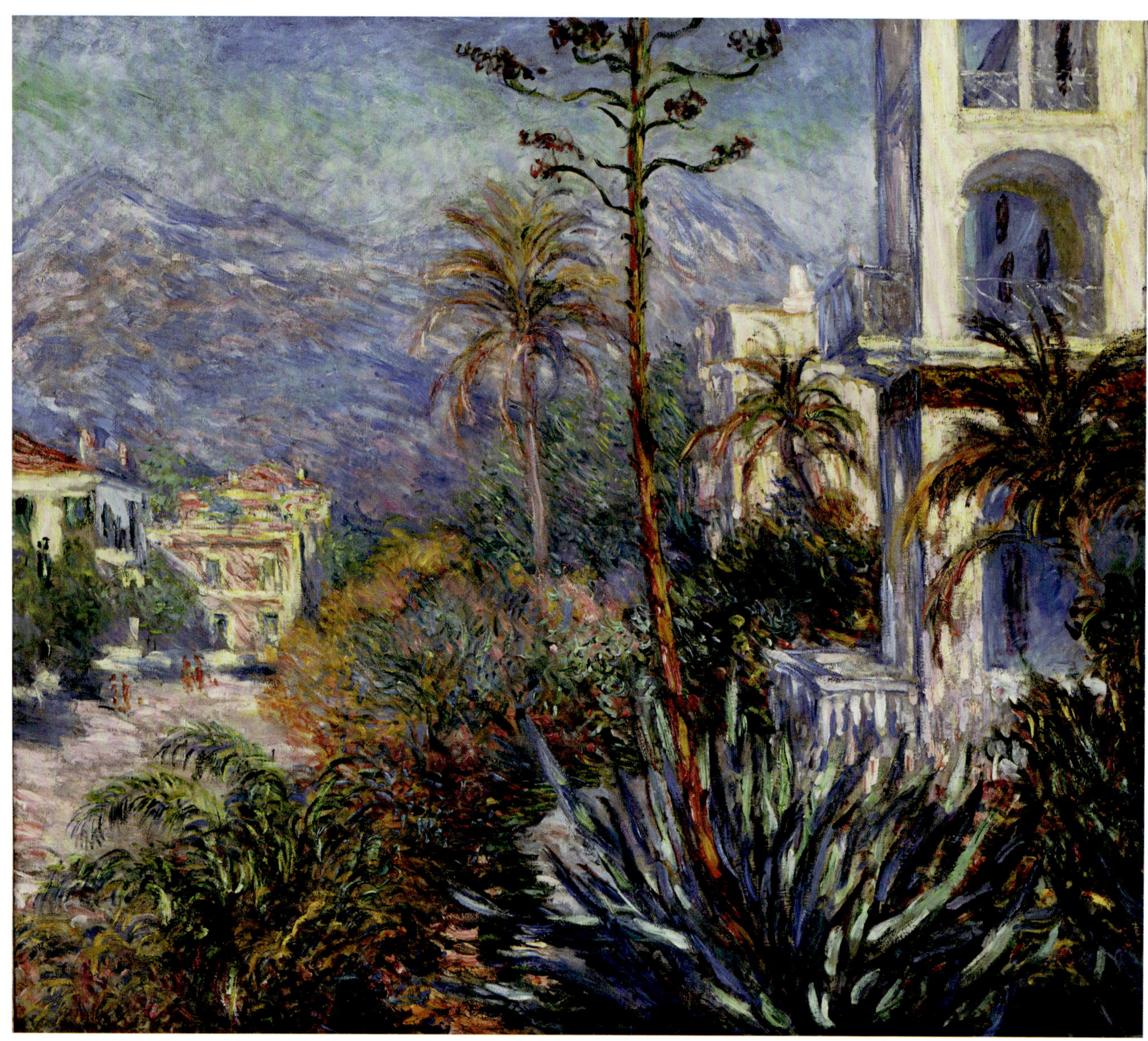

Claude Monet (1840–1926)

Villas at Bordighera

Les Villas à Bordighera

Die Villen in Bordighera

Las villas en Bordighera

Le Ville a Bordighera

De Villa's in Bordighera

1884, Oil on canvas/Huile sur toile, 116,5 × 136,5 cm

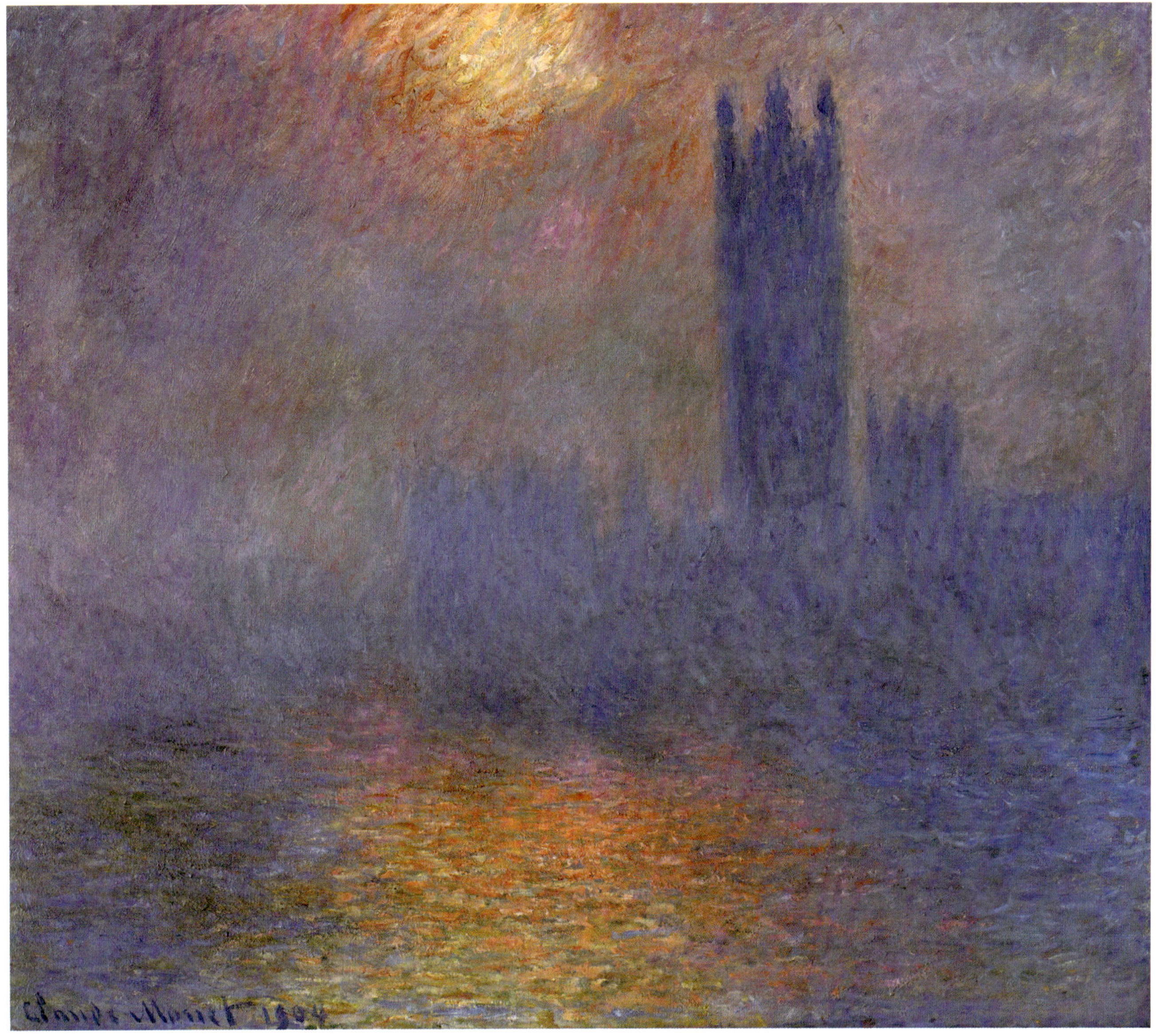

Claude Monet (1840–1926)
The Houses of Parliament (Effect of Fog)
Londres, le Parlement. Trouée de soleil dans le brouillard
London, das Parlament, Sonnenloch im Nebel
Londres, el Parlamento. Boquete de sol en la niebla
Londra, Il Parlamento. Effetto di sole nella nebbia
Londen, parlementsgebouwen. De zon dringt door de mist
1904, Oil on canvas/Huile sur toile, 81,5 × 92,5 cm

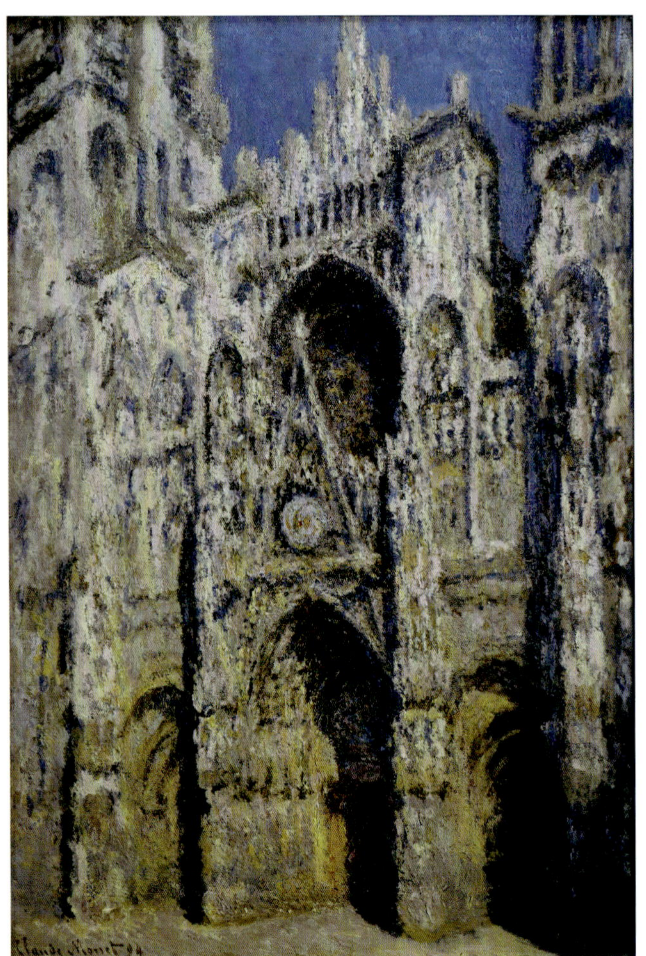 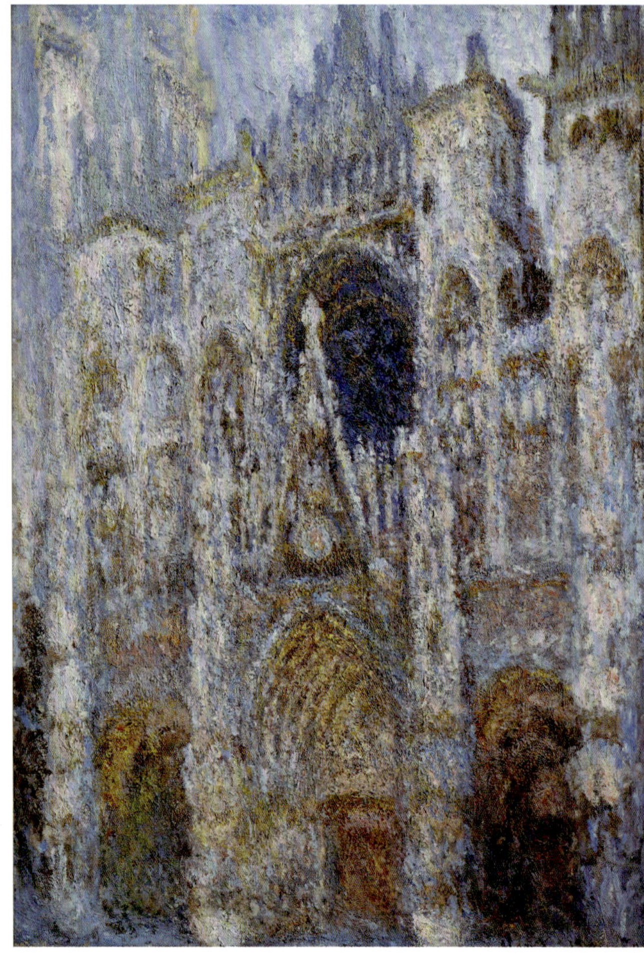

Claude Monet (1840–1926)
Rouen Cathedral in Full Sunlight
La Cathédrale de Rouen. Le portail et la tour Saint-Romain, plein soleil
Portal der Kathedrale von Rouen mit Turm Saint-Romain in voller Sonne
La catedral de Rouen. Portada y la torre Saint Romain, pleno sol
La cattedrale di Rouen. Il portale e la torre Saint-Romain, pieno sole
De kathedraal van Rouen. Het portaal en de Saint-Romain toren, volle zon
1893, Oil on canvas/Huile sur toile, 107 × 73,5 cm

Claude Monet (1840–1926)
The Portal of Rouen Cathedral in Morning Light, Harmony in Blue
La Cathédrale de Rouen. Le portail, soleil matinal. Harmonie bleue
Die Kathedrale von Rouen im Morgenlicht; Harmonie in Blau
La catedral de Rouen. Portada, sol matinal. Armonía azul
La cattedrale di Rouen. Il portale, sole del mattino. Armonia in blu
De kathedraal van Rouen, Het portaal bij morgenzon. Harmonie in blauw
1893, Oil on canvas/Huile sur toile, 92,2 × 63 cm

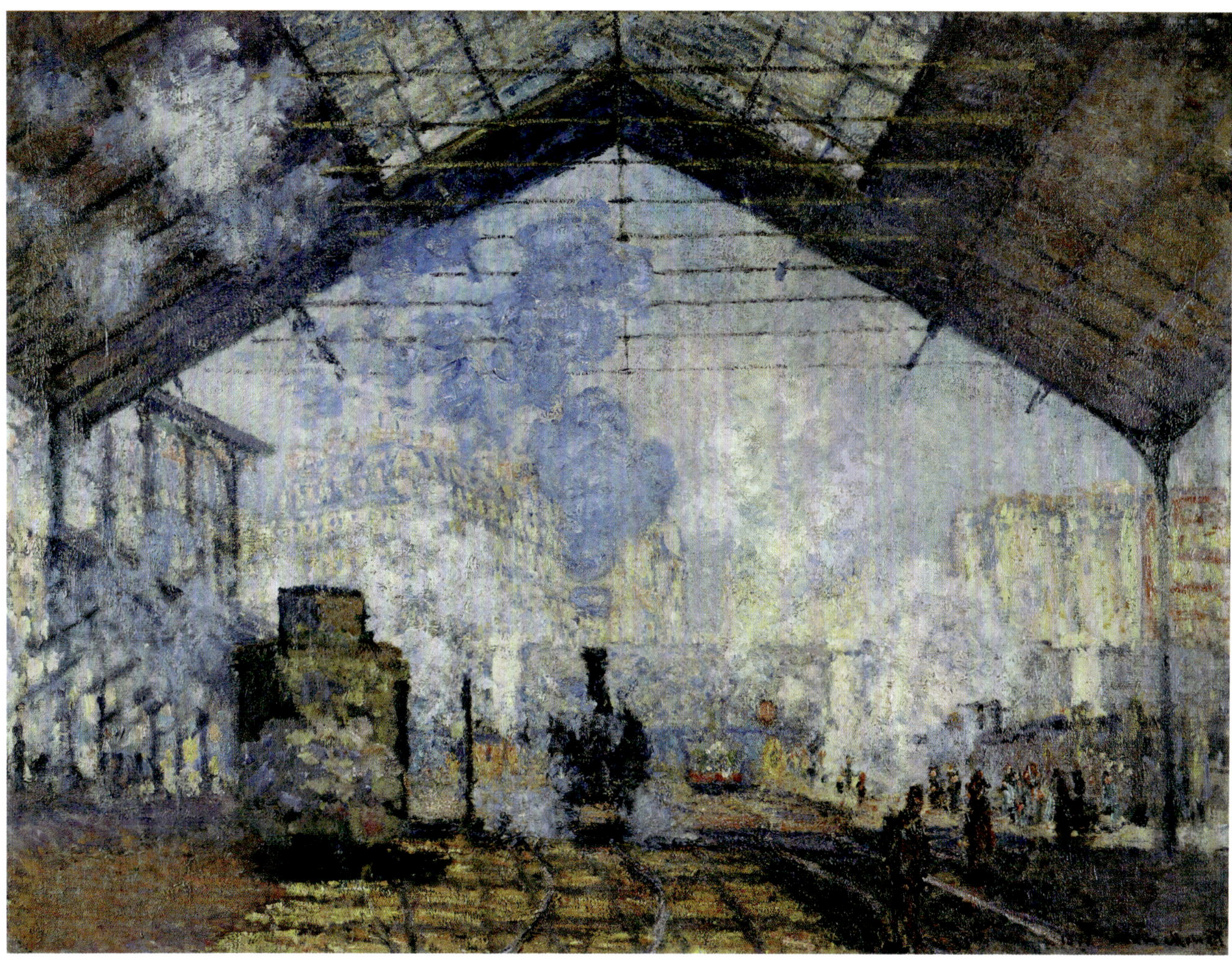

Claude Monet (1840–1926)
The Gare Saint-Lazare
La Gare Saint-Lazare
Der Bahnhof Saint-Lazare
La estación Saint-Lazare
La stazione Saint-Lazare
Het station Saint-Lazare
1877, Oil on canvas/Huile sur toile, 75 × 105 cm

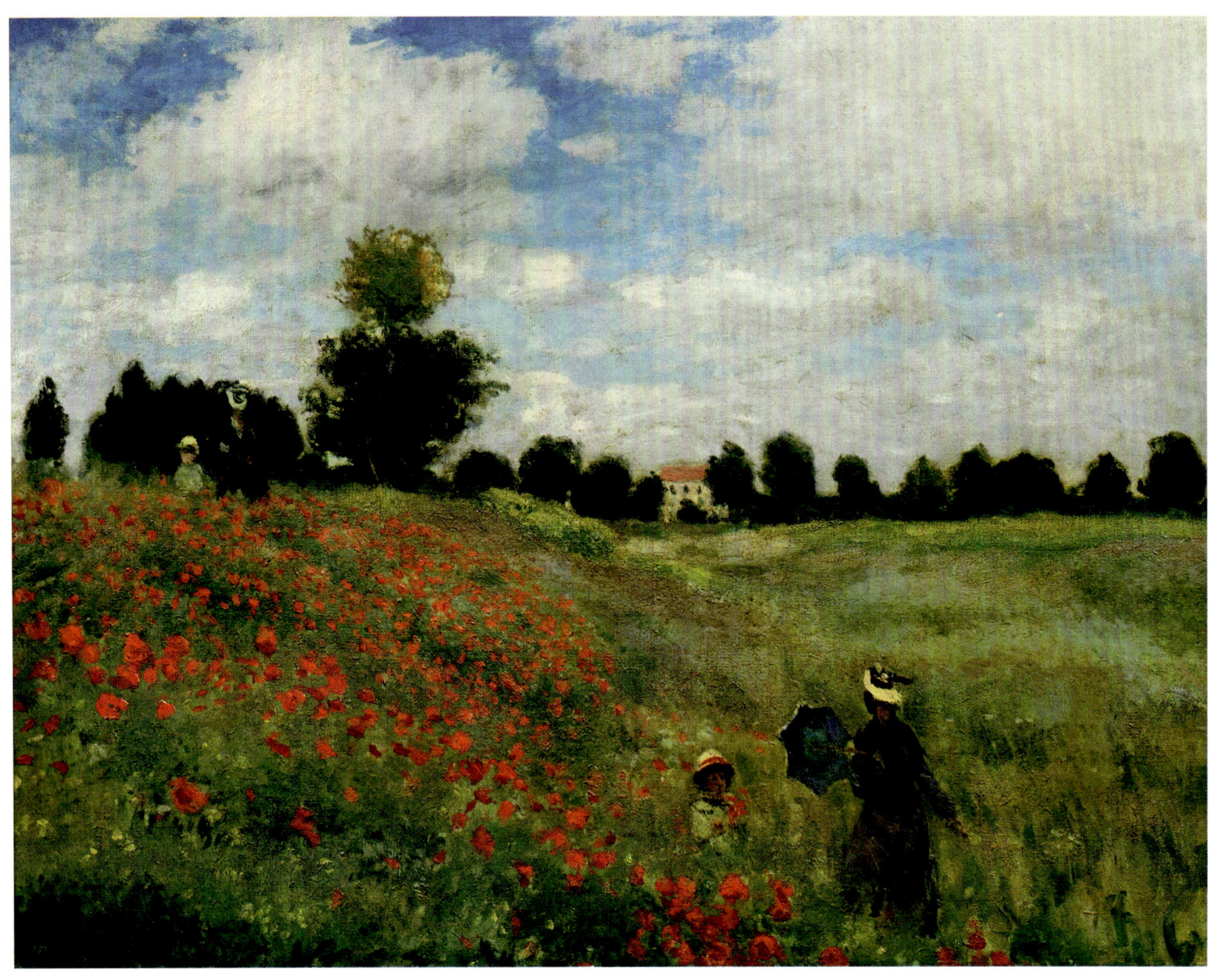

Claude Monet (1840–1926)

Poppies

Coquelicots

Mohnfeld bei Argenteuil

Amapolas

I Papaveri

Klaprozen

1873, Oil on canvas/Huile sur toile, 50 × 65,3 cm

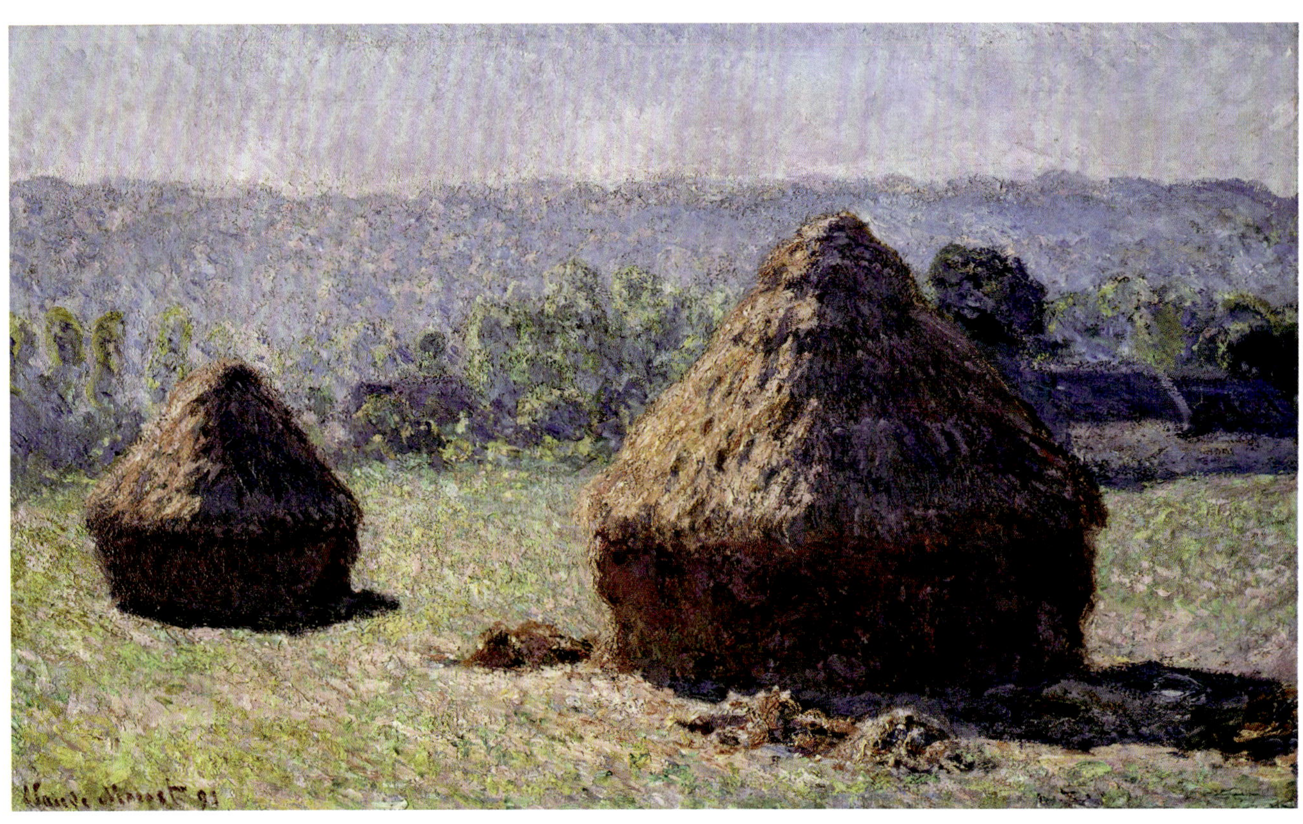

Claude Monet (1840–1926)

Haystacks. End of the Summer

Meules, fin de l'été

Heuhaufen, Spätsommer

Almiares, fin del verano

Covoni, fine dell'estate

Hooibergen, nazomer

1891, Oil on canvas/Huile sur toile, 60,5 × 100,8 cm

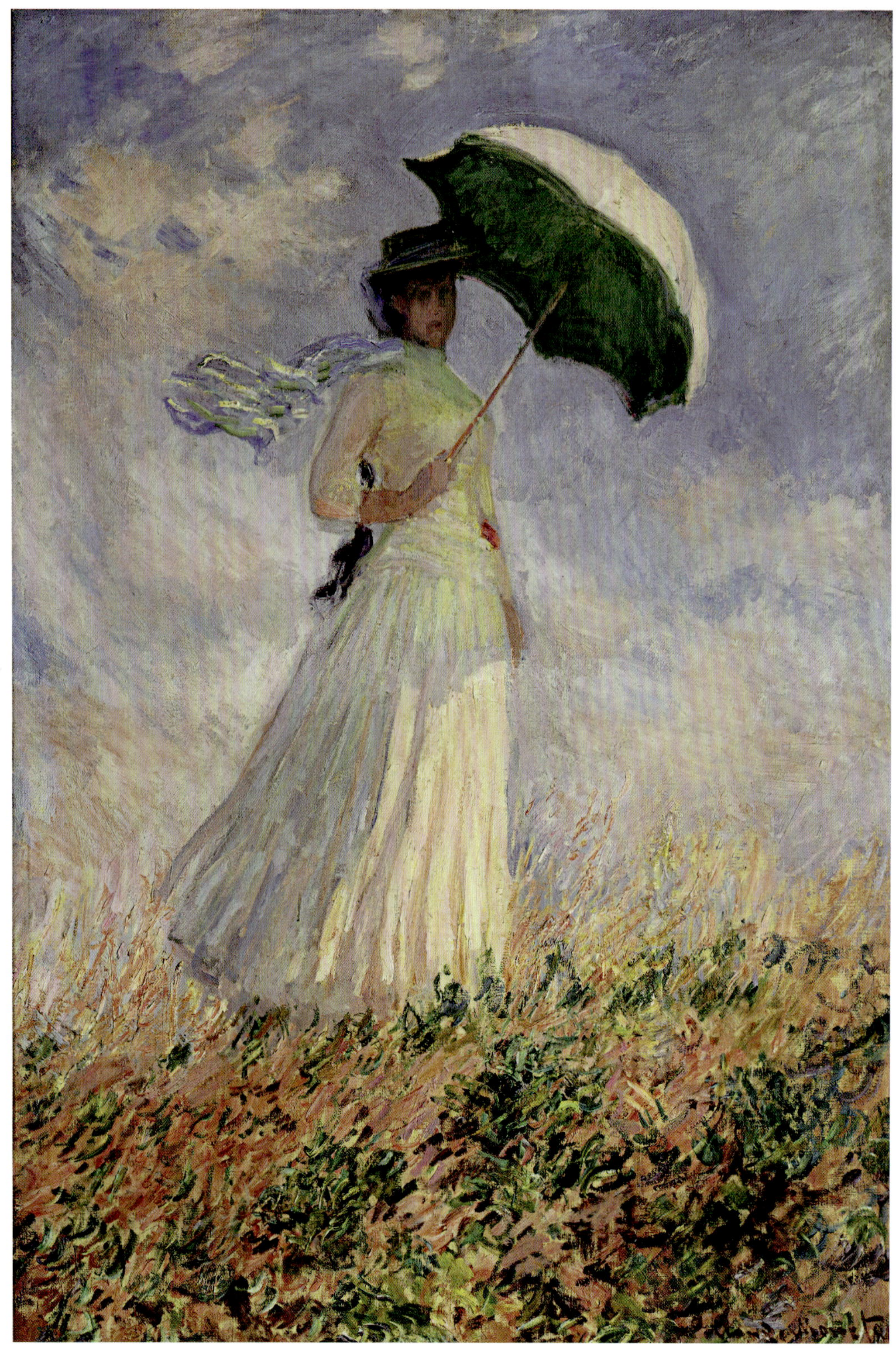

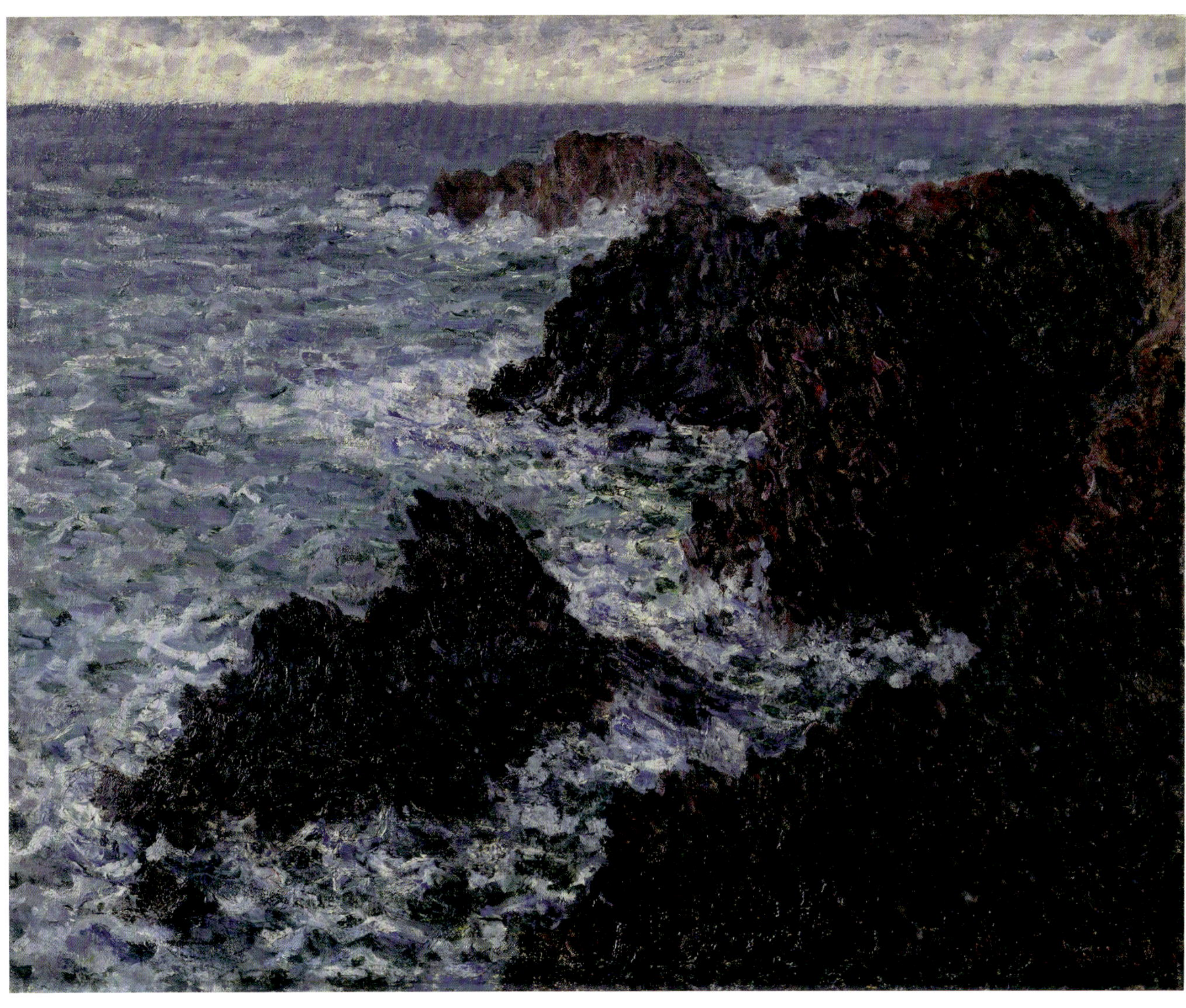

Claude Monet (1840–1926)

The Rocks At Belle-Île, the Wild Coast

Les Rochers de Belle-Île, la Côte sauvage

Die Felsen von Belle-Île; die wilde Küste

Las rocas de Belle-Île, la costa salvaje

Gli scogli di Belle-Ile, la Côte sauvage

De rotskust van Belle-Île, Côte sauvage

1886, Oil on canvas/Huile sur toile, 65,5 × 81,5 cm

Claude Monet (1840–1926)

Woman with a Parasol Turned to the Right

Femme à l'ombrelle tournée vers la droite

Frau mit Sonnenschirm

Mujer con sombrilla girada hacia la derecha

Donna con il parasole girata verso destra

Vrouw met parasol gedraaid naar rechts

1886, Oil on canvas/Huile sur toile, 130,5 × 89,3 cm

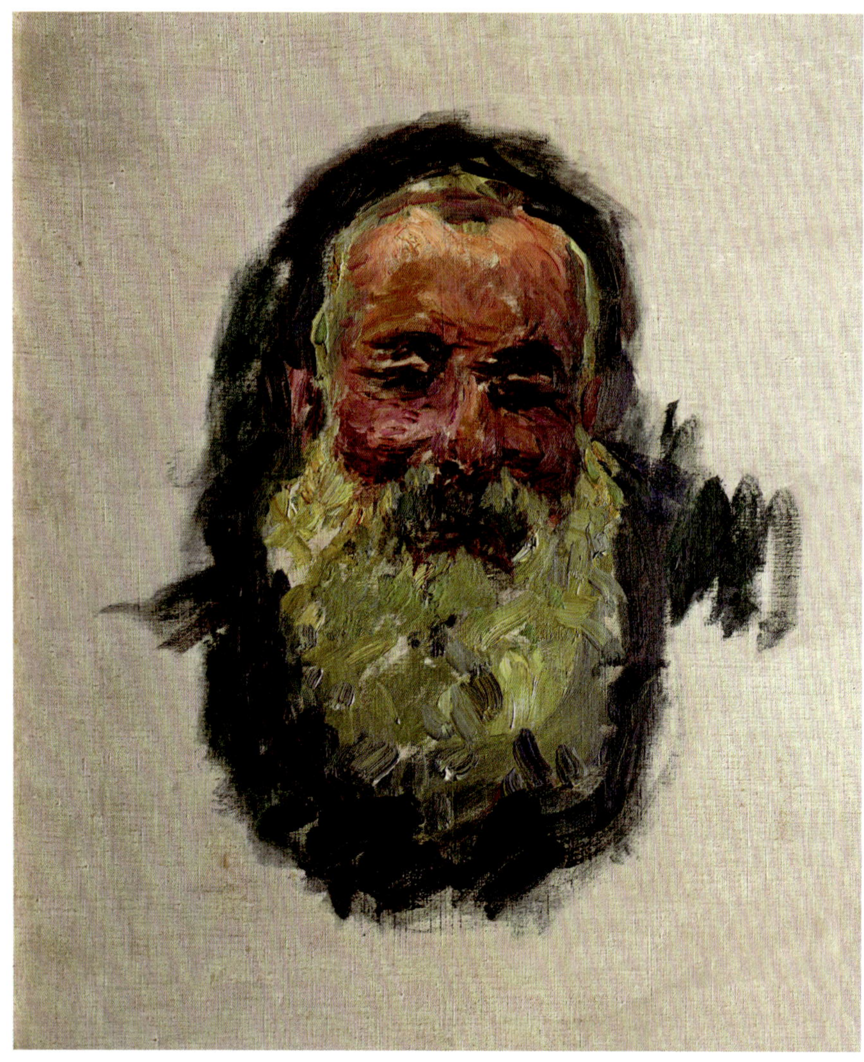

Claude Monet (1840–1926)

Self Portrait	Selbstbildnis	Autoritratto
Portrait de l'artiste	Autorretrato	Portret van de kunstenaar

1917, Oil on canvas/Huile sur toile, 70,5 × 55 cm

Self Portraits of Claude Monet are very rare—the best known being *Self Portrait with a Beret* of 1886—and this one counts among the last few painted by the artist in 1917. The medallion-framed face, traced in small touches that left the edges of the canvas blank, seems to stand out from the sketch, giving an unfinished impression that makes the work so touching.

Les autoportraits de Claude Monet sont très rares – le plus connu étant l'*Autoportrait au béret* de 1886 –, et celui-ci compte parmi les derniers que l'artiste ait peints, en 1917. Le visage en médaillon, tracé par petites touches en laissant les bords de la toile vierge, semble relever de l'esquisse, avec cette impression d'inachevé qui rend l'œuvre si touchante.

Selbstbildnisse von Claude Monet sind selten – das bekannteste ist *Selbstbildnis mit Baskenmütze* von 1886 – und dieses zählt zu den letzten, die der Künstler gemalt hat und zwar im Jahr 1917. Das Gesicht in einer Medaillonform ist mit kurzen Pinselstrichen gemalt und lässt den Rand der Leinwand frei. Es scheint einer Skizze gleichzukommen und hinterlässt einen Eindruck des Unvollendeten, was das Werk so berührend macht.

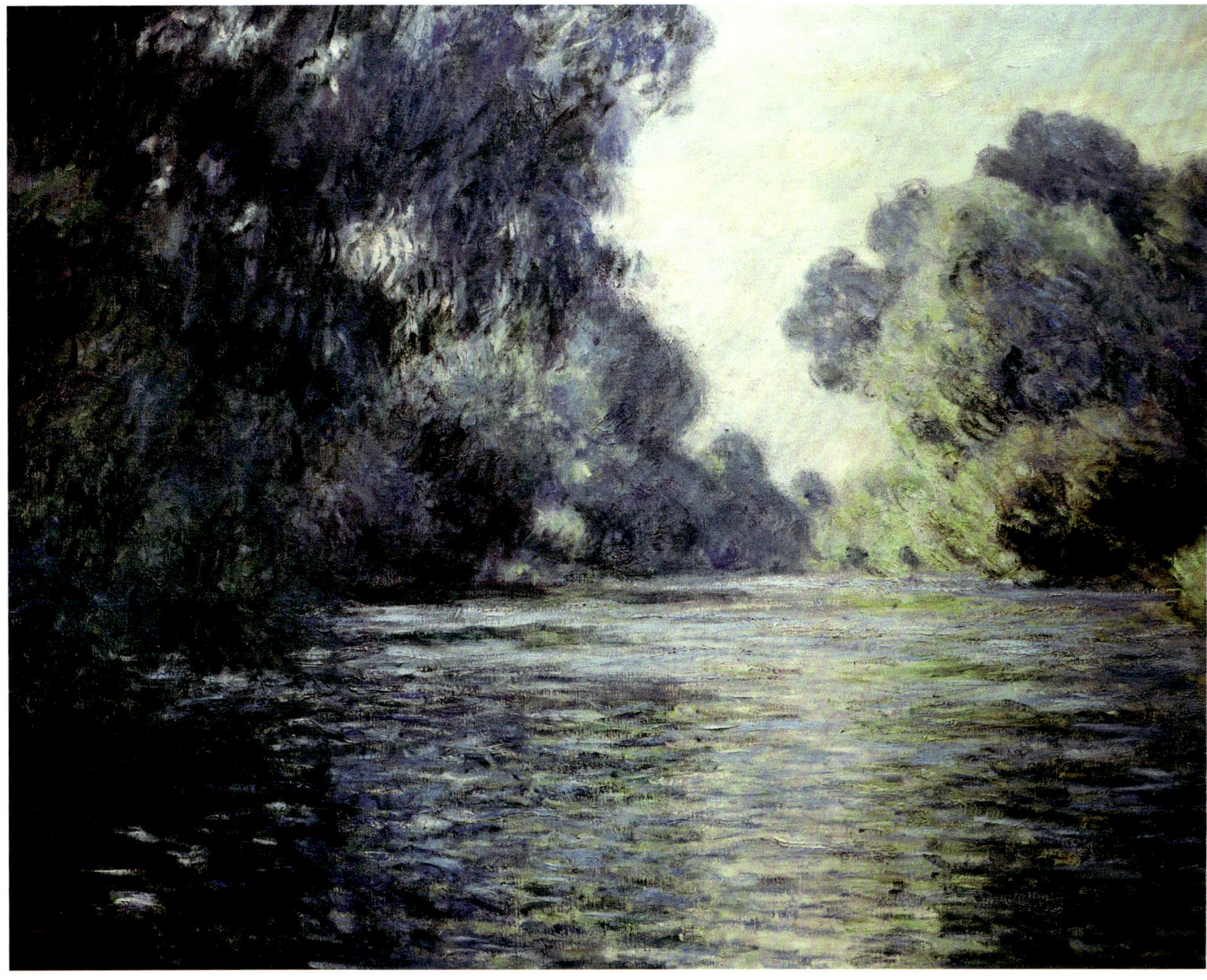

Claude Monet (1840–1926)

Arm of the Seine near Giverny	Arm der Seine bei Giverny	La Senna a Giverny
Bras de Seine près de Giverny	Brazo del Sena cerca de Giverny	Seine-arm bij Giverny

1897, Oil on canvas/Huile sur toile, 73,2 × 93 cm

Los autorretratos de Claude Monet son muy raros – siendo el más famoso el *Autorretrato con la boina* de 1886 –, y éste es uno de los últimos que el artista pintó en 1917. La cara en medallón, trazada por pequeñas pinceladas dejando los bordes del lienzo en blanco, parece ser el boceto sin terminar, pero esta impresión inacabada es la que confiere a la obra ese carácter conmovedor.

Gli autoritratti di Claude Monet sono molto rari (il più famoso è l'*Autoritratto con berretto* del 1886), e quello qui rappresentato è tra gli ultimi dipinti dall'artista, nel 1917. Il volto a medaglione, dipinto con piccole pennellate lasciando i bordi della tela in bianco, sembra essere piuttosto uno schizzo e possiede un'aria di incompiutezza che lo rende estremamente toccante.

Zelfportretten van Claude Monet zijn zeer zeldzaam. De bekendste is zijn *Zelfportret met een baret* uit 1886, een van de laatste die de kunstenaar in 1917 schilderde. Het medaillonportret, dat met kleine penseelstreken is neergezet en de randen van het doek onbedekt laat, lijkt uit de schets te treden. Juist deze indruk van onvoltooidheid maakt het werk zo vertederend.

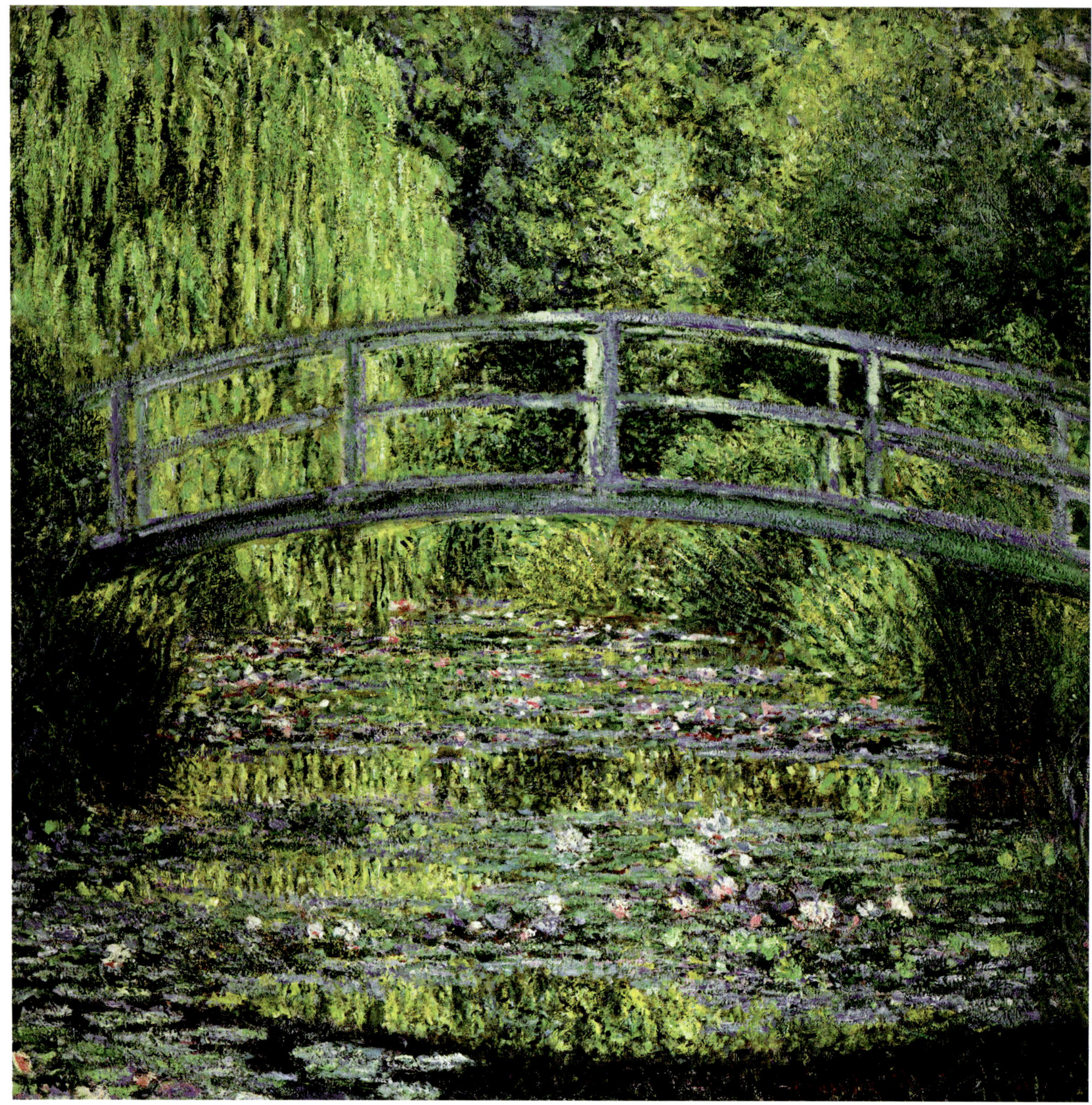

Claude Monet (1840–1926)
The Water Lily Pond: Harmony in Green   Der Seerosenteich, Harmonie in Grün   Lo stagno di ninfee, armonia verde
Le Bassin aux nymphéas, harmonie verte   El estanque de los nenúfares, armonía verde   De vijver met waterlelies, harmonie in groen
1889, Oil on canvas/Huile sur toile, 89,5 × 92,5 cm

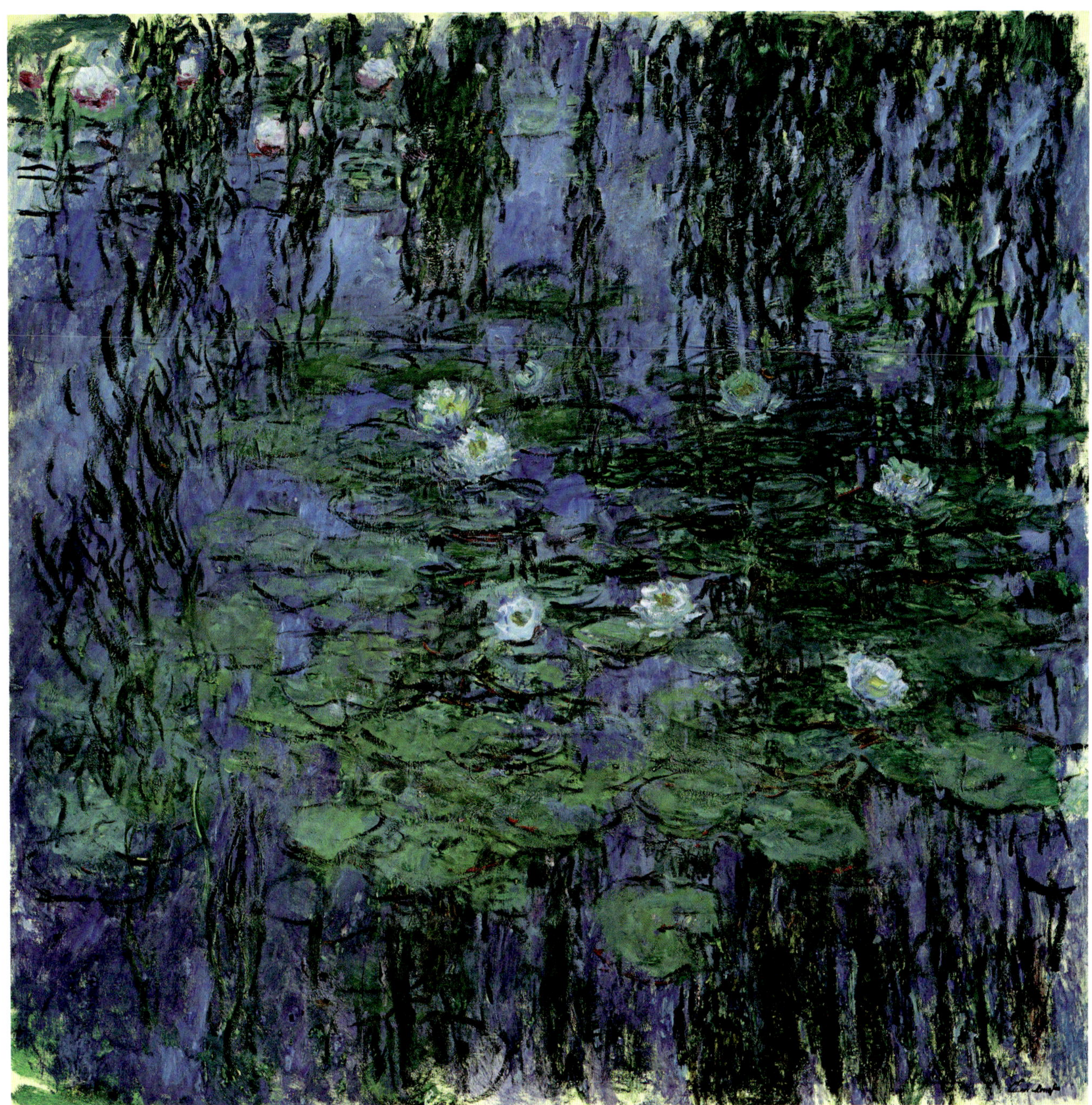

Claude Monet (1840–1926)

Blue Water Lilies   Blaue Seerosen   Ninfee blu

Nymphéas bleus   Nenúfares azules   Blauwe waterlelies

c. 1916–1919, Oil on canvas/Huile sur toile, 204 × 200 cm

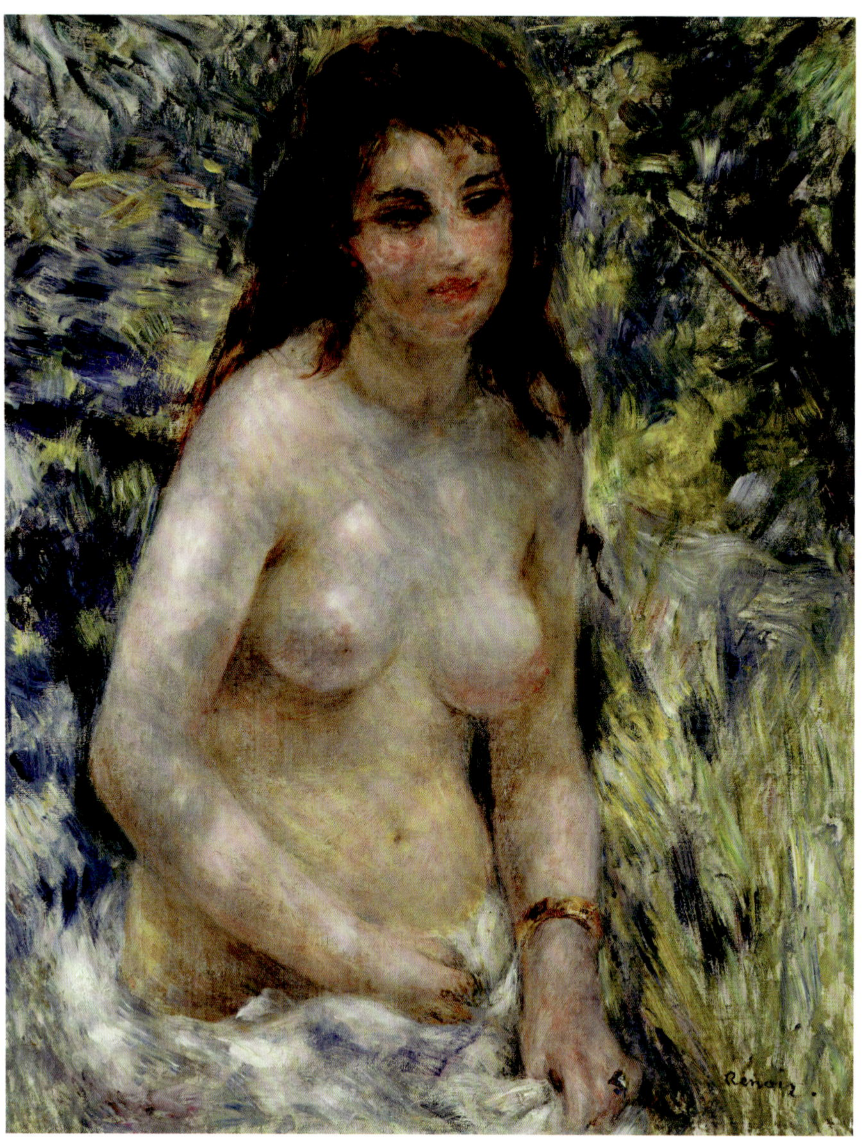

Other than the artist's classic and recurring subjects, this delicate study charms by the perfect blend of the figure in bust form and the décor in shades of blue-green and reminds us of the extent to which Auguste Renoir was a great landscape artist. Here, the artist is interested in the representation of light. The beams of sunlight passing through the unseen foliage and dappling in small touches the young lady's skin, make the composition vibrate.

Au-delà de son sujet, classique et récurrent chez l'artiste, cette délicate étude séduit par l'osmose parfaite entre le personnage en buste et le décor en camaïeu de bleu-vert qui rappelle à quel point Auguste Renoir est un grand paysagiste. L'artiste s'est intéressé ici à la représentation de la lumière. Les éclats de soleil, traversant l'invisible feuillage des arbres, éclairant la peau de la jeune femme par petites touches, font vibrer la composition.

Diese feinfühlige Studie geht über das klassische und wiederkehrende Motiv des Künstlers hinaus und begeistert durch die perfekte Osmose zwischen der Person als Brustbild und dem blau-grünen Camaieu-Dekor, das daran erinnert, welch ein großartiger Landschaftsmaler Auguste Renoir ist. Der Künstler hat sich hier für die Darstellung des Lichts interessiert. Die Sonnenstrahlen durchdringen das unsichtbare Blattwerk der Bäume, erhellen mit kleinen Flecken die Haut der jungen Frau und lassen die Komposition flimmern.

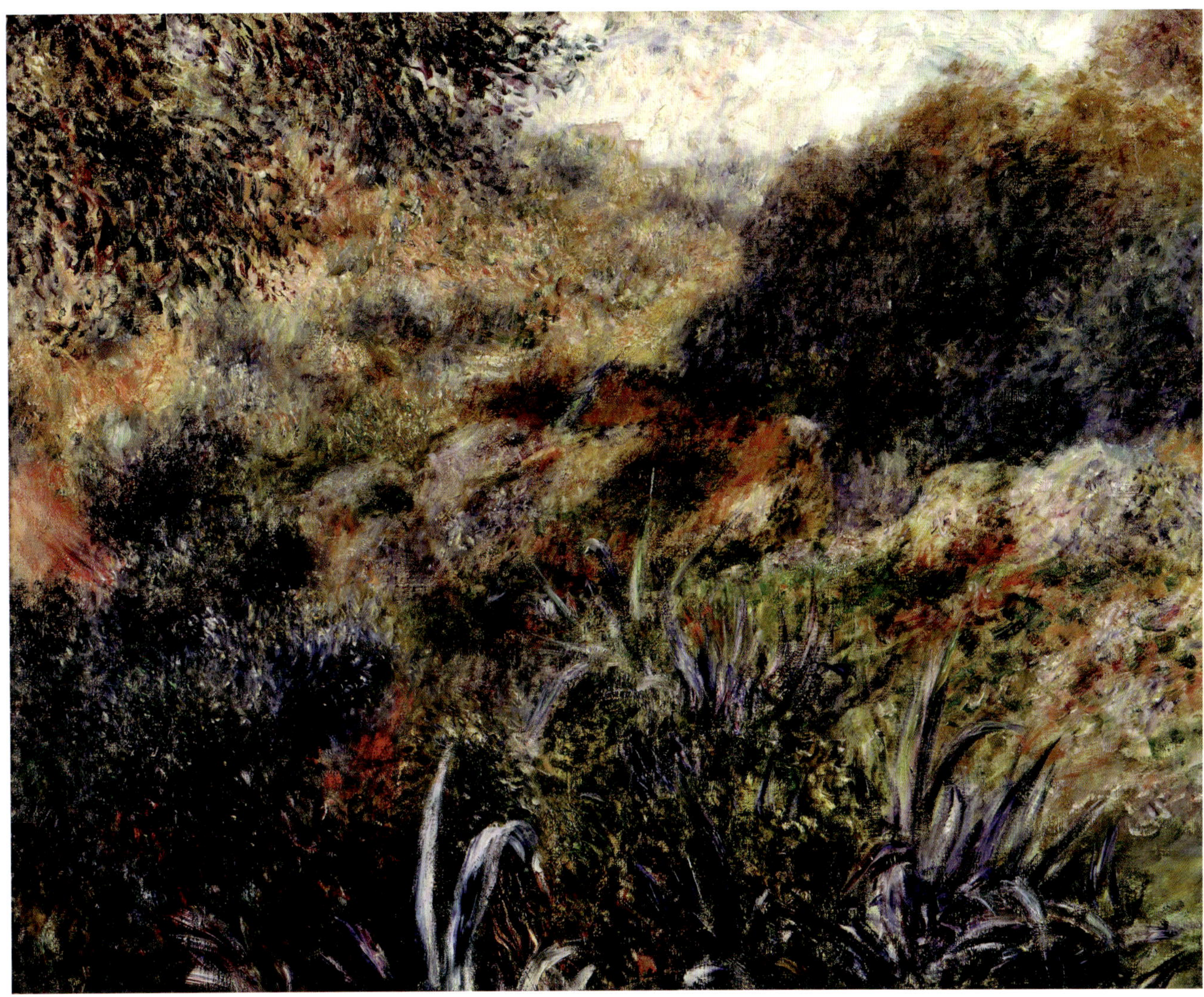

Más allá de su objeto, clásico y recurrente en el artista, este delicado estudio seduce por la perfecta armonía entre el busto del personaje y la decoración en claroscuro de tonos azul-verde que recuerda el gran paisajista que es Auguste Renoir. El artista se interesó aquí por la representación de la luz. Las ráfagas de sol, atravesando el invisible follaje de los árboles, iluminan la piel de la joven mujer con pequeños toques, que hacen vibrar la composición.

Oltre che per il soggetto, classico e ricorrente nell'opera dell'artista, questo studio delicato seduce con la sua perfetta armonia tra il personaggio, raffigurato a busto intero, e la decorazione in tonalità blu e verdi che ricorda le grandi qualità di Auguste Renoir come paesaggista. L'artista è interessato qui alla rappresentazione della luce. I raggi di sole attraversano il fogliame invisibile degli abiti e illuminano la pelle della giovane donna con piccole pennellate, facendo vibrare la composizione.

Afgezien van het klassieke en zich herhalende onderwerp is de charme van deze fijnzinnige studie de perfecte osmose tussen het personage in de buste en het decor in de blauwgroene camee die eraan herinnert hoezeer Auguste Renoir een groot landschapsschilder is. Hier gaat de interesse van de kunstenaar uit naar de weergave van het licht. Door de zonnestralen die door het onzichtbare loof van de bomen breken en met kleine toetsen de huid van de jonge vrouw doen oplichten krijgt de compositie iets zinderends.

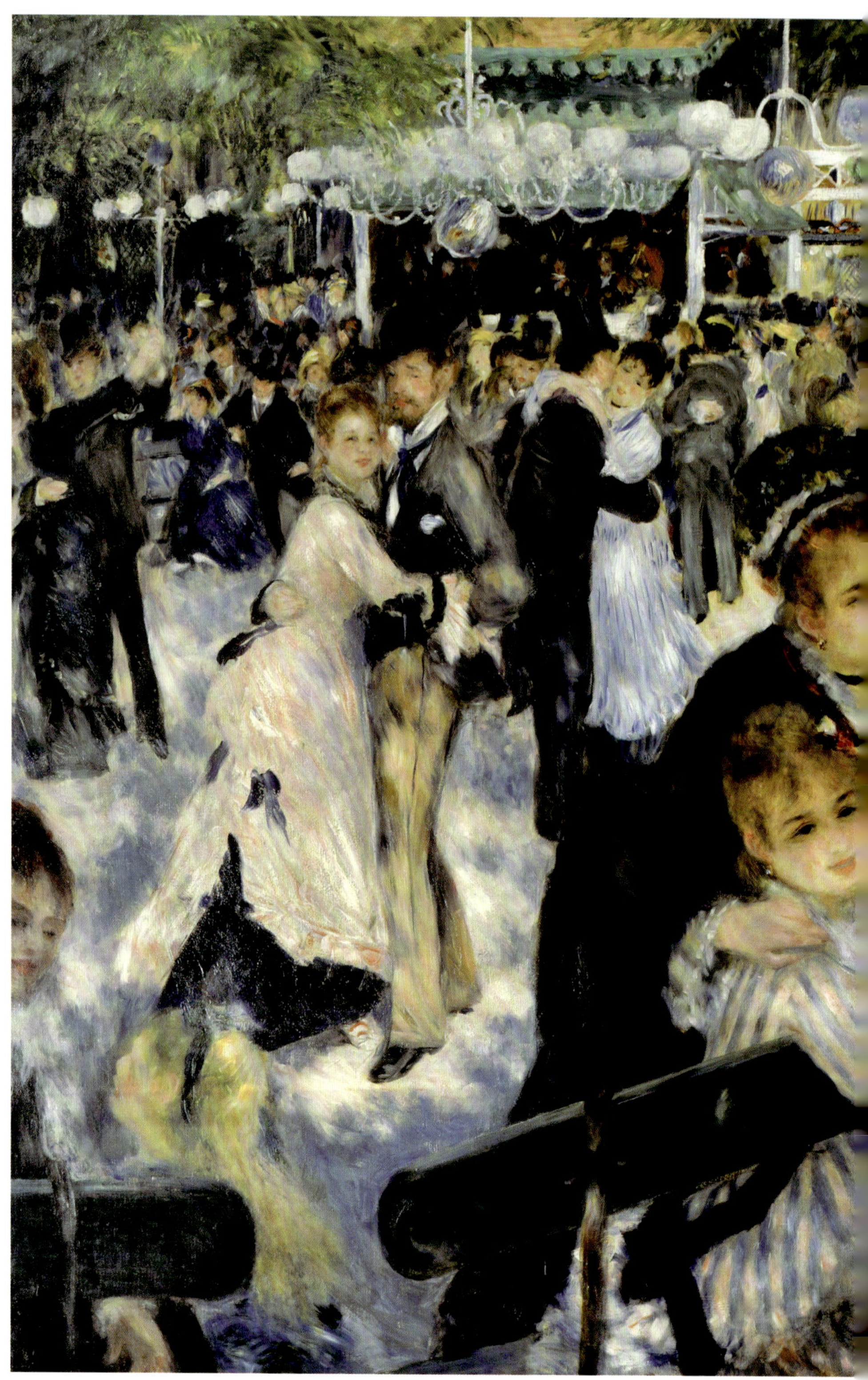

Auguste Renoir (1841–1919)
Dance at Le Moulin de la Galette
Bal du moulin de la Galette
Tanz im Moulin de la Galette
Baile en el Moulin de la Galette
Ballo del moulin de la Galette
Bal bij Le Moulin de la Galette
1876, Oil on canvas/Huile sur toile, 131,5 × 176,5 cm

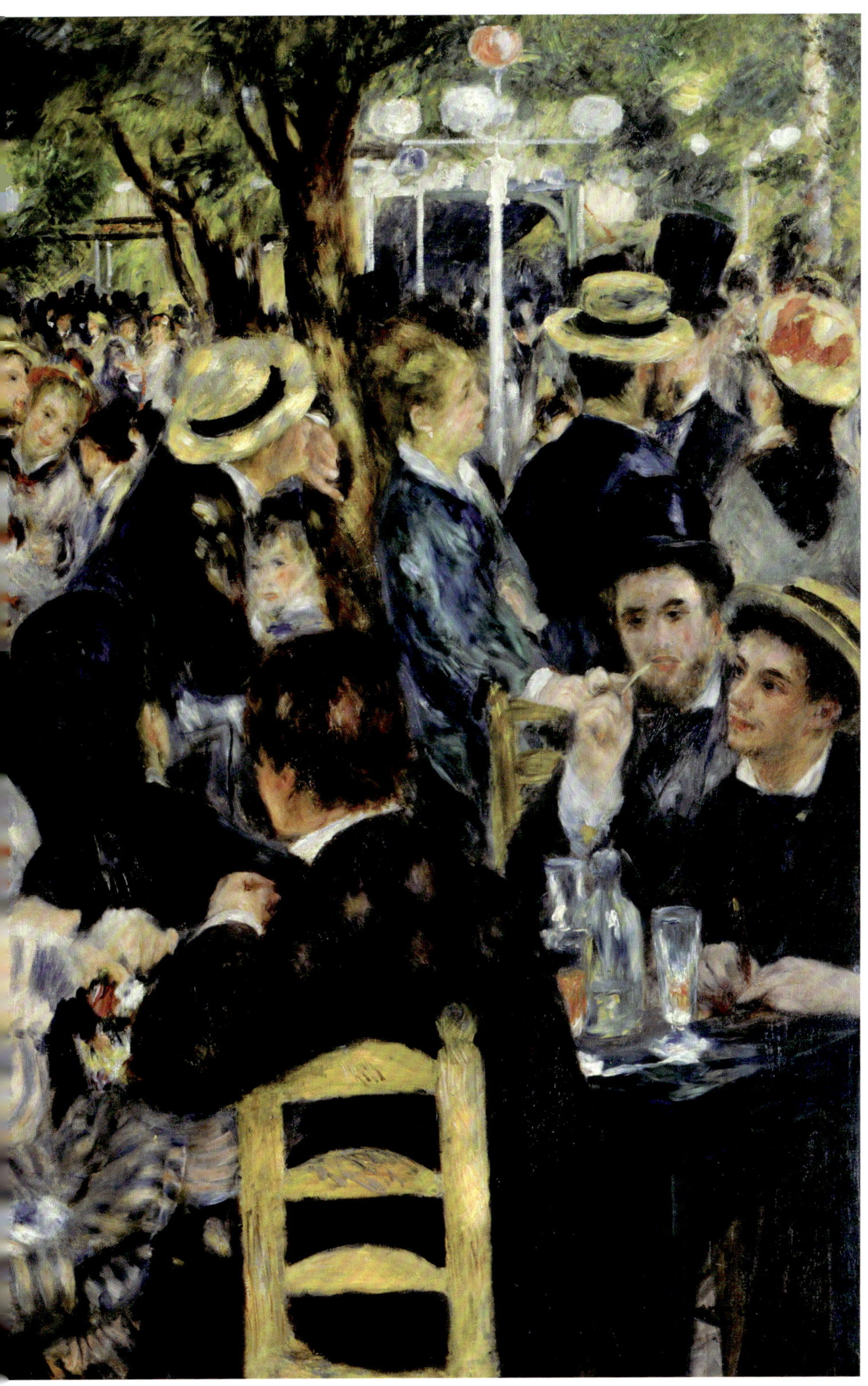

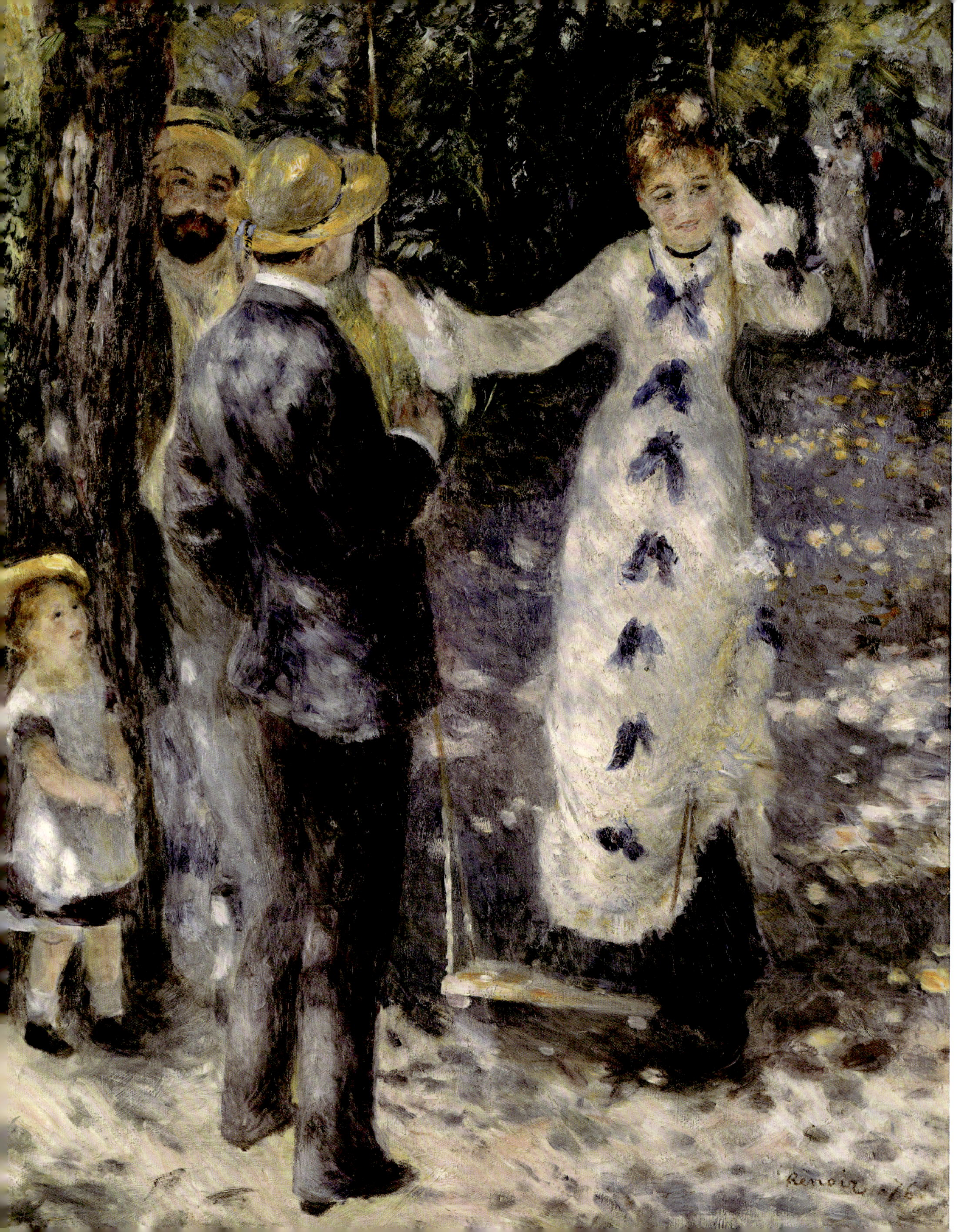
Renoir 1876

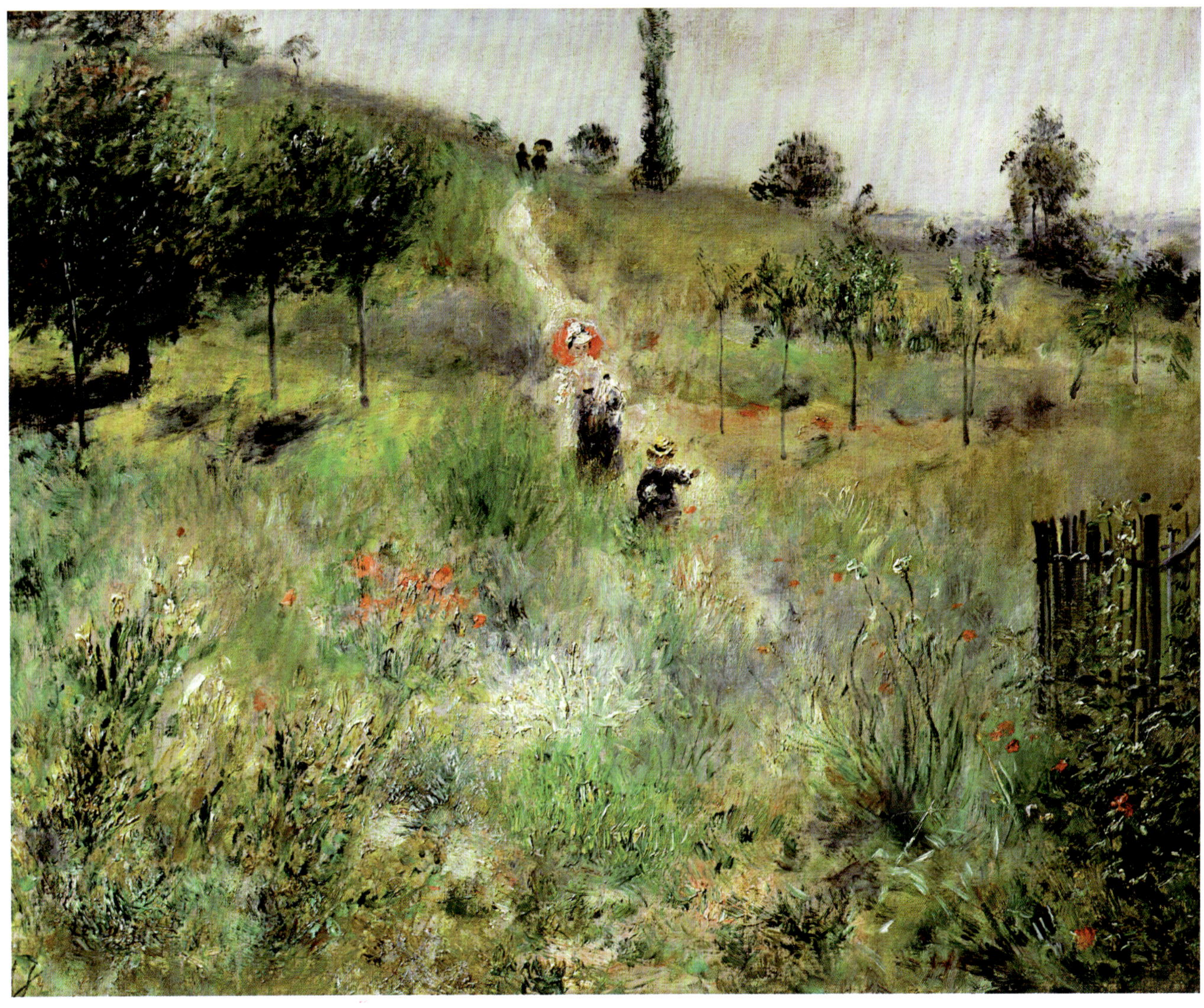

Auguste Renoir (1841–1919)
Path Leading Through Tall Grass
Chemin montant dans les hautes herbes
Ansteigender Weg durch hohes Gras
Sendero entre las hierbas
Il sentiero nell'erba alta
Weggetje omhoog door het hoge gras
c. 1875, Oil on canvas/Huile sur toile, 60 × 74 cm

Auguste Renoir (1841–1919)
The Swing
La Balançoire
Die Schaukel
El columpio
L'altalena
De schommel
1876, Oil on canvas/Huile sur toile, 92 × 111 cm

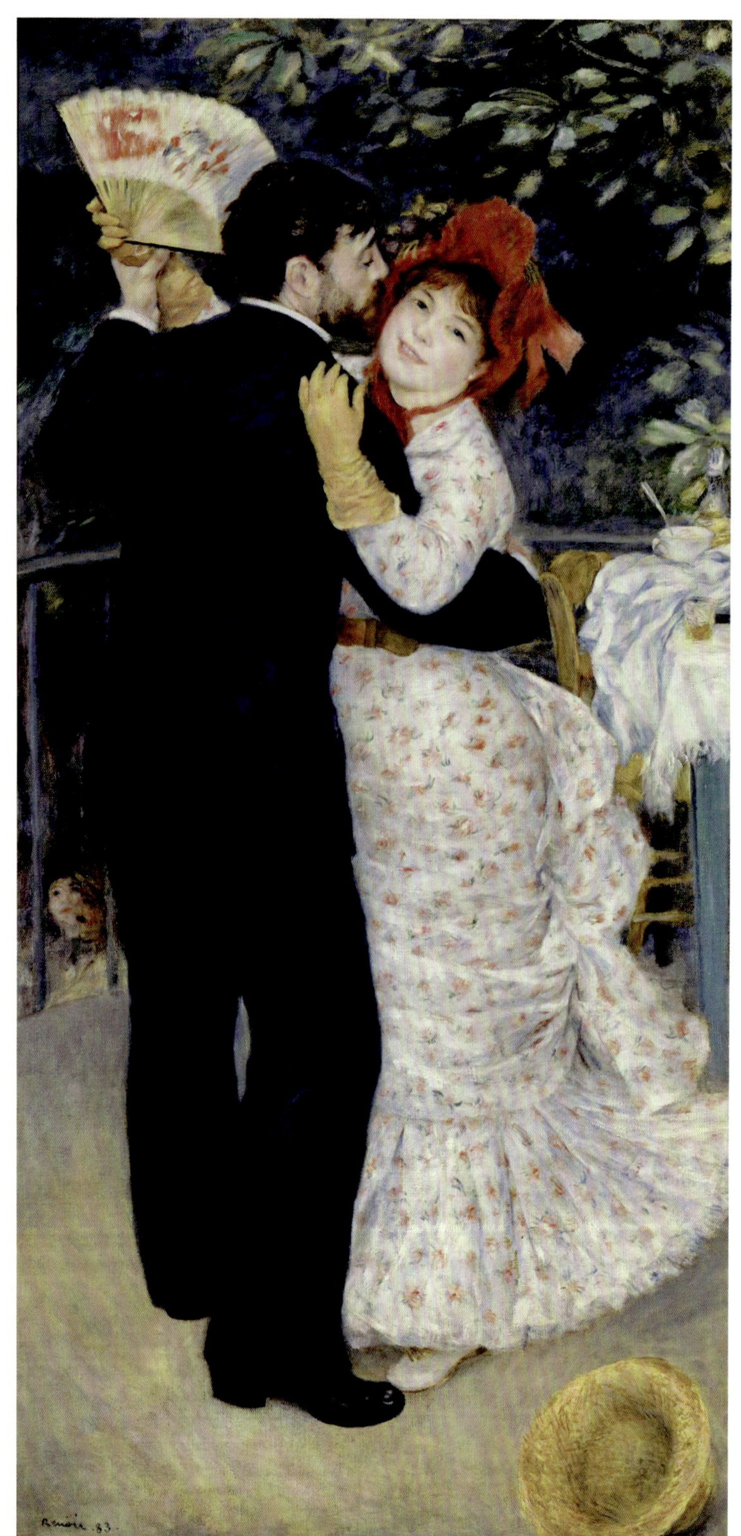

Auguste Renoir (1841–1919)

Dance in the Countryside
Danse à la campagne
Tanz auf dem Lande
Baile en el campo
Ballo in campagna
Dans op het platteland

1883, Oil on canvas/Huile sur toile, 180,3 × 90 cm

Auguste Renoir (1841–1919)

Dance in the City
Danse à la ville
Tanz in der Stadt
Baile en la ciudad
Ballo in città
Dans in de stad

1883, Oil on canvas/Huile sur toile, 179,7 × 89,1 cm

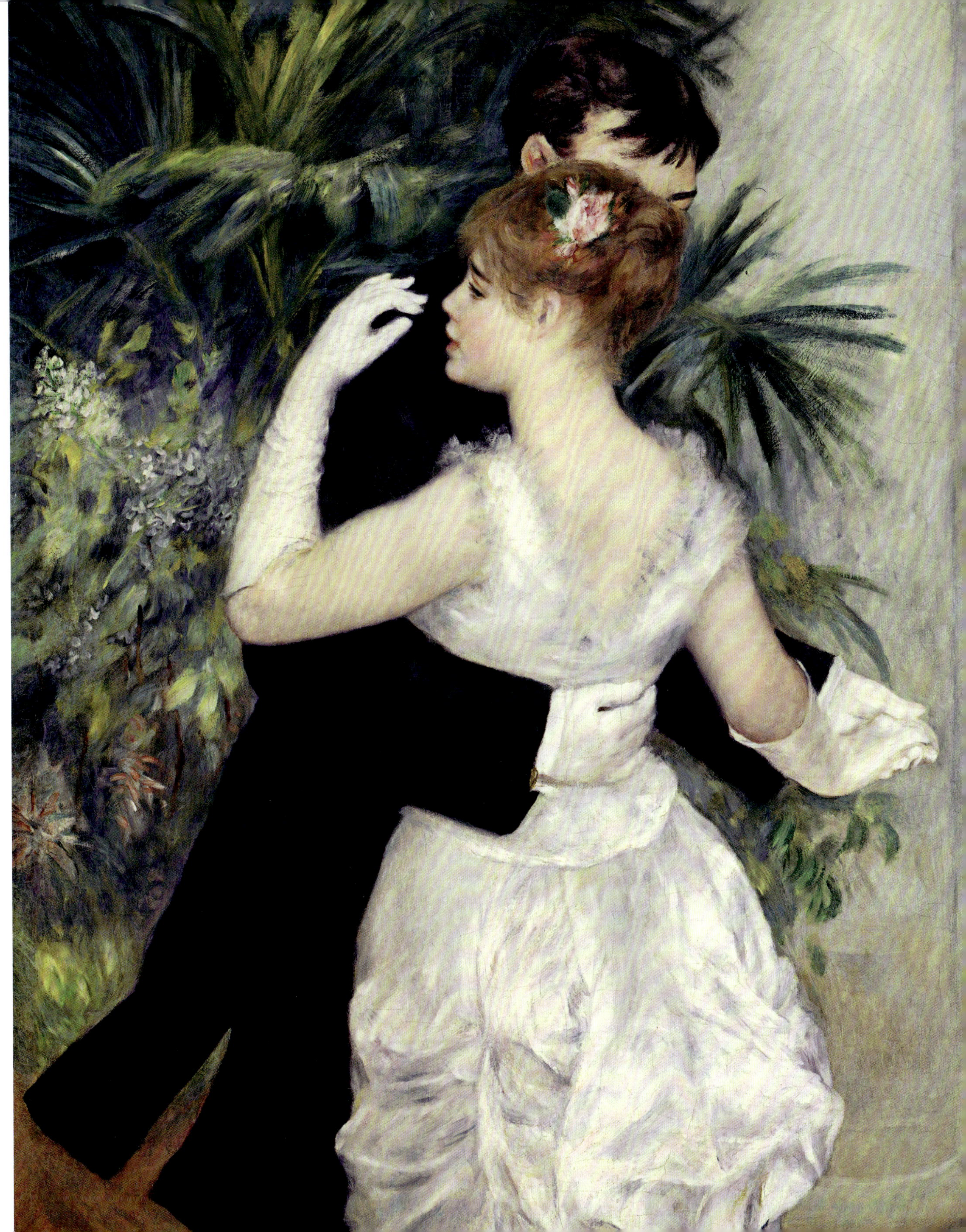

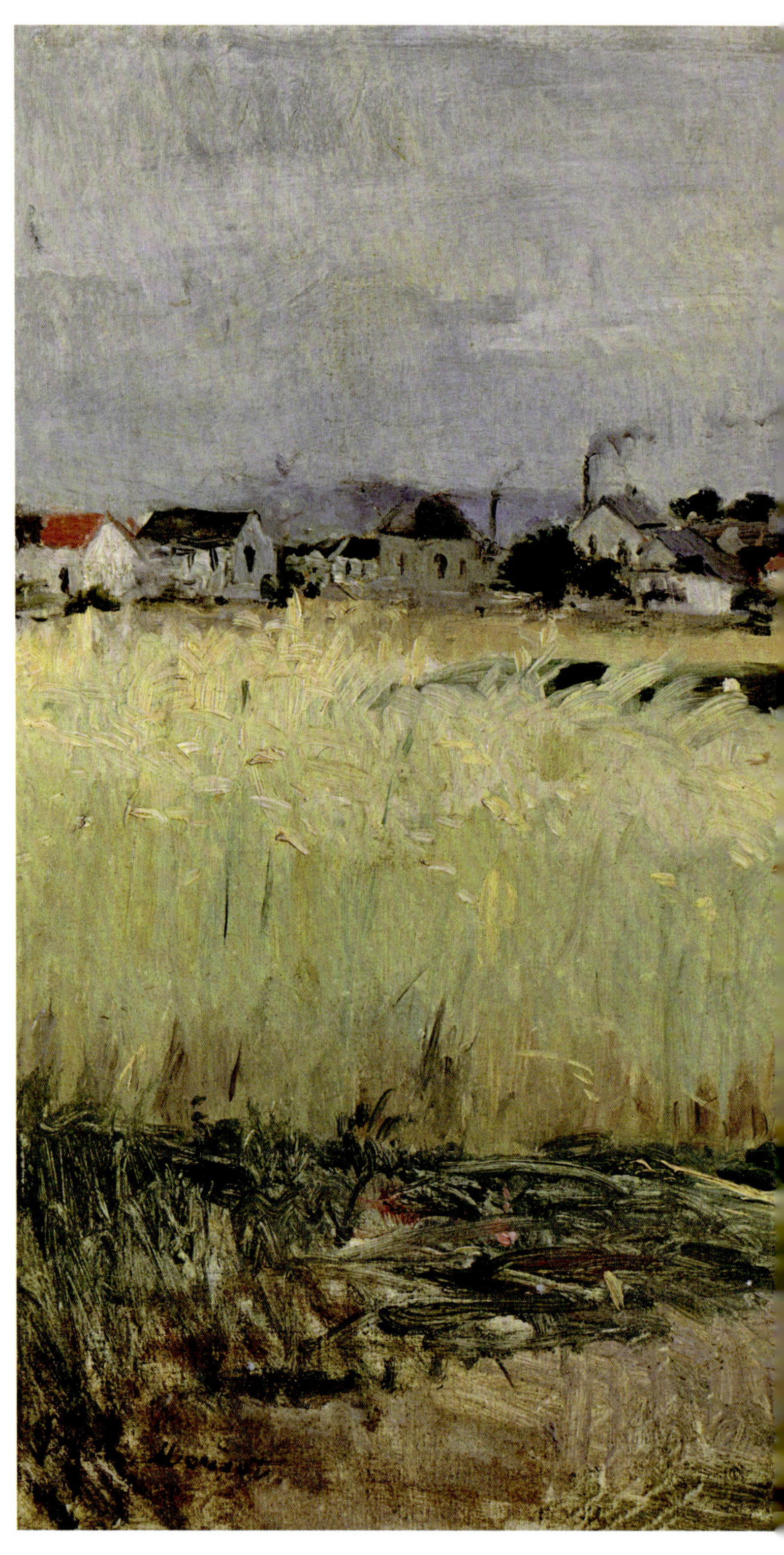

Berthe Morisot (1841–1895)
In the Wheatfield
Dans les blés
In den Kornfeldern
En el campo de trigo
Nel campo di grano
In het korenveld
1875, Oil on canvas/Huile sur toile, 46,5 × 69 cm

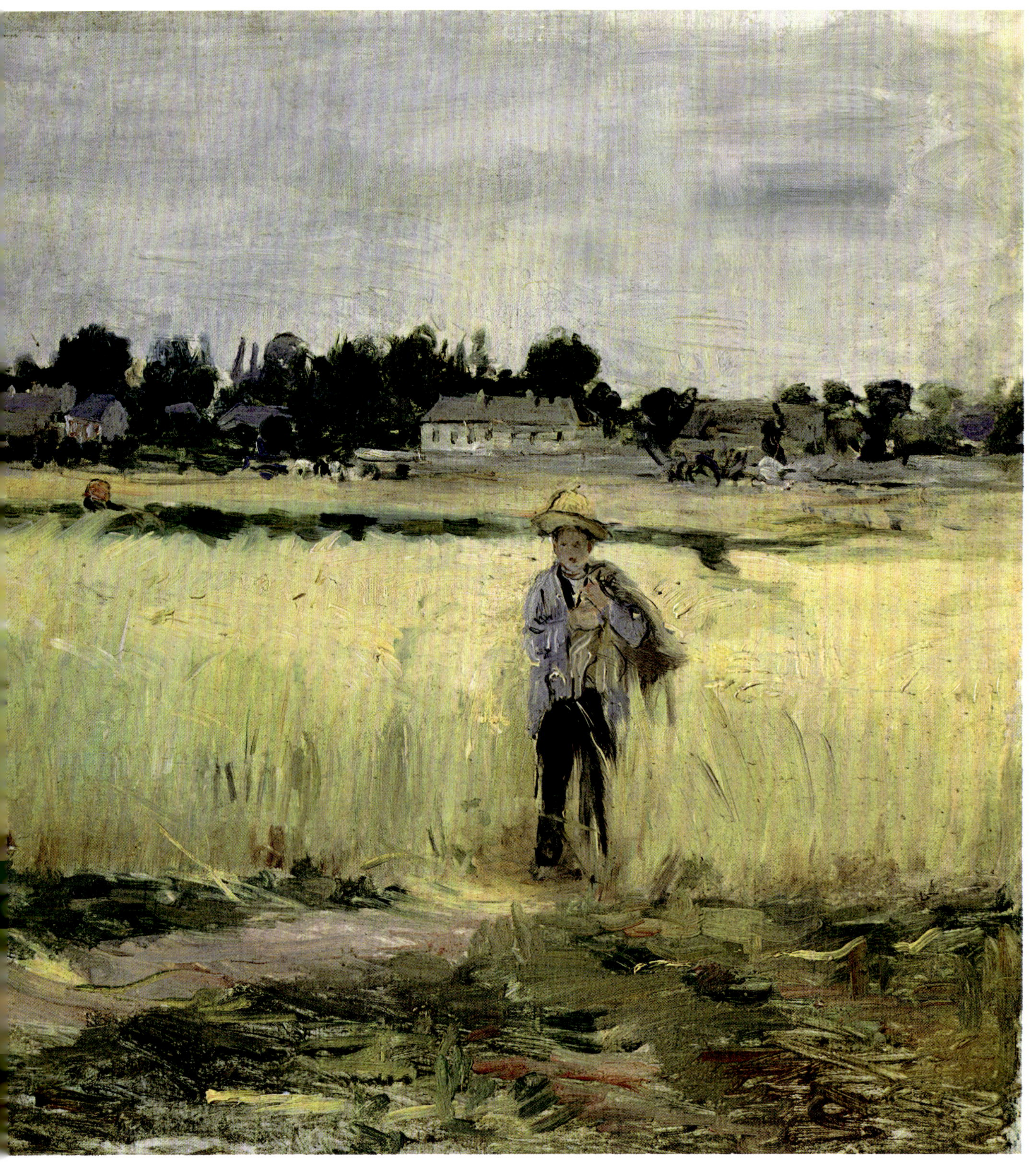

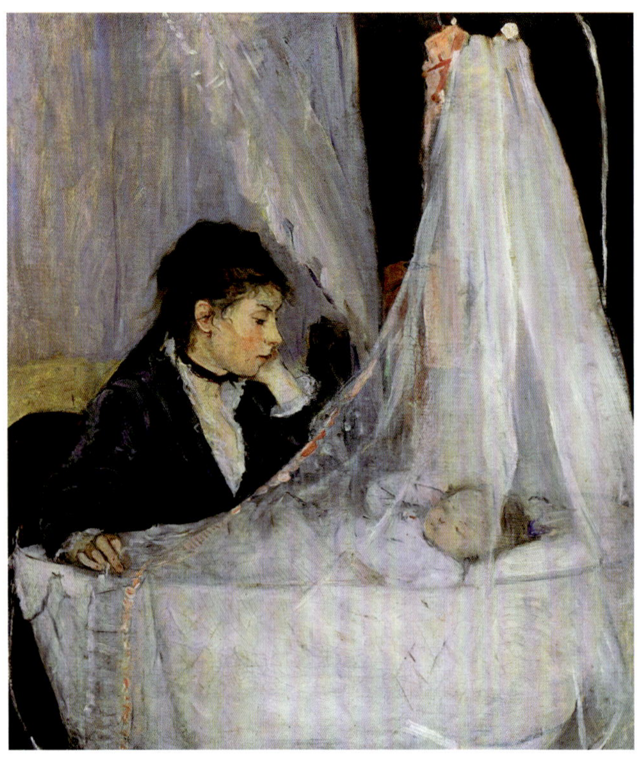 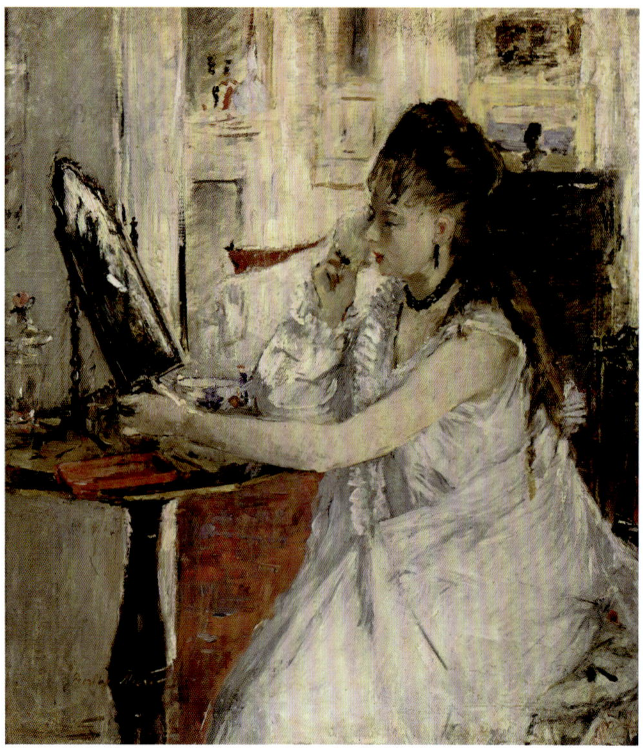

The Cradle   Die Wiege   La culla
Le Berceau   La cuna   De wieg

1872, Oil on canvas/Huile sur toile, 56 × 46,5 cm

Berthe Morisot, who was the pupil of Édouard Manet, excels in representing intimate moments. *Young Woman Powdering Her Face* seduces through the care imparted to the décor, painted with a lively touch in a thousand shades of silvery white. *The Cradle* is among one of the artist's most famous paintings. It shows his sister Edma watching over her sleeping little girl who appears through the subtle transparency of the curtain.

Berthe Morisot, qui fut l'élève d'Édouard Manet, excelle à représenter des moments d'intimité. *Jeune femme se poudrant* séduit par le soin porté au décor, peint d'une touche vive, en mille nuances de blancs argentés. *Le Berceau* compte parmi les tableaux les plus célèbres de l'artiste. Il montre sa sœur Edma veillant sur sa petite fille endormie, qui apparaît dans la transparence subtile du voilage.

Berthe Morisot, Schülerin von Édouard Manet, brilliert mit der Darstellung intimer Momente. Die Attraktivität des Werkes *Junge Frau, sich pudernd* liegt in der Sorgfalt des Dekors, das mit flinker Pinselführung in Tausenden von silbrig-weißen Farbtönen gemalt ist. *Die Wiege* zählt zu den berühmtesten Gemälden der Künstlerin. Es zeigt ihre Schwester Edma, die über ihre schlafende kleine Tochter wacht, welche durch die subtile Transparenz des Schleiers zu erkennen ist.

Berthe Morisot, quien fue alumna de Édouard Manet, sobresale en la representación de momentos de intimidad. *Joven mujer maquillándose* seduce por la atención prestada a la decoración, pintado con una pincelada viva, en mil tonalidades de color blanco plateado. *La cuna* es una de las más famosas pinturas de la artista. La autora muestra a su hermana Edma velando por su niña dormida, que aparece a través la sutil transparencia del velo.

Berthe Morisot, che fu allievo di Édouard Manet, eccelse nel rappresentare momenti di intimità. Il quadro *Giovane donna che si incipria* seduce con la sua cura della decorazione, dipinta con pennellate vivaci e migliaia di sfumature di bianco argento. *La culla* è uno dei dipinti più famosi dell'artista, in cui raffigura sua sorella Edma mentre guarda dormire la figlioletta, visibile attraverso la sottile trasparenza del velo.

Berthe Morisot, een leerlinge van Édouard Manet, kan meesterlijk intieme momenten weergeven. *Jonge vrouw die haar gezicht poedert* ontleent zijn charme aan de aandacht die is besteed aan het decor dat met een levendige toets in duizend zilverwitte tinten is opgebracht. *De wieg* is een van de bekendste doeken van de kunstenares. Het toont haar zus Edma die waakt bij haar slapende dochtertje achter een subtiel doorschijnende hemel van voile.

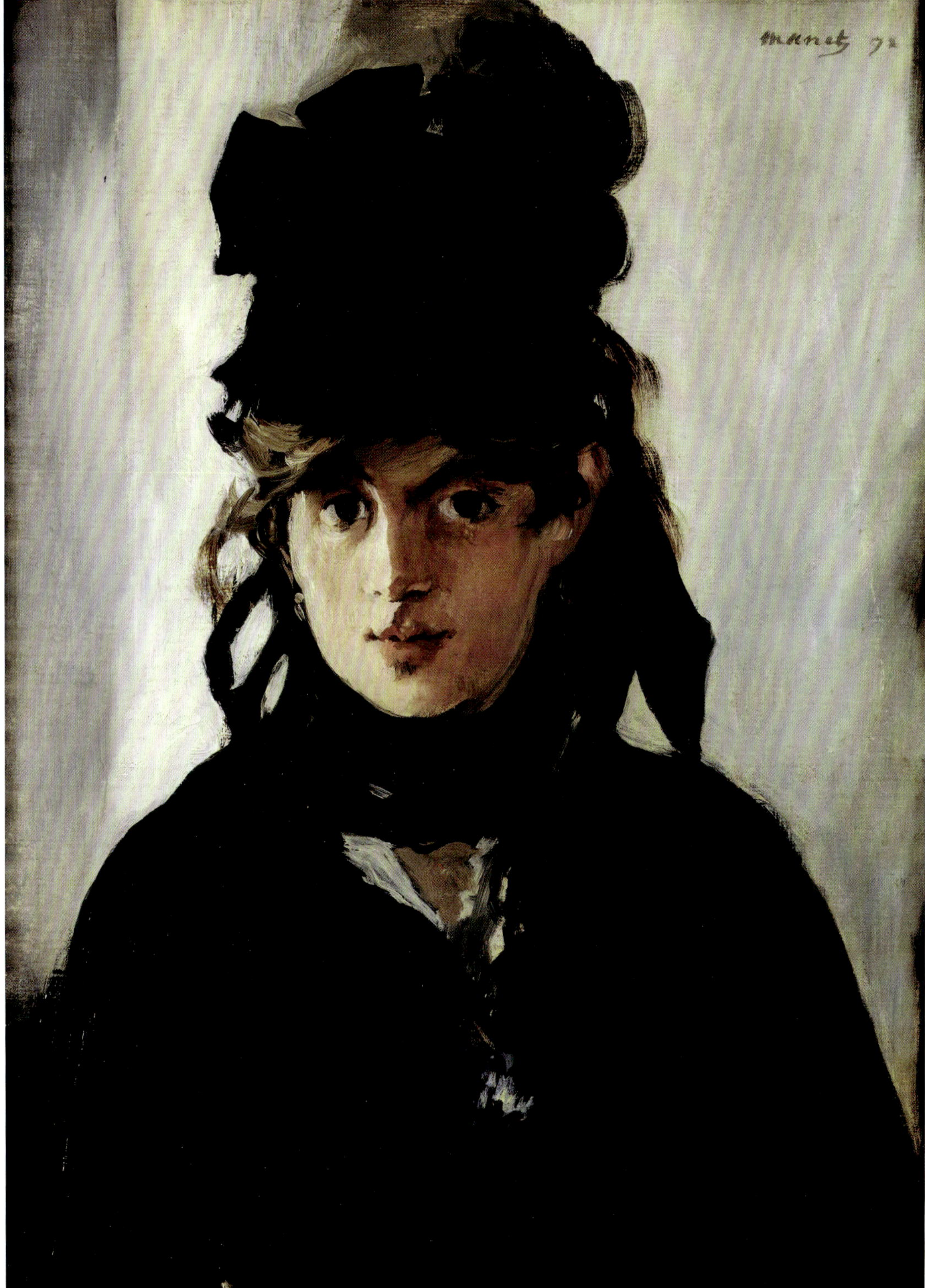

Berthe Morisot
(1841–1895)

Young Woman
Powdering Her Face

Jeune femme se poudrant

Junge Frau, sich pudernd

Joven mujer maquillándose

Giovane donna
che si incipria

Jonge vrouw die haar
gezicht poedert

1877, Oil on canvas/Huile
sur toile, 46 × 39 cm

Édouard Manet
(1832–1883)

Berthe Morisot with a
Bouquet of Violets

Berthe Morisot au
bouquet de violettes

Berthe Morisot mit
Veilchenstrauß

Berthe Morisot con
ramillete de violetas

Berthe Morisot con un
mazzo di violette

Berthe Morisot met
een bosje viooltjes

1872, Oil on canvas/Huile
sur toile, 55,5 × 40,5 cm

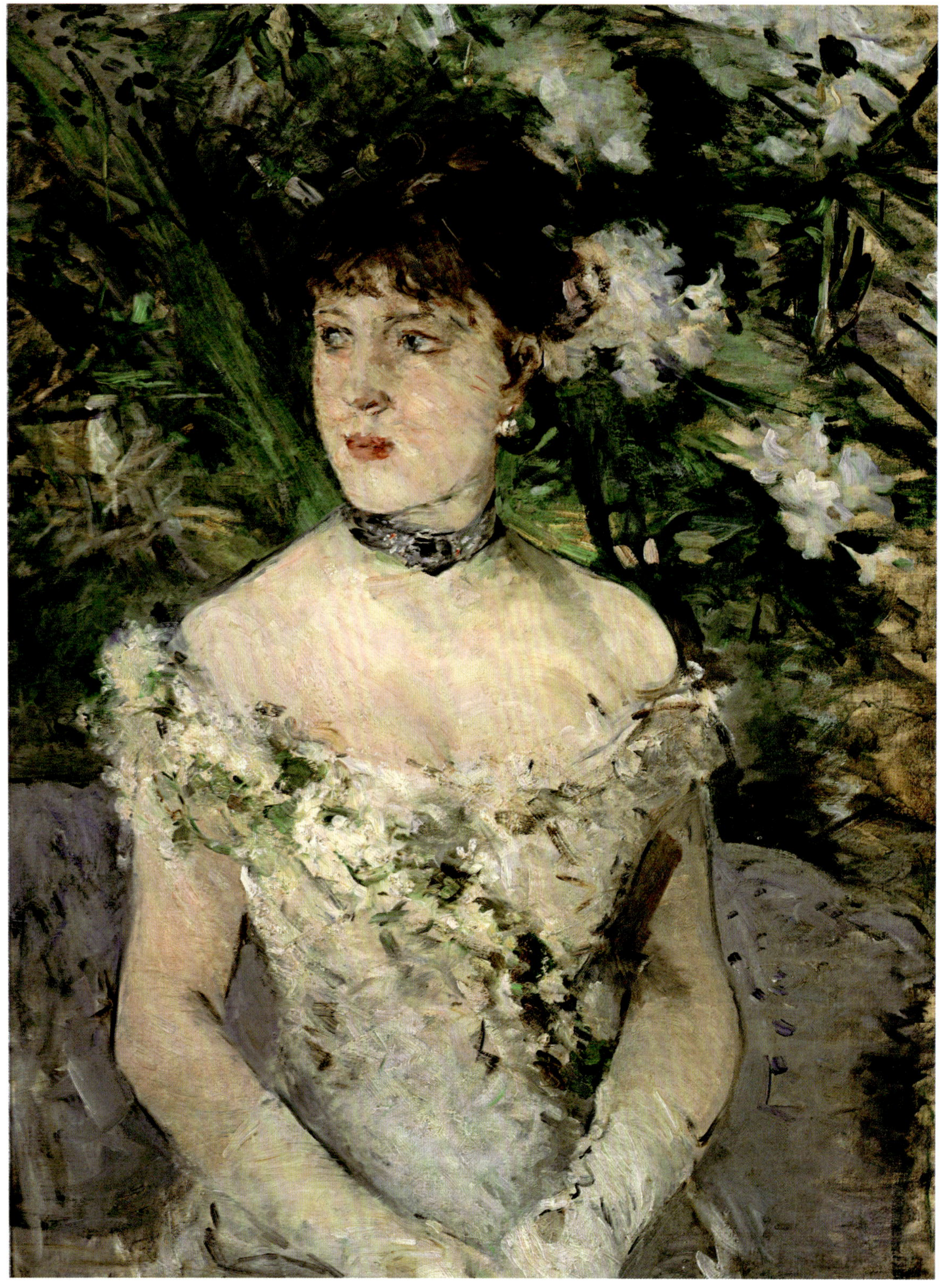

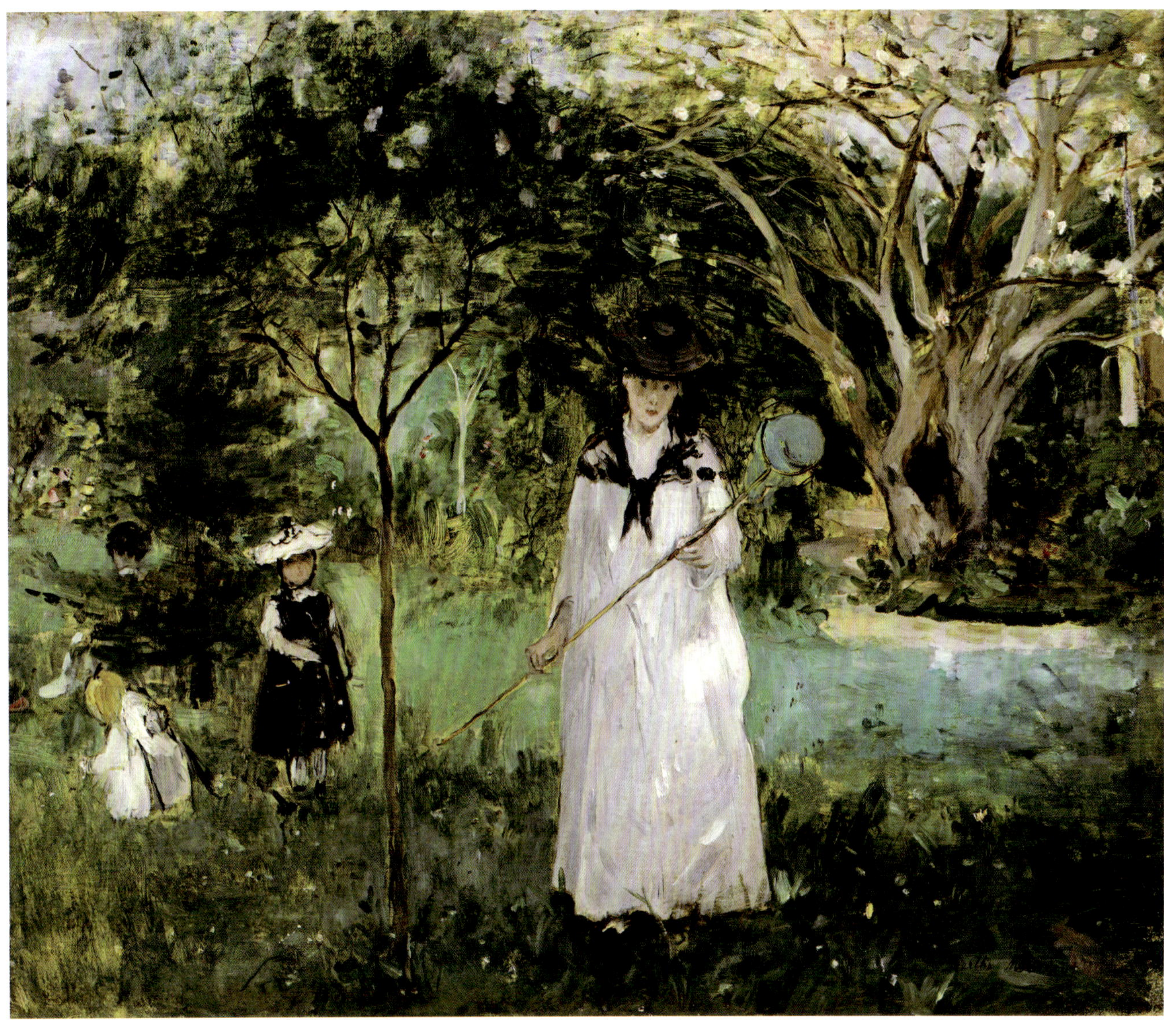

Berthe Morisot (1841–1895)

Young Woman Dressed for the Ball

Jeune Femme en toilette de bal

Junge Frau im Ballkleid

Joven mujer en traje de baile

Giovane donna in tenuta da ballo

Jonge vrouw in baljurk

1879, Oil on canvas/Huile sur toile, 71,5 × 54 cm

Berthe Morisot (1841–1895)

The Butterfly Hunt

Chasse aux papillons

Die Schmetterlingsjagd

La caza de mariposas

Caccia alle farfalle

De vlinderjacht

1874, Oil on canvas/Huile sur toile, 46 × 56 cm

This work puts Gustave Caillebotte more on the side of realism than of impressionism. One discerns the weight of his academic training under Léon Bonnat. The technique is perfect, the rendering impeccable. But the subject, unparalleled in painting, will be described as vulgar during the presentation of the work at the Salon of 1874. The bold framing and the slightly angled view make it a very modern work of almost photographic precision.

Cette œuvre place davantage Gustave Caillebotte du côté du réalisme que de l'impressionnisme. On reconnaît ici le poids de sa formation académique auprès de Léon Bonnat. La technique est parfaite, et le rendu irréprochable. Mais le sujet, inédit dans la peinture, sera qualifié de vulgaire lors de la présentation de l'œuvre au salon de 1874. Le cadrage audacieux et la vue en légère plongée en font une œuvre très moderne, d'une précision quasi photographique.

Dieses Werk stellt Gustave Caillebotte mehr auf die Seite des Realismus als des Impressionismus. Zu erkennen ist hier seine akademische Ausbildung bei Léon Bonnat. Die Technik ist perfekt und die Wiedergabe einwandfrei. Aber das in der Malerei neuartige Thema des Werkes wird auf dem Salon von 1874 als „vulgär" bezeichnet. Der gewagte Bildausschnitt und der Blickwinkel leicht von oben herab machen das Gemälde zu einem sehr modernen Werk von nahezu fotografischer Genauigkeit.

Esta obra sitúa a Gustave Caillebotte más del lado del realismo que del impresionismo. Reconocemos aquí el peso de su formación académica con Léon Bonnat. La técnica es perfecta y la representación impecable. Pero el tema, nuevo en la pintura, será calificado como vulgar en la presentación de la obra en 1874. El encuadre audaz y la vista en ligera perspectiva de pájaro hacen de este un trabajo una obra muy moderna, de una precisión casi fotográfica.

In quest'opera Gustave Caillebotte è più vicino al Realismo che all'Impressionismo. In essa è visibile il peso della sua formazione accademica presso Léon Bonnat. La tecnica è perfetta e la resa impeccabile, ma il soggetto, nuovo nella pittura, sarà additato come volgare in occasione della presentazione del quadro al Salon del 1874. L'inquadratura audace e la vista leggermente dall'alto rendono il dipinto un'opera molto moderna, con una precisione quasi fotografica.

Op grond van dit werk is Gustave Caillebotte eerder een realist dan een impressionist. Het getuigt onmiskenbaar van het stempel dat zijn academische opleiding bij Léon Bonnat op zijn werk drukt. De techniek is perfect, de weergave onberispelijk. Maar het nooit eerder in de schilderkunst verbeelde onderwerp wordt bij de presentatie op de Salon van 1874 als 'vulgair' afgedaan. Door de gedurfde kadrering en het lichte duikersperspectief is dit werk zeer modern en bijna fotografisch precies.

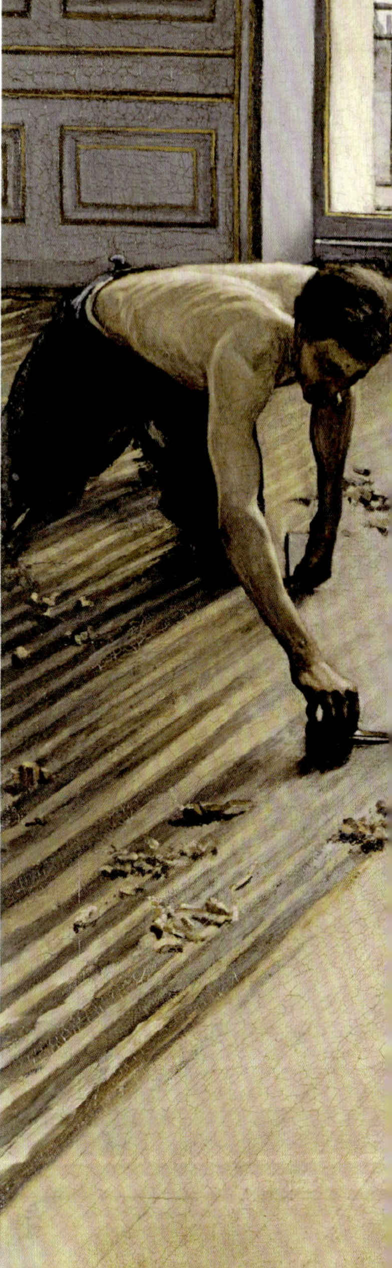

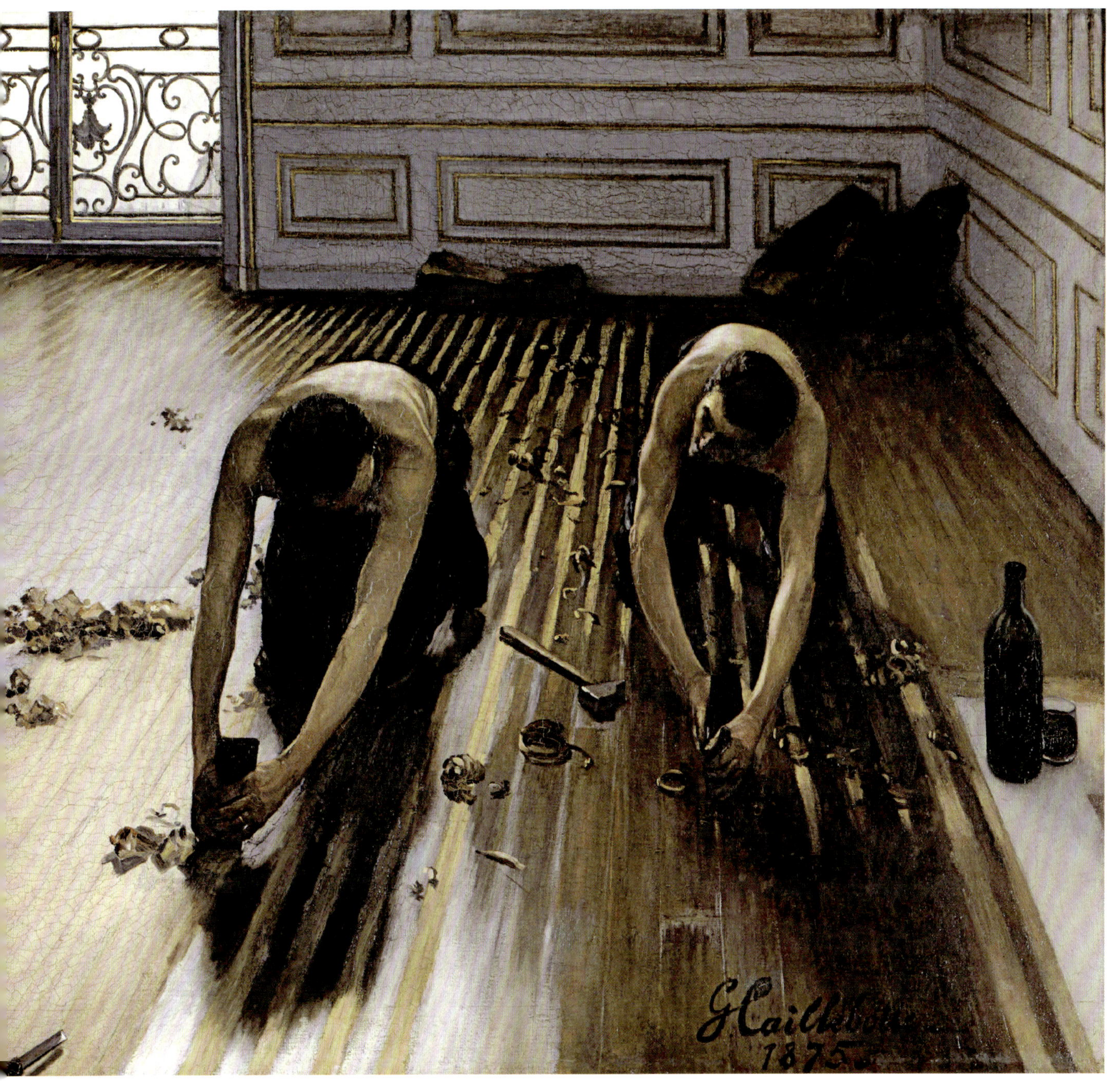

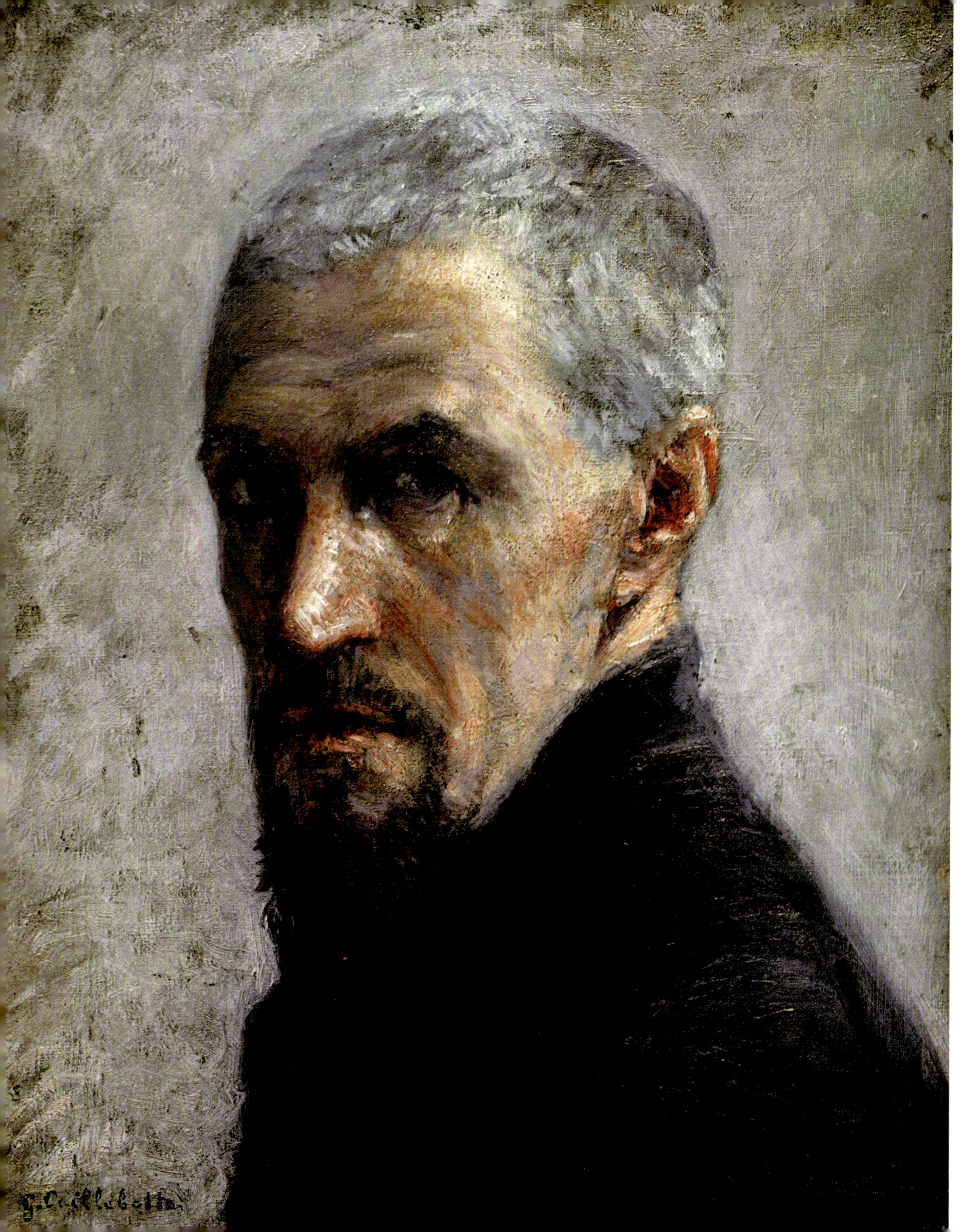
G. Caillebotte

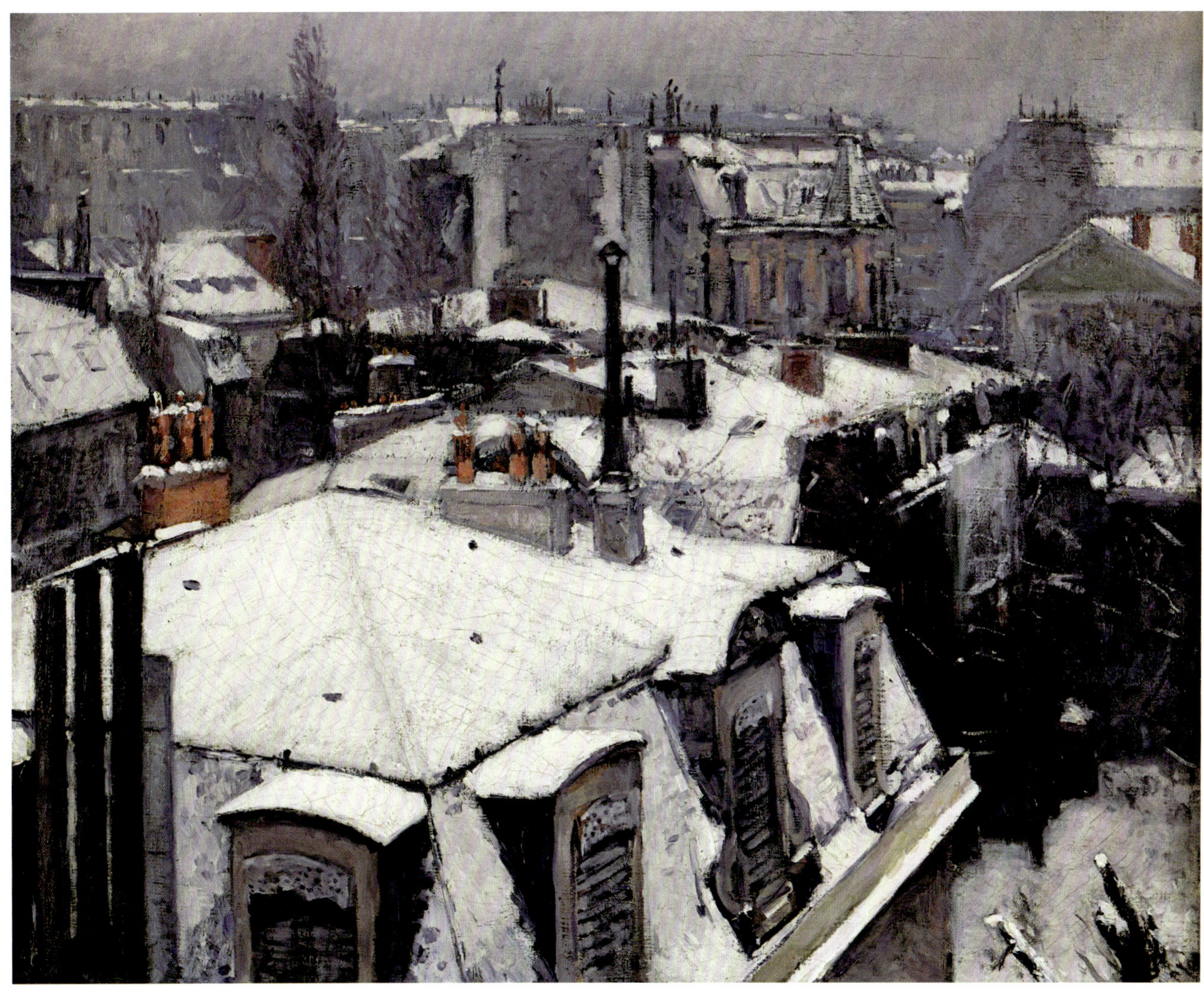

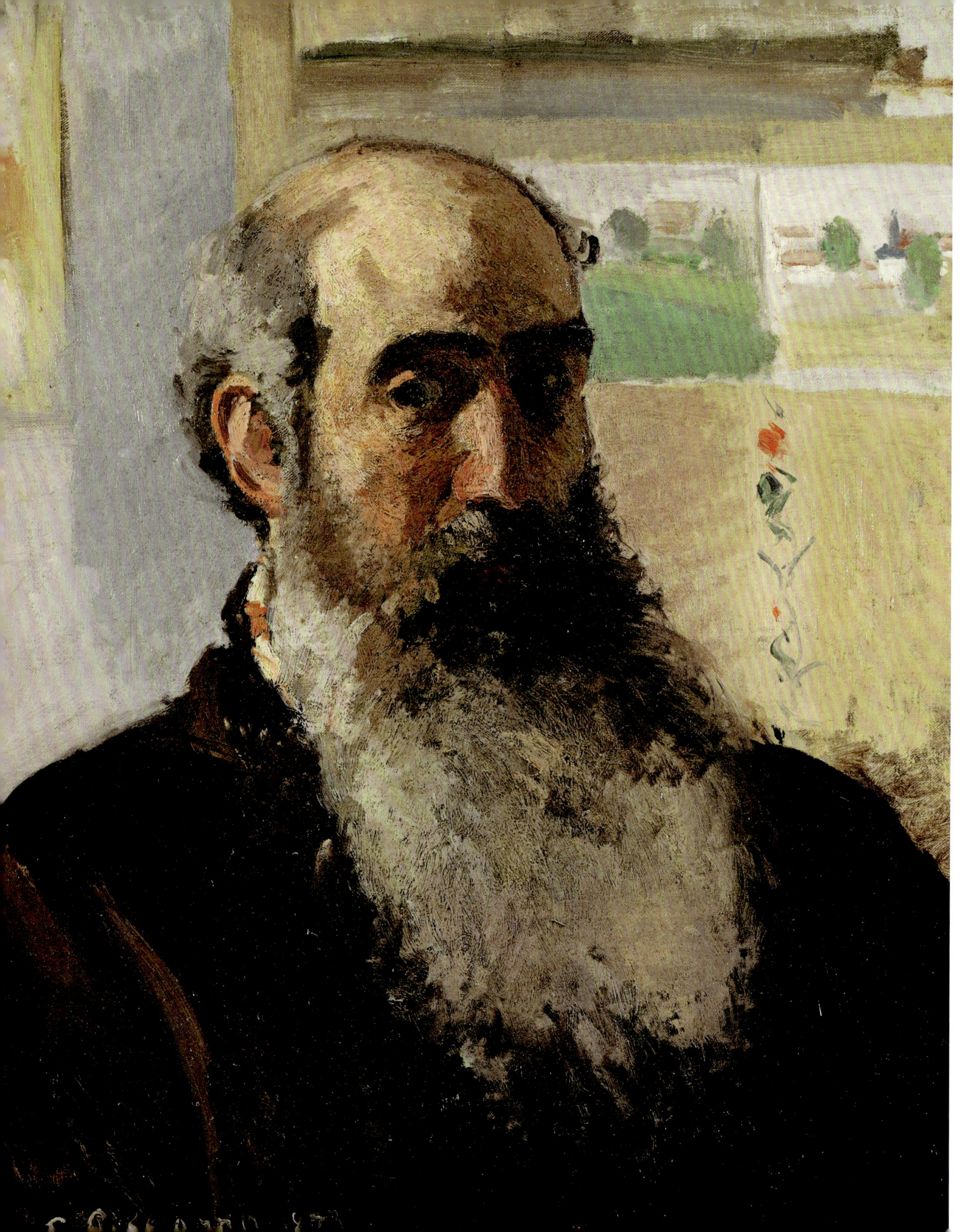

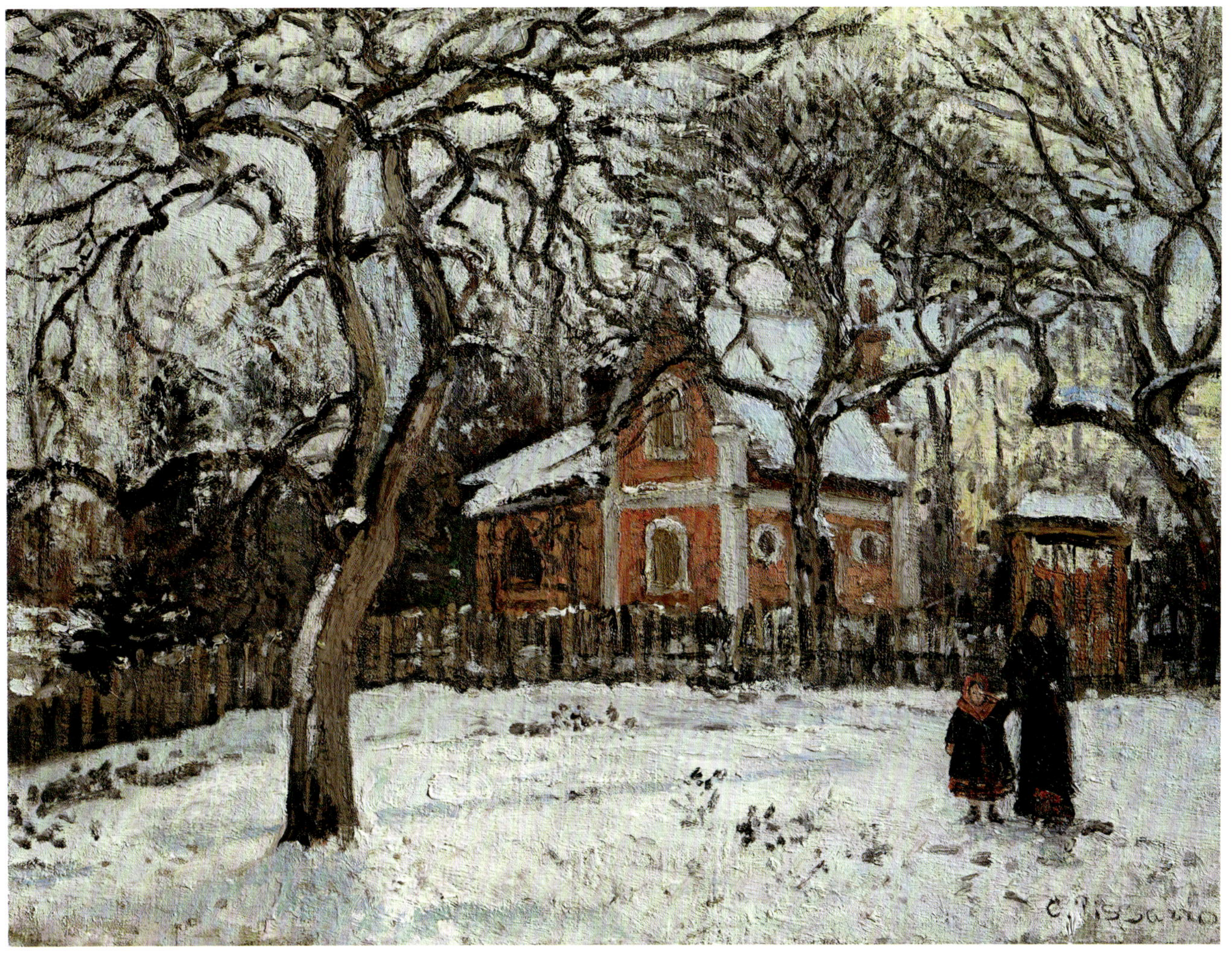

Camille Pissarro (1830–1903)

Self Portrait

Portrait de l'artiste

Selbstbildnis

Autorretrato

Autoritratto

Portret van de kunstenaar

1873, Oil on canvas/Huile sur toile, 55,5 × 46 cm

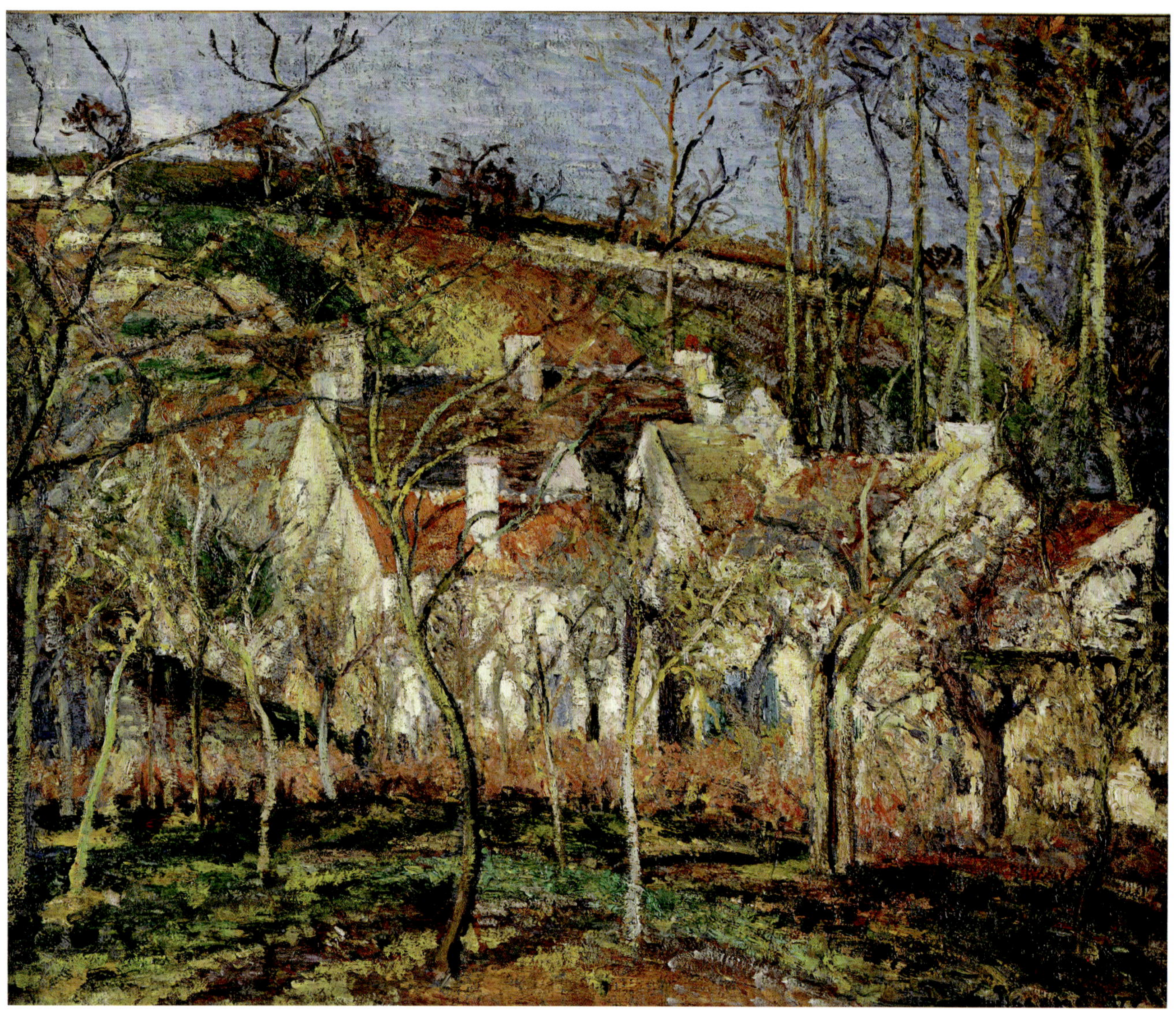

Camille Pissarro (1830–1903)

| The Red Roofs, Corner of a Village, Winter Effect | Les Toits rouges, coin de village, effet d'hiver | Rote Dächer, Dorfrand, winterliche Stimmung | Los tejados rojos, rincón de pueblo, efecto de invierno | I tetti rossi, un angolo del villaggio, effetto d'inverno | Rode daken, hoek van dorp, winter |

1877, Oil on canvas/Huile sur toile, 54 × 65 cm

The great achievement of this painting of a simple subject resides in the richness of its palette and in its harmony of beiges, browns, ochres, and greens which make the composition vibrate without violent contrasts. The effect of depth arises from a skillful succession of planes—first the tree trunks devoid of foliage, then the group of houses, and finally the slope of the hill cutting into the blue sky.

La grande réussite de cette toile au sujet simple réside dans la richesse de sa palette, et à ses harmonies de beiges, de bruns, de rouges, d'ocres et de verts, qui, sans jamais opérer de contrastes violents, font vibrer la composition. L'effet de profondeur naît d'une habile succession de plans, les troncs d'arbres dépourvus de feuillage d'abord, puis le groupe de maisons, et enfin, la pente du coteau qui se découpe sur le ciel bleu.

Der große Erfolg dieses Gemäldes mit einfachem Motiv liegt in der reichhaltigen Farbpalette und in der Harmonie der Beige-, Braun-, Rot-, Ocker- und Grüntöne, die ohne starke Kontraste die Komposition flimmern lassen. Die Tiefenwirkung wird durch eine geschickte Aufeinanderfolge von Ebenen erreicht: zunächst die kahlen Baumstämme, danach die Ansammlung von Häusern und schließlich der Hang, der sich vom blauen Himmel abhebt.

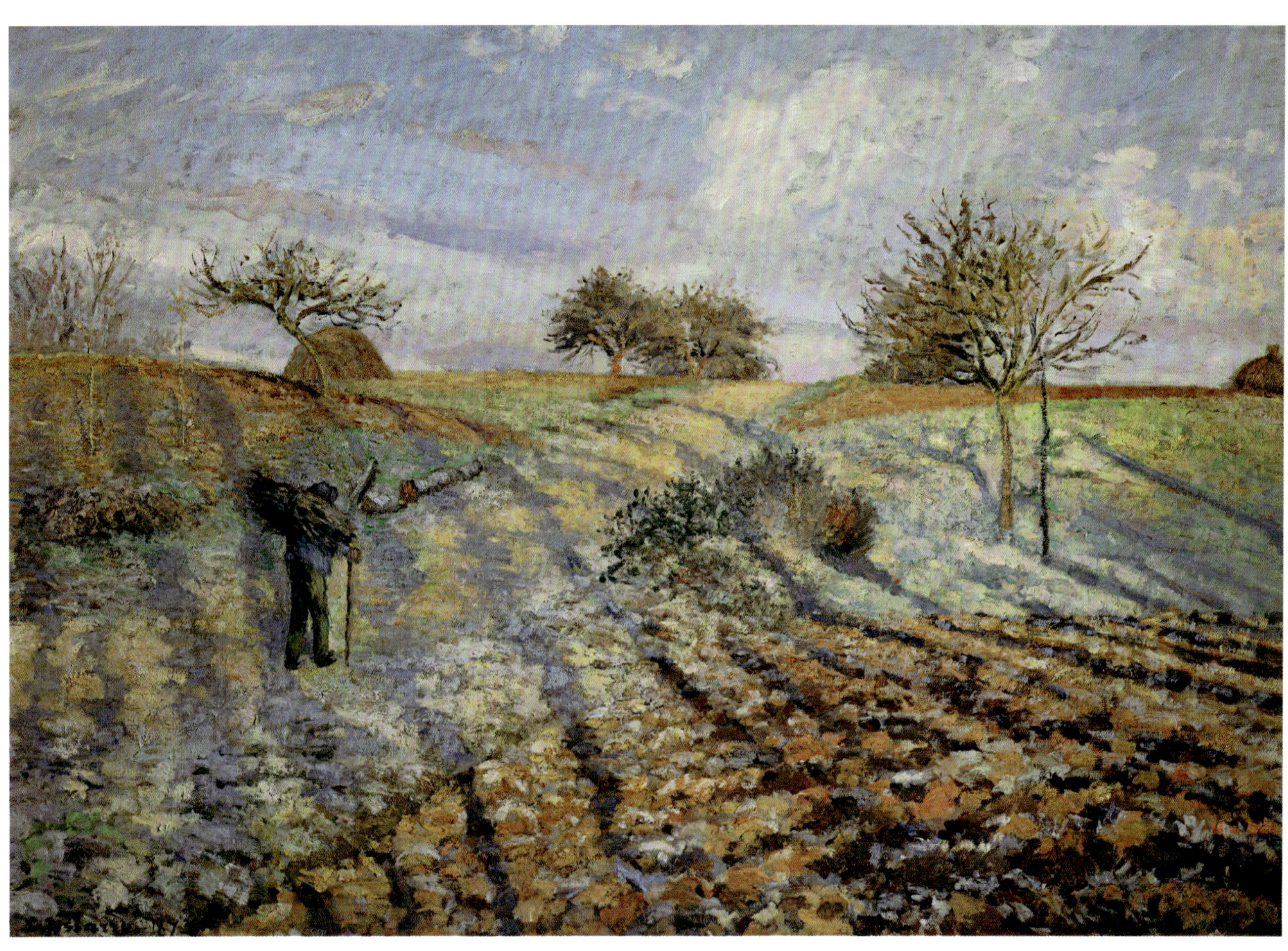

Camille Pissarro (1830–1903)

White Frost   Gelée blanche   Raureif   La escarcha   Gelata bianca   Rijp

1873, Oil on canvas/Huile sur toile, 65,5 × 93,2 cm

El gran éxito de esta pintura de un tema simple reside en la riqueza de su paleta y sus armonías de color beige, marrón, rojo, ocre y verde, que operan sin contrastes violentos y hacen vibrar la composición. El efecto de profundidad surge de una hábil sucesión de planos, los troncos de los árboles desprovistos de hojas, después el grupo de casas, y finalmente la pendiente de la colina que se destaca contra el cielo azul.

Il grande successo di questo dipinto dal soggetto semplice risiede nella ricchezza della sua tavolozza e nelle sue armonie di beige, marroni, rossi, ocra e verdi, che fanno vibrare la composizione senza creare contrasti violenti. L'effetto di profondità è ottenuto mediante un'abile successione di piani: i tronchi privi di foglie dapprima, seguiti dal gruppo di case e, infine, la pendenza della collina che si staglia sul cielo azzurro.

Het grote succes van dit doek met een eenvoudig thema schuilt in de rijkdom van het kleurenpalet en de harmonie van beige-, bruin-, rood-, oker- en groentinten, die nergens op het doek felle contrasten vormen maar de compositie iets zinderends geven. Het schilderij heeft diepte door de vakkundige opbouw van de kale bomen op de voorgrond, gevolgd door de huizen en tot slot de helling van de heuvel die zich aftekent tegen de blauwe lucht.

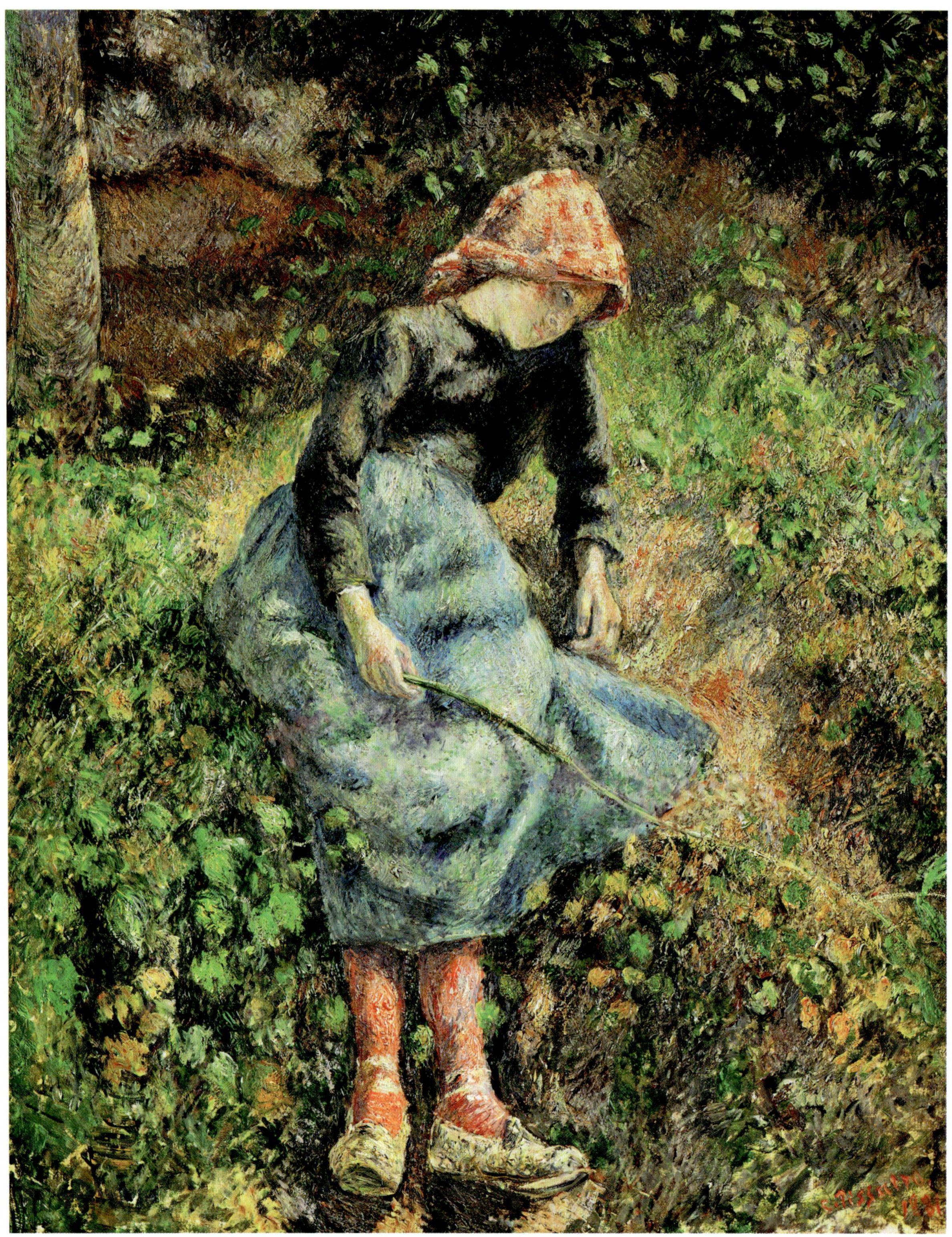

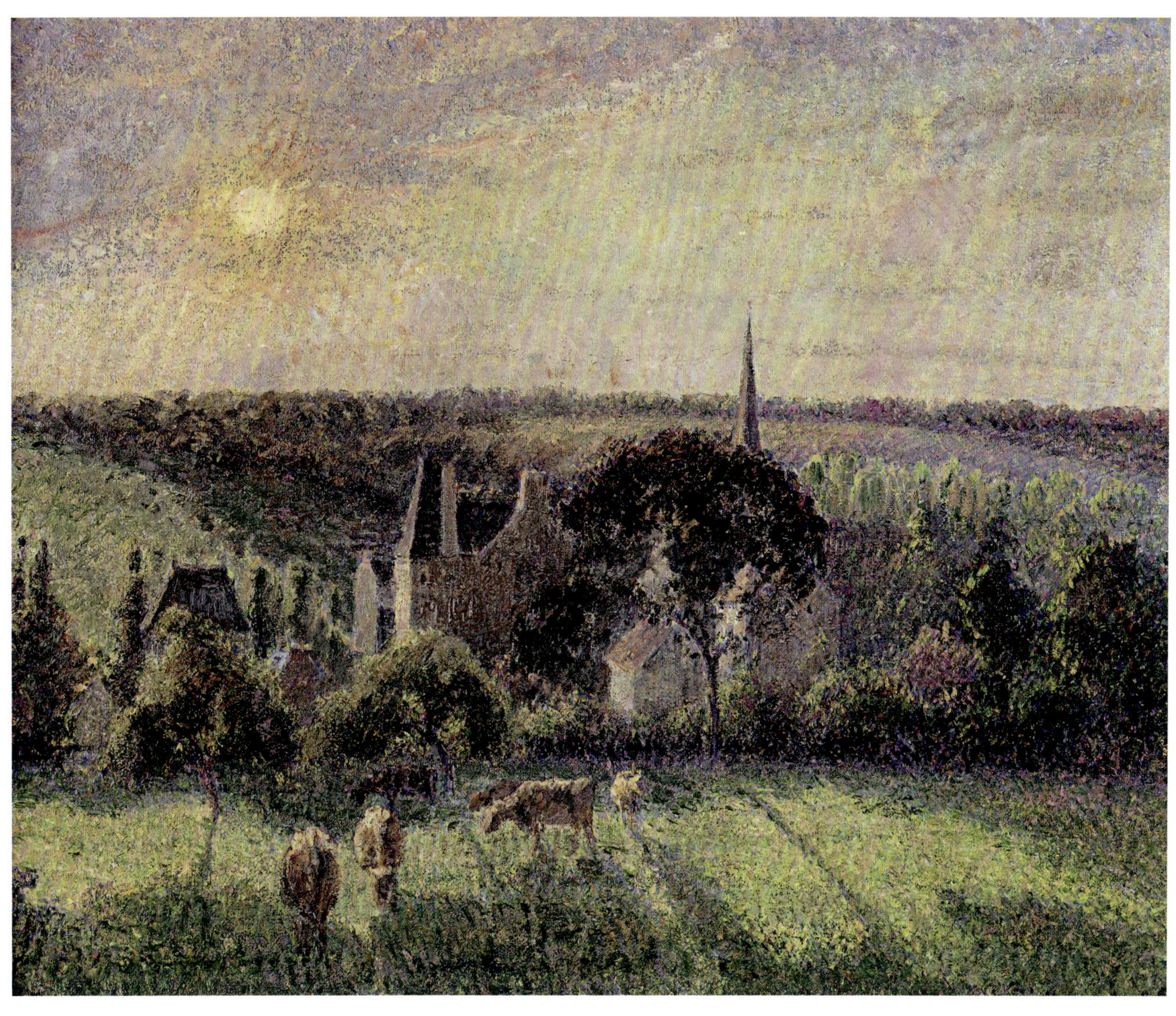

Camille Pissarro (1830–1903)

Landscape at Éragny

Paysage à Éragny

Landschaft bei Éragny

Paisaje en Éragny

Paesaggio a Éragny

Landschap in Éragny

1897, Oil on canvas/Huile sur toile, 60 × 73,5 cm

Camille Pissarro (1830–1903)

The Shepherdess

La Bergère

Die Schäferin

La pastora

Ragazza con bastoncino

De herderin

1881, Oil on canvas/Huile sur toile, 81 × 64,8 cm

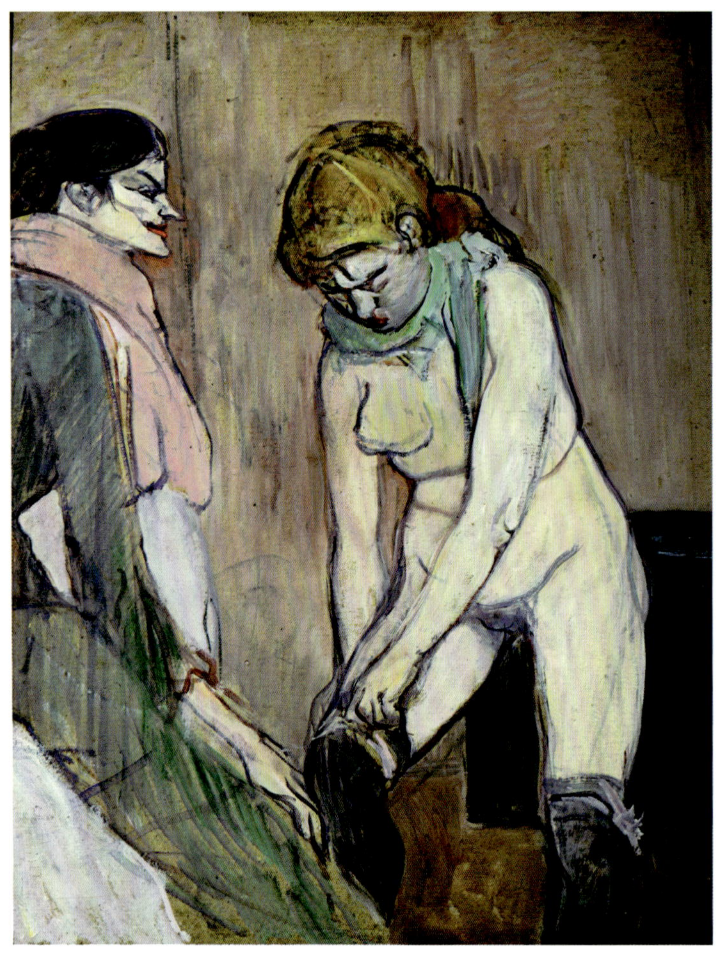

Henri de Toulouse-Lautrec (1864–1901)

Woman Pulling up Her Stockings

Femme tirant son bas

Frau, sich die Strümpfe anziehend

Mujer subiéndose las medias

Donna che si infila una calza

Vrouw die haar kous optrekt

1894, Oil on canvas/Huile sur toile, 58 × 46 cm

Henri de Toulouse-Lautrec (1864–1901)

The Clown Cha-U-Kao

Clownesse Cha-U-Kao

Die Clownesse Cha-U-Kao

La payasa Cha-U-Kao

La clownessa Cha-U-Kao

De vrouwelijke clown Cha-U-Kao

1895, Oil on cardboard/Huile sur carton, 58 × 43 cm

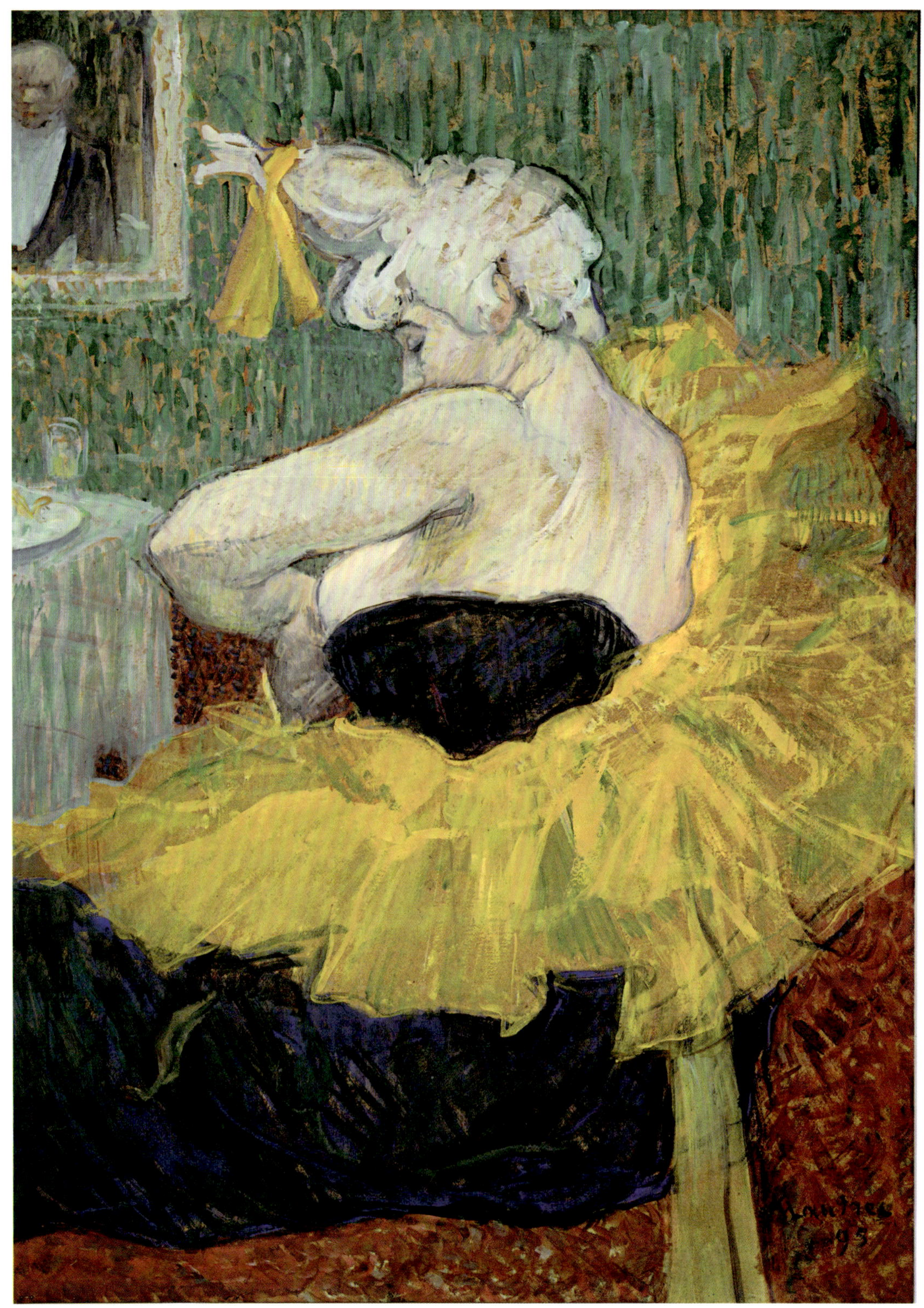

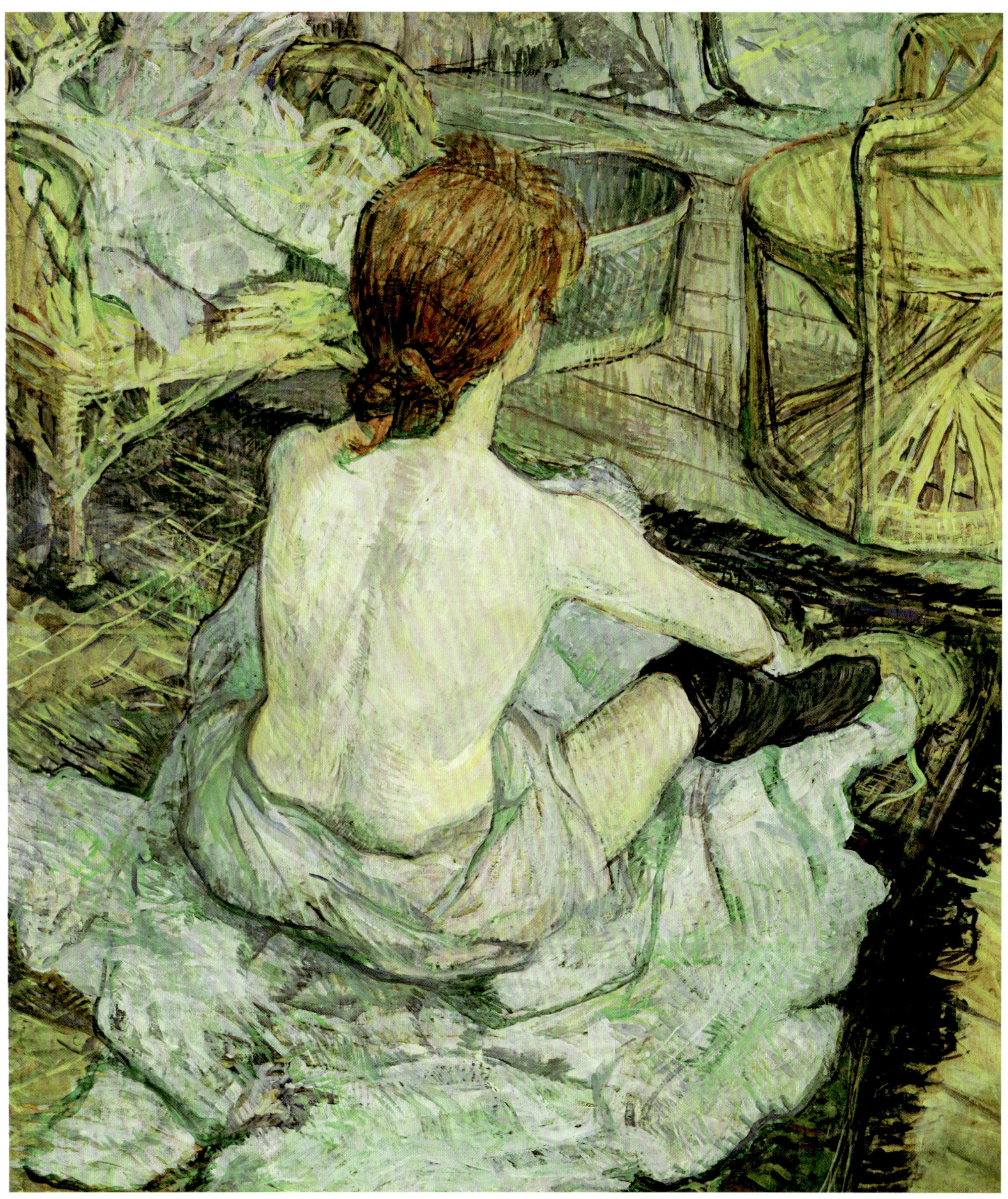

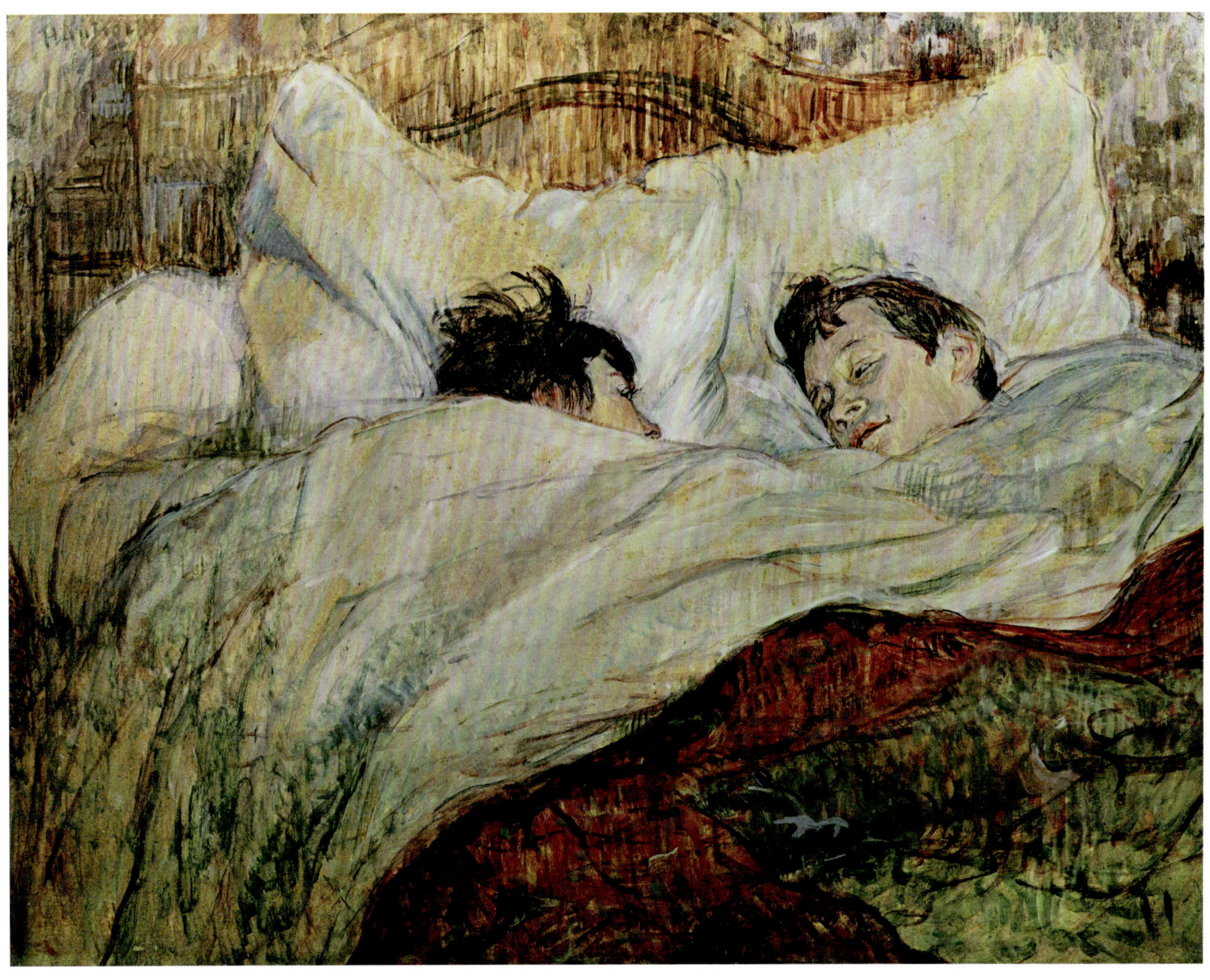

Henri de Toulouse-Lautrec (1864–1901)

Red-Haired Woman *or* The Toilette

Rousse *ou* La Toilette

Rothaarige *oder* Bei der Toilette

Pelirroja *o* El aseo

Rossa *o* La Toletta

Roodharige *of* La toilette

1889, Oil on cardboard/Huile sur carton, 67 × 54 cm

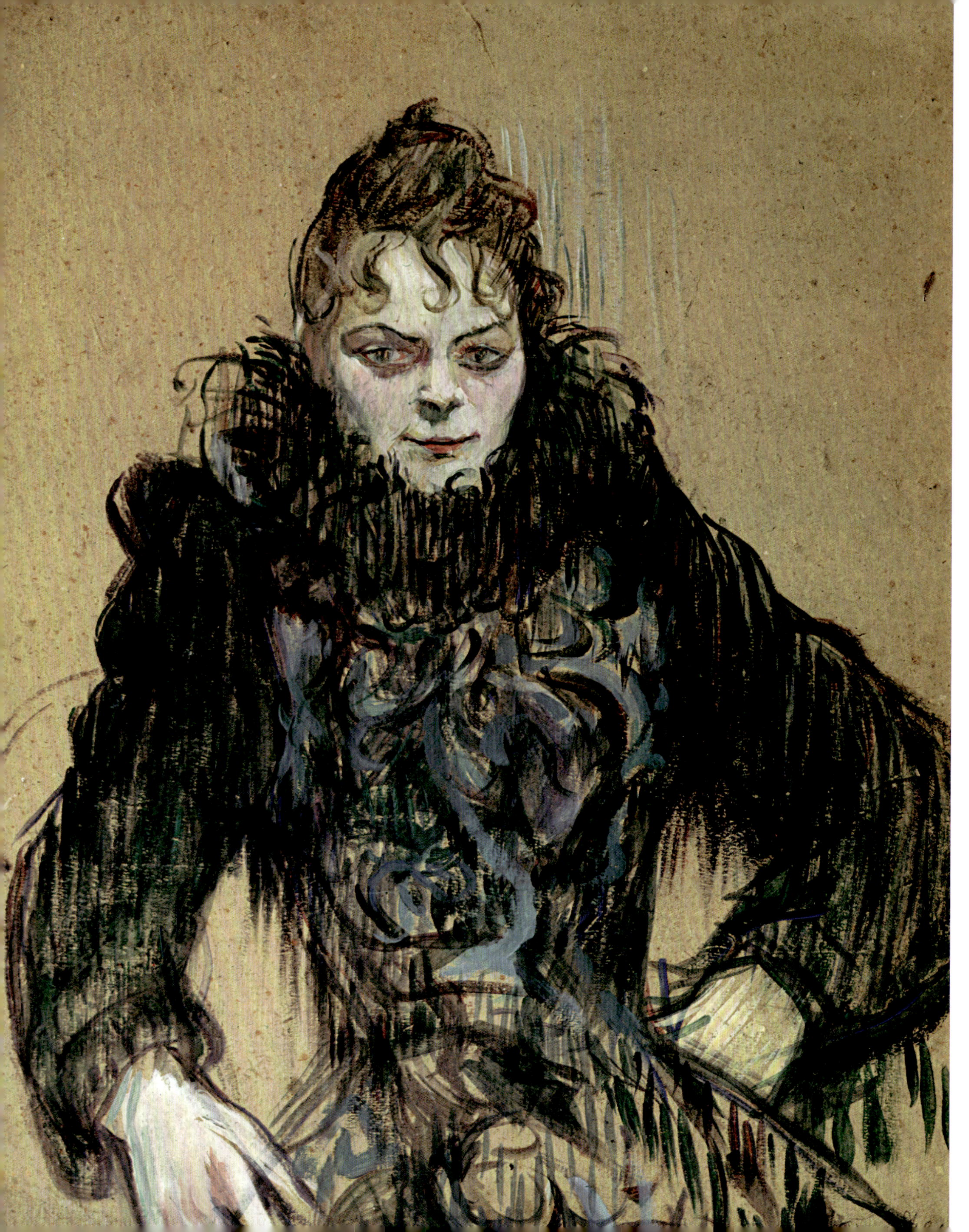

Henri de Toulouse-Lautrec (1864–1901)

Woman in a Black Boa

Femme au boa noir

Frau mit schwarzer Federboa

Mujer con boa negra

Donna dal boa di piume nero

De vrouw met de zwarte boa

1892, Oil on cardboard/Huile sur carton, 50 × 40 cm

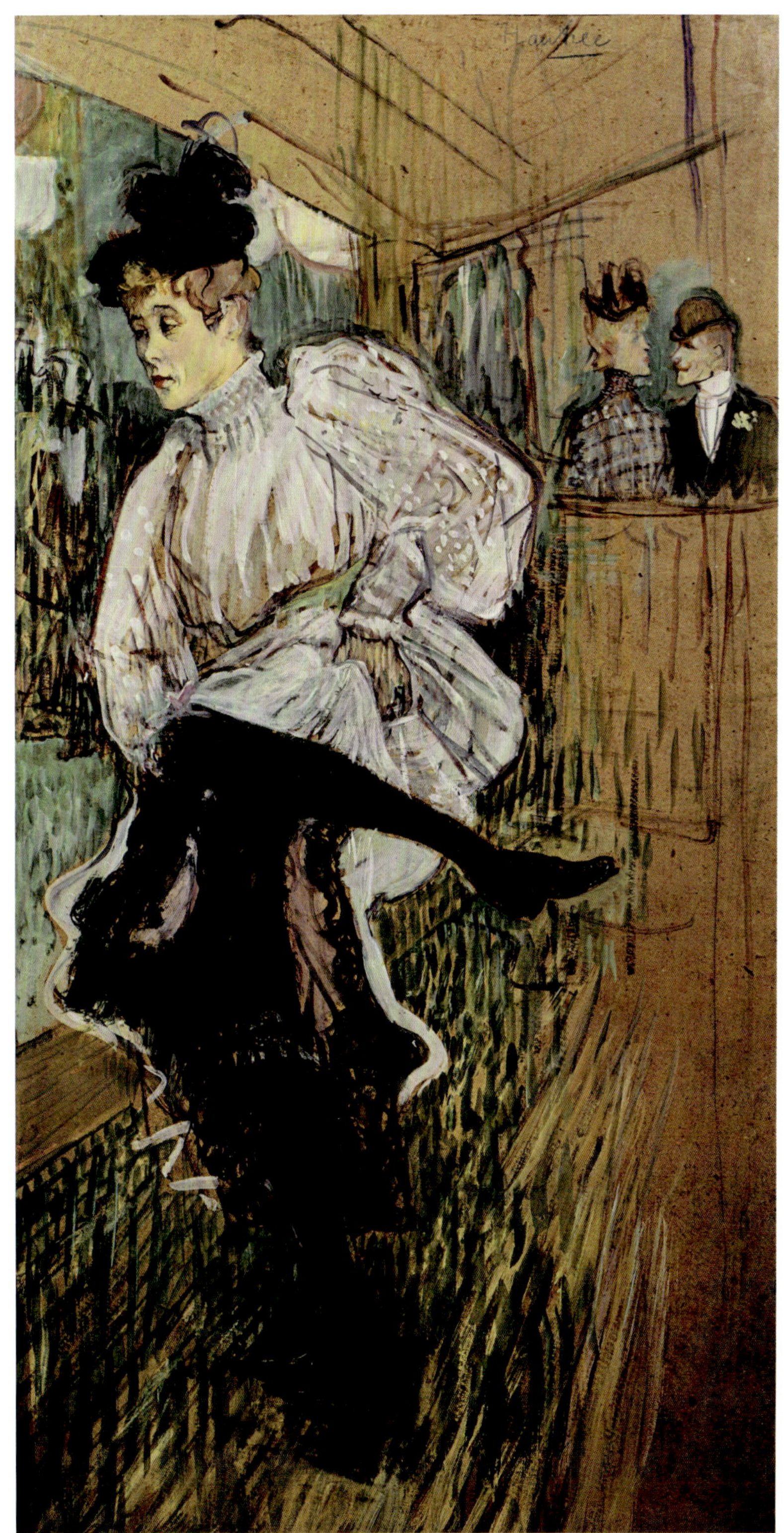

Henri de Toulouse-Lautrec (1864–1901)

Jane Avril Dancing

Jane Avril dansant

Die tanzende Jane Avril

Jane Avril bailando

Jane Avril che danza

Een dansende Jane Avril

1892, Oil on cardboard/Huile sur carton, 85,5 × 45 cm

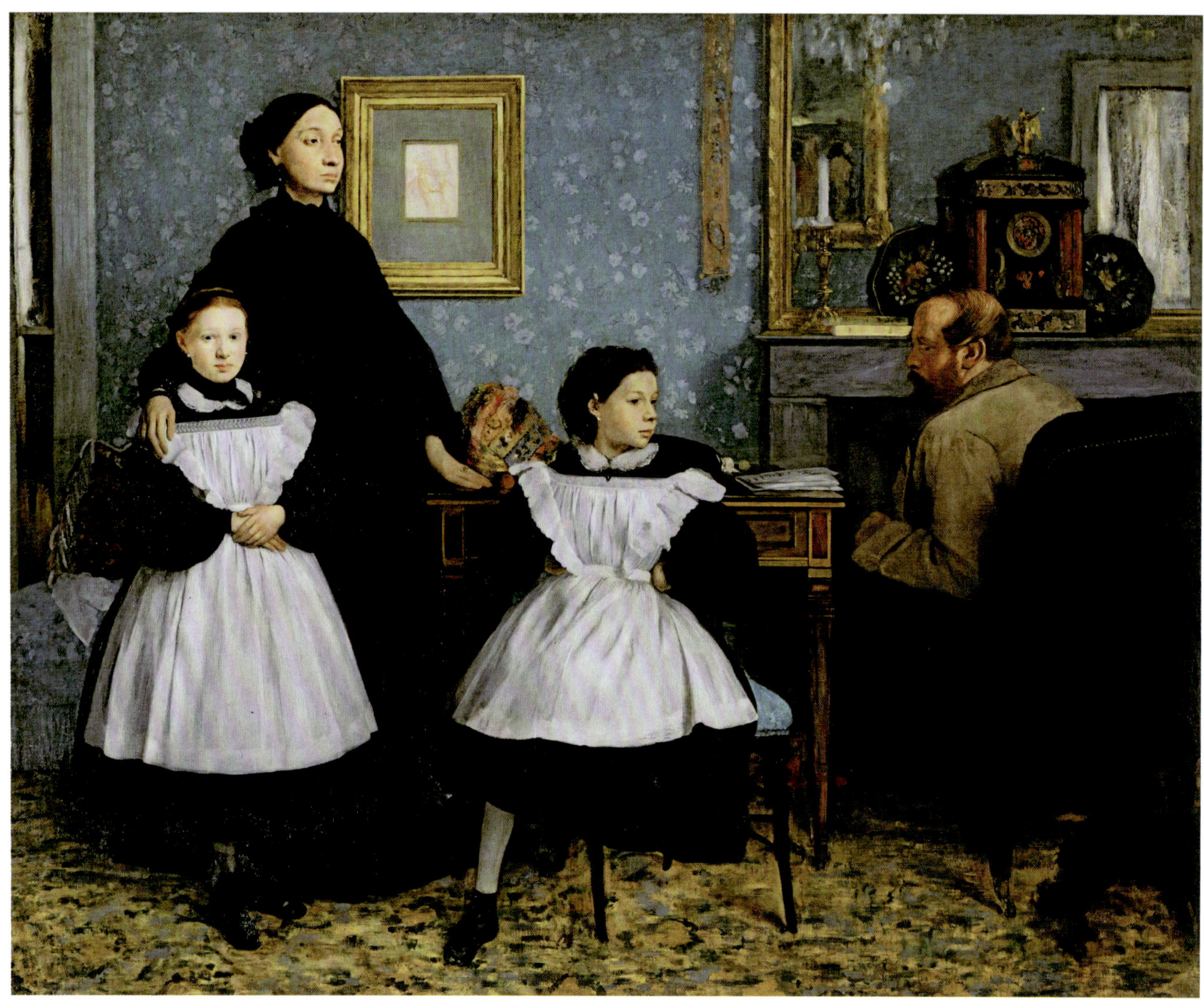

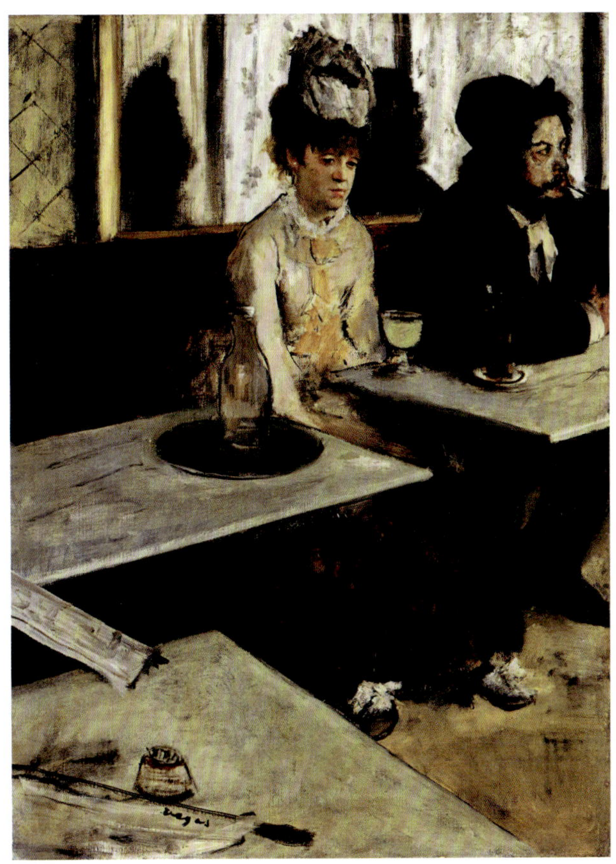

Edgar Degas (1834–1917)

In a Café *or* Absinthe

Dans un café *ou* L'Absinthe

In einem Café *oder* Der Absinth

En un café *o* La absenta

In un caffè *o* L'assenzio

In een café *of* De absint

c. 1875–1876, Oil on canvas/Huile sur toile, 92 × 68,5 cm

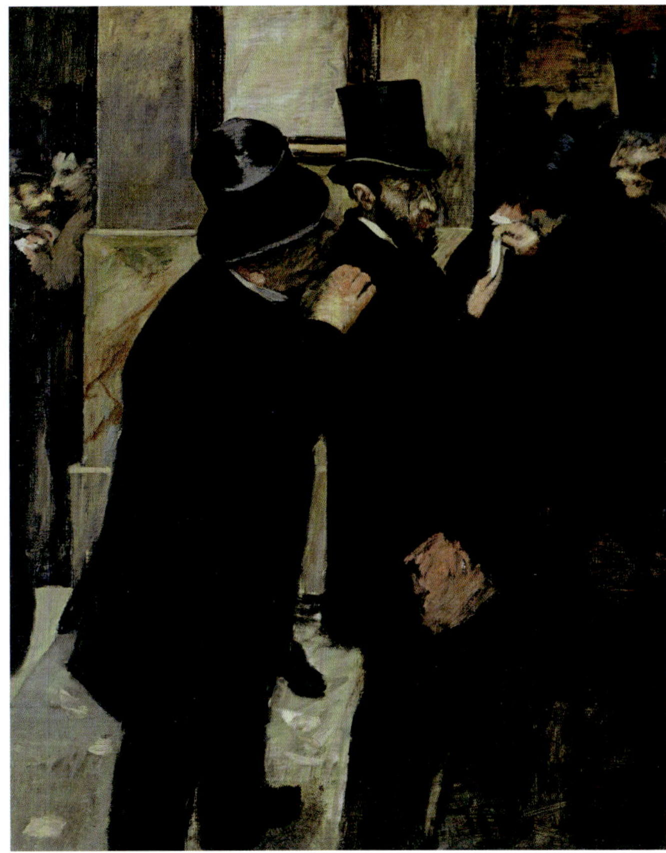

Edgar Degas (1834–1917)

Portraits at the Stock Exchange

Portraits à la Bourse

Porträts an der Börse

Retratos en la Bolsa

Ritratti alla Borsa

Portretten in de Beurs

c. 1878–1879, Oil on canvas/Huile sur toile, 100,5 × 81,5 cm

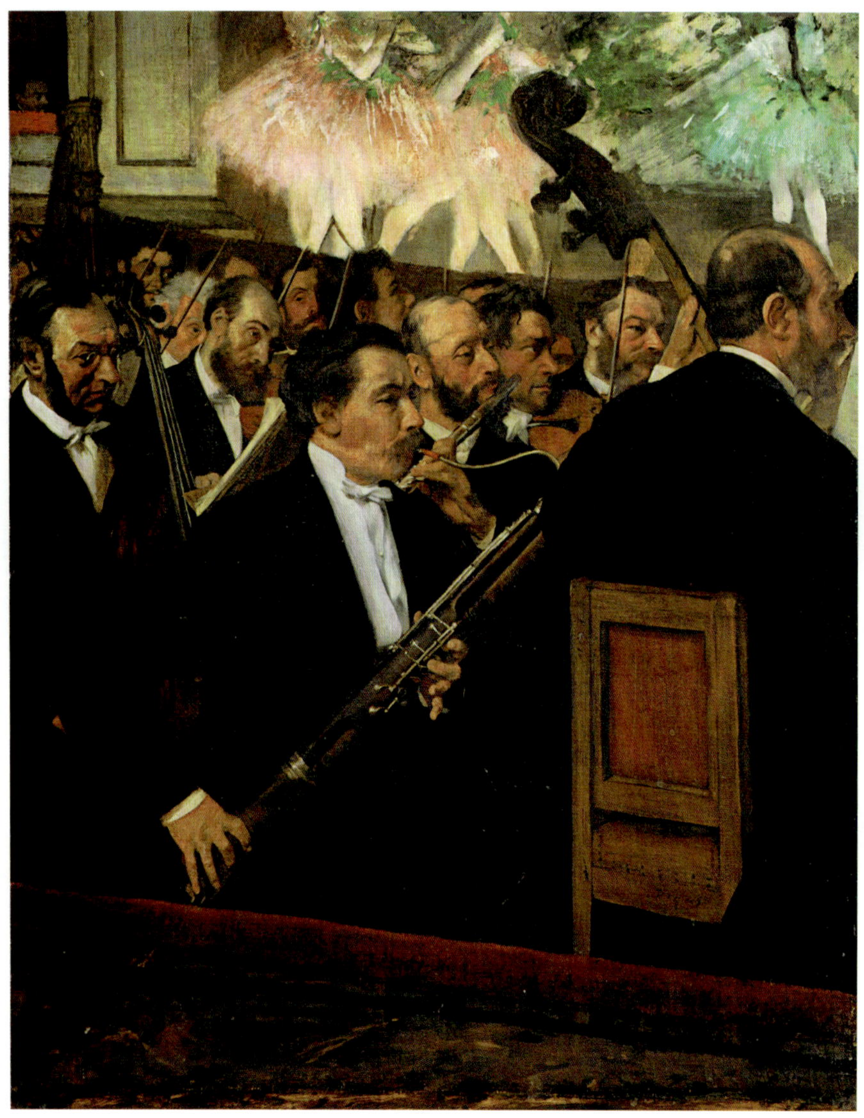

Edgar Degas (1834–1917)
The Orchestra at the Opera
L'Orchestre de l'Opéra
Orchester in der Oper
La orquesta de la Ópera
L'Orchestra dell'Opéra
Het orkest van de Opera
c. 1870, Oil on canvas/Huile
sur toile, 56,6 × 46 cm

As with the nude, scenes of life or of horses, dancing is a central subject for Edgar Degas, who multiplied variations of it in paint or pastel. The originality of this work rests in the fact that the artist dedicates the essential element of this painting to that which one normally does not see at the Opera—the orchestra pit.

Au même titre que le nu, les scènes de vie ou les chevaux, la danse est un sujet central chez Edgar Degas, qui multiplia les variations, en peinture ou au pastel. L'originalité de cette œuvre réside dans le fait que l'artiste consacre l'essentiel de son tableau à ce que l'on ne voit habituellement pas à l'Opéra, la fosse d'orchestre.

Genauso wie Akte, Szenen aus dem Leben und Pferde ist der Tanz ein zentrales Motiv bei Edgar Degas, von dem er viele Variationen mit Farbe oder Pastell anfertigte. Die Besonderheit dieses Werkes besteht darin, dass der Künstler in seinem Gemälde dem, was man normalerweise in einem Opernsaal nicht sieht, nämlich dem Orchestergraben, den größten Platz einräumt.

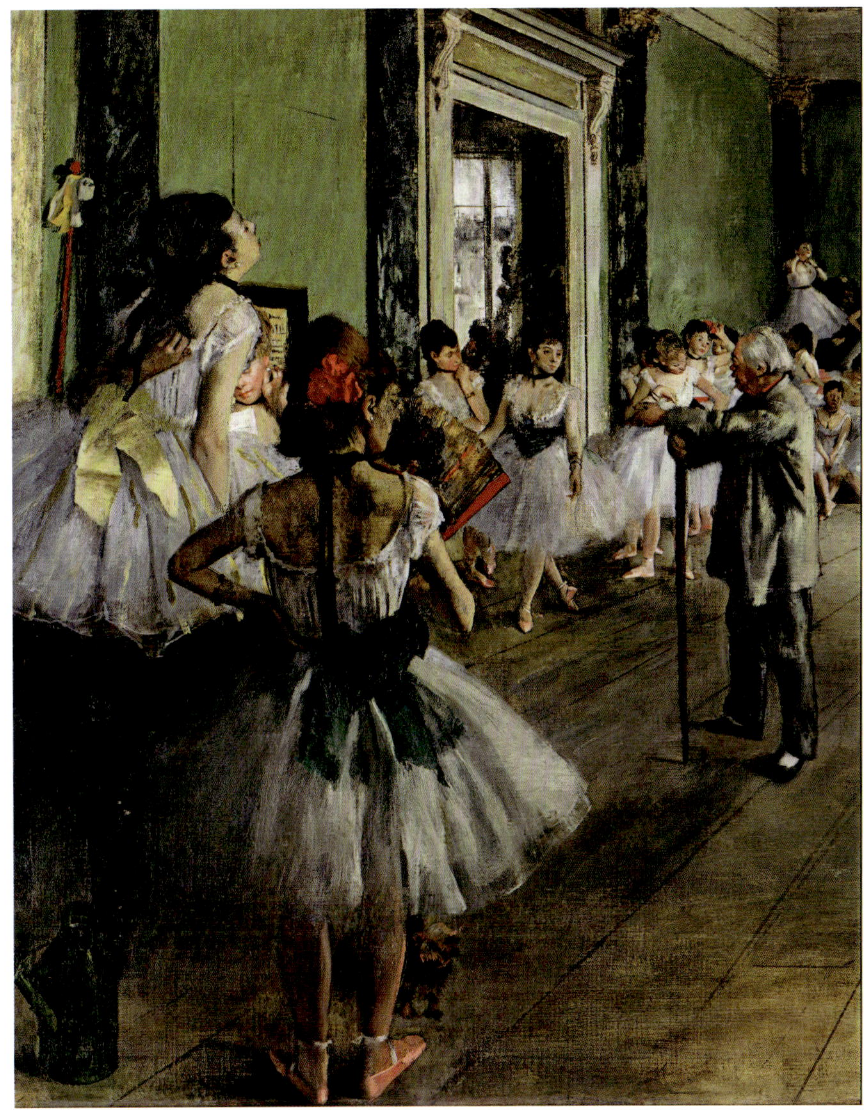

Edgar Degas (1834–1917)
The Dancing Class
La Classe de danse
Tanzunterricht
La clase de danza
La Classe di danza
De dansklas
c. 1873–1876, Oil on canvas/
Huile sur toile, 85,5 × 75 cm

Junto con los desnudos, las escenas de la vida o los caballos, el baile es un tema central de Edgar Degas, que multiplica las variaciones, tanto en pintura como en pastel. La originalidad de este trabajo radica en el hecho de que el artista consagra lo esencial de su pintura a lo que no vemos habitualmente en la ópera, el foso de la orquesta.

Oltre ai nudi, alle scene di vita e ai cavalli, anche la danza è un tema centrale dell'opera di Edgar Degas, che l'artista raffigura in molteplici modi, sia con pintura che a pastello. L'originalità di questo dipinto risiede nel fatto che l'artista consacra il quadro a un soggetto dell'Opéra che generalmente resta nascosto: la fossa degli orchestrali.

Naast naakten, alledaagse taferelen en renpaarden vormt dans een centraal thema op de doeken van Edgar Degas, die er zowel met verf als met pastelkrijt naar hartenlust op varieerde. Wat dit werk zo bijzonder maakt is het feit dat de kunstenaar het grootste gedeelte van zijn schilderij wijdt aan wat men in de Opera normaal gesproken niet ziet, namelijk de orkestbak.

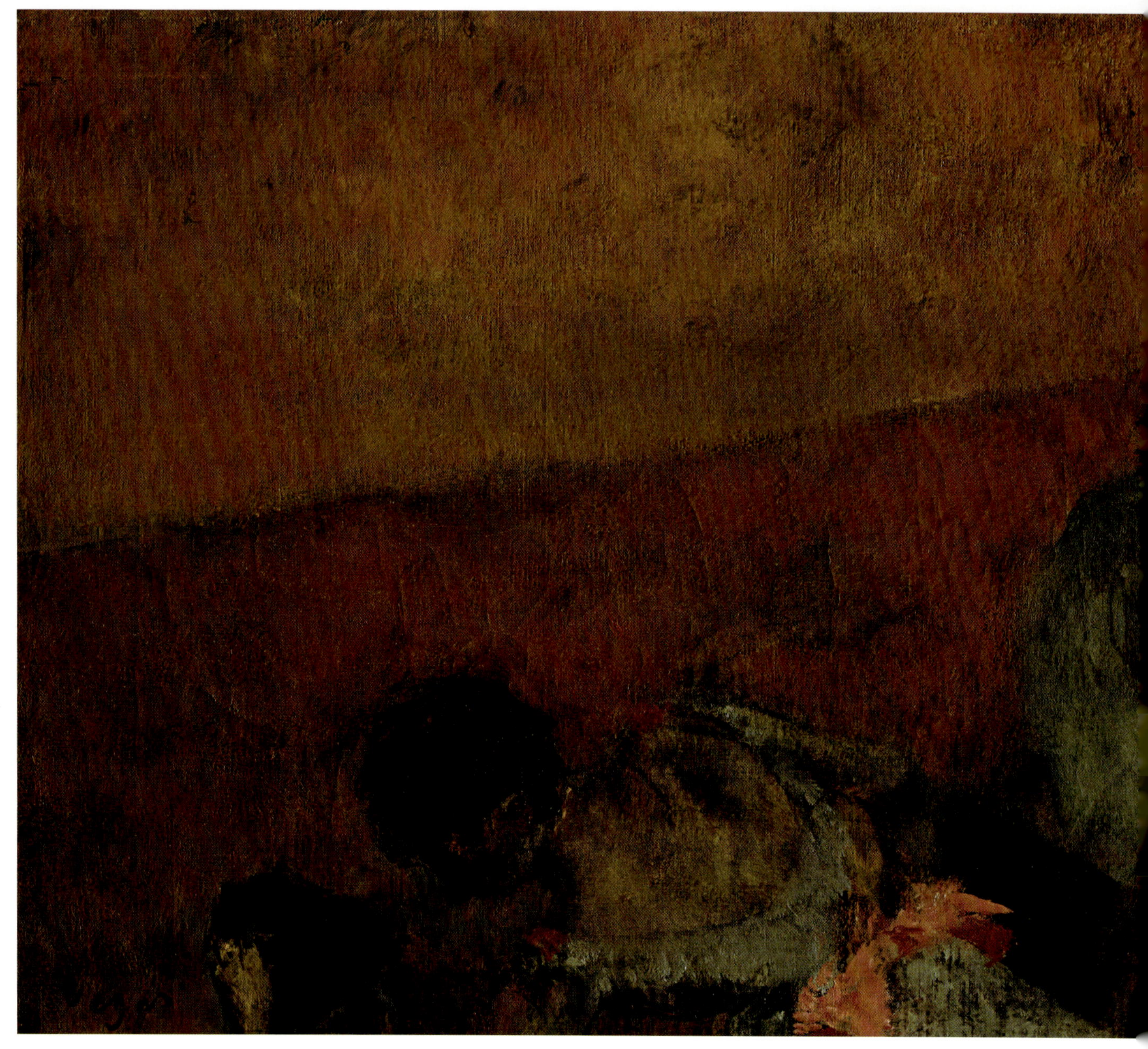

Edgar Degas (1834–1917)

Dancers Climbing the Stairs

Danseuses montant un escalier

Tänzerinnen, eine Treppe hinaufsteigend

Bailarinas subiendo la escalera

Ballerine che salgono una scala

Danseressen die een trap opkomen

c. 1886–1890, Oil on canvas/Huile sur toile, 39 × 89,5 cm

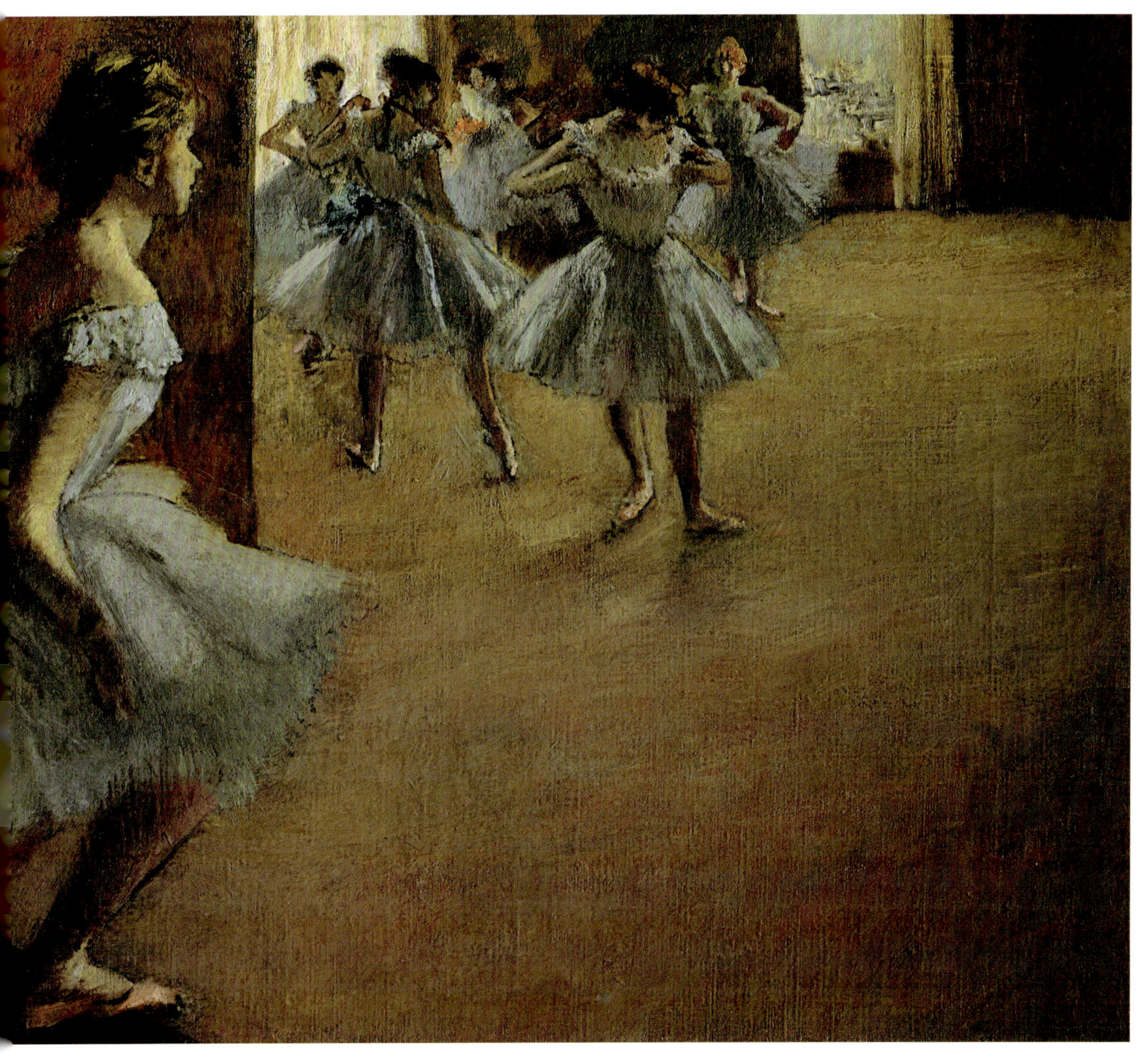

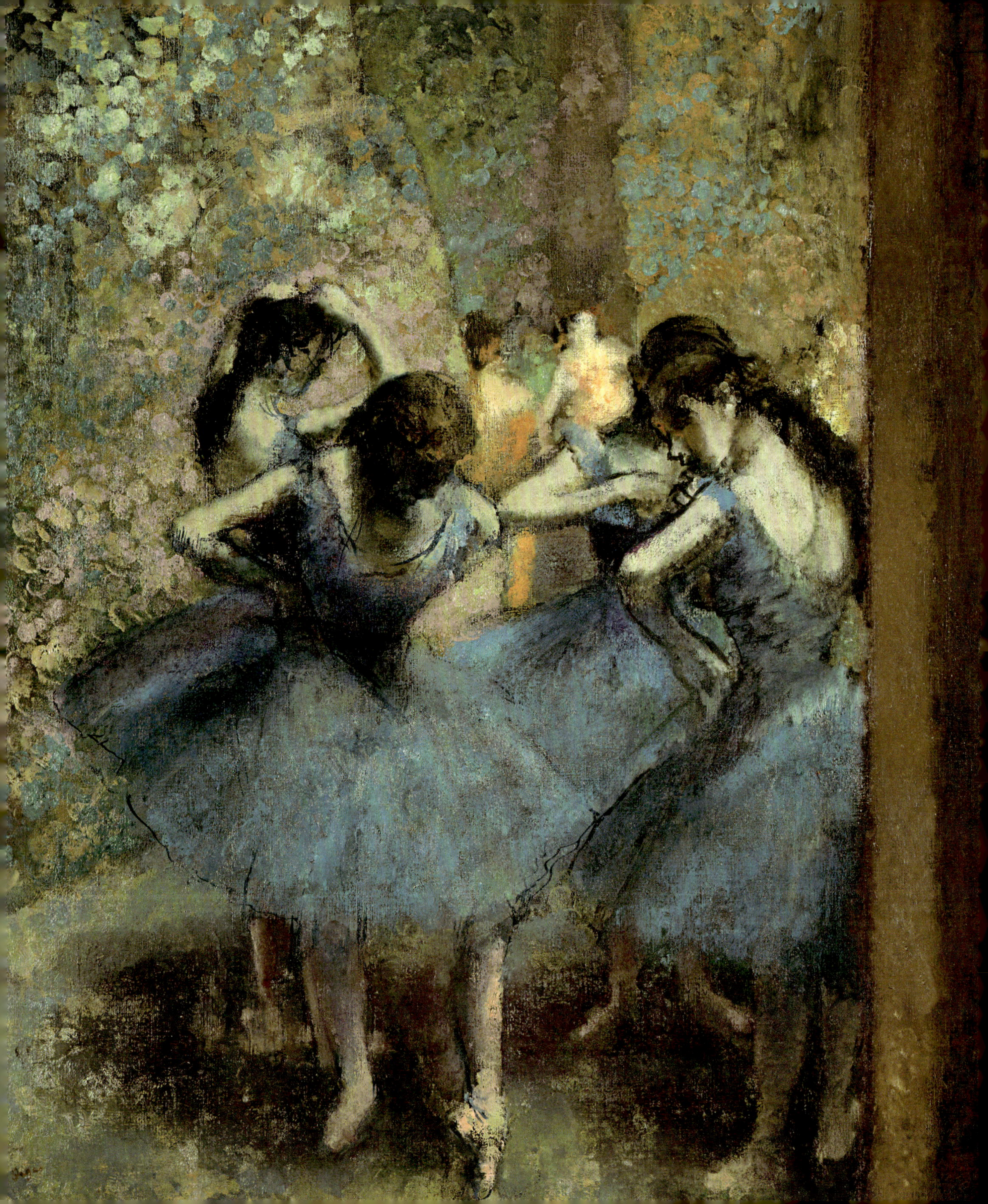

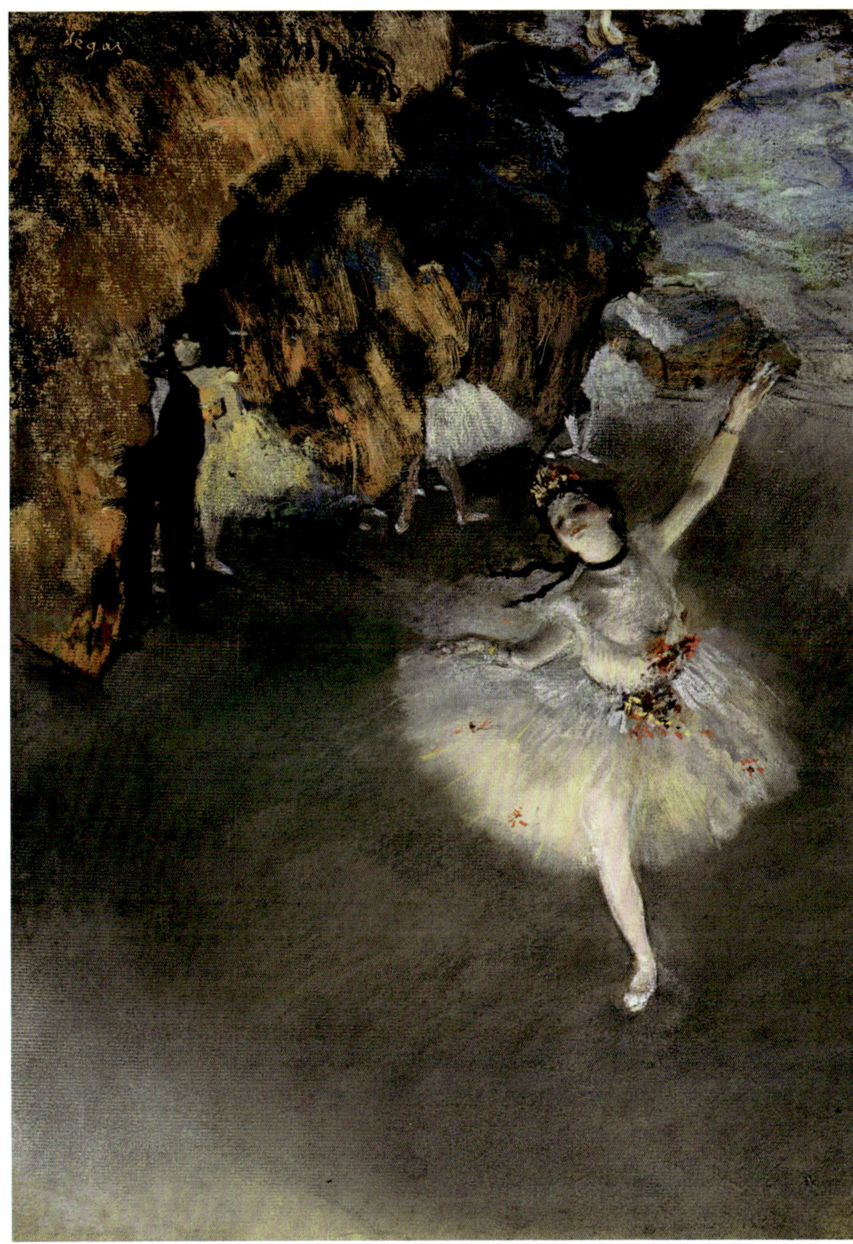

Edgar Degas (1834–1917)

Ballet

Ballet

Ballett

Balé

Baletto

Ballet

c. 1876, Monotype pastel/
Pastel sur monotype,
58,4 × 42 cm

Edgar Degas (1834–1917)

Dancers in Blue

Danseuses bleues

Tänzerinnen in Blau

Bailarinas en azul

Ballerine in blu

Blauwe danseressen

c. 1890, Oil on canvas/Huile sur toile, 85,3 × 75,3 cm

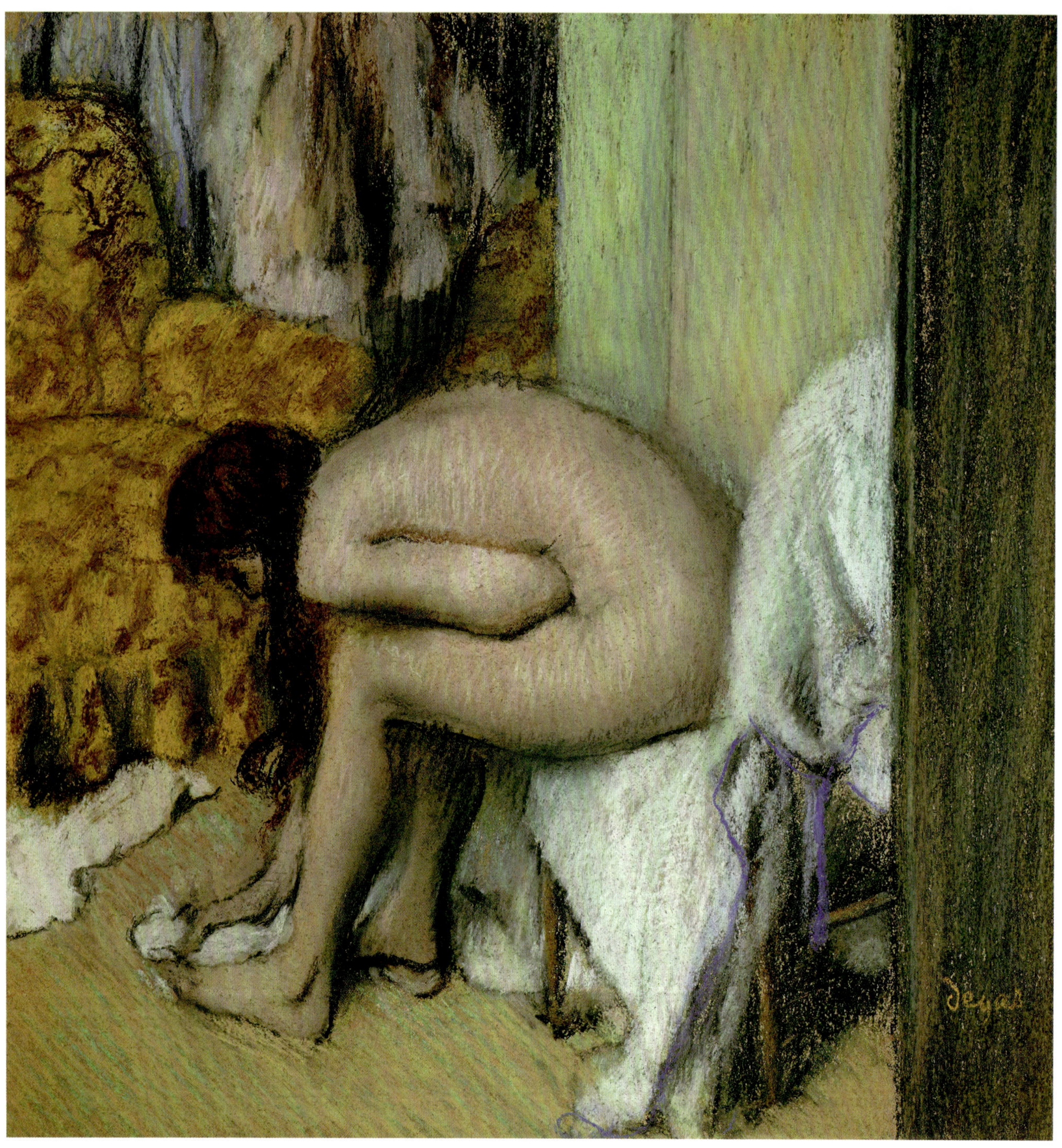

Edgar Degas (1834–1917)

After the Bath, Woman
Drying Her Left Foot

Femme à la toilette
essuyant son pied gauche

Sitzende Frau, sich den
linken Fuß abtrocknend

Mujer en el baño
secándose el pie izquierdo

Donna che si asciuga
il piede sinistro

Zittende vrouw die haar
linkervoet afdroogt

1886, Pastel on cardboard/Pastel sur carton, 54,3 × 52,4 cm

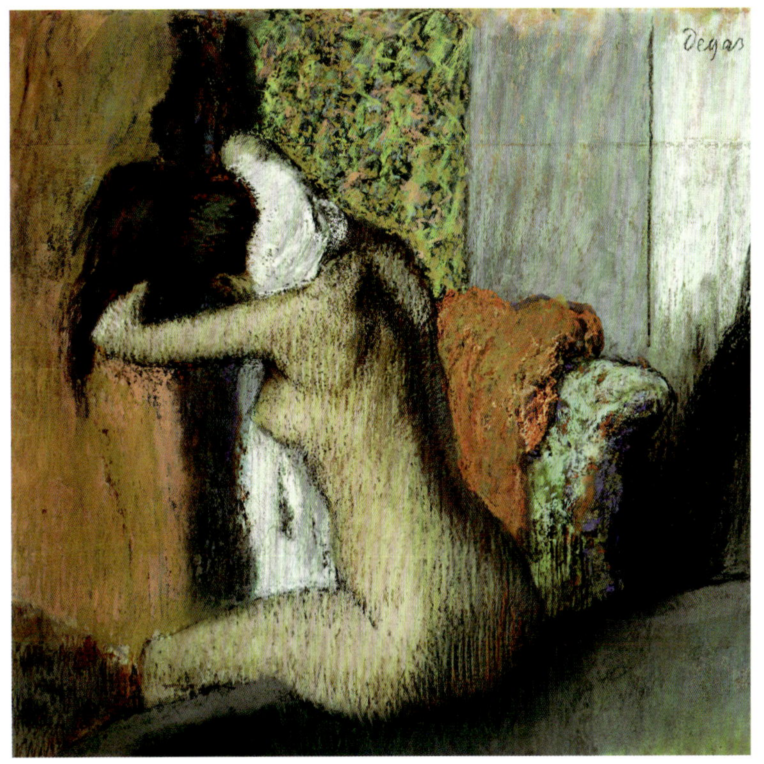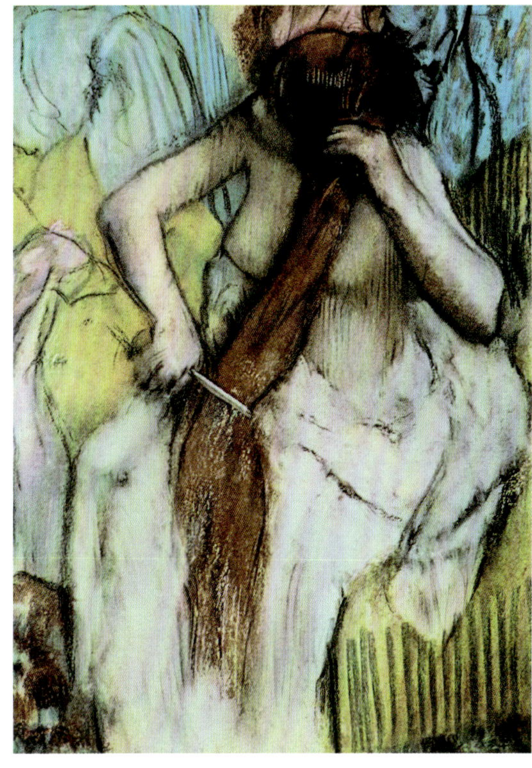

Edgar Degas (1834–1917)

After the Bath, Woman Drying Her Neck

Après le bain femme nue s'essuyant la nuque

Sich den Nacken abtrocknende junge Frau, von hinten

Mujer después del baño secándose la nuca

Donna che si asciuga il collo dopo il bagno

Na het bad, naakte vrouw die haar nek afdroogt

1898, Pastel on fine vellum on cardboard/Pastel sur vélin fin sur carton, 62,2 × 65 cm

Edgar Degas (1834–1917)

Woman Combing Her Hair

Femme se coiffant

Frau, sich frisierend

Mujer peinándose

Donna che si pettina

Vrouw die haar haar kamt

c. 1887–1890, Pastel on beige paper on cardboard/Pastel sur papier beige sur carton, 82 × 57 cm

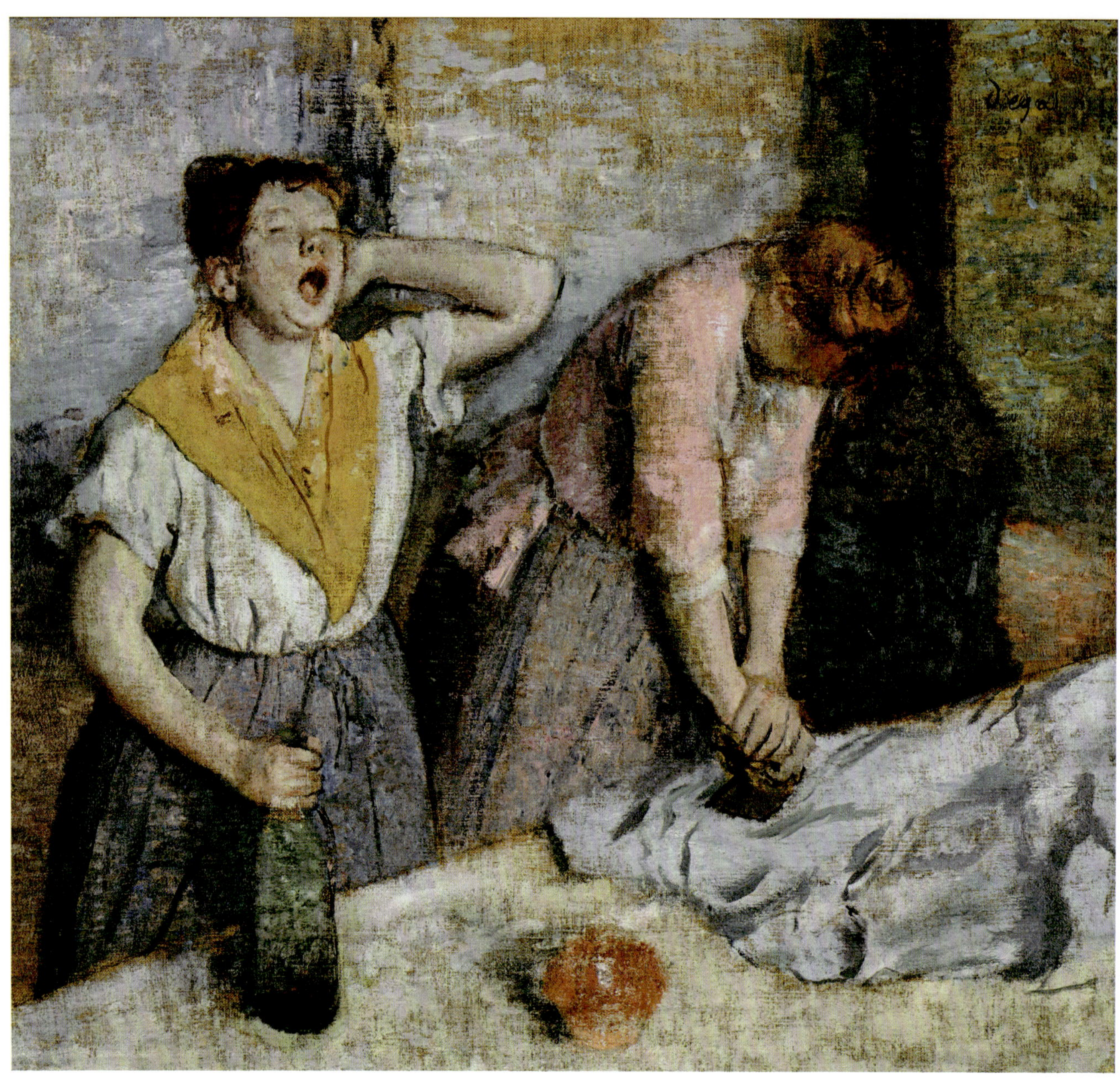

Edgar Degas (1834–1917)
Women Ironing
Repasseuses
Die Büglerinnen
Las planchadoras
Le Stiratrici
De strijksters
c. 1884–1886, Oil on canvas/Huile sur toile, 76 × 81,5 cm

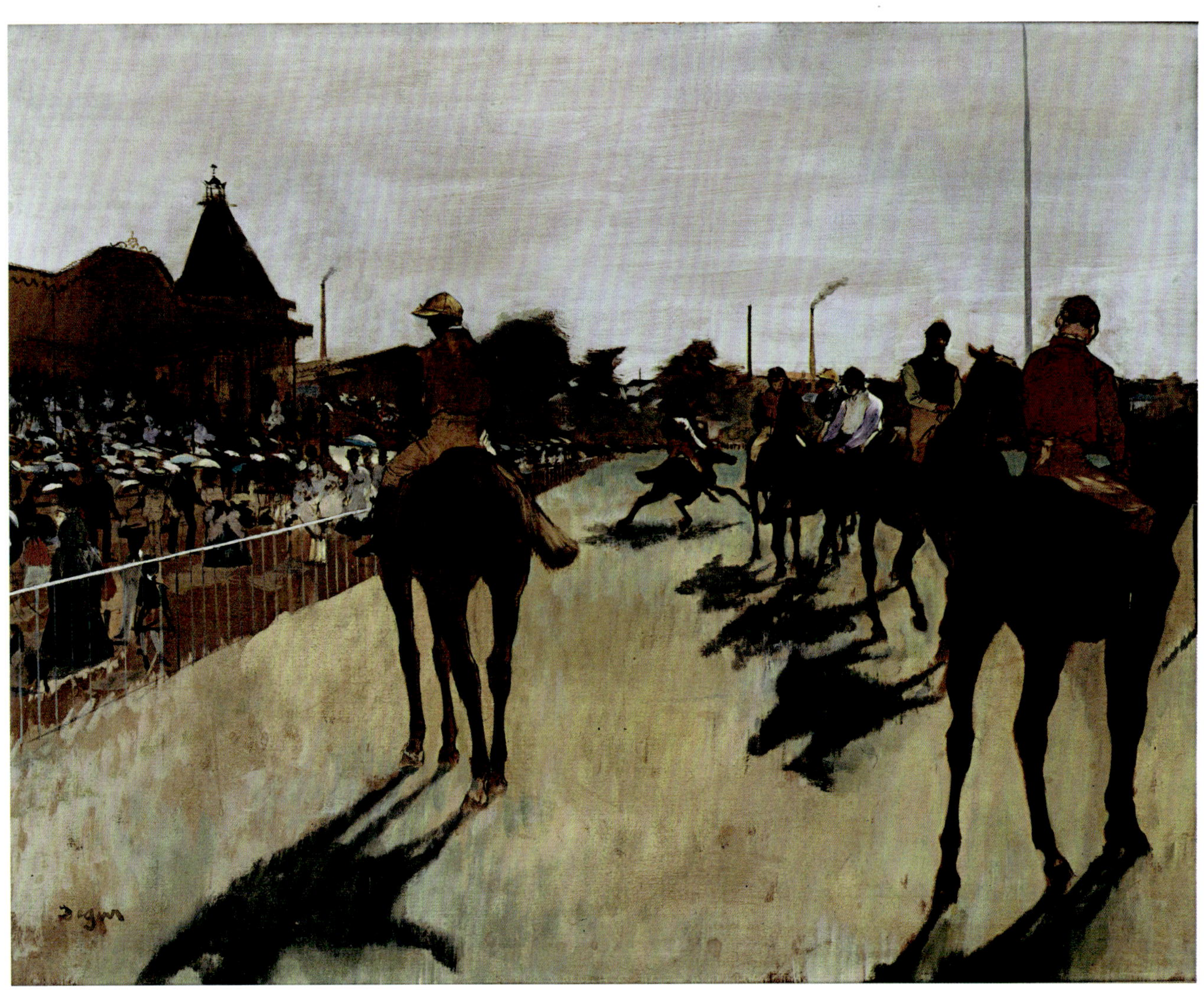

Edgar Degas (1834–1917)

The Parade *or* Race Horses in front of the Tribunes

Le Défilé *ou* Chevaux de courses devant les tribunes

Die Parade *oder* Rennpferde vor den Tribünen

El desfile *o* Caballos ante las gradas

La sfilata *o* Cavalli da corsa davanti alle tribune

De optocht *of* Renpaarden voor de tribunes

c. 1866–1868, Oil on paper on canvas/Huile sur papier sur toile, 46 × 61 cm

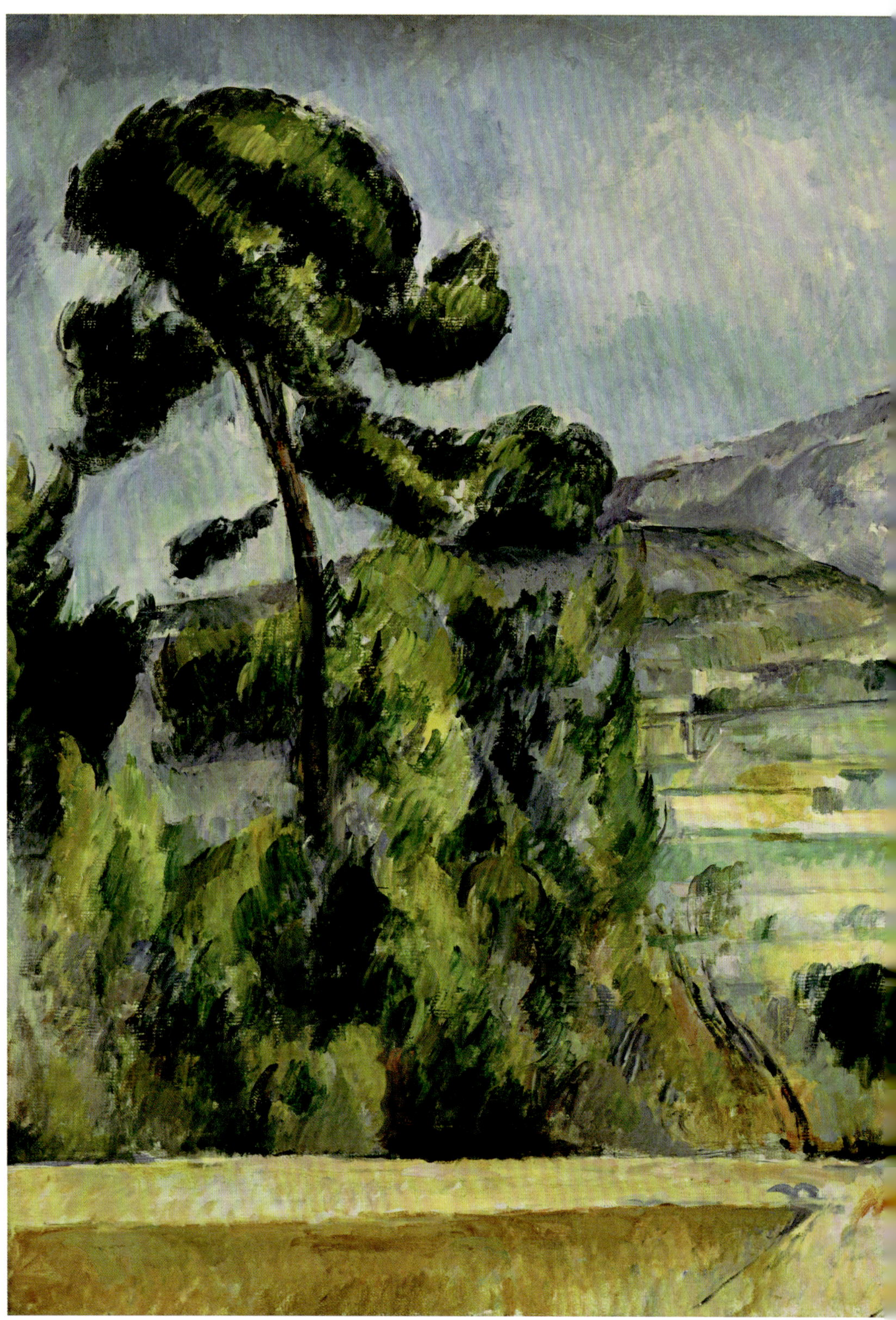

Paul Cézanne (1839–1906)

Mount Sainte-Victoire

Montagne Sainte-Victoire

Das Bergmassiv Sainte-Victoire

Montaña Sainte Victoire

La montagna Sainte-Victoire

De berg Sainte-Victoire

c. 1890, Oil on canvas/Huile
sur toile, 65 × 95,2 cm

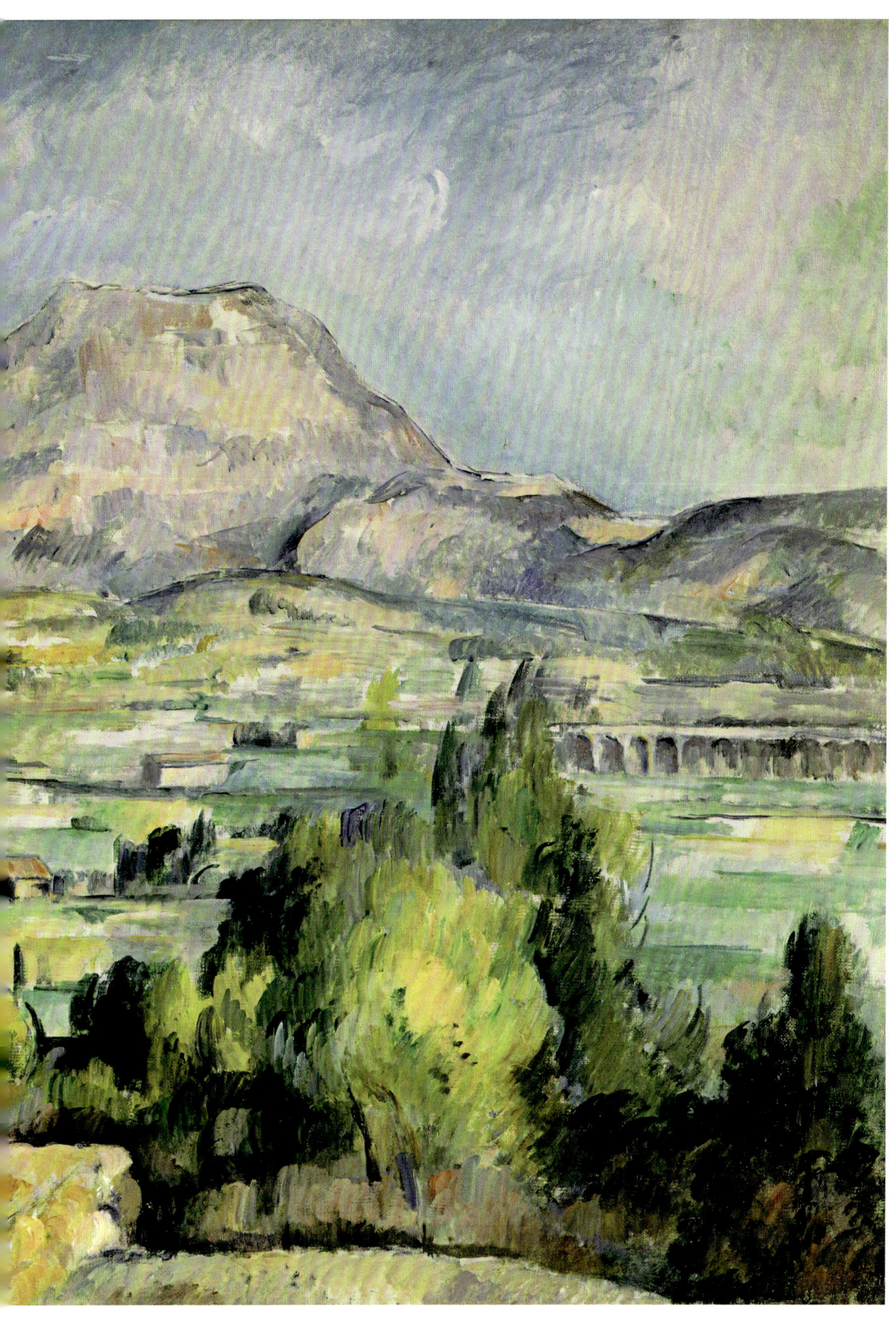

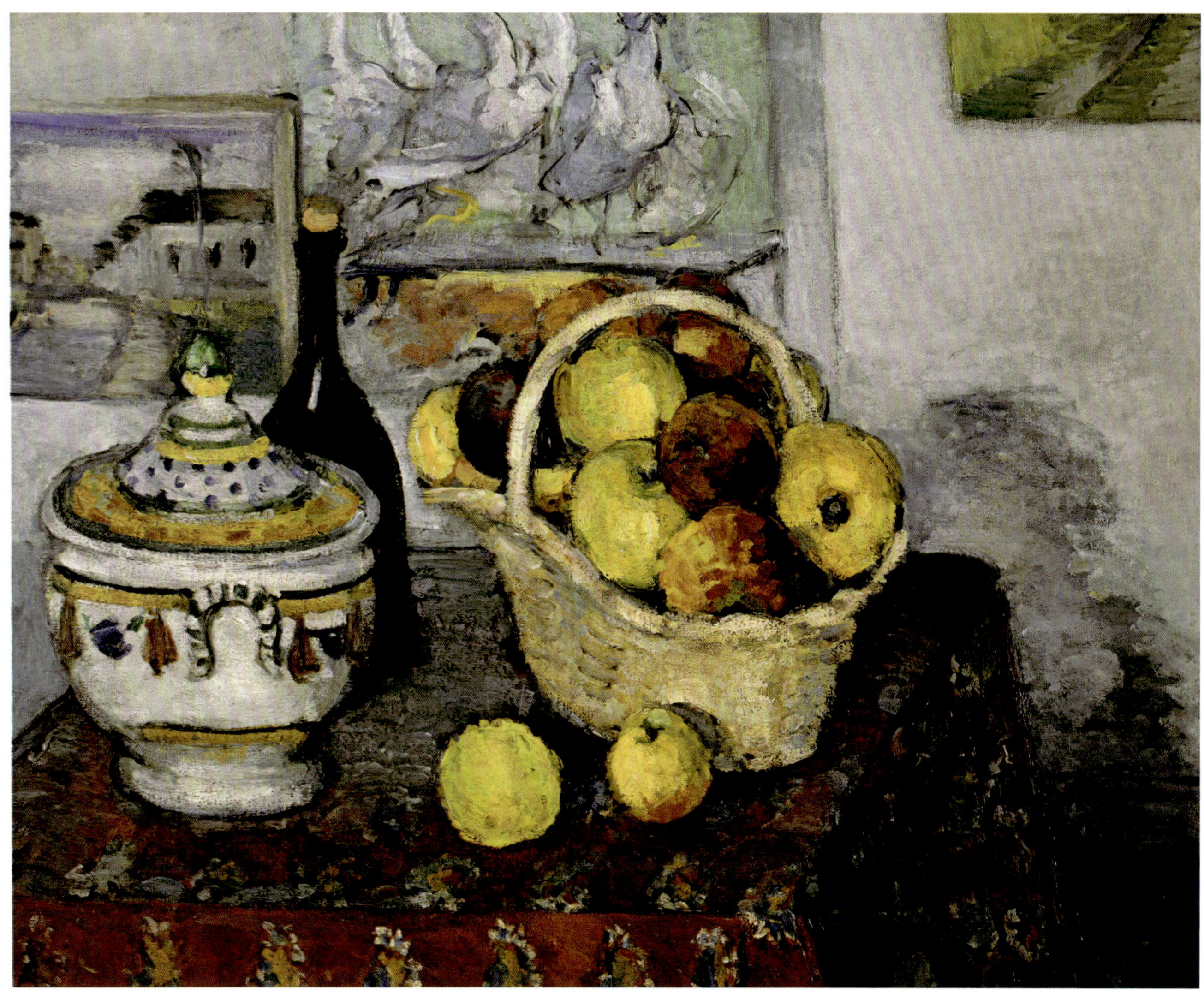

Paul Cézanne (1839–1906)

Still Life with Soup Tureen

Nature morte à la soupière

Stillleben mit Suppenschüssel

Naturaleza muerta con sopera

Natura morta con zuppiera

Stilleven met soepterrine

c. 1877, Oil on canvas/Huile sur toile, 65 × 81,5 cm

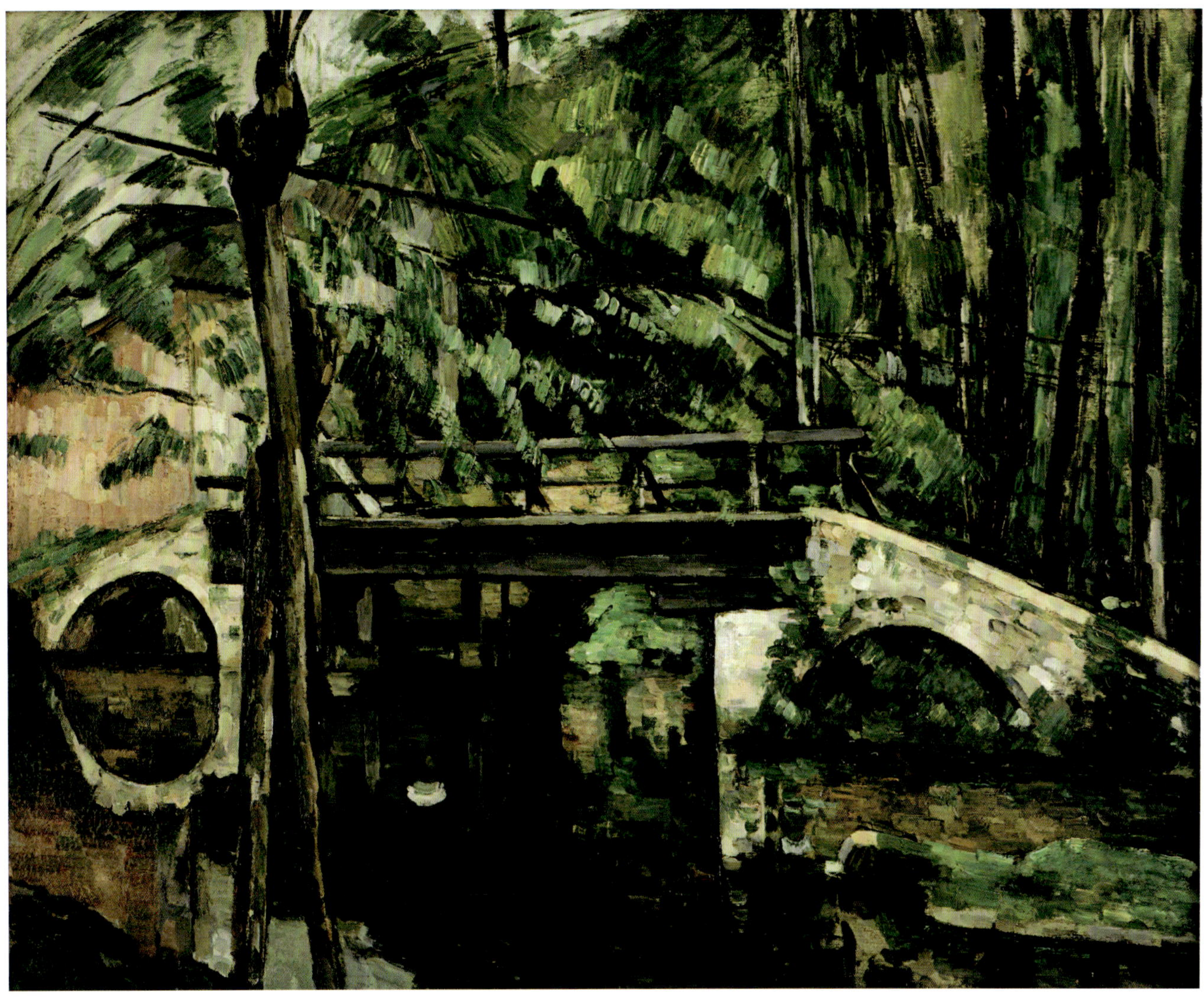

Paul Cézanne (1839–1906)

The Bridge at Maincy

Pont de Maincy

Brücke in Maincy

El puente de Maincy

Il Ponte di Maincy

De brug in Mancy

c. 1879, Oil on canvas/Huile sur toile, 58,4 × 72,4 cm

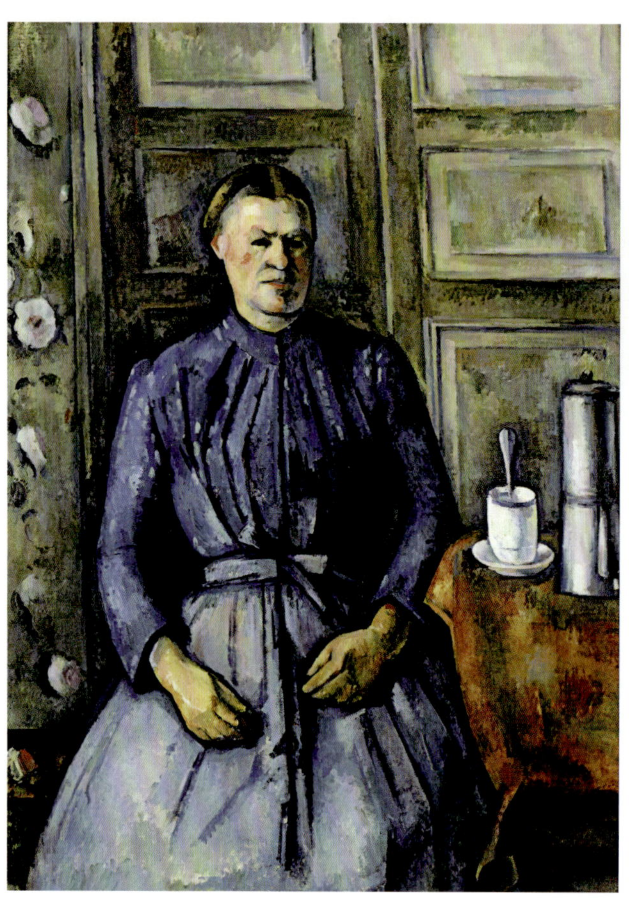

Paul Cézanne (1839–1906)

Woman with a Coffeepot

La Femme à la cafetière

Die Frau mit Kaffeekanne

La mujer con la cafetera

Donna con caffettiera

Vrouw met koffiepot

c. 1890–1895, Oil on canvas/Huile sur toile, 130 × 97 cm

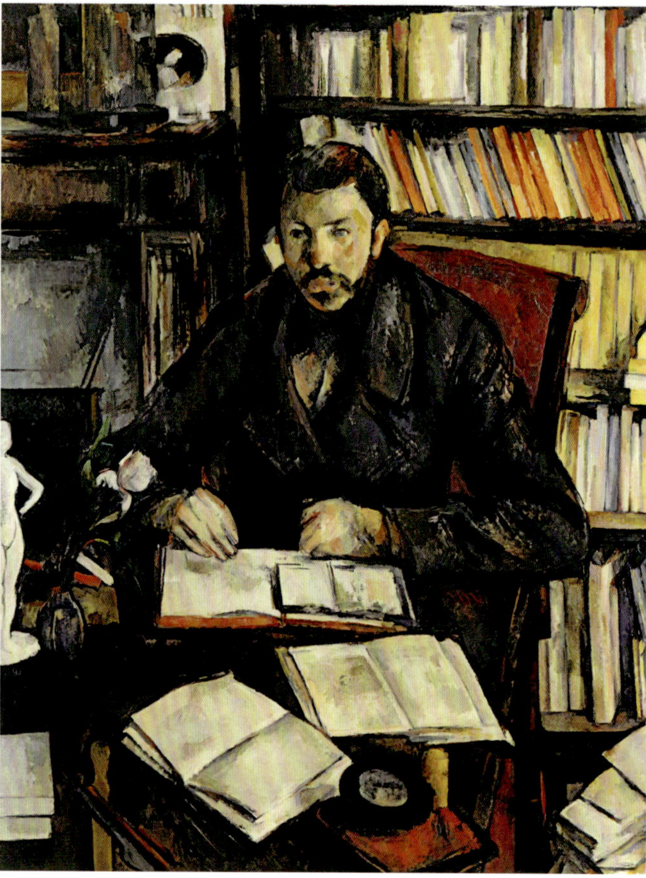

Paul Cézanne (1839–1906)

Gustave Geoffroy

c. 1895–1896, Oil on canvas/Huile sur toile, 117 × 89,5 cm

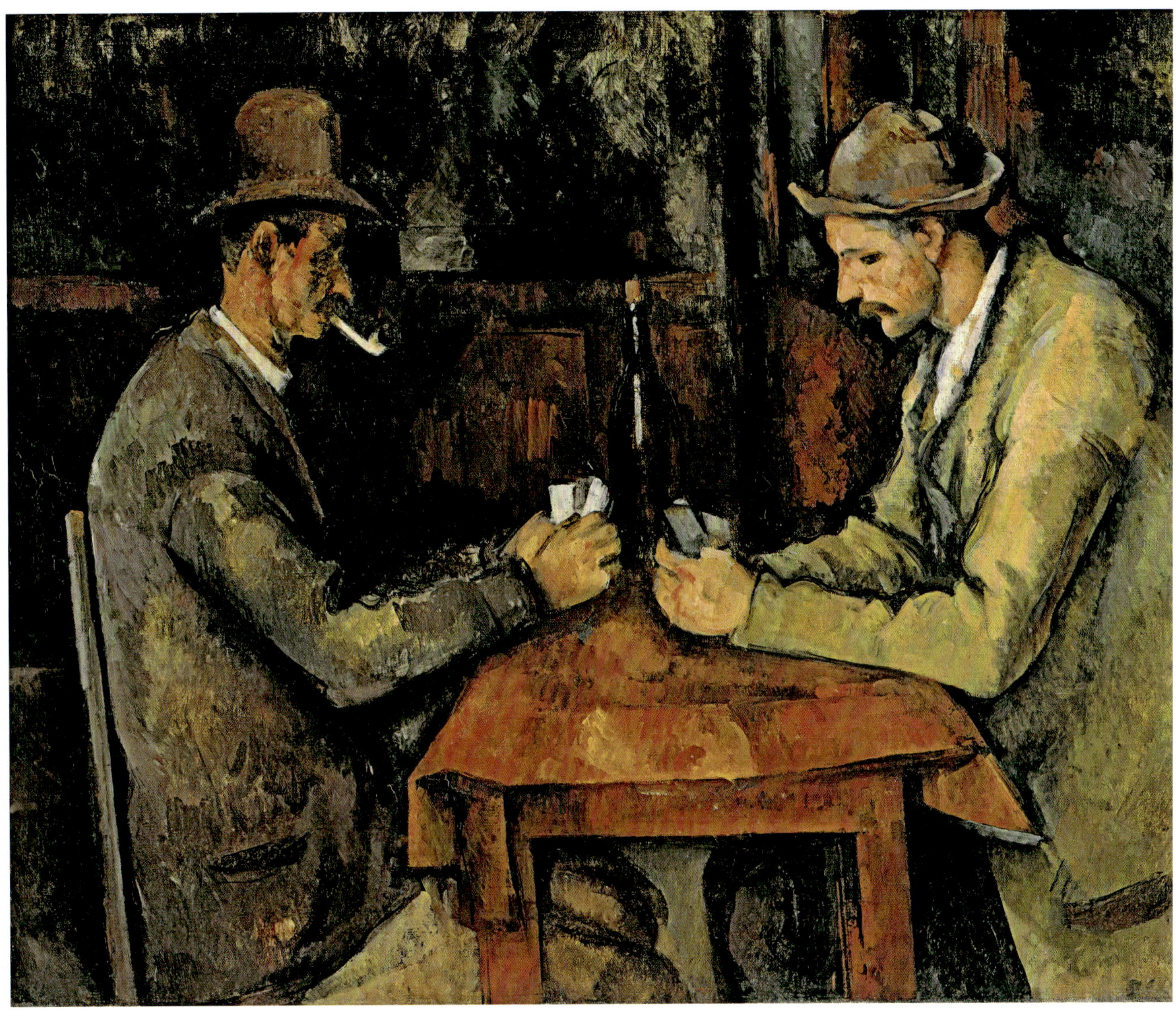

Paul Cézanne (1839–1906)

The Card Players

Les Joueurs de cartes

Die Kartenspieler

Los jugadores de cartas

I giocatori di carte

De kaartspelers

c. 1890–1895, Oil on canvas/Huile sur toile, 47 × 56,5 cm

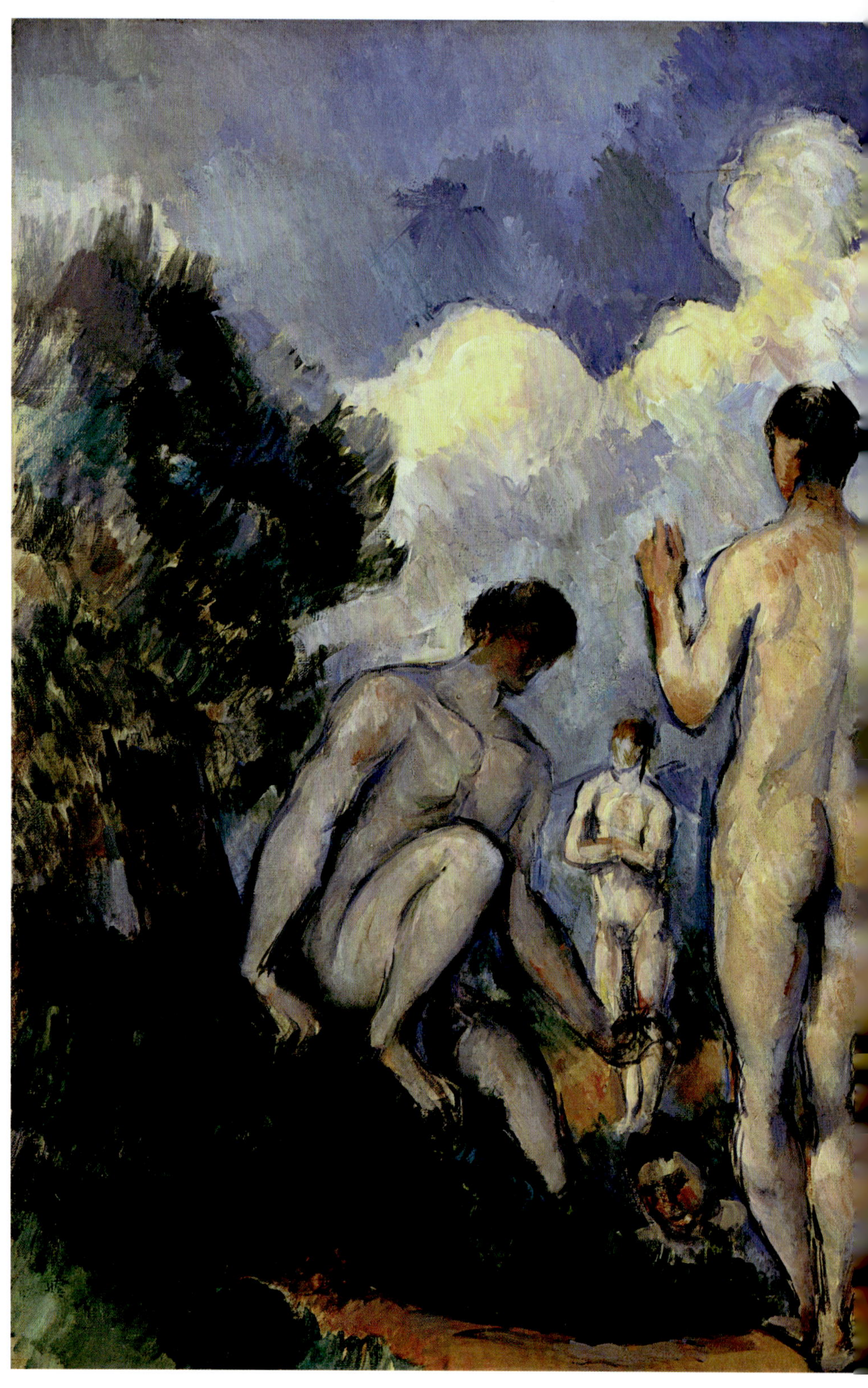

Paul Cézanne (1839–1906)

Bathers

Baigneurs

Badende

Bañistas

Bagnanti

Baders

c. 1890, Oil on canvas/Huile sur toile, 60,5 × 82,5 cm

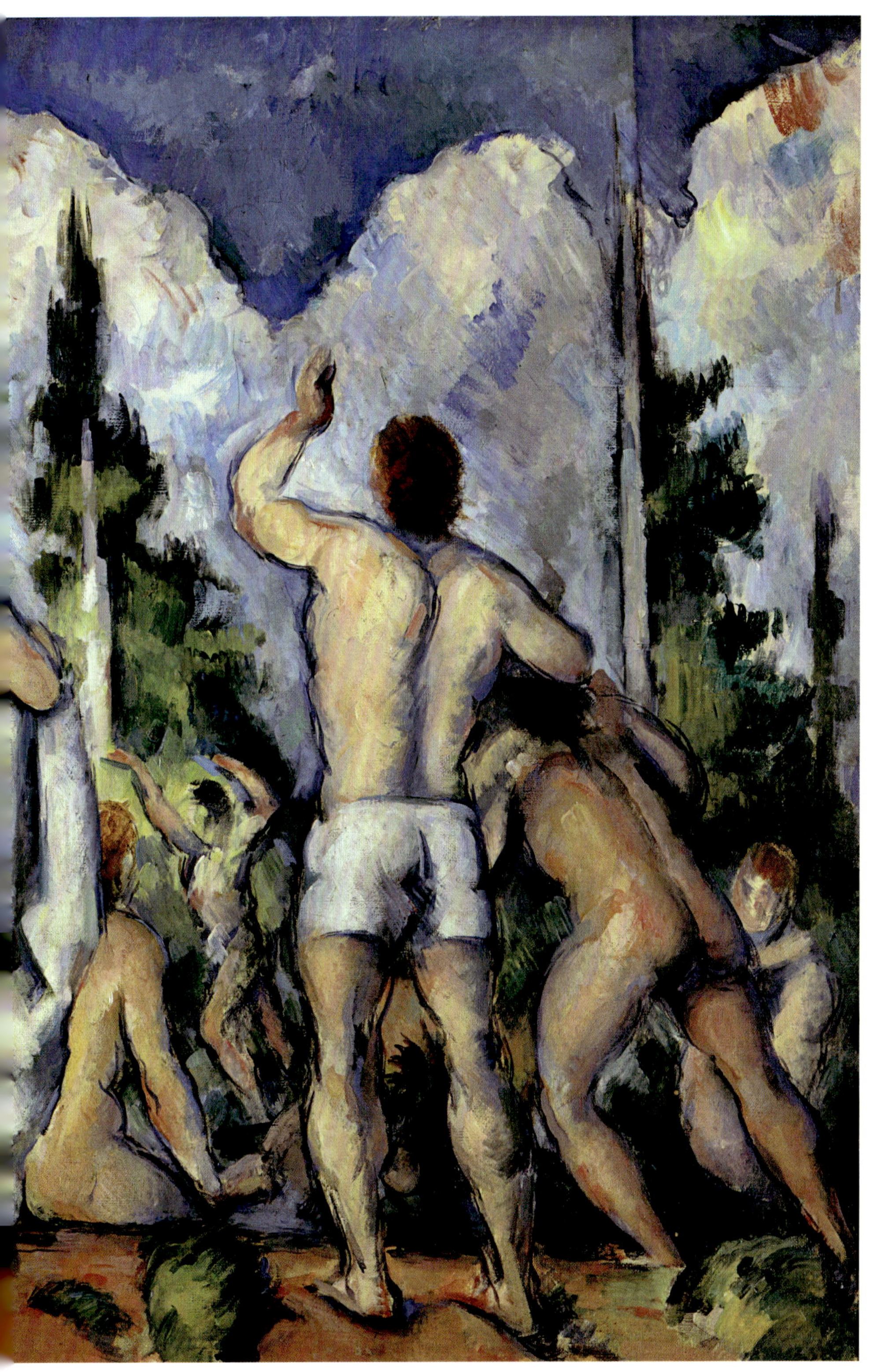

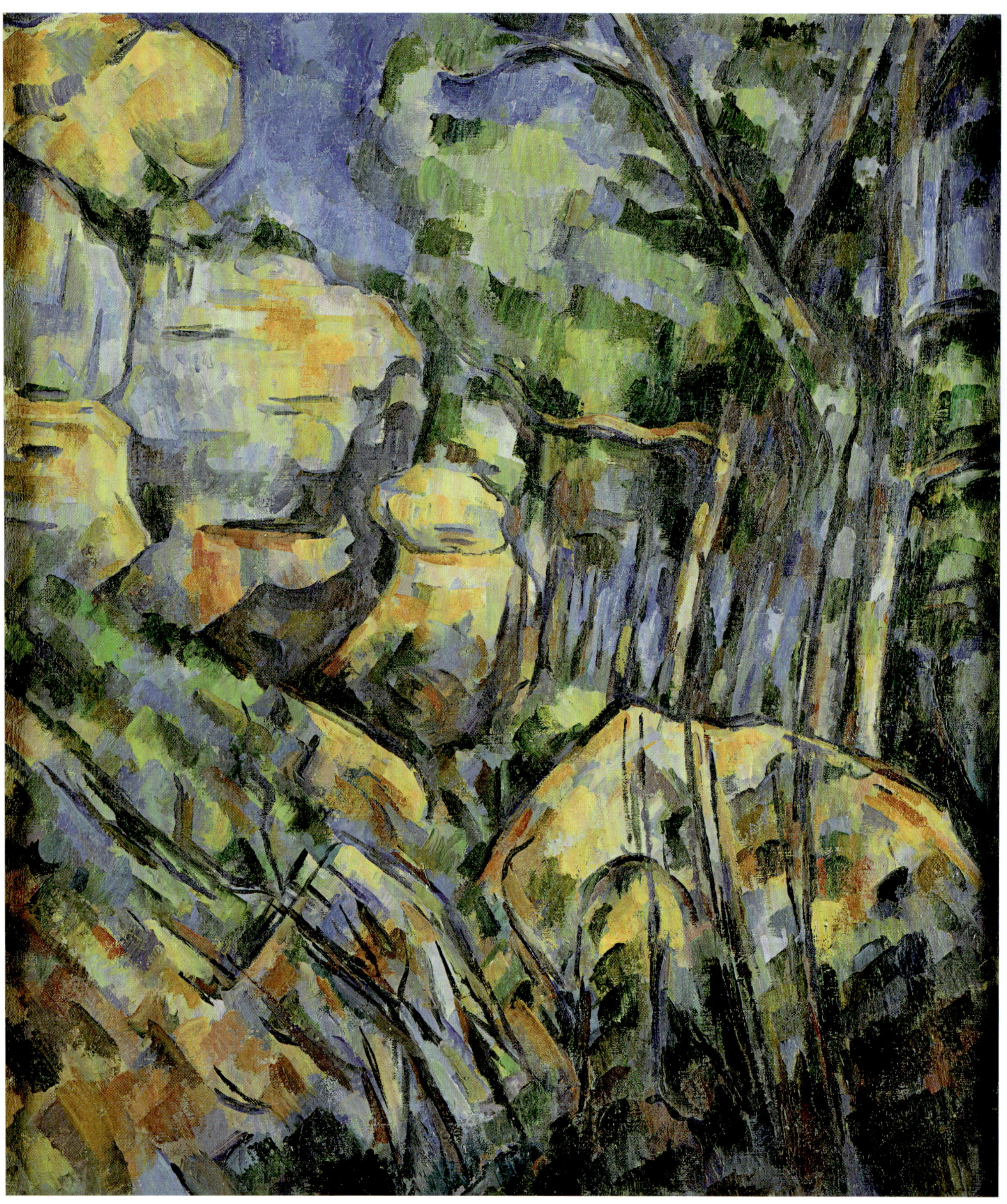

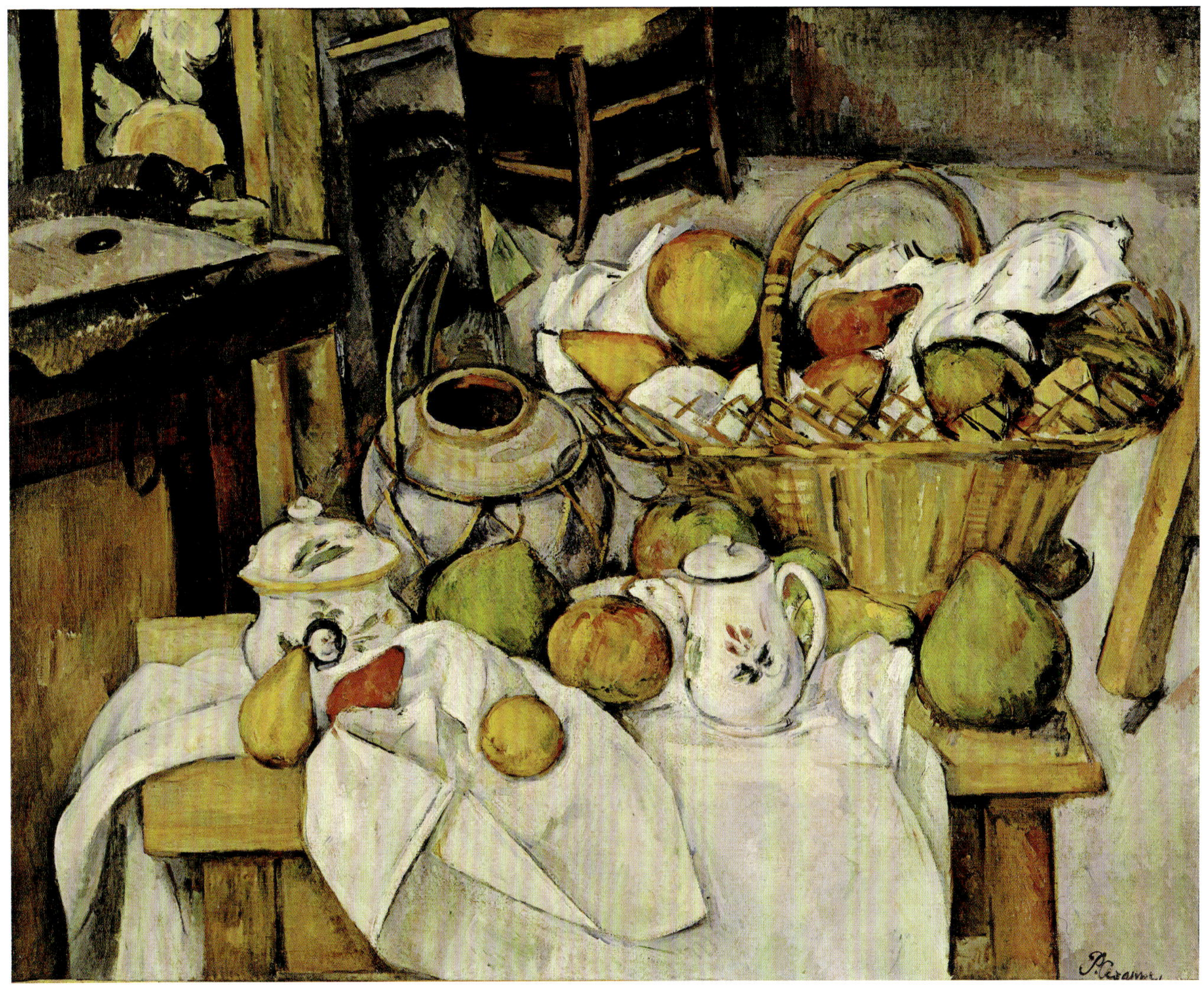

Paul Cézanne (1839–1906)
Kitchen Table
La Table de cuisine
Der Küchentisch
La mesa de la cocina
Il Tavolo da cucina
De keukentafel
c. 1888–1890, Oil on canvas/Huile sur toile, 65 × 81,5 cm

Paul Cézanne (1839–1906)
Rocks near the Caves above Château Noir
Rochers près des grottes au-dessus du Château-Noir
Felsen bei den Höhlen oberhalb des Château Noir
Rocas por encima del Château Noir
Rocce sopra lo Château-Noir
Rotsen bij de grotten boven het Château-Noir
c. 1904, Oil on canvas/Huile sur toile, 65,5 × 54,5 cm

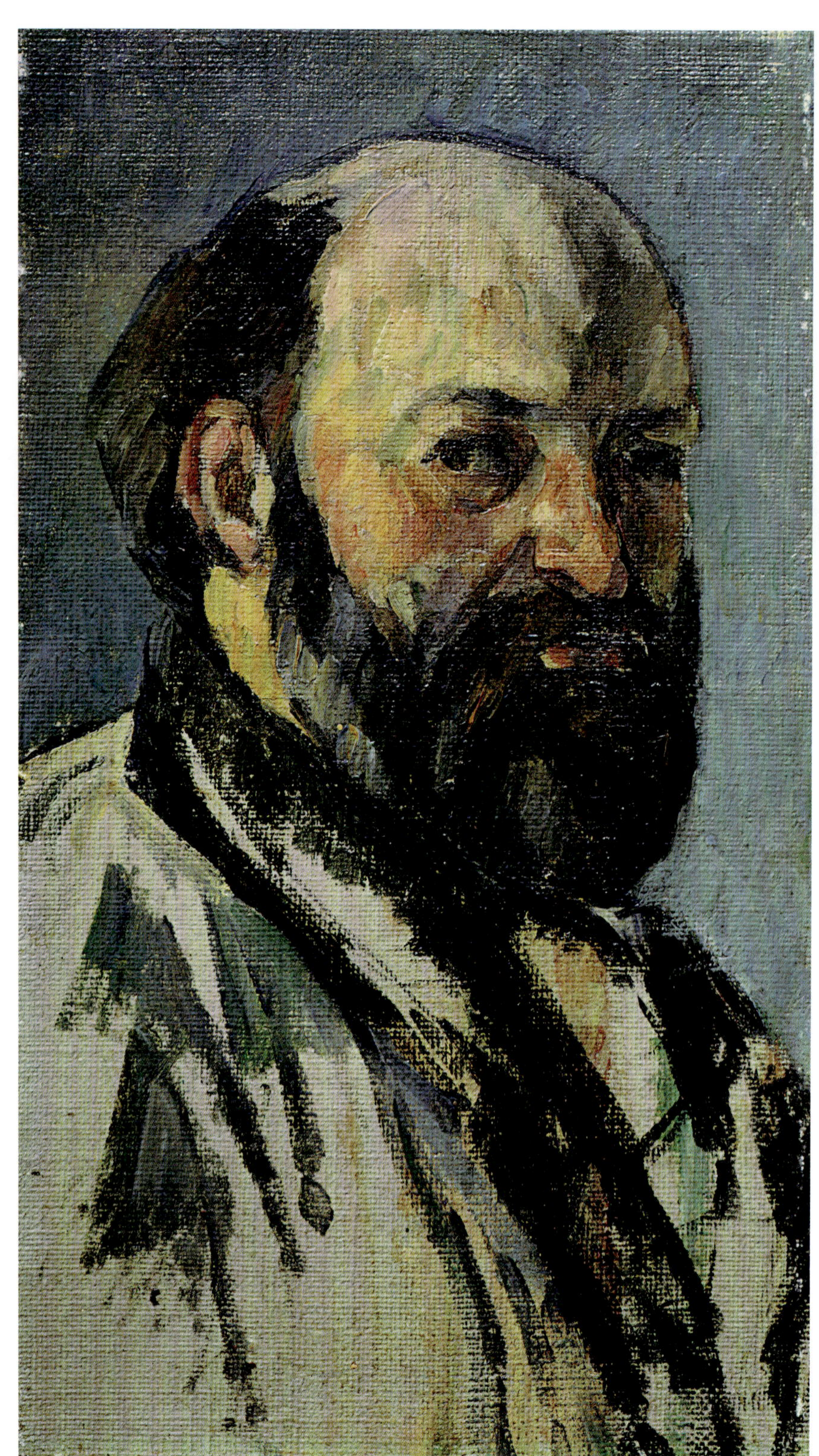

Paul Cézanne (1839–1906)
Self Portrait
Portrait de l'artiste
Selbstbildnis
Autorretrato
Autoritratto
Portret van de kunstenaar
c. 1877, Oil on canvas/
Huile sur toile, 25 × 14 cm

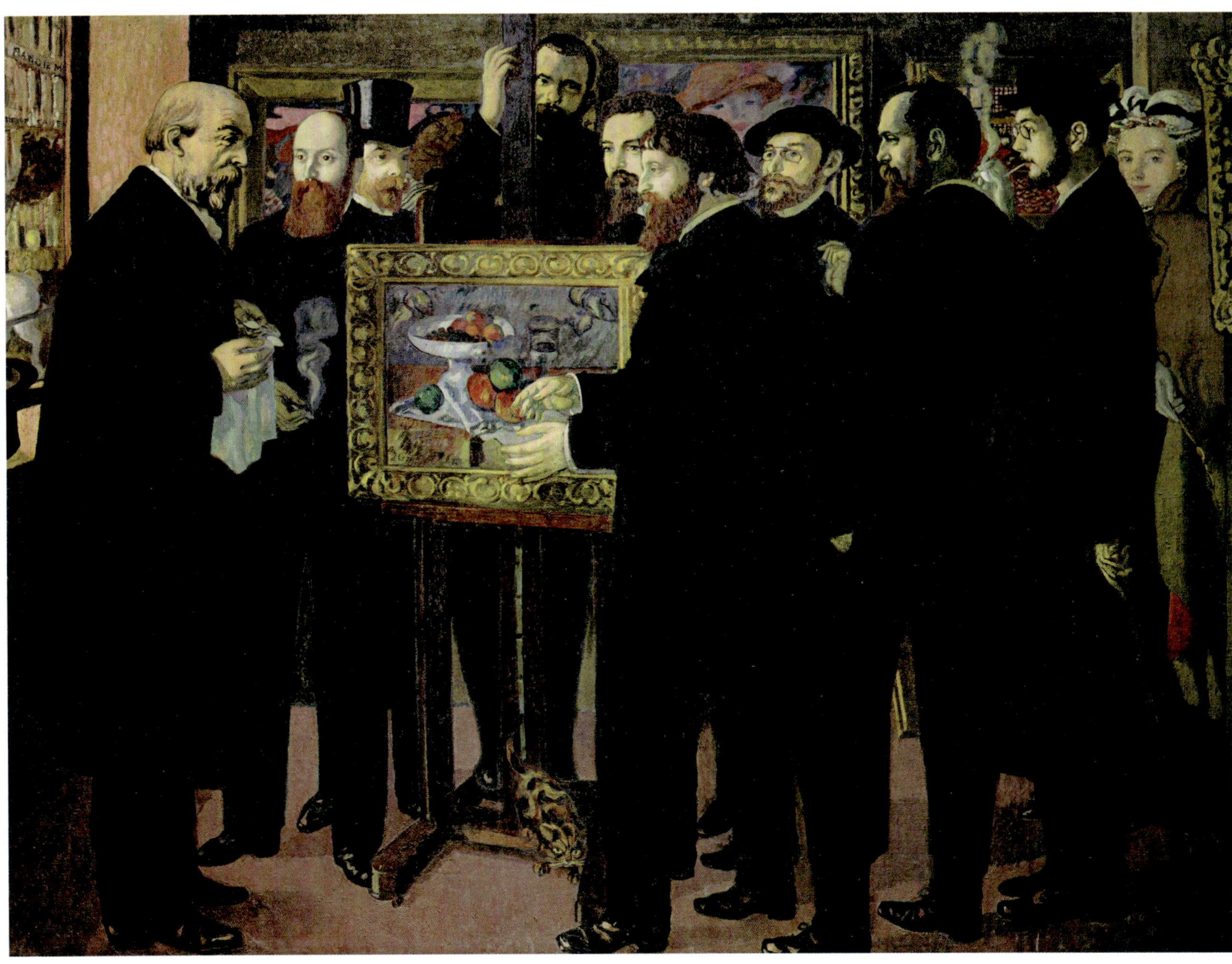

Maurice Denis (1870–1943)

Homage to Cézanne

Hommage à Paul Cézanne

Hommage an Paul Cézanne

Homenaje a Paul Cézanne

Omaggio a Cézanne

Hommage aan Paul Cézanne

1900, Oil on canvas/Huile sur toile, 182 × 243,5 cm

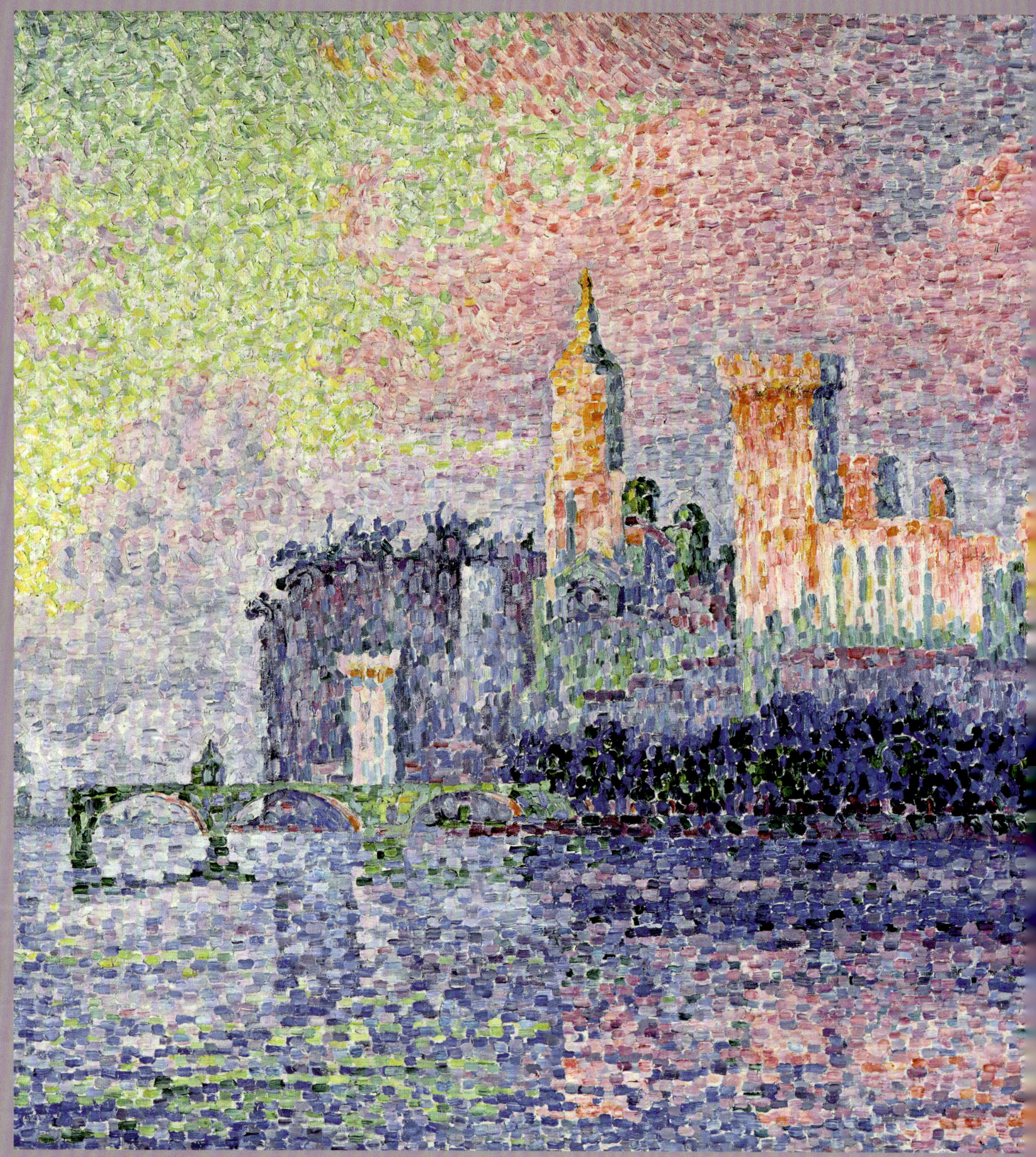

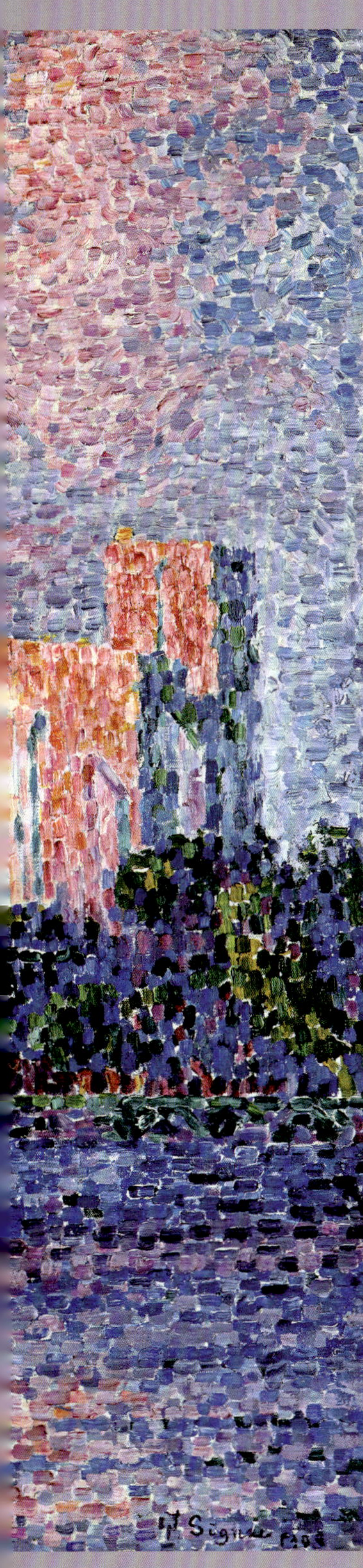

Postimpressionism

New trends emerged around 1886: neo-impressionism under the brush of Seurat, Signac or Cross, adepts of pointillism, and synthetism (or cloisonnism) developed at Pont-Aven by Gauguin, Sérusier and Bernard. At the same time, van Gogh was to impose his own style through landscapes and portraits, their expressiveness arising from a heavy and feverish touch.

Postimpressionnisme

Vers 1886, deux nouvelles tendances se dessinent, le néo-impressionnisme sous le pinceau de Seurat, Signac ou Cross, adeptes du pointillisme, et le synthétisme – ou cloisonnisme –, développé à Pont-Aven par Gauguin, Sérusier et Bernard. En parallèle, van Gogh va imposer son propre style, au travers de paysages et de portraits dont l'expressivité naît d'une touche épaisse et fiévreuse.

Postimpressionismus

Um 1886 zeichnen sich zwei neue Tendenzen ab: der Neoimpressionismus unter der Pinselführung von Seurat, Signac und Cross, allesamt Anhänger des Pointillismus, und der Synthetismus – oder Cloisonismus –, der in Pont-Aven durch Gauguin, Sérusier und Bernard entwickelt wird. Parallel dazu setzt van Gogh mit Landschaftsgemälden und Porträts, deren Ausdruckskraft durch eine dicke und unruhige Pinselführung erzielt wird, seinen eigenen Stil durch.

Postimpresionismo

Alrededor de 1886, surgen dos nuevas tendencias, el neoimpresionismo bajo el pincel de Seurat, Signac y Cross, seguidores del puntillismo, y el sintetismo – o cloisonismo – desarrollado en Pont-Aven por Gauguin, Sérusier y Bernard. En paralelo, van Gogh va a imponer su propio estilo, a través de paisajes y retratos cuya expresividad nace con una pincelada gruesa y frenética.

Post-Impressionismo

Intorno al 1886 emersero due nuove tendenze: il Neoimpressionismo, di cui furono esponenti Seurat, Signac e Cross, seguaci del Puntinismo, e il Sintetismo (o *Cloisonnisme*), sviluppato a Pont-Aven da Gauguin, Sérusier e Bernard. Nel frattempo, van Gogh impose il suo stile personale mediante paesaggi e ritratti la cui espressività era ottenuta mediante pennellate spesse e febbrili.

Postimpressionisme

Omstreeks 1886 raken twee nieuwe stijlen in zwang: het neo-impressionisme van Seurat, Signac en Cross, die het pointillisme aanhangen, en het synthetisme of cloisonnisme dat in Pont-Aven door Gauguin, Sérusier en Bernard werd ontwikkeld. Tegelijkertijd imponeert van Gogh met landschappen en portretten in een heel eigen stijl die zijn expressiviteit aan een dikke, nerveuze penseeltoets ontleent.

Paul Signac (1863–1935)
The Castle of the Popes
Le Château des Papes
Papstpalast in Avignon
El castillo de los Papas
Il Palazzo dei Papi
Het pauselijk npaleis in Avignon
1909, Oil on canvas/Huile sur toile, 73,3 × 91,9 cm

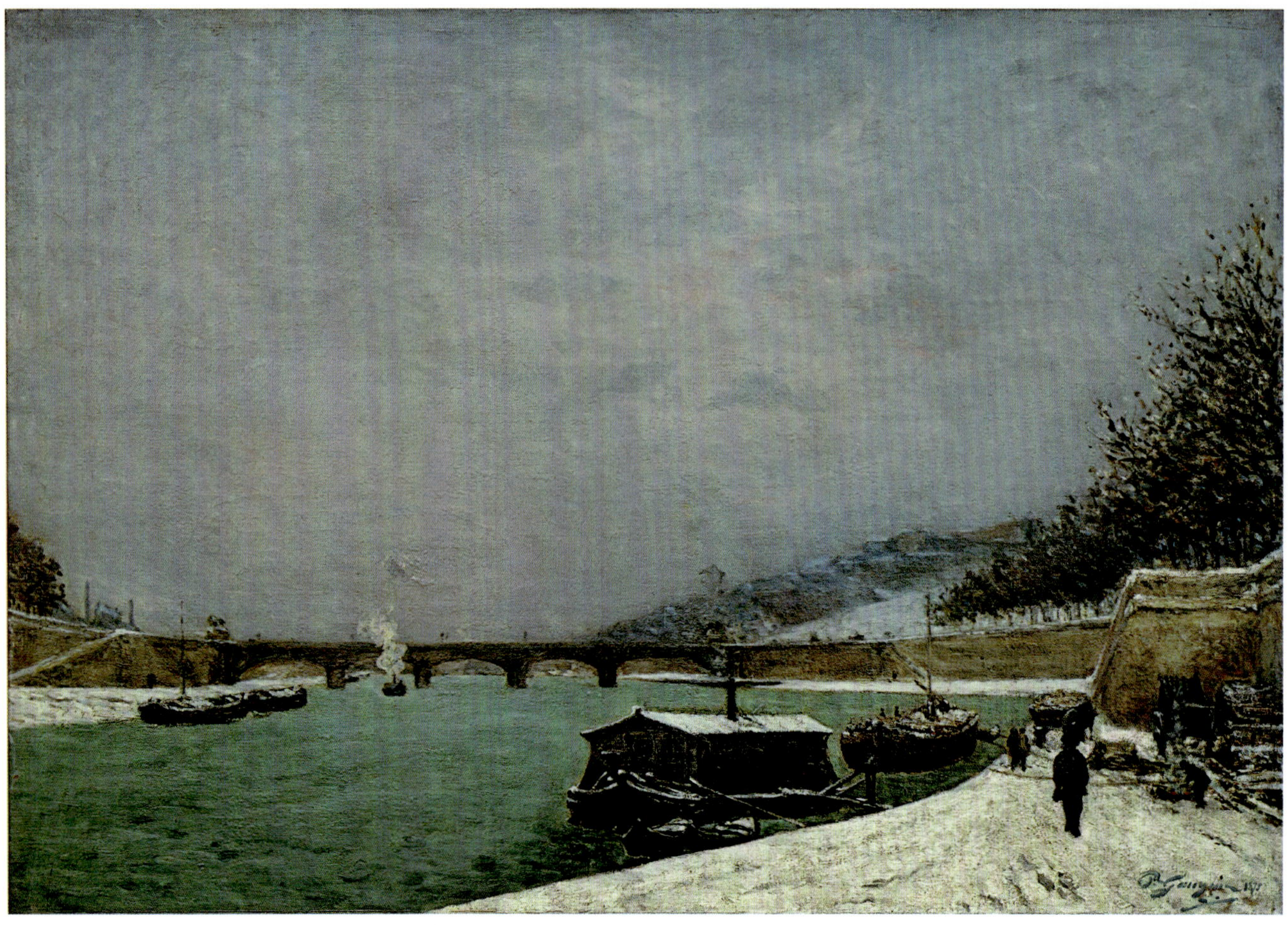

Paul Gauguin (1848–1903)

The Seine at the Pont d'Iéna. Snowy Weather
La Seine au pont d'Iéna. Temps de neige
1875, Oil on canvas/Huile sur toile, 65,4 × 92,4 cm

Die Seine beim Pont d'Iéna im Winter
El Sena en el puente de Jena. Tiempo de nieve

La Senna al ponte di Jena. Tempo nevoso
De Seine bij de Pont d'Iéna in de winter

Who could guess that this is a painting by Paul Gauguin? We are in 1875, about more than ten years prior to the invention of synthetism at Pont Aven. Gauguin has just started painting, after having met Camille Pissarro and joined the impressionist group. This beautiful view of the snow-covered riverbanks of the Seine owes to their outline, the application of a fragmented touch, and the regard paid to the landscape as well as the atmospheric conditions.

Qui pourrait deviner qu'il s'agit là d'une toile de Paul Gauguin ? Nous sommes en 1875, soit plus de dix ans avant l'invention du synthétisme à Pont-Aven. Gauguin vient de se mettre à la peinture, après avoir fait la connaissance de Camille Pissarro et s'être rapproché du groupe des impressionnistes. Cette très belle vue des bords de Seine sous la neige s'inscrit d'ailleurs pleinement dans leur lignée, par l'usage d'une touche fragmentée, et l'intérêt porté à la fois au paysage et aux conditions atmosphériques.

Wer könnte erraten, dass es sich hier um ein Gemälde von Paul Gauguin handelt? Wir befinden uns im Jahr 1875, also mehr als zehn Jahre vor der Entstehung des Synthetismus in Pont-Aven. Gauguin beginnt mit der Malerei, nachdem er Camille Pissarro kennengelernt und sich der Gruppe der Impressionisten angenähert hat. Dieser sehr schöne Blick auf das verschneite Seine-Ufer entspricht ihnen im Übrigen vollends durch die kurzen Pinselstriche und das Interesse für Landschaft und Witterungsverhältnisse.

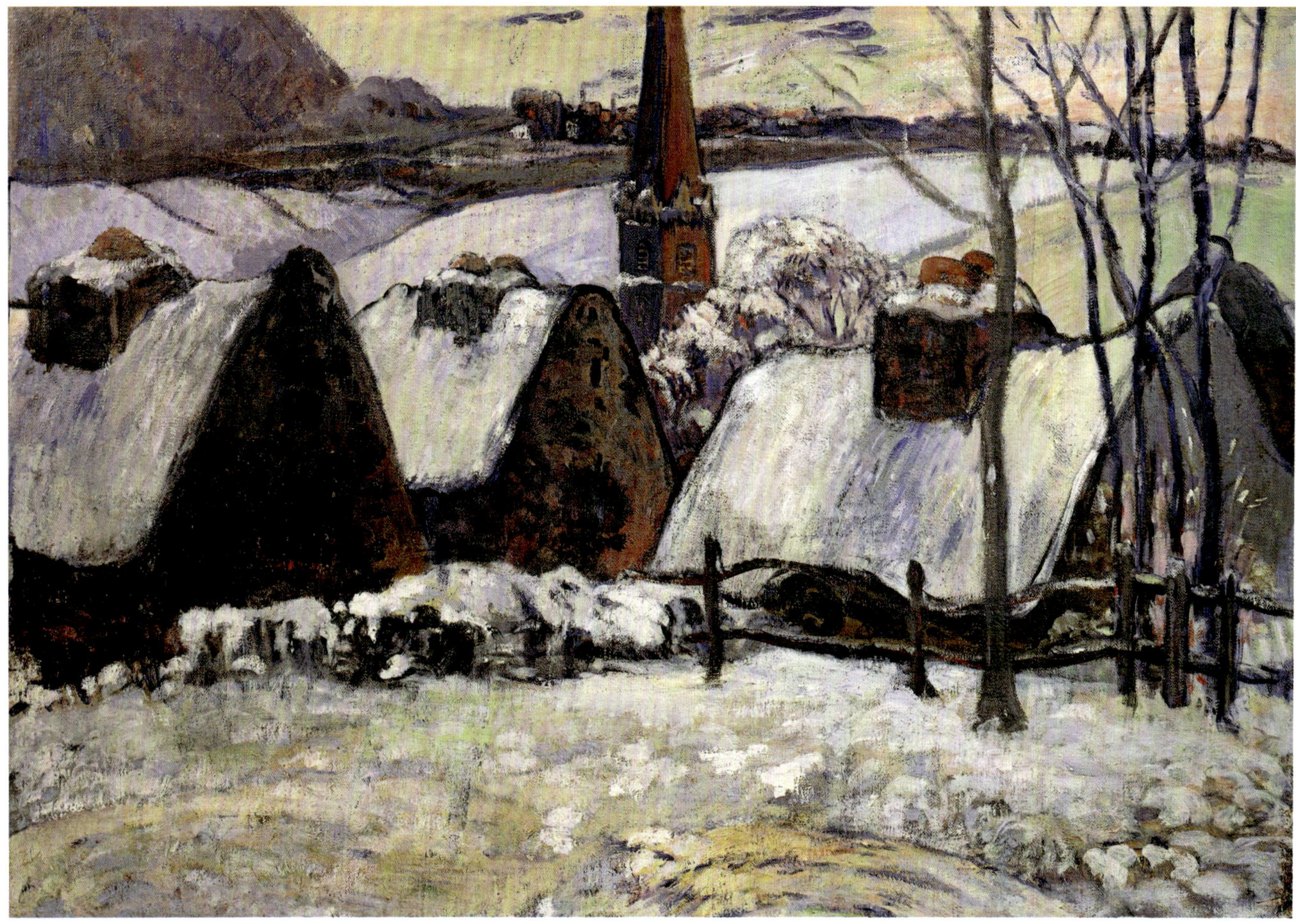

Paul Gauguin (1848–1903)

Breton Village in the Snow　　　Bretonisches Dorf im Schnee　　　Villaggio bretone sotto la neve

Village breton sous la neige　　　Pueblo bretón bajo la nieve　　　Bretons dorp in de sneeuw

c. 1894, Oil on canvas/Huile sur toile, 62 × 87 cm

¿Quién podría adivinar que se trata de un cuadro de Paul Gauguin? Estamos en 1875, más de diez años antes de la invención del sintetismo en Pont-Aven. Gauguin acaba de empezar con la pintura, después de conocer a Camille Pissarro y de acercarse al grupo impresionista. Esta hermosa vista del río Sena en la nieve está totalmente alineada con su estilo, por el uso de la pincelada fragmentada y el interés tanto por el paisaje como por las condiciones atmosféricas.

Chi direbbe che si tratta di un dipinto di Paul Gauguin? Siamo nel 1875, più di dieci anni prima dell'invenzione del Sintetismo a Pont-Aven. Gauguin ha appena iniziato a dipingere dopo l'incontro con Camille Pissarro e l'avvicinamento al gruppo degli impressionisti. Questa splendida vista della Senna sotto la neve segue pienamente il loro stile in virtù dell'uso di pennellate frammentate e dell'interesse mostrato sia per paesaggio sia per le condizioni atmosferiche.

Wie had kunnen denken dat dit een doek van Paul Gauguin is? We schrijven 1875, tien jaar na de uitvinding van het synthetisme in Pont-Aven. Gauguin is net begonnen te schilderen, nadat hij kennis heeft gemaakt met Camille Pissarro en toenadering tot de groep impressionisten heeft gezocht. Door het gebruik van korte kwaststreken en de waarde die zij toekennen aan landschap en weersomstandigheden, is dit prachtige zicht op de besneeuwde Seine-oevers overigens volledig in hun lijn.

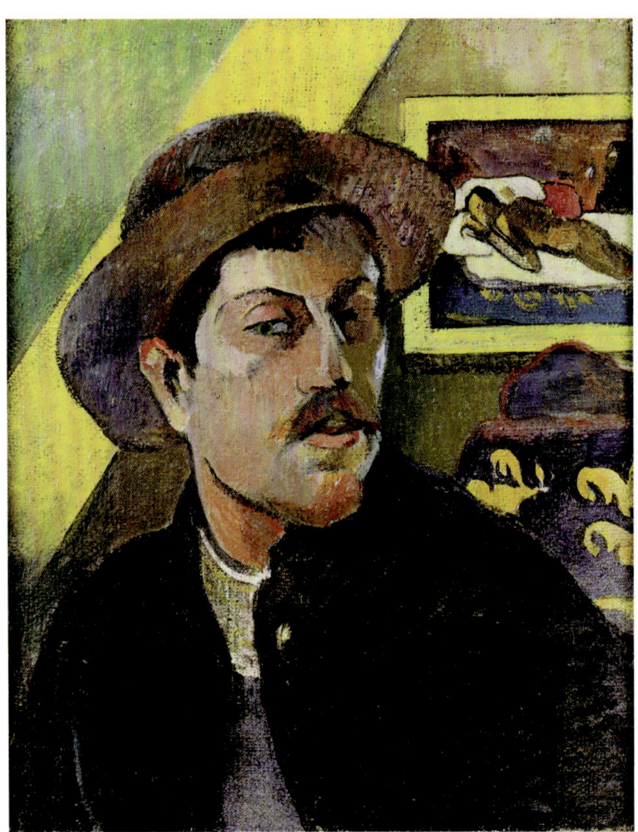

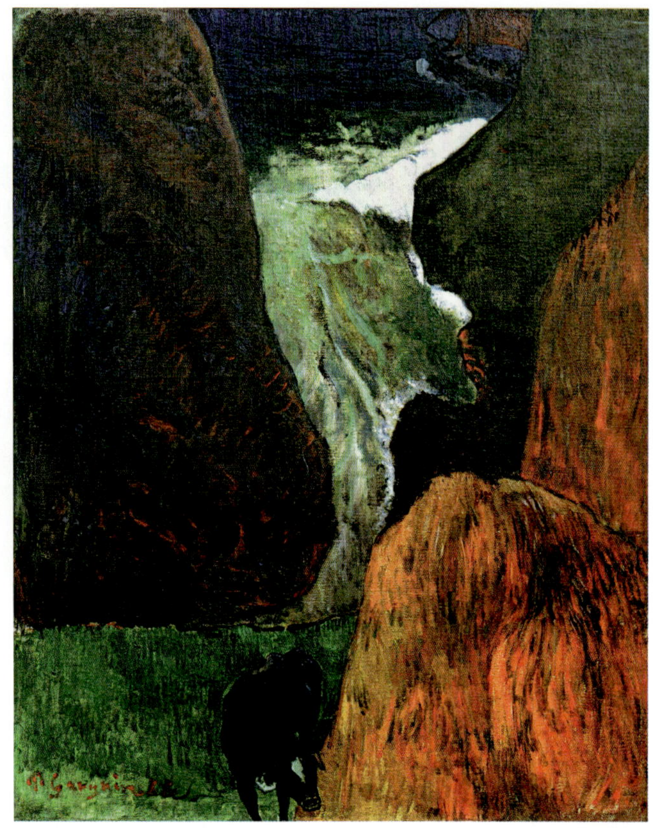

Paul Gauguin (1848–1903)

Self Portrait

Portrait de l'artiste

Selbstbildnis

Autorretrato

Autoritratto

Portret van de kunstenaar

c. 1893–1894, Oil on canvas, double-sided/Huile sur toile
double face, 46 × 38 cm (verso: *William Molard*)

Paul Gauguin (1848–1903)

Seascape with Cow

Marine avec vache

Landschaft mit Kuh zwischen Klippen

Marina con vaca

Paesaggio marino con mucca

Zeegezicht met koe

1888, Oil on canvas/Huile sur toile, 72,5 × 61 cm

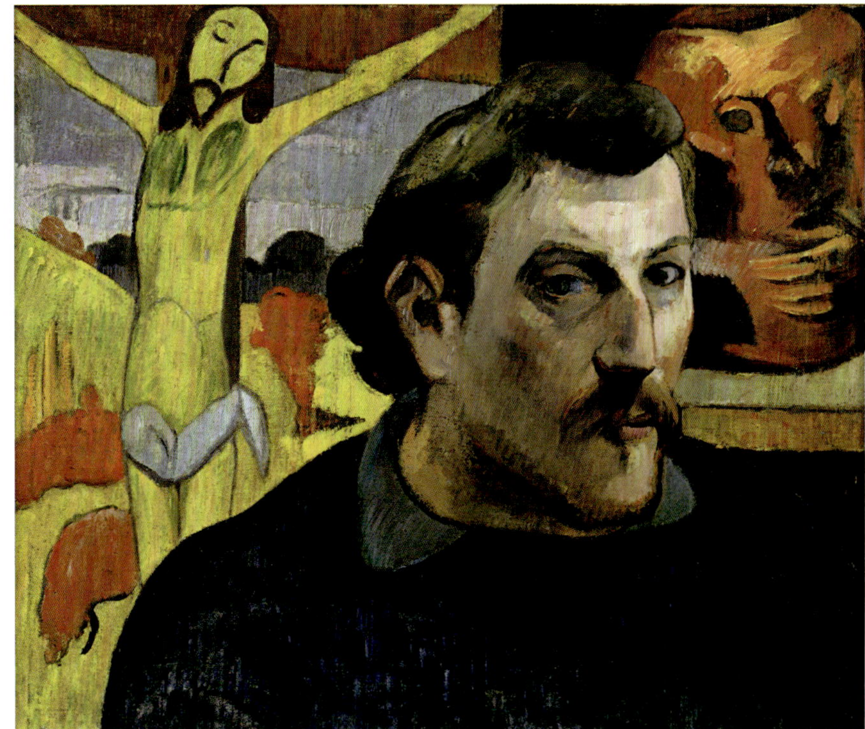

Paul Gauguin (1848–1903)

Self-Portrait with
Yellow Christ

Portrait de l'artiste
au Christ jaune

Selbstbildnis mit dem
gelben Christus

Autorretrato con
Cristo amarillo

Autoritratto con
Cristo giallo

Portret van de kunstenaar
met gele Christus

c. 1890–1891, Oil on canvas/
Huile sur toile, 38 × 46 cm

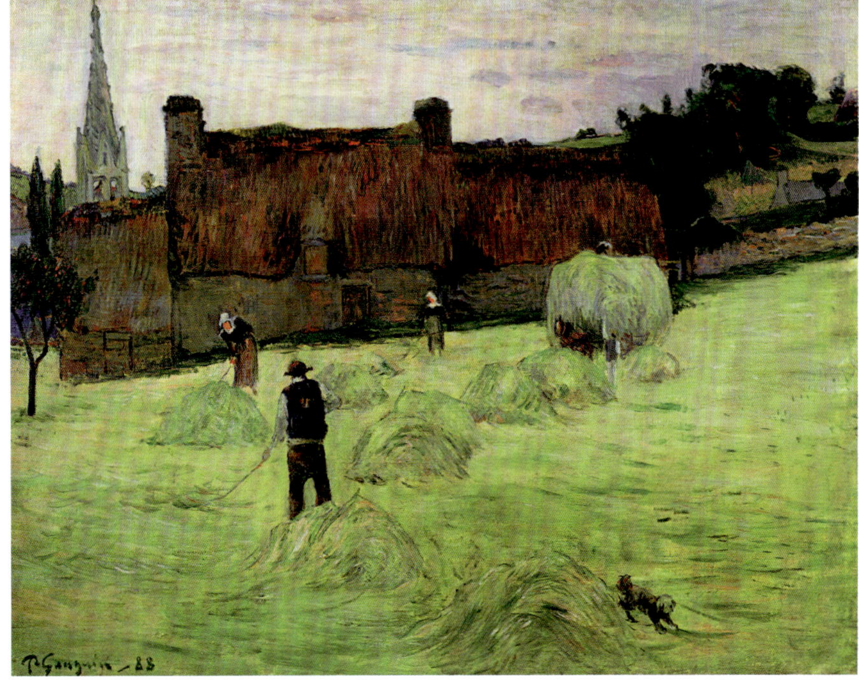

Paul Gauguin (1848–1903)

Haymaking in Brittany

La Fenaison en Bretagne

Heuernte in der Bretagne

Siega del heno en Bretaña

La raccolta del fieno
in Bretagna

Hooien in Bretagne

1888, Oil on canvas, double-
sided/Huile sur toile double
face, 72 × 92 cm (verso:
Bouquet of Flowers with a
Window Open to the Sea/
Bouquet de fleurs devant une
fenêtre ouverte sur la mer)

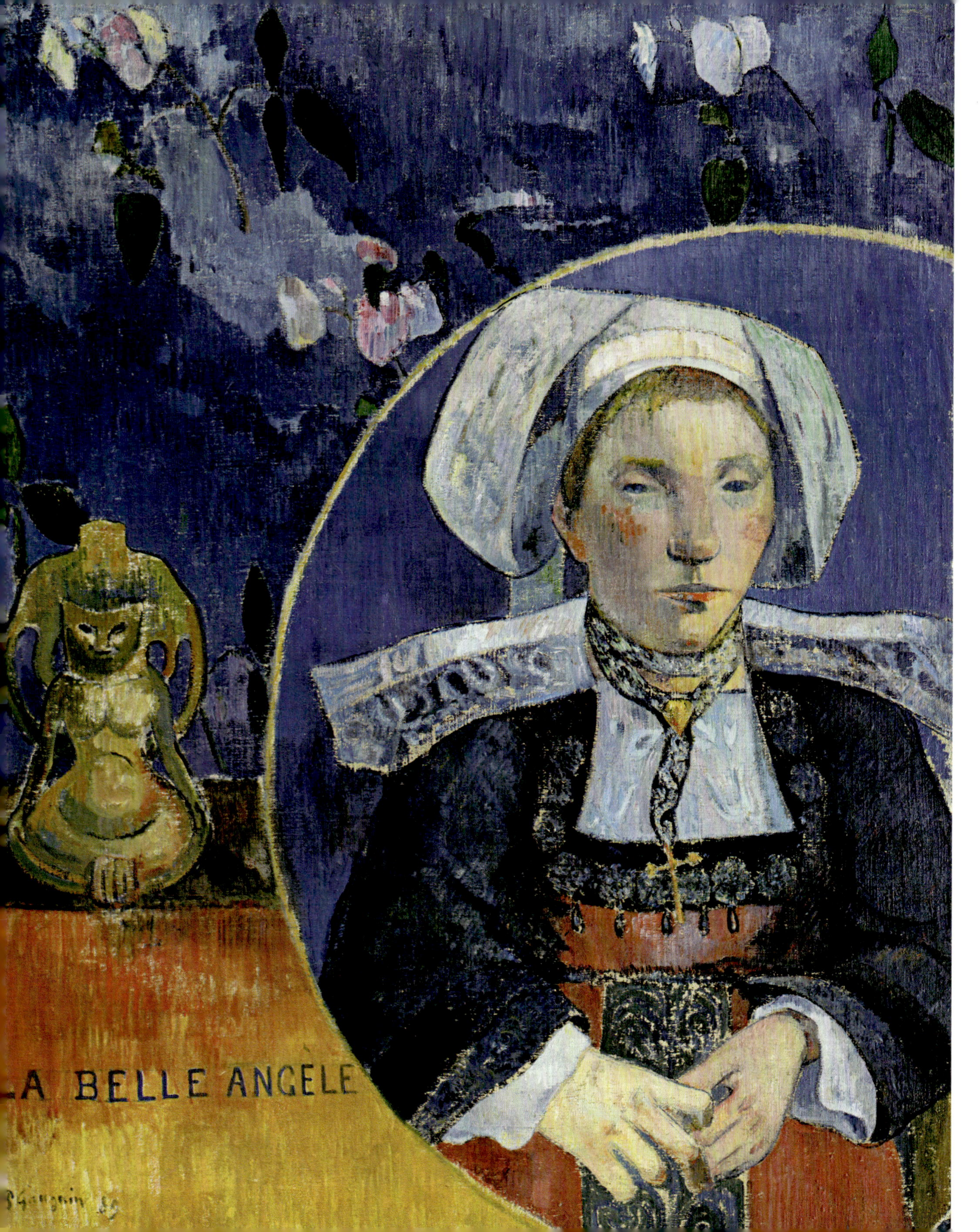

LA BELLE ANGÈLE

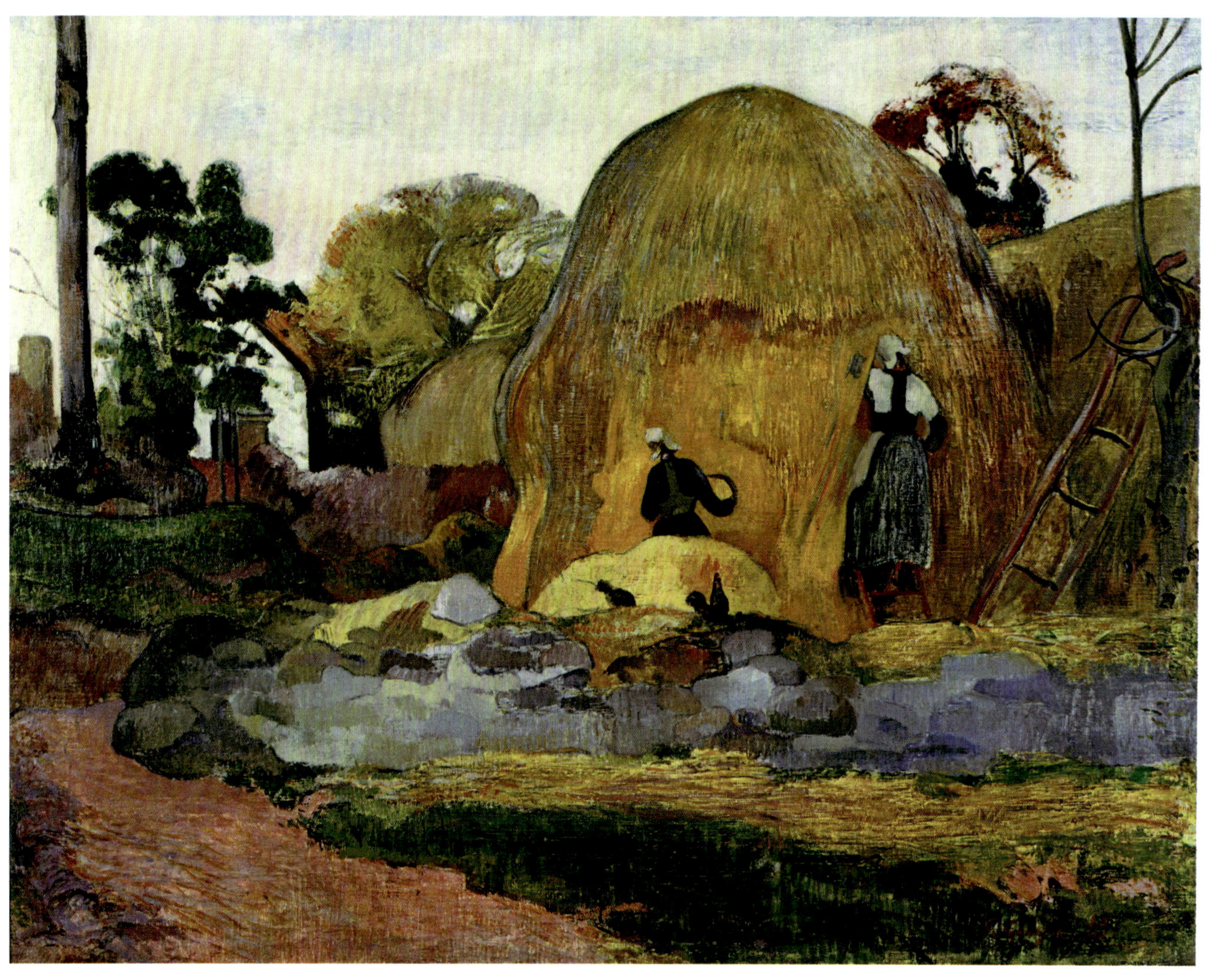

Paul Gauguin (1848–1903)
The Beautiful Angèle
La Belle Angèle
Die schöne Angèle
La bella Angèle
La bella Angèle
De mooie Angèle
1889, Oil on canvas/Huile sur toile, 92 × 73,2 cm

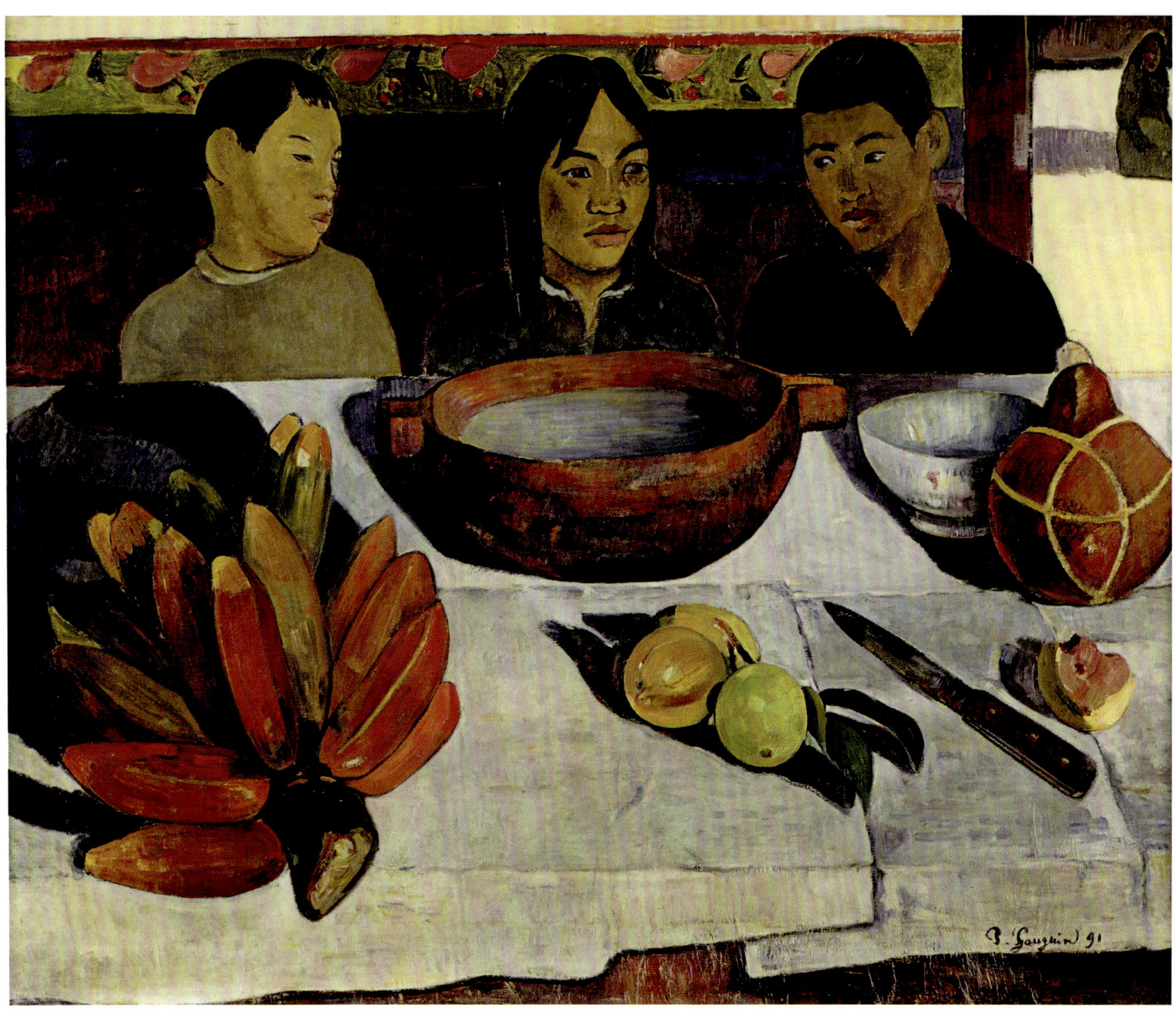

Paul Gauguin (1848–1903)

The Meal

Le Repas

Die Mahlzeit

La comida

Il Pasto

De maaltijd

1891, Oil on paper on canvas/Huile sur papier sur toile, 72,5 × 91,5 cm

Paul Gauguin (1848–1903)

Still Life with a Mandolin

Nature morte à la mandoline

Stillleben mit Mandoline

Naturaleza muerta con mandolina

Natura morta con mandolino

Stilleven met mandoline

1885, Oil on canvas/Huile sur toile, 61,7 × 51,3 cm

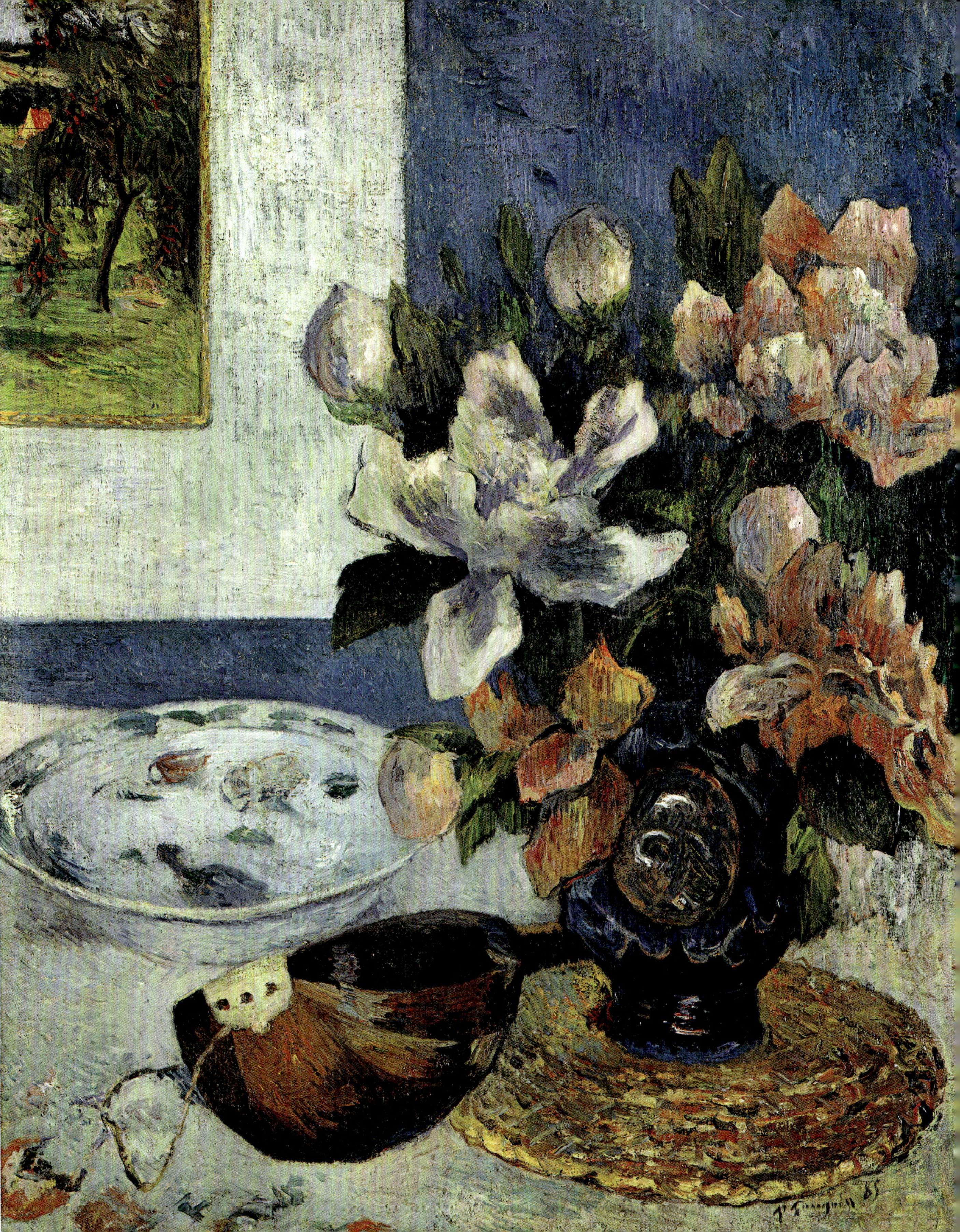

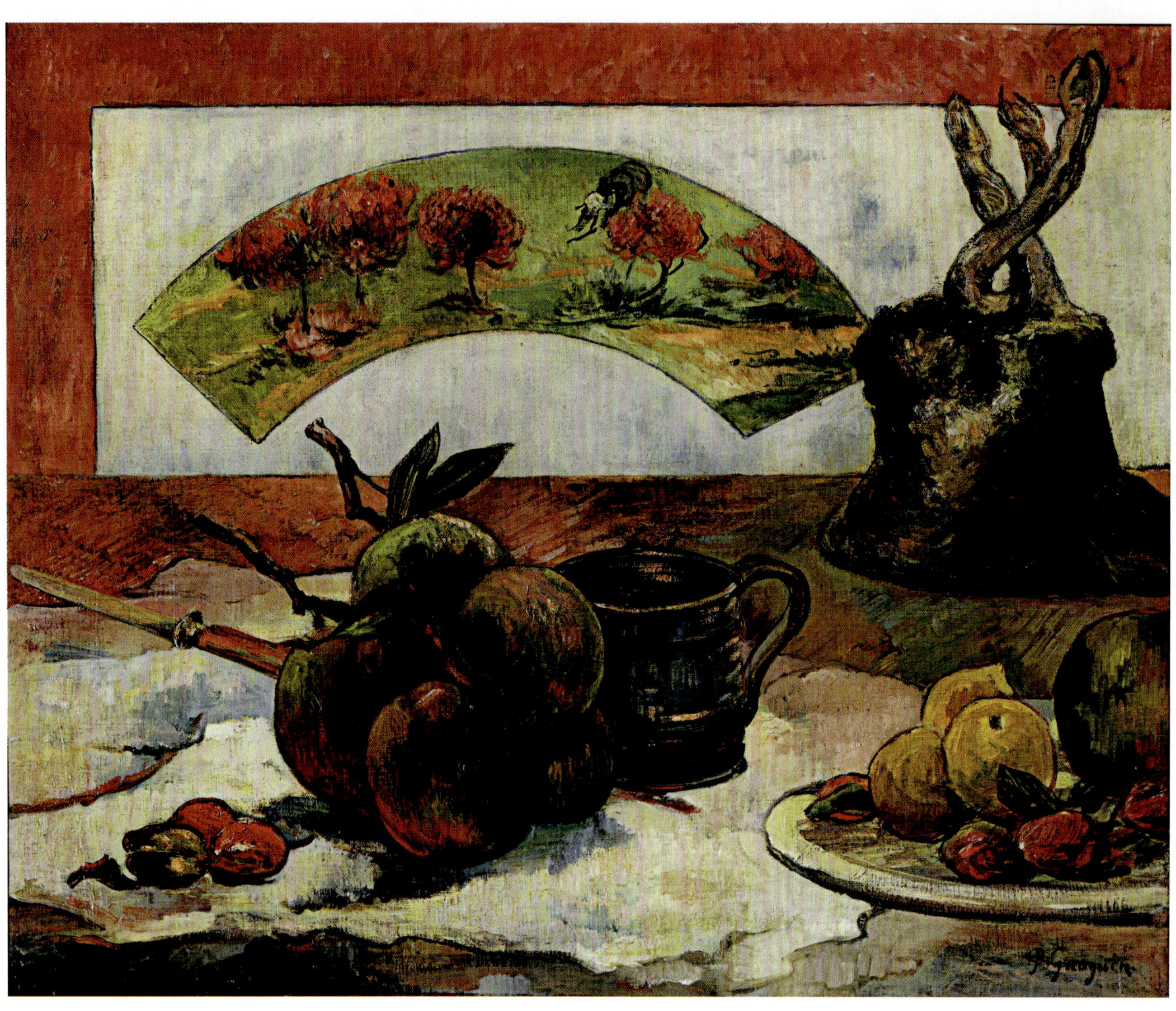

Paul Gauguin (1848–1903)

Still Life with a Fan

Nature morte à l'éventail

Stillleben mit Fächer

Naturaleza muerta con abanico

Natura morta con ventaglio

Stilleven met waaier

1889, Oil on canvas/Huile sur toile, 50,5 × 61,5 cm

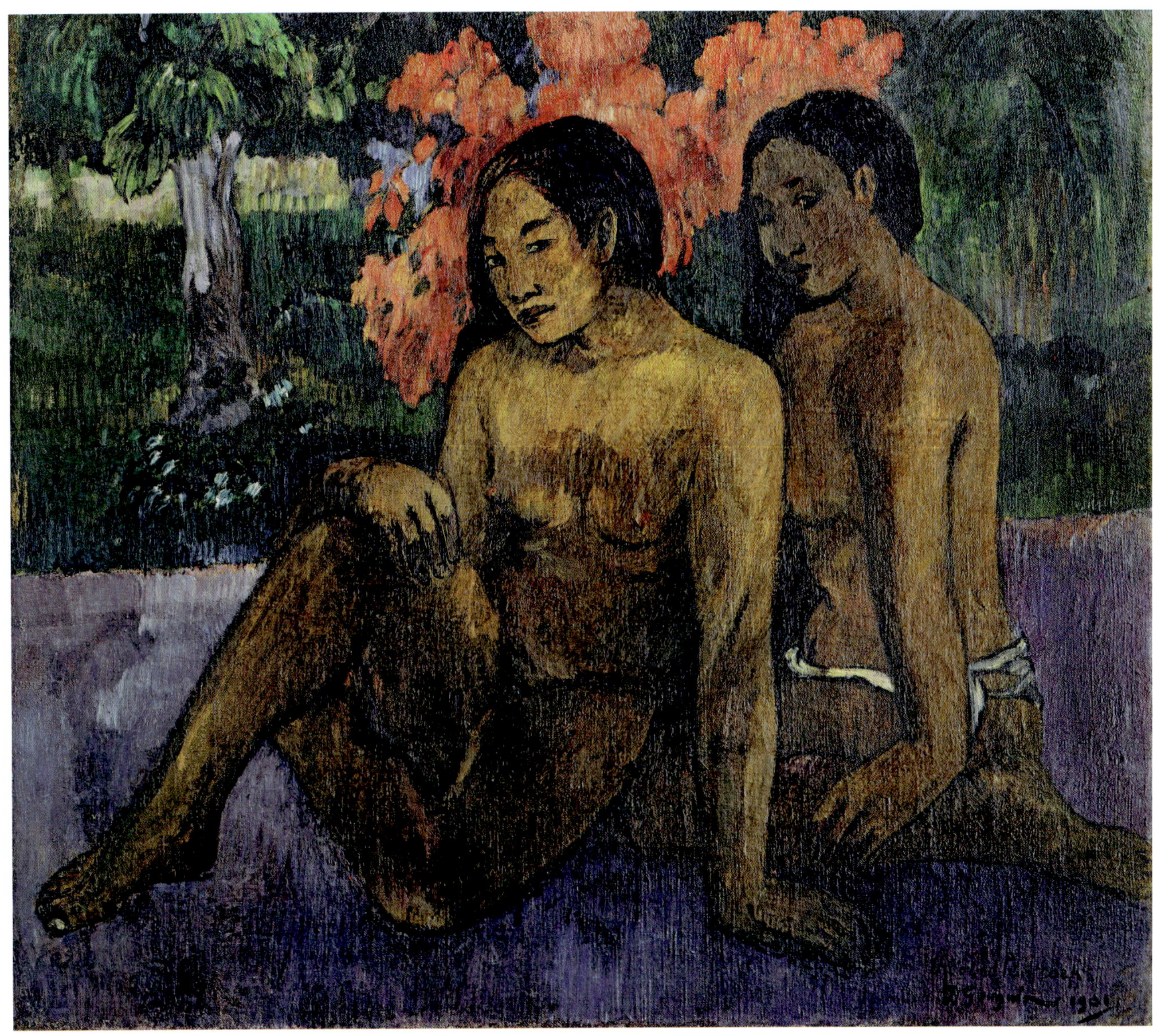

Paul Gauguin (1848–1903)

And the Gold of their Bodies

Et l'or de leur corps

Und das Gold ihrer Körper

Y el oro de sus cuerpos

E l'oro dei loro corpi

En het goud van hun lichamen

1901, Oil on canvas/Huile sur toile, 67 × 76,5 cm

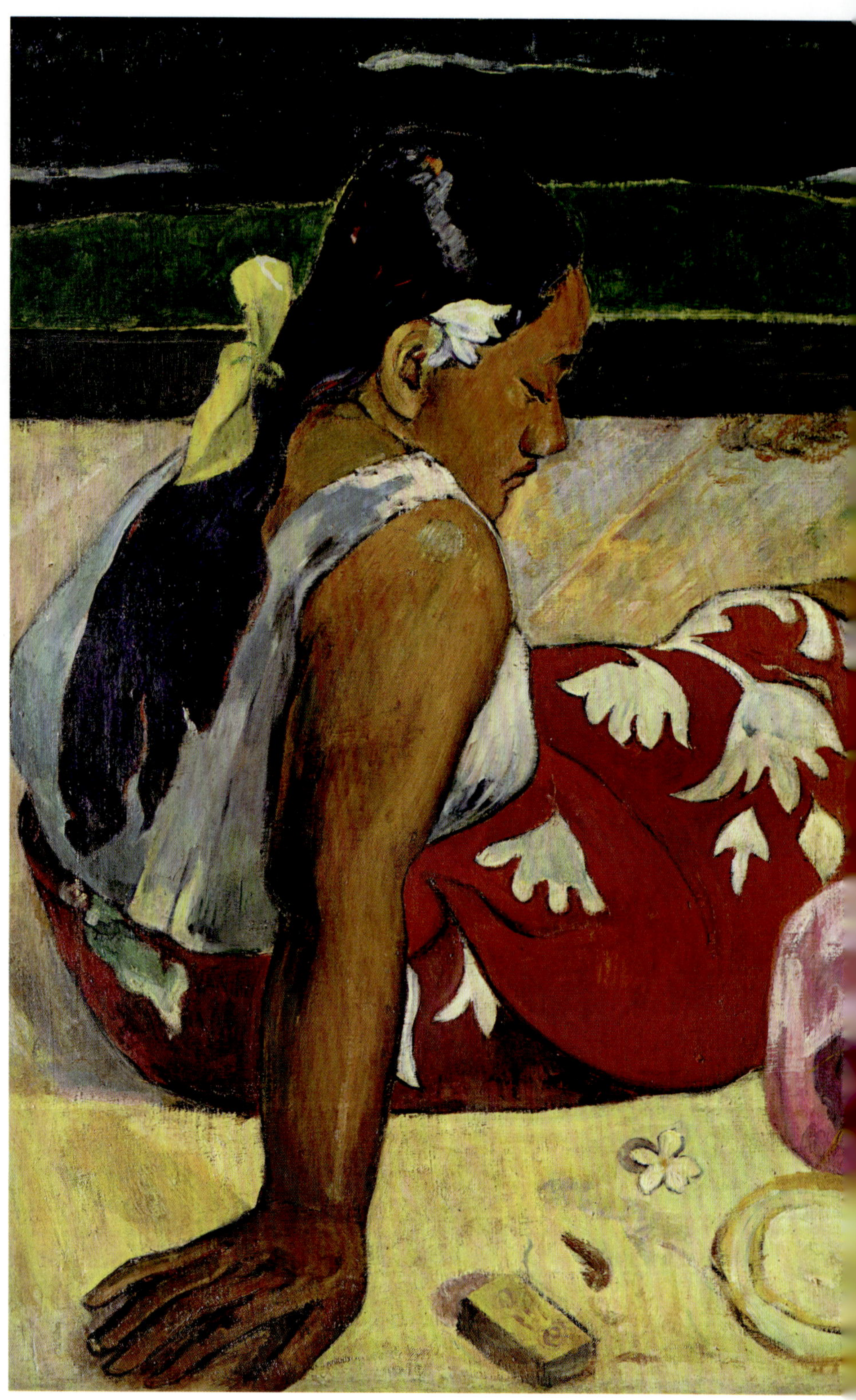

Paul Gauguin (1848–1903)
Tahitian Women
Femmes de Tahiti
Frauen auf Tahiti
Mujeres de Tahití
Due donne tahitiane
Vrouwen van Tahiti
1891, Oil on canvas/Huile sur toile, 69 × 91,5 cm

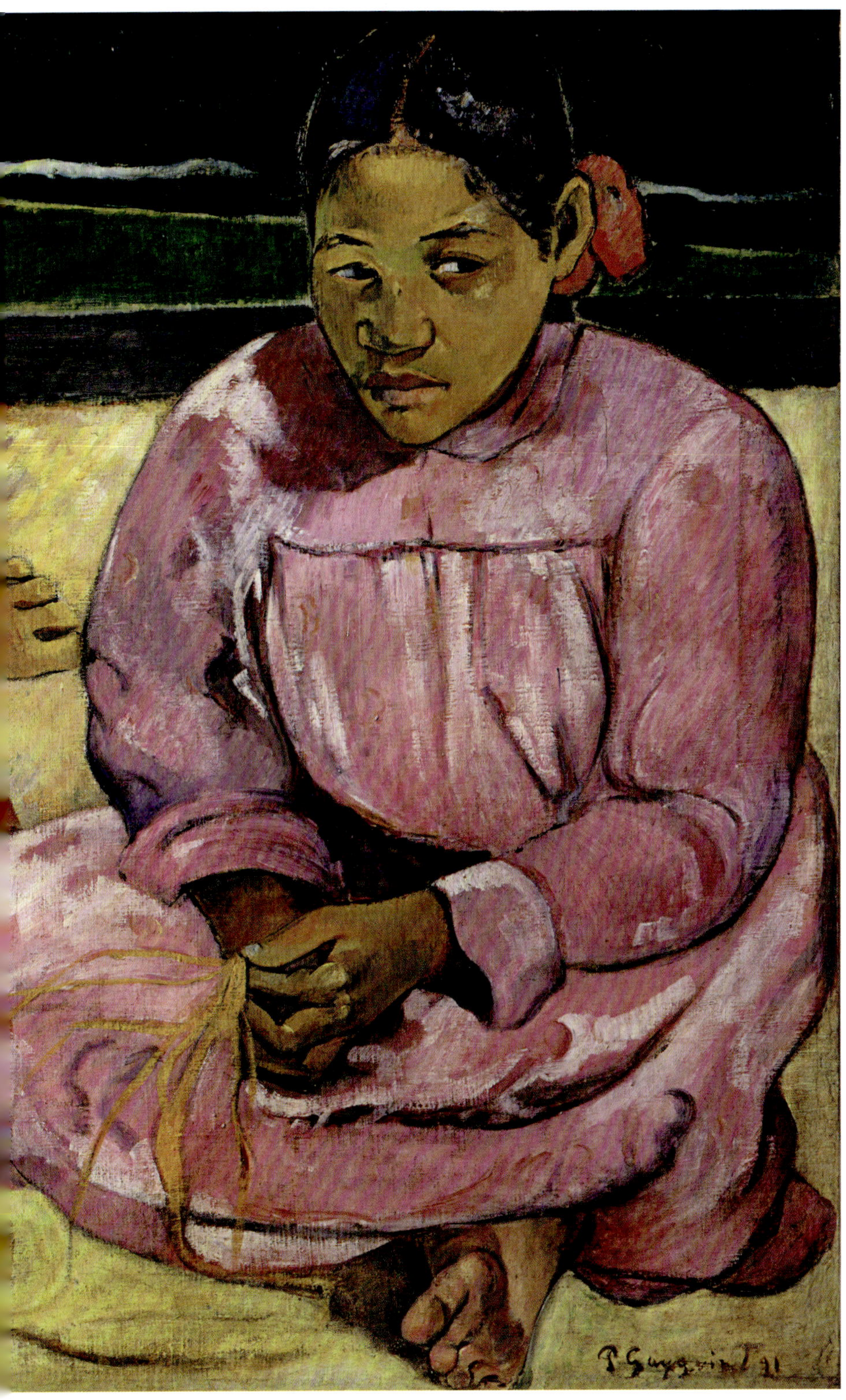

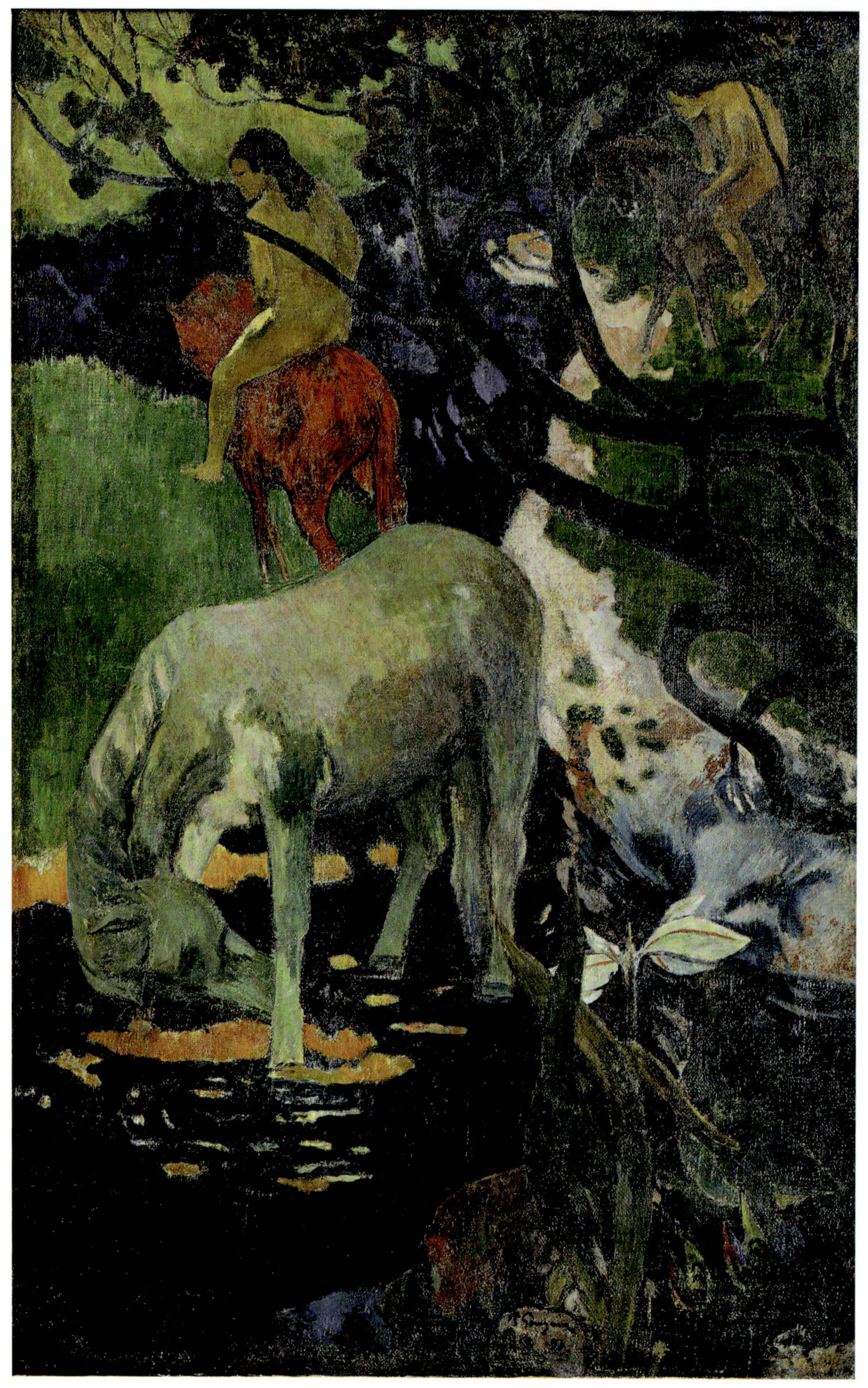

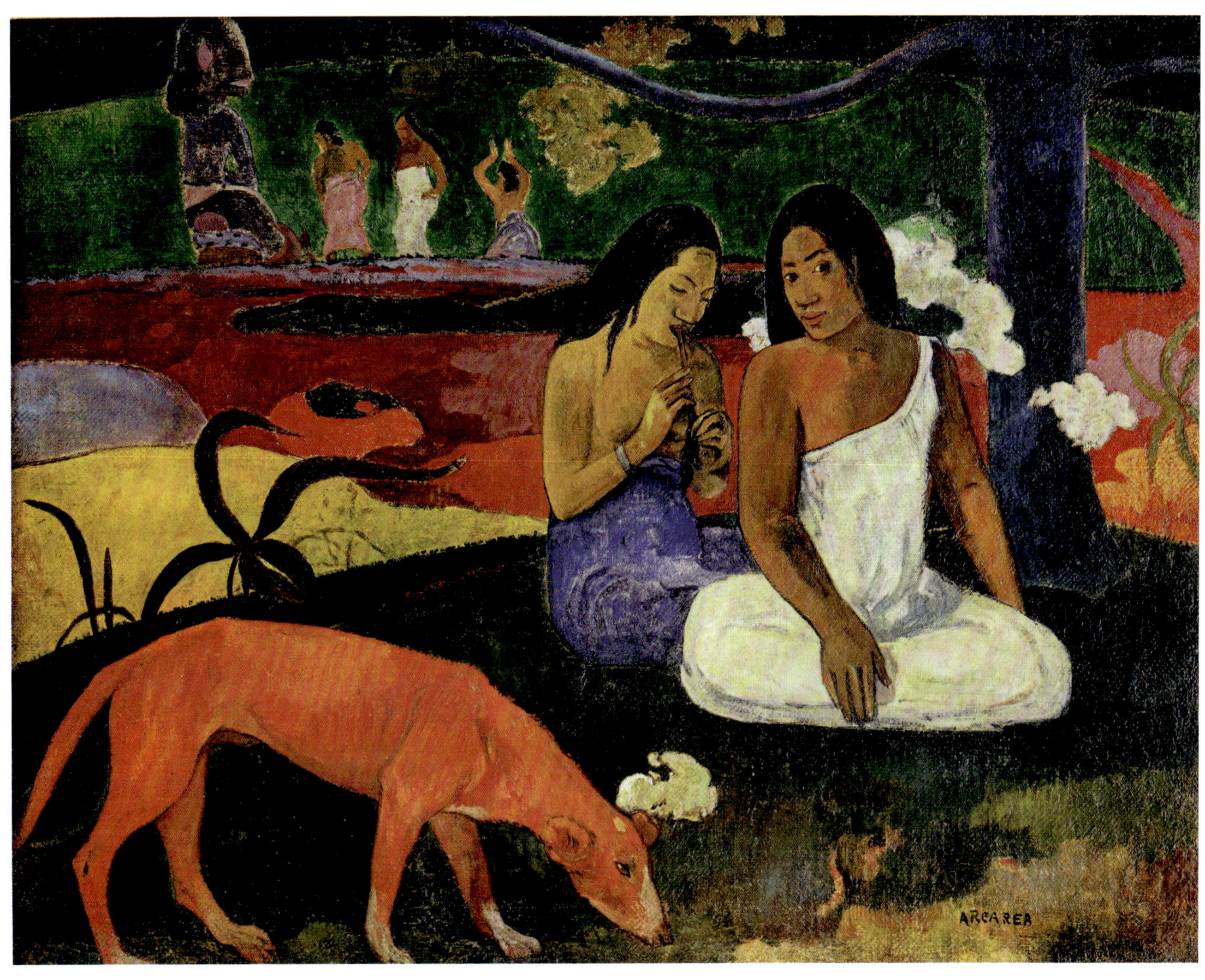

Paul Gauguin (1848–1903)
Arearea
1892, Oil on canvas/Huile sur toile, 74,5 × 93,5 cm

Paul Gauguin (1848–1903)

The White Horse

Le Cheval blanc

Der Schimmel

El caballo blanco

Il cavallo bianco

Het witte paard

1898, Oil on canvas/Huile sur toile, 140,5 × 92 cm

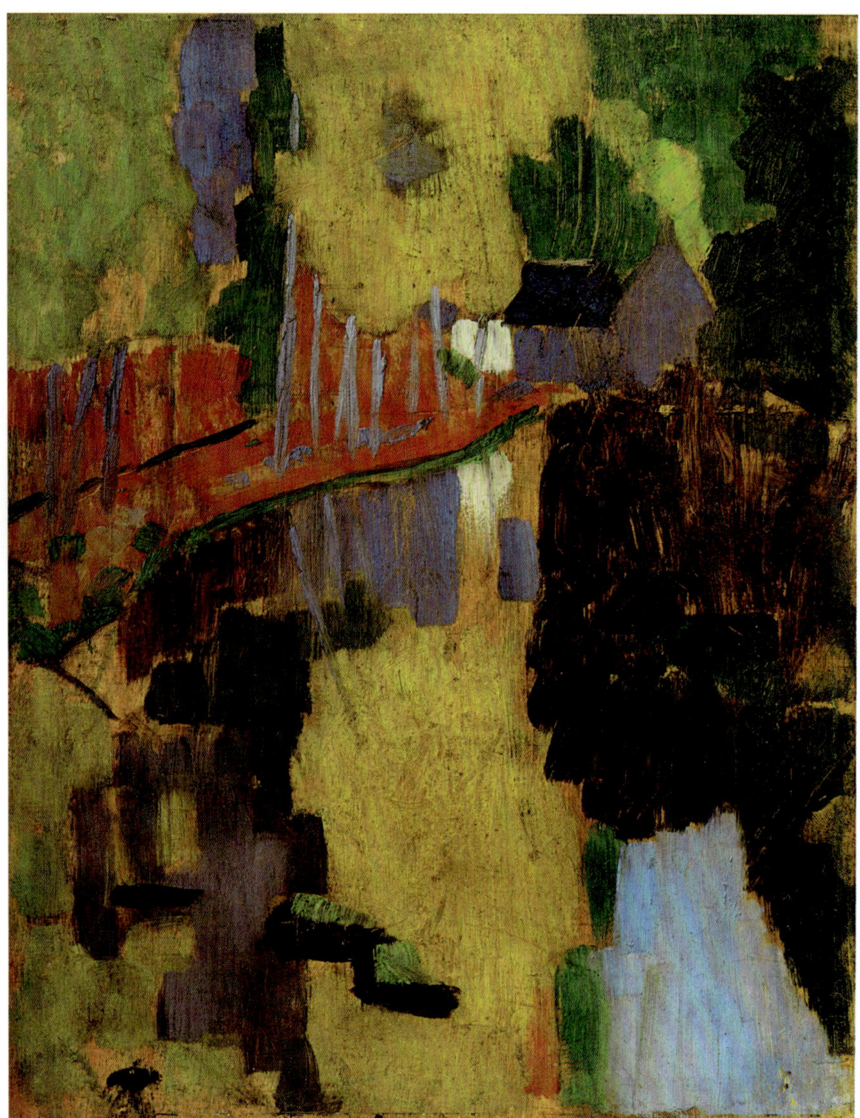

"How do you see these trees? They are yellow. Well then put on some yellow; this rather blue shadow—paint it with pure ultramarine; these red leaves? Apply some vermilion." Such was the lesson that Paul Gauguin gave to his friend Paul Sérusier while panting the Bois d'Amour at Pont-Aven in 1888. Thus was *The Talisman* born, a landmark painting where the sensation elicited by a landscape takes the place of the imitation of nature.

« Comment voyez-vous ces arbres ? Ils sont jaunes. Eh bien, mettez du jaune ; cette ombre, plutôt bleue, peignez-la avec de l'outremer pur ; ces feuilles rouges ? Mettez du vermillon. » Telle est la leçon donnée par Paul Gauguin à son ami Paul Sérusier en train de peindre le bois d'Amour, à Pont-Aven, en 1888. Ainsi naît *Le Talisman*, tableau manifeste où la sensation face au paysage prend le pas sur l'imitation de la nature.

„Wie sehen Sie diese Bäume? Sie sind gelb. Dann nehmen Sie Gelb; diesen Schatten, eher blau, dann malen Sie ihn in reinem Ultramarinblau; diese roten Blätter? Nehmen Sie Zinnoberrot." Diese Malstunde gibt Paul Gauguin seinem Freund Paul Sérusier, als der 1888 den Bois d'Amour in Pont-Aven malt. So entsteht *Der Talisman*, ein Manifest, in dem das Empfinden gegenüber der Landschaft die Imitation der Natur in den Hintergrund drängt.

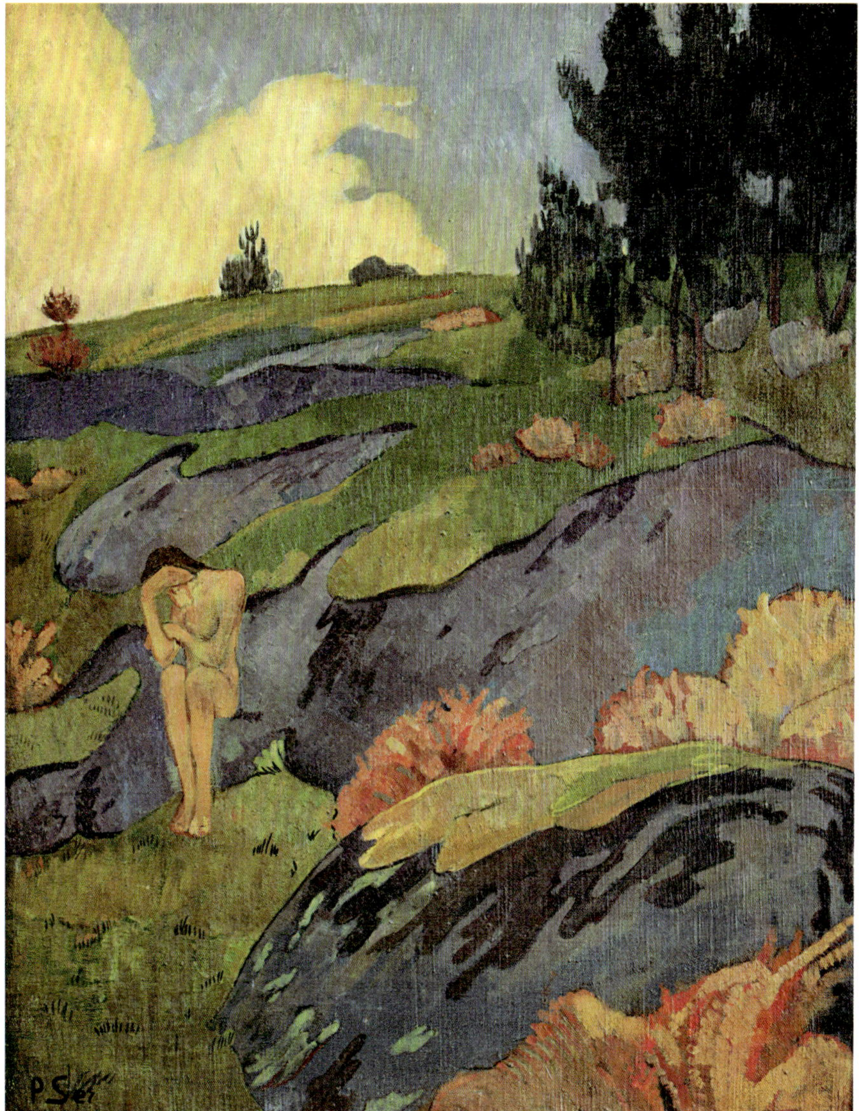

Paul Sérusier (1864–1927)
Breton Eve
Ève bretonne
Bretonische Eva
Eva bretona
Eva bretone
Bretonse Eva
1890, Oil on canvas/Huile
sur toile, 72,6 × 58,3 cm

"¿Cómo ve estos árboles? Son de color amarillo. Bien, ponga amarillo; esta sombra, más azul, pinte con azul ultramar puro; ¿estas hojas rojas? Ponga bermellón." Esta es la lección dada por Paul Gauguin a su amigo Paul Sérusier mientras pintaba el Bois d'Amour, Pont-Aven, en 1888. Así nació *El Talismán*, cuadro manifiesto donde sensación frente al paisaje se impone a la imitación de la naturaleza.

"Come vedete questi alberi? Sono gialli. Ebbene, metteteci del giallo; quest'ombra, decisamente blu, coloratela con una tonalità blu oltremare puro; queste foglie rosse? Dipingetele di vermiglio." Questo è il discorso che Paul Gauguin fece al suo amico Paul Sérusier quando quest'ultimo stava dipingendo il Bois d'Amour di Pont-Aven, nel 1888. Nacque così l'opera manifesto *Il Talismano,* in cui il sentimento verso il paesaggio prevale sull'imitazione della natura.

"Hoe ziet u die bomen? Ze zijn geel. Welnu, maak ze geel. Die ik zou zeggen blauwe schaduw, schilder die met zuiver ultramarijn. Die rode bladeren? Gebruik vermiljoen." Die les geeft Paul Gauguin zijn vriend Paul Sérusier in 1888 in Pont-Aven tijdens het schilderen van het Bois d'Amour. Zo ontstaat Talisman, een schilderij waarop de emotie die het landschap teweegbrengt het wint van de imitatie van de natuur.

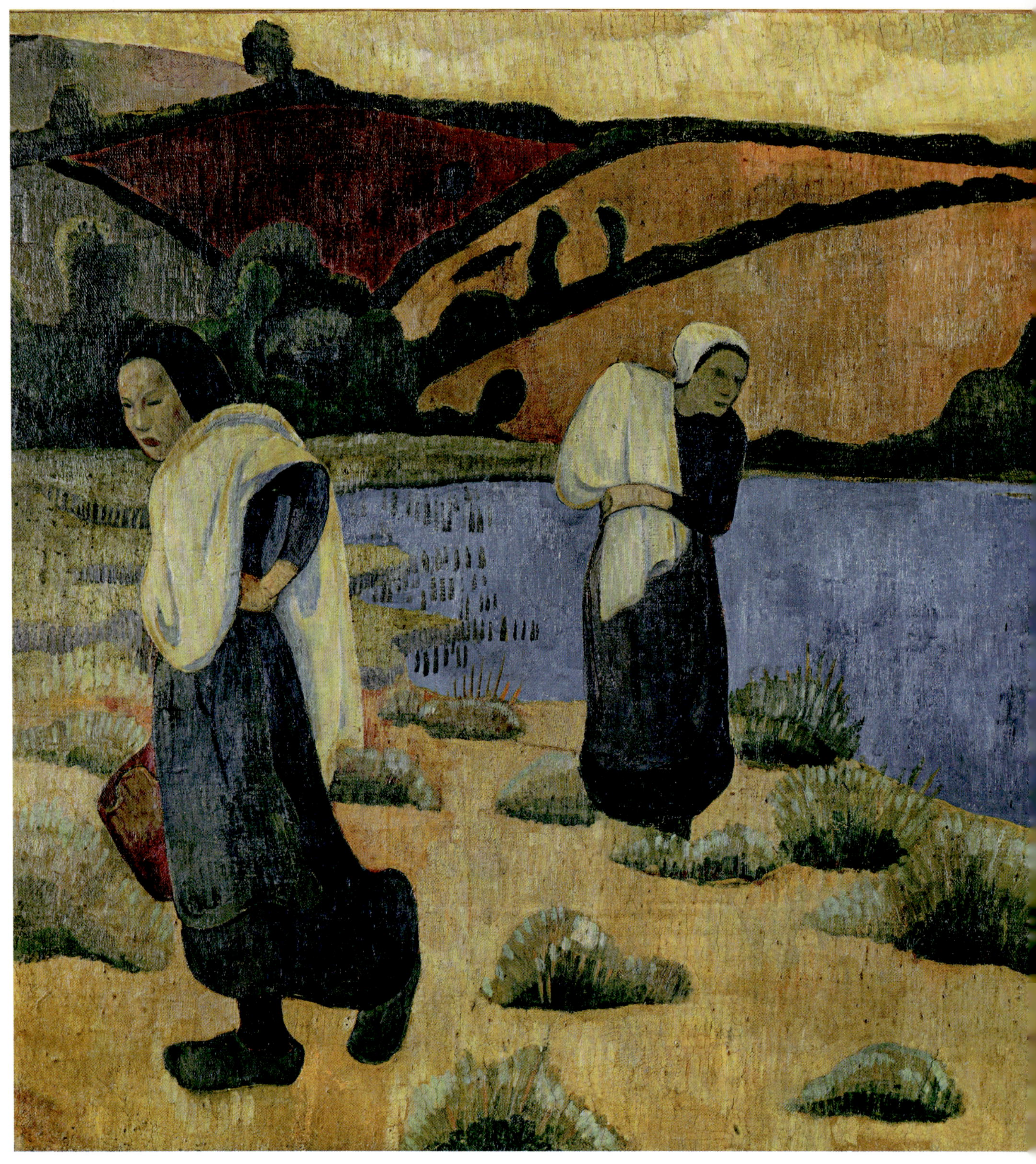

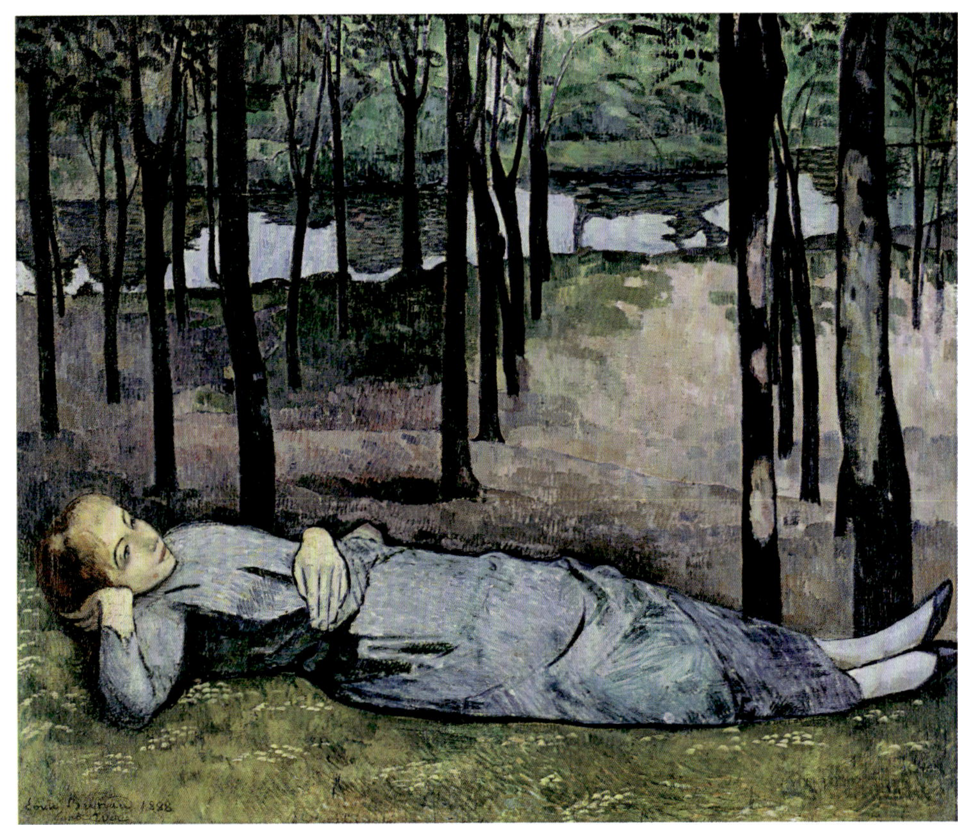

Émile Bernard (1868–1941)
Madeleine in the Bois d'Amour
Madeleine au Bois d'Amour
Madeleine im Bois d'Amour
Madeleine en el Bois d'Amour
Madeleine nel Bois d'Amour
Madeleine in het Bois d'Amour
1888, Oil on canvas/Huile sur toile, 137 × 163 cm

Paul Sérusier (1864–1927)
The Washers at the River Laïta
Les Laveuses à la Laïta
Wäscherinnen an der Laïta
Lavanderas en el río Laïta
Le lavandaie presso la Laïta
Wasvrouwen bij de Laïta
1892, Oil on canvas/Huile sur toile, 73,2 × 92,2 cm

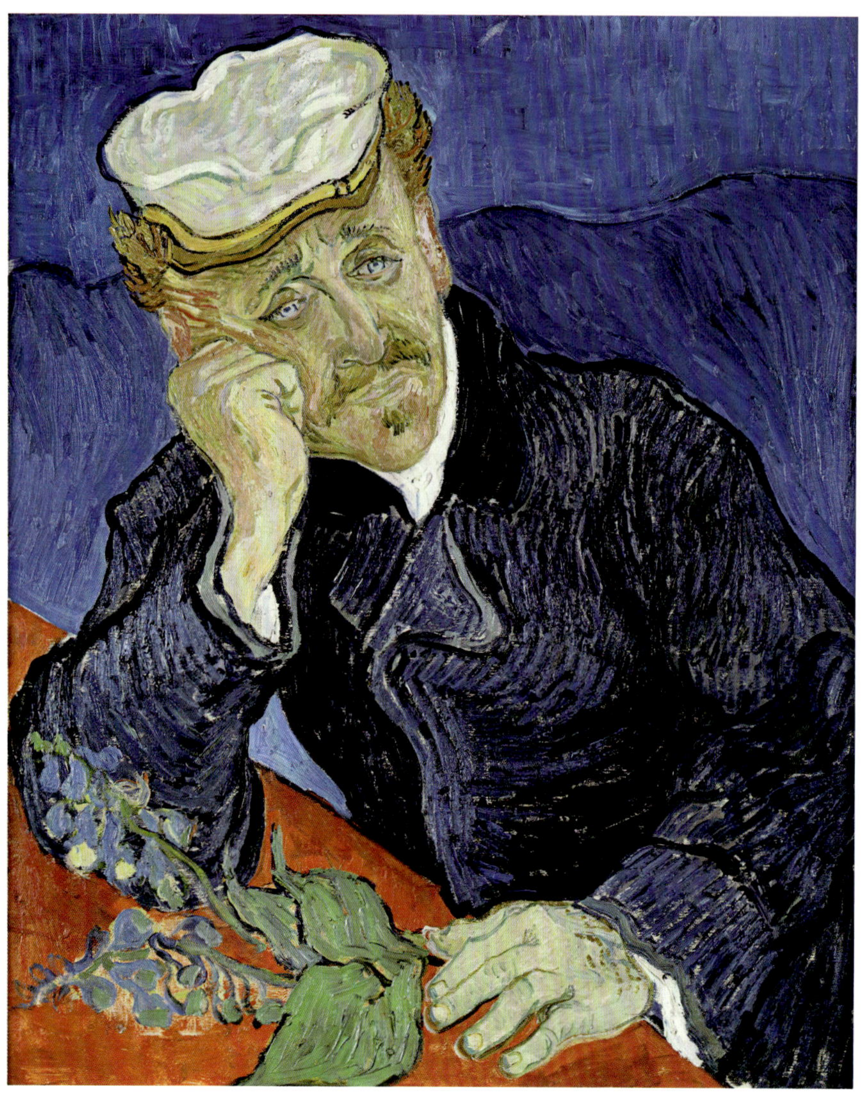

Vincent van Gogh (1853–1890)

Portrait of Dr. Gachet

Le Docteur Paul Gachet

Der Doktor Paul Gachet

El doctor Paul Gachet

Il dottor Paul Gachet

Dokter Paul Gachet

1890, Oil on canvas/Huile sur toile, 68,2 × 57 cm

Vincent van Gogh (1853–1890)

The Church in Auvers-sur-Oise

L'Église d'Auvers-sur-Oise

Die Kirche in Auvers-sur-Oise

La iglesia de Auvers-sur-Oise

La Chiesa di Auvers-sur-Oise

De kerk van Auvers-sur-Oise

1890, Oil on canvas/Huile sur toile, 93 × 74,5 cm

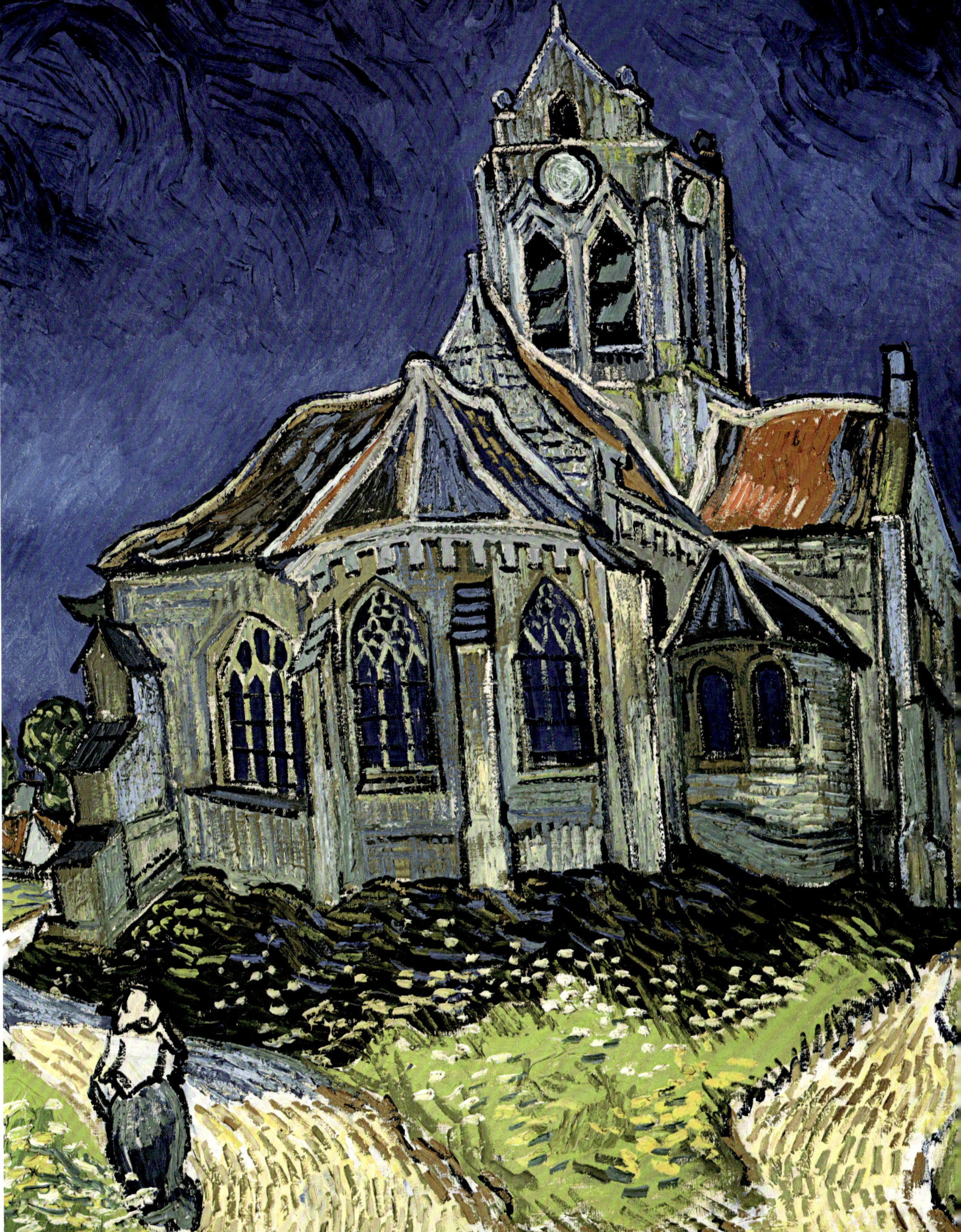

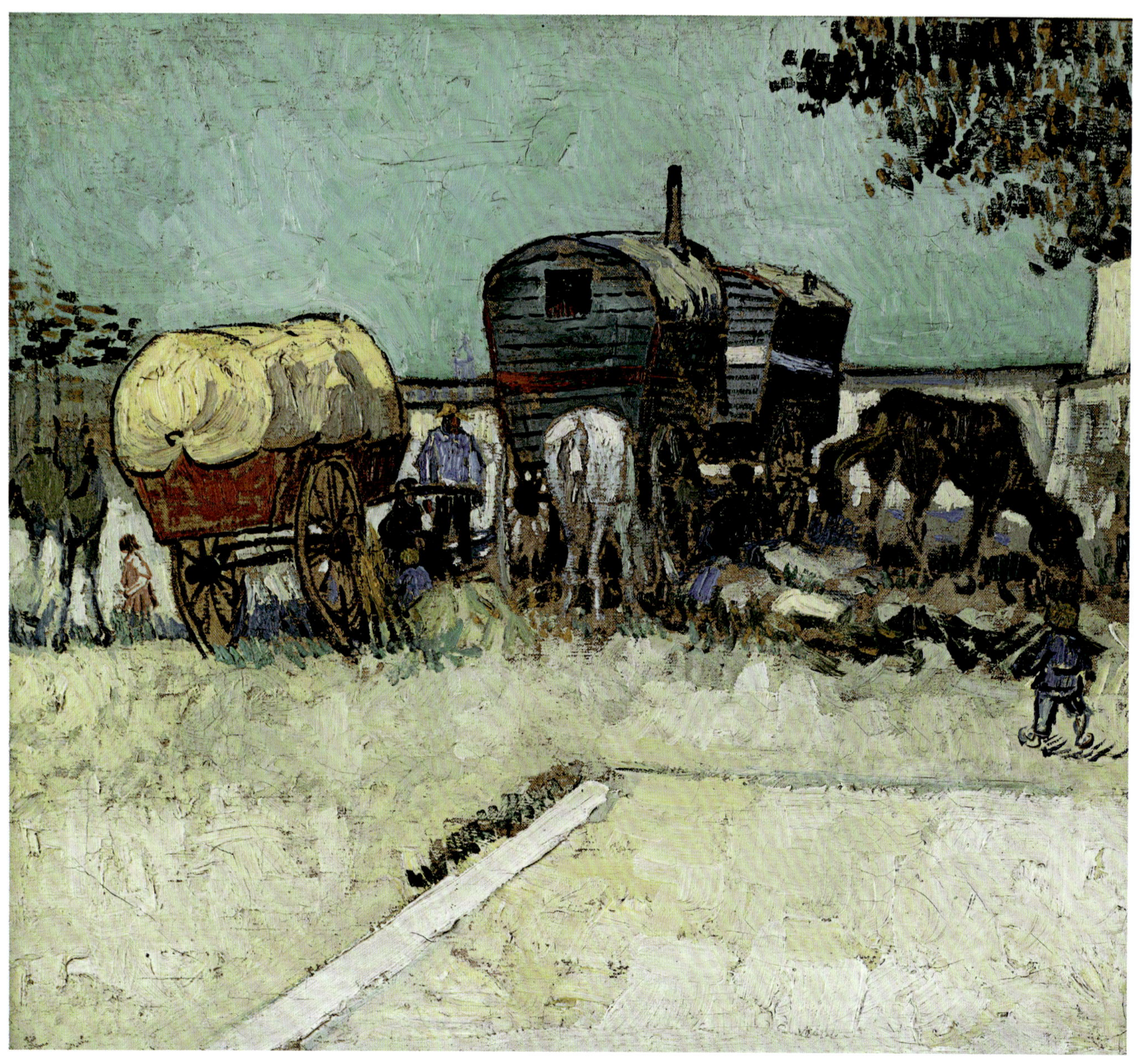

Vincent van Gogh (1853–1890)

The Caravans, Gypsy Camp near Arles

Les Roulottes, campement de bohémiens aux environs d'Arles

Zigeunerlager mit Pferdewagen nahe Arles

Campamento de gitanos con caravanas cerca de Arlés

Le roulotte, campo nomadi intorno ad Arles

De woonwagens, zigeunerkamp in de buurt van Arles

1888, Oil on canvas/Huile sur toile, 45 × 51 cm

Vincent van Gogh (1853–1890)

Saint-Paul Hospital at Saint-Rémy-de-Provence

Hôpital Saint-Paul à Saint-Rémy-de-Provence

Hospital Saint-Paul in Saint-Rémy-de-Provence

Hospital Saint-Paul en Saint-Rémy-de-Provence

Ospedale Saint-Paul di Saint-Rémy-de-Provence

Ziekenhuis Saint-Paul in Saint-Rémy-de-Provence

1889, Oil on canvas/Huile sur toile, 63,4 × 49 cm

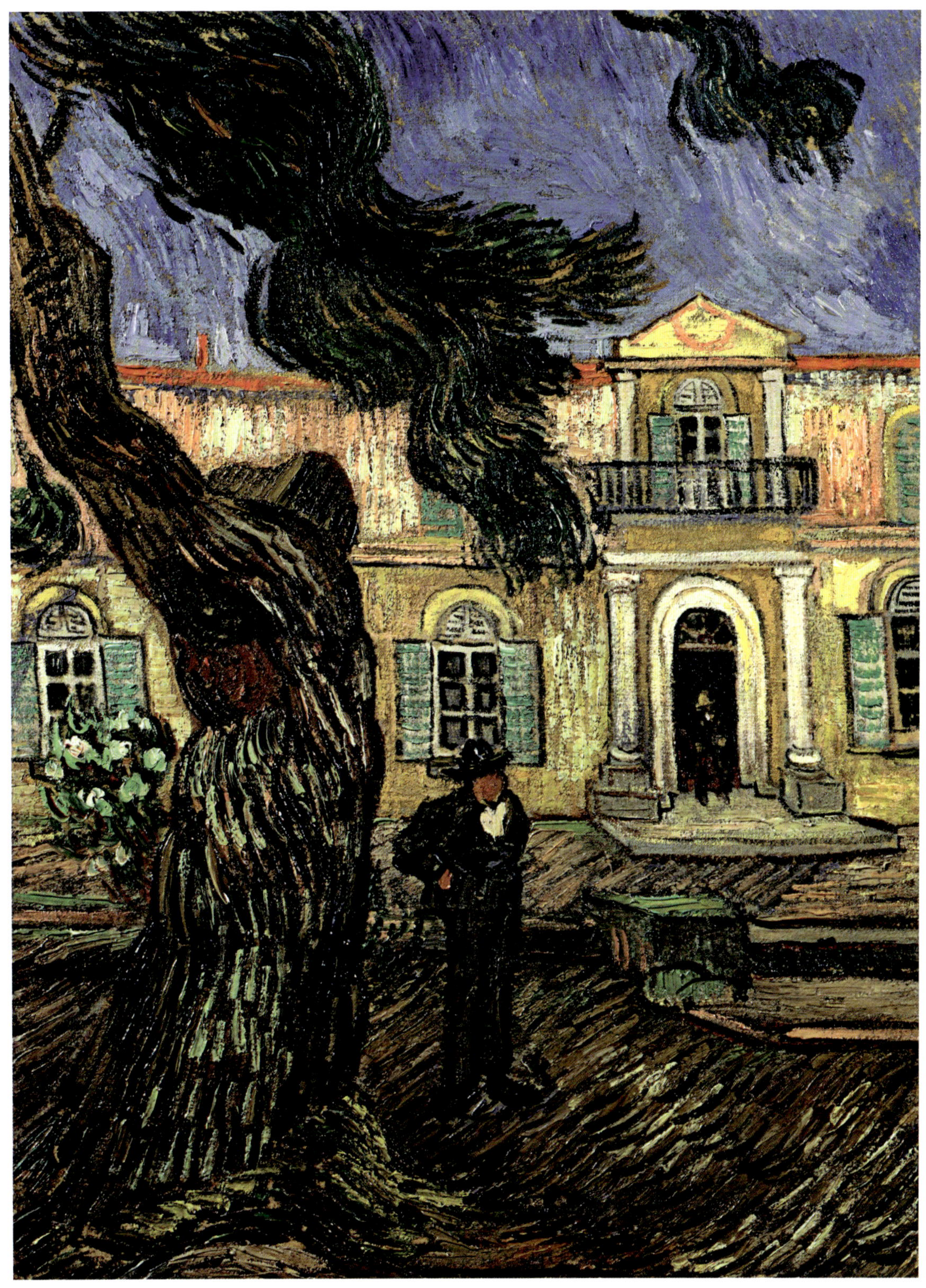

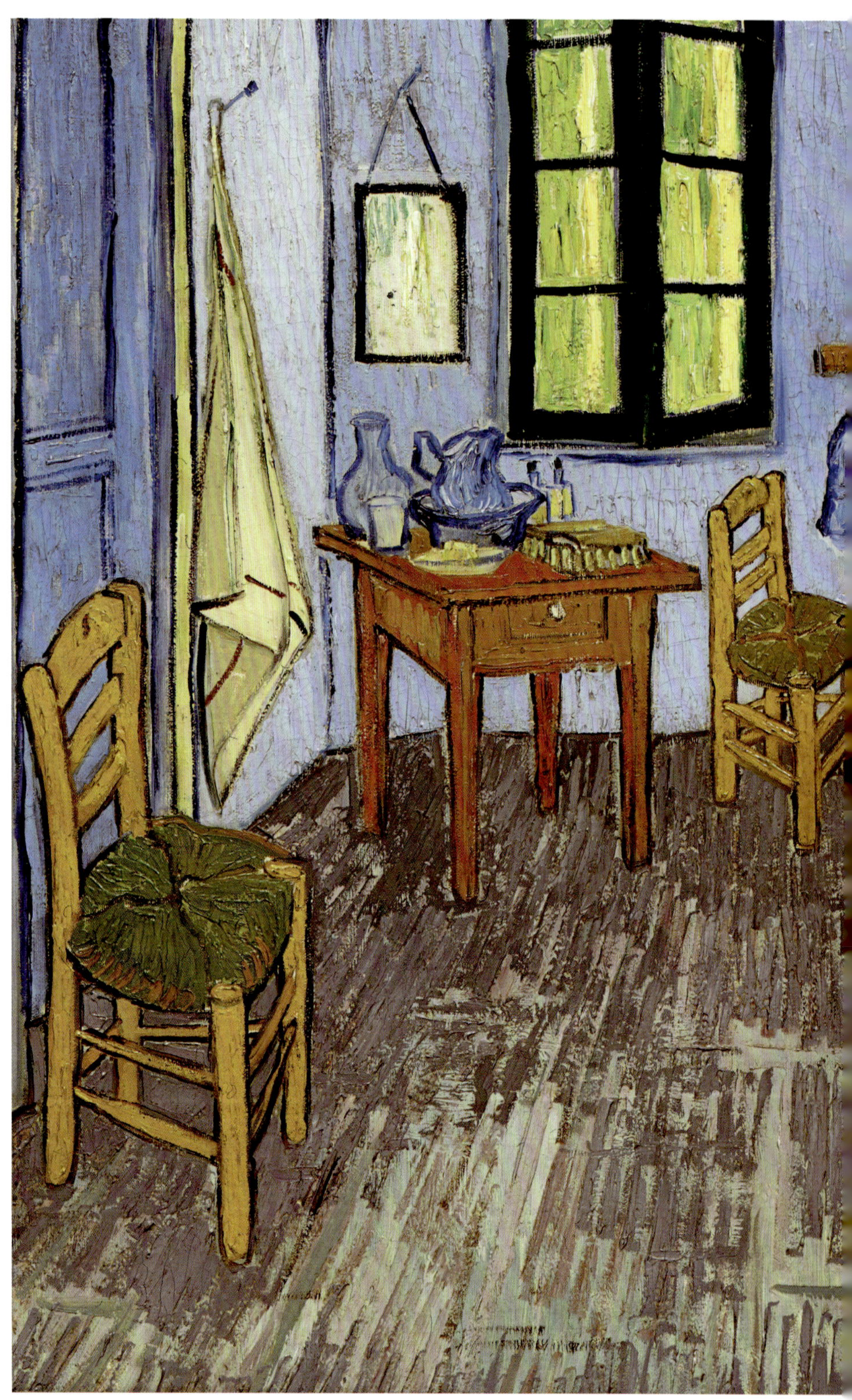

Vincent van Gogh (1853–1890)
The Bedroom in Arles
La Chambre à Arles
Das Schlafzimmer in Arles
La habitación en Arlés
La stanza ad Arles
De kamer in Arles
1889, Oil on canvas/Huile sur toile, 57,3 × 73,5 cm

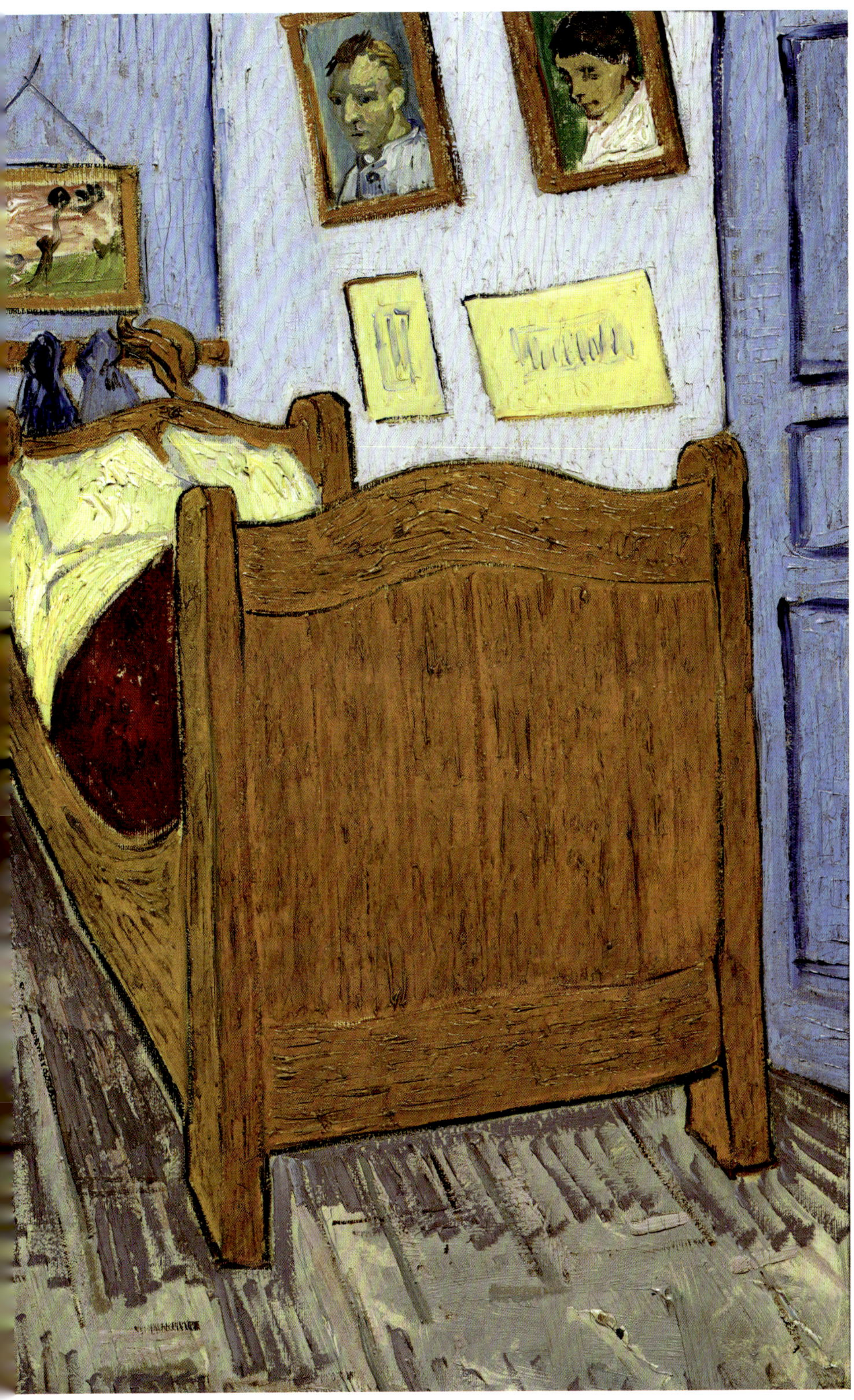

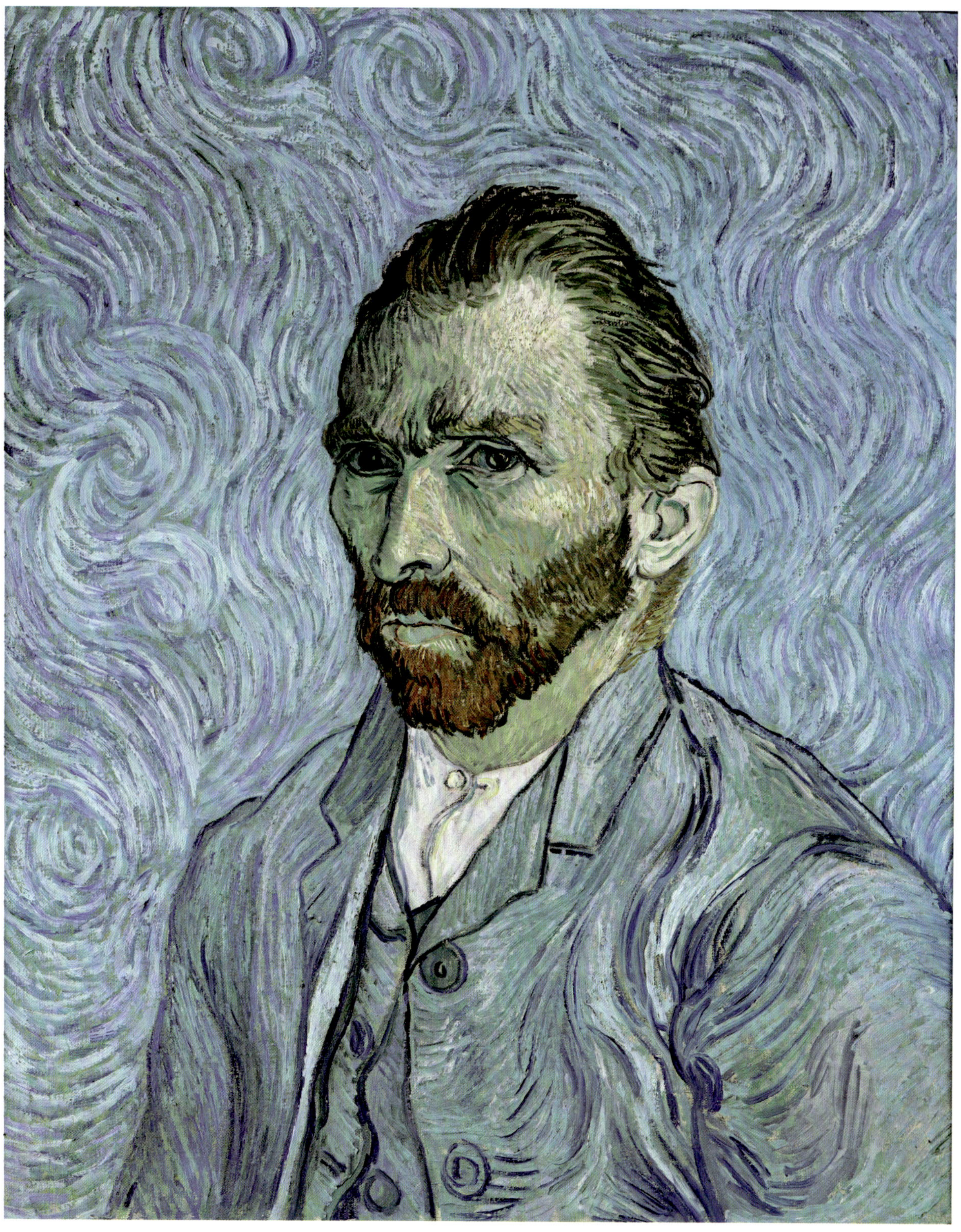

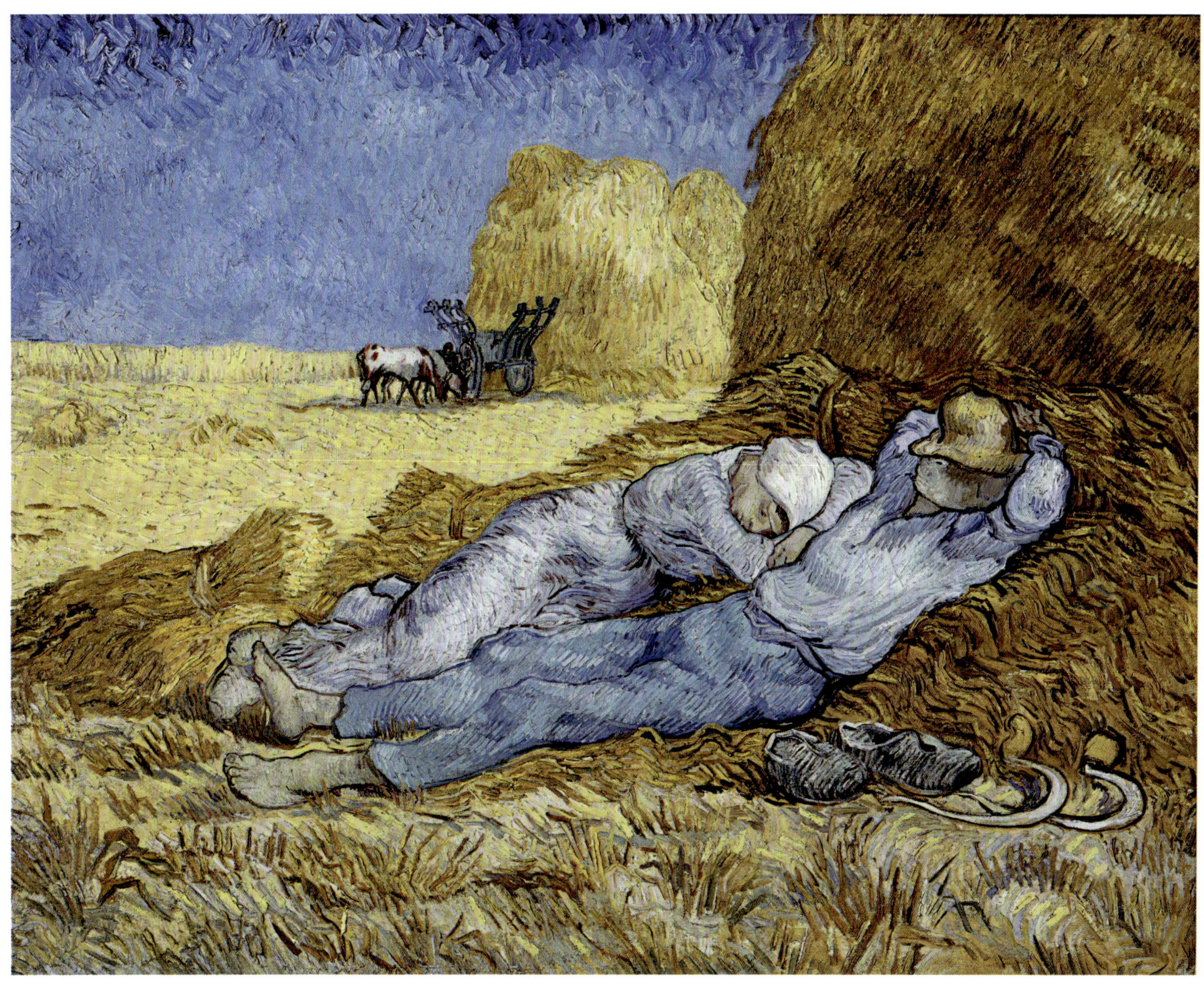

Vincent Van Gogh (1853–1890)
Noon, Rest from Work
La Méridienne *ou* La sieste
Mittagsschlaf
La meridiana *o* La siesta
La Meridiana *o* La Siesta
Middagrust
c. 1889–1890, Oil on canvas/Huile sur toile, 73 × 91 cm

Vincent van Gogh (1853–1890)
Self-Portrait
Portrait de l'artiste
Selbstbildnis
Autorretrato
Autoritratto
Portret van de kunstenaar
1889, Oil on canvas/Huile sur toile, 65 × 54,2 cm

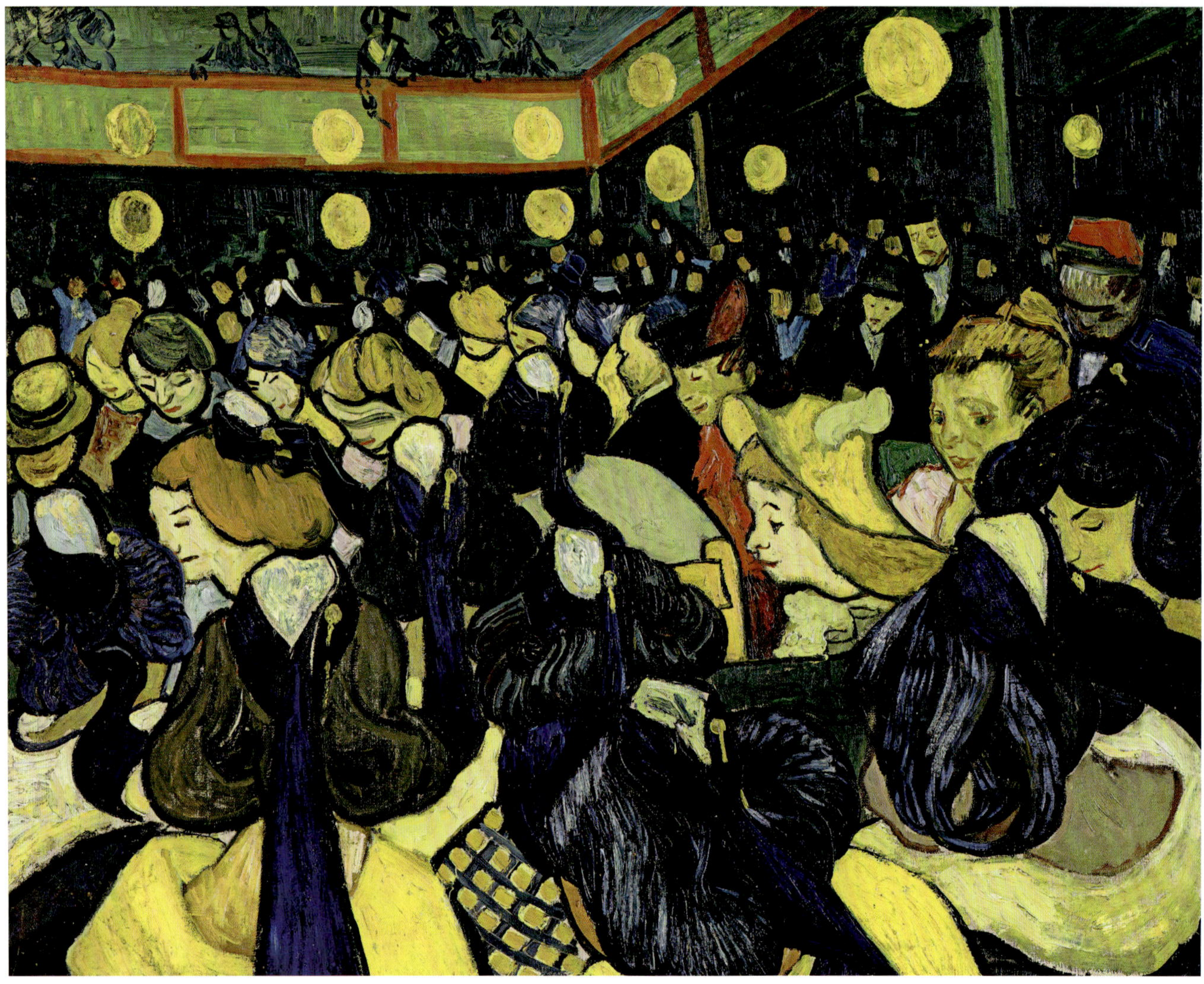

Vincent van Gogh (1853–1890)

The Dance Hall in Arles   La Salle de danse à Arles   Der Tanzsaal in Arles   El salón de baile en Arlés   La sala da ballo ad Arles   De danszaal in Arles

1888, Oil on canvas/Huile sur toile, 65 × 85,5 cm

"I now want to definitely paint a starry sky. It often seems to me that night is more richly colored than day", wrote Vincent van Gogh in a letter to his sister Wilhelmina. Here the artist offers an extraordinary symphony of blues and greens illuminating a constellation of stars (among which one can recognize the Big Dipper) and the light of the quay's street lamps, which is reflected in the dark waters of the Rhone.

« Je veux maintenant absolument peindre un ciel étoilé. Souvent, il me semble que la nuit est encore plus richement colorée que le jour », écrivait Vincent van Gogh dans une lettre à sa sœur Wilhelmina. L'artiste offre ici une extraordinaire symphonie de bleus et de verts, qu'illumine une constellation d'étoiles (on reconnaît entre autres la Grande Ourse) et la lumière des réverbères du quai, qui se reflète dans les eaux sombres du Rhône.

„Ich möchte nun unbedingt einen Sternenhimmel malen. Es will mir oft scheinen, dass die Nacht noch farbiger ist als der Tag", schreibt Vincent van Gogh in einem Brief an seine Schwester Wilhelmina. Der Künstler bietet hier eine außergewöhnliche Symphonie aus Blau- und Grüntönen dar, welche erleuchtet wird von den Sternbildern (man erkennt unter anderem den Großen Bären) und dem Licht der Laternen am Kai, das sich im dunklen Wasser der Rhône spiegelt.

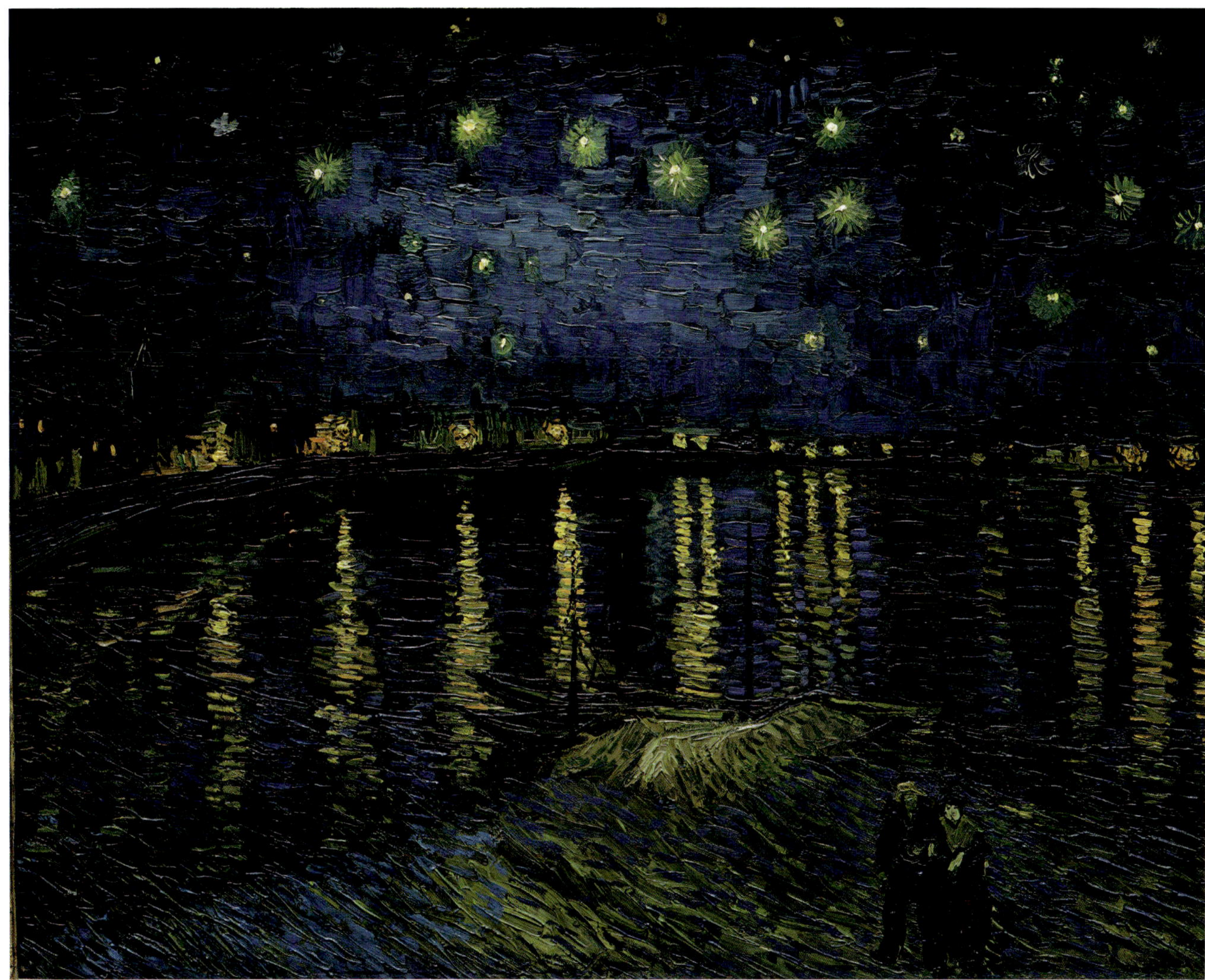

Vincent van Gogh (1853–1890)

The Starry Night | La Nuit étoilée | Sternennacht | La noche estrellada | La notte stellata | Sterrennacht

1888, Oil on canvas/Huile sur toile, 73 × 92 cm

"Ahora definitivamente quiero pintar un cielo estrellado. A menudo me parece que la noche es aún más rica en colores que el día", escribió Vincent van Gogh en una carta a su hermana Wilhelmina. El artista ofrece aquí una extraordinaria sinfonía de azules y verdes, que ilumina una constelación de estrellas (se reconoce entre otras la Osa Mayor) y la luz de las farolas del muelle, que se reflejan en las aguas oscuras del Ródano.

In una lettera alla sorella Wilhelmina, Vincent van Gogh scrisse: "Adesso voglio assolutamente dipingere un cielo stellato. Spesso, ho l'impressione che la notte sia più ricca di colori se paragonata al giorno." L'artista propone in questo quadro una straordinaria sinfonia di tonalità blu e verdi illuminata da una costellazione di stelle (si riconosce tra le altre l'Orsa Maggiore) e dalla luce dei lampioni del molo, che si riflette nelle acque scure del Rodano.

"Ik wil nu echt een sterrenhemel schilderen. Vaak lijkt me de nacht kleurrijker dan de dag", schreef Vincent van Gogh in een brief aan zijn zus Wilhelmina. De kunstenaar creëert op het doek een bijzondere symfonie van blauw- en groentinten, die hij verlicht met een sterrenstelsel (met duidelijk herkenbaar de Grote Beer) en het licht van de straatlantaarns op de kade die weerspiegelen in het donkere water van de Rhône.

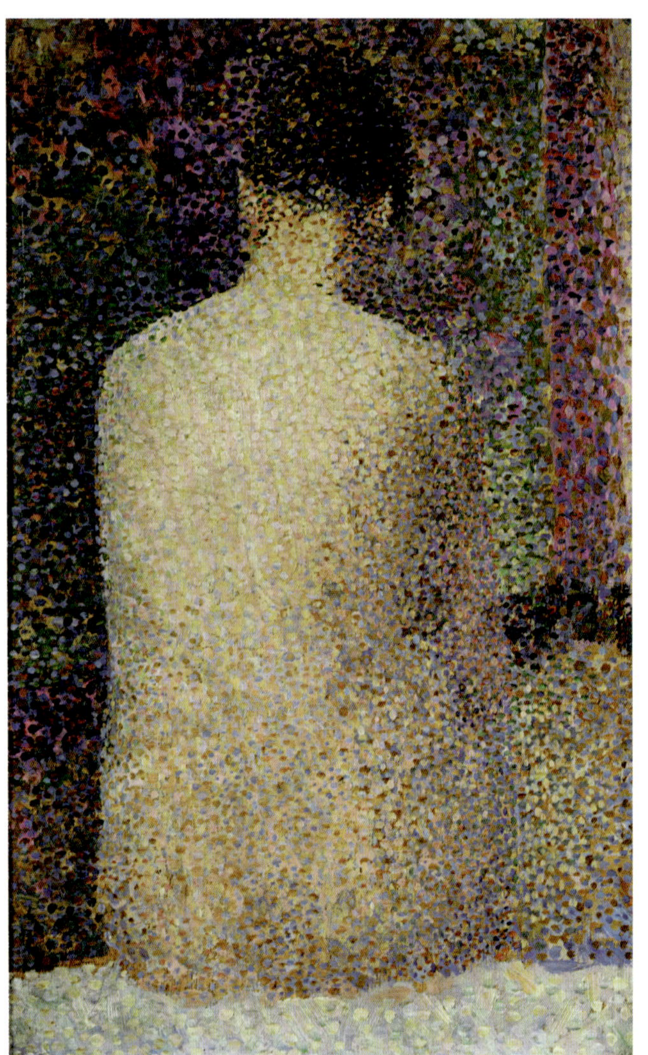

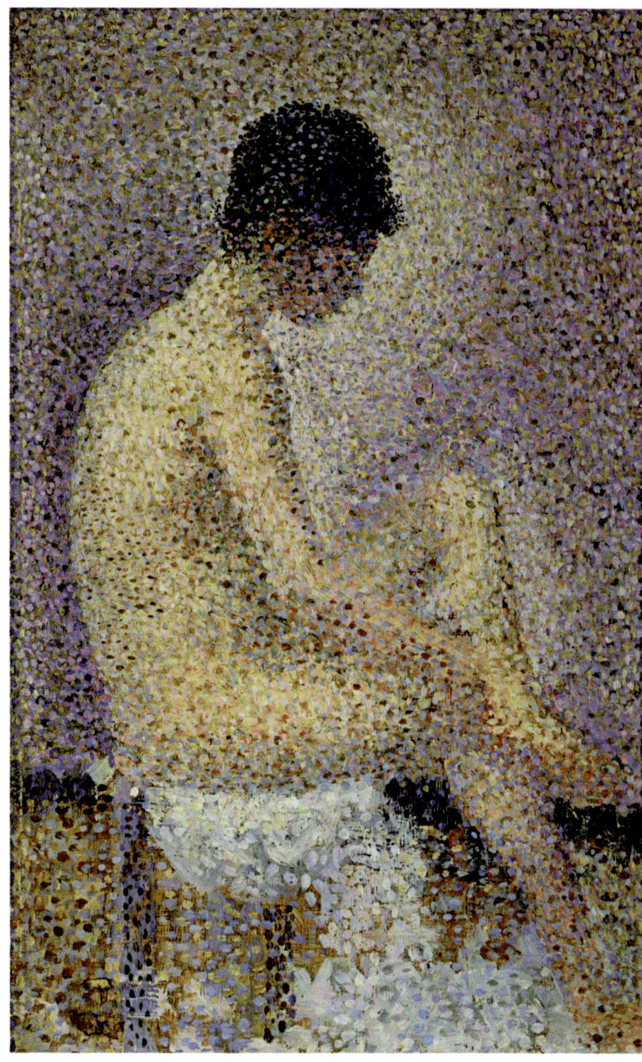

Georges Seurat (1859–1891)

Model from the Back

Poseuse de dos

Sitzendes Modell, Rückenfigur

Pose de espalda

Modella di spalle

Model, op de rug

1887, Oil on wood/Huile sur bois, 24,3 × 15,3 cm

Georges Seurat (1859–1891)

Model in Profile

Poseuse de profil

Modell sitzend, im Profil

Pose de perfil

Modella di profilo

Model, en profil

1887, Oil on wood/Huile sur bois, 24,7 × 15,5 cm

Georges Seurat (1859–1891)

The Circus

Le Cirque

Der Zirkus

El circo

Il circo

Het circus

1891, Oil on canvas/Huile sur toile, 186 × 152 cm

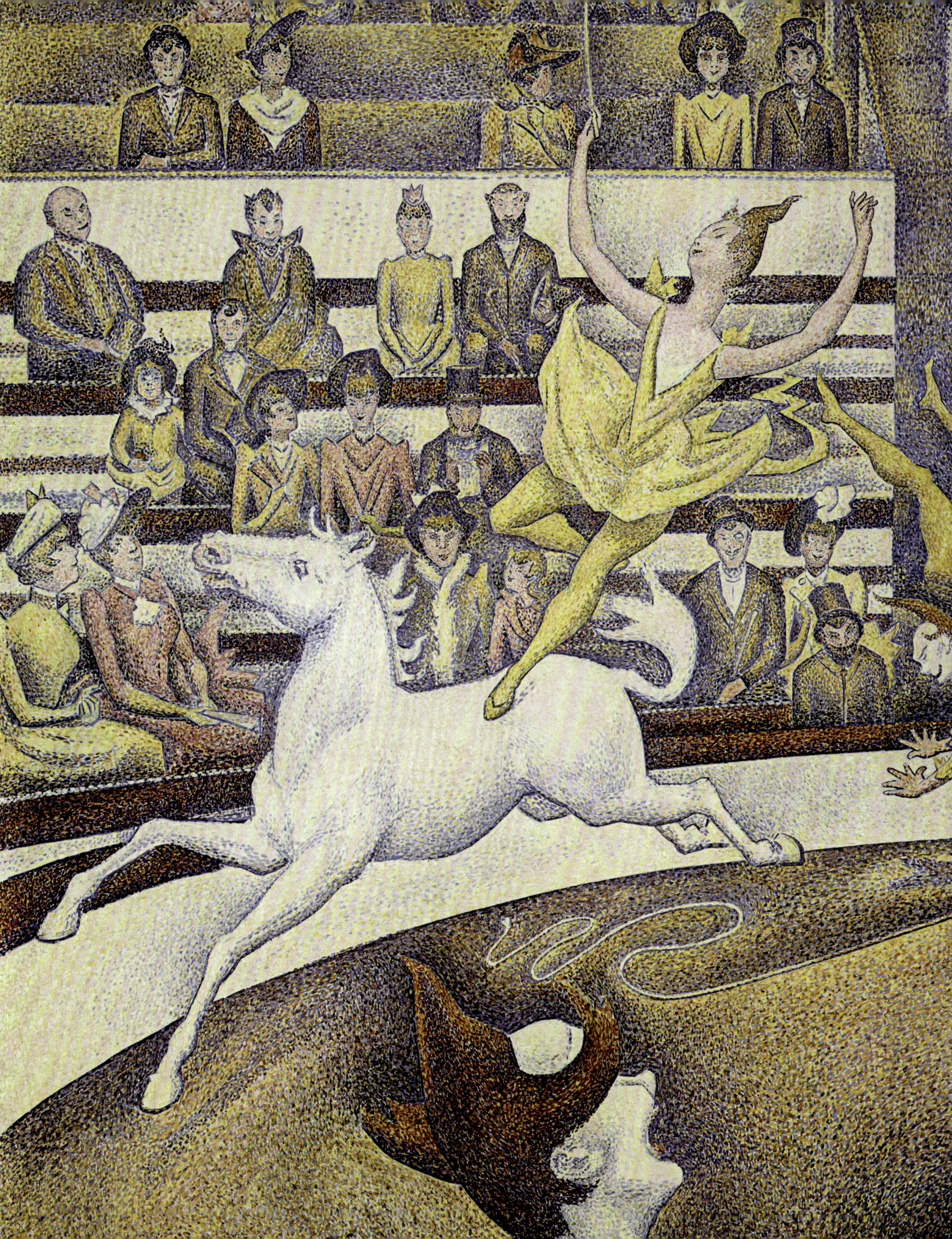

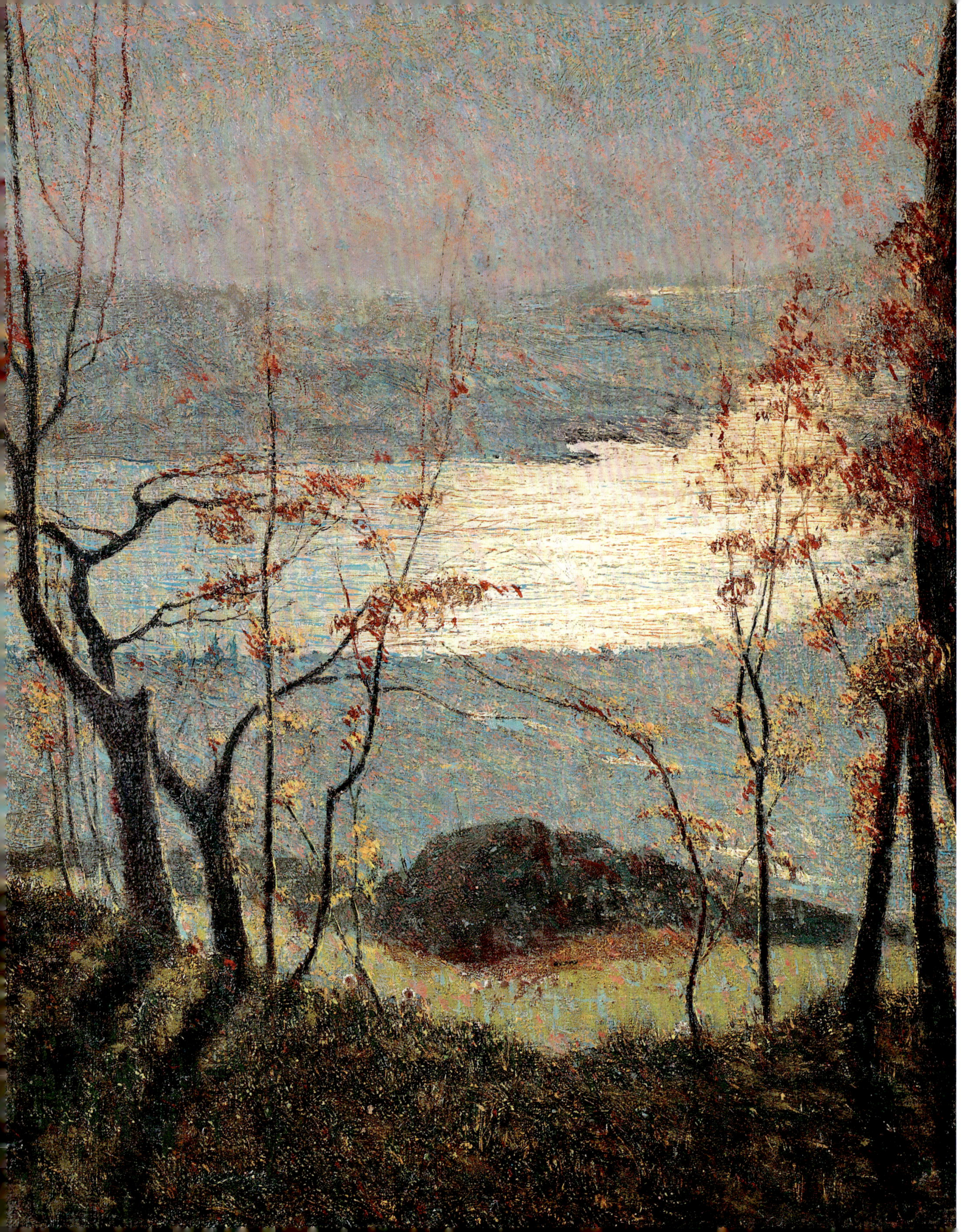

Vittore Grubicy di Dragon (1851–1920)

Morning

Matin

Morgen

Mañana

Mattino

Ochtend

c. 1896–1897, Oil on canvas/Huile sur toile, 47 × 41 cm

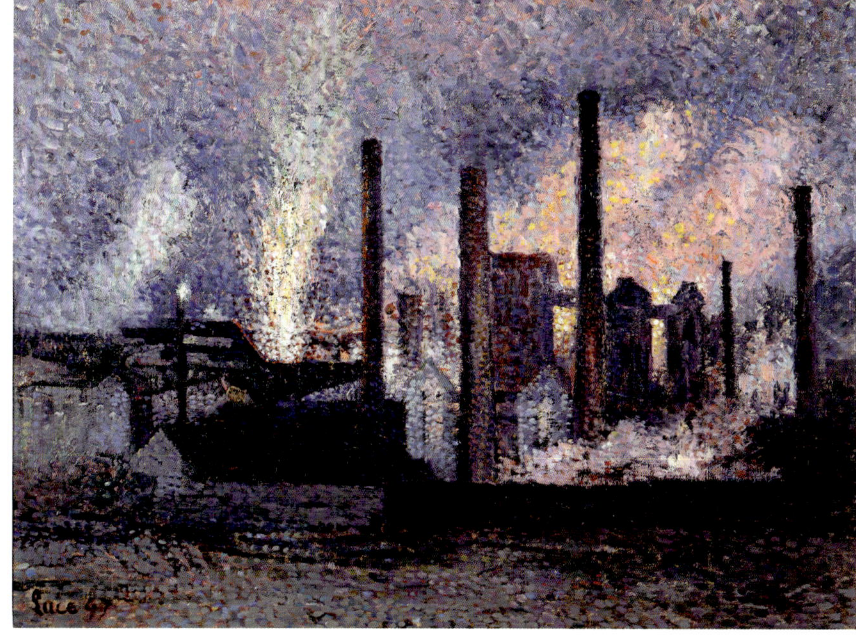

Maximilien Luce (1858–1941)

Factories near Charleroi

Usines près de Charleroi

Fabriken bei Charleroi

Fábricas cerca de Charleroi

Fabbriche vicino a Charleroi

Fabrieken, niet ver van Charleroi

1897, Oil on canvas/Huile sur toile, 51,2 × 38,5 cm

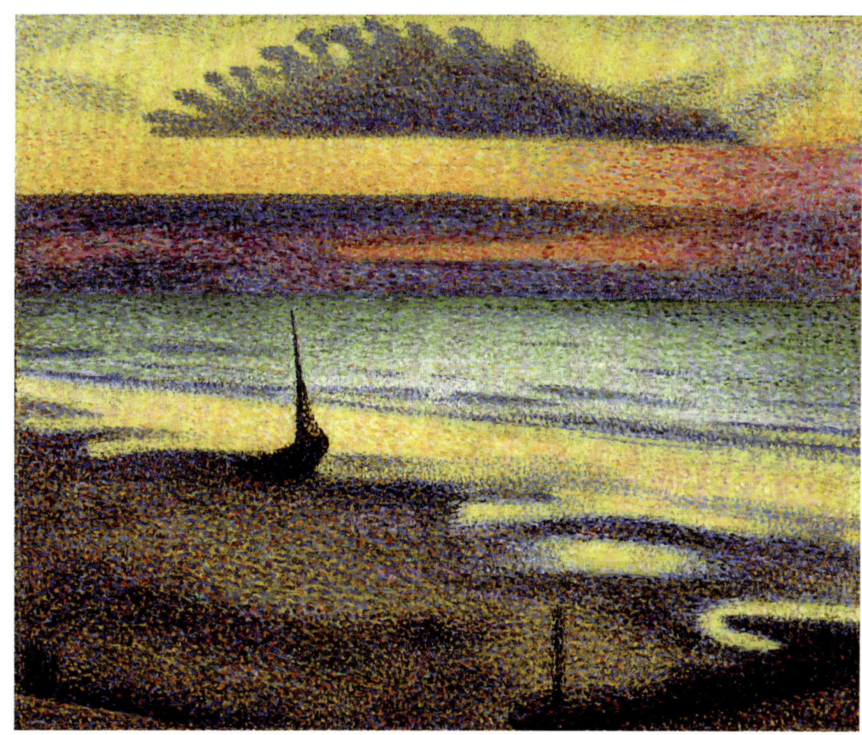

Georges Lemmen (1865–1916)

The Beach at Heist

Plage à Heist

Strand bei Heist

Playa en Heist

Spiaggia a Heist

Strand bij Heist

1891, Oil on wood/Huile sur bois, 37,5 × 46 cm

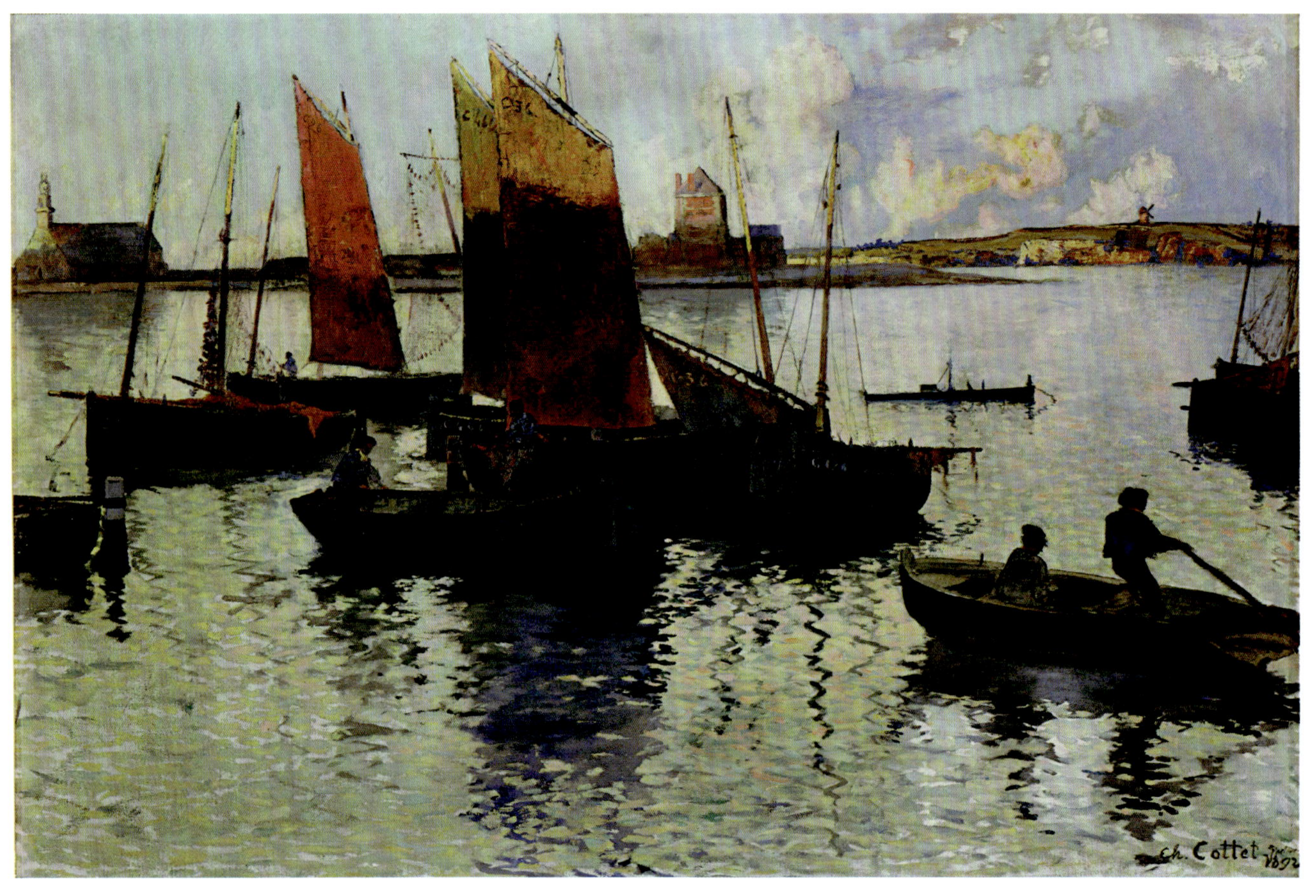

Charles Cottet (1863–1925)

Evening Light at the Port of Camaret
Rayons du soir, port de Camaret
1892, Oil on canvas/Huile sur toile, 74 × 110 cm

Der Hafen von Camaret im Abendlicht
Rayos de noche, puerto de Camaret

Raggi della sera, il porto di Camaret
De haven van Camaret bij avondlicht

Beginning in the 1880's the American Winslow Homer turned his back on the first part of a career dedicated to illustration (during the Civil War) and to rural scenes in a naturalistic vein. He painted numerous marine subjects and paintings bordering on realism and symbolism. Hence this bewitchingly poetic *Summer Night*.

À partir des années 1880, l'Américain Winslow Homer tourne le dos à une première partie de carrière dédiée à l'illustration (pendant la guerre de Sécession) et à des scènes rurales dans une veine naturaliste. Il peint de nombreuses marines, et des tableaux à la frontière du réalisme et du symbolisme. Ainsi de cette *Nuit d'été* d'une poésie envoûtante.

In den 1880er-Jahren wendet sich der Amerikaner Winslow Homer von seiner ersten Karriere ab, die der Illustration (während des Sezessionskriegs) und ländlichen Szenen im naturalistischen Stil gewidmet gewesen war. Er malt zahlreiche Seestücke und Gemälde an der Grenze zwischen Realismus und Symbolismus. So das Gemälde *Sommernacht* von bezaubernder Poesie.

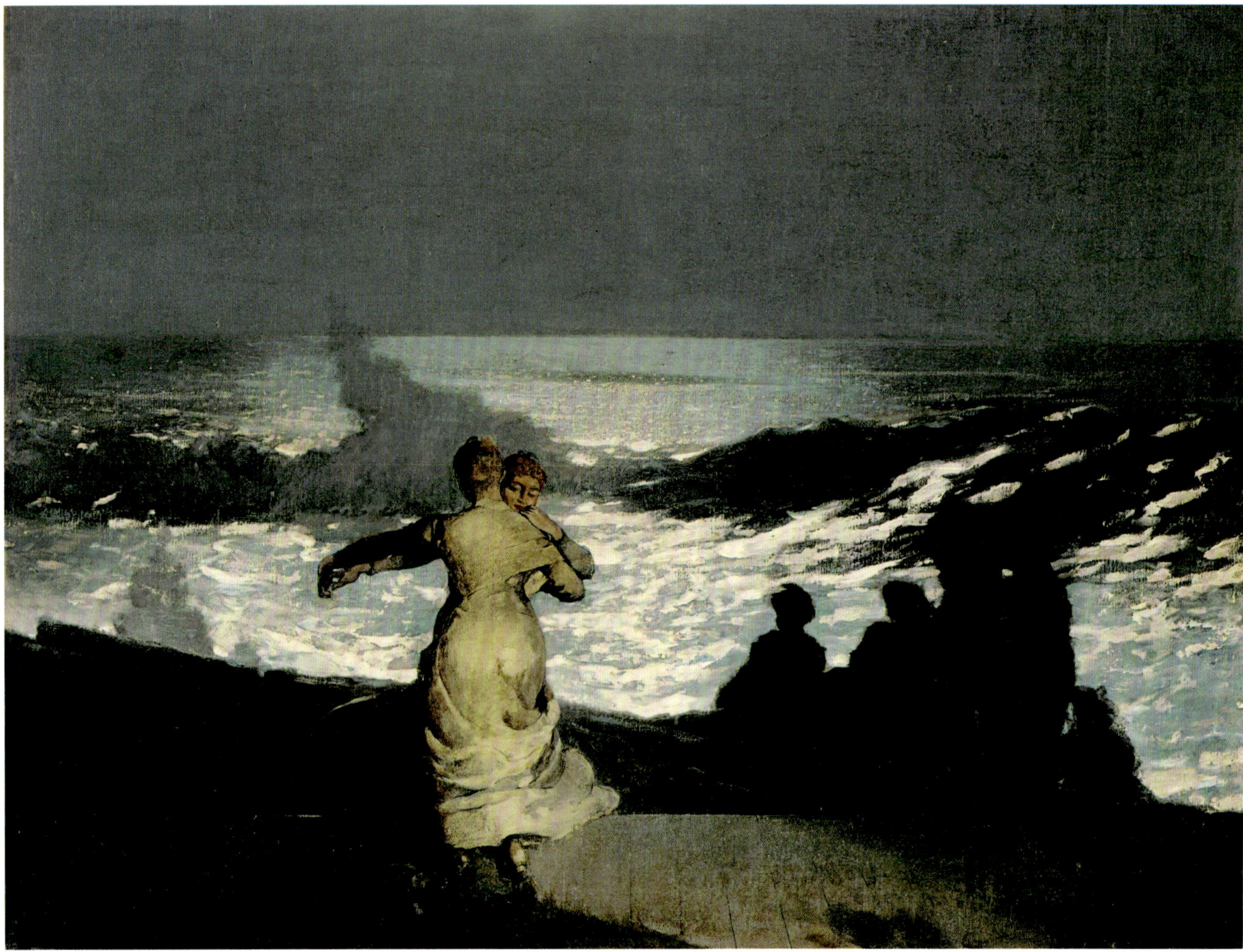

Summer Night   Sommernacht   Notte d'estate

Nuit d'été   Noche de verano   Zomernacht

1890, Oil on canvas/Huile sur toile, 76,5 × 102 cm

Desde la década de 1880, el estadounidense Winslow Homer da la espalda a la primera parte de su carrera dedicada a la ilustración (durante la Guerra de Secesión) y a las escenas rurales con una vena naturalista. Pintó numerosas marinas y cuadros que se encuentran en la frontera entre el realismo y el simbolismo. Así como esta *Noche de verano,* de una poesía inquietante.

A partire dal 1880, l'americano Winslow Homer voltò le spalle alla prima parte della sua carriera dedicata all'illustrazione (durante la Guerra di successione) e alle scene rurali in stile naturalistico per dipingere numerosi paesaggi marini e quadri al confine tra Realismo e Simbolismo. Nacque così questa *Notte d'estate,* che esprime una poetica struggente.

Vanaf de jaren 1880 zet de Amerikaan Winslow Homer een punt achter waarmee hij zijn schilderscarrière begon: illustratiekunst (tijdens de Burgeroorlog) en plattelandstaferelen met een naturalistische inslag. Hij schildert een groot aantal zeegezichten en schilderijen op de grens van realisme en symbolisme. Waaronder deze betoverend poëtische *Zomernacht.*

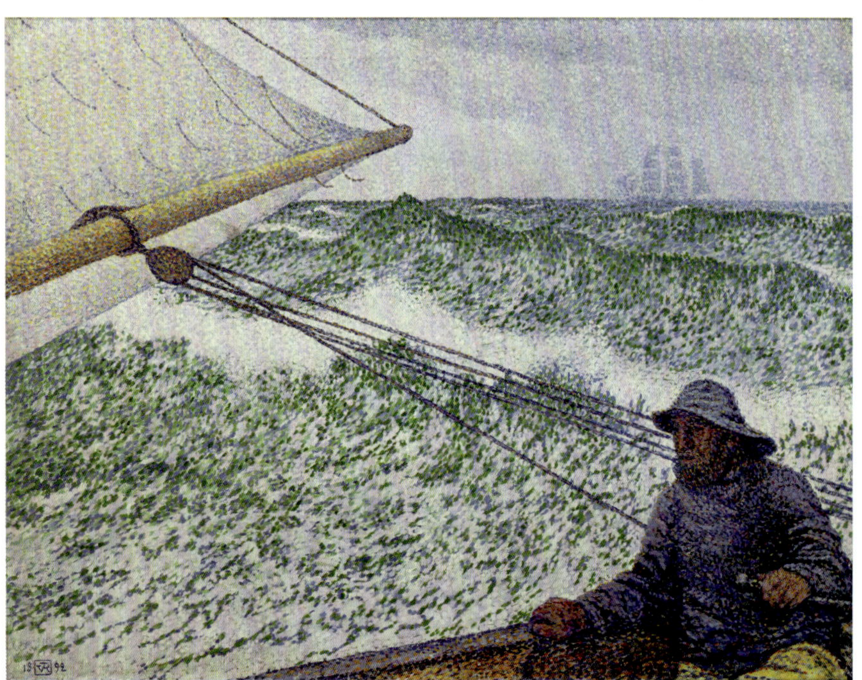

Théo van Rysselberghe (1862–1926)

The Man at the Helm

L'Homme à la barre

Der Mann am Ruder

Hombre al timón

L'uomo al timone

De man aan het roer

1892, Oil on canvas/Huile sur toile, 60,2 × 80,2 cm

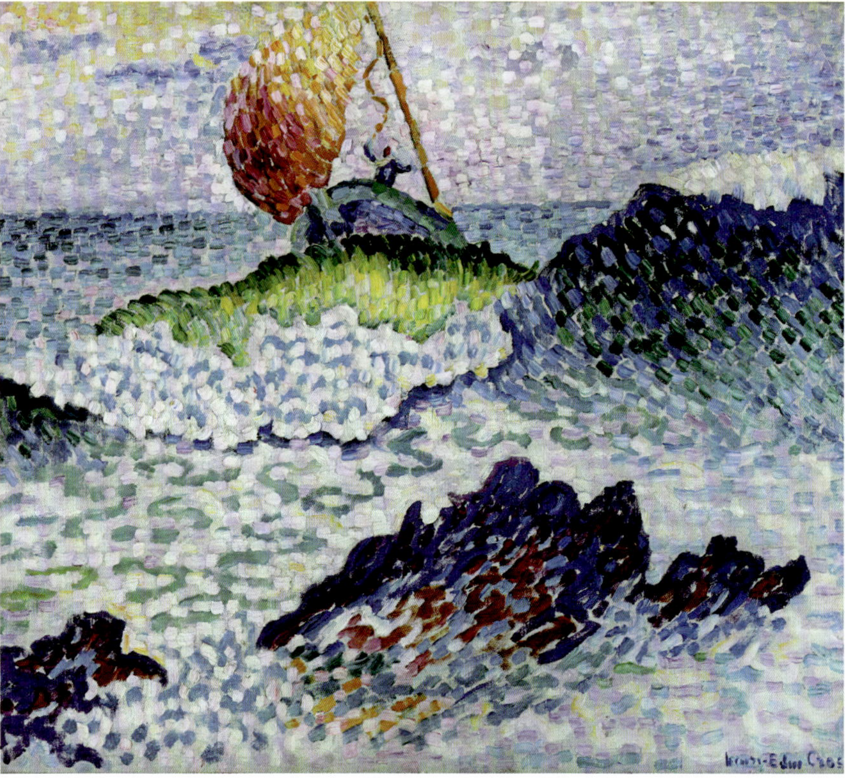

Henri-Edmond Cross (1856–1910)

The Shipwreck

Le Naufrage

Der Schiffbruch

El naufragio

Il Naufragio

De schipbreuk

c. 1906, Oil on canvas/Huile sur toile, 46 × 55 cm

Henri-Edmond Cross (1856–1910)

The Golden Isles

Les Îles d'Or

Die Goldenen Inseln

Las islas de Oro

Le Isole d'Oro

De Gouden Eilanden

c. 1891–1892, Oil on canvas/Huile sur toile, 59,5 × 54 cm

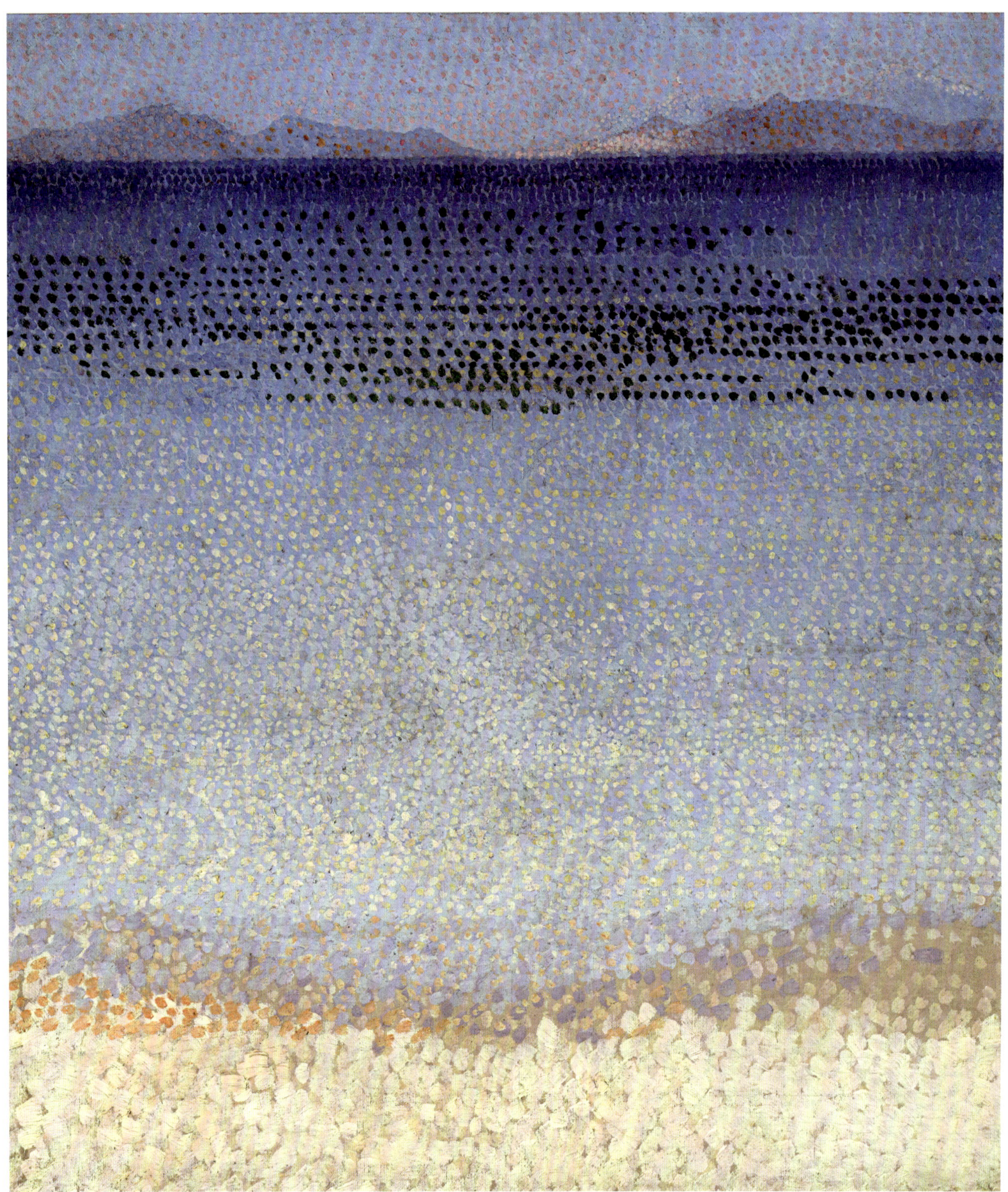

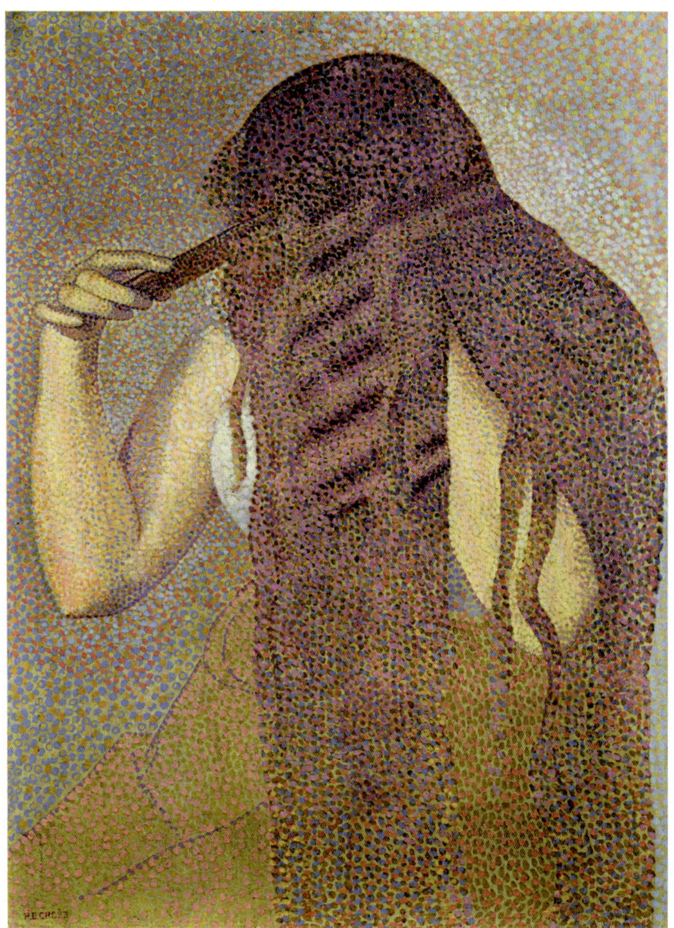

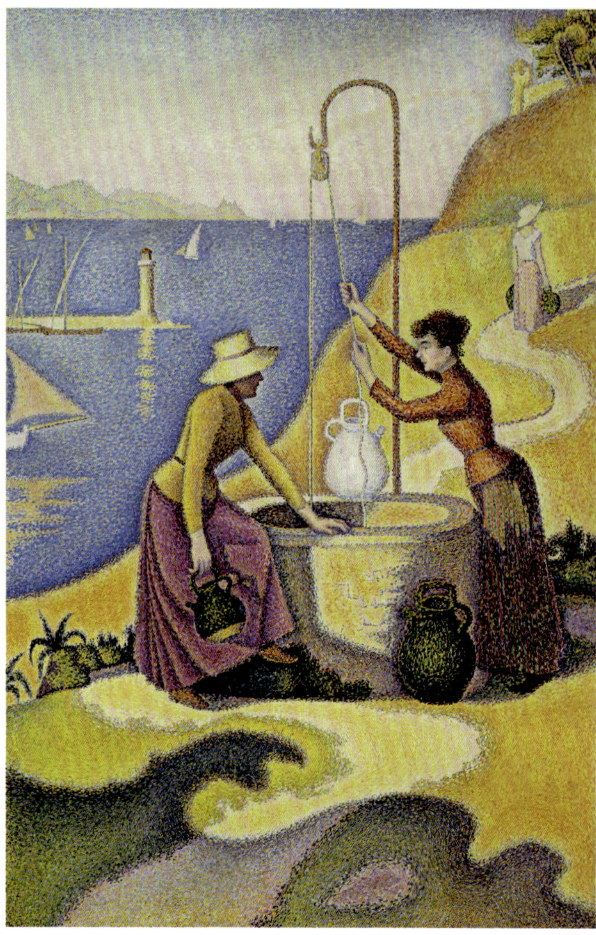

Henri-Edmond Cross (1856–1910)
The Hair
La Chevelure
Das Haar
El cabello
La capigliatura
Het haar
c. 1892, Oil on canvas/Huile sur toile, 61,5 × 46 cm

Paul Signac (1863–1935)
Women at the Well
Femmes au puits
Frauen am Brunnen
Mujeres en el pozo
Donne al pozzo
Vrouwen bij de put
c. 1892, Oil on canvas/Huile sur toile, 194,5 × 130 cm

Maritime or fluvial, ports never ceased to inspire Paul Signac. This spectacular work reveals a colorist who dares everything. While the portrayed locality may be immediately recognizable, the genius of the artist is to make a real fireworks of it with exploding reds and flaming roses, purples, blues and greens of a wild intensity.

Maritimes ou fluviaux, les ports n'ont cessé d'inspirer Paul Signac. Cette œuvre spectaculaire révèle un coloriste qui ose tout. Si le site représenté reste immédiatement reconnaissable, le génie de l'artiste est d'en faire un véritable feu d'artifice où explosent des rouges et des roses flamboyants, des violets, des bleus et des verts d'une intensité fauve.

Ob am Meer oder am Fluss – Häfen haben Paul Signac immer wieder inspiriert. Dieses spektakuläre Werk verrät einen wagemutigen Koloristen. Der dargestellte Ort bleibt sofort erkennbar, die Genialität des Künstlers besteht darin, aus ihm ein wahres Feuerwerk aus explodierenden knalligen Rot- und Rosatönen, aus Violett-, Blau- und Grüntönen fauvistischer Intensität zu machen.

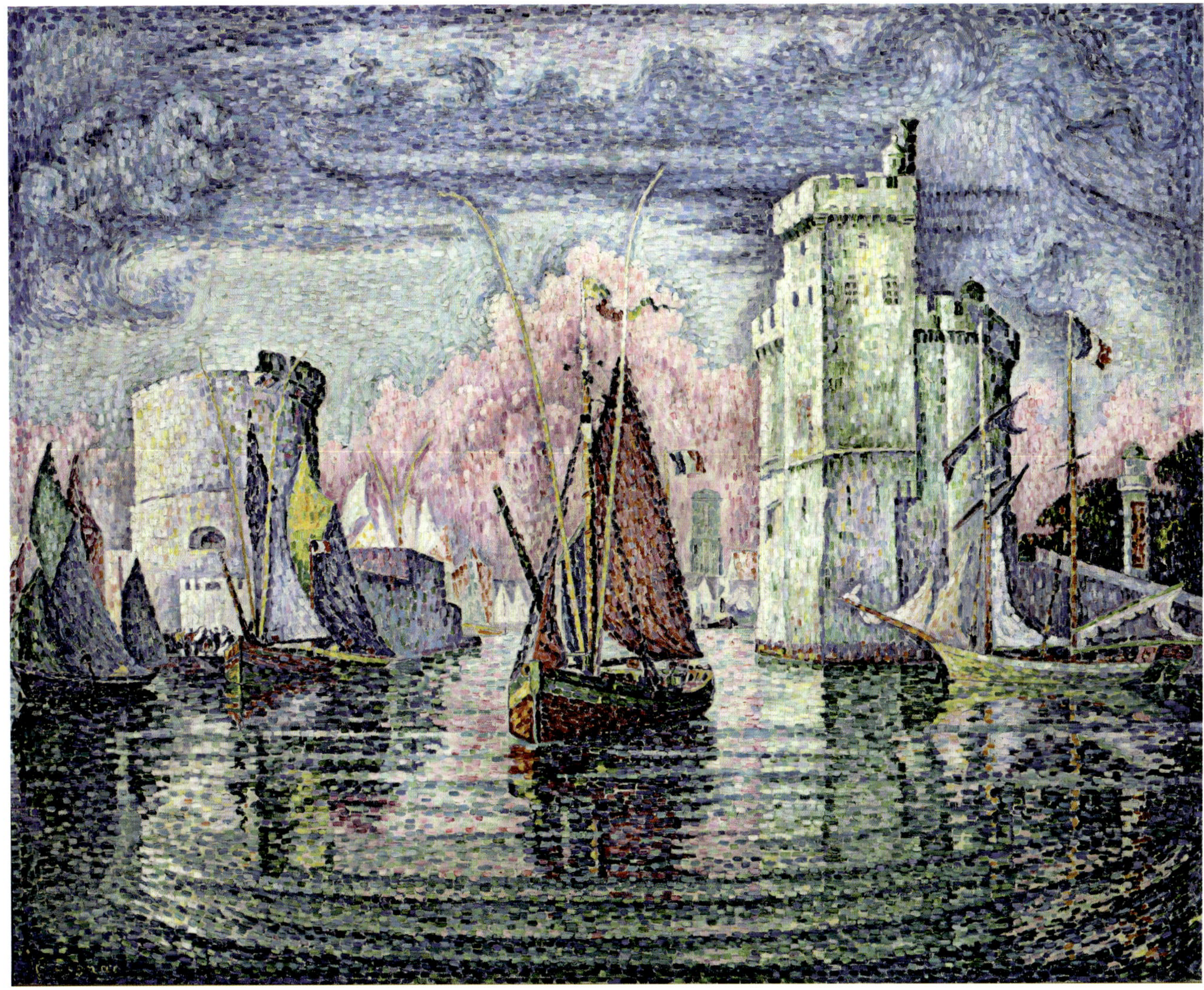

The Port at La Rochelle
Entrée du port de La Rochelle

Hafen von La Rochelle
El puerto de La Rochelle

Entrata del porto di La Rochelle
Ingang van de haven van La Rochelle

1921, Oil on canvas/Huile sur toile, 130,5 × 162 cm

Los puertos, marítimos o fluviales, no han dejado de inspirar a Paul Signac. Esta espectacular obra revela a un colorista que se atreve con todo. Si el sitio representado resulta inmediatamente reconocible es por el genio del artista que crea verdaderos fuegos artificiales que explotan en llamas rojas y rosas, púrpuras, azules y verdes de una intensidad salvaje.

I porti, sia marittimi che fluviali, furono sempre fonte di ispirazione per Paul Signac. Quest'opera spettacolare rivela un colorista che non ha pausa di osare. Sebbene il luogo rappresentato resti immediatamente riconoscibile, il genio dell'artista si palesa nella trasformazione del posto in un vero e proprio fuoco d'artificio in cui esplodono rossi e rosa fiammeggianti insieme a viola, blu e verdi dall'intensità selvaggia.

Zee- en rivierhavens zijn Paul Signac altijd blijven inspireren. Dit spectaculaire schilderij illustreert wat een durfal Signac als colorist is. De plek die hij weergeeft blijft onmiddellijk herkenbaar, maar zijn talent schuilt in het ware vuurwerk dat hij ervan maakt: een explosie van tinten vuurrood en roze, paars, blauw en groen met een fauvistische intensiteit.

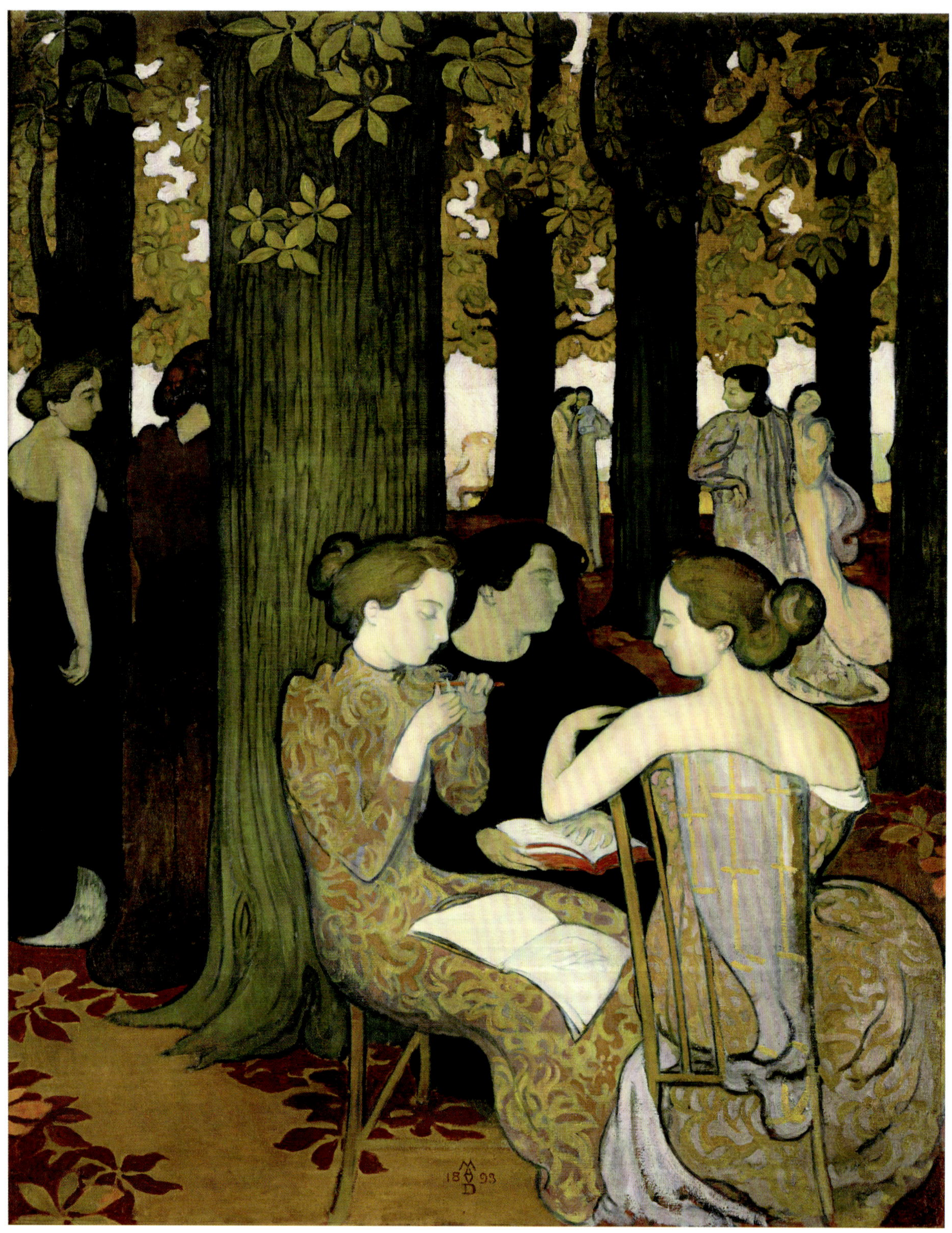

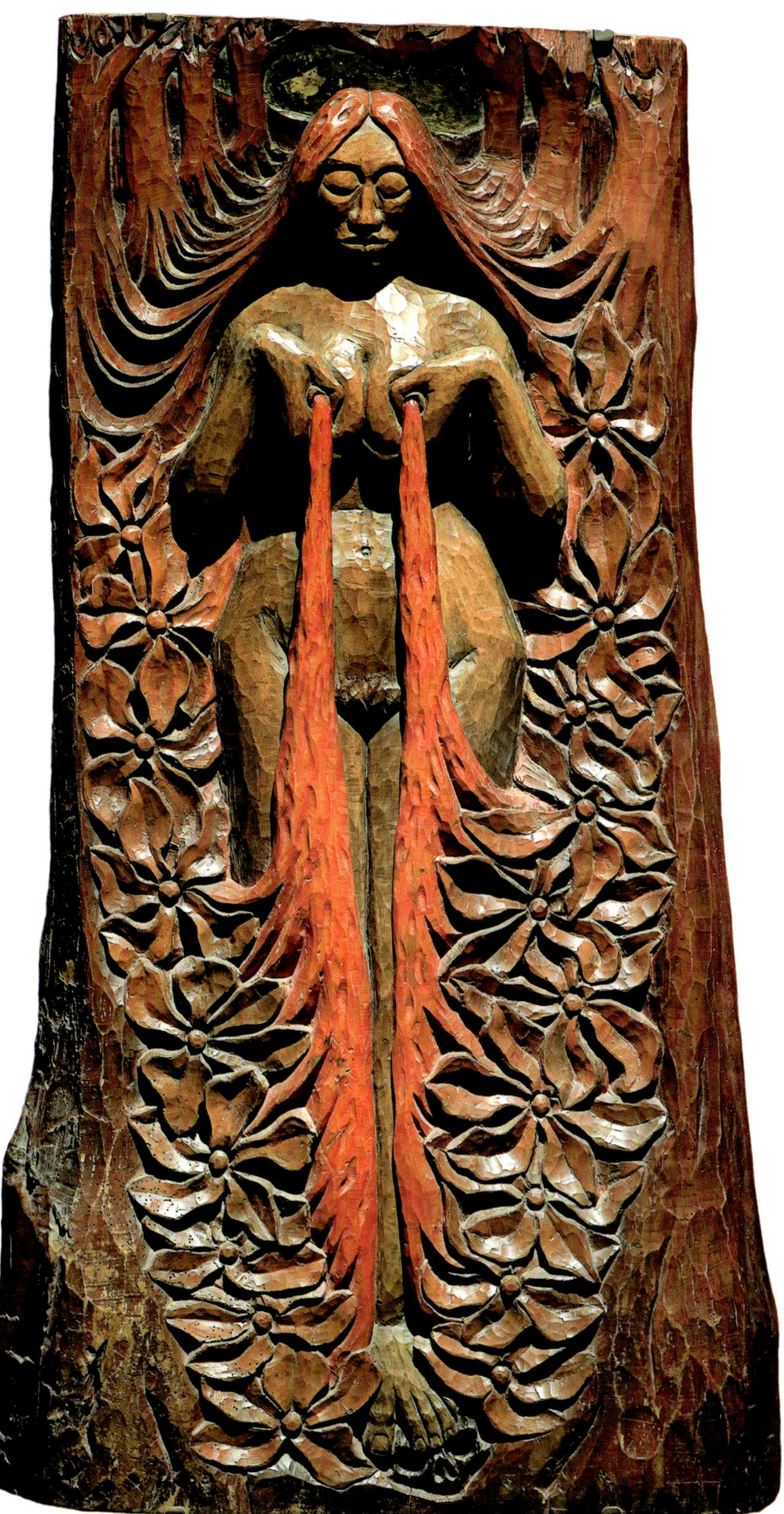

Maurice Denis
(1870–1943)

The Muses

Les Muses

Die Musen

Las musas

Le Muse

De muzen

1893, Oil on canvas/Huile
sur toile, 171 × 137,5 cm

Georges Lacombe
(1868–1916)

Isis

Iside

1895, Bas-relief in
mahogany/Bas relief en
acajou, 111,5 × 62 cm

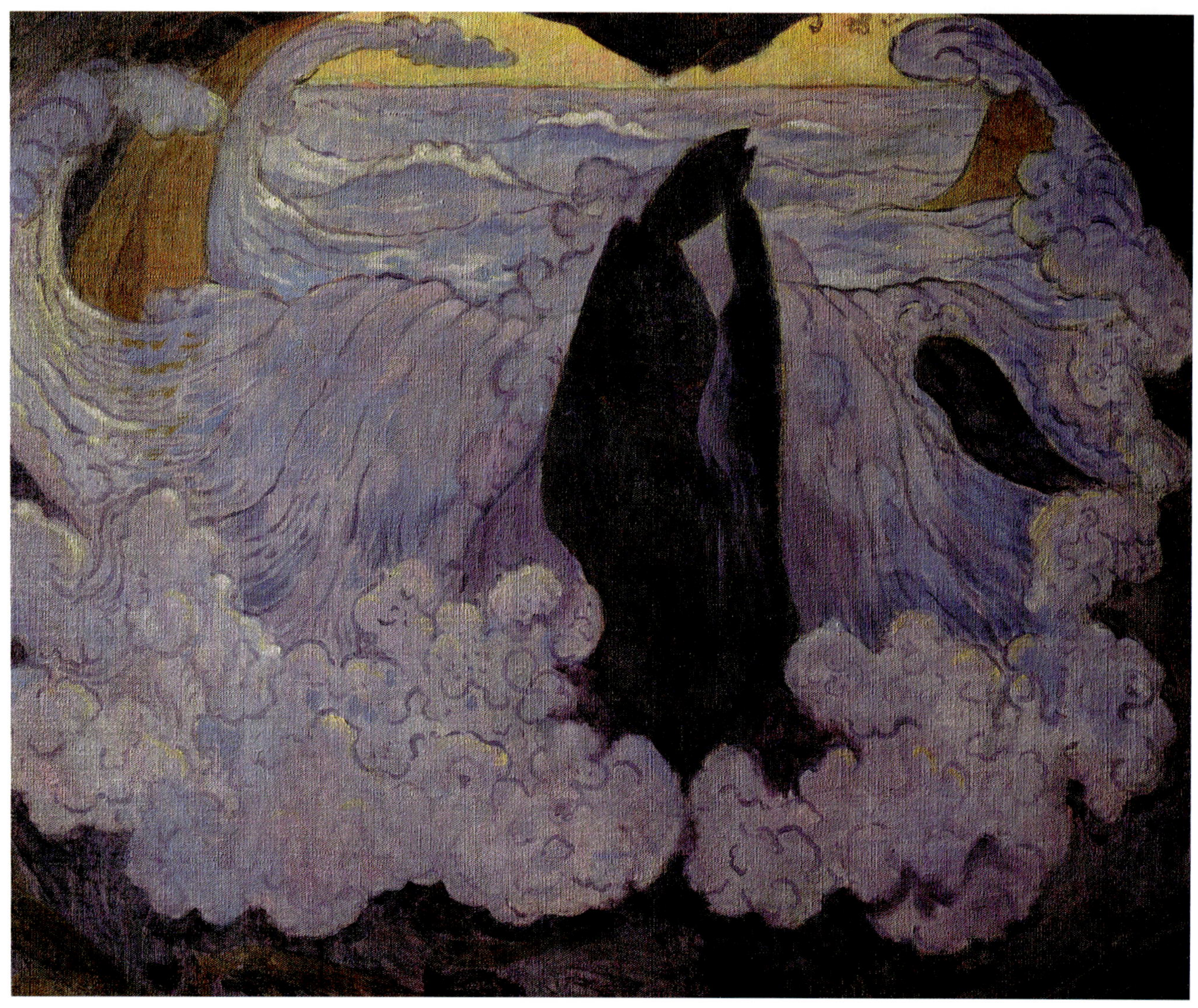

Georges Lacombe (1868–1916)

The Violet Wave

La Vague violette

Die violette Woge

La ola violeta

L'onda viola

De paarse golf

c. 1895–1896, Oil on canvas/Huile sur toile, 73,5 × 92,5 cm

Paul Ranson (1861–1909)

Lustral

Lustral

Lustration

Lustral

Lustrale

Lustral

1891, Tempera on canvas/Tempera sur toile, 35 × 24 cm

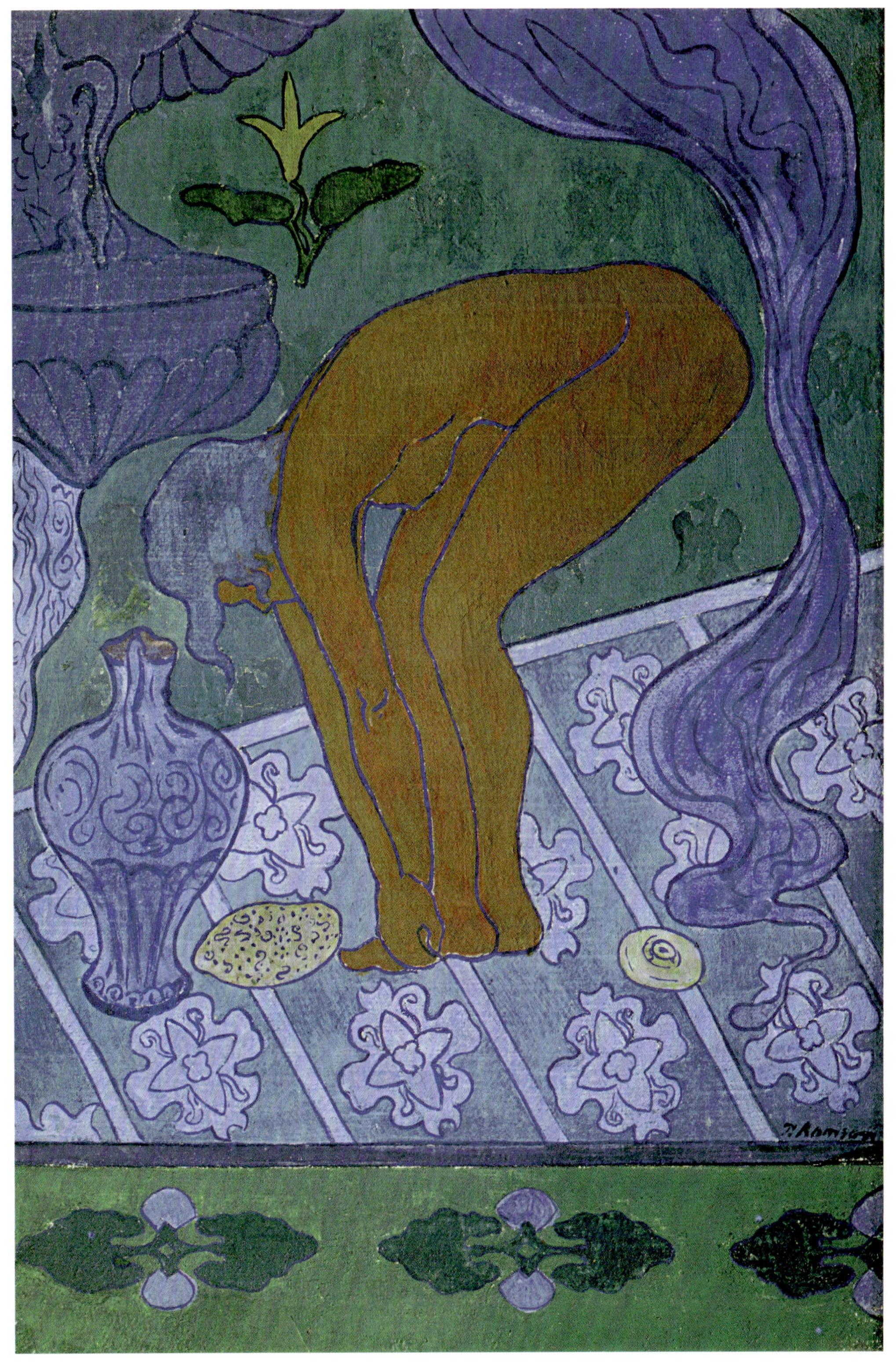

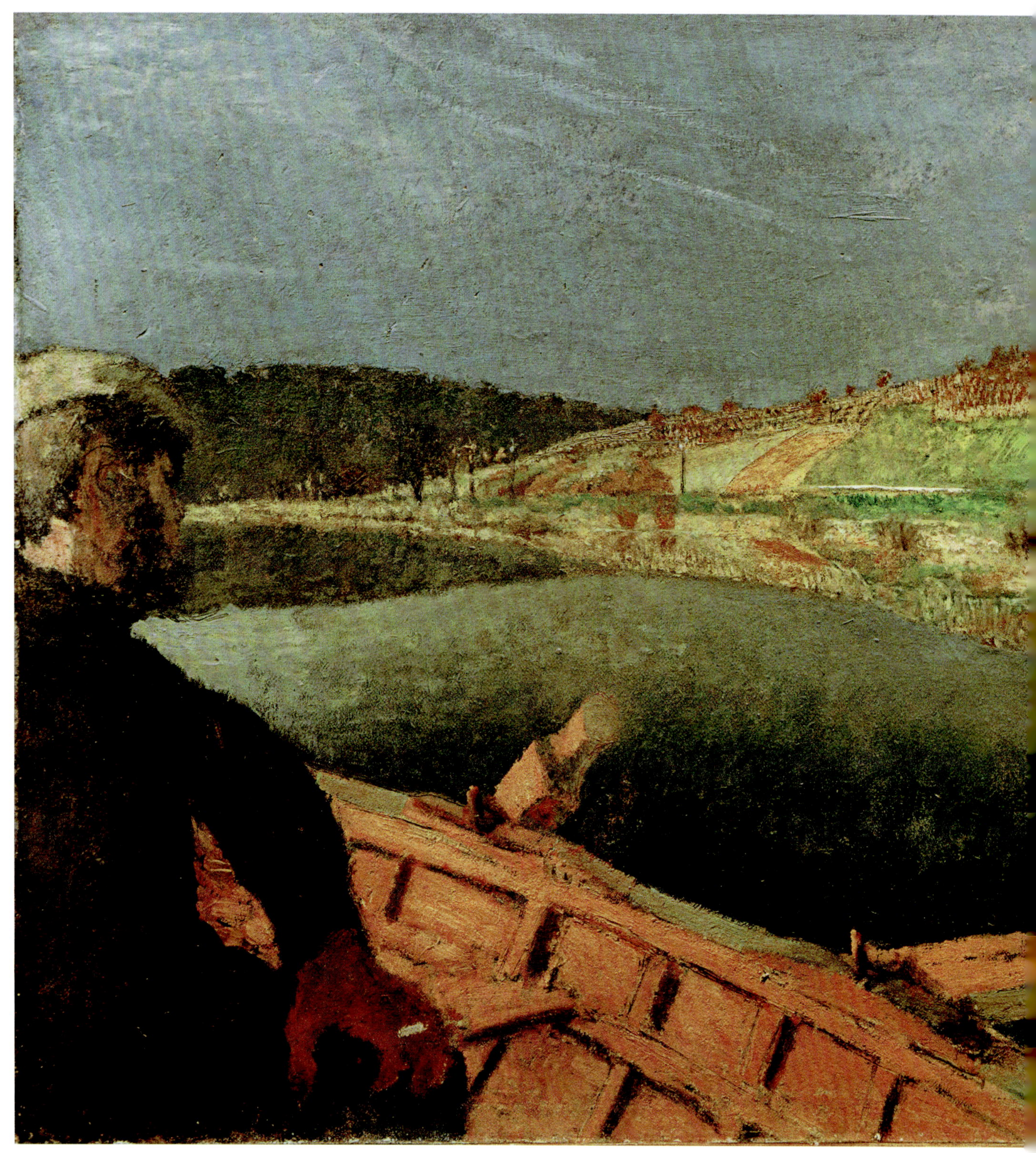

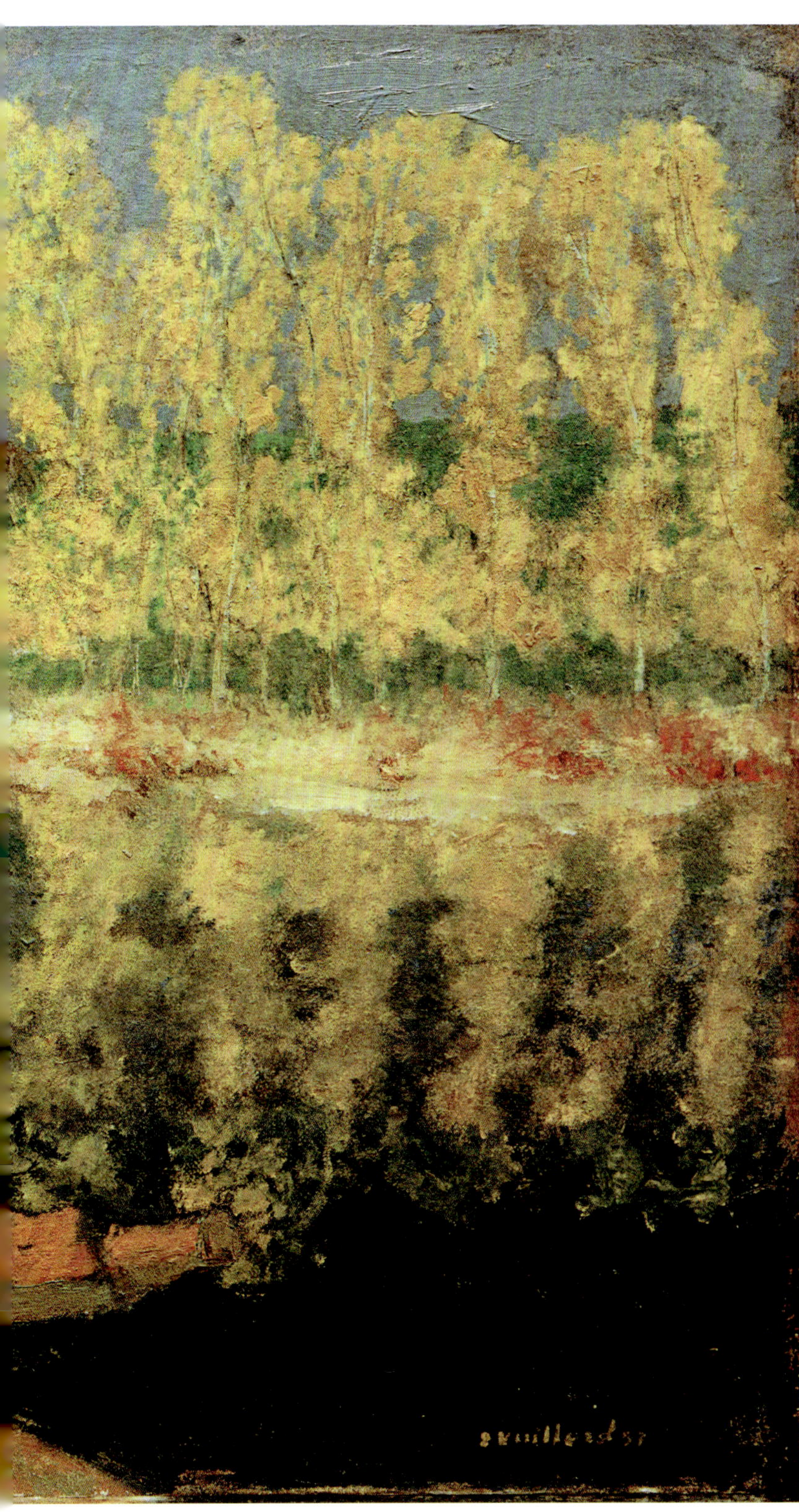

Édouard Vuillard (1868–1940)

The Oarsman

Le Passeur

Der Fährmann

El barquero

In barca

De veerman

1897, Oil on cardboard on plywood/Huile sur carton
sur panneau contreplaqué, 51,5 × 76 cm

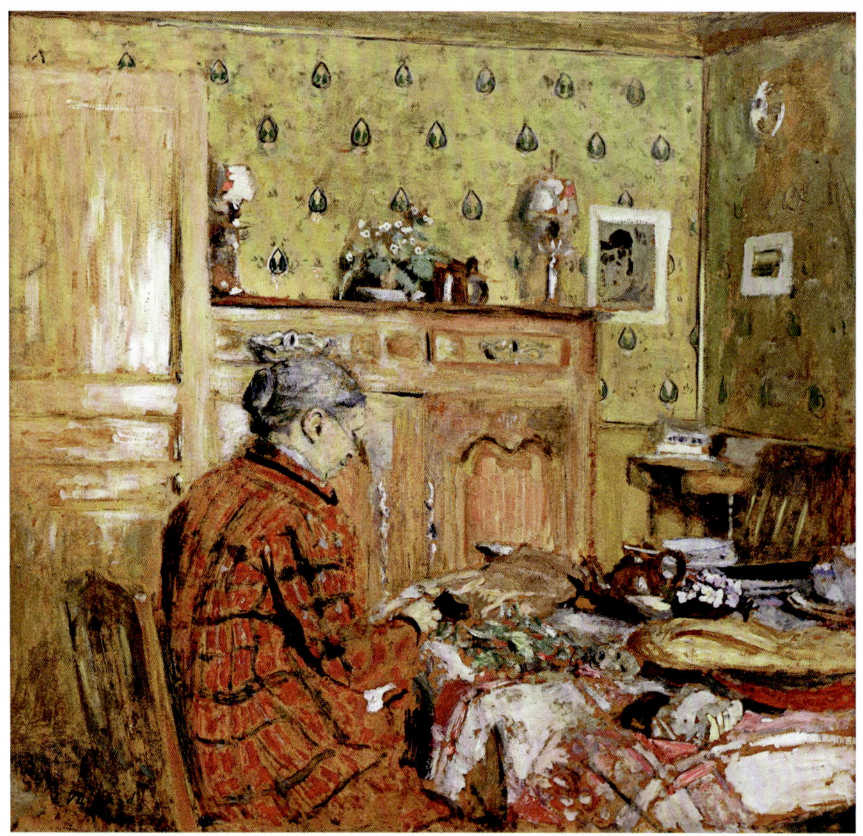

Édouard Vuillard (1868–1940)
Morning Breakfast
Le Déjeuner du matin
Das Frühstück
El desayuno de la mañana
La prima colazione
Het ontbijt
1903, Oil on cardboard/Huile sur carton, 58 × 60 cm

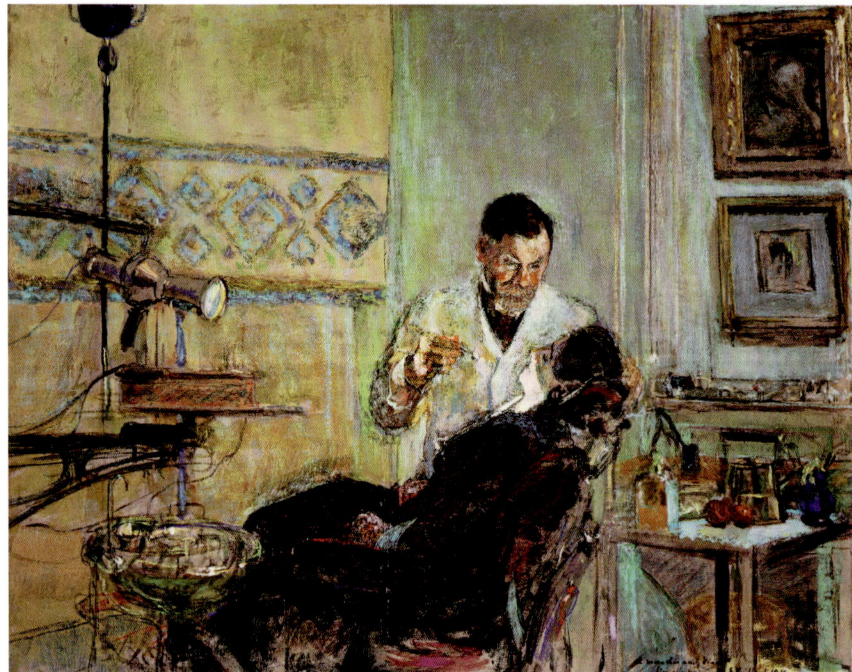

Édouard Vuillard (1868–1940)
Doctor Viau in his Surgery
Le Dr Viau dans son cabinet dentaire
Dr. Viau in seiner Zahnarztpraxis
El doctor Viau en su consulta
Il dottor Viau nel suo studio dentistico
Dr. Viau in zijn tandartspraktijk
1914, Glue and pastel highlights on canvas/Colle
et rehauts de pastel sur toile, 107,7 × 137,5 cm

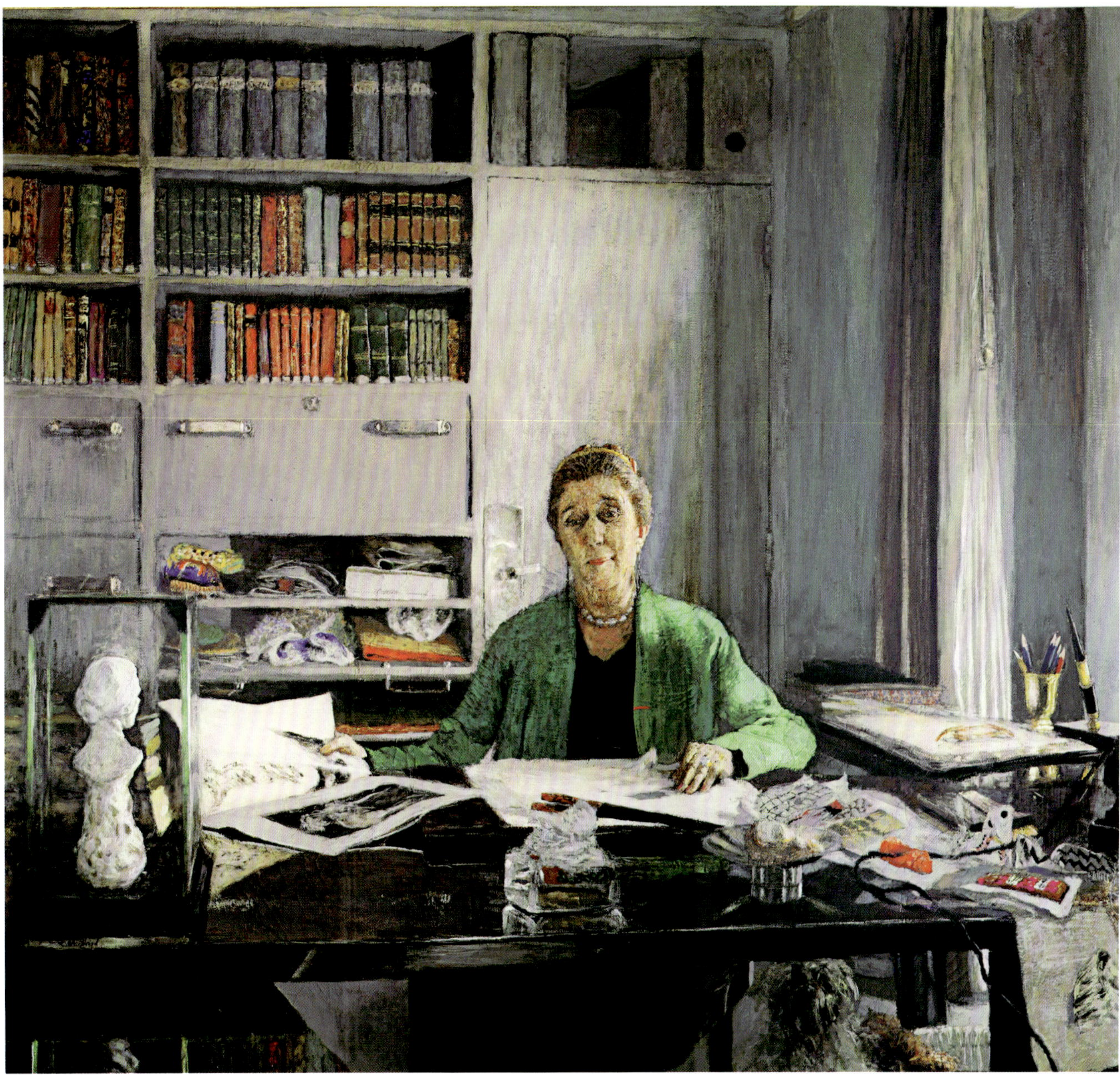

Édouard Vuillard (1868–1940)
Jeanne Lanvin in her Studio
Jeanne Lanvin dans son atelier
Jeanne Lanvin in ihrem Atelier
Jeanne Lanvin en su taller
Jeanne Lanvin nel suo studio
Jeanne Lanvin in haar atelier
1933, Glue on canvas/Colle sur toile, 124,5 × 136,5 cm

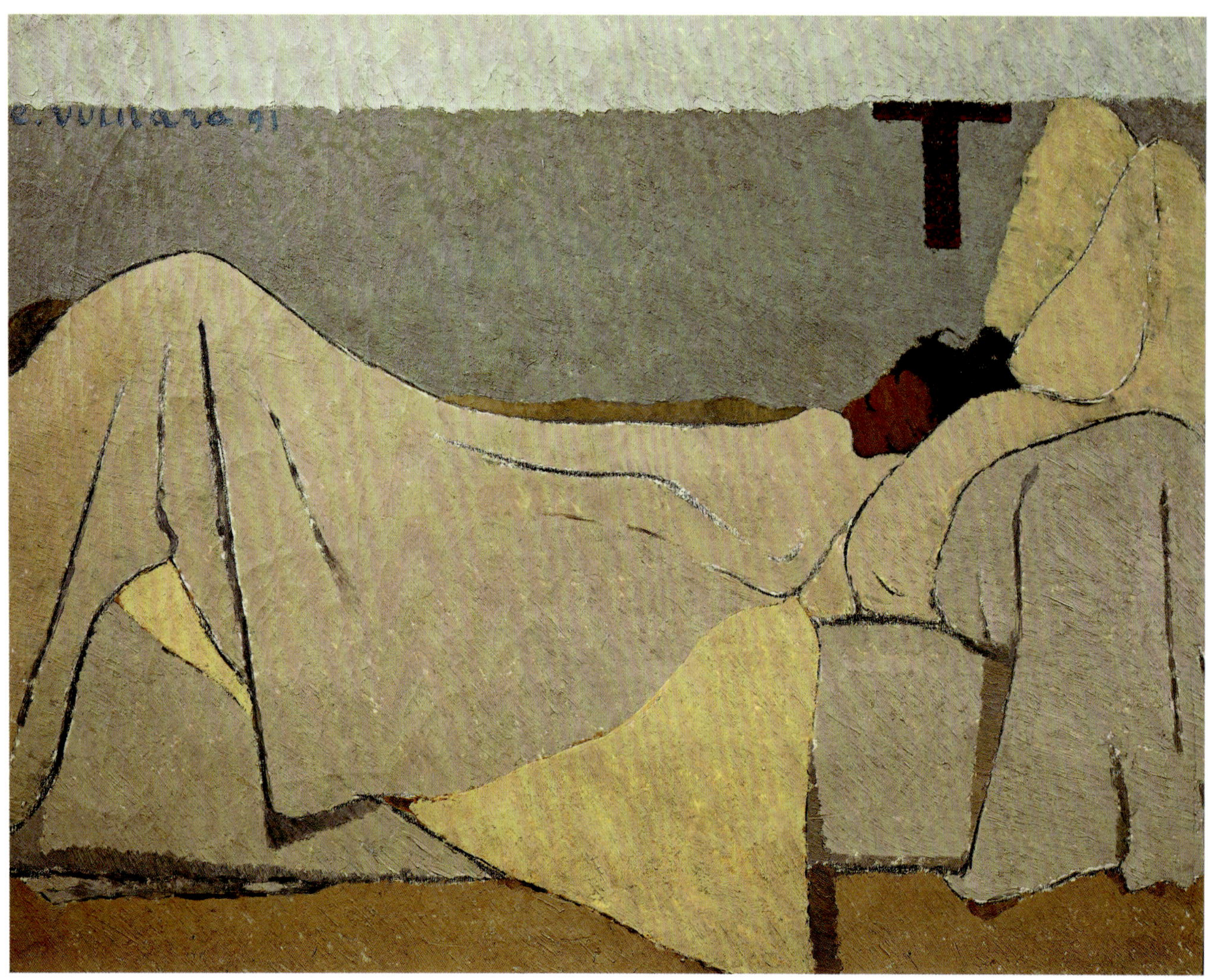

Édouard Vuillard (1868–1940)

In Bed	Im Bett	A letto
Au lit	En la cama	In bed

1891, Oil on canvas/Huile sur toile, 74 × 92 cm

Influenced on the one hand by Gauguin's lessons on synthetism and by the aesthetics of Japanese prints, this work by Édouard Vuillard is a masterpiece of simplification and stylization. Against a background patterned by three colored stripes, the bed and the lying figure are represented by a set of juxtaposed areas and some straight and oblique lines which suffice to bring them into existence.

Marquée à la fois par les leçons du synthétisme de Gauguin et par l'esthétique des estampes japonaises, cette œuvre d'Édouard Vuillard est un chef-d'œuvre de simplification et de stylisation. Sur un fond structuré par trois bandeaux de couleurs, le lit et le personnage couché ne sont figurés que par un jeu d'aplats juxtaposés, et quelques lignes droites et obliques qui suffisent à les faire exister.

Dieses Werk von Édouard Vuillard ist sowohl von den Synthetismus-Lehren Gauguins als auch von der Ästhetik japanischer Holzschnitte geprägt und ein Meisterwerk der Simplifizierung und Stilisierung. Vor einem in drei Farbstreifen gegliederten Hintergrund werden das Bett und die liegende Figur nur mittels nebeneinanderliegender farbiger Flächen und weniger gerader und schräger Linien dargestellt, die ausreichen, um sie existieren zu lassen.

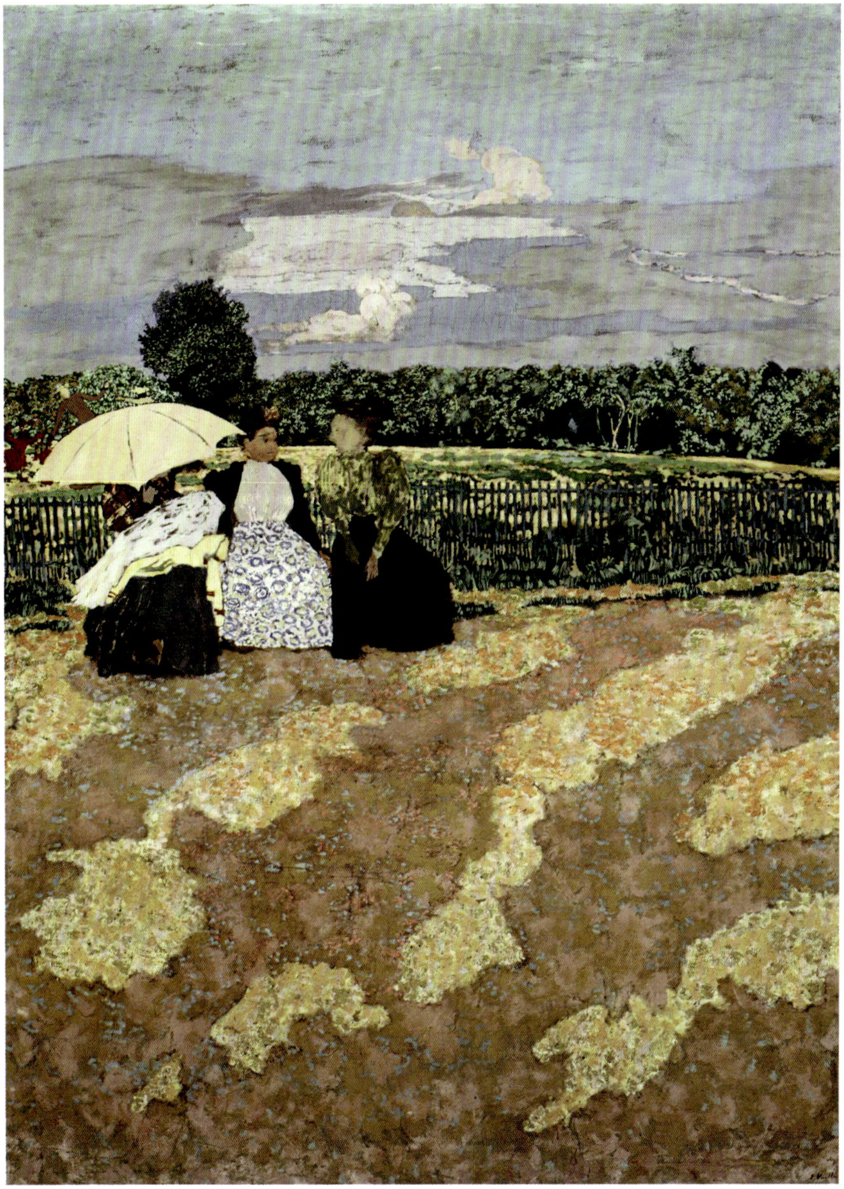

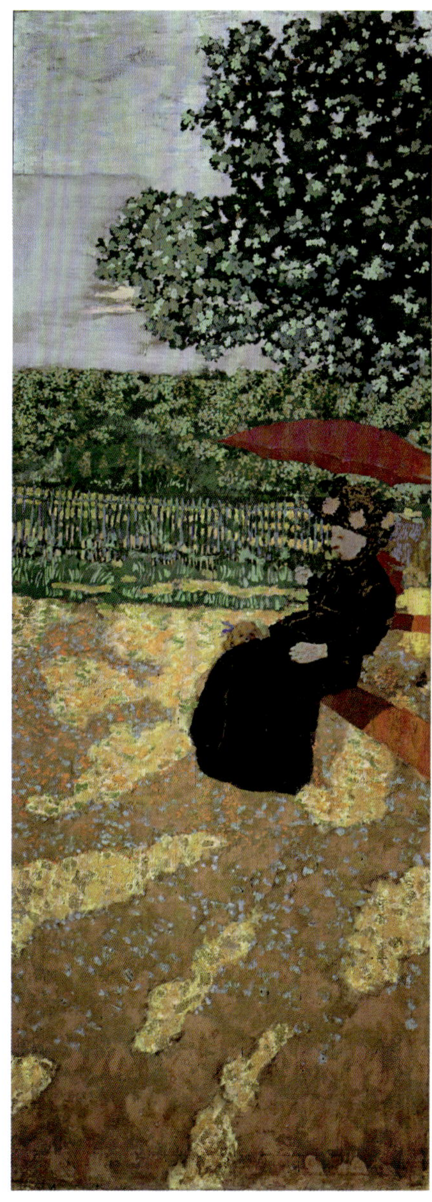

Marcada tanto por las lecciones de sintetismo de Gauguin como por la estética de los grabados japoneses, este cuadro de Édouard Vuillard es una obra maestra de la simplicidad y la estilización. Sobre un fondo estructurado por tres bandas de colores, la cama y el personaje acostado están representados tan solo por un juego de sólidos yuxtapuestos y algunas líneas rectas y oblicuas que son suficientes para hacerlos existir.

Influenzata sia dagli insegnamenti del Sintetismo di Gauguin sia dall'estetica delle stampe giapponesi, quest'opera di Édouard Vuillard è un capolavoro di semplicità e stilizzazione. Su uno sfondo strutturato con tre fasce di colori, il letto e il personaggio disteso sono rappresentati semplicemente mediante un gioco di aplat giustapposti e alcune linee rette e oblique sufficienti a farli esistere.

In bed van Édouard Vuillard, dat zowel van de invloed van Gauguins synthetisme als van de esthetiek van Japanse prenten getuigt, is een meesterwerk van eenvoud en stilering. Tegen een achtergrond van drie kleurenbanen worden het bed en het personage in bed slechts vormgegeven door een spel van naast elkaar geplaatste vlakken tinten en enkele rechte en schuine lijnen die volstaan om ze te laten bestaan.

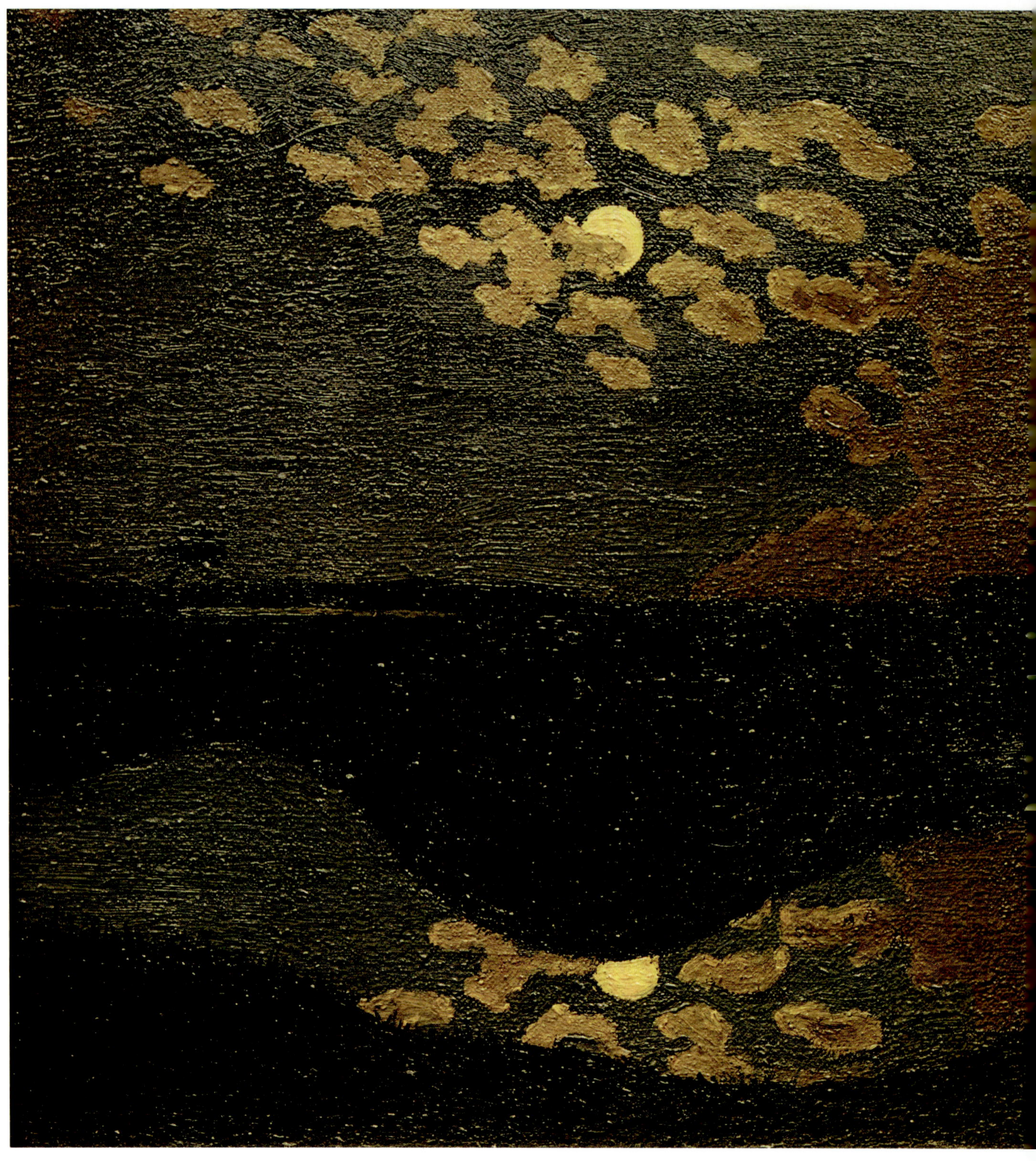

p 239 L

Édouard Vuillard (1868–1940)

Public Gardens: Conversation *(central panel)*

Jardins publics: La Conversation *(panneau central)*

Park in Paris: Die Ammen *(Mittelteil)*

Jardines públicos: La conversación *(panel central)*

Giardini pubblici: la conversazione *(pannello centrale)*

Openbare tuinen: Het gesprek *(middenpaneel)*

1894, Glue on canvas/Colle sur toile, 213,5 × 154 cm

p 239 R

Édouard Vuillard (1868–1940)

Public Gardens: The Red Parasol *(right panel)*

Jardins publics: L'Ombrelle rouge *(panneau droit)*

Park in Paris: Frau in Schwarz *(rechter Teil)*

Jardines públicos: La sombrilla roja *(panel derecho)*

Giardini pubblici: l'ombrello rosso *(pannello destro)*

Openbare tuinen: De rode parasol *(rechterpaneel)*

1894, Glue on canvas/Colle sur toile, 214 × 81 cm

Félix Vallotton (1865–1925)

Moonlight

Clair de lune

Mondlicht

Claro de luna

Chiaro di luna

Maanlicht

c. 1895, Oil on canvas/Huile sur toile, 27 × 41 cm

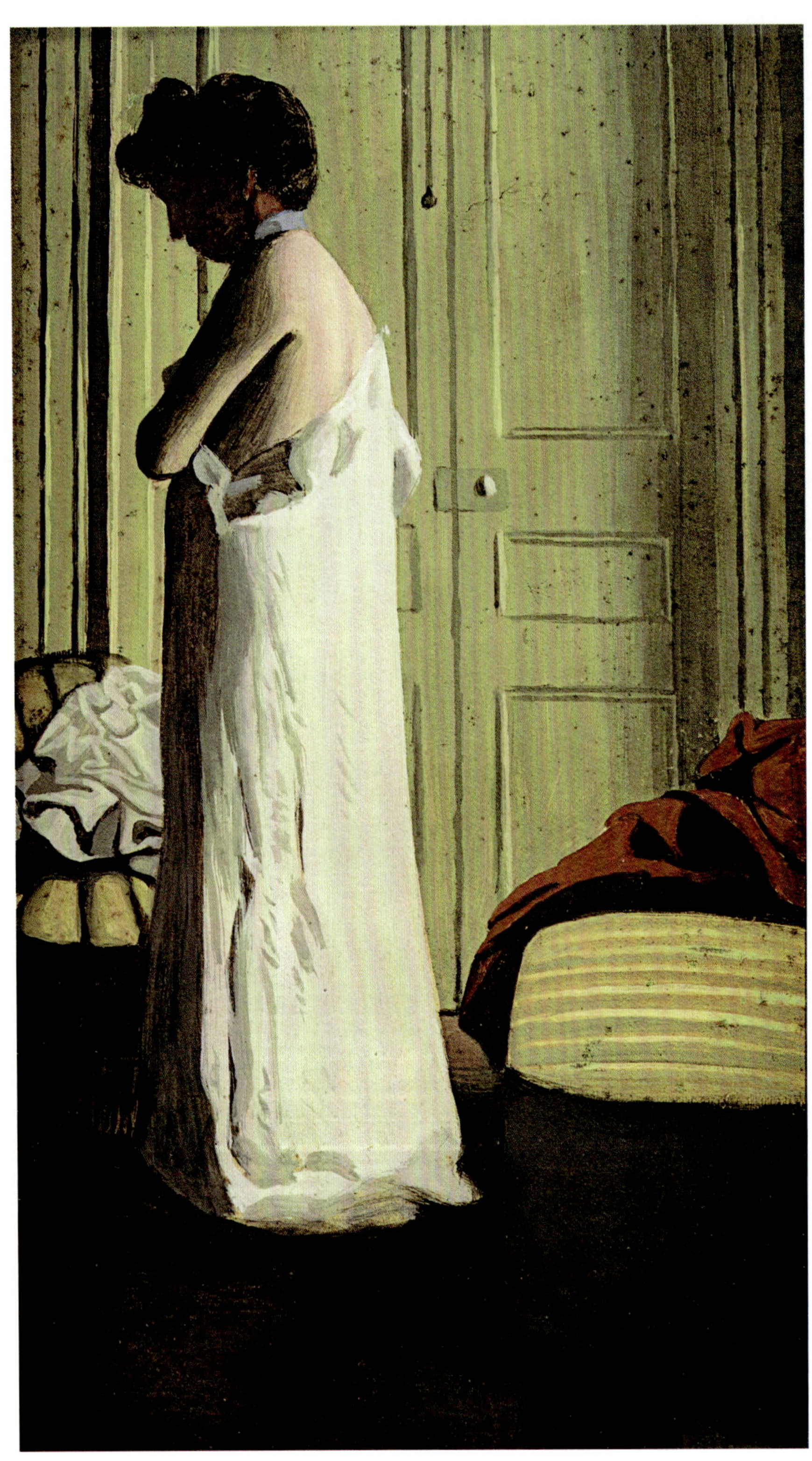

Félix Vallotton (1865–1925)

Woman Removing
Her Shirt

Femme retirant sa chemise

Frau ihr Hemd ausziehend

Mujer quitándose
el camisón

Donna che si toglie
la camicia

Vrouw die haar
nachthemd uittrekt

1900, Oil on cardboard/Huile
sur carton, 55,5 × 30,5 cm

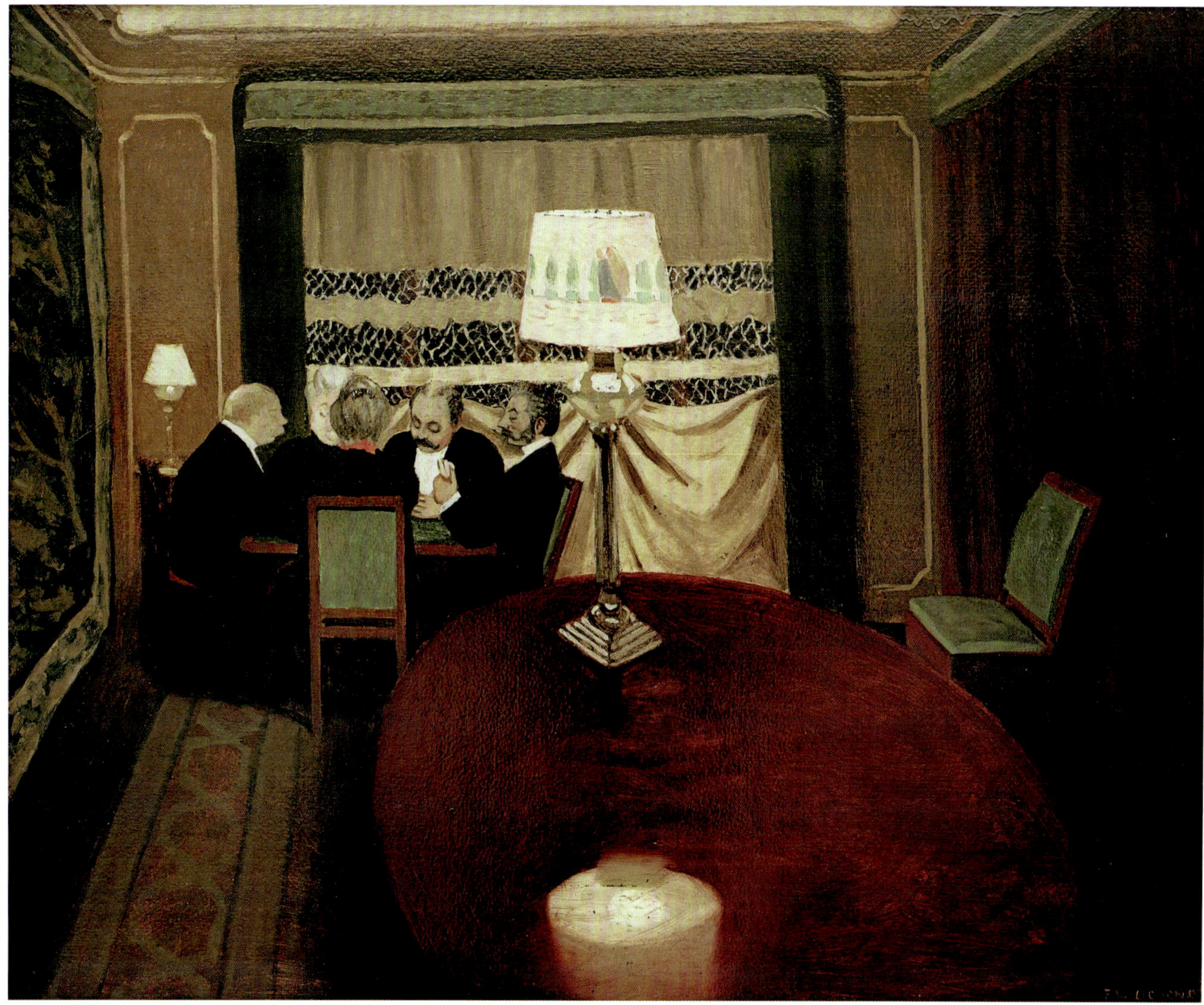

Félix Vallotton (1865–1925)

The Poker Game

Le Poker

Die Pokerspieler

El póker

Il poker

De pokerspelers

1902, Oil on cardboard/Huile sur carton, 52,5 × 67,4 cm

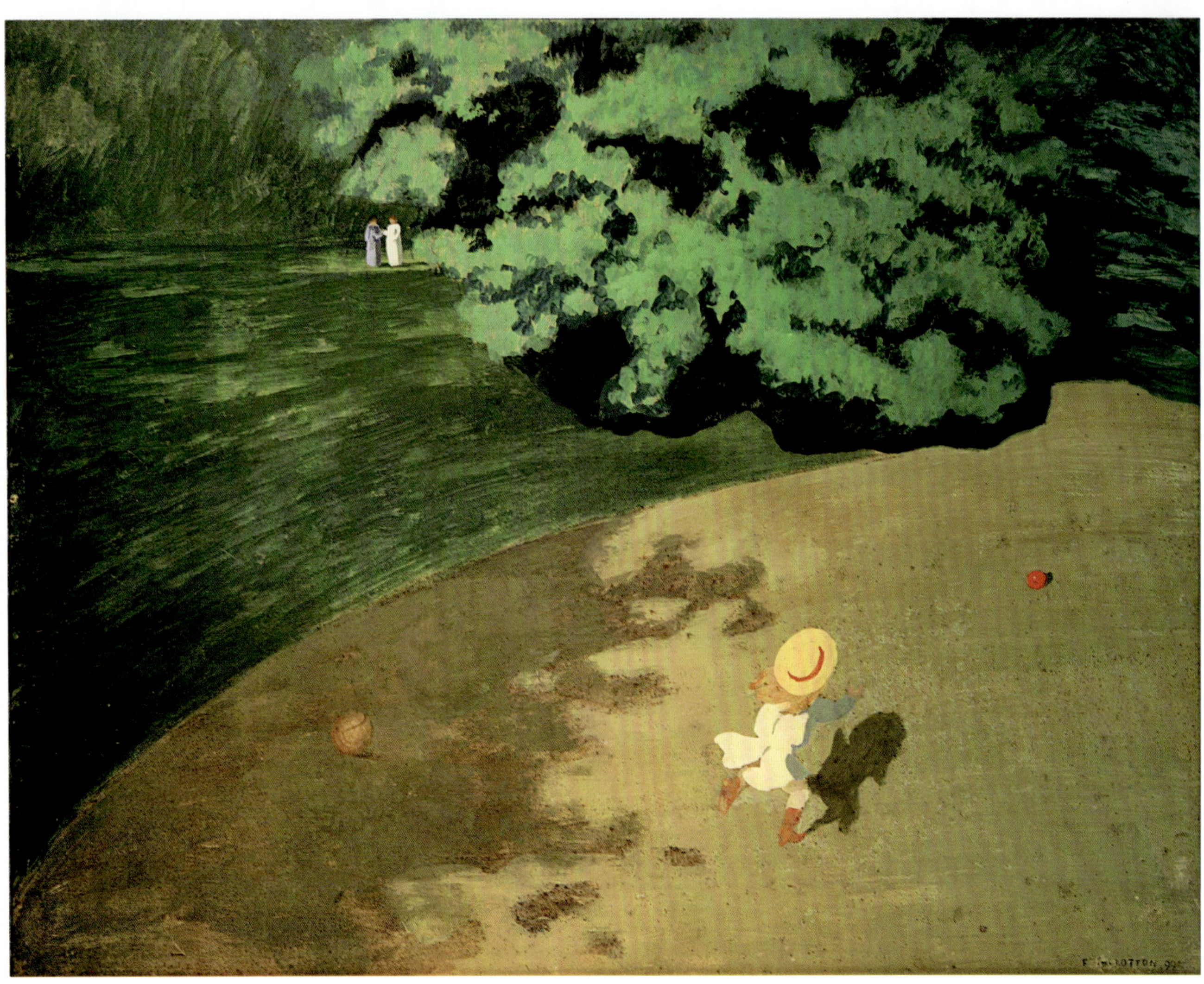

Félix Vallotton (1865–1925)

The Ball

Le Ballon

Der Ball

La pelota

Il pallone

De bal

1899, Oil on cardboard on wood/Huile sur carton sur bois, 49,2 × 62 cm

244

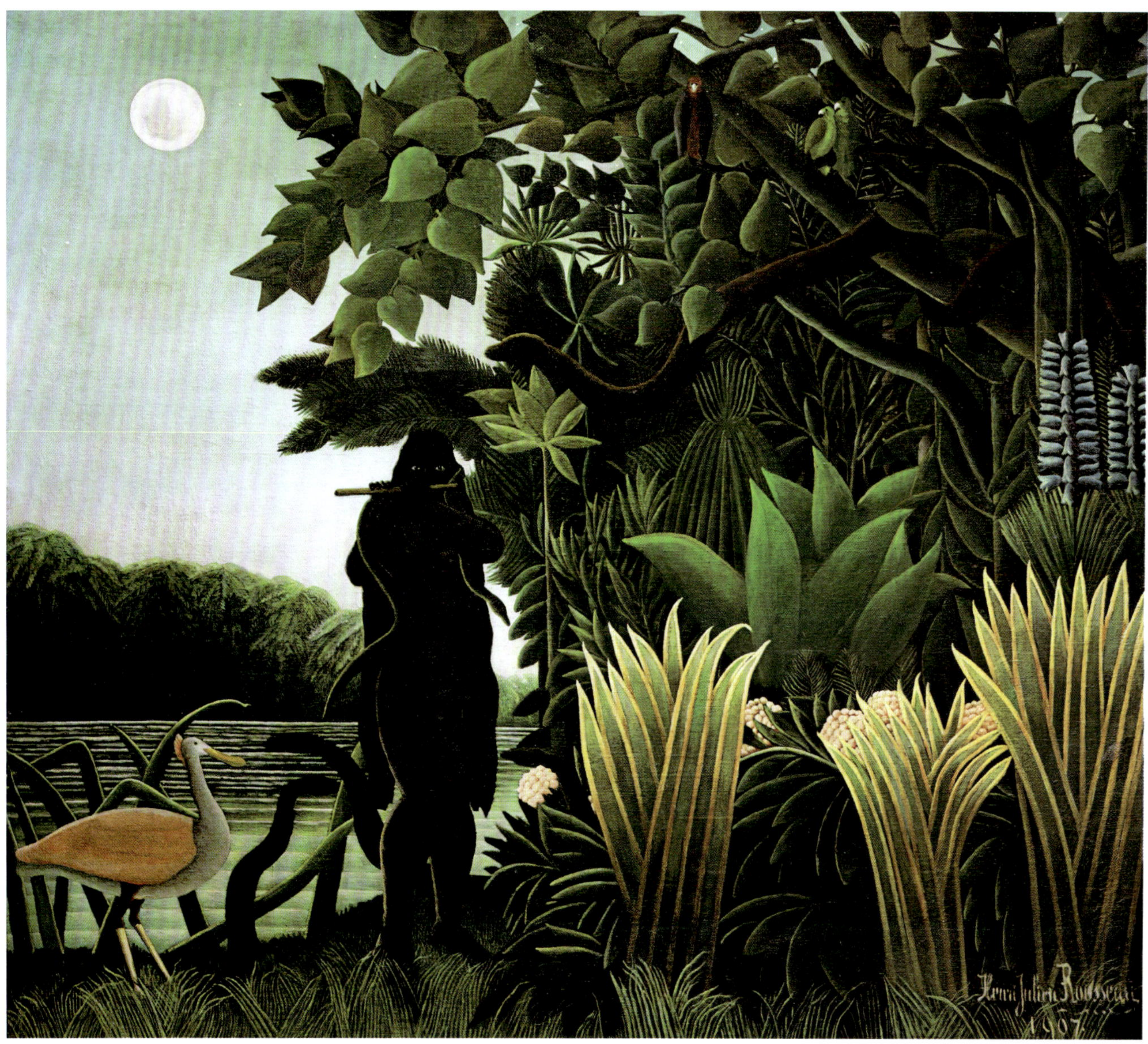

Henri Rousseau (1844–1910)

The Snake Charmer

La Charmeuse de serpents

Schlangenbeschwörerin

La encantadora de serpientes

L'Incantatrice di serpenti

De slangenbezweerster

1907, Oil on canvas/Huile sur toile, 167 × 189,5 cm

József Rippl-Rónai (1861–1927)
A Park at Night
Un parc la nuit
Ein Park bei Nacht
Un parque de noche
Un parco di notte
Een park bij nacht
c. 1892–1895, Oil on canvas/Huile sur toile, 38,4 × 46,2 cm

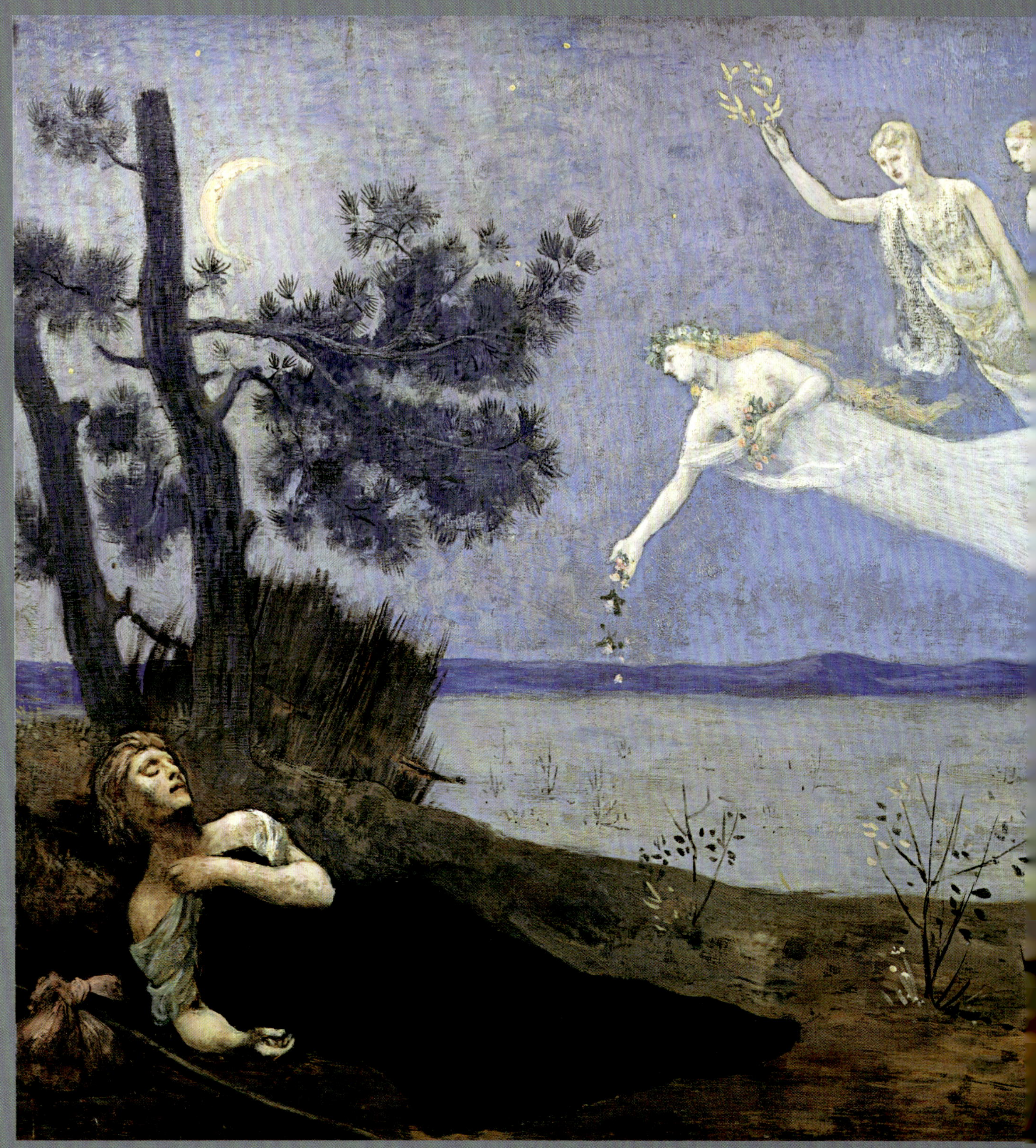

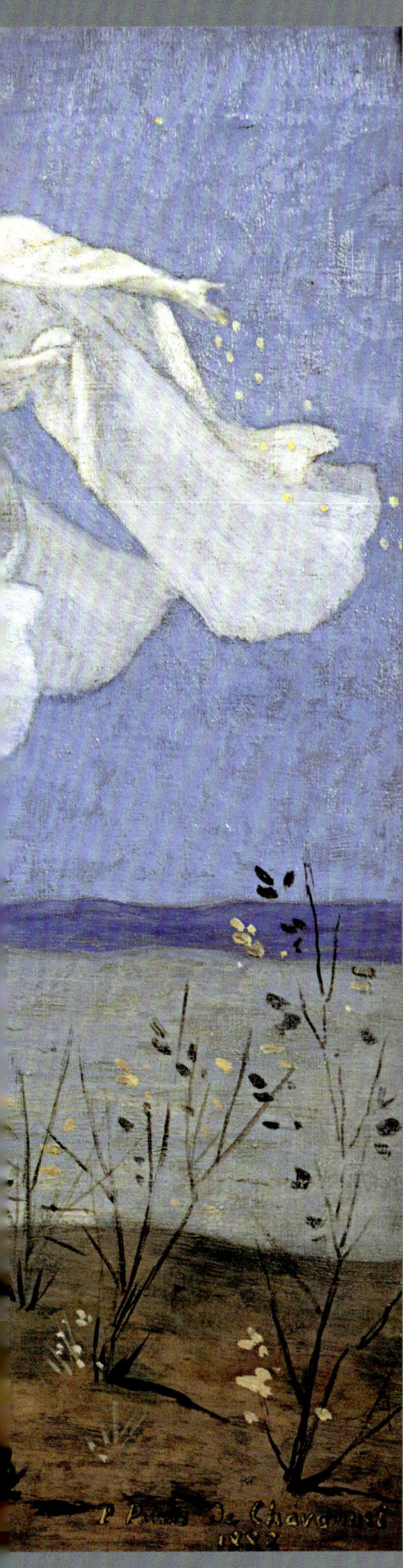

Symbolism and Art Nouveau

Symbolism has given birth to a number of "visions" which are more an expression of an interior world of the imagination, dreams, and the like, rather than the strict representation of the visibile. Puvis de Chavannes, Gustave Moreau, Odilon Redon or Gustave Doré knew how to give form and color to the mysterious and the miraculous. This was done with a sense of decoration and nature that would inspire Art Nouveau.

Symbolisme et Art nouveau

Le symbolisme a donné naissance à une quantité de « visions », qui relèvent davantage de l'expression d'un monde intérieur, de l'imagination, du rêve…, que de la stricte représentation du visible. Puvis de Chavannes, Gustave Moreau, Odilon Redon ou Gustave Doré ont su donner formes et couleurs au mystère, et au merveilleux. Avec un sens du décoratif et de la nature qui inspirera l'Art nouveau.

Symbolismus und Jugendstil

Der Symbolismus führte zu einer Vielzahl von „Visionen", die mehr dem Ausdruck einer Innenwelt, einer Fantasie, eines Traums gleichkommen als der strikten Abbildung des Sichtbaren. Puvis de Chavannes, Gustave Moreau, Odilon Redon und Gustave Doré wussten dem Geheimen und Wunderbaren Form und Farbe zu geben. Und dies mit einem Sinn für das Dekorative und die Natur, der später den Jugendstil inspirierte.

Simbolismo y modernismo

El simbolismo dio lugar a una serie de "visiones", que son más una cuestión de la expresión de un mundo interior, de la imaginación, de sueños… que de la representación estricta de lo visible. Puvis de Chavannes, Gustave Moreau, Odilon Redon y Gustave Doré fueron capaces de dar forma y color al misterio y a lo maravilloso. Con un sentido de la decoración y la naturaleza que inspirará al modernismo.

Simbolismo e Art Nouveau

Il Simbolismo generò una serie di "visioni" che esprimono un mondo interiore, della fantasia e dei sogni, invece di rappresentare rigorosamente il mondo visibile. Puvis de Chavannes, Gustave Moreau, Odilon Redon e Gustave Doré riuscirono a dar forma e colore a quanto c'è di misterioso e meraviglioso, con una sensibilità verso la decorazione e la natura che fu fonte d'ispirazione per l'Art Nouveau.

Symbolisme en nieuwe kunst

Het symbolisme gaf aanleiding tot een aantal 'visies', die eerder voortkwamen uit de expressie van innerlijke ervaringen, verbeelding en dromen dan uit de strikte weergave van het zichtbare. Puvis de Chavannes, Gustave Moreau, Odilon Redon en Gustave Doré wisten vorm en kleur te geven aan het onverklaarbare en het bovennatuurlijke. Met een gevoel voor decoratie en natuur dat tot de nieuwe kunst inspireert.

Pierre Puvis de Chavannes (1824–1898)
The Dream
Le Rêve
Der Traum
El sueño
Il sogno
De droom
1883, Oil on canvas/Huile sur toile, 82 × 102 cm

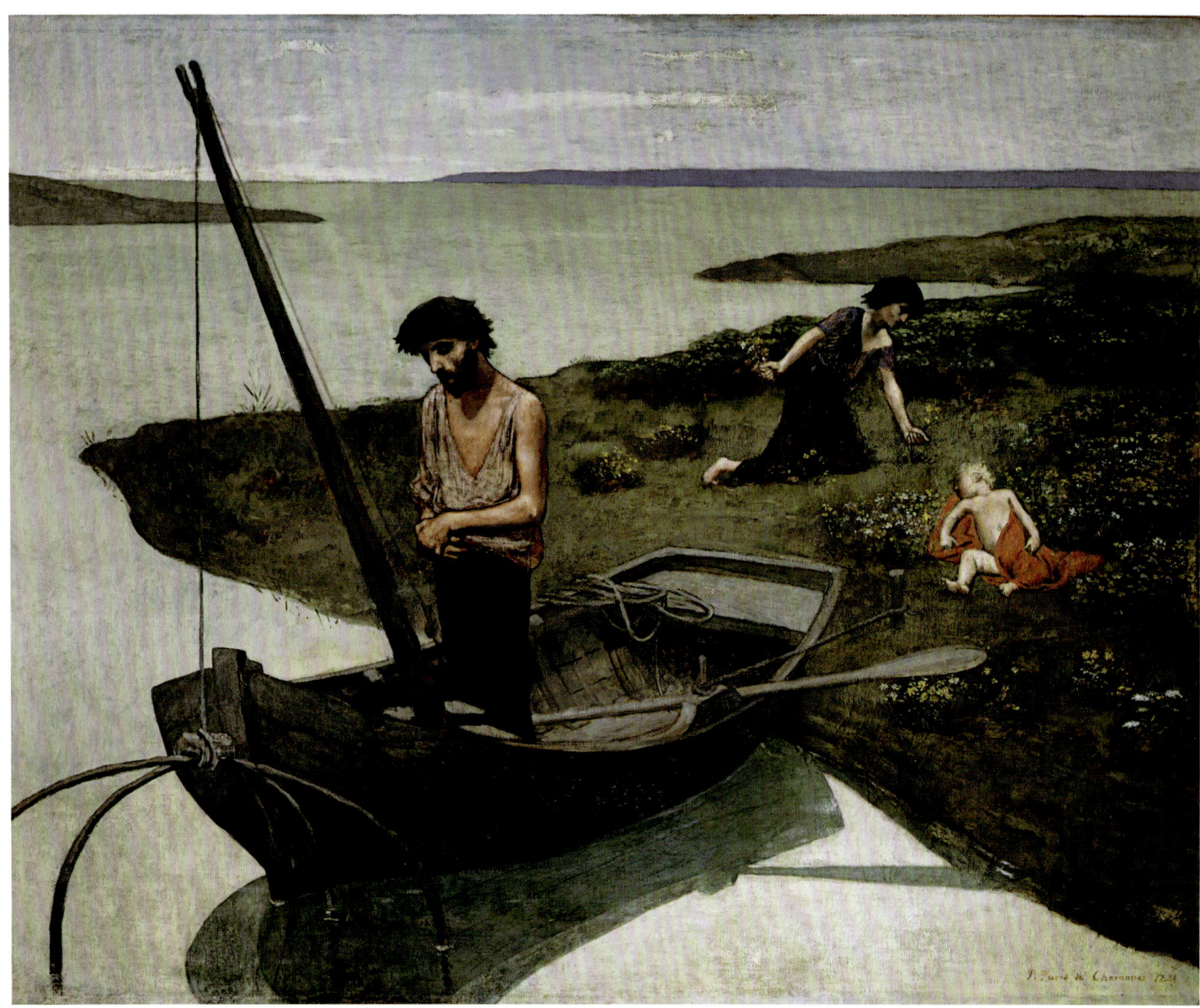

Pierre Puvis de Chavannes (1824–1898)

The Poor Fisherman

Le Pauvre Pêcheur

Der arme Fischer

El pobre pescador

Il povero pescatore

De arme visser

1881, Oil on canvas/Huile sur toile, 154,7 × 192,5 cm

Pierre Puvis de Chavannes (1824–1898)

Young Girls by the Seaside

Jeunes Filles au bord de la mer

Junge Frauen am Meer

Las jóvenes al borde del mar

Ragazze in riva al mare

Jonge vrouwen aan zee

c. 1879, Oil on canvas/Huile sur toile, 61,5 × 47,3 cm

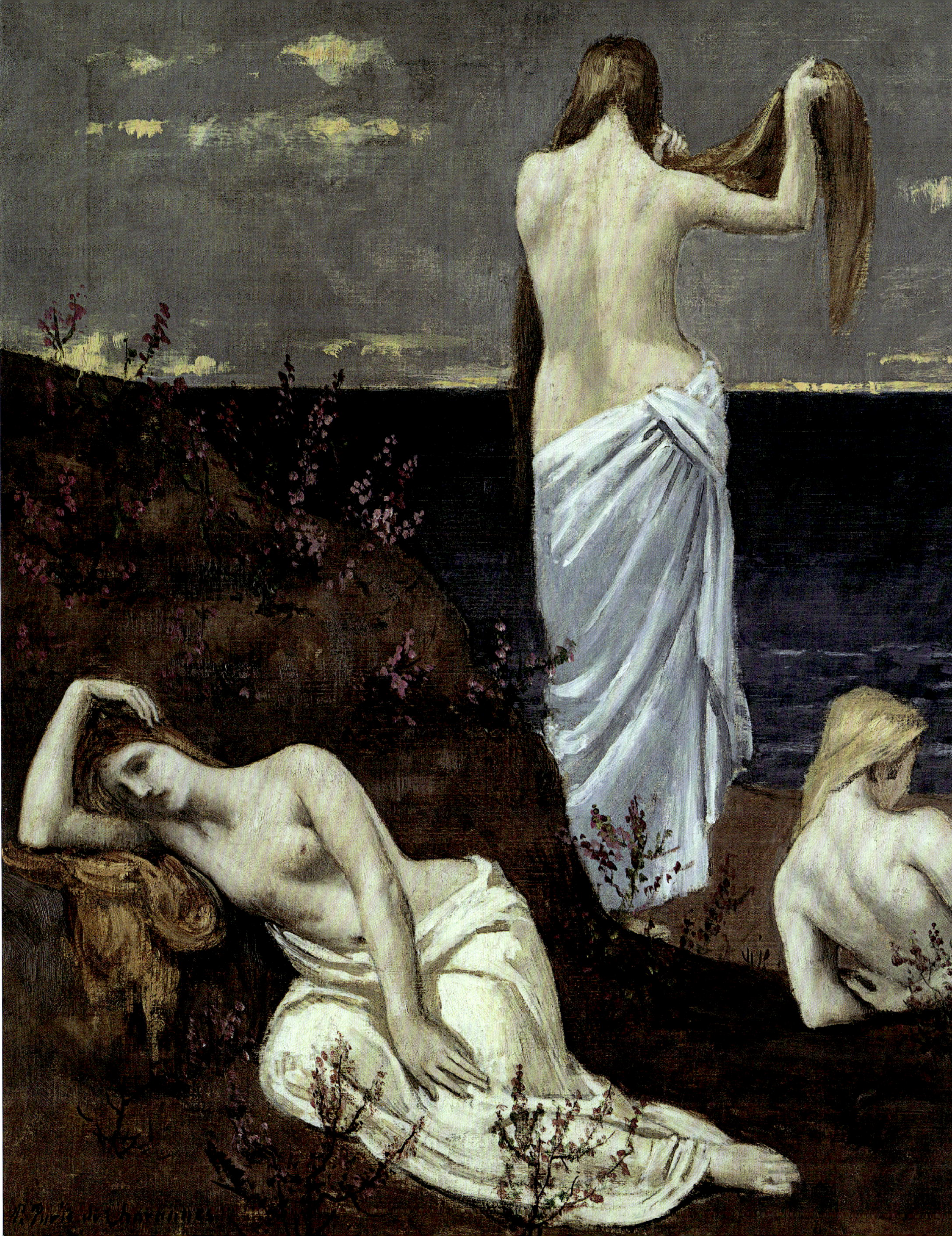
P. Puvis de Chavannes

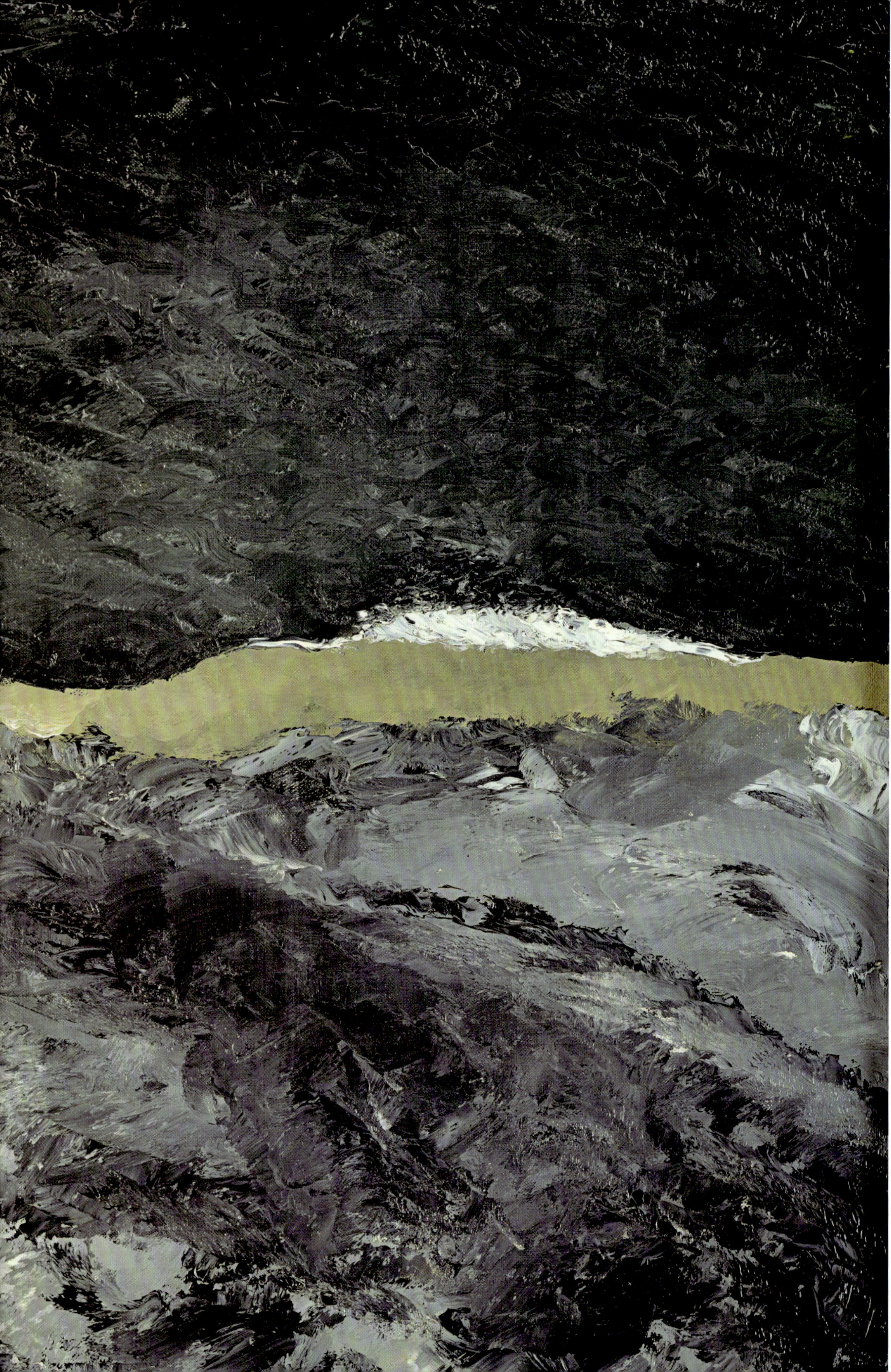

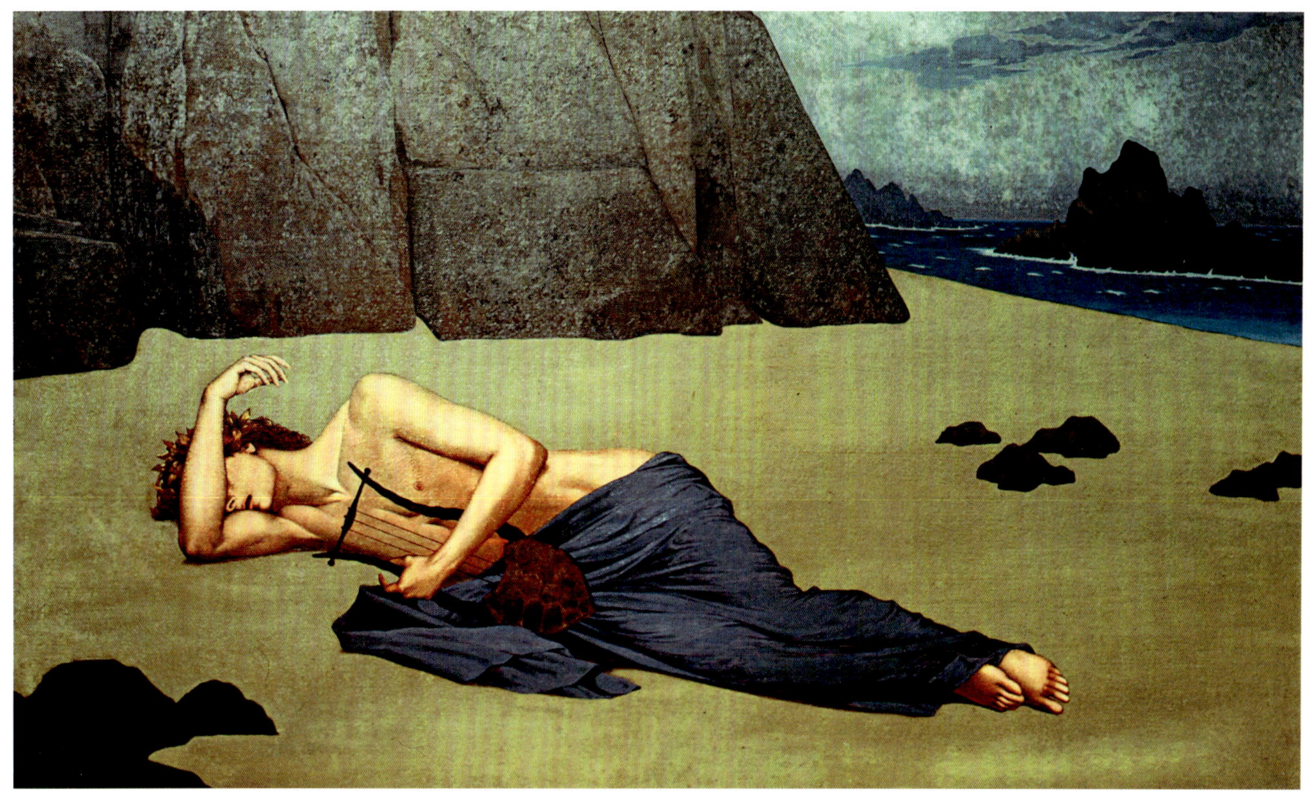

In *Orpheus' Lament,* the symbolist painter Alexandre Séon, a pupil and assistant to Puvis de Chavannes, shows the disconsolate poet and musician from Greek mythology mourning his vanished Eurydice in the heart of a ghostly and extremely simplified Breton landscape. It is undoubtedly Bréhat island where the artist stayed many times since 1894.

Dans cette *Lamentation d'Orphée,* le peintre symboliste Alexandre Séon, élève et assistant de Puvis de Chavannes, montre l'inconsolable poète et musicien de la mythologie grecque pleurant son Eurydice disparue, au cœur d'un paysage breton fantomatique, simplifié à l'extrême. Il s'agit sans doute de l'île de Bréhat, où l'artiste séjourna à de nombreuses reprises à partir de 1894.

In der *Wehklage des Orpheus* stellt der symbolistische Maler Alexandre Séon, Schüler und Assistent von Puvis de Chavannes, den untröstlichen Dichter und Musiker der griechischen Mythologie dar, der inmitten einer gespenstischen und bis ins Extreme vereinfachten bretonischen Landschaft um seine verschwundene Eurydike weint. Es handelt sich zweifellos um die Insel Bréhat, wo sich der Künstler ab 1894 wiederholt aufhielt.

En esta *Lamentación de Orfeo,* el pintor simbolista Alexandre Séon, alumno y asistente de Puvis de Chavannes, muestra al poeta y músico inconsolable de la mitología griega llorando a su desaparecida Eurídice, en el corazón de un paisaje fantasmal bretón, simplificado al extremo. Se trata sin duda de la isla de Bréhat, donde el artista se quedaba en numerosas ocasiones desde 1894.

In questo quadro il pittore simbolista Alexandre Séon, allievo e assistente di Puvis de Chavannes, raffigura Orfeo, poeta inconsolabili e musicista della mitologia greca che piange la scomparsa della sua Euridice nel cuore di un paesaggio bretone desolato e semplificato al massimo. Si tratta probabilmente dell'isola di Bréhat, dove l'artista soggiornò in numerose occasioni a partire dal 1894.

Op deze *Klaagzang van Orpheus* toont de symbolist Alexandre Séon, leerling en assistent van Puvis de Chavannes, de ontroostbare dichter en musicus uit de Griekse mythologie die zijn verdwenen Eurydice beweent, midden in een spookachtig en tot het uiterste vereenvoudigd Bretons landschap. Het betreft waarschijnlijk het eiland Bréhat, waar de kunstenaar vanaf 1894 herhaaldelijk verbleef.

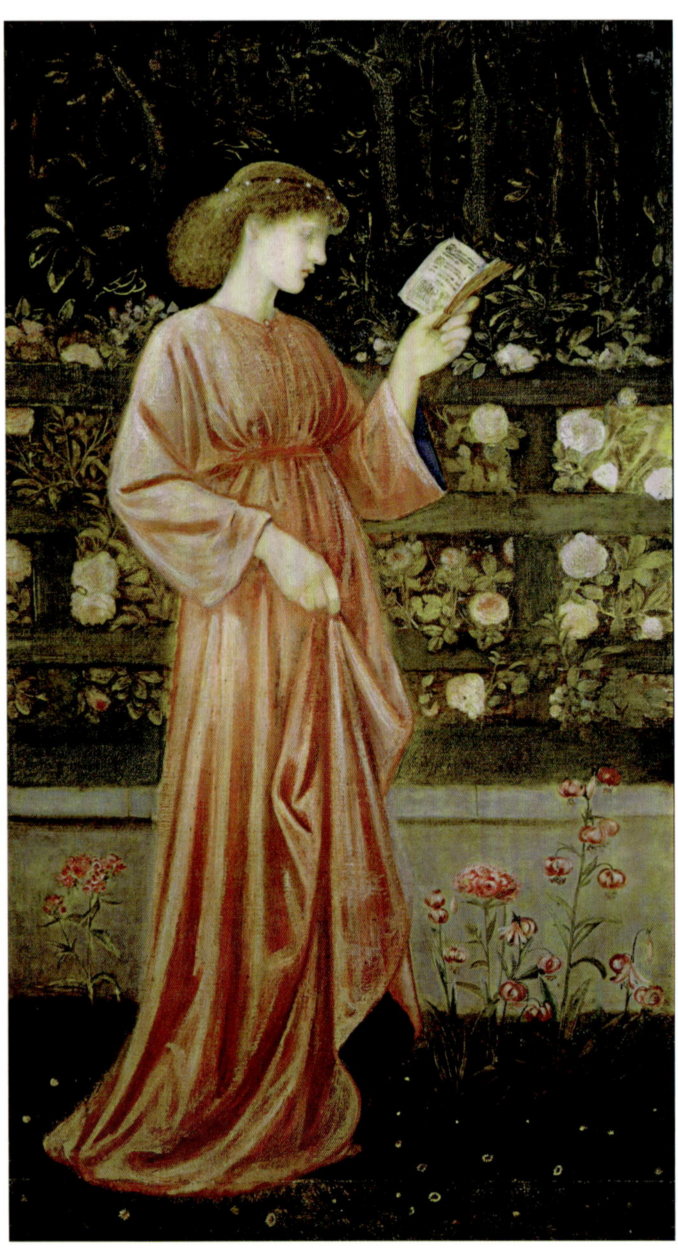

Edward Burne-Jones (1833–1898)

Princess Sabra

Princesse Sabra

Prinzessin Sabra

Princesa Sabra

La Principessa Sabra

Prinses Sabra

1865, Oil on canvas/Huile sur toile, 107,2 × 61,5 cm

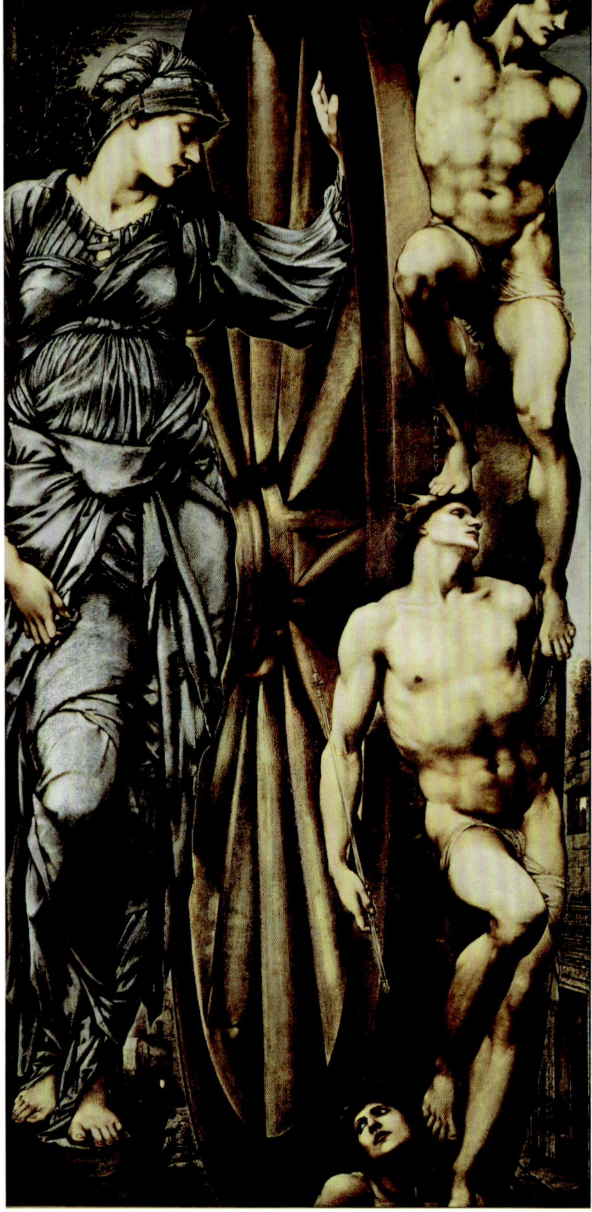

Edward Burne-Jones (1833–1898)

The Wheel of Fortune

La Roue de la Fortune

Das Rad der Fortuna

La rueda de la fortuna

La Ruota della Fortuna

Het rad van Fortuin

c. 1875–1883, Oil on canvas/Huile sur toile, 200 × 100 cm

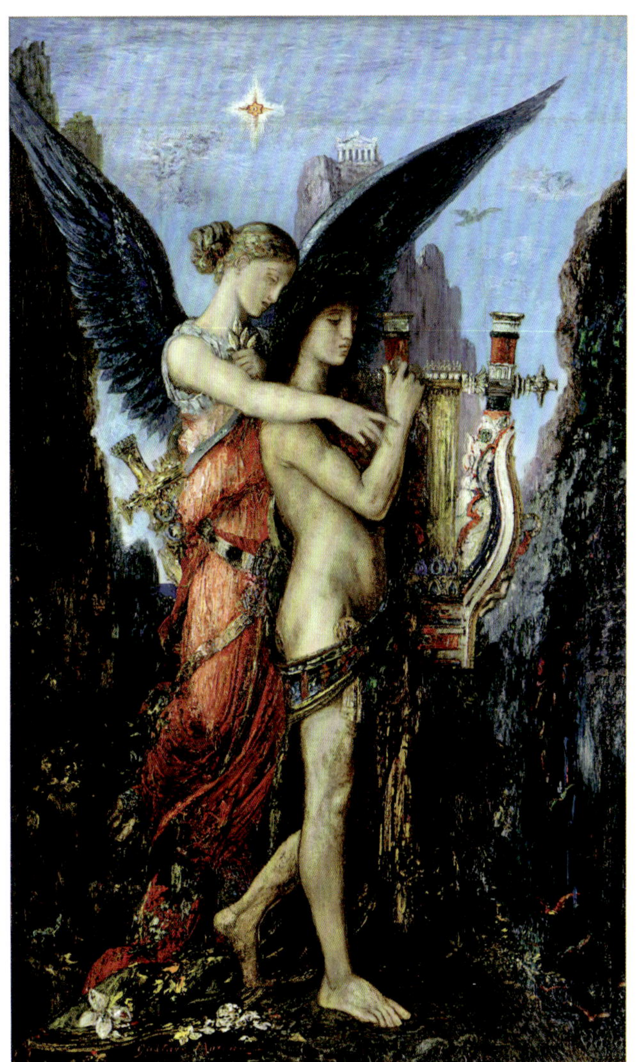 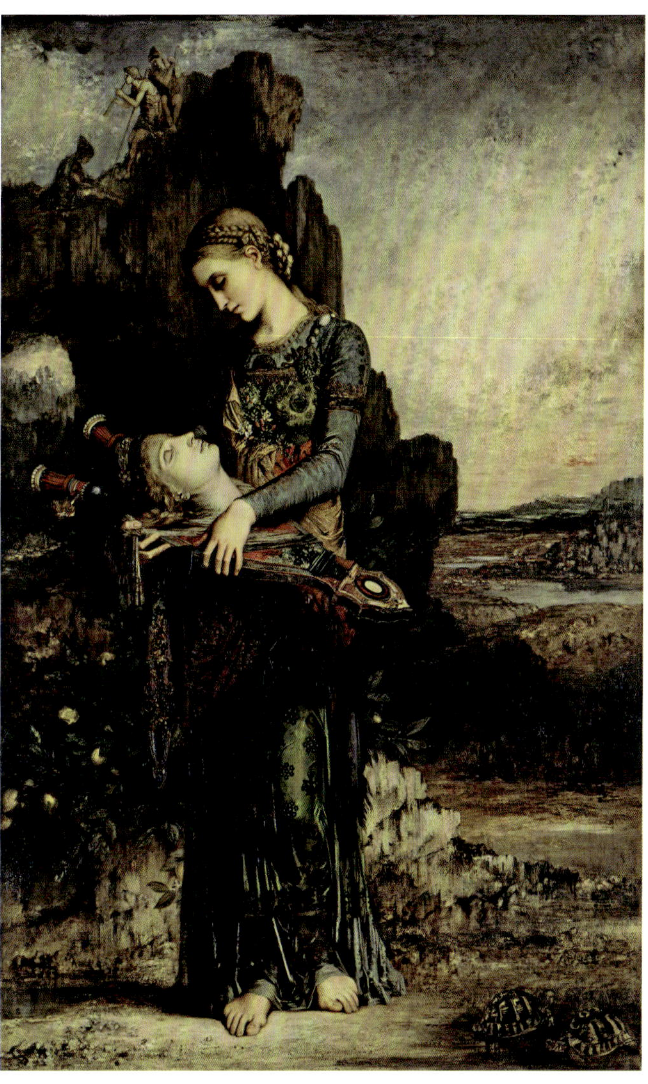

Gustave Moreau (1826–1898)

Hesiod and the Muse

Hésiode et la Muse

Hesiod und die Muse

Hesíodo y la musa

Esiodo e la Musa

Hesiodos en de muze

1891, Oil on wood/Huile sur bois, 59 × 34,5 cm

Gustave Moreau (1826–1898)

Orpheus

Orphée

Orpheus

Orfeo

Orfeo

Orpheus

1865, Oil on wood/Huile sur bois, 154 × 99,5 cm

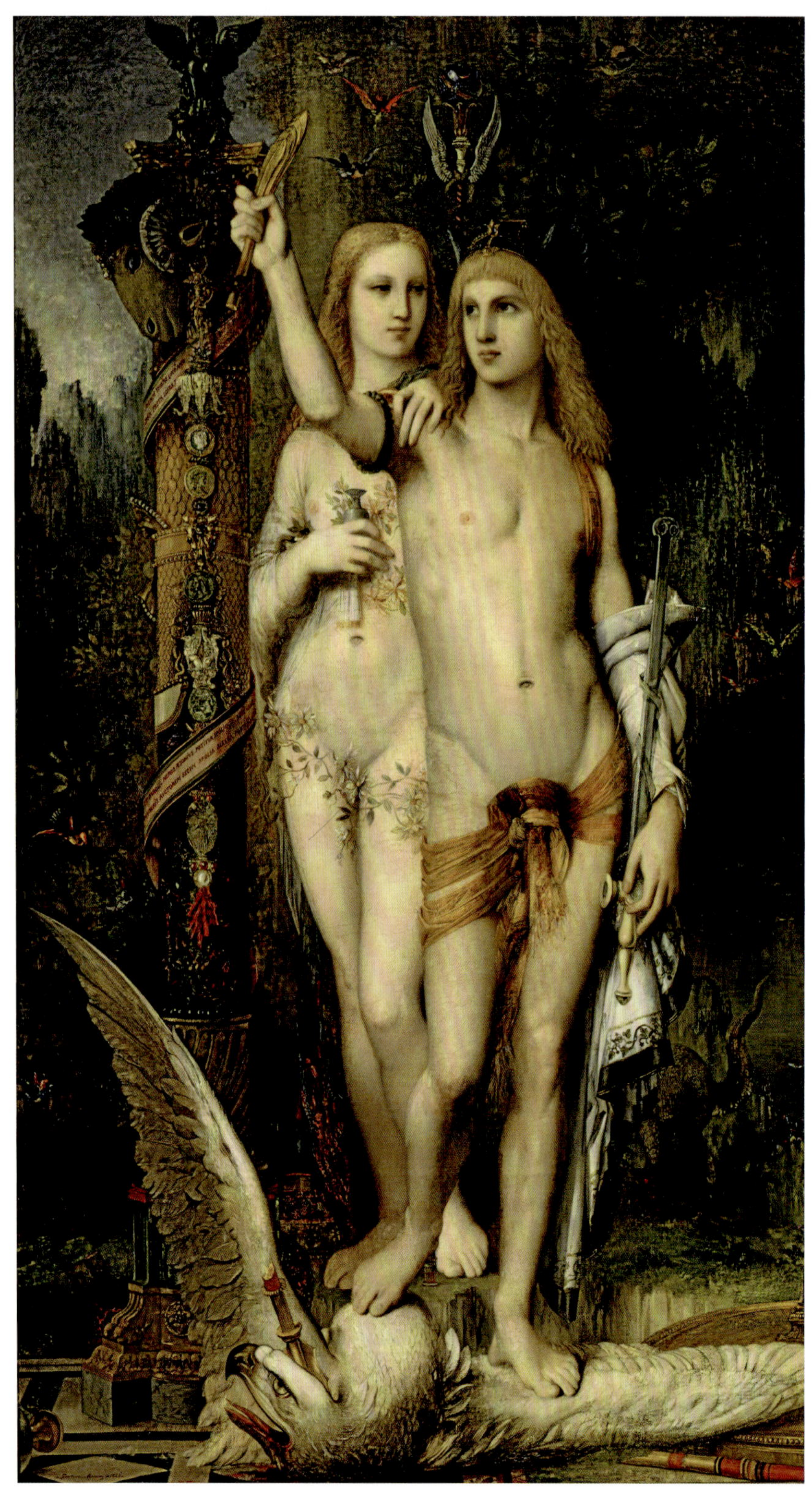

*Gustave Moreau
(1826–1898)*

Jason and Medea

Jason et Médée

Jason und Medea

Jasón y Medea

Giasone e Medea

Jason en Medea

1865, Oil on canvas/Huile
sur toile, 204 × 115,5 cm

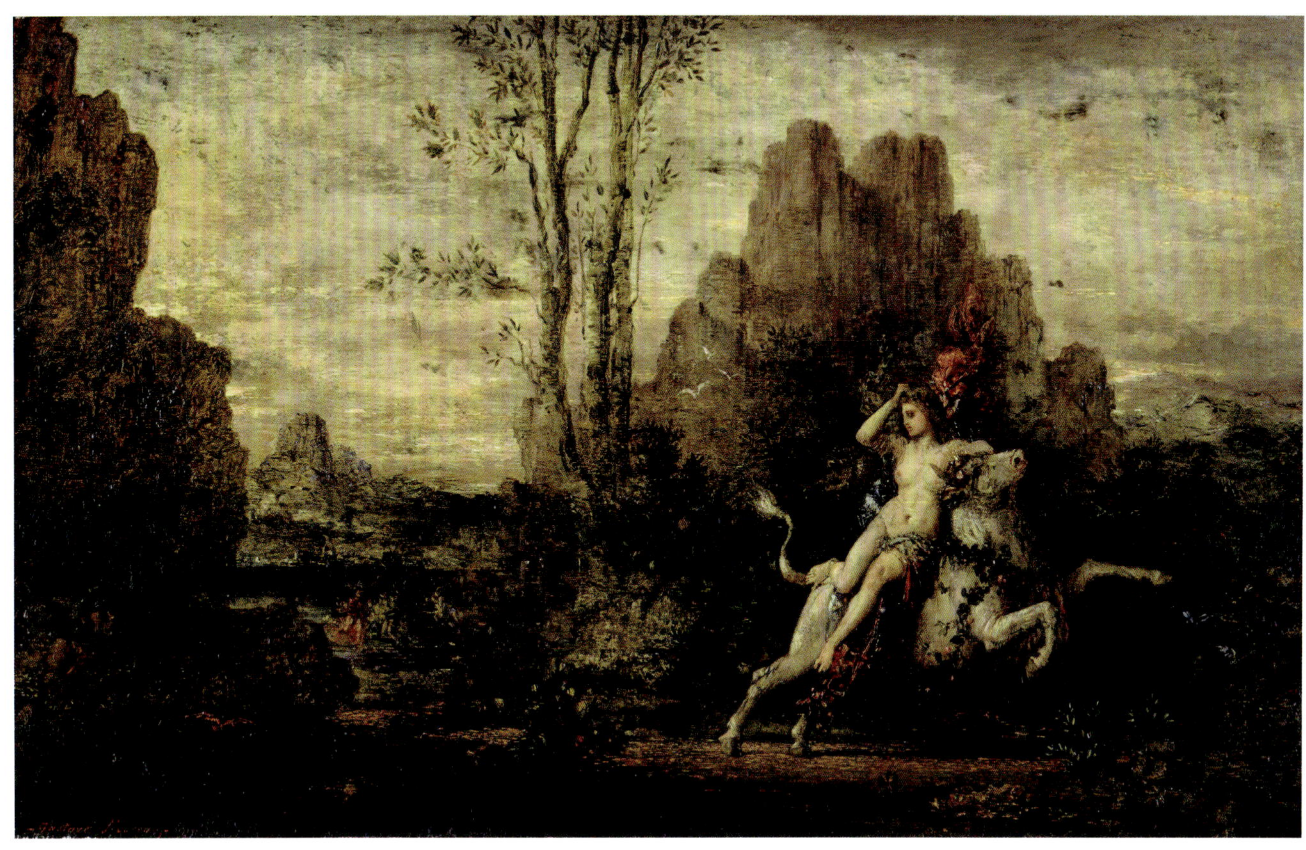

Gustave Moreau (1826–1898)

The Abduction of Europa

L'Enlèvement d'Europe

Die Entführung der Europa

El rapto de Europa

Il ratto di Europa

De ontvoering van Europa

c. 1869, Oil on wood/Huile sur bois, 26 × 42 cm

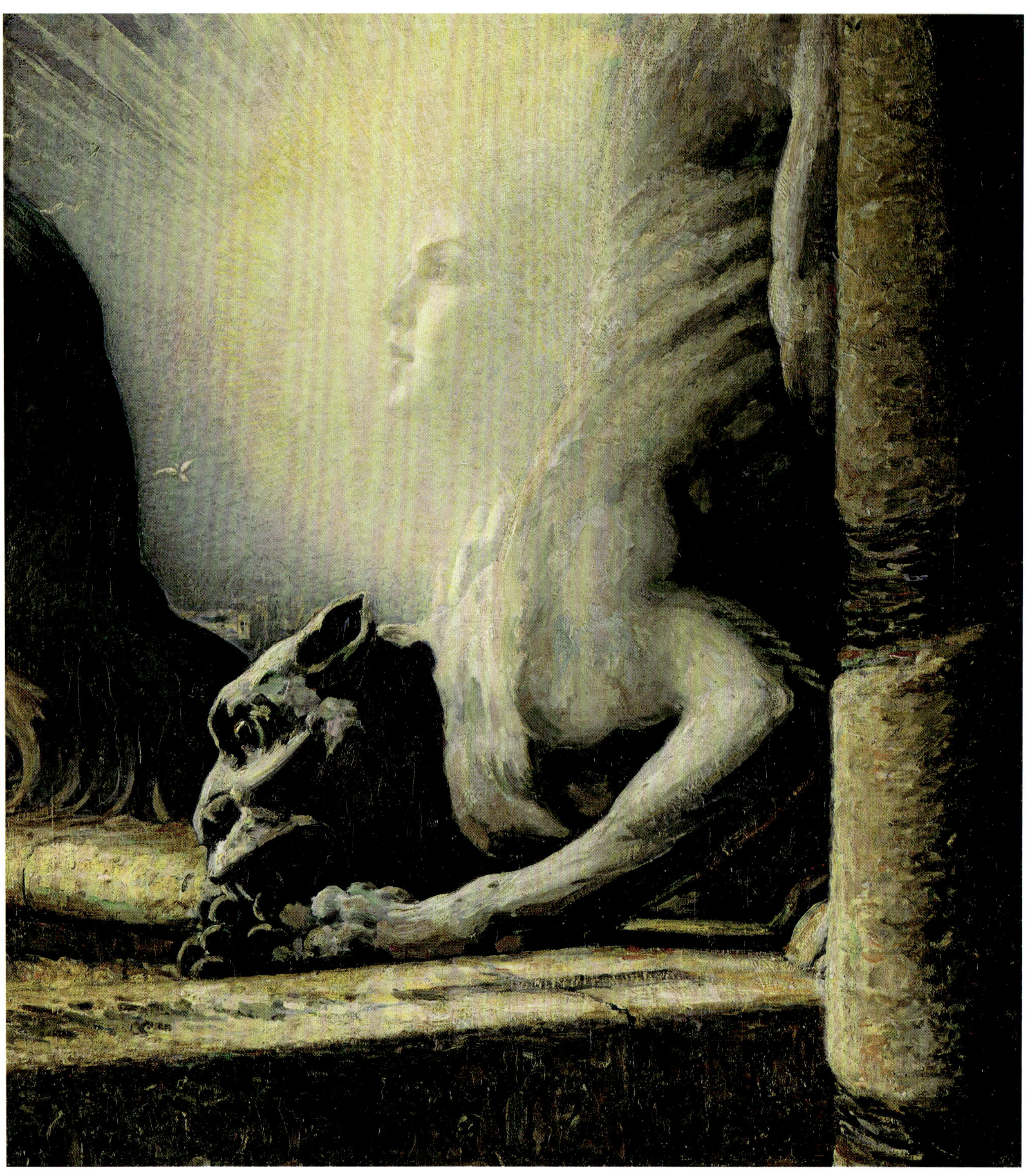

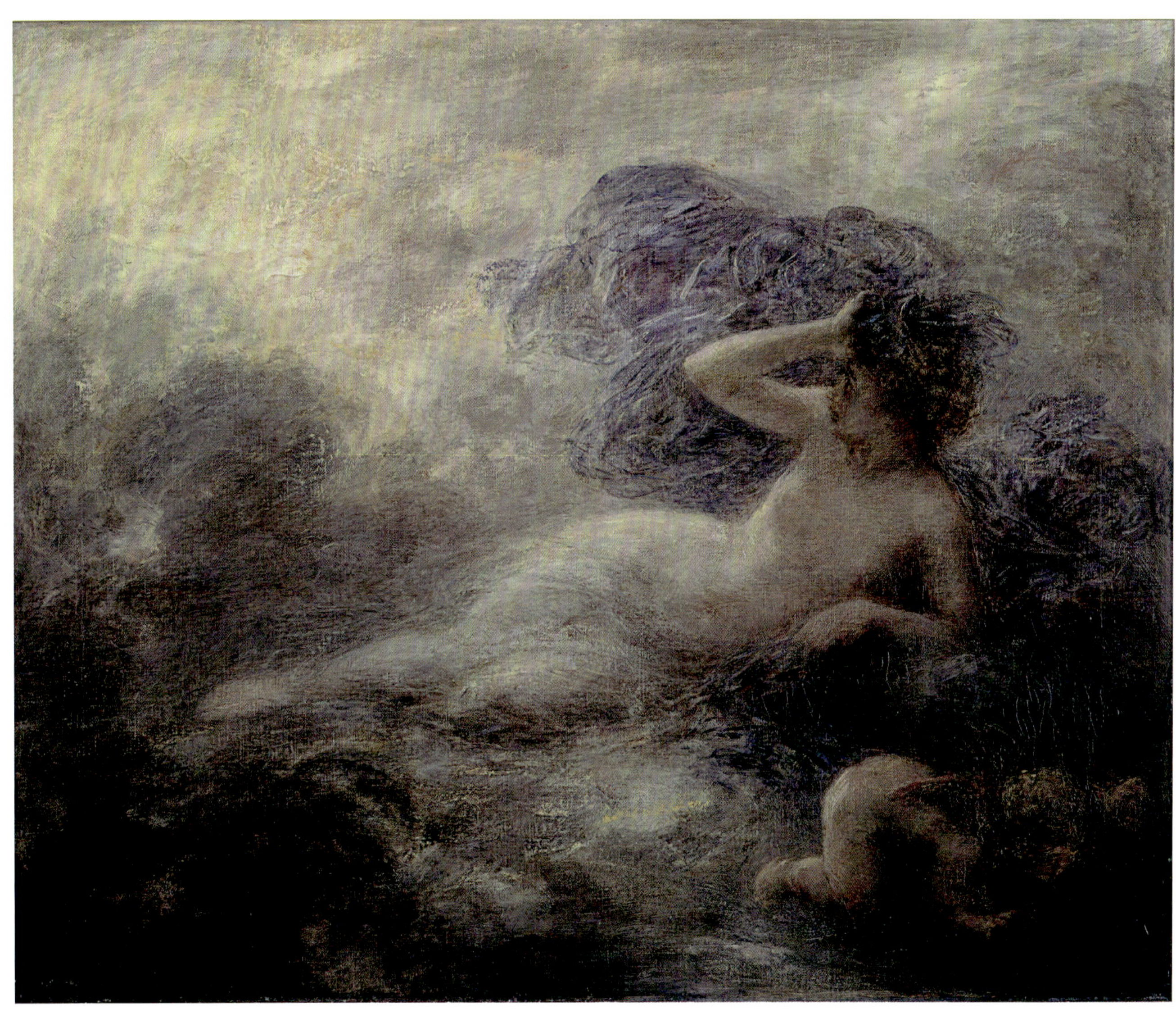

The Sphinx and the Chimera

Le Sphinx et la chimère

Sphinx und Chimäre

La esfinge y la quimera

La Sfinge e la chimera

Sfinx en Chimaera

1906, Oil on canvas/Huile sur toile, 81 × 73 cm

Henri Fantin-Latour (1836–1904)

Night

La Nuit

Die Nacht

La noche

La Notte

De nacht

1897, Oil on canvas/Huile sur toile, 61 × 75 cm

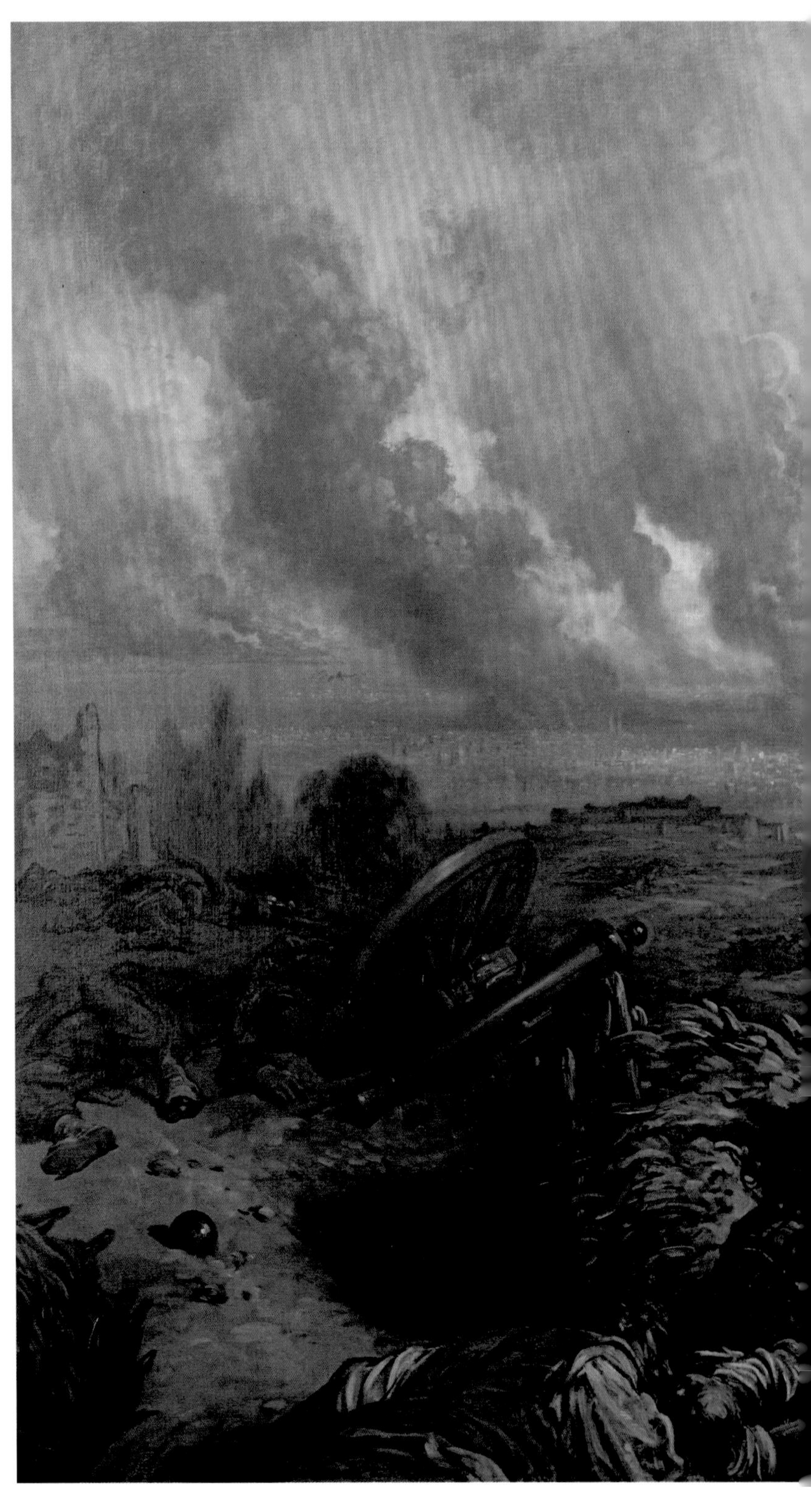

Gustave Doré (1832–1883)
The Enigma
L'Énigme
Das Rätsel
El enigma
L'enigma
Het raadsel
1871, Oil on canvas/Huile sur toile, 130,4 × 195 cm

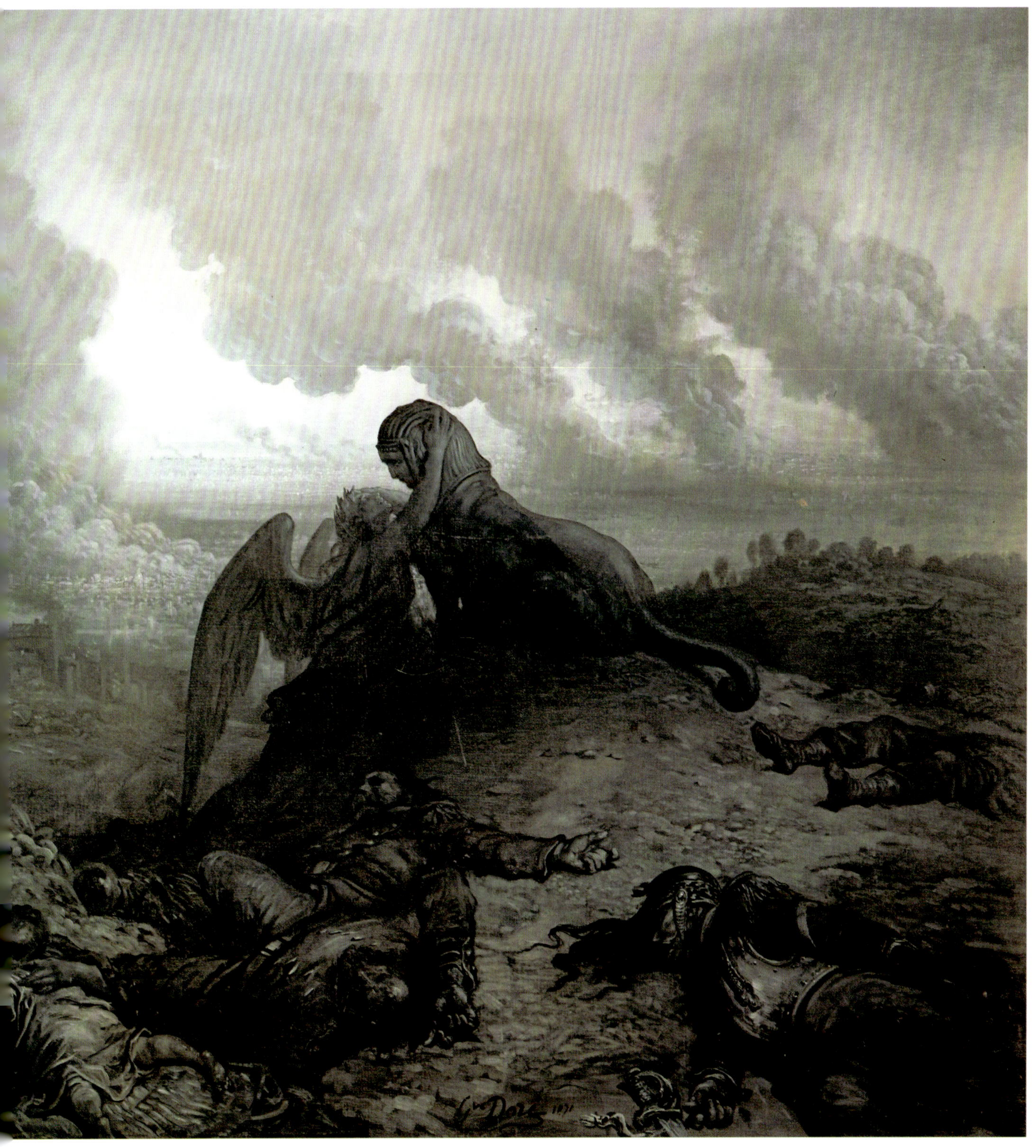

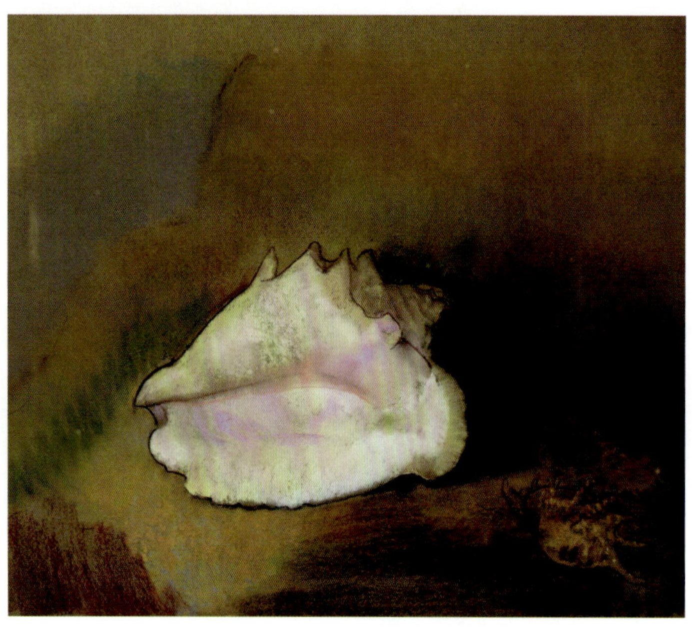

Odilon Redon (1840–1916)

The Seashell

La Coquille

Die Muschel

La concha

La conchiglia

De schelp

1912, Pastel on paper/Pastel sur papier, 52 × 57,8 cm

Odilon Redon (1840–1916)

The Sleep of Caliban

Sommeil de Caliban

Calibans Schlaf

Sueño de Calibán

Sonno di Calibano

De slaap van Caliban

c. 1895–1900, Oil on wood/Huile sur bois, 48,2 × 38,5 cm

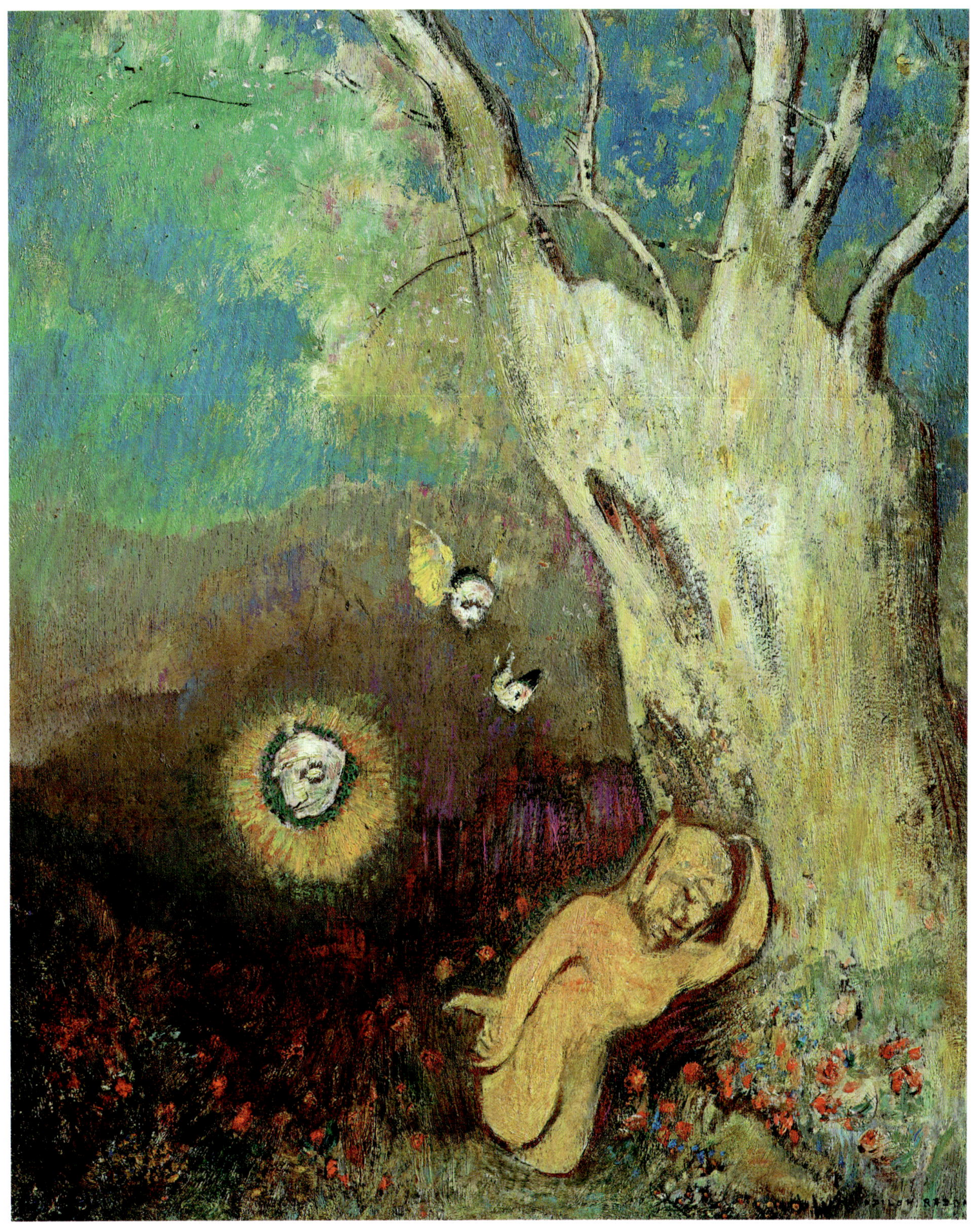

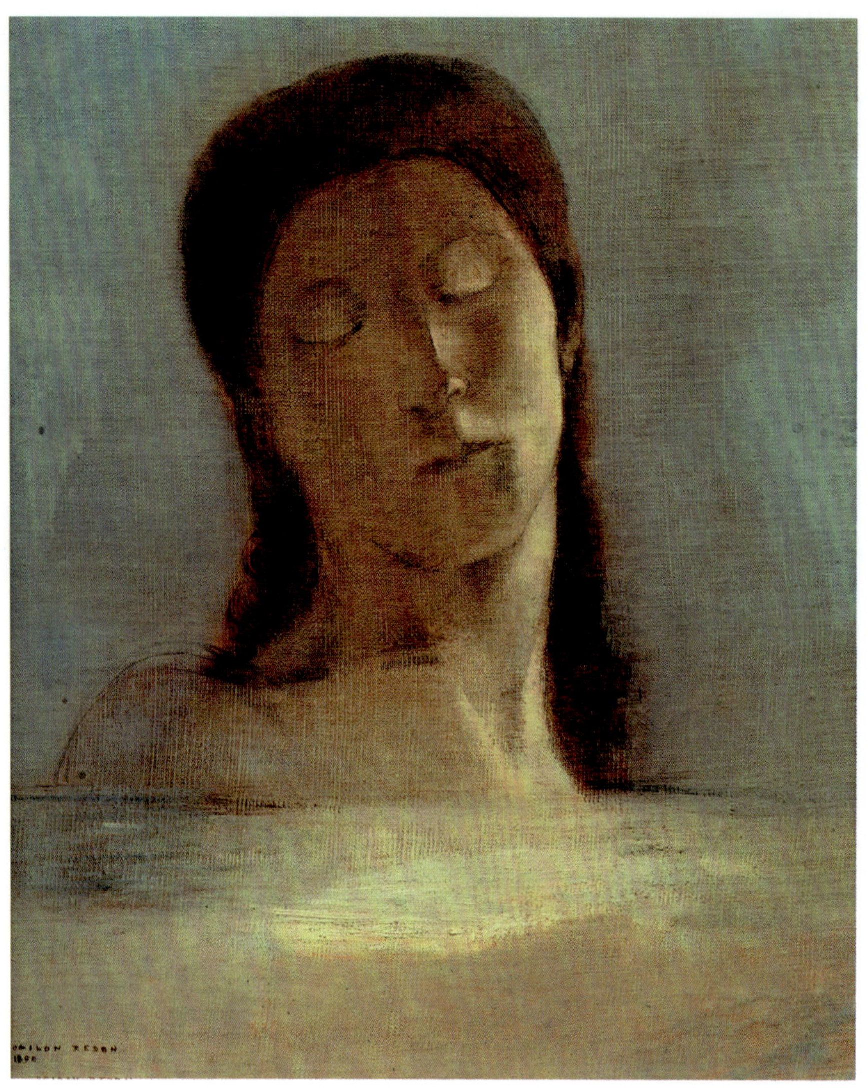

Odilon Redon (1840–1916)

Closed Eyes

Les Yeux clos

Geschlossene Augen

Los ojos cerrados

Gli occhi chiusi

Gesloten ogen

1890, Oil on canvas on cardboard/Huile sur toile sur carton, 44 × 36 cm

Odilon Redon (1840–1916)

The Buddha

Le Bouddha

Der Buddha

El Buda

Il Buddha

De Boeddha

c. 1906–1907, Oil on beige paper/Pastel sur papier beige, 90 × 73 cm

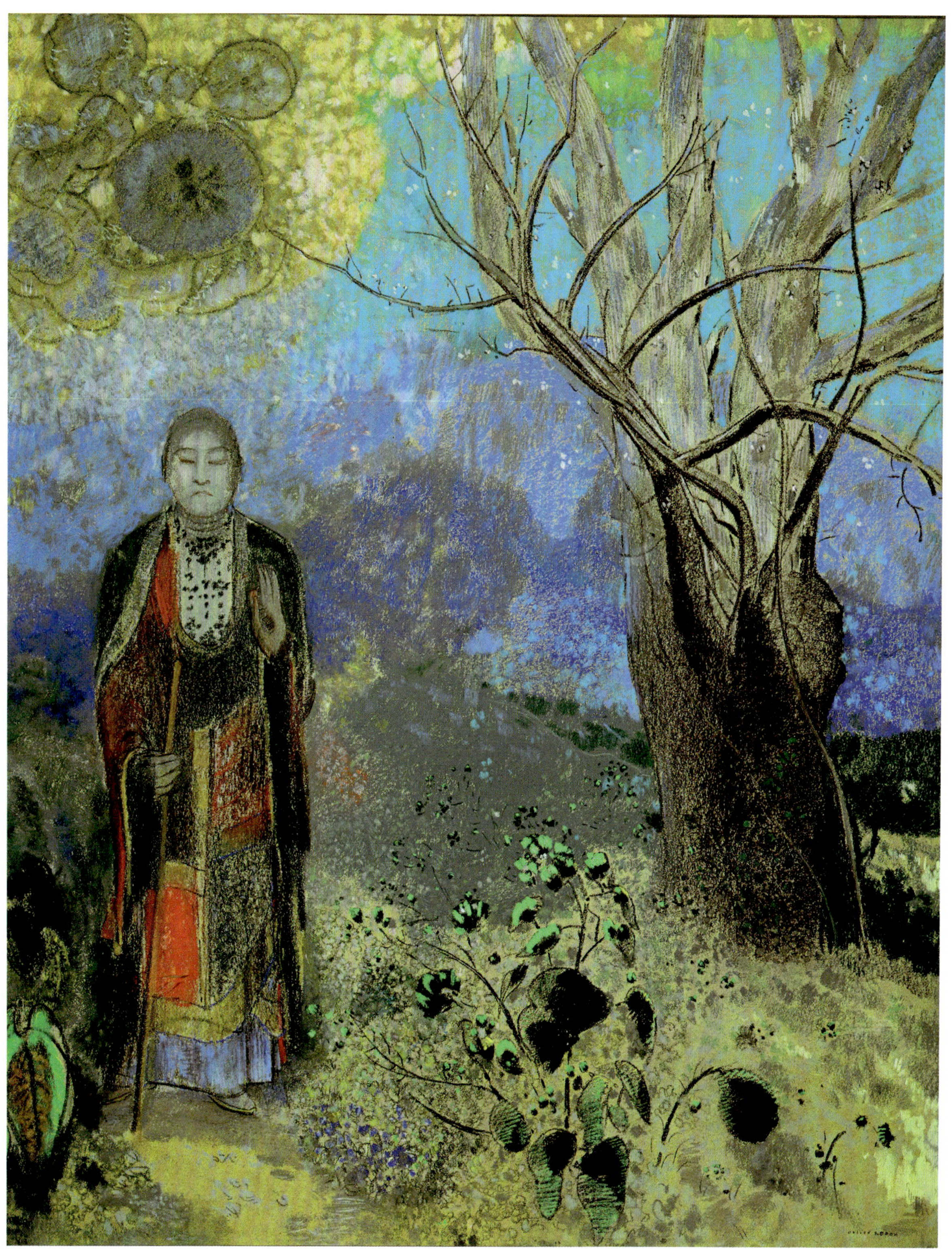

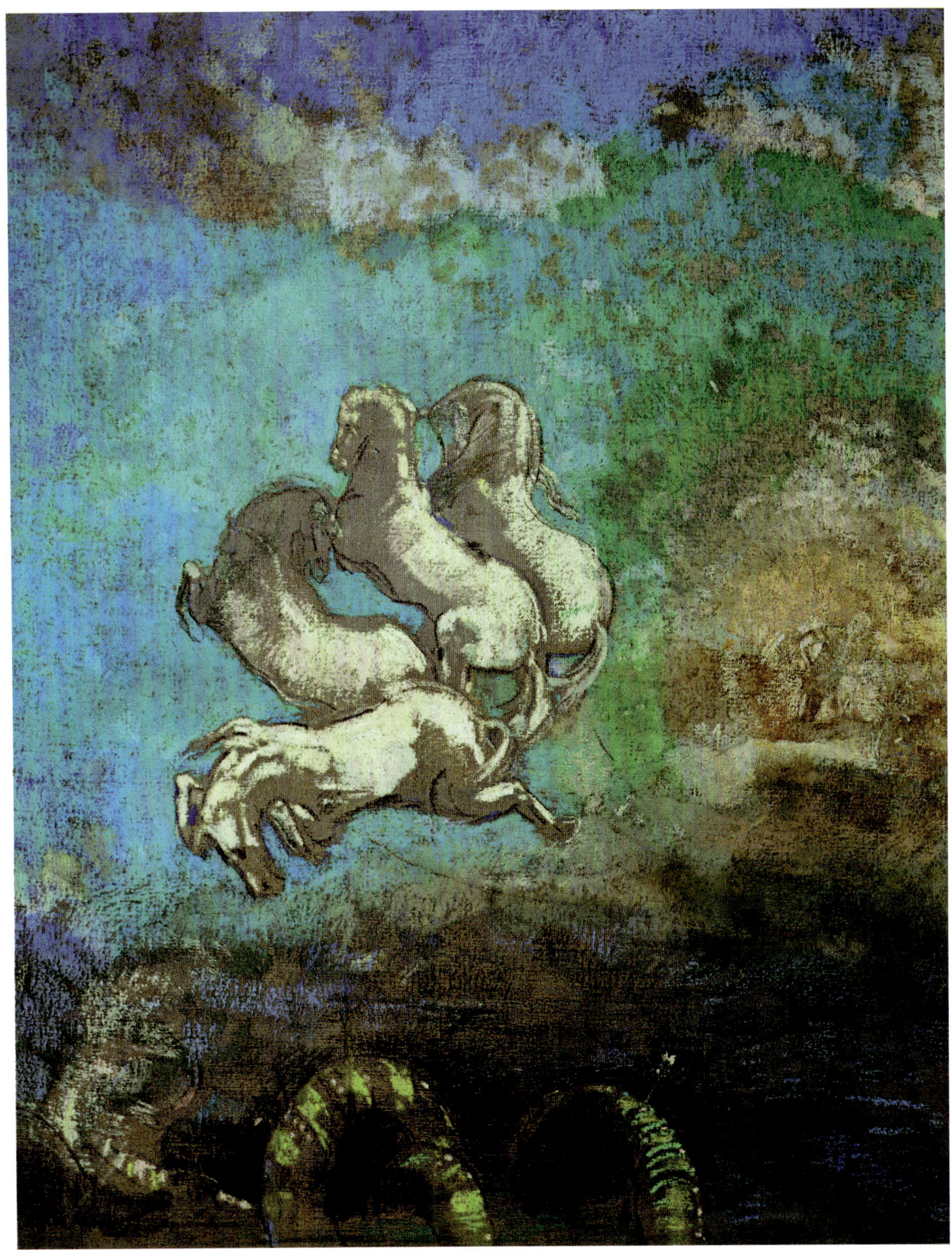

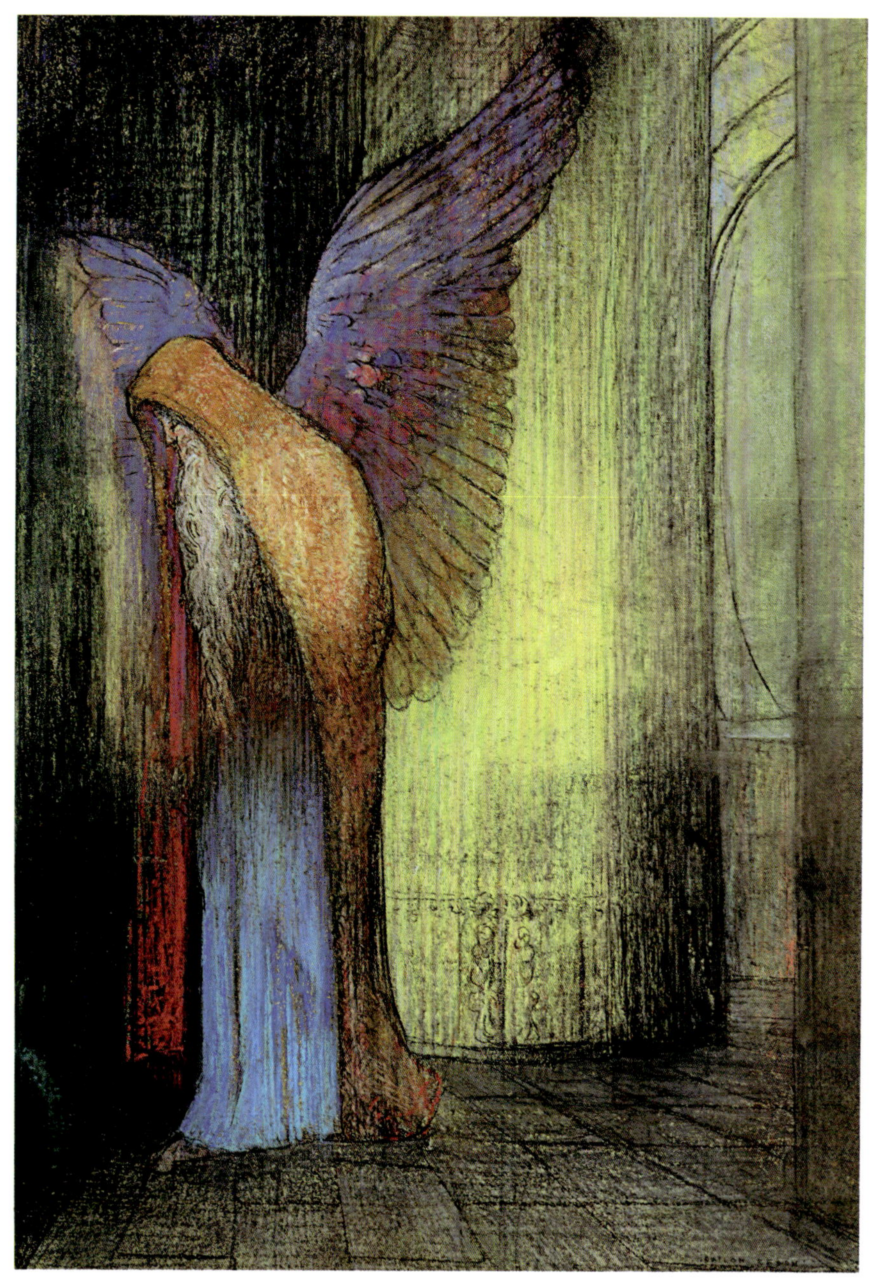

Odilon Redon (1840–1916)
Apollo's Chariot
Le Char d'Apollon
Der Wagen des Apoll
El carro de Apolo
Il carro di Apollo
De strijdwagen van Apollo
c. 1910, Pastel and
tempera on canvas/
Pastel et détrempe sur
toile, 91,5 × 77 cm

Odilon Redon (1840–1916)
Winged Old Man with a Long White Beard
Vieillard ailé barbu
Geflügelter Alter
Viejo alado con larga barba
Vecchio barbuto alato
Gevleugelde grijsaard met baard
c. 1895, Pastel on grey-beige paper/Pastel sur papier gris-beige, 56,9 × 39,7 cm

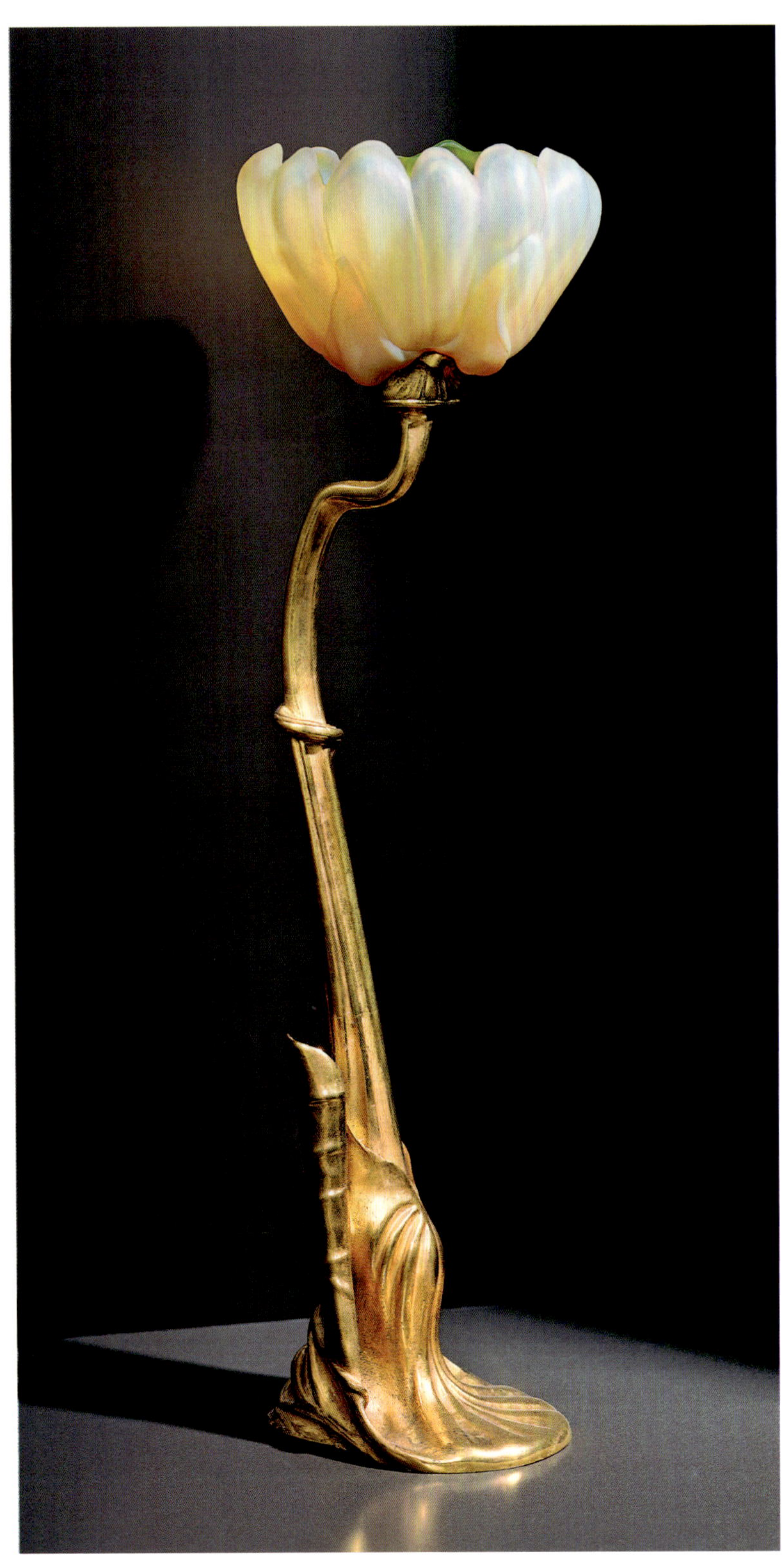

Louis Majorelle (1859–1926)

Nenuphar _lamp_

Lampe Nénuphar

Lampe Seerose

Lámpara Nenúfar

Lampada Nenufaro

Lamp Waterlelie

c. 1902, Gilded and chiseled
bronze, glass paste/Bronze doré et
ciselé, pâte de verre, 60,5 × 16,5 cm

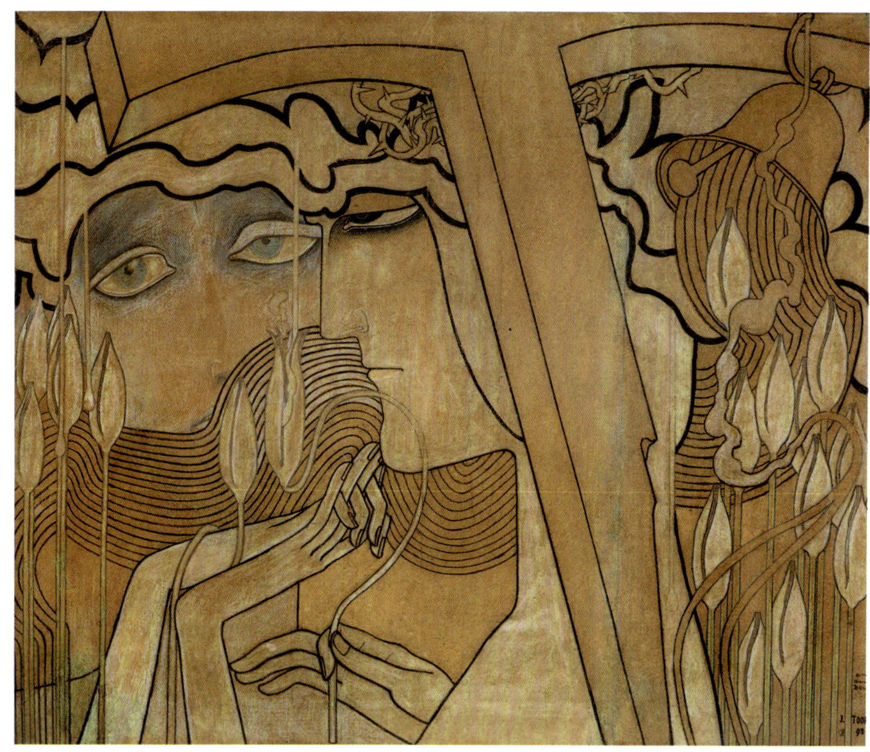

Jan Toorop (1858–1928)

Desire and Satisfaction

Le Désir et l'Assouvissement

Verlangen und Befriedigung

El deseo y la satisfacción

Il Desiderio e l'Appagamento

Verlangen en bevrediging

1893, Pastel on two sheets of beige paper on cardboard/
Pastel sur deux feuilles de papier beige sur carton, 76 × 90 cm

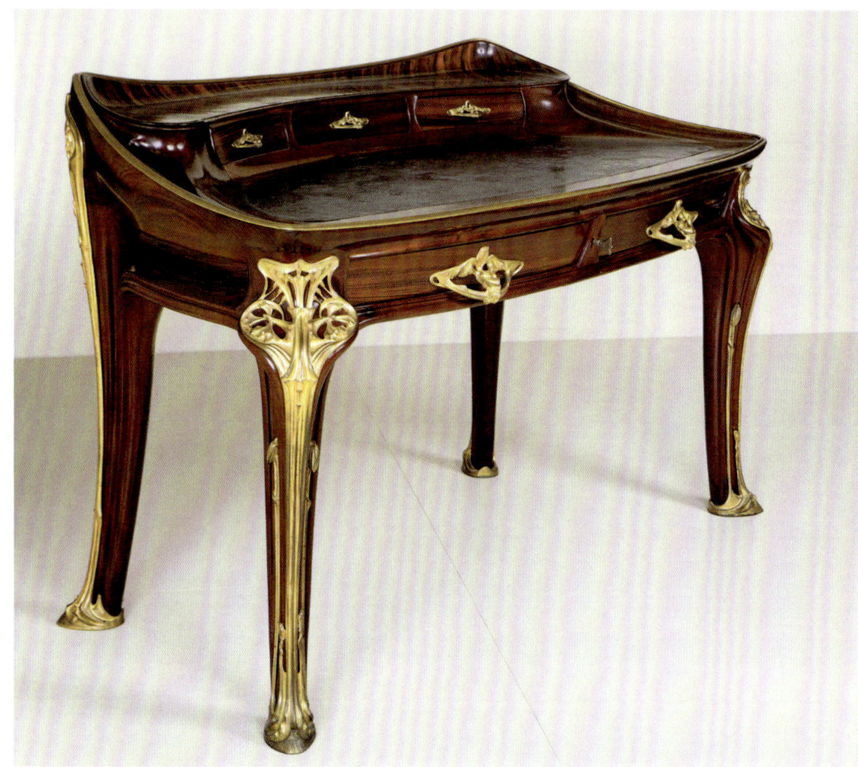

Louis Majorelle (1859–1926)

Orchids *desk*

Bureau Orchidées

Schreibtisch Orchideen

Escritorio Orquídeas

Scrittoio Orchidee

Bureau Orchideeën

c. 1905–1909, Mahogany, snakewood, gilded and
chiseled bronzes, copper, coated and embossed
leather/Acajou, amourette, bronzes dorés et ciselés,
cuivre, cuir coselé et repoussé, 95 × 70 cm

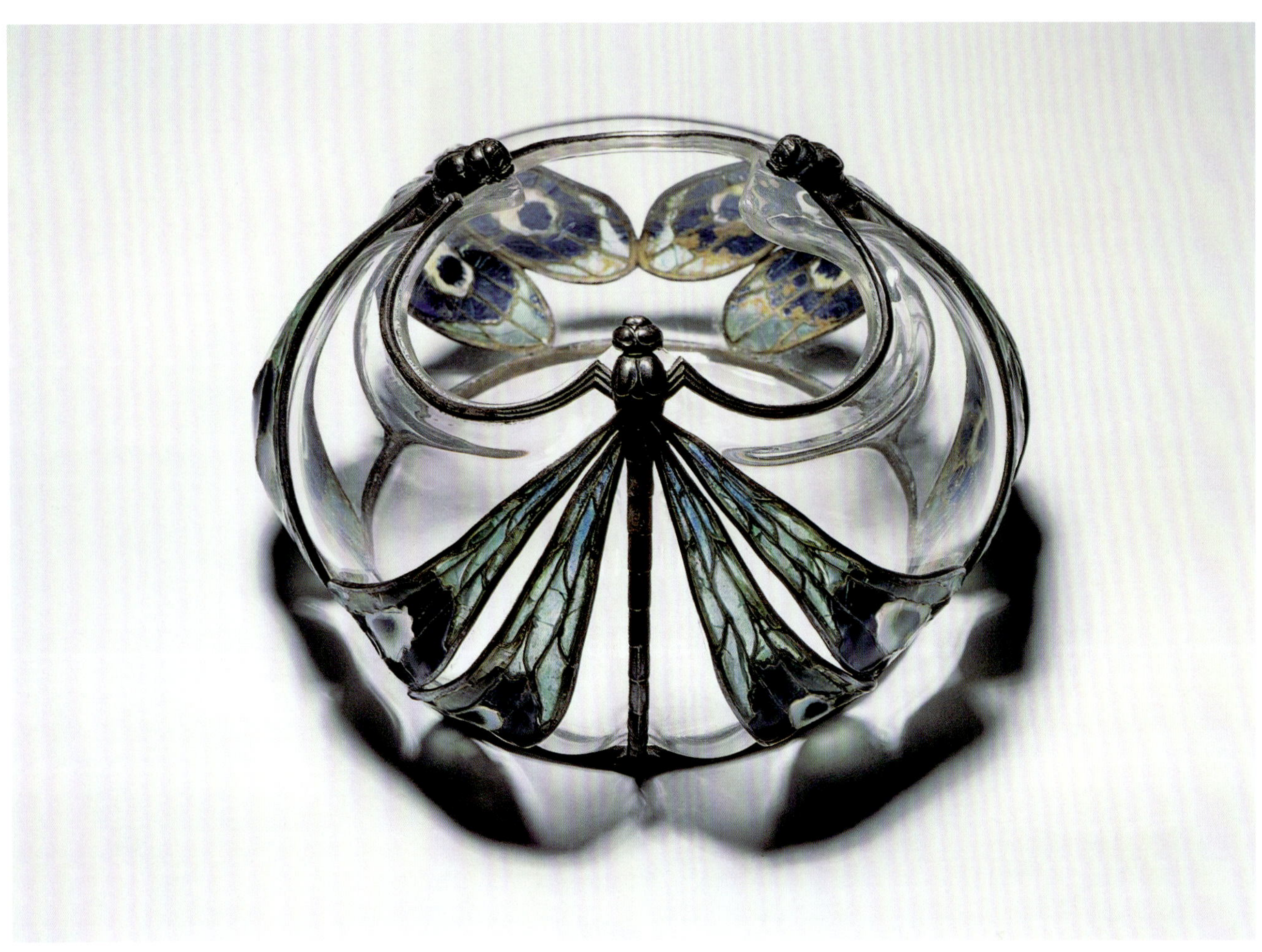

Eugène Feuillâtre (1870–1916)

Bonbon dish

Drageoir

Bonbonniere

Drageoir

Confettiera

Schaal

1903, Fused silver, forged and chiseled, cloisonné a jour enamel with spangles, blown glass/Argent fondu, forgé et ciselé, émail cloisonné à jour avec paillons, cristal soufflé, 8,3 × 14,5 cm

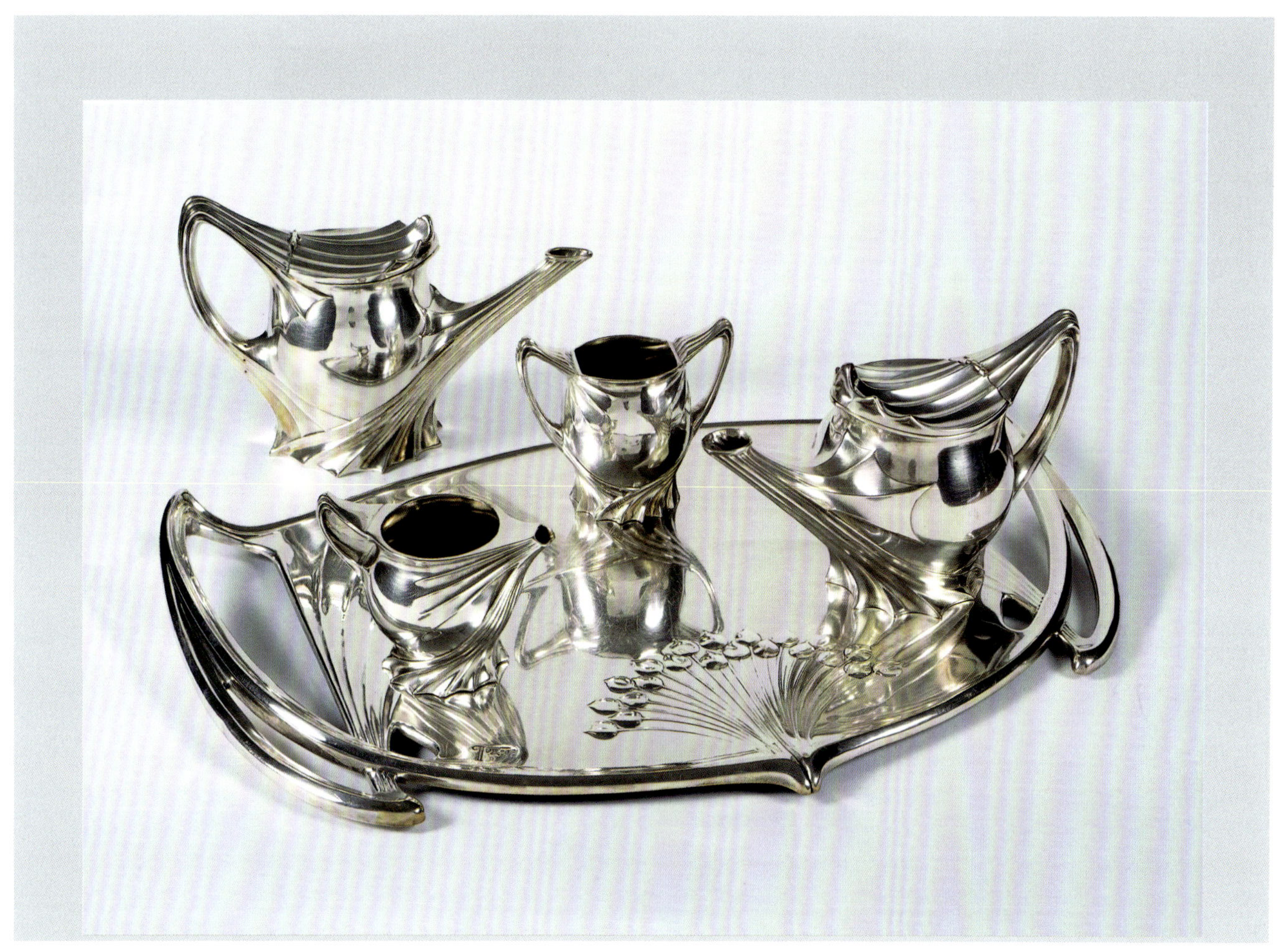

Paul Follot (1877–1941)

Tea service: sugar bowl, milk jug, teapot, tray

Service à thé : sucrier, pot à lait, théière, plateau

Teeservice: Zuckerdose, Milchkanne, Teekanne, Tablett

Servicio de té: azucarero, lechera, tetera, bandeja

Servizio da tè: zuccheriera, lattiera, teiera, vassoio

Theeservies: suikerpot, melkkan, theepot, theeblad

1903, Silver-plated metal/Métal argenté

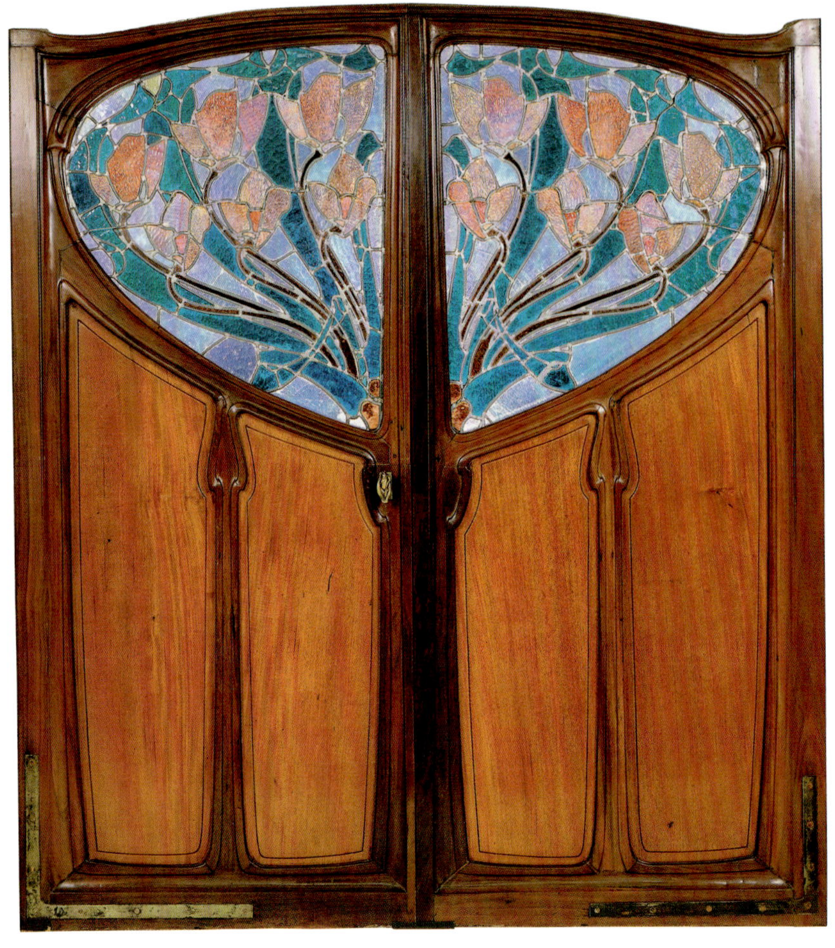

Émile André (1871–1933)

Double door

Porte à deux battants

Flügeltür

Puerta doble

Porta a due ante

Dubbele deur

1901, Mahogany, American chenille-like glass, opalescent glass, chiseled gilded bronzes/Acajou,
verres américains chenillés, verres opalescents, bronzes dorés ciselés, 198 × 182 × 6,5 cm

Henri de Toulouse-Lautrec (1864–1901)

At the Nouveau Cirque, Papa Chrysanthemum

Au Nouveau Cirque, Papa Chrysanthème

Im Nouveau Cirque, Papa Chrysantheme

En el Nouveau Cirque, Papá Crisantemo

Al Nouveau Cirque, Papa Chrysanthème

In het Nouveau Cirque, Papa Chrysant

c. 1894, Stained glass: "American" glasses, cabochons/Vitrail : verres "américains", cabochons, 120 × 85 cm

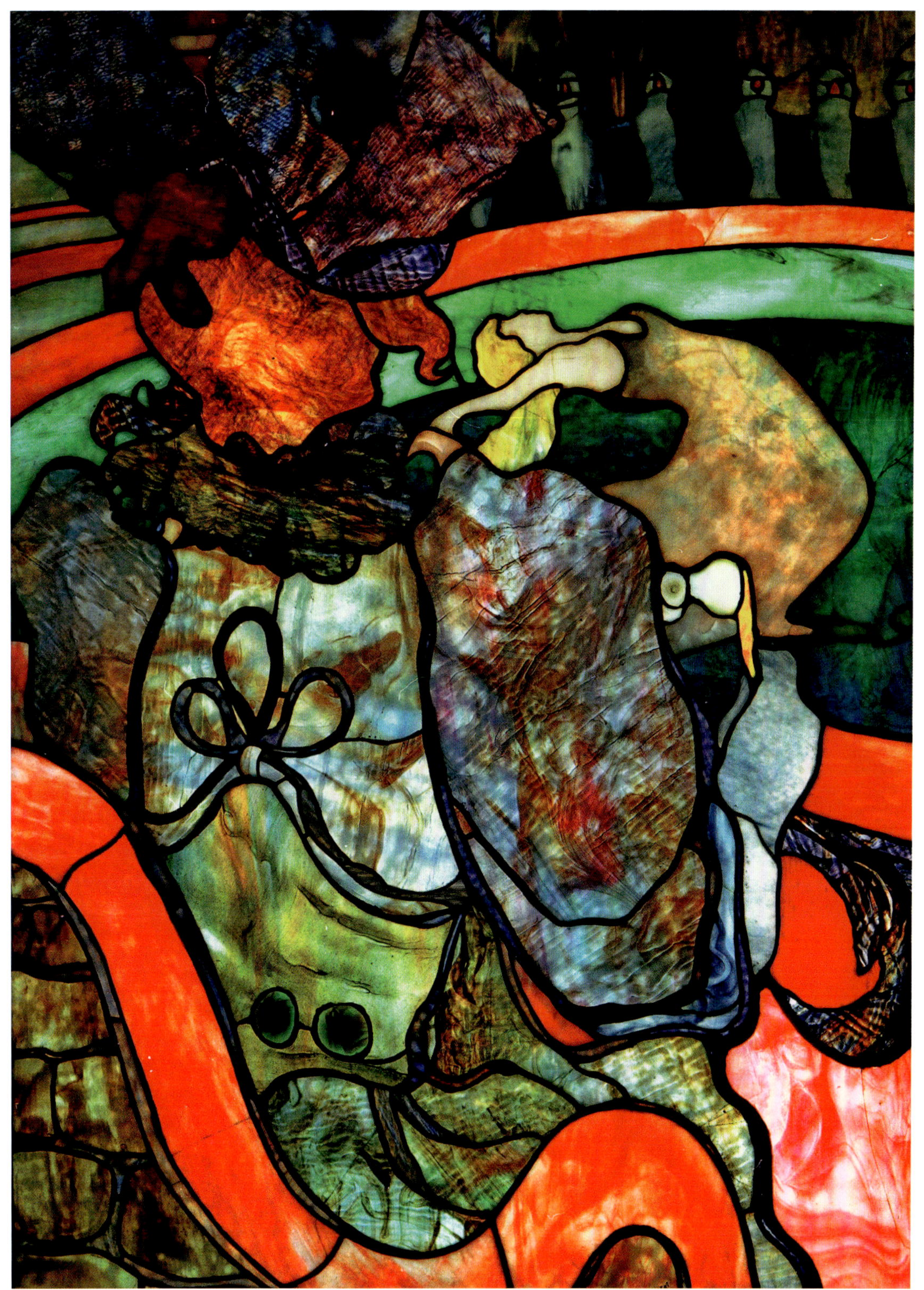

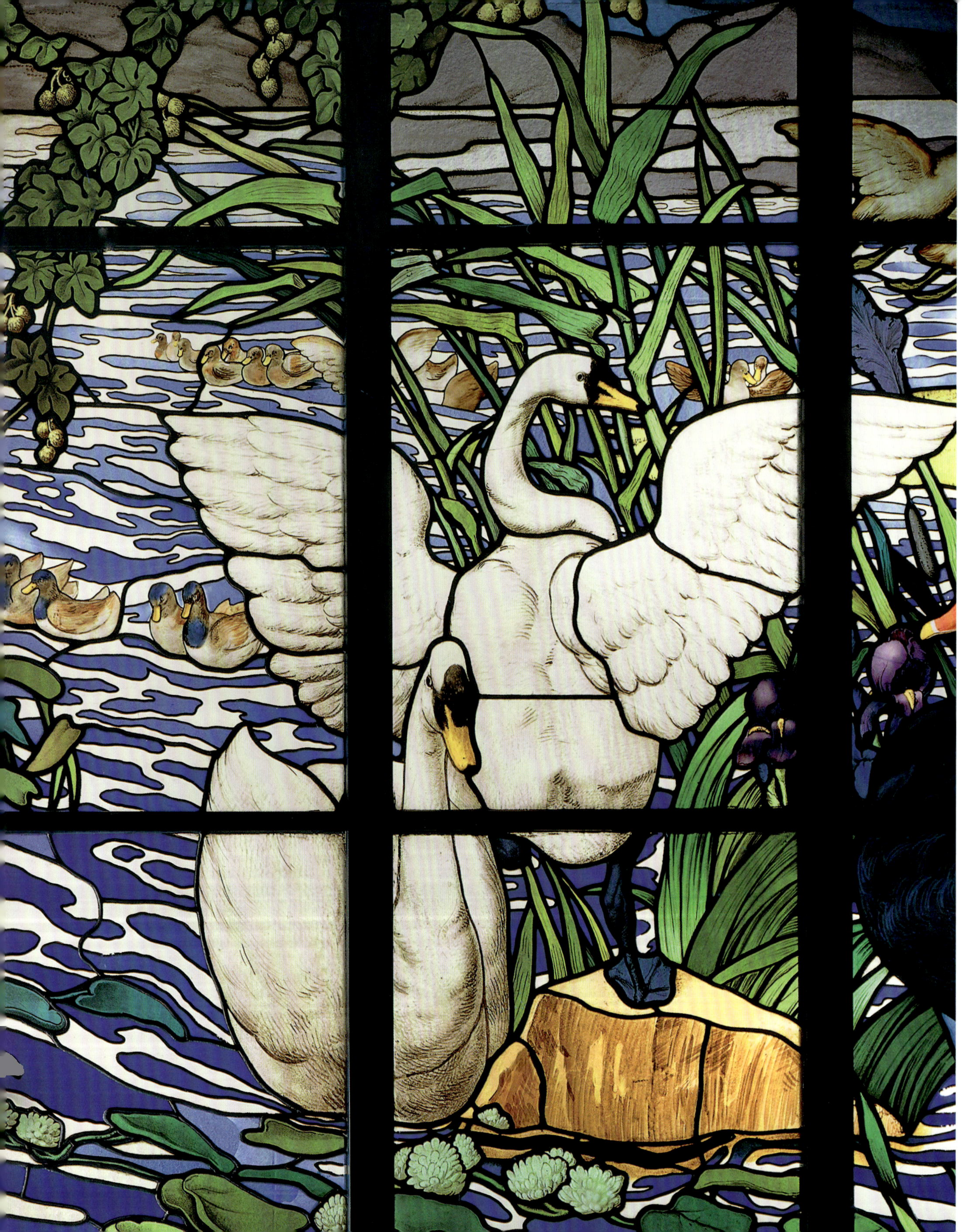

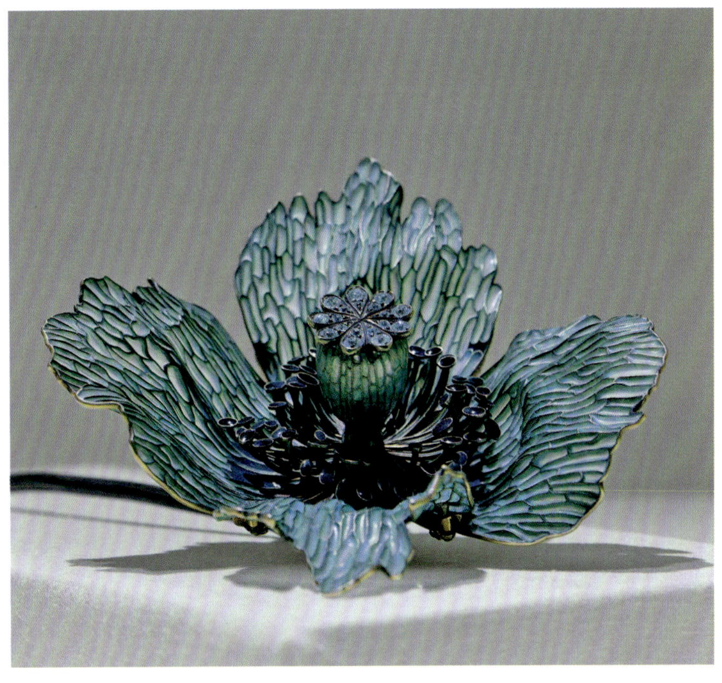

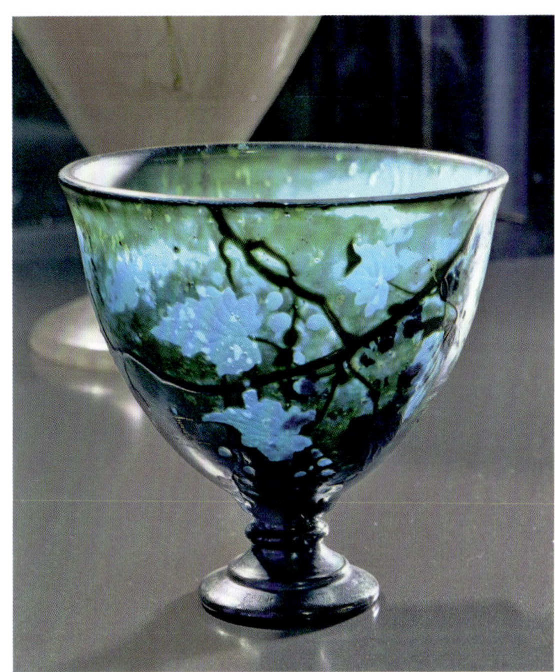

Albert Besnard (1849–1934)

Swans on Lake Annecy

Cygnes sur le lac d'Annecy

Schwäne auf dem Lac d'Annecy

Cisnes en el lago de Annecy

Cigni sul lago di Annecy

Zwanen op het meer van Annecy

1890, Acid-etched and painted glass/Verres gravés à l'acide et peints, 250 × 200 cm

René Lalique (1860–1945)

Peacock

Pavot

Mohnblume

Amapola

Papavero

Papaver

1897, Gold, silver, diamonds, enamel/Or, argent, diamants, émail, 7,5 × 23,5 cm

Émile Gallé (1846–1904)

On Such A Night

Par une telle nuit

An einem solchen Abend

En una noche como esta

In una notte come questa

Op een nacht als deze

1894, Crystal with metallic inclusions, partially gilded/Cristal, inclusions métalliques, partiellement dorée, 13,3 × 13,5 cm

The French glass painter Henri Carot worked with Maurice Denis (on the stained glass windows of the church of Sainte-Marguerite du Vésinet), but also alongside Albert Besnard, one of whose preparatory drawings he has transposed here. This stained glass, whose naturalistic subject and colors evoke the Art Nouveau style, was intended to decorate the vestibule of the private Parisian mansion of the artist Henry Lerolle.

Le peintre verrier français Henri Carot a œuvré avec Maurice Denis (les vitraux de l'église Sainte-Marguerite du Vésinet), mais aussi au côté d'Albert Besnard, dont il transpose ici un carton. Ce vitrail, dont le sujet naturaliste et les couleurs évoquent le style Art nouveau, était destiné à décorer le vestibule de l'hôtel particulier parisien de l'artiste Henry Lerolle.

Der französische Glasmaler Henri Carot arbeitete mit Maurice Denis zusammen (die Fenster der Kirche Sainte-Marguerite du Vésinet), aber auch mit Albert Besnard, von dem er hier einen Karton umsetzt. Dieses Fenster, dessen naturalistisches Motiv und Farben an den Jugendstil erinnern, war zur Dekoration des Vestibüls des Pariser Stadtpalais des Künstlers Henry Lerolle bestimmt.

El pintor de vidrio francés Henri Carot trabajó con Maurice Denis (las vidrieras de la iglesia de Sainte-Marguerite de Vésinet), y también junto a Albert Besnard, del que incorpora aquí un cartón. Este vidrio, donde el tema naturalista y los colores evocan el modernismo, fue pensado para decorar el vestíbulo de la mansión parisina de Henry Lerolle.

Il pittore francese di vetrate Henri Carot lavorò insieme a Maurice Denis (autore delle vetrate della chiesa di Sainte-Marguerite du Vésinet) e ad Albert Besnard, del quale traspone qui un cartone. La vetrata ha un soggetto naturalistico, presenta colori che evocano lo stile Art Nouveau ed era destinata a decorare la hall della proprietà parigina di Henry Lerolle.

De Franse glasschilder Henri Carot werkte samen met Maurice Denis (glas-in-loodramen van de kerk Sainte-Marguerite du Vésinet), maar ook met Albert Besnard, van wie hij dit ontwerp uitvoerde. Dit venster, waarvan het naturalistische onderwerp en de kleuren aan de nieuwe kunst doen denken, was bedoeld ter versiering van de hal van het Parijse herenhuis van Lerolle.

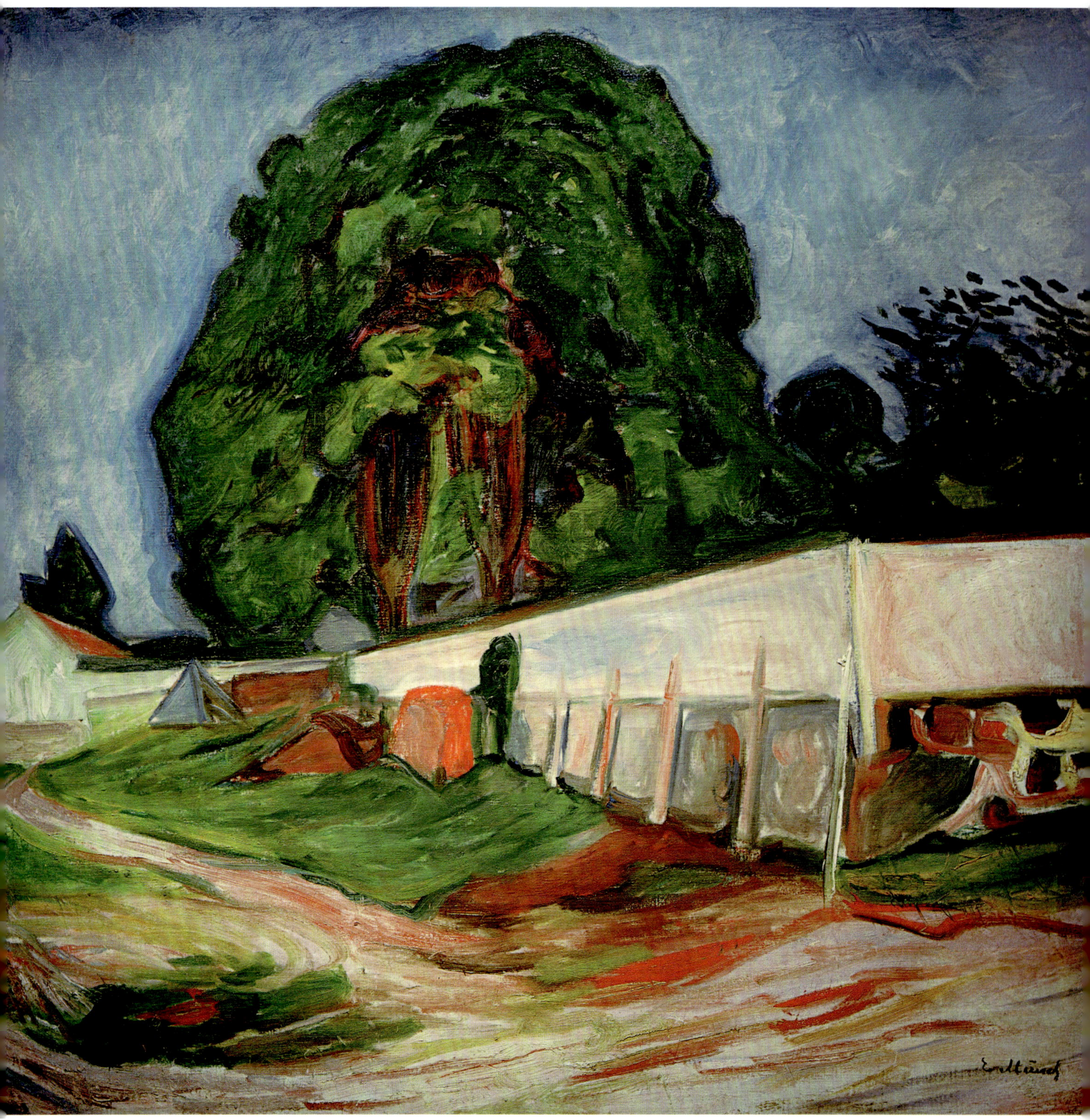

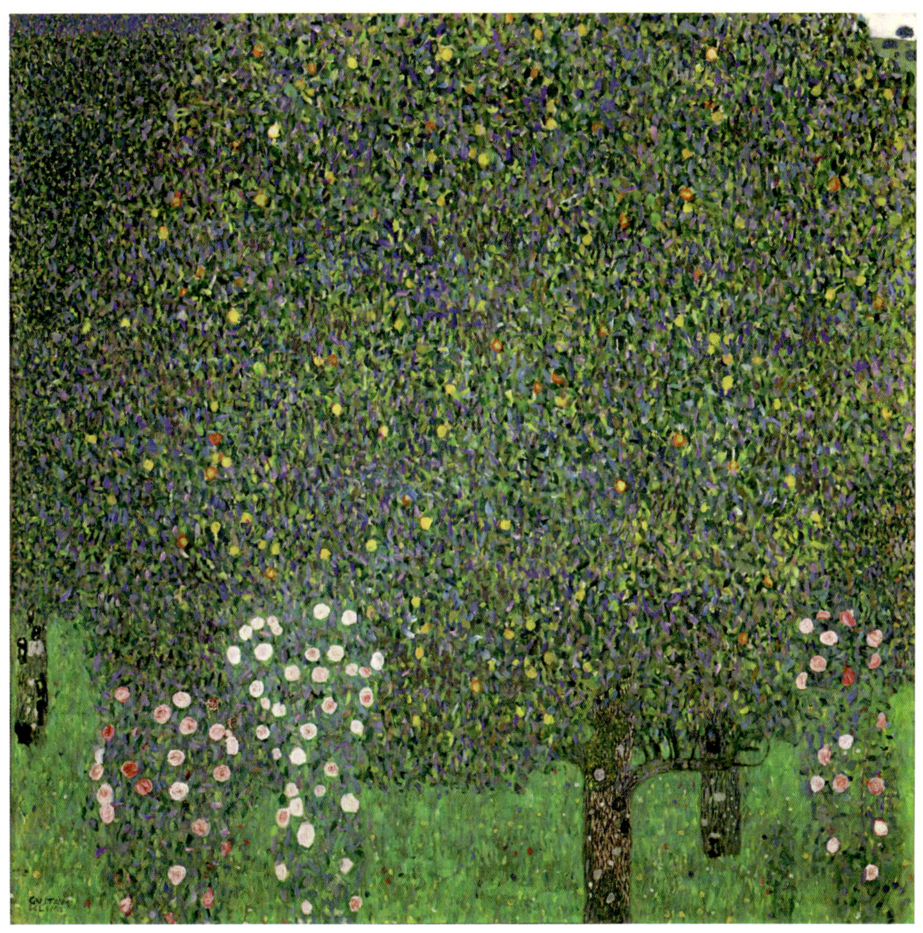

Edvard Munch (1863–1944)

Summer Night at Åsgårdstrand
Nuit d'été à Åsgårdstrand
Sommernacht in Åsgårdstrand
Noche de verano en Åsgårdstrand
Notte d'estate a Åsgårdstrand
Zomernacht op het Åsgårdstrand

1904, Oil on canvas/Huile sur toile, 99 × 103,5 cm

Gustav Klimt (1862–1918)

Rosebushes under the Trees
Rosiers sous les arbres
Rosensträuche unter Bäumen
Rosales bajo los árboles
Rose sotto gli alberi
Rozenstruiken onder de bomen

c. 1905, Oil on canvas/Huile sur toile, 110,2 × 110,2 cm

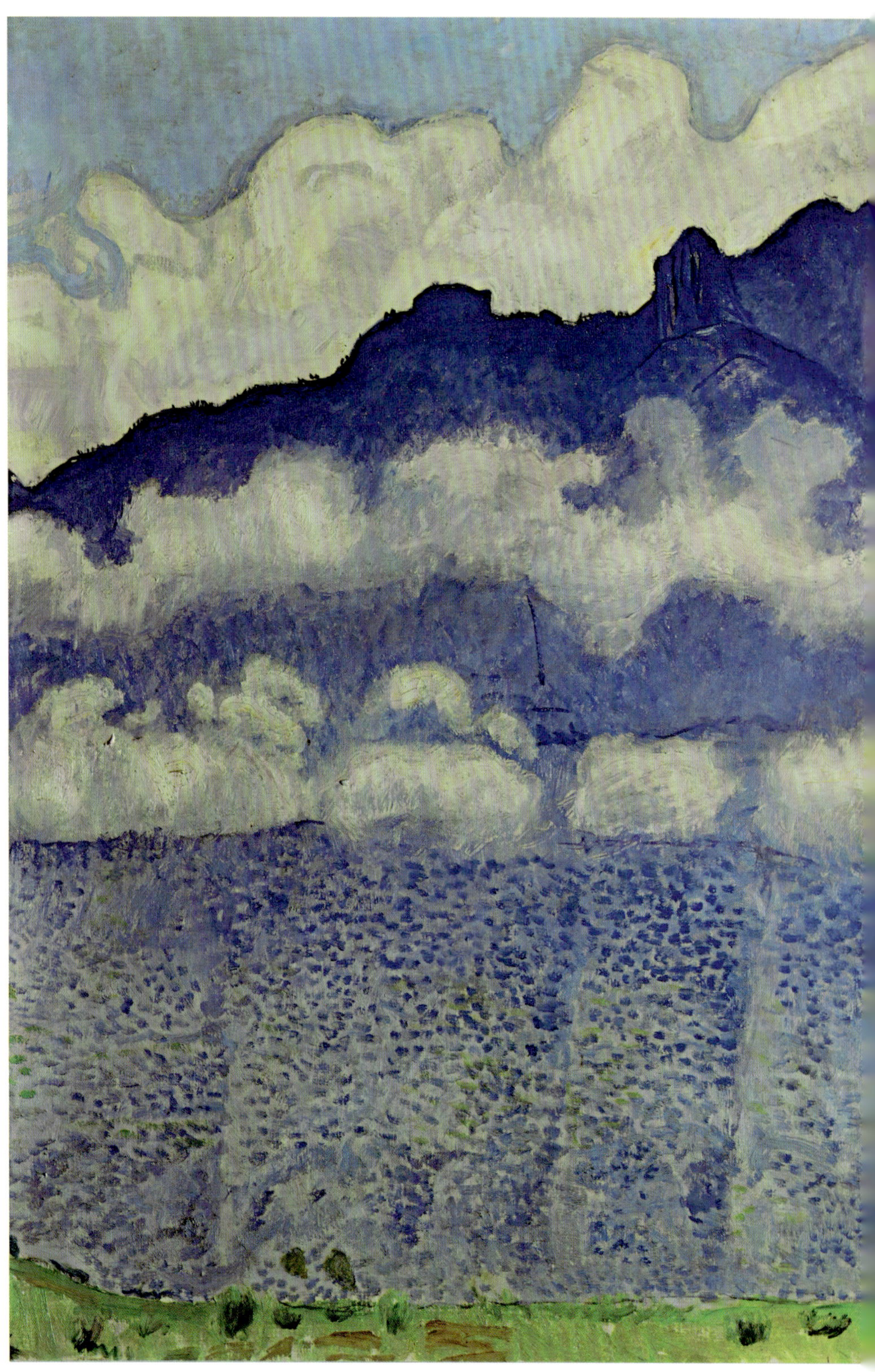

Ferdinand Hodler (1853–1918)
Landscape *(Pointe d'Andey, Arve Valley)*
Paysage *(la Pointe d'Andey, vallée de l'Arve)*
Landschaft *(Pointe d'Andey, Tal der Arve)*
Paisaje *(Pointe d'Andey, valle del río Arve)*
Paesaggio *(Pointe d'Andey, valle dell'Arve)*
Landschap *(de Pointe d'Andey in het dal van de Arve)*
1909, Oil on canvas/Huile sur toile, 67,5 × 90,5 cm

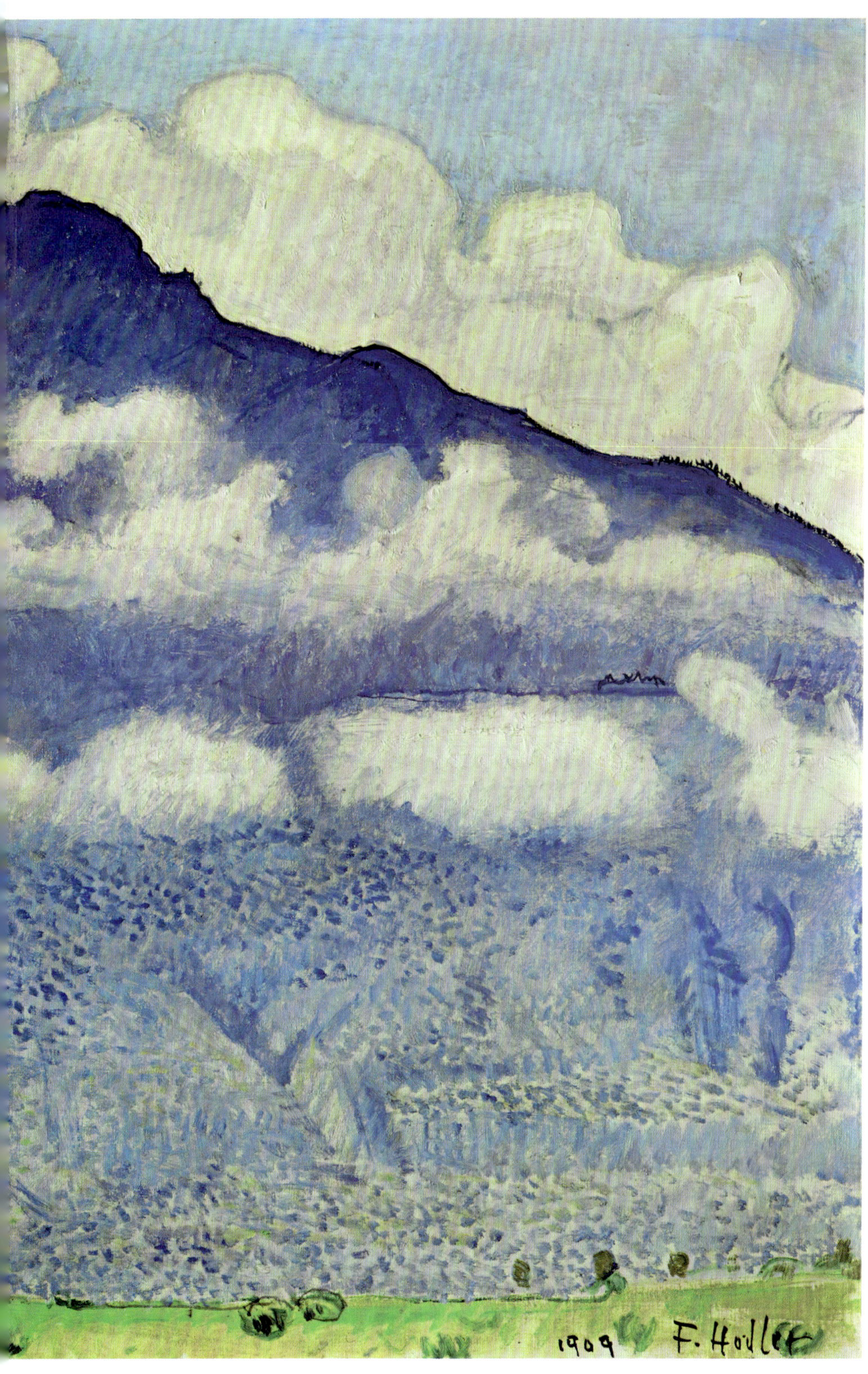

1909 F. Hodler